P9-CMW-062

STUDIES IN HISPANIC AMERICAN AFFAIRS

Edited by
A. CURTIS WILGUS

Volume III 1934

ARGENTINA, BRAZIL AND CHILE
SINCE INDEPENDENCE

Argentina, Brazil and Chile since Independence

ARGENTINA by J. Fred Rippy
BRAZIL by Percy Alvin Martin
CHILE by Isaac Joslin Cox

Edited by
A. CURTIS WILGUS

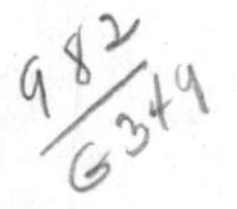

NEW YORK
RUSSELL & RUSSELL · INC
1963

reissued, 1963, by Russell & Russell, Inc.
by arrangement with George Washington University
L. C. Catalog Card No: 63—8373

Printed in the United States of America

PREFACE

THE third annual Seminar Conference on Hispanic American Affairs at The George Washington University was held from July 2 to August 10, 1934. During this period the lectures contained in this volume were delivered. As in the two previous Seminar Conferences, the class consisted chiefly of advanced students. The order in which the lectures were originally given by the chief speakers has been changed to conform to the sequence indicated in the title. The lectures included in the Appendices were given at intervals rather than at the end of the course. Professors Rippy, Martin, and Cox have aided in reading their respective proofs. Others who have given assistance to the editor are Professor George Howland Cox, Mr. Raul d'Eca, and Miss Catherine Phelps. Mr. Henry W. Herzog, in charge of the University Press, has again borne the burden of guiding the manuscript through the various stages of printing. The index has been prepared by Mr. Raul d'Eca. Editorial work has been confined chiefly to securing uniformity of presentation.

A. CURTIS WILGUS,
Director of the Center of Inter-American Studies.

TABLE OF CONTENTS

I. INTRODUCTION

II. ARGENTINA

III. BRAZIL

IV. CHILE

By ISAAC JOSLIN COX, *Northwestern University*

V. APPENDICES

I. INTRODUCTION

CHAPTER ONE

COLONIAL ANTECEDENTS OF THE A B C COUNTRIES

By A. Curtis Wilgus

I

ALTHOUGH Argentina, Brazil, and Chile, the so-called A B C States, are not a geographical or a political unit, they can be conveniently grouped for the purpose of detailed study.

At first glance they may appear to the student very different in many fundamental respects. The language of Brazil is Portuguese, while the language of Argentina and Chile is Spanish. However, the intellegentsia of each country can understand the other's language and can quite easily learn to speak it.

In political organizations the countries are different. Argentina and Brazil are federal republics while Chile has a unitary republican government. Their political history in the modern period has differed widely, each having passed along different paths which are marked by certain definite and individualistic characteristics. Argentina and Chile began their independence as republics, while Brazil continued from 1822 to 1889 as a monarchy with an emperor. The nineteenth century political life of Brazil paralleled in some respects that of our own. Secession movements began early, and the rising Republican Party adopted an anti-slavery attitude shortly after the middle of the century. Argentine political history since independence was marked by sectionalism, the city of Buenos Aires quarrelling with the interior provinces for political dominance, until this difficulty was settled about the time that our Civil War began. Chile passed through a critical period of anarchy shortly after independence, and early in the last decade of the nineteenth century experienced a revolution which has been known ever since as "The Civil War."

Both Argentina and Chile have had Indian problems similar to those of the United States in which the natives had first to be subdued and then reduced to an uncertain semi-civilization. The frontier in all three countries was pushed back during the nineteenth century, more or less successfully, about the time that we were expanding toward the Pacific.

Like the United States, each country has been a melting pot for European nationals with Indian or African elements to be assimilated. Climatic factors, and the lack of certain necessary minerals, have led to the early development of basic agrarian civilizations in each of the present-day states.

But because the subsequent chapters deal with the modern period since independence, one need not dwell longer on the nineteenth and twentieth centuries. Instead, one may examine briefly the colonial background in each of these states in order that their recent life may be better understood.

II

The Spanish and Portuguese age of exploration in America was characterized by three distinct and separate motives. The first was a fanatically religious crusading zeal, which was carried over from the mother lands where the Moslem invaders had been recently expelled by the forces of the Iberian Catholic Kings. The second was a national greed for gold, which was desired and needed because of the impoverishing peninsular wars which had reduced the peoples of the countries to poverty. The third was a lusty and bellicose love of freedom and a desire for promoting personal prestige.

Through an astute use of gunpowder and horses, a few scattered groups of European conquerors were able to cow and reduce to vassalage large numbers of natives, some of whom were cannibals, and many of whom were sedentary rather than nomadic Indians. In Chile, however, the fierce liberty loving Araucanians fought the Spaniards successfully for over three hundred years, while in Argentina the natives found the earliest European invaders tender morsels for their cannibalistic palates.

The earliest explorations along the Argentine coast date from the beginning of the sixteenth century when Vespucci, Vicente Yáñez Pinzón, and Solís were in the region. The latter, however, was so unfortunate on his second trip to the country as to be captured and eaten by the Indians in 1515. Subsequent explorers were more careful. Between 1516 and 1525 some survivors of the Solís party explored the *gran chaco* toward Peru looking for the rumored kingdom of the Incas. Later, in 1527, Sebastian Cabot, the son of a famous father, was in the region looking for mythical places and things. Not until 1534, however, did Spain actually begin the establishment of a colony in the Plata region when Pedro de Mendoza was appointed *adelantado*. In 1535 this gentleman built a fort on the present site of Buenos Aires, but it was shortly abandoned due to Indian opposition, and the settlers moved up the river to the present Asunción in Paraguay. Not until 1580 was Buenos Aires finally established as a permanent colony. Meanwhile, other scattered settlements had been made in the interior of what is now Argentina.

Chile was settled later than Argentina. After the discovery of the Pacific by Balboa, the Spaniards were interested chiefly in occupying Peru and in enriching themselves at the expense of the natives. In 1531, before the conquerors of Peru had seriously considered the conquest of Chile, Charles V granted the region between the Straits of Magellan and Peru to the German banking house of Fugger in payment for money borrowed. Fortunately for the history of Chile this company was never able to take advantage of its grant. In 1534 an attempt was made to occupy Chile by Simón de Alcazaba, who set out from the Argentine side in the hope of reaching the country across the Andes. This expedition failed. The next year Diego de Almagro, who had been granted territory by the crown in what is now northern Chile as a reward for his share in the conquest of Peru, set out from the latter country to occupy his possession. In two years of labor he succeeded in getting as far south as the present City of Santiago, but his adventure brought him nothing but hardship and ill-luck. Finally in 1540 the intrepid Pedro de Valdivia was sent by Pizarro to conquer the region. With great foresight and careful planning he succeeded in occupying the middle half of Chile as far south as the Biobio River. But he was never able to satisfactorily quiet the Araucanian Indians who defended every inch of their land. However, the town of Santiago was founded in 1541, Valparaiso was settled in 1544, and Concepción was established in 1550 at the mouth of the Biobio. Several Chilean expeditions were sent across the Andes into present-day Bolivia and Argentina but these were of little importance. Chile having been settled from Peru remained a political division of that territory until independence. In 1557 the region was consolidated under Hurtado de Mendoza who had the title of Captain-General of Chile.

Brazil's early history was a checkered one. The Spaniards preceded Cabral on the Brazilian coast by one year, having explored a part of the region in 1499. After Cabral in 1500, came Vespucci, who claimed to have taken home a load of Brazilwood thus giving a name to the region. At first only renegades settled in Brazilian territory. These individuals under a stifling sun and a high humidity soon went native; and by intermarrying with the Indians a numerous half-breed element early appeared along certain sections of the coast. The first serious Portuguese attempt to occupy the region came in 1530 when Martim Affonso de Sousa was sent to establish a colony which immediately became a dumping ground for undesirables from Portugal. The feudal system, current in Europe, was transplanted with some modifications to the colony, and many of the docile Indians were enslaved and gradually exterminated. It was not until late in the century that the government allowed negroes from its African colonies to be introduced into the country. In 1549, finally, Thomé de Sousa was sent to rule Brazil, and the capital was established at Bahia. Then began a period of precarious prosperity.

In all three of these colonies, agriculture formed the basis of wealth. Practically no minerals were found in Argentina, and comparatively few were mined in Chile. In the seventeenth century gold and diamonds were found in great abundance in Brazil, and a shifting of centers of population from the north to the south resulted. Sugar, tobacco, cotton, Brazilwood, and spices formed the basis of Brazil's agricultural life, while Chile produced grapes and other fruits, and Argentina produced grains and some cattle. Ranches and plantations in all three of the colonies were generally owned by absentee landlords, thus creating a none too efficient economic life.

Political affairs in these countries were similar during the three centuries of the colonial period. From 1580 to 1640 Brazil was united with the other Spanish colonies under the Spanish Crown, and some of her Portuguese institutions were brought into harmony with those of her neighbors. At the end of this period Brazil regained her political identity but she suffered more from political corruption than did the Spanish colonies. In all countries, public offices were sold, officials were corrupt, and the church constantly influenced political affairs. More than the other colonies, Brazil constituted an experimental laboratory for political ideas. In 1645 the country was given to the Portuguese heir presumptive as a patrimony. After this experiment the colony was ruled over by a viceroy. For a while in the sixteenth century there had been two capitals, one for north Brazil and one for south Brazil, but in 1763 a permanent capital for the colony was established at Rio de Janeiro. At any time the Portuguese King might interfere in local government, and his prime minister could make reforms or not at will.

Argentina was a part of the Viceroyalty of Peru until 1776, when a viceroy was appointed to reside at Buenos Aires. This step was taken largely to combat smuggling which was carried on in the Plata region by foreign merchants who were refused legal trading rights because of the monopolistic Spanish mercantile laws which compelled the people of Argentina to trade with the mother country by way of Lima and Panama.

Chile was quite logically attached to the Viceroyalty of Peru until the end of the colonial period. Her commerce, however, was restricted, for she could not trade directly with any part of the world except through Peru and usually through Spain.

Colonial society was honeycombed by corruption and characterized by insincerity. The upper class (Peninsulars) were natives of the mother countries who came to the colonies chiefly to rule. Their children and their descendents, if they remained of pure European stock, were known as Creoles. Both the classes were in reality castes and were continually antagonistic toward each other. In Brazil this caste system was accentuated by the existence of a local nobility. Beneath these persons of European descent were the mixed white and Indian elements, the *mestizos,* who had no political and few social rights. Below this group were the mulattoes, and at the bottom were free Indians and negroes, and enslaved Indians and negroes. Generally speaking, these groups mutually hated and feared each other, and social coöperation was effected only by force.

Music and the arts were influenced in the colonial period by the aspects of nature, by the Indian, and by the negro. European characteristics, however, were intermingled in many instances. Literature was largely European, for the lack of printing presses prevented what otherwise would doubtless have been a prolific output of poetry, drama, novels, and serious prose writings. Education was in the hands of the clergy who taught only what they wished in the elementary schools and in the universities in Argentina and Chile. Brazil had no schools of higher learning. The church used both the Index and the Inquisition—although to a lesser extent in Brazil than elsewhere—to promote its aims. Culture in the rural sections and in some municipalities has aptly been defined as "raw," and illiteracy was high in all parts of the colonies.

From a social and intellectual morass it was difficult for the colonists of both Spain and Portugal to lift themselves to a level of intellectual understanding where they might grasp the ideas in contemporary thought that gradually seeped into the colonies from the revolutions of the eighteenth century in Europe and in English North America. But some among the colonists, chiefly those Creoles who had travelled or who had been educated abroad, were able to take advantage of the extensive external contemporary mental ferment and turn it into channels which eventually led to independence from the mother countries. Thus in Argentina and Chile, Creole revolts brought independence between 1816 and 1818. In 1808 Brazil, finding herself with a Portuguese monarch in her midst and in the relation of the mother country to Portugal, which had for the moment turned colony, was unable to successfully throw off European influences until 1822, and even in that year the change was simply from one monarch to another instead of from monarchy to republicanism as was the case with her neighbors.

For all three colonies the three century long colonial period was one of poor preparation for what was to follow. The wonder is that out of such chaotic colonial inexperience and disorganization the rising young states were able to establish such relatively effective governments, and to meet the exacting responsibilities required from them by the world of nations into which they had been so suddenly born. Undoubtedly without the aid, encouragement, and example of the United States they would have succeeded less well.

CHAPTER TWO

THE POLITICAL HERITAGE OF SPANISH AMERICA

By N. Andrew N. Cleven

THE political heritage of a people does not lend itself easily to analysis. No heritage does, for a heritage is generally much too complex for that. Yet there can be no adequate understanding of the political theories and practices of a people without a comprehensive analysis of their political legacy. This is particularly true of the people of Spanish America. There are few people who have a richer and a more varied political heritage than they.

I

Political heritages are, by and large, the product primarily of ethnological and environmental factors. Iberia and America have been Nature's ethnological experimental laboratories from time immemorial. Streams of blood from many different ethnological sources have gone into the making of the Spaniard in the Old World and in the New: the blood of the Celts, Iberians, Greeks, Phœnicians, Carthaginians, Hebrews, Romans, Teutons, Arabs, Berbers, negroes, and Mongolians.[1] Ethnological admixtures began long before there was any recorded history of Iberia. The biological process of admixture has gone on down throughout the ages, and will no doubt continue to do so "until the crack of doom." It is the way of all flesh. This statement may sound trifling: a mere truism, a mere commonplace. But truisms and commonplaces must not blind one to the fundamental significance of this biological process. It is necessary to have an eye to fundamentals in order to understand the political theories and practices of the Spanish Americans.

---

[1] The list is obviously incomplete. The term "race" is a very illusive one. It may mean almost anything. It is well, accordingly, to be careful in its use, and not to make conclusions concerning ethnological admixtures lightly. The list given includes those peoples who are generally held to have contributed of their blood to the making of the Spaniard. That there were other ethnological factors involved in the biological process may be taken for granted. The reader should also be cautioned against accepting the arrangement of the names of peoples as indicating any *final* solution as to the time the people entered the peninsula.

By the end of the fifteenth century, when Spain began discovery, exploration, and colonization in the New World, the Spaniard had developed his amatory proclivities to a very high degree. America offered him a virgin field for his amatory instincts, and he made good use of his opportunity. He had no sooner landed in Española than he began procreating a new human being. He had brought no women with him from Spain. The native women became, accordingly, the mothers of a new human species. The *mestizos,* the fruit of that union, began, in due time, to procreate other human beings, intermixing freely with ethnological groups coming within their sphere of amatory interests. The Spanish in them saw to that. The introduction of the African negro added yet another ethnological factor. He, too, began early procreating another species. The negro intermixed freely both with the Indians and with the whites, as well as with the mixed castes. The importance of the introduction of negroid blood into the biological process in America should not be underestimated. The *zambo,* the fruit of the union between a negro and an Indian, will bear close study, politically as well as biologically. Complex as the ethnological mosaic had become, it was to become still more so, for another ethnological element was injected into the biological process. In the Philippines, the Spaniard came in contact with the Mongolians. Here, too, the ethnological admixture was fairly general.[2] The introduction of the *mongoloid* strain into Spanish America, while on a small scale, did, nevertheless, occur. Thus the process of ethnological intermixture, begun in the Old World and continued in the New, has complicated the socio-political life of America to a very remarkable degree. The end is not yet, however, for the ethnological intermixture process is still continuing. The result can better be imagined than described.

The effect upon the political life of Spanish America of the presence of mixed castes has been of profound social and political importance. Spain began the practice, in the New World, of forcing the offsprings of a union of two socially unequal individuals into the so-called inferior parent class. The progress of the mixed caste, not to mention the native peoples, has been greatly hampered. It has made the mixed castes bitter opponents of white rule. The *mestizos* have played a very important rôle in the political life of Mexico, Guatemala, Ecuador, Peru, Bolivia, Paraguay, and Chile. In Peru and Bolivia the *mestizo* is

[2] Consult the monumental work of Blair and Robertson on *The Philippine Islands* for a detailed account of the relations between the Spaniards and the Mongolians in the Philippine Islands during the Spanish rule.

known as a *cholo,* a term by no means always complimentary. Much of the chaotic and the unstable, politically, in those two countries, has been laid at the door of the *cholos.*[3] There are those who believe, and the number of those who so believe is by no means small, that the *cholo* is anxious to secure not only wealth, power, and prestige through wielding public authority, but that he desires much more than that. He desires such authority in order to help redress the grievances of his group against white domination, and ultimately to rid his people of the hated white rule altogether.

The *cholos* have contributed several very able men, some of whom deserve to rank among the great leaders of their day and age. Among them may be mentioned the celebrated General Andrés Santa Cruz, Grand Marshal of Zepita.[4] Santa Cruz traced his descent, on his maternal side, back to the ruling Inca—a fact of which he was not only inordinately proud, but of which he made a very great deal. Upon the death of Simón Bolívar in 1830, the mantle of leadership, as far as the fruition of the idea of a United States of Spanish America is concerned, fell upon the shoulders of Santa Cruz. He began experimenting with the idea of creating a Spanish American nationality. To this end he founded the celebrated Peru-Bolivian Confederation which was, no doubt, to be the nucleus of the confederation of all of Spanish America. It was a grandiose idea, but it failed.[5] Short-lived though it was—it lasted less than three years—the struggle for its overthrow disrupted the institutional life of Peru and Bolivia, and retarded the cultural progress of those two countries for more than a half century. The opposition to the late President Sanchez Cerro of Peru, resulting in his assassination, was largely due to the fact that he was a *cholo.* As such he was genuinely hated by many of the whites of Peru; and

---

[3] Consult Edward A. Ross's illuminating work entitled *South of Panama* for an account of the amatory proclivities of the Spanish Americans. Arguëdas, the celebrated Bolivian historian, is especially critical of the political activities of the *cholos.*

[4] Consult the writer's brief biographical sketch of Santa Cruz in *The Encyclopædia of the Social Sciences.*

[5] The failure cannot be attributed to the weakness, or lack of ability, of the Marshal of Zepita. The Peru-Bolivian Confederation (1836-39) was considered by what is now called the A B C Powers, all three of whom were opposed to it on the ground that it would be a menace to the peace and security of South America. Those who desire more information on this very interesting period of the history of South America will find the despatches of our diplomatic agents in Chile, Peru, and Ecuador illuminating.

there were among these whites some who were not above resorting to assassination to get rid of him.[6]

Complicated as the biological process has been and is, the influences of environment have been and are no less so. Again there are homely truths to be held constantly in mind. The Spaniard could have been produced nowhere but in the Iberian Peninsula. A trite, homely, commonplace observation? Perhaps. Many a fundamentally important truth may seem, offhand, to be homely, commonplace, and trite. But no student of the political life of Spanish America, and certainly of old Spain itself, can brush aside so easily these fundamental facts. It is worth repeating that the Spaniard could have been produced in no other country in the wide, wide world but in Iberia. He is the product of the topography, the soils, and the climates found only in Iberia. That which is essentially Spanish in him is the product of the African peoples of Spain, primarily the Celtiberians. The mentality, the attitude toward man and nature, and the physique which are called Spanish are all the product of Iberia of prehistoric times. The exaggerated individualism, the inordinate love of particularism, and the brilliantly imaginative mysticism known as Spanish are essentally the product of prehistoric Iberia.[7] The different contributing elements which have been dealt with above have also had their effect, of course, upon the formation of these Spanish characteristics; but the fundamentals have remained very much the same. The Spaniard is African, not European, because Spain is African. Geographically, Africa begins and Europe ends with the Pyrenees, or Europe begins and Africa ends at the Pyrenees, depending upon the angle from which the matter is considered.

The Spaniard of the Americas has, very naturally, been tremendously influenced by the ethnological and environmental factors affecting him in the new world—so much so, that the product is claimed to be a new race, and a race the like of which the world has never seen. Dr. José Vasconcellos, the celebrated Mexican scholar, holds to this opinion, and has given the idea wide currency. The youth of Spanish America find the idea an excellent one; and many of them firmly believe that the

---

[6] Among efforts to assassinate him was the one in Miraflores as he was leaving the Cathedral after high mass.

[7] Consult for a discussion of these matters: Rafael Altamira y Crevea's *Historia de España y de la civilización española* (Chapman's *History of Spain* is based on this work); R. B. Merriman's *Rise of the Spanish Empire;* S. de Madariaga's *Spain* and the *Genius of Spain;* E. D. Salmon's *Imperial Spain;* J. P. Oliveira Martin's *Iberian Civilization;* Havelock Ellis' *The Soul of Spain;* the *Cambridge Mediæval History;* and others.

Spanish genius will again illumine the world through the medium of this new race. This idea has great effect upon the development of a nationality in each of the eighteen republics. It also has its effect upon the movement to mould these peoples into one people. A spiritual rapprochement has been established between Spain and Spanish America largely as a result of this leavening idea. Annually on Columbus Day, called by them the *Día de la Raza* (the Day of the Race), Spanish people in many different parts of the world gather together to recount past glories, past achievements, and the past grandeur of the Spanish race. They do not content themselves with such a recounting merely, but urge the sons and daughters of Spain everywhere to achieve even greater things in the future. For Columbus is taken by the Spaniard to epitomize the genius of the Iberian race.[8] This rapprochement between the Spaniards of the Old and those of the New World may foreshadow a renaissance similar to, or even greater than, that which is now overhauling Italy. It may not be too much to say that the liberal movement which overthrew the Bourbon monarchy in Spain and which resulted in the establishment of a republic in its place in 1931 was affected by this rapprochement between the Spaniards of the two hemispheres.

II

From out of these ethnological and environmental factors in Europe and in America have come influences shaping the political ideology of the Spanish people. These same factors have largely determined the efforts to put that political ideology into practice. There is not a single one of the several parent peoples of Spanish America of today but has played its part in the political development of Spanish America. Institutions, even political ones, do not have the habit of springing full-grown into being and without warning. The origins of the political life of Spanish America lie, accordingly, deeply rooted in the past. There is hardly a single political institution in Spanish America that is not Euro-African in origin. Nor is there a single political institution in Spanish America superior to its prototype.

The passing of Frederick Jackson Turner naturally calls to mind his great work, that of emphasizing the significance of the frontier in

---

[8] Consult the works of Andrés Bello, Rubén Darío, and Manuel Chocano for expositions of this cultural and spiritual rapproachement. Also see the works of Vasconcellos and Manuel Ugarte. The latter's work on *The Destiny of a Continent* (translated by J. Fred Rippy) will give a good idea of causes that tend to mould this spirit of racial unity.

United States history.[9] That which is of interest in this discussion is not merely the significance of the frontier in the history of the United States, or even the significance of the frontier in the history of greater America. The interest lies rather in the significance of the frontier in universal history. Our concern in the here and the now is apt to cause us to forget, or to minimize, the history of the larger whole. The Iberian, like the Englishman, has in the final analysis done little but transplant the institutional life of his own native land, and haltingly to attempt to keep pace with the progress which the Old, not the New World, is making in an effort to democratize human society.

The significance of the frontier in the political life of Spanish America must not be underestimated. This region, too, had free lands, rich mineral wealth, rich grazing and agricultural lands. It has played a rôle not unlike that of its Anglo-Saxon neighbors of the north. The main difference lies, probably, in the fact that Spain transplanted into the New World, which England did not, the feudal régime. Since the Crown of Spain alone owned the lands acquired by its *conquistadores* in America, it divided those lands as it saw fit. There were large sections of the newly-conquered lands divided into *encomiendas*—fiefs they would be called in feudal language—which were granted to such subjects as had rendered conspicuous services for God and king. The Crown of Spain thereby created a new class of nobility, for the *encomenderos,* as those were called to whom an *encomienda* was given, were feudal lords, as well as feudal vassals. Hernán Cortés, Francisco Pizarro, and Ximénes de Quesada,[10] conquerors respectively of Mexico, Peru, and Colombia, were given princely grants of land, with large numbers of Indians, in the countries of their conquests. The grant of an *encomienda* did not confer ownership upon the *encomendero;* nor was the grant hereditary. The *encomienda* was granted only for one life. Upon the death of the *encomendero* the *encomienda* reverted to the Crown of Spain. This method of procedure is of profound im-

---

[9] Since the passing of Professor Turner, certain scholars have revamped the idea of the frontier in history. The result has been a healthful one, for it has directed attention to the rôle of the frontier in world history. Out of this revamping has come an appreciation of the *commonality* of human socio-political life on the frontiers of the world.

[10] Consult Sir Clements Markham's excellent work on *The Conquest of New Granada* for the manner in which the land was parcelled out to the *conquistadores.* Also consult F. A. MacNutt's work on *The Letters of Cortés to the Emperor,* and his work on Cortés.

portance to an understanding of landownership in Spanish America, as many of our people, living in regions which were once under the control of Spain or Mexico, can testify. No one *owned* land but the king, and men held land *of* the king. This principle of landownership, residing in the sovereign alone, finds expression in the celebrated Constitution of the United States of Mexico of 1917.[11] The Mexicans, believing in the principle that sovereignty rests in the nation, lay down the principle, in Article 27 and Article 130 of that instrument, that ownership of the lands of the republic inheres in the nation, which alone has the power to dispose of the lands. The Crown of Spain took great care to see that no one might go to the Indies[12] whose religious faith, or whose loyalty to the king, was questioned. Spain strove to send to her possessions in America her best people, and succeeded, to a remarkable degree, to create a second self in America.[13] From these facts may be deduced the conclusion that, while the wildernesses of the original frontiers affected Spanish life in America, the customs and usages of the upper social stratum were affected less than were those of the English in America. The tremendous importance of the Roman Catholic Church in conserving and preserving Spanish life in Spanish America must not be ignored. This statement must not be allowed to blind us to the degree to which the *religiosos,* whether of the mission or of the see, adapted their life to the new environment. But the life of the cities was not greatly affected by pioneering conditions. The more important cities in the Indies were built either upon the site of native cities, such as Mexico City, Cuzco, Quito, Manila, or in localities which made it relatively easy to conserve intact Spanish life, such as Lima, Buenos Aires, Santiago de Chile, Santa Fé de Bogotá, and others which could be named. The life in these cities was almost an exact reproduction of life in cities of Old Spain. Nowhere in America could cities be found, in the period between 1600 and 1800, equalling those of Lima, Mexico City, and Charcas. Life in these cities rivalled in brilliancy even those of Old Spain itself. This is not at all strange when one considers the

---

[11] Consult H. M. Branch's work comparing the Constitution of Mexico of 1857 with that of 1917.

[12] Consult E. G. Bourne's work on *Spain in America.*

[13] Consult the several works by Bernard Moses on Spanish South America. Also see Blair and Robertson *The Philippine Islands* and H. I. Priestly *The Mexican Nation: A History.* The Philippine Islands should be included because they formed a part of the Viceroyalty of New Spain shortly after their conquest by Legaspi.

great wealth of these three cities and of the aristocratic nature of its people and their institutions.[14]

III

There will be no time to consider all the political institutions and practices introduced into America by Spain. Attention will be centered on two of the more important political institutions evolved in the peninsula which have had a most pronounced influence upon political life in Spanish America. The earliest of these was the municipality. The Spanish people are an urban people, and have been so throughout the period of the recorded history of Iberia. In fact, the municipality was a creation of the prehistoric period of the peninsula. Historians still differ as to the origin of the Spanish municipality. But all are agreed that the main features of the institution were developed prior to 238 B. C. This is the date of the arrival of the Carthaginians in Iberia. It is also the date of the beginning of the written history of the peninsula. That is to say, the municipality in Spain is a creation of the Celtiberians. The date of their beginnings is, however, as stated above, not known. Nor is it known from whence the Celtiberians derived their notion of a municipality. It is not at all improbable that the municipality was an indigenous creation, although the Celtiberians may have borrowed the idea from other Mediterranean peoples. All that we know definitely is that by the time the curtain of history rises on Iberia, the municipality had already become a complex organism. In fact, the larger municipalities of the peninsula were city republics by 238 B. C. They had evolved the principle of representation and the division of powers in government. Sovereignty was vested in the freemen of the municipality, known as *vecinarios*. Sovereignty was exercised by them as a body, or by agents, or agencies, selected by them. The method of selection was usually some form of election. The municipality had full control not only of its immediate self, but of the larger territory over which it exercised jurisdiction. The muncipality was still in a democratic state and continued to be so for centuries. It was the municipality which jealously guarded democracy and which tenderly nurtured it. When the Spaniard speaks of Spain and the Spaniards as having always been democratic, the most democratic people

---

[14] Consult Bernard Moses' work on *The Spanish Dependencies in South America*. Juan Ulloa's *Noticias secretas* and Alexandre von Humboldt's *The Political Essay on the Kingdom of New Spain* also contain interesting data on this head.

in the world, he refers to the democracy as evolved and nurtured in the municipality.[15]

The achievements of the municipalities of Iberia are many. It was the municipality that developed that thing which we call Spanish, and which conserved and intensified that thing on down through the centuries. Especially important were the services of the municipalities in resisting foreign invasion. It was the municipality that offered the most successful resistance to the invaders during the Carthaginian conquest. The same was true to an even greater degree during the Roman, Teutonic, and Mussulmanic conquests. The greatest success was achieved by them in the northwest, in the north, and in the northeast of the peninsula. It was in Austria, Cantabria, the Basque Provinces, and in Cataluña that the invaders made the least progress. Leaving out of account Cataluña, it may be said that the municipalities of those regions were never really reduced to the status of conquered territories. These territories, therefore, came to be the very *heart* of Iberia. And from out of these territories came the ideas and the forces which ultimately enabled Iberia to come into its own.

Throughout the long rule of the Romans, more than six hundred years, these municipalities preserved intact that which was in reality their very selves. The same can be said for them also in the period of the Teutonic domination, a period lasting over two hundred years. Modifications there were, to be sure, and not unimportant, but no modifications of really fundamental importance. It is customary to speak of the Spanish municipal system as being Roman in origin. The influence of the Romans in that part of the peninsula over which they ruled, and that included by far the greater portion of Iberia, was unquestionably very great. But two things should be borne in mind in this connection. The first is the cardinal fact that Rome was very tolerant towards a conquered people in that she did, frequently, permit them to retain their own laws and forms of government. The second is, as already noted above, that the territories in the northern part of Spain were never really reduced to the status of conquered colonies, and this in spite of the fact, so often stated, that Spain was more Roman than Rome itself. There can be no question, therefore, of the influence of Rome upon the political life of the Iberians. Neither must it be for-

[15] Consult J. P. Oliveira Martins' *A History of Iberian Civilization* (translated by A. F. G. Bell). While this work is not cited often by present-day historians, yet it is an excellent study of the very essence of Spanish civilization, and will bear careful study.

gotten that a conquered people will, on regaining emancipation, revert to the customs, manners, and institutions of the period when they were free. Again, there will be modifications; but the point here is that it was the Celtiberian, not the Roman, municipal system which came to the fore upon the fall of the Roman rule. The same was true of the Teutonic rule. It may even be said that the influence of the Teutons upon Iberia was greater than that of Rome, as far as the municipalities are concerned. The Teutons were lovers of democracy and hence appealed to the Celtiberians through their love of democracy. That which is to be noted, therefore, is that the latent democracy in the Celtiberian municipaliy found expression in the democracy of the invading Teutons. Even the languages of these regions of Iberia have remained less affected by outside influences than any of the other languages of the peninsula.

The municipalities played even a more important rôle during the Mussulmanic invasion. It was in Asturia that the Mussulman met defeat. For it was to Asturia that the Teutons fled from the Mussulmanic inundation. The court of Toledo—Toledo was the capital of Visigothic Spain—fled to Asturia. It was here under the leadership of Pelayo, a descendant of the Teutonic monarchs, that they joined with the Asturians against the common enemy. And it was in Asturia that the idea of the Christian reconquest took form, and where the reëstablishment of the Visigothic monarchy was determined upon. It took, to be sure, more than seven hundred years to achieve this end; but the *end* was achieved. And the achievement is the thing to note. The Teutonic idea of monarchy was taken as the *norm* for the *new* monarchy. It is probably more accurate, historically, to say that, as has been stated above, it was the Visigothic monarchy that was reëstablished. Historians are, naturally, not agreed on this point. The Latin school is inclined to minimize the influence of the Teutonic factor and point to the influence which Rome must have had upon the development of monarchial institutions in the peninsula. This school of historians is strengthened in its position through the fact that the Roman Catholic Church had such a very powerful influence upon the political life of Iberia. There can be no denying the fact that the ecclesiastical institutions, as developed by the Roman Catholic Church, had a very definite effect upon the development of political institutions in Iberia both during the Visigothic period and the period of the Christian reconquest. The Teutonic school, on the other hand, claims that it was the Visigothic idea of a monarchy that was introduced in the peninsula following the downfall of the Roman rule, and that it was that monarchy which formed the norm for

Pelayo and his followers in the formative period of the Spanish monarchy, and was a means of driving the Mussulman out of the peninsula. The members of this school point to the fact that all the kingdoms of western Europe took from the Teutons the idea of kingship and developed it along the lines demanded by the needs of their people. While the writer himself feels that the Teutonic school has the better of the argument, he has no intention whatever to pass judgment upon a question about which such great controversies have raged in the past and which are quite likely to continue in the future.[16]

A word should be said further about the nature of the rule of the Visigoths in Iberia. While they possessed themselves of nearly all of the peninsula, they were in the minority, numerically, and never really Germanized Iberia. The same can be said for the Suevi, the Teutonic people who played such a large rôle in the formation of the Portuguese kingdom. It is indeed more accurate to say that both the Visigoths and the Suevi, and not the Iberians, were conquered. The Visigoths, Arians though they were in their interpretation of Christianity, had never been able, either in Gaul or in Iberia, to overcome the Athanasians. They were defeated by the Roman Christians in Gaul under Clovis and by him driven out of Gaul; and they surrendered to the Roman Christians in Spain at the Third Council of Toledo in 586 when their King Reccared gave up Arianism for Roman Catholicism. This act of King Reccared was very generally followed by his subjects, although the struggle between the followers of Arius and Athanasius in Spain did not cease until eighty years later. This strife between them merely tended to weaken the Visigothic rule in Iberia. But despite that fact, it was the Teutonic idea of monarchy that prevailed and it was preserved and strengthened throughout the turbulent and chaotic period of the reconquest.

On the west of the Iberian range the kingdoms of Oviedo, Asturia, León, Castilla, and Sevilla were established gradually, and were finally merged into the Kingdom of Castilla. On the east of that range the

---

[16] Rafael Altamira in his *History of Spanish Civilization,* M. Colmeiro in his *Cortes de los antiguos reinos,* F. Martínez Marina in his *Teorias de los cortes,* etc., and M. Bofarull y Romanña in his *Las antiguas cortes,* etc., all support, in the main, the Teutonic Origin of the *Cortes.* R. B. Merriman in his *The Rise of the Spanish Empire in the Old World and in the New* on page 205, volume I, declares that the Castilian monarchy descended from the Visigothic monarchy. He holds that Pelayo claimed that he was a descendant of the ancient Visigothic monarchs. In fact, Dr. Merriman accepts the Teutonic theory of the origin of the Spanish monarchy.

kingdoms of Aragón, Navarra, Valencia, and Cataluña were gradually established, and were finally merged into the Kingdom of Aragón. It was not until 1516, however, upon the accession of Charles I, that the kingdoms of Castilla and Aragón were merged into the Kingdom of Spain. And it was not until 1709 that the *Cortes,* the national legislature of Spain, if it may be so called, was summoned for the whole of the Kingdom of Spain. And even then the Spanish nation was not definitely formed. There are still Spains within Spain.

The municipality early secured a *fuero.* This term *feuro* has different meanings.[17] It may mean a set of privileges for a particular municipality, or it may mean a constitution or a code of laws. Of peculiar interest is the variety in the *fueros,* for rarely were two principalities given exactly the same *fuero.* In general, the purpose of the *fuero* was the same, namely, the granting of special privileges to a municipality by the monarch. But whatever may have been the purpose or the nature of the *fueros,* they were guarded with a zeal and a determination to defend them that made the *fuero* of a given municipality something inalienable and almost sacred. It was doubtless the possession of a *fuero* and the struggle for its possession that made the municipality of Iberia the school of "all that was the highest and best in the political life of the time." [18] The variety of the *fueros* was also of very great significance. The importance of this variety for the Castilian cities is thus explained by Dr. Merriman: [19]

> "The number and variety of these local *fueros* which were given out at different times by different sovereigns, and also, through delegated or usurped authority, by the greater lords and higher clergy, was probably the most fruitful cause of the social and constitutional diversity of mediæval Castile."

As the municipality grew larger and became economically more powerful, the crown sought its aid against a rebellious nobility and an ambitious clergy. The latter had early become a political factor in Iberia. This was natural for its members were not infrequently intellectually very able men and often very highly educated. The monarchs came to lean on the clergy, making use of its members as ministers and advisers. This was true not only of Iberia but throughout Roman Catholic Chris-

---

[17] The word *fuero* comes from the Latin *forum.* It was the term meaning tribunal or court among the Romans, but had other meanings. There is of course a great deal of material on the Spanish *fueros.* Mention may be made of Altamira, Lozano and Pidal, Sacristán y Martínez, and Hinojosa.

[18] R. B. Merriman, *The Rise of the Spanish Empire,* I, p. 184.

[19] *Ibid.,* I, p. 185.

tendom up until our own times. In fact, one of the several practices transplanted into the Indies was that of employing members of the higher clergy as officers of the crown. In order to curb the political power of the clergy, the crown assumed control of the relations between itself and the pope. By 1600 this control was about absolute including the right to control appointments to positions in the church, the right to permit or refuse to admit papal documents into the kingdom, the right to permit or refuse to permit the establishment of religious orders in the kingdom, and many other rights.[20]

In return for the services rendered the king by the towns in his struggle with the nobility and the clergy, the king granted additional rights and privileges. The larger cities, like Burgos, Toledo, León, Barcelona, Valladolid, Saragossa, Sevilla, Córdoba, and Valencia, exerted a powerful influence in the political life of their respective territories and even in the affairs of the whole peninsula. The eleventh, twelfth, and thirteenth centuries were the golden age of the municipalities in Spain. As the municipalities grew more powerful, especially through their representation in the *Cortes,* they began to want a larger share in the affairs of state. They wanted a share in the government of the kingdom.

This end the municipalities strove to reach through unions known as *hermandades,* or brotherhoods. The more powerful of these *hermandades* were doubtless those organized in Castilla and Aragón. The *hermandad* of Castilla was at its height in 1315, and it practically ruled the kingdom at that time. In 1520 the *hermandad* of Castilla actually took up arms against the king. It demanded that Charles I, then Emperor Charles V of the Holy Roman Empire, should return to Spain to reside there permanently, that he should rid himself of all his foreign advisers and officers, that he should agree not to employ foreigners in any capacity in the kingdom, and that he should put an end to the abuses of his ministers.[21] But the *hermandad* had overreached its power and was definitely defeated. But while it was defeated, it left an example

[20] The subject of the relation between church and state in Spain, as well as in Spanish America, is a large one. Consult Cleven's *Readings in Hispanic American History* and his monograph on "The Ecclesiastical Policy of Maximilian of Mexico" in *The Hispanic American Historical Review* for 1928. The recent book by Professor Mecham on the relation between the Hispanic American republics and the Vatican treats of this whole subject in detail.

[21] Consult volume III of Dr. Merriman's work on *The Rise of the Spanish Empire* for a detailed account of this final clash between Charles I and the municipalities of his kingdom.

of what the municipalities could do in the hour of a great crisis. There are instances in which the examples of the *comuneros* of 1520 were used both in Spain and in Spanish America.

With the defeat of the *hermandad* in Castilla in 1520 began the decline of the municipalities in that country. The king triumphed over the municipalities there as he had over the nobility and over the clergy. Out of the struggle came the hatred of the foreigner which is so pronounced in many of the eighteen Spanish American republics today. There resulted also the struggle between the church and the state. This hatred toward the foreigner and this struggle between the church and the state constitute a legacy of no mean importance. No account, however brief, of the political life of Spanish America is possible without some attention to this legacy. The decline of the municipalities in Spain in the sixteenth century was a natural result of the conditions of the age. It was an age in which a highly centralized national government was essential. The election of Charles I to the position of Emperor of the Holy Roman Empire made such a centralization of the national government necessary. But even more important than that was the prevailing notion of the rights of kings and the position of the people in relation to the kings. It must also be added that the work of the Catholic Monarchs of Spain had laid the groundwork for such centralization of power. The House of Austria and the House of France could not allow, of course, such nurseries of political democracy as the cities to continue. There have rarely been greater champions of the divine right theory of monarchs than the Haspburgs and the Bourbons.

The municipality was one of the most important political institutions transplanted in the Indies. And it was the first political institution to be so transplanted. Cristóbal Colón was empowered, as were the leaders of all authorized expeditions to the New World, to found municipalities. Colón founded Isabella in 1493, the first European municipality to be set up in the New World. Other municipalities were founded by him in *Española*. *Conquistadores* very naturally followed his example. By the end of the eighteenth century Spain had founded hundreds of municipalities in America. Even where there was no appointed leader, any group of ten men (heads of families) was authorized by Spanish law to found municipalities, and to organize and govern them in the name of the crown. The most conspicuous example, perhaps, of this law was the founding of Vera Cruz in 1519 by Hernán Cortés and his men.[22]

---

[22] It is difficult to understand why Cortés should have organized Vera Cruz for the purpose for which it is claimed he organized the municipality, namely, to give

The American municipalities were organized and governed according to the Old World model. The one marked difference, if difference it can be called, lay in the fact that the membership of the *cabildo,* or *ayuntamiento,* as the municipal council was called, might be, and very often was, selected from the Creole class. This fact is of tremendous importance since the Creoles were very generally excluded from the offices of the state and of the church. The *cabildo,* including the *cabildo abierto,* or open town meeting, was the one body to which the Creoles were eligible, and in which they found a school of practical politics. The Creoles made good use of their opportunities. They soon became critical of the colonial administration and were not slow to seek reforms. This training in municipal government, even after most of the offices of the municipality became vendible, was invaluable to the Creoles; for it was the Creoles who were, ultimately, to take charge of the formation of new governments upon the overthrow of the rule of Spain.[23] The fact, before alluded to, that the capital city of a viceroyalty, a captaincy general, or a *presidencia,* enjoyed jurisdiction over the entire colony of which it was the capital, with the obligation of assuming charge of the government thereof until the regularly appointed representatives of the crown were duly installed, made the *cabildos* and the *cabildos abiertos* very important indeed. There is no time for details, but evidence is on record showing that Mexico City, Lima, Bogotá, and Buenos Aires ruled over the entire viceroyalty *ad interim,* awaiting the installation of the newly appointed viceroy. The same can be shown to have been the case with Santiago de Chile, Asunción, Caracas, and Guatemala City.[24]

The municipality was also the seat of the ecclesiastical institutions, except the missions, but including the universities and colleges. Obviously the ecclesiastical institutions exercised no mean influence upon the political affairs of the Indies. Here again it is necessary to have in mind that the government of the church was a rather complicated matter,

legality to his acts, as the officer of this municipality, on the expedition into Mexico. Cortés was an outlaw, and his men who helped organize Vera Cruz were his accomplices. It seems more nearly accurate to say that Vera Cruz was organized by Cortés as the leader of the original plan.

[23] The student of Spain in America is struck with the failure of the mother country to conciliate the Creoles. The Creoles were not infrequently one of the most exclusive classes in the Indies, and should have been invested with a larger share in the government.

[24] The student of the Spanish municipalities in America will find the *Actas de los cabildos* of the several cities of Spanish America unusually illuminating and instructive.

and, as such, demanded men trained to manage it. The ecclesiastical *cabildo* was a center of activity for the Creoles, even to a greater extent than the civil *cabildo* of the city, or municipality, for the government of the church was more democratic and nearer the people than the civil *cabildo*. The church was an avenue through which even a fisherman's son might attain to the highest church offices. That is to say, the Roman Catholic Church, even in aristocratic Spanish lands, practiced the rugged democracy for which it has always been noted. The reward of merit may have come slowly, but evidences show that merit, irrespective of birth and class membership, did receive its reward.

The importance, politically, of the universities and colleges in the Indies is evident to all who have any knowledge of the subject. Two of the most powerful universities in the Indies, that of San Marcos at Lima and that in Mexico City, were founded in the fifties of the sixteenth century. Others followed, until by the end of the eighteenth century there were twenty universities in operation in the Indies, all of them modeled upon the celebrated University of Salamanca. To attempt to dismiss the universities as engaged only in a study of the classics and of theology is to admit the greatest ignorance. The leading universities were noted for their brilliant work in law and jurisprudence. Among the most powerful of these was the University of Saint Xavier of Charcas, now Sucre. It must be admitted, of course, that much of the renown of this university comes from its close relationship with the famous and celebrated *Academia Carolina*. To this university came thousands of the young men from all the different parts of the Indies. The fact of the wonderfully invigorating climate, the distance from the viceregal power, the wealth and power of Potosí, and the presence of powerful men as *oidores* of the *Audiencia* of Charcas, all have a bearing upon the making of this powerful educational institution.[25] The rôle of the universities, therefore, in moulding the political life of Spanish America cannot be overestimated. The universities, too, were schools of practical politics, for the students did not confine themselves merely to a study of the theories of government, but were not above, even as the students of many of the universities of Spanish America today, taking an active part in openly opposing the government.

[25] Consult Gabriel Mariano Moreno's excellent work on *Los últimos días de la colonia* for a detailed account of the work of the University of Charcas and of the *Academia Carolina*. Charcas, the city of eternal springtime, was a fit place for intellectual vigor. Not only the climate but its scholastic traditions—it was a Jesuit institution—fostered this intellectual activity. The people of Sucre have just cause for being proud of their school.

We are very apt to overlook, or minimize the work of the universities of Lima, Mexico City, Charcas, Córdoba, Bogotá, Guatemala (*La Antigua*), and Santiago de Chile in the formative period of the new Spanish American states. It was men trained in these institutions, many of whom subsequently travelled and studied in Spain and elsewhere in Europe, and many of whom were great students of political government, who became the leaders of the period.[26]

The wars of emancipation were, of course, the work of the Creoles. The *mestizos* gave them much assistance, in the large, but it was primarily the Creoles who took the leadership, and who remained in charge throughout the wars, and who took the lead in the formation of independent governments. It should also be borne in mind, in this connection, that the wars of emancipation had their beginnings in universities. It was young Bernardo Monteagudo, one of the most celebrated sons of Charcas and of the University of Saint Xavier and of *La Academia Carolina,* who was one of the prime leaders in the events of May 25, 1809 which ushered in the wars of emancipation in the Indies. But he is only one of hundreds, for each of these several universities had alumni among the leaders of the period. The university buildings were not infrequently the meeting places of revolutionary activities. The *Aula Major* of the University of Saint Xavier is an almost sacred place now because in it many of the most important events in the formative period of Bolivia took place. The Bolivians justly consider the *Aula Major* as a national shrine of hallowed memory.[27] The conclusion is, accordingly, warranted that the municipality in the Indies took a major rôle in all the more important political crises in Spanish America, and that the *cabildos abiertos* were especially useful as vehicles of expressions of the sentiments of the people. It may also be said that the public town meetings of the British American colonies were, relatively speaking, no whit more important in moulding the political life of its people than the *cabildo abierto* of Spanish America.

---

26 Consult the writer's chapter on "Modern Political Life in Hispanic America" in volume I of this series of studies.

27 The writer had the great privilege of visiting the *Aula Major* of the old University of Saint Xavier and must own to a feeling of great admiration for it, not only as a national shrine, but as a great university auditorium. It retains some of the old grandeur that belonged to this great institution, and is a concrete example of the power and influence of the Jesuits who established it and made it one of the greatest universities in the New World for more than two hundred years. This *aula* and the university of *La Antigua,* Guatemala impressed the writer as the two finest examples of the universities of the Indies.

IV

The other powerful institution affecting the political activities of the Spaniards of America was the *Cortes.* The legacy of the development, power, and influence of this institution is of even greater importance to us in this connection than the municipality itself. For it must be noted that while the municipality was reduced to a very subordinate position shortly after independence was achieved, the legislative bodies of the new governments have grown in importance with the passing of time. Of course they have suffered at times in their struggle with the national chief executives, but the people sooner or later regain their control through the legislative branch of their government.[28]

Like the British Parliament, the *Cortes*[29] was never transplanted to America. The question of the origin of the *Cortes* need not detain us, for it is still shrouded in the deepest mystery. Here again we find two distinct schools of thought regarding its origin—the same schools in fact which are concerned with the origin of the Spanish monarchy. The Teutonic school believes, of course, that the *Cortes,* like the English Parliament, are Teutonic in origin. The Visigoths, whom we have seen in control of Iberia immediately following the Romans and before the Mussulmans, evolved, as did the Angles, Saxons, and Jutes in England, and the Franks, the Burgundians, and the Lombards in France, a great national assembly as well as a great national council. The national assembly was composed of the freemen. Later the monarch surrounded himself with advisers from the upper class and from the clergy. This body came in time to be the national council. The date of this division in the government power and in the composition of the different bodies is not known. As in the case of the English Parliament, so in the case of the *Cortes* of Spain, there is no definite proof that either grew out of these earlier governmental bodies. The Latin school believes of course, that the development of the legislative bodies of the countries of western Europe is an independent growth, and that the origin of those bodies lies rather in Rome than in the lands of the Teutons. It must be admitted that neither school is able to point to the connecting link between the bodies from which the national legislature may have sprung

---

[28] The leaders of the formative period of the independent states of Spanish America looked upon the municipalities as dangerous to their right of domination, and opposed them. The municipalities have had few opponents more powerful than Simón Bolívar. Consult the work by C. Parra-Pérez on *Simón Bolívar: An Introduction to His Political Ideas* translated by the writer.

[29] The word *Cortes* is the plural of the Spanish word *Corte,* and is used by the Spaniards only in the plural.

and the national legislature as it came to be. The problem, therefore, of the origin of the *Cortes,* like that of the English Parliament, remains unsolved. The writer, having in mind what has been said on the origin of the municipalities of Iberia, must own that he leans toward the Teutonic origin of the *Cortes;* and that the reasons are about the same in the case of both the municipality and the *Cortes.*[30] The student of the origin of the Spanish *Cortes* must not ignore the national councils of the Visigoths. These were called the Councils of Toledo, having been held in Toledo, the capital of Visigothic Spain. At least seventeen of these Councils of Toledo were held before 711, and all are rather well accounted for.[31] And during the ninth, tenth, eleventh, and most of the twelfth centuries, that is during the period of the restoration of the monarchy in Iberia, councils were held similar to those held in Toledo in the pre-Mussulmanic period. The nobility and the clergy seem to have been members of these councils as in the Councils of Toledo.

The question of the representation of the third estate in this national legislature is even still more complicated. The origin of the representation of the third estate in the *Cortes* is fully as difficult to determine as is the representation of the same estate in England. Historians, such as Colmeiro and Altamira, are however agreed upon two definite dates marking the precise time when there can be no question of the presence of members of the third estate in the *Cortes.* These dates are 1163 for Aragón and 1188 for León and Castilla. It is, of course, to be remembered that representatives from the third estate were sent to meetings of the *Cortes* in each kingdom before these dates. Even at that, the Spanish people achieved the right of representation for the third estate almost a hundred years before the people of England.[32] The students of the English parliamentary system are agreed, it seems, that the date 1276 marks the definite datc when the third estate received summons from the king to send representatives to the English Parliament. Again

---

[30] The authorities cited in connection with the discussion of the origin of the municipality may be referred to here. Consult also R. B. Merriman's "Cortes of the Spanish Kingdoms in the Later Middle Ages" in the *American Historical Review,* XVI, pp. 476-495. Also see R. Altamira's "Magna Carta and Spanish Medieval Jurisprudence" in H. E. Malden's *Magna Carta Commemoration Essays,* and the work by M. Colmeiro. Consult Merriman for further bibliographical references.

[31] Consult M. Colmeiro on the work of the Councils of Toledo.

[32] Dr. Charles McIllwain has much material of great value in his chapter on the rise of the third estates in Europe in volume VII of the *Cambridge Mediæval History.* Consult *Cortes de los antiguos reinos de León y de Castilla,* especially the *Introducción* by M. Colmeiro.

it must be noted that the third estate in England may have had representation in Parliament prior to 1276.

A word should be written about the operation of the Spanish *Cortes*. The right to summon members to that body, except in the case of the nobles, and the right to determine the date and place of meeting, as well as the right to determine what business was to be transacted in the *Cortes* were the exclusive prerogative of the monarch. The right to determine the number of representatives from the second and third estates belonged to the monarch. The third estate was represented by *procuradores* from the municipalities. The summons came to the *cabildo,* in the form of a royal writ, commanding it to select a certain number of *procuradores* to the *Cortes,* leaving the manner of selection to the *cabildo.* There was a variety of ways of selecting the *procuradores,* but the more common form was some form of election. The number of *procuradores* from each municipality also varied: one, two, three, or even four were chosen, depending upon the size of the municipality. The third estate never reached the stage where it could demand a summons from the monarch to the *Cortes,* to determine the number of its own representatives, or to determine the frequency of the meetings of the *Cortes.* The monarch never surrendered the right to determine these matters. Nor was any municipality ever chosen as the permanent meeting place of the *Cortes.*

Despite these limitations, the municipalities played an important rôle in the *Cortes* during the twelfth and thirteenth centuries, the period in which the *Cortes* was at the height of power and influence. The *cabildo* guarded jealously the right, which seems to have been granted it from the beginning, of controlling the action of its *procuradores* in the *Cortes.* This control was secured through the *poderes,* or instructions issued to the *procuradores.* The *poderes* were both general and specific, often describing in great detail what the *procuradores* might and might not do. If business were introduced in the *Cortes* for which the *procuradores* had no specific *poderes,* they were obliged to await new *poderes* from the *cabildo.* In no case were the *procuradores* permitted to deviate the slightest from this rule. Instances are on record of *procuradores* who, acting contrary to their *poderes* were prosecuted as traitors to the country, and of some who were even executed for this crime.[33]

[33] Consult R. Altamira's *A History of Spanish Civilization,* page 135. This is the work edited by J. R. Trend. Altamira states that a *procurador* from Segovia had been hanged because he had voted for certain taxes in the *Cortes* against the instructions of the *cabildo.*

The *cabildo* also appears to have acquired the right, from the very first, of presenting petitions to the king in *Cortes*. Needless to say this right was held, as it has been held throughout the existence of the present Spanish American republics, as almost a sacred right. Elaborate *cuadernos de peticiones,* as the collections of petitions to the king in *Cortes* were called, were prepared for all the meetings of the *Cortes*. Such *cuadernos* were presented to the *Cortes* when that body met merely to give the oath of allegiance to the heir to the throne, or to a new ruler; and to receive in return from the heir or the ruler a promise to preserve, protect, and defend the rights, liberties, and laws of the kingdom.[34] It must be evident that the *poderes* and *cuadernos* were very useful to the men who created new governments in Spain and in the Indies.

Of even greater importance, perhaps, was the work of the *Cortes* in codifying laws. The more important of these were the *Lex Romana Visigothorum* of Aleric, the *Fuero Juzgo* of Kings Chindaswinth and Recceswinth, the *Fuero Real* or the *Fuero de las Leyes,* the *Espéculo,* and the *Siete Partidas*. The first antedates, of course, the Spanish *Cortes,* for it was really a work of Aleric of Italy. Nor can the second be said to have been the work of the *Cortes* as such. The two are important, however, to the student of the history of the Spanish *Cortes,* because it gives an idea of the tremendously fierce struggle between the men who favored the Teutonic and the men who favored the Roman elements of law. The result was largely a compromise, as a study, at least, of the *Siete Partidas* will reveal. That the people through the *Cortes* had a part in the final codification of the *fueros* and laws of Spain, can hardly be denied. The only point at issue might be the degree of share the people had in the process of such codification.

The three estates also clung tenaciously to the right to accept or refuse to accept a new ruler, to the right to depose an unworthy ruler and to select his successor, and to the right to establish a new dynasty when the dynasty had become extinct or had been deposed. Even Charles I, much as he disliked the idea, had to appear before four different *Cortes* in as many different kingdoms to receive the oath of allegiance and to give in return the usual oath of the monarch assuming the reigns of government; that is, he was obliged to appear in Burgos for Castilla, in Sara-

---

34 These *cuadernos* and *poderes,* a large number of which are still in a good state of preservation, contain, as do the *actas de cabildos,* a great deal of very valuable source material. No student of the period would be able to give an adequate picture of the life of the times, social, ecclesiastical, as well as political, without recourse to these materials.

gossa for Aragón, in Valencia for Valencia, and in Barcelona for Cataluña. And Philip V, too, was obliged to have the *Cortes* consent to his claims to the throne of Spain. He called the famous *Cortes* of Madrid of 1713 for that express purpose. It was at this *Cortes* that he appeared as the King of the whole of Spain, the first example of its kind in the history of the country.

V

The memory of the achievements of the *cabildos* and of the *Cortes* in the day of their greatness served the people admirably well during the period of the Napoleonic invasion. It was this legacy, this inheritance, this heritage, call it what you will, of the great lore of a glorious past that guided the men of the peninsula, as it did the men of the Indies, in an effort to establish a government capable of driving the French from Spanish soil, and of restoring Ferdinand VII. The people of France never studied the *cahiers* with greater interest than did these Spaniards in the hour of their great struggle against the sinister designs of the Little Corsican. It was during this period that the Spanish people determined to put an end to absolute government in Spain as well as in America. That there were relapses into absolutism in Spain was to be expected, but too much emphasis should not be placed on that phase of our story. After all, these lapses from the grace of liberalism were not of long duration. It is true, however, that more than a century was to pass before the republican form was substituted in Spain for the monarchical form of government, the precise date of that event being 1931.

The period of the Napoleonic invasion saw the *cabildo abierto* play an unusually important rôle in Spain no less than in Spanish America. Throughout Spain and Spanish America, whenever such a thing was possible, the *cabildos abiertos* took up the common cause. The process very naturally began in Spain, then spread to the colonies in America. In 1809 the National Provisional *Junta* of Spain declared, in a moment of idealistic impulse, that there was no longer any dividing line between Spaniards of America and those of Spain. They were *all* Spaniards.

But laudible as this act undoubtedly was, it was an act which the mother country was soon to rue, for the Spaniards of America proceeded to put the new policy into practice. They justly claimed that since they had a larger population than Spain they had a right to the larger share in the government of the larger Spanish Kingdom. The Spaniards of Spain very naturally declined to agree to such a proposition. The members of the *Deputación Americana* in the sessions of the *Cortes* of 1810-1813 may have overreached itself; but it can hardly be blamed for desiring to inaugurate a new era in governmental affairs.[35] The attitude of Spanish America began gradually to change as soon as it sensed the unwillingness of the home government to institute the reforms in the government which the Spanish American leaders felt essential to larger success. Instead of aiding merely in restoring Ferdinand VII to his throne in Spain, Spanish America began to work for complete political independence. The leaders of Spanish America proceeded on the assumption that the sovereignty had reverted to the people on the overthrow of the old monarchy, and that the people had an unquestioned right to determine their own form of government.[36] And they proceeded to establish such governments.

VI

There are those, and among them are found many of the scholars and publicists of Spanish America, who state that the form of government established in Spanish America was based upon existing forms of government. This seems to be founded on rumors rather than on facts. It is, of course, not to be denied that the founders of the new governments in America drew heavily upon existing political institutions. It is claimed that they drew very heavily upon the political institutions of the United States of America. One may bluntly ask, in passing, why the Fathers of the Spanish American republics should have imitated our forms of government? Others declare that the leaders of Spanish America imitated France. There would appear to be much more truth in the latter assertion than in the former. After all, the Constitution of the United States was hardly suitable to the purposes of the leaders of Spanish America. The constitutions of France were, of course, more democratic than our constitution and for that reason appealed more to them than our instrument did.

But why believe that it was necessary for these leaders to imitate? There were among them great students of political theory, men who knew, as few of our Fathers did, most of the known political theories, ancient, medieval, and modern, of Europe and America. Francisco de Miranda and Simón Bolívar are only two of many men who were thor-

---

[35] Consult the *Actas of the Cortes* of Cádiz of 1810-1813. They contain materials of great interest as well as of great importance.

[36] This phase of the narrative has been dealt with by the writer in his chapter on "Modern Political Life in Hispanic America" in volume I of this series.

oughly familiar with the political theories of England, France, and the United States, as well as those of Greece and Rome. All of them sought not merely for forms to blindly imitate, but sought for ideas useful to them in forming a government suitable for their own peculiar needs. These leaders went to the same sources that the Fathers of our country did, and to which those of France did a little later. The several constitutions which were produced in Spanish America after 1811, are proofs of the sincere efforts of the leaders to evolve a form of government believed to be suitable for their purposes. A careful study of the several fundamental laws drawn up after 1812 will reveal how largely the Spanish Americans drew upon Spanish sources for the form as well as the content of those instruments. It was the Constitution of Spain of 1812,[37] modified to suit the needs of the new republics, and not the Constitution of the United States or the constitutions of France, that served as the prototype of the earlier fundamental laws, at least.

VII

A word should also be written about federalism as a heritage from Old Spain. The struggle between federalism and unitarianism in Iberia began long before the history of that country was written. The struggle was pronounced in the age of the Celtiberians, and it has continued down through the centuries. And the end is not yet, as the conduct of the Catalonians under the republican régime will show. The struggle between federalism and unitarianism in England and in the United States has been no whit more important, as far as the struggle itself is concerned, than the struggle between these principles in Spain and in Spanish America.

Regionalism has been, and still is, one of the most important single political factors in the political life of the Spanish people in the New World, as well as in the Old World. The monarchy as finally established in Spain was a federal monarchy. And even a cursory acquaintance with the political history of Spanish America will reveal the rôle of rampant regionalism there. It is not necessary to dwell upon a fact that is so well known. Argentina is probably the best example of regionalism at its worst in Spanish America. In the struggle that lasted in that country for more than sixty years there was developed the *caudillo* at his worst. During that period the *gaucho caudillo*, the cowboy mili-

[37] Consult the author's translation of *The Constitutions of Spain of 1808 and 1812.* While the Constitution of 1812 was monarchial in charter, it furnished many democratic features.

tary chieftain, as he might be called, played a very important rôle. Juan Manuel de Rosas may still be said to have the best claim to be considered the *gaucho caudillo par excellence;* and the *caudillaje* developed by him must be taken as the essence of *personalismo caudillo.*

VIII

What shall be said, in conclusion, of the capacity of the Spanish Americans for political government? Before passing judgment we should note that many of the malpractices of the leaders of Spanish America are also due to the heritage of the mother country. Graft, inefficiency, indifference, and downright dishonesty in government were not foreign to the Fathers of the Spanish American republics. The colonial government throughout the Indies was replete with such things. And matters were no better in Spain itself. Bluntly stated, this attitude toward government, this feeling that government is run not for the good of the people but for professional politicians, is a legacy from Old Spain. One thing seems perfectly evident, and that is that this seeming lack of political ability is not due merely to the ignorance of political theory and political practice. This is another of the myths which it would be well to discard at once. The Spanish Americans cannot be excused so easily.

There is, to be sure, no dearth of ignorance or lack of political experience among many who manipulate politics in Spanish America. The governmental malpractices and the political ills of Spanish America, as elsewhere, are due rather to the perverted nature of men in public office. Not all men in public office are thus afflicted, to be sure; but, even at that, the number of such men is far too large. That politics have a way of poisoning good men, even among the finest people in the world, is a well-known fact. This statement that the political inability of the Spanish Americans is due to the perverted nature of professional politicians may sound quite commonplace. But its commonplaceness does not alter the facts, and must not blind us to its importance. Politics is all too often a game with the men of Spanish America, a profession, a means of livelihood. The professions, including politics, are very generally overcrowded. The contest degenerates, therefore, not infrequently, into a struggle of the *outs* to dislodge the *ins.* The proverbial love of adventure of the Spaniards does not improve matters. It rather makes the situation all the more important.[38] Most, if not all, of the

[38] Consult the writings of Dr. Charles E. Chapman, especially his *History of the Cuban Republic,* for an intelligent and courageous account of politics in operation in Spanish America. His recent article in *The Hispanic American Historical Review* on the age of the *caudillos* is also very illuminating.

professional politicians make a sport of civic virtue; men exploit the worse side of a gullible citizenry, and leech upon the very vitals of the nation. This may seem intemperate language, and an exaggeration of the facts in the case. Observation of the manner in which professional politicians operate in several of these republics, coupled with a rather intimate acquaintance with their history, convinces the writer that the language is hardly strong enough.

There can be no doubt but that professional politics is the bane of Spanish America, as it is in all countries in which it operates. It is not ignorance, but rather too much knowledge of how to manipulate politics to one's own personal advantage that is to blame for this state of affairs. The professional politician of Spanish America, as elsewhere, looks upon political government as something to be controlled by him in the interest of himself and his henchmen. Nowhere do professional politicians know better the gentle art of packing the political pork barrel, and the equally gentle art of dipping the fingers deftly into that barrel, than in Spanish America.

We make a peculiarly serious misake, too, in looking upon these people as young and inexperienced. They are not a young people, but an old people, a people enmeshed in the traditions of the past. Society is stratified, socially and economically; and this is also a heritage of the past. Nor does it seem that the people are really very anxious to get from under this stratification, for such stratification is much too useful for the professional politician for that. The governmental malpractices and the social ills of Spanish America are, so it would seem, the result, rather, of a senile old age. The encrustating slime of red tape, the senseless multiplication of political offices to give some henchmen of the political boss a fat sinecure, the contemptible flaunting of the interests of the people and the welfare of the state, are all evidences of a senile old age.

Is an improvement in their political government possible? The remaking of human nature is not an impossibility! Miracles do happen even in politics. But nothing short of a thorough overhauling of the warped political mindedness of the professional politicians of Spanish America, other than their complete removal altogether from the arena of political life, will do the job. The Augean stables of Spanish American politics most certainly need a thorough cleansing. Who is there to do the job? The citizens, the great majority of whom are earnestly wishing for such a purging. But it is no easy task, for eternal vigilance is the price of liberty in Spanish America as elsewhere. We may conclude, finally, therefore, that the political ills and governmental malpractices of Spanish America are by no means the innocent things that we are likely to think that they are. They are, rather, the product of the age-old struggle between efficiency and liberty, a struggle which seems to know no end.

II. ARGENTINA

By J. Fred Rippy

CHAPTER THREE

THE ENVIRONMENT AND THE NATIVE RACES

I

IN A SENSE, the history of "modern" Argentina may be said to begin with the discovery of this region by the Europeans, for the discovery took place after the beginning of the epoch which is usually termed "modern." In these lectures, however, the period since 1810 will be emphasized, for two reasons: (1) time and space is limited, and (2) the events which have transpired in this region since 1810 are considered more important.

History is concerned for the most part with the relations of men and groups of men with each other and with their natural environment. Their environment, human and nonhuman, is both immediate and remote. In the modern period of history no group of human beings has been left free to deal exclusively with each other and with the geographical area delimited by their national boundaries. The destiny of any given group is influenced by the destiny of many other groups, whether these be neighbors or whether they dwell across distant seas. Modern history has been characterized by an interchange of ideas, techniques, and commodities throughout a vast area which may be denominated as western civilization. In fact, during much of this epoch the interchange has been world-wide.

Argentine history has been influenced by the history of its American neighbors, by events and developments in Europe, and at times by the activities of groups of men outside of Europe and America. During the modern era there has existed a considerable degree of political isolation under the creed of national sovereignty, but economic isolation has been more limited. Argentina's economic destiny has been closely linked with that of the leading western nations—that is, those of western Europe and America—and it has also been connected to some extent with world economy. New ideas, new tastes, changes in the purchasing power of consumers, progress in science and technology, no matter where they have occurred, have usually exerted a profound influence on Argentine civilization.

These assertions may appear commonplace, but it is necessary to emphasize them if the history of modern Argentina is to be understood. The desire for democracy and liberty probably originated in Europe, but it soon reached the people of Argentina and caused important political movements. The idea of progress also had its genesis in modern Europe, but it soon permeated Argentina. The humanitarian spirit did not develop spontaneously among men dwelling on the Río de la Plata, but it nevertheless found lodgment in their minds and stimulated various activities. Certain ideas regarding religious toleration and the relationship of church and state first took form in Europe, but they later had great weight among Argentine statesmen. The steamboat was invented in the United States, but the invention profoundly influenced the destiny of the men of the *pampa.* The steam locomotive and the railway originated in England and the United States, but they finally reached the Argentine and transformed the economic life of the country. The invention and mass production of agricultural machinery in the United States eventually revolutionized Argentine agriculture. Most of the discoveries in modern medicine were not made in southeastern South America, but the people of Argentina have benefited by them. The Argentines did not invent steel windmills, hydraulic pumps, gasoline engines, barbed wire fences, macadamized and cement roads, and processes of refrigeration, but these inventions made important contributions to the development of their country. The inhabitants of the Río de la Plata area did not originate the industrialization of Europe and the United States, with its attendant rapid growth of population and food demands, but these factors had much influence upon the economic development of Argentina. No thinker of the *pampa* wrote *Das Kapital,* but Marxism has tended to unsettle the relations between capitalists and laborers in the Argentine nation. And finally, the destiny of Argentina has been profoundly affected by the migration of peoples and investments.

II

One must not, however, minimize the influence of the immediate environment. The physical geography of Argentina has been a primary influence in the development of the nation.

The area, climate, and natural resources of the Argentine nation possibly justify the expectation that it will eventually become one of the world's first-rate powers. It possesses a territory of more than a million square miles, an area more than three times as large as both France and Germany and somewhat larger than that portion of the United States which lies east of the Mississippi River. It is almost exactly the size of the following states combined: Mississippi, Indiana, Illinois, Wisconsin, Louisiana, Arkansas, Missouri, Iowa, Minnesota, Texas, Oklahoma, Kansas, Nebraska, South Dakota, and North Dakota. And its soil, climate, and topography are more like those of this portion of the United States than of any other region of the world.

About one-fourth of the area of Argentina consists of the great central *pampa;* the ranges and spurs of the Andes, with their intermediate valleys, comprise another fourth; and the other half is about equally divided between the plateaus of Patagonia to the south and the rolling and often wooded plains of the north and northeast. It is estimated that about eighty-two per cent of Argentina's land has economic value either for tillage, pasture, or forests. About one-third of the country is classed as forest land, but it is likely that no more than a sixth contains timber of considerable value. With the exception of a comparatively small region in the north, the entire area of the republic is in the temperate zone. Patagonia, although disagreeable in winter, is by no means as cold as Minnesota and the two Dakotas. More than a third of Argentina is arid or semiarid; somewhat more than a third receives a mean annual rainfall of between sixteen and forty inches; and the rest, mainly in the northeast, receives in excess of forty inches. The potential water power of the country is comparatively small, being estimated at only some five million horsepower. Subterranean water, however, is fairly abundant.

Argentina is a land of small mineral wealth. It contains comparatively little coal and iron, two minerals which are thought to be so vital in the development of manufacturing that any country which does not possess them or have access to them in a neighboring region is supposed to be placed under a serious handicap industrially. Tungsten deposits are abundant, but the country's resources in gold, silver, copper, lead, zinc, borax, and antimony, so far as now known, are rather unimportant; and petroleum is apparently far less plentiful than in many other regions of the world. Salt appears to have been sufficiently abundant to take care of the livestock and the meat industry.

The availability of fluvial means of transportation is somewhat limited. Although the rivers which empty into the Plata estuary form one of the great drainage systems of the world, they furnish convenient water transportation for only a small portion of Argentina. Most of the terrain offers few difficulties, however, to railway building, although scarcity of stone in many regions renders the construction of hard-surfaced highways rather expensive. The republic contains several good harbors, and the major part of its territory is comparatively close to the sea.[1]

The heart of Argentina, as well as its most striking physical feature, is the *pampa,* which extends from a thousand to fifteen hundred miles north to south, and from three hundred to five hundred miles east to west. One traveler from the United States was struck with its resemblance to the steppes of "the south of Russia." "Both exhibit," he says,

> "the same boundless, unbroken expanse, the same fertility of the soil during the rainy season, and dry, parched appearance in the heat of summer; the total absence of trees; the streams few, flowing with a sluggish current, and brackish to the taste; the lakes and ponds of both encrusted with salt. . . ."[2]

Another writer of the same period (the second decade of the nineteenth century) describes these plains more vividly:

> "Over this immense space there is not a tree, not a shrub, not a single perennial plant to be seen, save only those few which here and there lift their heads near a herdsman's hut. There are no hills nor eminences, and the undulations are so gentle as only to be perceived by taking a long view over its surface; and then the eye passes round . . . the horizon as over the face of the undulating ocean in a calm. . . . The keen blasts called the pamperos sweep over the . . . unsheltered plain without the least obstruction; and the fierce rays of the sun are felt in all their unmitigated fervor. . . . This interminable plain [is] one of the most expanded and awful solitudes on earth. . . . The pampas are exceedingly productive in grass, and a great portion of them are beset with a species of thistle, which grows from two to seven feet high, and is not unlike our garden artichoke. The only tree that seems to flourish everywhere . . . is the embudo [*ombú*] . . . ; its trunk, however, is a mere watery pulp, and the growth is utterly useless for everything but shade. . . . There is no tradition that, in all this immense extent of territory, . . . one single stick of good timber has been ever found growing at the distance of one mile from the rivers. . . . The pampas are sometimes afflicted with the most wasteful droughts; when vegetation is parched up, the ponds and streams . . . dried. . . ."[3]

---

[1] R. H. Whitbeck, *Economic Geography of South America* (New York, 1926), pp. 207-283; Clarence F. Jones, *South America* (New York, 1930), pp. 301-397; Gaston F. Tobal, *Lecciones de geografía argentina* (Buenos Aires, 1931), pp. 1-117.

[2] Poinsett to Adams, November 4, 1818, in Manning, *Diplomatic Correspondence* (New York, 1925), I, p. 462.

[3] Theodorick Bland to J. Q. Adams, November 2, 1818, in Manning, *op. cit.,* I, pp. 400-402.

Hudson, who lived for years on the *pampa* and knew it as few men did, adds a few interesting touches:

> "We see all around us a flat land, its horizon a perfect ring of misty blue colour where the crystal-blue dome of the sky rests on the level green world. Green . . . from April to November, but not all like a green lawn or field: there were smooth areas . . . , but the surface varied greatly and was mostly more or less rough. . . . There were other breaks and roughnesses on that flat green expanse caused by the vizcachas, a big rodent the size of a hare, a mighty burrower in the earth. . . . The earth thrown out of these diggings formed a mound, and being bare of vegetation it appeared in the landscape as a clay-coloured spot on the green surface. . . . The . . . change in the aspect of the plain would begin in November: the dead, dry grass would take on a yellowish-brown colour, the giant thistle a dark rust brown. . . . It was then, when the water-courses were gradually drying up and the thirsty days coming . . . , that the mocking illusion of the mirage was constantly about us. . . . By the end of November the thistles would be dead, and their huge hollow stalks as dry and light as the shaft of a bird's feather. . . . The roots were not only dead but turned to dust in the ground, so that one could push a stalk from its place with one finger, but it would not fall since it was held up by scores of other sticks all round it, and these by hundreds more, and the hundreds by thousands and millions. . . . At any moment a careless spark . . . might kindle a dangerous blaze . . . [Now] the one desire and hope of every one was for the *pampero*—the southwest wind, which in hot weather is apt to come with startling suddenness, and to blow with extraordinary violence . . . , and there would be thunder and lightning and a torrent of rain. . . . In an hour or two it would perhaps be all over, and the next morning the detested thistles would be gone, or at all events levelled to the ground. [Sometimes these *pamperos* were accompanied by a hail storm.]"[4]

Such were the vast plains of Argentina. For ages they were the haunt of roving Indians, the guanaco, and the rhea (American ostrich); for three centuries they were occupied by wild or semiwild horses and cattle preyed upon by Spanish and half-Indian *gauchos;* and during the last fifty years they have furnished pasture for blooded animals and become one of the important granaries of the world. They have thus been the scene of one of man's most interesting contests with nature.

III

Although the aborigines of Argentina were less numerous than in many other countries of Spanish America, probably never numbering

[4] W. H. Hudson, *Far Away and Long Ago* (New York, 1918), pp. 63-71.

more than two hundred and fifty thousand, they have exerted considerable influence on the history of the country. On Wissler's map of the native cultures of America most of Argentina falls within the guanaco area. A portion of the northeast is in the Amazon area and a part of the northwest may form a part of the Inca area.

Classified according to their speech, the Indians of the region embrace the following important linguistic stocks: the Calchaquian in the mountains and forests of the northeast; the Guaycuruan of the *gran chaco;* the Charruan and Tupian along the great rivers; the Puelchean, spoken by those who roamed over the *pampa;* the Tsonekan, Onan, and Yahganan in Patagonia and Tierra del Fuego; and the Araucanian, which was the language of the natives who lived mainly in Chile but who had some relatives along the eastern slopes of the Andes, in northwestern Patagonia, and in the southwestern part of the *pampa.*

Some of the linguistic stocks embraced several tribes, only a few of which need be mentioned here. The Tupi-speaking Guaranís dwelt in Paraguay and along the northeastern border of Argentina; the Abipones, Chiriguanos, Matacos, and Tobas were the leading Guaycurua-speaking tribes; the Tsonekan stock of Patagonia is often referred to as the Tehuelches; and the Querandís, who dwelt along the lower western bank of the Río de la Plata, probably belonged to the Puelchean stock.

All these aborigines lived mainly upon the products of the chase. The guanaco and the American ostrich (rhea) were the most important game of the area, but the deer and the fox were also plentiful. Monkeys could be found in the forests of the northeast, and the vicuña, useful mainly for its wool, dwelt in the mountains of the northwest. In the extreme south the natives tended to live more on fish and seals. Although some of them cultivated a little maize, their diet of flesh was usually supplemented mainly by wild vegetable products, such as pine nuts, the seed of the mesquite tree, prickly pears, berries, and a few edible grasses. In short, the Argentine aborigines were hunters and not agriculturalists, nomadic and not sedentary; and, with few exceptions, the Spaniards never succeeded in inducing them to change their habits. In the far northwest some of the tribes were more domestic.

Aside from the culture traits which have to do with food, certain others are worth noting. Some of the tribes wove cloth, but work in skins was more extensively developed. The most widely used weapons were the lance, the *bolas,* and the lasso, although the bow and arrow were employed in the north. Pottery was made by the tribes of the northwest and the littoral. The Patagonian boot, made of skin, was widely used, but many of the tribes went barefoot. Most of them smoked tobacco and drank some kind of strong beverage, usually *chicha.* While their habitations varied a great deal, they were usually "simple affairs of skins or mats supported by a ridge pole, in many cases without smoke holes." The common form was "a kind of skin-covered lean-to." "The culture of the typical group reminds one of the North American plains area." After the Spanish colonists introduced horses and cattle, the natives soon developed an intense horse-culture, as did the plains Indians of North America. Hunting wild cattle on horseback with *bolas* and lasso speedily became a means of procuring food, as well as a sport; and the horse was employed in warfare, the warriors often riding naked into battle.

Owing to the nature of these Indians, comparatively little miscegenation occurred in Argentina. As already suggested, no large number of the natives was ever induced to adopt sedentary habits, the important exceptions being those of the far northwest, a few of the tribes of the *gran chaco,* and the Argentine Guaranís. It should be noted, however, that many of the *gauchos* (cowboys of the *pampa*) were *mestizos.* In addition to the Indians were the negroes, some thirty or forty thousand of whom were introduced into Argentina during the colonial period. But the census of 1914 lists only four hundred thousand inhabitants as "*mestizos* with vestiges of inferior races," and an estimate of 1930 places the number at only three hundred thousand out of a population of more than eleven million.

Until after the middle of the nineteenth century the Indian population diminished but slowly. The census of 1869 listed ninety-three thousand one hundred thirty-eight. Subsequently, however, the number rapidly decreased. It was only some thirty-eight thousand in 1914 and less than twenty-four thousand in 1920.

The Indians of Argentina thus met the fate which they encountered in the United States. Slightly more miscegenation occurred, but only a hundred thousand or so of any generation were ever incorporated into Argentine society. In Argentina, as in the great republic of North America, their influence was felt mainly as warriors and raiders who harrassed the frontiers and spread terror among the white settlers. Some of them fought on one side or the other during the struggle for emancipation and in subsequent civil wars. They made necessary the erection of frontier forts and provoked many campaigns designed to subdue or exterminate them. Their power was not completely shattered until

General Julio Roca undertook his expeditions in 1878 and 1879. The Roca campaigns brought to an end more than three centuries of intermittent warfare and skirmishes between the Europeans and the aborigines of Argentina.[5]

Such was the environment, geographical and human, in which Europeans were to develop their civilization in the southeastern portion of South America: vast arid and semi-arid plains bounded by the sea and the Río de la Plata on the east and by the Andes on the west; rolling meadows and woodlands and occasional swamps toward the north, and bleak plateaus in the south; inadequate fluvial transportation save in the northeastern section; comparatively little minerals and rather deficient water power; but a fertile soil, an area imperial in its extent, a delightful climate save in the far north and in the far south, and a scanty primitive population destined neither to furnish an adequate labor supply nor to destroy the racial homogenity of the people who were later to form the Argentine nation.

---

[5] For the native races, see George E. Church, *Aborigines of South America* (London, 1912), pp. 206-301; Clark Wissler, *The American Indian* (New York, 1928), p. 249 *passim;* Ricardo Levene, *Lecciones de historia argentina,* I, pp. 69-80. Population statistics are taken from Tobal, *op. cit.,* pp. 134-135.

CHAPTER FOUR

THE COLONIAL BACKGROUND

THE geographical setting described in the previous chapter refers to the area of Argentina of the recent period. The colonial history of the area, however, is closely linked with that of a much wider region embracing Chile, Peru (particularly Upper Peru, or Bolivia), Paraguay, and Uruguay (or the *Banda Oriental*).

I

The conquest and settlement of the Argentine proper proceeded in the main from three centers: Spain, Upper Peru, and Chile. The first efforts, advancing from the Spanish base, were made along the margin of the Plata estuary and the Paraguay River, but the first permanent settlement within the limits of present-day Argentina was established by settlers who came from Upper Peru.

All of the important towns of the colonial period were founded during the course of the sixteenth century, the permanent occupation of Buenos Aires coming rather late. These settlements, twelve in number, were as follows:

Santiago del Estero (1553)	Buenos Aires (1580)
Mendoza (1561)	Salta (1582)
San Juan (1562)	Corrientes (1588)
Tucumán (1564)	La Rioja (1591)
Córdoba (1573)	Jujuy (1593)
Santa Fé (1573)	San Luís (1596)

Six of these towns: Santiago del Estero, Tucumán, Córdoba, Salta, La Rioja, and Jujuy were founded by settlers who came from Upper Peru. Three were occupied from the Chilean base: Mendoza, San Juan, and San Luís. The remaining three: Santa Fé, Buenos Aires, and Corrientes, were founded by settlers proceeding either directly from Spain or from some town in the riverine area. The first permanent town established in the fluvial region was Asunción (1536), which became the capital of Paraguay and the base from which Santa Fé and Buenos Aires were occupied.

These twelve towns were to constitute the nuclei of twelve out of the fourteen provinces which were later to constitute the Argentine Republic. Before the end of the sixteenth century the area was organized into three provinces: Tucumán, which embraced the six towns occupied by settlers from Upper Peru; Cuyo, which included the three settlements of Chileans; and Paraguay, which embraced all of the middle and lower basin of the River Plate system. In 1617, however, the Province of Buenos Aires was detached from Paraguay.

Delay in the occupation of the lower basin of the Río de la Plata was due largely to the character of the Indians found in the region, for they were intrepid warriors who could not easily be conquered and reduced to serfdom. In 1516 the Charruas of Uruguay ambushed and killed Juan Díaz de Solís, the discoverer of the Río de la Plata. In 1528 the Guaranís destroyed the fort constructed by Sebastian Cabot on the Paraná River some two hundred miles above its mouth. And in 1541 the Querandí Indians forced the complete abandonment of Buenos Aires, which had been founded by Pedro de Mendoza some five years before. Already they had killed many of the settlers, including Mendoza's brother whom they had captured by means of the *bolas*. Perhaps the occupation of the area would have been further delayed if the Guaranís of Paraguay had not proved more docile and useful as laborers. Juan de Garay, who founded Santa Fé and refounded Buenos Aires, brought his settlers from Asunción, and the little group who permanently occupied the town that was destined to become the capital of the Argentine nation consisted of sixty Spaniards, of whom fifty were Creoles, and some two hundred Guaraní families.

The Indians of the provinces of Cuyo and Tucumán, however, were almost as difficult to manage. They frequently menaced the security of the colonists, and those who were subdued and reduced to serfdom on the *encomiendas* were hardly sufficient to supply the need for laborers in the region. To a greater extent than in any of the other Spanish colonies of America, the white inhabitants of Argentina were forced to do their own work.

II

Until the year 1776, when the viceroyalty was established, the cities of the region led a more or less autonomous existence. In fact, this part of the colonial period may be denominated the Era of the City States. The royal governors in the capitals of the provinces, and their deputies in the other towns, had superior authority; but the deputies were often fellow-townsmen virtually chosen by the municipalities.

Ambitious and active governors of the provinces might interfere in the politics of the towns, but in normal times, so far as internal affairs were concerned, the leading urban centers were largely self-contained communities.

The towns even divided between themselves the jurisdiction over the intervening rural territory. The government of Buenos Aires, for instance, extended nearly three hundred miles toward Córdoba, more than half as far in the direction of Santa Fé, southward to the shifting Indian frontier, and across the wide Río de la Plata into the *Banda Oriental*. The jurisdiction of every town extended to that of its nearest neighbor.

Every municipality had the right, which it often exercised, to send agents or deputies to lay complaints and petitions before the king and the Council of the Indies. They also negotiated with each other with reference to such matters of common concern as the hunting of wild cattle and defense against the Indians. In short, notwithstanding the lack of democracy in their elections and the occasional interference of the central authorities, the towns had "all the conscious dignity of political communities." The *corregidores* who represented the crown and the central authorities in the other colonies were absent from this region.[1] Owing to the lack of minerals, and the consequent feeling in Spain that these three provinces were unimportant, the area which later became the Argentine Republic was not as rigidly governed as were most of the other Spanish colonies in America. To the twelve municipalities already mentioned were added Colonia in 1680, Catamarca in 1683, Montevideo in 1726, and a few other settlements of minor importance.

The governing body of the towns was the *cabildo,* composed of from four to eight, and sometimes even of twelve, *regidores* (town councilmen), the number varying with time and the importance of the municipality. The first groups of councilmen were chosen by the conquerors or founders. Thereafter, for several decades, the retiring members of the *cabildo* selected their successors. Beginning with the year 1618, however, these offices were sometimes sold to the highest bidder. The term of a *regidor* who did not secure his office by purchase was only a year. The purchased seats on the town council endured for life.

The *cabildos* had charge of local administration and justice, choosing certain municipal officials to perform these duties. They were supposed

[1] The deputy governors were sometimes called *corregidores.*

to look after all the local interests and needs of the inhabitants, and the people under their jurisdiction were always free, theoretically at least, to lay before them their requests and complaints. They distributed town lots; issued permits for grazing, cutting wood, and extracting tallow; licensed retail storekeepers, inspected stores, and fixed prices and wages; levied taxes and promoted public works; arranged processions and attended to all public celebrations; inspected jails and hospitals; collected contributions for the relief of the poor; and supervised public morals. The influence of the *cabildos* was thus important in social matters, as well as in local military, economic, and political affairs.

In times of emergency the council might summon the principal residents under its jurisdiction to a civic assembly known as the *cabildo abierto*. Such town meetings sometimes merely listened to a royal message asking for money. On other occasions, however, they were called upon to concert measures of defense against Indian marauders or foreign invasion.

Municipal government in the Río de la Plata area furnished almost the only opportunity for the Creoles, or Americans, to participate in political and administrative affairs. Although such participation was confined to a very small group elected in a quite undemocratic fashion, many of the townsmen appear to have developed an intense interest in local affairs. A somewhat exaggerated regional or local sentiment everywhere prevailed and found expression in the lively municipal action of every separate town. "From the beginning, the cities of Buenos Aires, Sante Fé, and Corrientes, as well as the six cities of [the Province] of Tucumán and the three of Cuyo, were virtually and consciously the capitals of separate regions." [2]

Some writers have contended that the town councils served as cradles of liberty and schools of democracy. To a very limited extent this appears to have been the case. The method of securing membership in the *cabildo* was far from democratic, and the elections had to be sanctioned by the governor who sometimes refused to approve them; questions of high politics and administration were decided by the superior officials of Spain and America; but the importance of these local centers of political and administrative life can not be denied.

Without subscribing unreservedly to the extreme views of Sarmiento and Alberdi, Levene describes certain municipal activities of the period

[2] F. A. Kirkpatrick, *A History of the Argentine Republic* (Cambridge, 1931), p. 23.

now under consideration as "democratic movements." In 1577 the leading residents of Mendoza deposed a dissolute governor, and three years later the Creoles of this village attempted in vain and not without bloodshed to obtain a larger participation in the municipal government. In 1583 the Creoles of Buenos Aires, who constituted a majority of the population, demanded an open *cabildo* in order to choose a successor to the deceased founder of the town, and exerted some influence on the election. In 1589 the council of the same town declared that the lands and wild cattle under their jurisdiction belonged to the sons of the conquerors and not to the king of Spain. In 1588, when the governor of the Province of Tucumán attempted to control the choice of *regidores* and *alcaldes* in the city of Córdoba, the *cabildo* protested and proceeded with the elections, and the governor felt obliged to approve them. Similar disturbances took place before the end of the century in Corrientes and Tucumán, and Asunción was from the beginning a turbulent municipal republic.

Movements of a like nature occurred during the eighteenth century, at least two of them of considerable significance. One took place at Asunción, and the other in Corrientes.

For more than a decade, namely, from 1721 to 1732, Paraguay was disturbed by a spirit of insurgency. Although motivated in part by animosity toward the Jesuits, it was in the main an expression of the desire for local autonomy. Under the leadership of José Antequera, the *cabildo* and populace of Asunción deposed one governor and attempted to prevent another from taking charge of his office. After the execution of Antequera by the Spanish authorities, Fernando Mompó took up the banner of the fallen chief and rallied the inhabitants by an appeal to popular sovereignty. The uprising has become known as the *comunero* revolt, and in its last stages it attracted the sympathy of the residents of Corrientes, who refused to serve against the Paraguayan insurgents, raised the cry of "*Viva el común*," and deposed their deputy governor.

Serious trouble was averted in Corrientes on this occasion, but between 1762 and 1764 new difficulties arose. They were caused by the unreasonable exactions of an autocratic, stubborn, and pro-Jesuit governor of Buenos Aires, who conscripted the inhabitants of Corrientes for heavy military duties in the *gran chaco* and in the *Banda Oriental*. When several of them finally deserted, he demanded that others be sent to take their places. The leaders of the town refused to comply, elected a governor of their own in open *cabildo* (1764), and declared their intention of defending their country against the provincial governor, and, for that matter, "even against the king." The revolt, which may be considered a precursor of the independence movement at the opening of the next century, was soon suppressed by armed force. Numerous arrests were made and several death sentences were pronounced, but before the executions took place a new viceroy arrived (in Peru) bringing amnesty and peace.[3]

III

The intense spirit of localism, which expressed itself in, and was at the same time nurtured by, an active municipal life, was destined to make the consolidation of the Argentine nation extremely difficult. Various counterpoises tended, however, to hold the spirit in check and finally to put an end to the city republics within the Argentine proper. These counterpoises consisted of geographical factors, which contributed to the growing power of the littoral and riverine area and eventually compelled all of the settlements to face toward the Atlantic; the iron rule of Juan Manuel de Rosas; the nationalism of certain other leaders; and the construction of railways.

The *audiencia,* and other institutions of the later colonial period, were also centralizing influences. Until 1783, most of the area was subject to the *Audiencia* of Charcas (Bolivia) established at Chuquisaca in 1559;[4] thereafter it was under the jurisdiction of the *audiencia* set up in Buenos Aires in 1783. During the last thirty-four years of the colonial epoch, namely, from 1776 to 1810, the entire Río de la Plata area, including Upper Peru, Paraguay, and *Banda Oriental,* was under a viceroy. After 1783 the viceroyalty was divided into eight intendancies, three of which[5]—by far the largest of the group—embraced present-day Argentina and Uruguay.

The viceroys and the "intendant-governors" almost prostrated municipal autonomy, while the *audiencia* and the viceroyalty, especially the former, tended to induce the people to think in terms of a larger unity. The members of the *audiencia,* who corresponded directly with the king,

---

[3] For an excellent discussion of local government in the Spanish colonies, see Herbert I. Priestley, "Spanish Colonial Municipalities," in *The Louisiana Historical Quarterly* (April 1922). A longer treatise is presented by J. A. García in *La ciudad indiana.* Consult also Levene, *op. cit.,* I, Chs. VIII and XIV. A satisfactory discussion of the *comunero* revolt will be found in Bernard Moses' *The Spanish Dependencies in South America,* II, pp. 281-311.

[4] An *audiencia* also existed in Buenos Aires between 1661 and 1671.

[5] These were Buenos Aires, Córdoba del Tucumán, and Salta.

not only constituted a high court of appeal, but also possessed administrative functions of the greatest importance. No political body in the colonies was more influential. The people were accustomed to look to the *audiencia* for relief from the oppressions of their local functionaries and even of the viceroy himself. The fact that nearly all of the Hispanic American republics were once the seat of distinct *audiencias* seems to indicate that this institution was an integrating factor of no little importance. The new nations were unities defined during the colonial epoch rather than aggregations formed after independence. The *audiencias* thus appear to have represented the most compact groups of colonial association, units strong enough to resist within their limits the dissolving forces which destroyed Spain's American empire. Within the *Audiencia* of Buenos Aires, however, sectionalism was so potent that a portion of the Plata basin was eventually lost.[6]

IV

The economic and social development of the Río de la Plata was a very slow process. Despite its seductive name, the region furnished almost no precious metals during the colonial period. The birth and growth of the colony took place amidst hunger and misery. It presented the only important example in South America of a Spanish society based almost entirely upon the ranch and the farm.

Population increased at a snail's pace. The civilized and semicivilized inhabitants of the area later embraced within the Argentine Republic probably numbered little more than three hundred thousand in 1800, of whom perhaps somewhat more than a third dwelt in the suburbs and on the open *pampa.* The population of the whole viceroyalty may have totaled nearly a million and a half.[7]

The region as a whole lacked homogeneity in interests, customs, sentiments, and ideas. Buenos Aires, Montevideo, and Santa Fé, together with the rural areas largely dominated by them, were populated in the main by whites who had considerable direct contacts with Europe. The upper portion of the great basin of the Plata, including Corrientes, Misiones, and Paraguay, was occupied mainly by Indians. The vast area stretching from Córdoba to the borders of Charcas was inhabited

---

[6] José N. Matienzo, *El gobierno representativo federal en la república argentina* (Madrid, 1917), pp. 41-63; Carlos Pereyra, *El pensamiento político de Alberdi* (Madrid, n. d.), pp. 25 ff.

[7] Argentine Republic, *Censo nacional* (1869), *passim;* Ernesto Tornquist, *The Economic Development of the Argentine Republic* . . . (New York, 1918), p. 7.

by semi-civilized Indians, *mestizos,* and whites, while Charcas itself was largely Indian; and both regions were a sort of prolongation of Peru. The old province of Cuyo, near the eastern border of the Andes and still in economic and social contact with Chile, also contained a considerable element of subdued Indians and *mestizos.* In general, the proportion of Europeans decreased with the distance from the estuary of the Río de la Plata. Everywhere the civilization was urban and the semicivilization, consisting of *gauchos* and reduced Indians, was rural. Moreover, nomadic natives entirely untouched by European culture still roamed over fully half of the viceroyalty.

The cowboys, or *gauchos,* who were later to become a potent factor in the history of the country, were already beginning to attract attention at the close of the colonial era. The writers of the period describe their peculiar dress; their arms, consisting of the lasso, the *bolas,* the lance—a long stick with a half-moon blade attached to the end—and a large knife; their songs and bloody encounters; and their method of rounding up, hamstringing, killing, and skinning the cattle. The *gauchos* valued the animals mainly for their hides and, in some cases, their tallow, devouring half-raw and sometimes unsalted only such choice bits of the meat as their immediate needs required, and leaving the remainder for the vultures. They were the product of bad government and the plains environment. Without stimulus for agriculture or commerce, without any schools or inducements for culture, repelled by the rudimentary civilization of the cities, they were abandoned to the wild life of the *pampa,* where they engaged in an open contest with the semidesert and with misery. Here they reverted to a primitive and almost barbarous life. No physician assuaged their infirmities and no shepherd of the church comforted them in their grief.[8] Perhaps no less than eighty thousand of them were roaming these plains in 1800.

[8] Levene, *op. cit.,* I, pp. 359-362, and authorities there cited. W. H. Hudson, the naturalist, has attempted to explain the "downward drag" of the *pampa:* "The first colonists who made their homes in this vast vacant space . . . came from a land where the people are accustomed to sit in the shade of trees, where corn [namely, cereals] and wine and oil are supposed to be necessaries, and where there is salad in the garden. Naturally they made gardens and planted trees, both for shade and fruit, wherever they built . . . a house on the pampas, and no doubt for two or three generations they tried to live as people live in Spain, in the rural districts. But now the main business of their lives was cattle-raising, and as the cattle roamed over the vast plains and were more like wild than domestic animals, it was a life on horseback. They could no longer dig or plough the earth or protect their crops from insects and birds and their own animals. They gave up their oil and wine and bread, and lived on flesh alone. They sat in the shade and ate the fruit of trees planted by their fathers or their grandfathers

As already suggested, the economic pursuits of the inhabitants of Argentina proper were agricultural and pastoral, mainly the latter, although the soil was cultivated to a considerable degree near the principal settlements, and industries developed on a tiny scale, despite numerous restrictions, in the leading towns. The first horses were turned loose on the *pampa* in 1537; the first cattle, sheep, and goats were brought into the region from Upper Peru between 1550 and 1552. These animals multiplied so rapidly that a few years later the hunting of wild horses and cattle became the leading sport and the chief means of livelihood of the inhabitants. Immense herds roamed over the plains and could be appropriated to the extent of several thousand by anyone who had the ability to seize and kill or tame them. The horses were valued chiefly for their hides and as mounts for *gauchos* and travelers. The cattle were used as draft animals, or were killed for hides and tallow, and for fresh, jerked, and salted beef. Goats and mules were confined mainly to the old provinces of Cuyo and Tucumán, where the mules were exported (when this was permitted) or employed as pack animals on the mountain trails. Agriculture, carried on in a rather primitive fashion and seldom extending far beyond the neighborhood of the leading towns, was confined mainly to maize and wheat, although grapes were grown in Cuyo, sugarcane and tea in areas adjacent to Tucumán and Santiago del Estero, some tobacco around Corrientes, and hemp and flax in the neighborhood of Buenos Aires and Santa Fé. In general, the cultivation of fruits and vegetables was neglected. Industries were limited to the fabrication of simple household necessities: linen, woolen, and cotton cloth, *ponchos,* blankets, *mantillas,* shoes, saddles, sandals, a little silverware, and so forth—all manufactured surreptitiously or under severe restrictions. Toward the end of the colonial period, boats were constructed in Corrientes.

The clergy, both regular and secular, became rather numerous during the late colonial era; but, despite the fact that many solid temples, churches, and convents existed in the leading towns, especially in Córdoba and Buenos Aires, the church was by no means as wealthy as in Mexico and Peru. Tucumán (1570), Buenos Aires (1620), and

---

until the trees died of old age, or were blown down or killed by the cattle, and there was no more shade or fruit.

"It thus came about that the Spanish colonists on the pampas declined from a state of agricultural people to that of an exclusively pastoral and hunting one; and later, when the Spanish yoke, as it was called, was shaken off, the incessant throat-cutting wars of the various factions . . . confirmed and sunk them deeper in their wild and barbarous manner of life." (*Far Away and Long Ago,* pp. 65-66.)

Salta (1731), as well as Asunción, were the seats of bishoprics. There were numerous religious holidays and processions, and frequent quarrels either between the religious and civil authorities or among the various religious organizations themselves.

Primary education, such as existed, was in charge of the religious orders, the "schools of the king," and the municipal authorities. Needless to say, it was quite inadequate. Probably no more than one or two per cent of the people, and these almost entirely townsmen, could read and write. The teachers in the primary schools were ignorant. "Each child read the book which he could bring from home: profane histories understood neither by pupils nor teachers; books of chivalry; . . . lives of the saints. . . ." [9]

The main object of secondary education was the training of the clergy. Toward the close of the eighteenth century, secondary schools existed in Buenos Aires and Córdoba, and possibly in some of the other towns. An academy *(colegio)* founded by the Jesuits in Córdoba in 1613 was transformed into a university shortly before 1700 and soon became the intellectual center of the colony. Theology, obsolete philosophy, and law were emphasized in the courses of study. A few of the young men were able to attend the universities of Spain or an institution of higher learning in Santiago de Chile, Chuquisaca, or Lima. The colonial mind was familiarized with three characteristic and converging concepts: "political absolutism, economic absolutism, and religious absolutism." [10]

The tardy development of the colony was due largely to the policy of the mother country, the lack of precious metals, the character of the Indians, and the somewhat shiftless habits of the European population. Only a very limited use of the ports of the region was permitted prior to 1778 for commerce and industry were subjected to rigid controls. With few exceptions, trade with foreigners was always illegal, and commerce was in the hands of a small group of monopolists and smugglers. The whites looked somewhat scornfully upon manual labor; of the Indians, who perpetually harassed the frontiers, probably no more than a hundred thousand in Argentina proper ever contributed at any given period to the scanty supply of workers; and, as already observed, only a few thousand negro slaves were ever introduced into the colony. The *mestizos* and poor whites became the more or less skilled artisans

---

[9] Levene, *op. cit.*, I, p. 326.

[10] José Ingenieros, *La evolución de las ideas argentinas* (Buenos Aires, 1918), I, p. 77.

of the towns, the suburban small farmers, and the cowboys of the plains.

During the second half of the eighteenth century, the Río de la Plata area profited by the more liberal policies of the Bourbons, who were influenced by the age of enlightenment in Europe and desired to counteract the advance of the Portuguese from Brazil. The colony, especially its eastern portion, experienced a sort of economic and intellectual renaissance. However, the close of the colonial epoch still found it undeveloped and backward, and one of the poorest regions of South America.[11]

---

[11] For a good discussion of conditions toward the end of the eighteenth century, see Ricardo Levene, "La política económica de España en América durante el siglo XVIII y la revolucíon de 1810," in *Anales de la facultad de derecho y ciencias sociales,* IV, pt. I (1914), pp. 594 ff.

CHAPTER FIVE

THE WINNING OF INDEPENDENCE AND THE DELIMITATION OF THE NATIONAL BOUNDARIES

THE Río de la Plata was the first of the Spanish American colonies to win its independence. In most of the other colonies the struggle lasted some ten or fifteen years, but Argentina achieved its emancipation in six years, and its soldiers and leaders then assisted in the liberation of Chile and Peru.

I

The causes of the revolt against the rule of the mother country were internal and external, economic and political: the revolution of the thirteen English colonies in North America; the French Revolution of 1789 and the political and economic ideas upon which it was based; the British invasions of the Río de la Plata in 1806 and 1807; the Napoleonic attempt to conquer Spain; discriminations against the Creoles; irksome restraints upon colonial life, economic as well as intellectual; and the impetuous and intrepid character of the colonists themselves. The success of the revolt was due to the absorbing preoccupations of the mother country and to the bold and energetic qualities of the people and leaders of the colony.

The North American revolution was not without influence in the Plata region. It served as an example; it was supported by Spain, the mother country of Argentina; and the outcome suggested to humiliated Englishmen the idea of fomenting a revolution in the Spanish colonies, an idea which motivated action on more than one occasion.

French influence was even more potent. Most of the leaders of the emancipation movement in Argentina were inspired by the liberal ideas of the Encylopedists and the Physiocrats: liberty, equality before the law, natural rights, popular sovereignty, free trade, and *laissez faire*. The Declaration of the Rights of Man, the most important document formulated by the French revolutionary leaders, profoundly stirred the intellectuals of the *pampa*.

British attempts to conquer the region in 1806 and 1807 were also an important factor in stimulating the movement for independence. The popular defense of Buenos Aires and the final expulsion of the English gave the people a consciousness of their power. A Creole party was immediately organized, as well as permanent corps of colonial militia; an open *cabildo* conferred the command of the troops upon Santiago Liniers; and a *junta* of war deposed the viceroy because of his inefficiency and cowardice. Moreover, the British popularized the doctrine of free trade and gave a practical illustration of its benefits by introducing cheap goods in the wake of their invading army.

The Napoleonic invasion of Spain in 1808 and subsequent events in the mother country were likewise influential. The leaders of the Spanish nation, unwilling to submit to the rule of the French Emperor, organized *juntas* and a provisional government in the absence of their monarch. The leaders of the Río de la Plata followed suit, taking advantage of the occasion to enunciate the doctrine of residuary sovereignty. The Spanish King was in prison, let the people of the colonies rule! They were the ultimate repository of authority.

The inhabitants of the colony, and especially those of the littoral and riverine areas, had long been restive under the economic fetters imposed by Spain. To all the rigid controls of the Middle Ages, the mother country had added those of the mercantilist system administered in the interest of a small group of merchant parasites. Prices and wages were fixed by the *cabildos,* and trade was controlled by Spanish monopolists. While intermittent traffic with smugglers, and occasional legalized trade with foreigners during the commercial disturbances occasioned by the wars of the late eighteenth century, were demonstrating the practical benefits of a more liberal policy, the Physiocrats were furnishing the arguments in its support.

Agitation for a new economy was not long delayed. In 1793 the farmers of the province of Buenos Aires petitioned the king, begging him not to hinder the export of their products. They declared that the tillers of the soil were the producers of the wealth of the country; that the land was fertile and the people anxious to cultivate wheat and other provisions; that there was no other occupation for the people of the towns; and that the inhabitants of these broad and fertile plains were living in abject misery because they had no outlet for their surplus commodities. Six years later they sent another petition to the *cabildo* of Buenos Aires asking for freedom of trade so long as the price of wheat did not exceed four *pesos* per *fanega,* that is, about two dollars per bushel.

The establishment of the *consulado*—a group of officials who served both as a tribunal for dealing with mercantile complaints and as an institution for the protection and encouragement of commerce—at Buenos Aires in 1794 furnished an opportunity for discussion of the new economic ideas. Some of its members urged greater freedom both in domestic and in foreign trade, and its secretary, Manuel Belgrano, expounded the new political economy at great length.

Belgrano had studied in the Spanish universities and was familiar with the most progressive ideas of the Spanish and French economists. A few years later, his efforts were reinforced by those of Mariano Moreno, who was likewise a careful student of the new economic doctrines. Moreno soon became the attorney of the *hacendados* of the Río de la Plata.

As early as 1794 the big landowners of Buenos Aires and Montevideo had sent a memorial to one of the ministers of the king in which they had requested permission to export to Africa and Asia not only salted meats, lard, and tallow, but hides, skins, and furs of all kinds as well. In 1809 both the poverty of the treasury of the viceroyalty and economic disturbances due to the war in Spain led the colonial authorities to consider the expediency of trading with British merchants. The Spanish monopolists, who were influential both in the *cabildo* and the *consulado,* opposed the step. They were actuated mainly by the desire to defend their own interests, but they argued that trade with the English would injure the Spanish merchant marine and strike a mortal blow at the small manufacturers of the region—the shoemakers, the iron workers, the carpenters, and others. But the farmers and large landlords of both banks of the Río de la Plata, perceiving in British trade an outlet for their surplus products, were determined to defend their cause, and they employed Moreno to present their argument.

Moreno's "Representation" was a lengthy and important document, filled with the economic doctrines of the French Physiocrats and containing allusions to the political philosophy of the Encyclopedists. His attitude was not so much that of an attorney. He rather assumed the rôle of a statesman directing or defending a great national cause. With perfect mastery of the new political economy, he demonstrated the convenience and necessity of permitting free trade. He showed how the prohibitions had led to smuggling; pointed out the commercial exigencies caused by the profound political changes in Spain; argued that the viceroyalty should stand on a basis of equality with the Spanish provinces; demonstrated that the mother country could not consume all of the commodities of the fertile fields of Argentina; and emphatically insisted that duties levied on trade with foreigners, especially with England, were the only means of improving the state of the treasury. He examined one by one the fiscal expedients offered by his opponents and rejected them all.

The manner in which he replied to one of the arguments of the monopolists is noteworthy. The attorney of the merchants of Cádiz had declared that free trade with the English would result in the course of a few years in breaking the bonds which bound the American colonies to the mother country. Meeting the contention with energy and boldness, Moreno declared that rich and powerful colonies would not wish to emancipate themselves. Happy under the easy and gentle yoke of their metropolis, they would not attempt to cast it off, for they would realize the need of the protection of the mother country against foreign conquest, against the intrigues of powerful citizens and the dangers of anarchy.

Having dismissed as futile all the remedies proposed by his antagonists, Moreno declared, in conclusion, that freedom of commerce remained as the sole practical measure capable of restoring the treasury, furnishing an outlet for the surplus commodities of the region, reducing the cost of living, improving the miserable state of the inhabitants, and opening an unlimited horizon for the future. Let this reform be adopted, and the coffers of the treasury would be filled, the poor and impoverished classes would obtain immediate relief, existence would be made bearable if not comfortable, and a genuine social transformation would be initiated. Let it be rejected, and misery, contraband, and fiscal poverty would continue.[1]

After listening to the various arguments on both sides, the viceroy decided to permit the trade with England as a "necessary evil," but under restrictions which all but nullified its benefits. Even this limited concession was revoked by the Spanish provisional government; but before news of the revocation reached Buenos Aires the colony was already in revolt.[2]

II

The emancipation movement in the Río de la Plata was initiated in May 1810. The date usually given for its completion is that of July

[1] Moreno's "Representation" may be consulted in Norberto Piñero's *Escritos de Mariano Moreno* (Buenos Aires, 1894), I, pp. 89-224.

[2] An excellent discussion of the causes of the revolution, with useful citations, may be found in Levene, *Lecciones,* I, pp. 380-456.

9, 1816, when the congress assembled at Tucumán declared the independence of the area included in Argentina proper. The national destiny of the region was not secure, however, until the royalists were driven from the two Perus by the battles of Junín and Ayacucho in 1824.

It was on May 25, 1810 that the first colonial government was set up in the Plata area. The work of a small group of leaders of Buenos Aires backed by the residents of that little city, its establishment was preceded by an open *cabildo* consisting of the Spanish authorities of the capital and a small number of *vecinos,* or citizens. Four hundred and fifty were invited to attend, but only 251 persons were present, and only 224 cast their votes. The decision was overwhelmingly in favor of deposing the viceroy, Baltázar Hidalgo Cisneros, and establishing a provisional government *(junta gubernativa),* but the will of the leading citizens might have been defeated if the people of Buenos Aires had not given the demands of the open *cabildo* their strong support. The dominant members of the provisional government established on May 25 were Cornelio Saavedra, Manuel Belgrano, and Mariano Moreno.

The *junta* at once confronted two problems: the extension of its authority over the former viceroyalty and the maintenance of its power against the royalists with their bases of operation in Peru and Montevideo. These tasks proved quite difficult, and were rendered even more so by divisions among the Buenos Aires patriots themselves.

The course of events in Paraguay was not entirely favorable. An expedition sent by Belgrano to liberate this portion of the ancient viceroyalty was defeated by the Paraguayans themselves, but they soon proceeded to set up a government of their own. For the leaders of Paraguay were in favor of casting off the Spanish yoke, but were not disposed to acknowledge the authority of the provisional government of Buenos Aires. Paraguay was soon totally lost by the Buenos Aires government, but the patriots in the viceregal capital might find comfort in the fact that Paraguay was not a center of royalist reaction.

A somewhat different situation developed in the *Banda Oriental.* There the rural sections and the villages could be raised against the Spanish authorities, but the royalists, aided and abetted by the imperial family now residing in Brazil, established a stronghold in Montevideo and menaced from that base the provisional government of Buenos Aires. The royalists of Montevideo were finally subdued in 1814, but by that time the Uruguayan patriot, José Artigas, had so aroused the autonomous aspirations of the people that they refused to submit to the rule of the government on the other side of the Río de la Plata. By

1828, after a long struggle involving the Argentines, the Brazilians, and the Uruguayans, this region also was definitely lost.

The northwestern portion of the viceroyalty presented a still more difficult problem. From Córdoba northward to the frontier of present-day Argentina many of the leaders were royalists, and Spanish sympathizers were even more numerous in Upper Peru, or the *Audiencia* of Charcas, which for thirty-four years had been a part of the Viceroyalty of Río de la Plata. This vast area became the scene of several bloody encounters in which the fortunes of the patriots were sometimes favorable and at others quite adverse. The war, in fact, was for several years a ceaseless pendulum. When the royalists, inured to the mountains, came down to the plains, the soldiers of Buenos Aires, with many *gauchos* among their number, usually defeated them. But when the plainsmen followed the enemy up into the Andes, the mountain royalists turned and hurled them back. By the end of 1815 Charcas had been definitely taken by the royalists, but the *gauchos* under their brave leader, Martín Güemes, were still holding them at the frontiers of the Argentine proper.[3]

The man who had the genius to see the futility of this indecisive struggle and to propose and execute a better plan was José de San Martín, who was La Plata's greatest contribution to the independence movement in South America. As early as March 22, 1814 he had written a friend that the war in the north would be endless so long as the Spaniards maintained their stronghold in Peru. He accordingly proposed that the defense of the northern frontier be left to the valiant *gauchos* of Salta, supported by a squadron or two of veterans from the loyal towns, and that preparations be made to cross the Andes into Chile and afterwards advance upon Lima by sea.

In August 1814, this great soldier, veteran of the Peninsula War, was appointed governor-intendant of the old Province of Cuyo, beneath the eastern shadow of the Andes. Its three towns—Mendoza, San Juan, and San Luís—had been among the first to recognize the provisional government set up in Buenos Aires on May 25, 1810, and its people were in general devoted to the patriot cause. Quite aside from the larger plan of moving upon Peru by way of the Pacific, the wisdom of the step was demonstrated a few months later when the royalist victory of Rancagua forced the Chilean insurgents to flee across the

[3] Two interesting sources for this period are Gregorio Aráoz de Madrid, *Memorias* (Madrid, n. d.) and José María Paz, *Memorias póstumas* (Madrid, n. d.).

mountains and take refuge at Mendoza; for a royalist threat was then confronted in this quarter.

In his new stronghold, San Martín set to work with utmost patience and thoroughness. Mobilizing the entire province, he had the people manufacture arms, munitions, and uniforms, while the soldiers were drilled and the horses and mules trained to climb the mountains with burdens on their backs. Printing presses were brought in and propaganda released to stir the patriots; and on one occasion the women of Mendoza contributed their jewels to the cause. By the beginning of the year 1817 he had an army of some four thousand men, supported by some twelve hundred militia ready to help with the equipment and supplies. It was one of the most perfect military instruments that South America had produced. At the proper moment it would cross the glaciers of the Andes and fall upon the Spaniards of Chile.

Several months before the expedition began its advance into the mountain passes, however, important events occurred at Tucumán. Protected on the west by San Martín and on the north by the intrepid Güemes and his valient *gauchos,* some thirty-two delegates, representing ten of the leading towns of Argentina proper and certain of the districts of Upper Peru, assembled at that city, and after considerable discussion unanimously declared the independence of the "United Provinces of South America" on July 9, 1816. In making this declaration they merely proclaimed an actual situation which had existed for some time and which future events were to confirm. It was, however, a bold step, for the emancipation movement had suffered severe reverses throughout Spanish America. Chile had been lost by the independents, the insurgents of Mexico had been suppressed, Peru was still loyal, and Venezuela and New Granada had been recaptured by veteran Spanish troops released from the Napoleonic Wars.

Nevertheless, time was to reveal that the Congress of Tucumán assumed no great risk. Within two years San Martín had driven the Spaniards out of Chile, and exactly five years later (1821) he occupied Lima. In the meantime, Bolívar and his lieutenants had routed the enemy in Venezuela and New Granada and were preparing to move southward toward Quito and Guayaquil. The decisive battle of Pichincha soon followed (1822), and before the end of 1824—the self-effacing San Martín having previously withdrawn from the field of honor—the royalists were crushed in Peru. With the organization of the old *Audiencia* of Charcas into the independent Republic of Bolivia, this region was definitely detached from Argentina, the loss of Charcas having preceded the final detachment of *Banda Oriental* by a brief span of three years. With these losses and that of Paraguay, however, Argentina had suffered its last important sacrifice of territory.

The final delimitation of its boundaries was a long process which was not completed until 1902. After the war with Paraguay (1865-1870), Argentina laid claim to a vast strip of territory lying along the west bank of the Paraguay River from Bahía Negra in the north to Río Bermejo in the south, as well as to another large area along the east margin of the Paraná, namely, the Misiones territory. By a treaty of February 3, 1876, she received a clear title to the latter region, but surrendered the northern portion of the former and agreed to submit its central portion, the area between the Pilcomayo and the Verde rivers, to arbitration. President Rutherford B. Hayes served as arbitrator and decided in 1878 that this strip of territory belonged to Paraguay. The eastern limits of the Misiones area continued to be disputed with Brazil until it was submitted to the arbitration of President Cleveland, who concluded in 1895 that the region in question belonged to Brazil. The Argentine-Bolivian boundary was definitely settled in 1893. Of the two areas in dispute with Chile, one, involving the *Puna de Atacama,* was settled by the arbitral decision of William Buchanan, minister of the United States in Buenos Aires, and the other, which related to the division of southwestern Patagonia and Tierra del Fuego, was terminated by the decision of King Edward VII of England in 1902. The Falkland Islands were seized by Great Britain in 1833 and have not been recovered.[4]

III

But let us return once more to the independence period. Soon left with only three of the eight intendancies of the ancient viceroyalty, and with the *Banda Oriental* detached from one of these, the central authorities in Buenos Aires had much difficulty in consolidating even this reduced area, still by no means small, into national unity. Politics were turbulent in the capital, the leaders quarreled among themselves and split the populace into factions, and the old municipal spirit reasserted itself in the provinces.

The central government suffered one crisis after another. The *junta gubernativa* was transformed into the *junta grande,* with frequent

[4] For a convenient summary of the disputes discussed in this paragraph, see Tobal, *Lecciones de geografía argentina,* pp. 10-15.

changes of personnel, and the latter finally gave way late in 1811 to a triumvirate. In a little more than a year the first triumvirate was followed by a second, which was soon succeeded by a supreme directorate (1814); whereupon supreme director followed supreme director in rapid succession until the national authority was virtually annihilated.

Meanwhile, the three intendancies of the late colonial period—those of Buenos Aires, Salta, and Córdoba—were breaking up into smaller units each dominated by its leading town. The sentiment of local autonomy was growing rapidly, and the region was drifting toward anarchy. Late in 1813, Mendoza, San Juan, and San Luís were detached from the Intendancy of Córdoba and erected into a separate intendancy with its capital at Mendoza. In September 1814, Entre Ríos and Corrientes were separated from the Intendancy of Buenos Aires and made separate provinces. In October 1814, the Intendancy of Salta was divided into two parts and the Province of Tucumán, composed of the towns of Tucumán, Santiago del Estero, and Catamarca, was formed. Already, in March 1814, the *Banda Oriental,* not yet permanently lost, had been given the status of a province. Thus by the time independence was declared in July 1816, the old threefold division had dissolved into five provinces and four intendancies.

Moreover, the local jurisdictions, and especially the towns, had long since begun to demand a voice in the national government. From the outset the *cabildos* had been centers of revolutionary action. The emancipation movement, it will be recalled, started with the open *cabildo* of Buenos Aires. In December 1811 the delegates from the towns of the upper riverine area and the western hinterland arrived in the capital and were incorporated into the *junta gubernativa.* With the formation of the first triumvirate late in 1811, the urban delegations became a *junta* of observation. In 1813 a constituent assembly, composed of representatives of the towns, was organized. And finally, the Congress of Tucumán (which continued its sessions in Buenos Aires until 1820) was composed of delegates from the towns, despite the fact that it had been convoked by the intendancies and the provinces. The towns were, therefore, the basis of political organization and the agencies of the emancipation movement, but the rural sections were beginning to be heard from. Artigas and Güemes were teaching the *gauchos* to be soldiers. Ere long they would gallop into the towns and take charge. The country would soon rule the city, and both the towns and the country would demand autonomous provinces. Federalism and the cowboys were looming on the horizon—federalism, the rural man on horseback, chaos, and barbarism.[5]

---

[5] José Nicolás Matienzo, *El gobierno representativo federal en la república argentina,* pp. 41-75. Levene, *Lecciones,* II, pp. 7-178, presents an excellent summary of the independence movement. For a detailed account, see the two excellent works of Bartolomé Mitre, *Historia de Belgrano* and *Historia de San Martín.* For a philosophical treatment of the subject, consult José Ingenieros, *La evolución de las ideas argentinas,* vol. I. Consult also M. A. Pelliza's, *Dorrego* (Buenos Aires, 1878), and Luís V. Varela, *Historia constitucional de la república argentina* (La Plata, 1910), Vols. I and II.

CHAPTER SIX

THE ANARCHY OF 1820-1829

"WHEN a people begins a revolution, two opposing interests enter into conflict from the outset: the revolutionary and the conservative. Among us the parties who supported these two causes have been denominated the patriots and the royalists. It is natural for the victorious party, after its triumph, to divide itself into two factions, the moderates and the extremists, the latter desiring to carry out the revolution in all its consequences and the former wishing to confine it within certain limits." [1]

Such were the reflections of Domingo F. Sarmiento in 1845. While most suggestive, as his statements usually are, they contain one important inaccuracy. The "revolutionary" party embraced two factions from the *very beginning* of the struggle for independence. One of them desired little more than an administrative secession from the Spanish provisional government and (later) from the restored monarchy; the other wished an entire change of régime, a complete regeneration for the whole viceroyalty.

For an enlightened minority of young *porteños* (residents of Buenos Aires)—afterwards joined by other small minorities of the upper riverine area and the interior—the revolution signified a total renunciation of the colonial system. Their creed was the *Social Contract,* their economic doctrine the free trade of the Physiocrats, their political philosophy that of the Encyclopedists, and their program essentially the program of the French Revolution. They demanded popular sovereignty, liberty of worship, equality before the law, freedom of commerce, secularization of education, and, in short, everything that was contrary to the ideals and principles of the old colonial system. In order to accomplish their purposes the young leaders of Buenos Aires had sent military expeditions to the more distant regions of the viceroyalty for the purpose of revolutionizing them. Their plan was to compel the *cabildos* to overthrow the functionaries appointed by the king and to assume the administration of the local jurisdictions until deputies could assemble from all parts of the viceroyalty and set up a new central government.

---

[1] *Vida de Facundo, ó civilizacóin y barbarie* (Buenos Aires, 1896), p. 58. In 1868 a translation of this work was published in New York by Mrs. Horace Mann.

For the conservatives of Buenos Aires and the municipal oligarchies of the interior the movement which began in May 1810 had a far more limited purpose. It was designed merely to effect a separation from the provisional government of Spain until the legitimate monarch could be restored to his throne, or until events in the peninsula could indicate some other course respectful to the vested interests they had managed to acquire under the old régime. Far from desiring any genuine and thorough change, many of them lacked at first even a definite separatist spirit. Later, it is true, they became reconciled to a permanent separation from the mother country, but they continued their opposition to any effective modification of the political, social, or economic life of the region. The group was composed in the main of moderately wealthy merchants and landowners—members of families long prominent in municipal government—and a number of the higher clergy.

Thus there were two groups of "patriots" and two phases of the revolution: (1) the struggle for independence from Spain, and (2) an internal contest between heterogeneous forces striving to establish a new social equilibrium. The first virtually ended by the close of the year 1816; the second dragged on from 1810 until 1829, when it resulted in the triumph of Rosas with the support of the conservatives and the *gauchos* of the Province of Buenos Aires.

Both factions of the patriots were led by the townsmen who presumed to think and act for the inhabitants of the contiguous rural sections. These countrymen had little knowledge of the significance of events going on about them. And the same was true, indeed, of the humbler residents of the provincial towns. Only in Buenos Aires, during the early years of the revolution, did the popular mass develop opinions and a desire to make their influence felt. The multitudes of the remainder of the ancient viceroyalty were mere rabbles without definite convictions, swayed by priests or demagogues, joining either side with indifference or being impressed into military service by any officer—royalist, conservative patriot, or revolutionary—who passed along, until the adventurers who commanded them were able finally to dominate every province and rule the entire country.

II

The main center of the struggle between the conservatives and the reformers was Buenos Aires, the seat of such national government as could maintain itself during this turbulent period. Many revolutions and counter-revolutions occurred, with consequent changes in personnel as well as in the names applied to the national authorities. The genuine revolutionists, or reformers, dominated the *Junta* of 1810, the Triumvirate of 1811-1812, the Constituent Assembly of 1813, some of the supreme directors, and two of the presidents who followed; and they numbered among their leaders such men as Mariano Moreno, Juan José Castelli, Bernardo Monteagudo, Manuel de Sarratea, Juan J. Paso, Nicolás Rodríguez Peña, Carlos M. de Alvear, Gervasio Posadas, José Manuel García, Manuel Dorrego, and Bernardo Rivadavia. The conservatives, or counter-revolutionists, controlled the *Junta Grande* of December 1810-September 1811, the *Junta de Observación* which followed, the Congress of Tucumán, two or three of the supreme directors, and one or two of the presidents, while among their leaders were found Cornelio Saavedra, Gregorio Funes, Gregorio Tagle, Juan Martín de Pueyrredón, José Rondeau, Juan and Marco Balcarce, and the theologians of the interior.

The confused history of the period will become more comprehensible if we examine the attitude and activities of the clergy, of the oligarchies of the interior towns, of the *caudillos* of the provinces, and of the conservatives of Buenos Aires, as well as the work of the Assembly of 1813, and the reforms of Rivadavia. The outcome of the contest between the opposing groups often turned upon the success or failure of Argentine armies in the northwest, where they continued to fight with the Spaniards until 1824, or in the *Banda Oriental,* where they first confronted the Spanish royalists and afterward the troops of Brazil.

For the three decades following 1810, the Argentine clergy may be classified in three groups based upon divergent attitudes towards independence from Spain and genuine reforms. At the outset, the majority were royalists, a small group favored separation from the metropolis, and an insignificant minority were truly revolutionary. The second group gradually increased at the expense of the first until July 1816, when most of the churchmen were reconciled to a definite administrative secession from the mother country. The third group, the genuine reformers, never experienced any considerable enlargement of its ranks. On the whole, the clergy were conservative and reactionary, eager to maintain their ancient prerogatives, functions, and influence, and even desiring to increase their power at the expense of the civil authorities. Most of the leaders of the revolutionary faction complained of the attitude of the secular and regular clergy, and were anti-Catholic in the sense of desiring to curtail the functions and prestige of the churchmen. They were so profoundly influenced by the ideas of the French philosophers that their disposition could not have been otherwise. Yet many of them assumed a cautious attitude, because they were fully aware of the influence which the friars and priests were able to exert upon the masses.

Most of the men of influence in the interior towns desired to take the place occupied by the peninsular-born Spaniards of the colonial period. They wished to continue the old régime and maintain for themselves a privileged status. The attitude of the *hacendados* and wealthy merchants of Buenos Aires was similar to that of the provincial oligarchies, but the interests of the conservatives of the capital and the interior clashed at two points. The counter-revolutionists of Buenos Aires desired (1) to dominate the provinces of the littoral and the interior, and (2) to have charge of the collection and expenditure of the customs revenues of the port of Buenos Aires; and the conservatives of the interior opposed them on both issues.

Thus while the conservative oligarchies were obstructing the reformers they were also having clashes with each other. The first concession made to the autonomy of the provinces was granted by the conservative *Junta Grande* under the domination of deputies of the hinterland. Indeed, the conservatives were on the whole more inclined toward federalism than were the reformers, although both revolutionaries and counter-revolutionaries were found in the federalist as well as in the centralist, or unitarian, ranks.

Members of the two groups were likewise ranged on both sides of another important issue—that of monarchy versus republic. While the majority of the conservatives favored monarchy, some of them were on the other side, and many of the genuine revolutionists were far from convinced that a republic was absolutely essential to the regeneration of Argentine society. The French *philosophes* not only did not insist upon this form but many of them considered the enlightened constitutional monarchy as an ideal system of government; and a number of Sarmiento's "extremists" were disciples of the philosophers in this respect also. They were often the most ardent advocates of the numerous monarchical projects which were under consideration throughout the period.[2]

The masses of the towns of the interior and the *gauchos* of the plains—men who slowly developed political sentiments and became conscious of their prowess during the course of their contests with the

[2] For an excellent discussion of the subject, see Adolfo Saldías, *La evolución republicana durante la revolución argentina* (Madrid, n. d.).

royalists and Spaniards—were either invited to participate in the internal struggle or else were compelled to do so by their *caudillos*. In less than a decade after 1810 the *gaucho* commanders, in most instances men who had been born in the towns but had spent much time among the cowboys of the ranches, held the balance of power. At the end of two decades they were dominant throughout the country, and between 1835 and 1852 one of their number subjected the nation to a ruthless dictatorship. Sarmiento has called these *gaucho* leaders barbarians, and in many respects they were. But they were uncompromising enemies of monarchy, and most of them were tenacious champions of federalism.[3] In these respects they influenced the destiny of Argentina more profoundly than did the intellectuals. On the third issue, however, the issue of reform, their power was employed in general against the ardent patriots who were insisting upon a fundamental change of régime. Pursuing the immediate objectives of plunder and adventure, the rural masses were usually blind to their best interests in the more remote future.

III

It is not necessary to consider the work of the conservatives in detail. It was the Congress of Tucumán, dominated by them, that declared the independence of the provinces of the Río de la Plata, but if it had not been for their influence this declaration might have come earlier. They also contributed to the cause of independence, furnishing such outstanding leaders as Saavedra, Belgrano, and San Martín, although their bitter contests with the reformers often hampered the independence movement. They gave a certain impulse to federalism, mainly with the view of frustrating reform, and were partially responsible for the rise of the *caudillos* in the provinces. They furnished in Pueyrredón a chief executive who was able to maintain himself in power for three years—a term unequalled in length between 1810 and the advent of Rosas. But his reactionary and monarchical tendencies roused the *gaucho* leaders against him, and his administration was followed by the terrible anarchy of 1820. Except for their support of

---

[3] David Peña, *Juan Facundo Quiroga* (Buenos Aires, 1906), pp. 52ff. Peña points out four reasons why the provinces tended to become federalist: (1) hostility to the Buenos Aires religious reforms; (2) opposition in La Rioja (home of Quiroga) to the control of its mines by the national government; (3) opposition to monarchy on the part of the provincial masses and *candillos;* (4) resentment at the autocratic procedure of La Madrid in raising troops for the war with Brazil.

the movement for national independence, the attitude and activities of the conservatives were contrary to the spirit of the age. In general, they were obstructionists.

It is more important to examine the work of the reformers, a work which they accomplished in two distinct periods separated by an interval of almost seven years. The first began with the meeting of the Revolutionary Assembly on January 31, 1813, and closed with its dissolution almost two years later, the executive power being successively in the hands of the Second Triumvirate and the first two of the supreme directors, Posadas and Alvear. The members of the Assembly of 1813 were stimulated by Napoleonic successes in Europe and patriot victories in Argentina. Genuine reformers for the most part, they stopped just short of a declaration of independence. They eliminated from the oath of office the clause which referred to vassalage to the king of Spain; ordered that the clergy should not only be placed under the control of the civil authority but that their prayers should be offered in behalf of the assembly instead of the king of Spain; sanctioned a law which required the removal of all European officials who had not obtained a title of citizenship; authorized the coining of national money; proclaimed freedom of commerce; and directed that the Argentine coat of arms should replace that of the king on all public buildings. They also passed significant social legislation, for they abolished slavery, Indian tributes, entails, primogeniture, and the torture of prisoners; and they not only ratified previous decrees granting freedom of the press, but encouraged the founding of new schools, as well as the reorganization of the courses of study from the primary grades through the university.

Some of these measures naturally offended many of the clergy, shocked pious laymen, and aroused the opposition of the municipal oligarchies. Moreover, the assembly made the mistake of refusing to receive the delegates of Artigas. The result was a combination of priests and other conservative townsmen, the advance upon Buenos Aires of the *gauchos* under the intrepid leader of the *Banda Oriental,* and the forced resignation of Alvear in April 1815.[4]

The genuine revolutionists were unable to resume their work until

---

[4] Ingenieros, *La evolución de las ideas argentinas,* I, pp. 229-303. This author presents an excellent discussion of the moving forces back of the events of the period. But the reader should also consult Alejandro Korn, "Las influencias filosóficas en nuestra evolución nacional," in *Anales de la facultad de derecho y sciencias sociales,* IV, Pt. I (1914), pp. 305ff.

1821 when Martín Rodríguez became governor of the Province of Buenos Aires and chose Rivadavia and García as members of his cabinet. Reforms were then undertaken in the narrower sphere of Argentina's most important province, with the hope that they might be extended to the remainder of the country as soon as the national government, which had expired during the anarchy of 1820, could be restored. A *junta* of representatives was assembled and significant legislation was passed. Tithes and the ecclesiastical *fuero* were abolished, various religious orders disbanded, the monasteries secularized, and religious toleration quietly granted. The customs were collected with greater honesty and efficiency, the finances reorganized, a bank of discount set up, and a loan floated in Europe. A system of long-term leases was substituted for the sale of public lands; the University of Buenos Aires was founded (1821) and important strides—the founding of Lancasterian schools among them—made in primary education; immigration was encouraged; and finally, a society for the administration of charity and the education of women *(Sociedad de Beneficiencia)* was established.[5]

When Gregorio Las Heras succeeded Rodríguez in 1824, he offered to continue Rivadavia in his post of minister of government, but the great reformer preferred a mission to Europe. Now that the United States and Great Britain were ready to recognize the independence of the former Spanish colonies, the main consideration was the restoration of the national government of Argentina and the extension of the reforms of the Province of Buenos Aires to a wider sphere. During the administration of Rodríguez, Rivadavia had sent delegates to the various provinces to urge the necessity of some form of union, and the most important act of Las Heras was the convocation of a general constituent congress which began its sessions in Buenos Aires in December 1824.

This congress remained in session for almost three years, but was able to accomplish very little either in the spreading of reforms or in strengthening the national authority. The new land system (long-term leases) was extended to the entire republic; a national constitution was drafted and submitted to the provinces; Rivadavia was elected national president, and the City of Buenos Aires was detached from the province bearing that name, but the reformers had divided into two factions—the federalists and the unitarians—with Manuel Moreno

[5] Ingenieros, *op. cit.,* I, pp. 365-507.

and Manuel Dorrego leading the federalists; a war had broken out against Brazil; the Province of Buenos Aires resented the loss of its leading town; and the interior provinces, dominated by their *caudillos,* were not disposed to submit to the rule of the central government. Belligerent churchmen and conservative laymen then seized the opportunity offered by the divided strength of their opponents, forced the resignation of Rivadavia, helped the federalists place Dorrego in power, and before the end of the year 1829 secured the election of Rosas as governor of Buenos Aires Province. Between December 1824 and the summer of 1827, the national government was little more than a broken reed, and between the latter date and 1830 it ceased to function entirely. The reforms of the revolutionary period were over; they had scarcely extended beyond the confines of the major province. The national chaos of 1820-1824 was followed by that of 1827-1829 and the conservative restoration under the bloody dictatorship of the *gaucho* from the plains of Buenos Aires.

IV

That picturesque element of Argentine society, the *gauchos* of the plains, must now be examined at some length. Already these cowboys have been observed in the ranks of the patriots: in the *Banda Oriental* under Artigas, in Salta under Güemes. By 1820 their leaders were dominant in almost every part of the country. We venture a few quotations from contemporary observers.

Joel R. Poinsett, who made two journeys across the *pampa* during the early years of the Plata independence movement, remarked:

> "It is not uncommon to see a proprietor of a league square of land owning several thousand heads of cattle, and sheep, and horses, living in a miserable hut, and having the bare necessaries of life. His house is covered with hides; his furniture is made of the same materials. His yard is enclosed by a few stakes, bound together with thongs; and he may be seen, with his herdsmen, seated by a fire, cutting off slices of beef from a spit stuck in the ground and eating it without bread or salt." [6]

Theodorick Bland, who visited the United Provinces of Río de la Plata in 1817, stated, however, that one rarely met "a country gentleman resident on his estate." The "grain and grazing farms" of the wealthy landowners were committed, he said, to the care of "peasants or slaves" while the *hacendado* resided in his city mansion and visited

[6] Poinsett to Adams, November 4, 1818, in W. R. Manning, *Diplomatic Correspondence,* I, p. 462.

his rural estate only "occasionally." Bland also pointed out that "the more wealthy, intelligent and better sort of people" were "universally found in the cities and the towns."

Bland's description of the *gauchos* at this period when they were just beginning to make their influence felt in Argentine history deserves to be quoted fully.

> "The herdsmen . . . of the . . . plains form a very considerable proportion of the population of the country. Thinly strewed over the great pastures, those residing at a distance from the cities . . . have little society, are totally illiterate, lead an indolent life, and dwell on an immense waste, in continual solitude. Their habitations are constructed in the simplest form; in general, they consist of low mud walls, thatched with the long grass of the plains, tied on a layer of reeds, with rawhide thongs, or stuck on with mud. . . . The bedding and clothing of the family, and the whole household furniture, exhibit a scene of laziness and dirt, yet mingled with apparent cheerfulness, great kindness, much natural intelligence, and an evident independence of character.
>
> "From infancy the herdsman is taught to ride, and there are, perhaps, no more expert horsemen in the world; much riding is required by his situation and mode of life; and to ride well is his pleasure and his pride. Either from the custom of his Spanish ancestors, or from its real and constant utility, the herdsman is never without a long butcher's knife, worn about his waist. His cloak . . . , or poncho, as it is called, is a square piece of cloth . . . with a slit in the middle, through which the head is put, leaving it to hang down all around. This poncho is his bed at night, and by day his cloak, a belt, a saddle cover, or a bag, as fancy or necessity may require . . . [His] lazo is a cord or thong, made of strong, well-prepared hide, about thirty yards long, with an iron ring or a loop at one end, through which a running noose . . . may be made in an instant; the other end is fastened to the cincho or broad surcingle, which secures the saddle. . . . The lazo is thrown . . . with unerring aim, either on foot, or on horseback, or at full speed, at a fleeing animal or retreating foe . . . [His] bola is an instrument made of three cords of about three feet each from the knot which unites them in the middle; to the end of which is fastened a ball of about two pounds weight. The bola, with a few twirls over the head, is thrown like a stone from a sling; and, entangling about the legs of the animal at which it is directed, instantly prostrates it at the mercy of the pursuer. . . . This instrument, like the lazo, is usually slung to the hinder part of the saddle. Mounted, and thus equipped, the herdsman is ready for a journey of a thousand miles, the protection or the seizing of his herd, or . . . the defense of his country.
>
> ". . . The wars that have been waged . . . have made the

> herdsmen of those plains as expert in the use of a gun on horseback, as of the lazo or the bola, all of which they now carry in their warlike excursions; and they may be considered as the most formidable guerrilla . . . soldiery that ever existed. In courage they are inferior to none; and the exploits that are related of their adroit and rapid horsemanship exceed what has been told of the Parthian, the Scythian, or the Cossack of the Don. Such are the herdsmen of the pampas . . . , who are usually called gauchos; an epithet, like that of the yankee, originally cast on them in derision, but one which has now ripened into a distinctive and common appellation that is no longer offensive. . . . Nothing is easier than to make a fine partisan soldier of the gaucho: those of the plains of the Banda Oriental, under Artigas, and those of Salta, under Güemes, are proofs how readily those peaceful herdsmen can be made terrible in war; they are a class of people who have a predisposition to an unrestrained, roving life."[7]

Sir Walter Scott remarked in 1827 that the vast plains of Buenos Aires were inhabited "only by Christian savages . . . , whose furniture consists chiefly of the skulls of horses, whose food is raw meat and water, and whose favorite pastime is running horses to death."[8] Sarmiento, who has written the classic description of *gaucho* life, has applied to this man of the vast Argentine plains Victor Hugo's characterization of the Arab and the Tartar. "He and his horse are but one person. He lives on horseback; trades, buys, and sells on horseback; drinks, eats, sleeps, and dreams on horseback."[9] The boys begin to ride as soon as they have learned to walk, exercising and amusing themselves by the use of the lasso and the *bolas,* "with which they constantly harrass and pursue the calves and goats. After they become stronger, they race over the country, falling off of their horses and mounting again, tumbling on purpose into *viscacha* burrows, scrambling over precipices, and making themselves thoroughly skilled in horsemanship. On reaching puberty, they take to breaking wild colts. . . ."[10] With early manhood comes complete independence and almost complete idleness, for the women look after the house, prepare the meals, shear the sheep, milk the cows, make the cheese, weave the coarse cloth used for garments, and are thankful when some of the men undertake the cultivation of a little maize for the family, bread not being in use as an ordinary article of diet.

---

[7] Bland to Adams, November 2, 1818, in Manning, *op. cit.,* I, p. 416 *passim.*

[8] As quoted by Sarmiento, *Vida de Facundo,* p. 27.

[9] *Ibid.,* p. 51.

[10] *Ibid.,* p. 33.

The *gauchos* spent much of their time in hunting, in reckless sports, and in quarreling and fighting at the country stores. Some of them became guides for the prairie caravans, others became wandering minstrels, and still others outlaws. "The *gaucho,*" says Sarmiento, "will be a malefactor or a military chief according to the course which things take at the moment when he attains celebrity." [11]

Most of the leaders got their first taste of military affairs as rural commandants appointed to protect the life and property of the country people, or as subordinate officers in the patriot armies. In both instances these honors were conferred upon them by the men of the towns, whom they viewed with more or less contempt, despising their "effeminate" dress and manner of life.

> "These men [says Sarmiento], Spaniards only in their language and in the confused religious notions which they preserve, must be seen in order to appreciate the indomitable and haughty characters which are born of this struggle of isolated man with his savage nature, of the rational man with the brute. It is necessary to observe these faces bristling with beard, these countenances as grave and serious as the Arabs of Asia, if one is to have a proper conception of the pitying scorn with which they look upon the sedentery denizen of the city, who may have read many books but is unable to throw and kill a wild bull, who knows not how, on foot and without assistance, to provide himself with a horse from the open *pampas,* who has never met a jaguar and received it with a dagger in one hand and a poncho wrapped around the other, to be thrust into the animal's mouth while he transfixes its heart and leaves its body stretched out dead at his feet. This habit of triumphing over difficulties, of constantly proving one's self superior to Nature, of defying and conquering her, develops prodigiously the consciousness of individual importance and superiority." [12]

Their mode of life tended also to inculcate habits of cruelty. Suffering was always present. Abuse of wild animals and game began with childhood. Blood flowed constantly. Men and boys were always slaying or witnessing the butchery of some dumb brute,[13] and from this to the

[11] *Ibid.,* p. 53.

[12] Sarmiento, *op. cit.,* p. 33.

[13] "The native manner of killing a cow or bullock at that time [*cir.* 1850] was peculiarly painful. Occasionally it would be slaughtered out of sight on the plain, and the hide and flesh brought in by the men, but, as a rule, the beast would be driven up close to the house to save trouble. One of the two or three mounted men engaged in the operation would throw his lasso over the horns, and, galloping off, pull the rope taut; a second man would then drop from his horse, and running up to the animal..., pluck out his big knife and with two lightning-quick blows severe the tendons of both hind legs. Instantly the beast would go down

spilling of human blood was but a step. Around the country stores knives twirled and flashed at the slightest provocation. Men were frequently wounded, and sometimes killed.

The long period of anarchy and civil war which followed on the heels of independence served to exaggerate these cruelties. The wounded received little care and prisoners were usually killed in short order, or else subjected to a long process of mental and physical agony in order to delight fiendish tormentors.[14] Hudson remarks that the *gaucho* did not cut throats like a gentleman but "did his business rather like a hellish creature revelling in his cruelty. He would listen to all his captive could say to soften his heart . . . and would reply: 'Ah, friend, . . . your words pierce me to the heart and I would gladly spare you for the sake of that poor mother of yours . . . , and for your own sake too, since in this short time I have conceived a great friendship towards you; but your beautiful neck is your undoing, for how could I possibly deny myself the pleasure of cutting such a throat—so shapely, so smooth and soft and so white! Think of the sight of warm red blood gushing from that white column!' And so on, with wavings of the steel blade before the captive's eyes, until the end." [15] A young soldier from the United States who fought in the armies of this epoch says that his

---

on his haunches, and the same man, knife in hand, would flit round to its front or side, and, watching his opportunity, presently thrust the long blade into its throat just above the chest, driving it in to the hilt and working it round;... when it was withdrawn a great torrent of blood would pour out from the tortured beast. . . .

"Slaughtering a cow was grand sport for them, and the more active and dangerous the animal, the more prolonged the fight, the better they liked it. . . . The crimson torrents of blood, the deep human-like cries, made the beast appear like some huge, powerful man caught in a snare by small, weak, but cunning adversaries, who tortured him for their delight and mocked him in his agony." (Hudson, *op. cit.*, pp. 40-41.)

A French writer has remarked: "In a country in which the only wealth of the inhabitants arises from the incessant destruction of innumerable flocks, it can be easily understood how their sanguinary occupation must tend to obliterate every sentiment of pity, and induce an indifference to the perpetration of acts of cruelty. . . . The first instrument that the infantile hand of the gaucho grasps is the knife—the first things that attract his attention as a child, are the pouring out of blood, and the palpitating flesh of expiring animals. . . . Thus the savage education of the estancia produces in the gaucho a complete indifference as to human life. . . . He lifts his knife against a man with the same indifference that he strikes down a bullock. . . ." (Quoted by William Hadfield, in his *Brazil, the River Plate, and the Falkland Islands,* pp. 302-303.)

[14] For a good description of *gaucho* methods of warfare, see: José Ramos Mejía, *Las multitudes argentina* (Madrid, 1912), pp. 137-250; and Lucás Ayarragaray, *La anarquía argentina y el caudillismo* (Buenos Aires, 1904), pp. 43-166.

[15] Hudson, *op. cit.*, pp. 125-126.

captors greeted him frequently with the consoling statement that he would be shot "bye and bye" or his throat would be cut "directly." [16] A favorite method of punishing a prisoner was to sew him up in rawhide and leave him to die.[17]

Such were the men who became involved in the civil wars of Argentina in less than a decade after the movement for independence got under way. They had risen against the king not so much because they hated him as because the battlefield offered an opportunity for perilous adventure and an outlet for superabundant energies. They soon became the agents of the opposing urban groups, mainly of the reactionaries. "It was a blind tool," said Sarmiento, "but one full of life and of instincts hostile to European civilization and to all regular organization. . . . This tool was employed by the opposing parties of the civilized cities, especially by the least revolutionary, until in the course of time the very men who summoned it to their aid yielded to it." [18]

It is not necessary to dwell upon the leaders of these *gaucho* hordes. Each province produced its *caudillo,* often several of them; and there were thirteen provinces by 1820, the fourteenth, Jujuy, being set up in 1834. The precursors of all the chiefs were Güemes and Artigas, and most conspicuous among the later group were: Estanislao López, dominant in the Province of Santa Fé from 1818 to 1838, but frequently extending his sway to Entre Ríos and Corrientes; Pedro Ferré, a man to be reckoned with in Corrientes at any time from 1821 to 1839; Francisco Ramírez, Ricardo López Jordán, and Juan León Solas in Entre Ríos and Corrientes; Juan Bautista Bustos (dominant from 1818 to 1829) and the Reinafé brothers in Córdoba; the Aráoz family in Tucumán; the Aldao brothers in Mendoza; Juan Felipe Ibarra, virtually supreme in Santiago del Estero during the period 1820-1851; and Juan Facundo Quiroga, whose power radiated from La Rioja.[19] Under such leaders the *gauchos* galloped into the towns or against each other. Rural barbarism menaced urban civilization; liberated Argentina became a land of chaos, and the initial responsibility for this terrible state of affairs rested mainly upon the municipal oligarchies who opposed reform.

---

[16] J. Anthony King, *Twenty-four Years in the Argentine Republic* (New York, 1845), pp. 36-37.

[17] Sarmiento, *op. cit.,* p. 60.

[18] *Ibid.,* pp. 58-59.

[19] *Cf.* Antonio Zinny, *Historia de los gobernadores de las provincias argentinas* (Buenos Aires, 1920-1921), *passim;* Peña, *Juan Facundo Quiraga, passim.*

Yet the inhabitants of the region were so prolific that, despite the slaughter of frequent battles, the population increased. It was estimated at 508,000 in 1818 and at 630,000 in 1826.[20] It is likely that a corresponding increase occurred in foreign trade, although accurate and complete statistics appear not to exist.

Indeed, at least one recent writer of Argentina has observed—probably not without some justification—that the disorders of the period have been exaggerated. The people did not live in perpetual convulsion. In spite of internal turbulence and foreign war, the inhabitants of the villages and the countryside still enjoyed their *siesta* and gazed luxuriously and dreamily, without serious uneasiness or preoccupation, upon the *pampa* and the mountains.[21]

---

[20] Bland, *op. cit.,* I, p. 438; Levene, *Lecciones,* II, p. 195.

[21] Norberto Piñero, "Crítica histórica," in *Anales de la facultad de derecho y ciencias sociales,* IV, Pt. I (1914), p. 248. Luís V. Varela presents a detailed account of this period of anarchy in his *Historia constitucional,* III, pp. 1-500.

CHAPTER SEVEN

THE DICTATORSHIP OF ROSAS

THE period of anarchy in Argentina terminated in the long dictatorship of Juan Manuel Rosas, who ruled the Province of Buenos Aires for more than twenty years and controlled most of the other provinces for nearly seventeen. His advent to power represented in the main a victory of the reactionary group over the genuine reformers.

I

It will be recalled that a counter-revolutionary movement had appeared at the very beginning of the struggle for independence, and that its supporters were the wealthy *hacendados* and the leading merchants of Buenos Aires, as well as the oligarchies of the interior and many churchmen of all the towns. Their longest lease on the national government extended from 1816 to 1819, when they controlled both the national congress and Supreme Director Pueyrredón. Although they favored federalism as long as the genuine revolutionists were in charge of the central government, they speedily forgot this tenet of their faith as soon as they themselves secured control of that government. Many of them were monarchists, and the centralist Constitution of 1819 was mainly their work. But it had been rejected by the provincial *caudillos,* who helped the reformers drive the reactionaries from power.

In 1820, as elsewhere noted, the national government was dissolved. During the period from 1821 to 1828 the genuine revolutionaries were in control of the government of the Province of Buenos Aires and were striving to extend their authority and their reforms to the littoral and the interior. Conservative landlords, merchants, and churchmen now became ardent supporters of the autonomy of the provinces. The merchants and the landowners wished to prevent the men of the interior from exercising authority over the leading port or sharing the customs receipts of the Province of Buenos Aires. The clergy were interested mainly in circumscribing the reforms of Rivadavia. And both groups, but especially the priests, encouraged revolts not only in the Province of Buenos Aires but in other provinces as well. In many sections of the country "Religion or Death!" became the battle cry of fanatics called *"apostólicos."* Men on horseback fought for the "holy cause" of church and federalism. In this manner the reactionaries defeated during this decade all the attempts of the genuine revolutionists to restore national unity, and confined the reform movement largely to the Province of Buenos Aires. This achievement was made less difficult by the fact that Manuel Dorrego and several other reformers became doctrinaire federalists; and the situation was further complicated by a war with Brazil (1825-1828) over the control of the *Banda Oriental.*

For more than ten years after 1820 the Province of Buenos Aires was never free from the menace of chaos and the threat of outside attack either from Brazil or the provincial *caudillos.* Tired and exasperated by the disturbances of the period, the wealthy conservatives finally added to the battle cry of religion and federalism still another slogan: "Order and *Patacones*" (silver dollars). Resentful of Rivadavia's nationalization (1826) of the city and port of Buenos Aires, determined not to submit to domination by the other provinces, unwilling to belong to any larger unity which they themselves could not dominate, eager to preserve their special privileges and promote their business interests, they developed a profound hatred for the radical intellectuals who sought to create a liberal commonwealth. Joining the *apostólicos* and enlisting the support of the federalist reformers, they soon proclaimed Juan Manuel Rosas as the man of the hour.

II

The choice was logical. Scion of a wealthy family, and now a millionaire in his own name, Rosas was duly conservative and at the same time the idol both of the plebs of Buenos Aires and of the cowboys of the *pampa.* Born in the capital in 1793, Juan Manuel entered upon his career with all the equipment necessary to master his environment: ancestry, fortune, a handsome physique (he was a *rubio* or blonde with blood free from any Jewish or Moorish mixture), industry, and talent for practical affairs. His formal schooling was brief, for from his early youth he spent most of his time on the ranch. Here he acquired all the qualities and defects of the *gaucho,* while escaping the revolutionary contamination of the capital. Devoting himself to rural affairs, he soon revealed the monopolistic spirit characteristic of his Spanish ancestors. Backed by wealthy relatives and friends in the City of Buenos Aires, he set out to monopolize the salt-meat industry and the produce market of the capital. The "trust" which they began to organize in 1815, soon found ways of obtaining cheap salt, reducing the *gauchos* to peonage, and evading the duties on exports. They organized an army, suppressed competition, and by 1819 set up a sort of feudal state of their own in the southern part of the Province of Buenos Aires.

Rosas first began to participate in political affairs in 1820 when he employed his *gaucho* army to restore order in the province. Thereafter he maintained his prestige by performing several missions for the provincial government until divisions in the ranks of the reformers and generals presented an opportunity for him to set up a governor of his own late in 1828. A year later, on December 8, 1829, with the strong backing of the *apostólicos* and the wealthy landowners and merchants of the capital, he became chief executive of the province, with extraordinary powers, for a term of three years. Although repeatedly urged to continue in power, he surrendered his office at the end of his term. He kept himself before the public eye, however, by retaining the command of his army and undertaking an expedition against the Indians in the southern part of the province. He also maintained his contacts with the *caudillos* of the other provinces; and his wife served the holy cause during his absence by keeping his interests to the fore in Buenos Aires. Finally, on April 13, 1835, he again took charge of the government of the Province of Buenos Aires, with supreme power conferred upon him not only by the assembly of the province but by a plebiscite as well. This position he continued to hold until February 1852, when he was driven into exile. Moreover, through devious machinations and several agreements, forced or voluntary, with the leaders of the other provinces, he soon assumed the rôle of supreme chief of all Argentina.[1]

III

It is difficult to arrive at a correct estimate of the character and work of Rosas. He ruled during a stormy and complicated period; unprejudiced and reliable witnesses are few, and the documentary evidence is inadequate. While he was in power, many sycophants glorified his

[1] The best discussion of Rosas' early career, in my opinion, is that of Ingenieros, in *La evolución de las ideas argentinas,* II, pp. 89-184. I have followed this author in my interpretation. Other writers think that Rosas represented a kind of democratic movement. *Cf.* Rowe, *The Federal System of the Argentine Republic,* pp. 19-21, 35-38, *passim,* and Levene, *Lecciones,* II, p. 345. José M. Ramos Mejía has written three interesting volumes on Rosas (*Rosas y su tiempo,* Buenos Aires, 1907).

talents and achievements, and numerous bitter enemies circulated violent attacks against him from their various places of exile. José Rivera Indarte, for instance, declared in 1843 that Rosas had already been responsible for the assassination of nearly six thousand persons. For almost fifty years after the dictator's downfall his name was anathema, Adolfo Saldías being one of the very few writers who dared record a sentence in his favor.[2] It was not until 1898 that the first dispassionate survey of his dramatic and bizarre career was published.[3] Since that date, other studies of a similar nature have appeared, but it is likely that the final judgment of history will not be enthusiastic.

Physicians have declared him a neurotic. Poets have denounced him as a creature so infamous that a proper portrait would require the soul of a Nero and the pen of a Tacitus. But the student of practical politics may see in him a clever demagogue, and the historian will probably conclude that he was a man of his time and environment. His cruelties should not be contemplated in the abstract, but rather in connection with the grave problems and the spirit of his age in Argentina. The reformers of the revolutionary period adopted not merely the ideas of the French revolutionists but their methods as well, and Rosas, in his youth, witnessed some of the executions, doubtless heard others discussed. He was accustomed to the rough life of the *pampa;* from the beginning to the end of his long rule, he experienced few hours of repose and security; and his rivals and enemies were not models of humanitarianism.[4]

He appears to have become more haughty and cruel with the continuance of his power. And this seems to have been natural. Extravagant praise and servilism nurtured his egotism; foreign menace, domestic revolution, and threats of assassination increased his ruthlessness.

At the outset, and indeed for several years, he appears to have been modest enough, often refusing to accept the honors which a subservient

---

[2] *La historia de Rosas, y su época* (Paris, 1881).

[3] Ernesto Quesada, *La época de Rosas.* There have been many subsequent editions of this work; perhaps the best is that of 1923 (Buenos Aires).

[4] In 1844 the "Argentine Commission" in Santiago de Chile issued the following "Maxims of Politics and War" over the signature of Sarmiento and two others: "It is necessary to employ terror in order to triumph in war. All prisoners and every enemy should be killed. . . . The capitalists who refuse to grant succor ought to be dealt with in the same way. It is necessary to display formidable rigor. All effective means of operation are good and should be employed without hesitation. The Jacobins of the epoch of Robespierre should be imitated." (Martín V. Lascano, *Rosas y su gobierno,* p. 193.) Levene, in his *Lecciones,* II, pp. 341-344, gives a sensible discussion of the terror of the Rosas period.

congress proposed to confer upon him. In 1832 he evinced what seems to have been a sincere reluctance to continue in power, resigning his office at the end of his three-year term. Again in 1834 and early in 1835 he repeatedly declined offers of a second administration. It is true that his enemies have asserted that on this occasion his diffidence was due to the determination to have supreme authority or none, and that he even fomented anarchy in order to make his resumption of dictatorial powers seem imperative; but it is not certain that such assertions are based on solid evidence. In power once more, he permitted his effigy to be carried along in the religious processions and his portrait to be hung in the churches, but this immodest extravagance may have been at first largely the work of fanatical partisans. If such procedure was later encouraged by the dictator himself, perhaps it was because of the conviction that such a policy was essential to the maintenance of his authority.

His terrorism cannot be denied or fully condoned, but it can be explained and partially excused. His proclamations were coarse and bloody;[5] the executions of his reign—by his orders and probably at times without his orders—were undoubtedly numerous; but he was dealing, in the main, with rough, brutal men—with *gauchos* and militarists. His initial acts of terror, in 1830 and 1831, were occasioned by the revolutionary attempts of Juan Lavalle, the stern general who had ordered Governor Dorrego to be shot; but the system of terror itself was first organized in 1833, when others were in charge of the government of the province and Rosas was away fighting on the Indian frontier. It was at this time that the rich merchants and landlords founded their Popular Restoration Society and the masses of the capital their *Mazorca*. Thereafter the society pointed out the victims, and certain brutal criminals of the *Mazorca* executed them.[6] Thus Rosas merely took over and continued a system inaugurated by others; and it should be noted further that his ruthless persecutions were confined largely to the periods when his government was most seriously menaced by internal revolt or foreign aggression.

Perhaps the most reliable evidence relative to the dictator's character and conduct is the record left by contemporary foreign observers. At any rate, a few quotations will be offered.

---

[5] A favorite slogan was "Federation or Death! Long live the Argentine Confederation! Death to the savage, loathsome, filthy Unitarians!"

[6] This is on the authority of Ongenieros (*op. cit.*, II, p. 289); several other writers seem to consider the two organizations synonymous.

The testimony of agents of the United States is somewhat fragmentary and contradictory. Rosas reminded John M. Forbes of our own "strong-minded farmers, . . . justly considered to be the best guarantees of our national liberty." Forbes noted that Rosas had adopted the manner of life of the *gauchos,* "their dress, their labors, and even their sports; and it is said that he excels in every gymnastic exercise, even the most active and adroit, of that half-savage race of men." [7] Writing in 1832, Francis Baylies referred to his great personal beauty and his scanty formal education.

> "Reared amongst the cattle and the gauchos, it is his influence over the latter and the patronage of the Anchorenas [a wealthy family of Buenos Aires] which elevated him to his high station. His disposition . . . is not bad, and his intentions are honest (. . . in this opinion I differ from many intelligent Americans here), but the tremendous power with which he is clothed would transform a patriot into a tyrant and an angel into a demon." [8]

An officer of the United States Navy who had intimate dealings with Rosas wrote in 1838:

> "He is a man who has much cunning as well as detemination, and I believe would not hesitate to commit any act to carry into effect his views. . . . To do the Governor justice, he has a policy which he makes respected, not only in Buenos Aires, but in every part of his Dominions. . . . You may traverse the streets of the Cities as well as the solitudes of the Pampas in perfect safety from his former ruthless subjects; they are tamed; for this he deserves the blessings and thanks of all good men. I must . . . acknowledge him to be a man well calculated for his country as it is. . . . He has Talents, Honesty, and firmness, and if he would enlighten his Countrymen by introducing Knowledge, Science, Agriculture, and Commerce, . . . He would . . . be another Cincinnatus." [9]

Minister W. H. Harris declared in 1851 that the Rosas government was the "most simple and vigorous despotism in the world . . . His actions appear to flow as much from a blind caprice, and distempered will, as from any settled system of policy." He then spoke of the dictator's "sanguinary deeds," "appalling acts of cruelty," and the "long and monotonous chapter of his life, filled with nothing but scenes of injustice, oppression, and death. . . ." [10]

---

[7] Forbes to Van Buren, December 9, 1829, Desp. Buenos Aires, Vol. 3.

[8] Baylies to Livingston, July 24, 1832, Desp. Argentina, Vol. 4.

[9] As quoted by John F. Cady, *Foreign Intervention in the Río de la Plata* (Philadelphia, 1929), p. 14, note.

[10] Harris to Webster, No. 65, May 4, 1861, Desp. Argentina, Vol. 7.

A French observer who wrote in 1841 avowed that Rosas still enjoyed the rough sports of the cattle range. He also added a few more intimate touches:

> "This man, who founded his power upon the affections of the people, did not feel that he was degrading himself when he engaged in diversions which they loved. But when he found himself in the presence of a distinguished foreigner, whose esteem he desired to gain, the rude gaucho disappeared. . . . The deep regret that seized him upon the death of his wife [1838], as well as the extreme solicitude which he displayed toward his daughter, seemed to indicate that tender feelings had not been altogether banished from his heart. He made this cherished daughter the depository of his most intimate thoughts and the heiress of his fortune. And because he laid up riches for her, he was accused of wishing to seat her upon a throne." [11]

Another French writer, who had resided for months in the Plata region, spoke (1843) of Rosas' disdain for life and liberty, but contended that the dictator might have rendered his country great service if Heaven had endowed him with more light and a more humane heart. Rosas knew how to command, he declared.

> "He possessed the secret of commanding obedience. By virtue of this quality he might have become the benefactor and savior of his country. He indeed saw that the evil was in the anarchy which devoured the land, . . . and in the insubordinate habits of soldiers and generals. Unfortunately, he over-emphasized the opposite tendency and gave to the power that had become irresistible in his hands an effect that was odious, destructive, and degrading. He substituted his personality for the existing institutions; he induced the entire population to adore his portrait; he had incense burned before that portrait in the churches; he had [an effigy of?] himself drawn in a carriage by women, and by the most distinguished persons in the capital city; and he desired that discourses be addressed to himself in public ceremonies. At least, if he did not direct this to be done, he encouraged these servile demonstrations which in their manifold forms have reduced the citizens of the capital to the moral condition of Asiatic people." [12]

A third French eyewitness, Baron Deffaudis, (1845) stresses Rosas' great industry and his emphasis on propaganda.

> "An indefatigable worker, he spends his days in supervising the smallest details of ministerial affairs, in corresponding directly with

---

[11] An officer of the French fleet which blockaded Buenos Aires in 1839-1840, as quoted by W. S. Robertson, "Foreign Estimates of . . . Rosas," in *The Hispanic American Historical Review,* X (May 1930), p. 129.

[12] *Ibid.,* X, p. 131.

the civil and military authorities of the provinces . . . , and finally in dictating and even correcting with his own hand an infinite number of articles destined for journals not only in his own country but also in foreign lands." [13]

A fourth Frenchman wrote of Rosas as follows in 1850:

"Endowed with a reflective and persistent will, Juan Manuel is essentially an absolute ruler. Although force—that is to say, the principle of persons who have no principles—is the basis of his government, and although he constantly consults in his policies the necessities of his personal position, yet he is much pleased to be considered a man of well-founded convictions. He professes a great horror for secret societies, even though the *Mazorca* . . . was nothing else than a secret society which became publicly known because of its excesses. . . .

". . . He busies himself with all the details of administration and carefully supervises them; he labors assiduously from fifteen to sixteen hours every day in the transaction of public business, and does not allow anything to pass without a minute inspection. Thus, as he has said, the entire burden of governmental responsibility falls upon himself. . . .[14]

"Raised to supreme power by astuteness, General Rosas has seen his domination violently attacked, and he has not known how to maintain himself except by force. Vindictive and imperious, by education and by temperament, he was precipitated into despotism. . . .

"General Rosas is much occupied with the means by which a government may influence the morale of a people. Thus it is that he attaches great importance to matters concerned with public education; for he considers both education and religion as means of political influence. This same motive causes him to intervene actively in the periodical press. He subsidizes periodicals in France, in England, in Portugal, in Brazil, in the United States, and directs his journals of Buenos Aires, the *Gazeta Mercantil,* the *Archivo Americano,* and the *British Packet.*" [15]

Such was the character of the Argentine dictator as sketched by the contemporaries who, although not entirely impartial, were perhaps best qualified to judge him. He was energetic, determined, industrious, and at times haughty and cruel; he was not insensible to public opinion

---

[13] *Ibid.,* X, pp. 132-133.

[14] Many other contemporaries refer to his great industry. For instance, a British diplomat, writing in 1842, marveled at Rosas' arduous manner of life. He reported that the dictator never left his house, had no regular hours for sleep, ate voraciously only once a day, usually between one and four in the morning. (Cady, *op. cit.,* p. 90, note.)

[15] Robertson, *op. cit.,* X, pp. 135-136.

at home or abroad. It should be added also, that he seems to have been strictly honest in the management of public funds. A millionaire when he first came to power, he carried little with him into exile and died almost in poverty years later (1877) in England.

It is possible that he began his career with the high motives of rescuing his country from anarchy and welding the recalcitrant provinces into a national unity. If so, he was in some sense the precursor of Bismarck and Cavour. Yet he never made any attempt to frame a national constitution, and it may be doubted whether these exalted objectives continued to be the inspiration of his political life. It may be that such worthy motives soon were subordinated to his insane love for prominence and power. It has been alleged that he even dreamed of founding a hereditary monarchy, with his son and his daughter as his successors.[16] Be this as it may, it is doubtful whether he revealed any genuine disposition to surrender his authority after the beginning of his second term of office.[17] Nor was he scrupulous with reference to the means he employed to retain power. The women of his family, household servants who obtained secrets from the inner precincts of the home, priests, rascals, and cut-throats all became his agents; spies, servile propagandists, and secret assassins were constantly in his service. At certain periods, to say the least, his government was a complete tyranny.

IV

In most respects, the men who assisted in elevating him to power must have been bitterly disappointed. The clergy who hailed him as a man of God were in the end hopelessly subjected to his iron rule. He began by assisting the ecclesiastical groups and ended by persecuting every clergyman who revealed a spirit of independence. The Jesuits were invited to return in 1836 but were expelled in 1847. Many of the priests and at least one bishop became his abject tools. In the persons of Rosas and Bishop Mariano Medreno of Buenos Aires "was realized," as Ingenieros has remarked, "the union of throne and altar." [18] The laymen who supported him, the merchants and landlords of Buenos Aires and

[16] Ingenieros, *op. cit.*, II, pp. 281-282.

[17] Once a ruler and his coadjutors have become guilty of tyranny and terrorism, the surrender of power will be regarded with great reluctance. It would expose them to retaliation and ostracism. Rosas naturally wished to retain his property and his residence in Argentina, and his satellites would naturally urge him not to abandon them.

[18] Ingenieros, *op. cit.*, II, pp. 519-520.

elsewhere, were served somewhat better. The *hacendados* and merchants of the leading province were protected from the greedy *caudillos* of the upper littoral and the interior, who were prevented from levying tribute and regulating the tariffs of the major port or sharing largely in its revenues; and influential supporters in all regions received gifts of land and live stock taken from the Indians or the unitarians.[19] But the price paid for protection and favors was very dear. The government was expensive, and the ruler involved the nation in trouble with France and England, whose blockades, lasting for almost a decade, greatly injured the progress of business and commerce. As for the *gauchos* of Rosas' native province and the masses of the capital (negroes and mulattoes in the main) who supplied the rank and file of his army, their rewards appear to have been somewhat scanty, although some of the soldiers received small allotments of land. Free ranges and the free hunting of cattle in the Province of Buenos Aires seem to have been stopped. The *gauchos* became mere hired hands on the *estancias* of the generals and the wealthy ranchmen of the capital.[20]

It has been asserted that Rosas laid broad and deep the foundations upon which the nation of Argentina was to be erected. In a somewhat limited sense, this is true. But the work was largely incidental.

Rosas and the reactionaries were not primarily interested in nation building. It will be recalled that the conservative clergy wished to avoid the spread of religious reforms, while the more or less opulent landlords and merchants of the Province of Buenos Aires desired to avoid the political and social transformation of the Río de la Plata at the expense of its largest and wealthiest province. What they demanded of the leaders of the other provinces, as already noted more than once, was that they leave Buenos Aires free to fix the tariffs, keep their hands out of the coffers containing the customs receipts, and delegate to the governor of that province the right to represent the whole area in all intercourse with foreign countries. Beyond this latter consideration they had no particular interest in national unity; and they were certainly unwilling to accept any form of unity that was not dominated by their own province.

While protecting the Province of Buenos Aires from the *caudillos* of the other provinces, and while frustrating the reforms of the uni-

---

[19] Antonio Zinny, *Historia de los gobernadores de las provincias argentinas,* II, pp. 141, 151-154; M. A. Cárcano, *Evolución histórico del régimen de la tierra pública* (Buenos Aires, 1925), pp. 71-99.

[20] Ingenieros, *op. cit.,* II, p. 112 and *passim.*

tarians throughout the country, Rosas incidentally made a contribution to Argentine nationality. Fortune was in some respects kind to him. José María Paz, an able leader of the unitarians, was captured by a *gaucho* with his *bolas* and imprisoned for years; Facundo Quiroga was assassinated, probably at the instigation of the Reinafé brothers, and the assassination furnished Rosas an excuse for executing them; Estanislao López died a natural death. Most of the other *gaucho* leaders were of smaller caliber, men who could be bought off by subsidies, won over by flattery, or exterminated. For several years only Juan Lavalle, Fructuoso Rivera, and Gregorio Aráoz de la Madrid were left to give him serious trouble. The swarming *gaucho* chieftains largely retired or disappeared, and the nation was held together during the crucial years when the ferment of Argentina's dissociated life might have riven it asunder. Rosas, the mighty *gaucho,* saved La Plata from the *gaucho* hordes who were cutting it to pieces. Only in this negative sense was he a nation-builder. His destructive work was probably necessary in order that constructive achievement might follow.[21]

This appears to have been his main contribution. He did little to foment the economic or cultural development of the country. The interior rivers were closed to commerce, the harbor of Buenos Aires became filled with sand, no railroads were built, many of the public schools ceased to function, the academies decayed, the university languished, and the writers and thinkers went into exile. Nor did the nation he ruled enjoy tranquillity by any means; for, as we shall observe later, within three years after the beginning of his second administration a series of "liberator" revolutions commenced, and thereafter the country, especially the littoral provinces, had few intervals of repose.

The unity which Rosas created was not satisfactory. It was a unity dominated by Buenos Aires, and it would cause bloodshed in the future. Rosas ostensibly rejected the centralizing system proposed by Rivadavia, but in reality his régime was equally centralistic. It differed from Rivadavia's proposal only in its brutality and in its maintenance of the integrity and dominance of the Province of Buenos Aires. Argentina would not find peace until a federal system was established and the major city was permanently detached from its province and made the national capital.

---

[21] The destruction or taming of the *gaucho* chiefs may have been merely a contribution to order. Levene (*Lecciones,* II, p. 309) points out that the provincial *caudillos* were nationalists. Of course Artigas and the *Banda Oriental* leaders were not so in the Argentine sense; they seceded from the ancient viceroyalty.

CHAPTER EIGHT

THE OVERTHROW OF ROSAS

I

ROSAS' popularity in his native province during the first years of his rule will hardly be questioned. His handsome physique, his skill in the management of horses and cattle, his dexterity in all rural sports, his courage, the prestige acquired from his family, and his astuteness in the management of the rough *gauchos,* made him the hero of the men of the cow country. His administrative ability and his conservatism commended him to reactionary clergymen and wealthy inhabitants of Buenos Aires. His condescension, bonhommie, rowdiness, and scorn for the élite of the capital won him the support of the proletariat, composed in large measure of negroes and mulattoes. His business patronage obtained for him the favor of the butchers, the small merchants, and the tavern keepers of Buenos Aires. Once in control of the leading port and province of Argentina, he was a man to be cultivated and feared. The *caudillos* of the riverine and interior provinces hastened to negotiate with him. In return for his support, or with the view of avoiding his terrible hostility, they granted him the management of foreign affairs. Good fortune, it will be recalled, soon relieved him of his most formidable rivals. Quiroga was assassinated in 1835, López sickened and died in 1838, and Paz languished for years in prison (1831-1839). Only Juan Lavalle, Fructuoso Rivera, and Gregorio Aráoz de la Madrid were at liberty to combat his rule during the early months which followed his second advent to power. He was therefore left comparatively free to consolidate his position.

Something already has been said about his technique. Briefly, it may be described as follows. He roused the passions of the half-barbarous masses by denouncing the unitarians; he established newspapers and subsidized a small coterie of writers; he suppressed the journals of the opposition and forbade the circulation of their works; he organized a spy system; and he appropriated a secret society composed in considerable degree of assassins. Sycophant priests displayed his handsome likeness above the altars; his effigy was carried in numerous processions; his name resounded in all public prayers; and he was held up for hero-worship in the schools. With the customs of Buenos Aires, the confiscated property of unitarians, the public lands, and a bank of issue at his disposal, he bought off the leaders he could not readily subdue, and sent into exile those he could not buy. If all these devices failed to sustain him, there still remained that "last resort of scoundrels," the appeal to patriotism. National neighbors could be provoked into hostility or else declared to be hostile. And, besides, France and England attempted opportune coercive measures, France from 1838 to 1840 and both England and France between 1845 and 1850. Their governments were engaging in high politics, exacting indemnity for abused nationals, protecting their commerce, or defending the integrity of Uruguay, which was being menaced by the dictator.[1]

II

His task was by no means easy. He was not ruling Plato's Republic! Although he never had a large army—at no time did it number more than twenty-five or thirty thousand men, half of them, perhaps, negroes and mulattoes of Buenos Aires—it was frequently employed. Ambitious *caudillos* must be watched and placated or intimidated, conspirators detected, opposition propaganda prevented in Argentina and counteracted abroad. He was eternally vigilant, eternally busy, and for years financially embarrassed because of French and British blockades.

His most dangerous enemies were the old unitarians, the young idealists, *hacendados* who had become his enemies in the days when he was establishing a monopoly of the hide and meat trade, and landlords and merchants of the provinces who were tired of paying tribute to Buenos Aires. The hostility of France and England may have been more of a help than a hindrance. Their blockades caused the loss of customs revenues, but they furnished a rallying cry for patriotic support.

Perhaps, indeed, the most potent factor in effecting his overthrow was economic. The leader of the final successful revolt—Justo José de Urquiza, one of the dictator's former lieutenants—was the champion of Entre Ríos and the dissatisfied elements in some of the other provinces whose leaders were resentful of the economic dominance of Buenos Aires. Rosas had pampered Buenos Aires and maintained its monopoly

[1] The best account of this coercive action is that of John F. Cady, *Foreign Intervention in the Río de la Plata,* already cited. Agents of the United States at Buenos Aires were convinced that Rosas was provocative and uncompromising in his dealings with foreign governments because he desired a perpetual crisis as a means of supporting his power (W. R. Manning, *Diplomatic Correspondence . . . Inter-American Affairs,* I, p. 457 and *passim*).

of the port revenues and international trade of the whole confederation. The objectives of Urquiza, the great *estanciero* of Entre Ríos, as well as the objectives of his followers from the other provinces, were the economic emancipation of the confederation from the yoke of the capital, and a national reorganization that would put the *porteños* in their place. In deposing the dictator, Urquiza had also the support of the leaders of Brazil and Uruguay, who feared the ambitions of Rosas with reference to the area east of the Río de la Plata.

III

The young intellectuals became active soon after Rosas began his second term in April 1835. The most effective leaders were Estéban Echeverría, Juan María Gutiérrez, Juan Bautista Alberdi, Vicente Fidel López, Bartolomé Mitre, Miguel Cané, Andrés Lamas, José Rivera Indarte, Juan Cruz Varela and his brother Florencio, and José Mármol. Although they harked back to the reformers of the revolutionary period in Argentina and hence to the French Encyclopedists, their inspiration was drawn more largely from the writers who furnished the ideology for the uprisings of 1830 and 1848 in France. In the main, they were disciples of Saint Simon, Pierre Leroux, and Robert de Lamennais; their doctrines were socialistic and passionately humanitarian. Their weapons were their pens; only Mitre and Sarmiento became soldiers, and although López later took some part in practical politics, and Alberdi and Gutiérrez made contributions to the Constitution of 1853, only Mitre and Sarmiento among their numbers became outstanding politicians and statesmen. Their literary works, however, not only influenced the men of their day in Argentina, but in many instances became true monuments of national culture.

Most of their writing was done in exile, whence they were soon driven by the dictator. Their main centers of residence were Santiago and Montevideo. Although some of them visited Europe, where they came in direct contact with the French thinkers, the Gallic associations of the majority were confined to Uruguay, where many French émigrés made their homes during the period. At least one of them, Sarmiento, visited the United States and was greatly impressed by its institutions.

They carried on their propaganda in Argentina by means of secret societies, such, for instance, as "Young Argentina," which was similar to the "Young Italy" of Mazzini and to other contemporary youth movements of Europe. The "Social Creed" of Young Argentina consisted of fifteen symbolic words and a statement of their significance.

The word *Association* signified the Argentine nation organized around the men of the youth movement. *Progress* was declared to be the legitimate destiny of all living creatures and all nations, each nation and each individual being entitled to live its own life. Unlimited progress was proclaimed as a law of the universe. Three other words much cherished in the creed were *Fraternity, Equality,* and *Liberty.* Under the word *God,* Christianity—not Roman Catholocism—was held up as a proper religious faith, absolute religious liberty was advocated, and the separation of church and state proposed. *Honor* and *Sacrifice* were declared to be the proper motive and norm of social conduct, and the youth of Argentina were urged to seek *Independence,* emancipation from retrograde traditions which were subjecting them to the ancient régime. Another slogan was the *Organization* of Argentine society upon the basis of democracy, but not upon the basis of universal suffrage. (A plebiscite had ratified Rosas' dictatorship in 1835!) Sovereignty should reside in the "collective reason of the people," namely, in an aristocracy of intellectuals. But everything should be for the people, and equality of classes the goal. "All social institutions should have as their aim the intellectual, physical, and moral improvement of the poorest and most numerous class." And finally, Young Argentina should dissociate itself from both of the old parties, the unitarians as well as the federals.

Such in outline was the creed of Young Argentina. It was the work of Echeverría and Alberdi (mainly the former), who wrote during the Rosas period many articles and pamphlets in which they stressed the importance of the sciences, moral philosophy, industry, improved methods of agriculture, and the encouragement of European immigration. At the same time, Sarmiento, who agreed with their views in the main, began his passionate advocacy of education as the prime duty of the state. The writings of other members of the group must be passed over here—Indarte's terrible attacks on Rosas have already been mentioned. Mitre, though publishing comparatively little during his exile, appears to have shared the views of Alberdi and Echeverría, for he was referred to as a socialist.

These young intellectuals—with their law of unlimited progress, their doctrine of class equality, their ardent humanitarianism, and their devotion to the fatherland whose ruler had cast them out—had their secret lodges, their friends and devotees, not only in the Argentine capital and the Province of Buenos Aires, but in many of the other provinces as well. But the influence they exerted in consolidating the opposition to Rosas is not easy to determine. Some of them were the instigators of the abortive conspiracy of Ramón Maza, who planned to raise the inhabitants of the Province of Buenos Aires early in 1839. Others had some connection with an uprising which took place in the southern part of that province later in the year. In fact, they were probably connected with almost every attempt made to depose the dictator for more than a decade, but their influence was hardly as great as that of the exiled unitarians who longed to recover their property and their power; and it was perhaps far less potent than that of the *estancieros* and merchants of the riverine and interior provinces who soon developed an intense resentment against the economic yoke fastened upon them by the fiscal policies of the dictator. The fruits of the efforts of the intellectuals were to be seen more in the national reorganization which followed the downfall of Rosas than in the events leading to the overthrow itself.[2]

IV

Aside from the revolution in southern Buenos Aires, five other attempts were made to overthrow Rosas between 1839 and 1847. The first was that of Colonel Genaro Berón de Astrada, governor of Corrientes, who issued a manifesto to the chiefs of the other provinces calling upon them to withdraw from the dictator the powers which they had delegated to him. Assembling an army of some five thousand, he got in touch with the unitarian émigrés of Montevideo and signed an agreement with Fructuoso Rivera, then president of Uruguay, in which the latter bound himself to extend his aid. General Pascual Echagüe, governor of Entre Ríos and a partisan of Rosas, immediately advanced upon Corrientes, however, and completely routed the army of Astrada, cutting the throats of the officers and a large number of the rank and file (March 31, 1839).

The second attack, which began late in 1839 and continued into the middle of 1840, was more formidable. Planned by the "Argentine Commission" composed of émigrés at Montevideo, supported by a detachment of the French navy which was trying to exact indemnity from Rosas because of his abuse of French subjects in Argentina, and led by Rivera and Lavalle, the liberating army invaded Corrientes and Entre Ríos and approached within a few miles of Buenos Aires. But because of friction among the chiefs and lack of any sympathetic dem-

---

[2] Ingenieros, *La evolución de la ideas argentinas,* II, pp. 605-754.

onstration within the capital, Lavalle suddenly fell back and afterwards retired to Santa Fé (September 1840).

Already, however, plans for a third onslaught were under way. On April 7, 1840, the governor of Tucumán had denounced the Rosas dictatorship as a scandal in the "eyes of South America and the world," expressed regret because of the postponement of a constitutional régime for Argentina, and prevailed upon many of the leaders of the province to take an oath to defend "the cause of liberty against absolutism, the cause of civilization against barbarism, and the cause of humanity against its bloody oppressors."[3] A "Coalition of the North," consisting of the provinces of Tucumán, Salta, La Rioja, and Jujuy, was soon formed; General Gregorio Aráoz de la Madrid was placed in charge of the allied army; and an agreement was made with Lavalle at Santa Fé. But Manuel Oribe and the other generals of the dictator outfought and outwitted their opponents, defeating them in several bloody engagements. Madrid fled to Chile and Lavalle was assassinated (October 1841) by a partisan of Rosas.

By this time a fourth uprising was under way in Corrientes and Entre Ríos. General Paz had made his escape from prison and was collecting an army for the purpose of overthrowing the dictator. Rivera also appeared upon the scene, and if the two had worked together harmoniously, they might have achieved their goal. But the envious Rivera soon began to intrigue against the more able general, causing him to retire to Montevideo in disgust. The former was then defeated by Oribe and afterwards by Urquiza (March 1845); and in 1843 the long siege of Montevideo began, the émigrés of Argentina and the *Colorados* of Uruguay organizing the defense with the aid of Paz, while the *Blanco* Oribe, aided by Rosas, led the attacking forces. The siege was not lifted until October 1851.

The fifth of the group of important uprisings against Rosas got under way in November 1845, when General Paz and the governor of Corrientes effected an agreement with Paraguay. Supported by the war vessels of England and France, as well as by some four or five thousand Paraguayans under the command of Francisco Solano López, Paz undertook to liberate the country. Once more, however, the intrigue and prowess of Urquiza proved too formidable for the insurgents. López was defeated and sent back across the Paraná; Paz withdrew from the scene and found refuge in Paraguay; General Joaquín Mada-

[3] Antonio Zinny, *Historia de los gobernadores de las provincias argentinas,* III, p. 303; Levene, *Lecciones,* II, pp. 356-358.

riaga, the governor of Correnties, was thoroughly beaten at the battle of Vencés in November 1847; and the allegiance of Corrientes was restored.

These numerous revolts, which disturbed the peace of the country almost constantly for nearly a decade, have been listed in detail in order to illustrate the difficulties which the dictator confronted. If the hostile operations of the French and British—those of France alone between 1838 and 1840, and those of both powers from 1845 to 1850—are given proper emphasis in connection with the movements of the insurgent chiefs, it will become quite evident that Argentina enjoyed little repose during the Rosas dictatorship.[4]

V

By the close of the year 1846 two facts were clearly revealed: Justo José Urquiza was the ablest military leader of Argentina, and he was becoming restive under the domination of Rosas, who had not been active in the field of battle since 1840. Nor was this restiveness due entirely to Urquiza's ambition; as already stated, it was also caused in part by the growing resentment of the people of his province against the political and economic yoke of Rosas. It was only a question of time until a complete break would occur.

The break came early in 1851, when Urquiza, doubtless confident of the support of Brazil, Paraguay, and the majority of the leaders of Uruguay, boldly renounced his allegiance to the dictator. Rosas had just repeated his annual farce of surrendering his power, alleging on this occasion that the state of his health was unsatisfactory. On May 1 Urquiza took the liberty of accepting the renunciation so far as the authority which Entre Ríos had delegated to the dictator was concerned. To do less, he declared, would be to evince a reprehensible lack of consideration for the physical state of Rosas, as well as for the national interests of Argentina!

On May 25, 1851, Urquiza issued his famous *pronunciamiento* which the writers of Argentina have often quoted with great pride.

> "People of the Republic: Twenty years ago, after a bloody fight, the comforting hope of order and national organization, nourished by the horrors of anarchy, germinated along the margins of the Paraná River. A man appeared upon the political scene, and af-

[4] For these various attempts to overthrow Rosas, see Levene, *op. cit.*, II, pp. 352-360 and authorities there cited; Martín García Merou, *Historia de la república argentina*, II, pp. 336-361; Antonio Díaz, *Historia política y militar de las repúblicas del Plata desde del año 1828 hasta el de 1866* (Montevideo, 1877-1878).

> fecting constitutional ideas as well as love for the confraternity of the Argentine provinces, was hailed by the people and honored with their unlimited confidence. And yet, this man harbored in his heart sinister designs, and no other thought possessed his head than that of exalting himself upon the ruins of the national dignity, shattering upon the altar of his ambition the rich aspirations of valor and glory which our fathers had bequeathed to us. . . . Confederated peoples: the heroic province which has honored me with the guidance of its destiny has made to resound in its every nook and corner the uniform cry of 'liberty, organization, and war against despotism.' Our sister, the illustrious Province of Corrientes, has joined its magnanimous resolution to that of Entre Ríos. The great Argentino-American alliance, liberator of the Plata republics, has in its favor the might of arms, the exalted justice of its cause, and the benedictions of all good men." [5]

Four days later the anticipated alliance was sealed. Brazil and the leaders of Uruguay, with the exception of those under the domination of Oribe, agreed to join the provinces of Corrientes and Entre Ríos in their effort to depose the dictator. Carlos López of Paraguay, the independence of which Rosas had refused to acknowledge, as well as most of the leaders of the remaining provinces of the Río de la Plata, failed to respond to the appeal. But this mattered not. The days of the dictatorship were numbered.

The Uruguayans supported the uprising because they were exasperated by Rosas's continuous interference in their domestic affairs. Brazil lent its aid because of uneasiness with reference to the imperialistic aspirations of the dictator on the east side of the Plata. López held aloof under the conviction that his best policy was one of cautious defense.

In the month of July Urquiza crossed the Uruguay River with an army of seventy-five hundred men, some five thousand of them inhabitants of Entre Ríos and the remainder from Corrientes. Oribe, who was still besieging Montevideo, soon capitulated. On October 8 the long siege was raised. Preparations were then carried forward for the invasion of the Province of Buenos Aires. With Entre Ríos again the base of operations, an army of more than twenty-eight thousand was soon assembled, sixteen thousand from the two Argentine provinces, some four thousand from Brazil, more than four thousand émigrés from Buenos Aires, and the remainder (less than two thousand) soldiers of the *Banda Oriental*. Near the end of the year the

---

[5] As quoted in Levene, *op. cit.*, II, pp. 390-391.

Paraná was crossed, and Urquiza advanced with his troops southward across the Province of Santa Fé toward the Argentine capital. On February 3, 1852, he met and defeated on the field of Caseros, a few miles north of Buenos Aires, the dispirited army of the dictator, who hastily wrote out his resignation and prepared to flee to England.[6]

In his quest for allies and recruits, Urquiza had made two important pledges. He had promised to organize a constitutional régime in Argentina and to throw open the Río de la Plata and its tributaries to the trade of the world. We shall soon observe how these pledges were fulfilled.

---

[6] Zinny, *op. cit.*, II, p. 165, says that the army of the dictator numbered about thirty thousand, but that many of them deserted shortly before the battle. Robert C. Schenck, minister of the United States to Brazil, but in Buenos Aires at the time, estimated Rosas' troops at between sixteen and twenty thousand (Manning, *Diplomatic Correspondence of the United States. Inter-American Affairs, 1831-1860,* I, p. 524). John S. Pendleton stated on January 2, 1852, that Rosas probably had twenty-five or thirty thousand soldiers but that they would probably "all go over" to the enemy (*Ibid.*, I, p. 518). *Cf.* also Varela, *Historia constitucional,* III, pp. 507-536.

CHAPTER NINE

NATIONAL REORGANIZATION, 1852-1880

I

WITH the overthrow of Rosas, Argentina entered a new epoch, that of national reorganization. Justo José Urquiza, although hardly a model statesman, stands forth as an influential leader in the difficult enterprise; but the work was not completed until years after he passed from the scene.

When he finally abandoned Rosas and took up arms against the dictator, Urquiza pledged himself, as already observed, to carry out two important enterprises: (1) the unification of the nation under a constitutional régime, and (2) the opening of its rivers to the commerce of the world. The second he accomplished fully through eleven treaties with various nations of Europe and America. In the first he was not entirely successful, owing largely to the obstinacy of the Province of Buenos Aires; but the eight years of his rule (1852-1860) were signalized by the adoption of a national as well as fourteen provincial constitutions, and by a considerable strengthening of the bonds of unity.

Nor was his work limited to these achievements. In the field of public education, he nationalized the University of Córdoba and the Academy of Monserrat in the same city, and by means of national subsidies, encouraged primary instruction in the provinces. He also encouraged immigration and colonization; for works describing the resources of the country were published and circulated at government expense, and agricultural colonies were founded during his administration in Entre Ríos and Santa Fé. Moreover, he made efforts to improve the transport system. It was during his term that T. J. Page accomplished his important explorations of Argentine rivers, that regular steamboat service was begun on these rivers, and that Allan Cambell and William Wheelright initiated their plans for the construction of the first railways in the republic.[1]

[1] Levene, *Lecciones,* II, pp. 429-434; Mariano Pelliza, *La organización nacional* (Buenos Aires, 1923), *passim;* Julio Victorica, *Urquiza y Mitre* (Buenos Aires, 1918), p. 87, *passim.*

This is not the place to discuss at length the constitutional régime established under the encouragement of Urquiza. On November 20, 1852, a constituent convention composed of delegates from every province except that of Buenos Aires met in Santa Fé. On May 1, 1853, the new constitution was completed, and on the anniversary of the beginning of the independence movement (May 25) it was proclaimed. Soon accepted by thirteen of the provinces, it eventually became the fundamental law of the Argentine nation. The work was done so thoroughly and satisfactorily that few amendments have been necessary (those of 1860 being the most important). It is now the oldest constitution in Latin America and one of the oldest in the world.

For the most part, the men of the constitutional convention were not the young idealists who set forth their views so impressively during their exile of the previous decade. One important member of this group, José María Gutiérrez, participated in the assembly, however, and the influence of Alberdi has been declared to have been of major importance.[2] Taking into consideration the provincial sentiment of the country, the framers of the constitution set up a federal system. Its guarantees to persons and property give this constitution rank among the most liberal fundamental laws of the world. To a very considerable extent it was a reproduction of the Constitution of the United States. Its most important variations were the virtual establishment of the Roman Catholic Church as the state church and the amount of interference in provincial affairs which has been found possible under its provisions.

By the terms of the new fundamental code, the fourteen provinces were authorized to draw up constitutions, and during the next few years they proceeded to do so. Thus, by the time Urquiza's term expired, Argentina, which had existed for nearly half a century without either an effective national constitution or effective organic laws for the provinces,[3] was fully equipped with the bases of a civil régime. A new

---

[2] Most Argentine writers assert that Alberdi's *Bases and Points of Departure for the Political Organization of the Argentine Republic,* together with his draft of a constitution, exerted a profound influence over the assembly. *Cf.* Paul Groussac, *Estudios de historia argentina* (Buenos Aires, 1918), pp. 261-371, for a different view. For a good brief sketch of Alberdi, see Carlos Pereyra, *El pensamiento político de Alberdi.*

[3] Between 1820 and 1852 legislatures had been established in all the provinces, but their sessions were irregular and turbulent and they were practically always the abject tools of the *caudillos.* In most instances, also, constitutions had been drafted, but all of these were now discarded and new ones substituted.

era was inaugurated in which executives were somewhat more respectful toward the law.[4]

II

For ten years Urquiza was constantly vexed by the recalcitrant conduct of the Province of Buenos Aires. Various factors gave rise to the problem. In the first place, Urquiza's background was not such as to inspire confidence. For years he had been the ruthless right-hand man of Rosas. Like the former dictator, he was a wealthy *estanciero* and a strong-willed *gaucho* leader. During the first months after Rosas' overthrow, Urquiza frequently evinced a capacity for stern conduct, at times suspending the customary rights of citizenship and imprisoning, expelling, or executing his political enemies. His spirit of moderation toward some of the old partisans of Rosas, and his willingness to accept their collaboration in government, likewise gave offense in some quarters. Many confessed a fear that he was to become another tyrant. His difficulties were also due in part to the ambition of some of the repatriated exiles—such men as Valentín Alsina, Dalmacio Vélez Sarsfield, Bartolomé Mitre, and Domingo F. Sarmiento—who were eager for place and power.

But more important than this personal factor, was the determination of many of the leaders of the province to maintain either their independence or the political and economic supremacy of their particular section over the entire Río de la Plata area. Foreign diplomats in the region saw clearly this phase of the problem. The British minister wrote late in 1852:

> "Buenos Aires for twenty years has governed and monopolized the power and patronage of the whole Confederation; she pretends to superior intelligence, and could not submit to take part in a Congress [namely the constituent congress] where her privileges would be attacked, and (as she views the matter) her population and wealth inadequately considered." [5]

Writing in 1856, the minister of the United States described the situation in similar terms. The Province of Buenos Aires, he noted, was for many years

> "charged with . . . all the rights pertaining to foreign relations—received and sent all the foreign Ministers, collected and disbursed

[4] L. S. Rowe, *The Federal System of the Argentine Republic* (Washington, 1921), pp. 64-68; Matienzo, *El gobierno representativa federal*, pp. 65-84, 193-213.

[5] As quoted by Pelham H. Box, in *The Origins of the Paraguayan War* (Urbana, 1929), p. 76.

> all the duties arising from the receipt of customs—and . . . permitted no other custom-houses, than those situated within it. The transit of foreign merchandise to and from the other provinces, passed through this. There was a nominal *Confederation* of Provinces, there was but one real Government, Buenos Ayres! ! ! These superior privileges, as they are called, together with a hatred of Urquiza, [were] the real cause of the difficulties. . . . This province struggled for a continuance of most of the same privileges and a retention of the ascendancy. The Confederation made counter-claims, and attempted to enforce them. . . ." [6]

In short, it was the old issue that had caused trouble since 1810 and had been largely responsible for the advent of Rosas, an issue which was far more important in determining the course of Argentine history than any theoretical questions of federalism or centralism. At this period, indeed, all were theoretically federals; but they disagreed violently with reference to the question of the division of the income of the only important customhouse in the nation.

> "The Province of Buenos Aires, in the name of federalism, believed that each state should be sufficient unto itself and manage its own revenues: *it professed the federalism of the rich.* The other provinces, in the name of the same political doctrine, believed that all the states should . . . divide equally the common revenues: *they professed the federalism of the poor.*" [7]

The political and economic motives were practically inseparable. The struggle was at once for political power and for the control of customs receipts. It was a contest between a large, comparatively populous, and wealthy coastal region and a group of small, poor, and scantily settled interior provinces. For the Province of Buenos Aires then embraced nearly half the area of the country, one-third of its population, and most of its wealth.

Aside from the personal and the regional issues, nothing else appears to have been at stake. Both contestants appear to have been equally liberal and equally conservative. The formerly ostracized intellectuals of the Rosas period, now grown more mature and more moderate, were found in both camps. One writer has observed in the confused history of the period a sort of incipient class struggle between the Buenos Aires bourgeoisie with the unawakaned proletariat of the growing city at their heels on the one hand, and the agrarian magnates and semifeudal *caudillos* of the provinces with their wild dependents, mainly

---

[6] Manning, *Dip. Cor. . . . Inter-American Affairs,* I, p. 587.

[7] Julio B. Lynch, "Introduction" to Victorica's *Urquiza y Mitre,* p. 9.

gauchos, on the other.[8] This may have been true in a very limited sense, but the contest was mainly personal and regional.

III

A satisfactory equilibrium was difficult to reach. A partial solution of the problem of the overwhelming preponderance of the Province of Buenos Aires could be found in its partition by the process of federalizing its capital city and its port; but such a solution was arrived at only after a prolonged fight. The intermittent contest lasted from 1852 to 1880 and included five brief civil wars. In summary, the main events were as follows.

The *Acuerdo de San Nicolás* (May 31, 1852) furnished the Buenos Aires leaders their first important opportunity for protest. This agreement provided, among other things, for the calling of a constitutional convention and the sharing of the national expenses in proportion to the income received by each province from the foreign customs dues. It also designated Urquiza as chief executive of the nation, conferring upon him extensive powers and the title of "Provisional Director." The legislature of the Province of Buenos Aires vigorously denounced this pact, refused to ratify it, declined to send delegates to the constitutional convention, and finally rejected the Constitution of 1853. Urquiza then tried to coerce the province, and a brief war followed; but in the summer of 1853, after his blockading squadron had gone over to the enemy, he withdrew, establishing his headquarters first at his ranch in Entre Ríos and later at Paraná, which was chosen as the temporary capital of the confederation.

Shortly afterwards a *modus vivendi* was established, but serious difficulties continued to arise. The main problem was that of obtaining revenues for the national government. Buenos Aires continued to be the leading port, almost to the exclusion of all others. Attempts to induce vessels engaged in the foreign trade to enter Rosario, and pay duties there, met with meager success. Differential duties in favor of that port and discrimination against Buenos Aires brought unsatisfactory returns while deepening the enmity of the province of which that city was the capital.

In 1859 another war occurred in which the national government was more successful. The forces of the confederation were led by Urquiza, now constitutional president; those of the Province of Buenos Aires were under the command of Bartolomé Mitre. On October 23, 1859,

[8] Box, *op. cit.,* p. 77.

the two armies met on the field of Cepeda, in the northern part of that province, and Mitre was routed. He then withdrew to Buenos Aires, and Urquiza advanced to San José de Flores where a pact was signed on November 11. The obstreperous province now agreed to surrender its productive customhouse and enter the confederation, provided an opportunity should be given to offer certain amendments to the constitution. Constitutional conventions speedily assembled, and by October 21, 1860, the revised fundamental law had been accepted by all parties.

But the settlement was far from satisfactory. Although the Province of Buenos Aires had agreed eventually to turn over to the nation the customs of its leading port, the major portion of its receipts were to be retained for five years. And the capital problem was still unsolved, for the amendments to the constitution provided that the national authorities could not reside in any province until the consent of the legislature of the province had been obtained.

In fact, Buenos Aires had hardly entered the national union before other difficulties arose and culminated in a third civil war. On this occasion the conflict was caused in part by disturbances in the provinces of the upper littoral and the interior. The strong-headed *caudillos* were not all dead. Between the date of the promulgation of the Constitution of 1853 and the end of his term, Urquiza intervened in the thirteen provinces no less than sixteen times for the purpose of suppressing disorders and restoring or supporting the "constitutional authorities." Santiago Derqui, who succeeded him as chief executive on March 5, 1860, was even more absorbed with provincial difficulties, intervening in local affairs nine times during the first eighteen months of his administration. Agents of Buenos Aires were suspected of fomenting some of these disorders, especially those which occurred in the Province of San Juan, the former home of Sarmiento, who now occupied a place in the ministry of Governor Mitre of the Province of Buenos Aires. The pretext for the third outbreak of hostilities between the latter province and the confederation was the refusal of the national congress to seat the Buenos Aires delegation because of alleged irregularities in its election; but the real causes were the San Juan outbreak, superimposed upon old enmities, and the struggle for power.

On September 17, 1861, the two armies, again led by Urquiza and Mitre respectively, met on the plains of Pavón, in the Province of Santa Fé; and although Mitre's losses were greater than those of Urquiza, the latter, now old—more than sixty—and discouraged, and out of sympathy with President Derqui, retired from the theatre of the war. He continued, however, to dominate Entre Ríos until he was assassinated in 1870. Derqui, with his term hardly begun, but without the support of the great *estanciero,* surrendered his office and proceeded to Montevideo, where he died two years later.

After the battle of Pavón, Mitre took charge of the national government while still retaining his post as governor of the Province of Buenos Aires. He convened the national congress at once and endeavored to settle the capital issue. At his suggestion, this body proposed to "federalize" the entire Province of Buenos Aires, but the *porteños* not only rejected this plan but also refused to consent to the federalization of their capital city. The best arrangement that could be secured was a compromise which permitted the national authorities to reside in Buenos Aires for five years. Mitre had turned "nationalist"!

The issue had been postponed, not settled. Now that the powerful province was a member of the national union—called the "Argentine Nation" after 1860—its leaders were determined to dominate it. The Paraguayan War (1865-1870) merely delayed the sectional conflict. In the election of 1868, however, the *porteños* were divided. Rufino de Elizalde and Adolfo Alsina, son of a former governor, both wished to be candidates, but the latter finally effected a combination with Sarmiento, who, although a native of San Juan, had for some time been identified with Mitre and the leaders of Buenos Aires. This greatly weakened the forces of the *porteños,* whose political efforts were further handicapped by an epidemic of cholera. The result was a victory for the provincial Sarmiento, who not only carried Buenos Aires but six of the other provinces. The new president broke with his old friend Mitre and proved to be more of a provincial than a *porteño*. In 1874 Mitre once more became a candidate for the presidency, but was defeated by Nicolás Avellaneda, a native of Tucumán who had the support of Alsina and was alleged also to have profited by the backing of Sarmiento, of whose Cabinet he had been a prominent member (minister of justice, cult, and public instruction). The imperious Mitre could restrain himself no longer. Denouncing the election as fraudulent, he rose in revolt. Doubtless there had been fraud—on both sides, for that matter—but the underlying motive for the uprising was the resentment of the Province of Buenos Aires at the loss of its dominant position, for although Mitre had a few followers in the interior provinces, his main support was in the great province of the littoral. Fortune, however, was against the general, and he was severely defeated.

As the election of 1880 approached, the politicians of the interior provinces, who were determined to maintain their supremacy, set up a strong organization known as the Córdoba League. They put forward as their candidate General Julio Roca, a *Tucumeño* who had achieved fame through his recent campaigns (1878-1879) against the Indians of the southern part of the republic. These campaigns had thrown open for land speculation and settlement a large area of fertile soil which the Province of Buenos Aires wished to retain as a part of its public domain. But the leaders of the interior provinces not only desired to retain the region for the nation but expressed the determination, as the election approached, to detach Buenos Aires from its province and make it the national capital. Thus, in addition to their desire to win the presidency, the *porteños* had another motive for vigorous action, namely, that of protecting the territorial basis of their power. Their candidate for the presidency was Carlos Tejedor, the popular governor of their province. The balloting for electors, which took place in April, revealed that only the electors of two provinces, Buenos Aires and Corrientes, had been instructed for Tejedor. It was therefore clear that the *porteños* had been defeated at the polls, but they now turned to another arbiter. They organized rifle clubs and planned a revolt. They would dominate the union or secede from it.

Civil war was again imminent. In June the national government withdrew to Belgrano; toward the end of July a brief, bloody struggle ensued, in which the *porteños* were defeated but treated rather mildly. The victorious party now proceeded, however, to settle the capital question once for all. New elections were ordered for both the national and the provincial legislatures, and the voting in the city and Province of Buenos Aires took place under military supervision! On September 21, 1880, the national congress passed a law separating the city from its province and declaring Buenos Aires to be the nation's permanent capital. Of course, the legislature of the Province of Buenos Aires voted to accept the measure—it had been renovated for that purpose!

The great city probably constituted the necessary fulcrum for the achievement of order and effective national organization. The lesson of history seemed to be that the nation could only be governed from the City of Buenos Aires, with all of its prestige and the extraordinary economic importance derived from its port. The provinces would be satisfied with nothing less. The settlement of the vexing issue marked the beginning of a new political era. The revolutions which followed the year 1880 did not constitute a real danger to national unity. The leaders of the Province of Buenos Aires accepted their defeat and acquiesced in the loss of their important city. In 1882 they founded a new capital at La Plata.

IV

The coming of the new epoch was not, however, entirely the result of the political and military events of 1880. Other factors were already in operation. The diffusion of culture, the spread of primary, secondary, and higher education, the influx of immigrants and capital, the construction of railways and telegraphs—movements which had begun in a small way under the patronage of Uriquiza—continued with accelerating pace under the able administrations of Mitre, Sarmiento, and Avellaneda—all of them effective patrons of cultural and economic progress—until a fundamental transformation was taking place in Argentine life. With the overthrow of Rosas, the nation moved rapidly into the orbit of Occidental culture and came directly under the influence of new ideas, a new technology, and a new impact of Western economy.

It should be noted also, in passing, that the civil wars of the period were not limited entirely to the contest between the rich province and its poor neighbors. The various provincial disturbances during the decade from 1852 to 1861 have, indeed, already been mentioned. They were likewise frequent during the nineteen years which followed. In September 1868, an Argentine senator declared that between June 1862 and the same month of 1868 some 117 conspiracies and revolts occurred, resulting in ninety-one battles and the death of 4,728 persons.[9] This may have been an exaggeration, but the records published by Manuel Alberto Urrútia reveal at least twenty-two instances of federal intervention in the provinces, not including that of Buenos Aires, between 1862 and the end of 1880.[10] Although some of these may have been instigated by the national government for political purposes, most of them probably represented the survival of the *caudillo* spirit of another epoch. The *caudillos* would not be suppressed until rapid communication and effective equipment had strengthened the arm of the central government, and applied science had diverted the attention of soldiers and officers from the spoils of war to the profits of agriculture and stock raising.

---

[9] Matienzo, *El gobierno representativo federal en la república argentina*, p. 254.

[10] *Intervenciones del gobierno federal en las provincias* (Buenos Aires, 1904), I, *passim*.

Moreover, it would be an error to assume that the influence of Buenos Aires, both city and province, greatly declined after 1880. Although the influence of the region was eclipsed for a decade, it was afterwards largely recovered. After 1886, city and province usually stood together in the national elections. Between them, they furnished the majority of the chief executives, and down to 1930, at least, there was not a single administration in which either the president or the vice president was not a native of the Province of Buenos Aires. Moreover, with very few exceptions, all the presidents not natives of the great province or its erstwhile capital were residents of the City of Buenos Aires at the time of their election, and all, with rare exceptions, filled their cabinets with men domiciled in the capital.[11] And the reason for this predominance does not seem obscure. The population of the province and the federal capital has increased more rapidly than that of the remainder of the republic (being one-third of the total in 1869 and approximately five-eighths in 1930); the two areas possess the vast majority of the national wealth; three-fourths of the nation's imports, as well as slightly more than a third of its exports, still pass through the port of Buenos Aires; and all railways converge in the capital city almost as completely as all roads ever led to ancient Rome.[12]

It has been asserted that the predominant influence of the great city and province soon ceased to be resented by the other political divisions of the nation. "After 1880," says Matienzo, "the regional dissidences between the *porteños* . . . and the provinces . . . vanished, because the City of Buenos Aires, governed directly by the national authorities," was "considered the common possession of all the Argentines." [13] This assertion can be supported only by demonstrating that the later struggle between the Córdoba League and the *Unión Cívica* or the *Unión Cívica Radical* was entirely nonregional—a subject that demands further investigation. At any rate, the possession of the great city gave the federal government increased strength and prestige and reduced the danger of Argentina's breakup into two or more nations until the expansion of its railways and telegraphs could entirely eliminate the possiblity of dissolution. In this respect, at least, the year 1880 marked the dawn of a new epoch in Argentine political history.

---

[11] Matienzo, *op. cit.*, pp. 135-139.

[12] Tobal, *Lecciones de geografía argentina*, pp. 168 and *passim*. The most complete work on the period of national reorganization is that of Arturo B. Carranza, *La cuestión capital de la república* (5 vols., Buenos Aires, 1926-1932). The best discussions in English are: Kirkpatrick, *The Argentine Republic*, Chs. XVI and XVIII, and C. E. Akers, *A History of South America*, pp. 37-61. See also Varela, *Historia constitucional*, III, pp. 537-579.

[13] *Op. cit.*, p. 108.

CHAPTER TEN

THE ECONOMIC REVOLUTION AND EDUCATIONAL PROGRESS

THE half-century which followed the elevation of Mitre to the presidency of the Argentine nation witnessed a remarkable transformation in its economic and social life. Its population grew rapidly, its herds not only increased [1] but improved in quality, and it became at the same time one of the leading agricultural regions of the world. Between 1862 and 1914 the area of land in cultivation expanded from some two hundred thousand to more than sixty million acres, and foreign trade grew in value from a little more than thirty-five million dollars to nearly seven hundred million dollars. National wealth increased rapidly, public revenue augmented, and significant progress was made in the field of public instruction.

The remarkable economic development was caused by the growing demand for meat and cereals in industrialized Europe, by the migration of European workers and capital to Argentina, and by the increasing application of technology to the Argentine environment. The first of these influences requires no elaboration; the second and third must be discussed at some length.

I

For three centuries after the discovery, European migration to the Río de la Plata region was a very tiny stream, at times hardly more than a mere trickle. Spain had little surplus population, and most of what there was preferred to go elsewhere. The entrance of foreigners into the colony was made exceedingly difficult, and the number who gained admittance was quite small. During the early years of independence, many of the reformers, especially Rivadavia and those who shared his ideals, sought to attract immigrants, but only a few came in, mainly from the British Isles and France. The Rosas period which followed may be compared with the colonial epoch, for he placed difficulties in the way of all immigrants, except (at times) the English.

[1] The sheep increased from fifty-four million in 1869 to seventy-four million in 1895. By 1914, however, the number had declined to forty-three million. Other species of livestock continued to increase throughout the period.

The era of national reorganization marked the beginning of immigration on a rather important scale. Alberdi's phrase "to govern is to populate" was generally accepted, and numerous attempts—many of them successful—were made to induce people from Switzerland, Germany, France, Italy, and elsewhere to settle on the land. Several agricultural colonies were established in Entre Ríos, Santa Fé, the Province of Buenos Aires, and elsewhere in the *pampa*. By 1857 almost five thousand immigrants were entering Argentina each year; in 1879 more than fifty-five thousand entered, although the net for that year was a little less than thirty-two thousand; while the largest group for the period came in 1873—a gross number of more than seventy-six thousand, with a net of over fifty-eight thousand.

During the next decade the stream increased rapidly, reaching a peak, for the period before the World War, in the year 1889, with a net immigration of 220,260. Shortly afterwards the "swallows," or temporary and seasonal immigrants, began to enter the country, so that while the maximum of arrivals was reached during the pre-war period in 1912, with 379,117, the net for that year was only 206,121,[2] or less than in 1889. Among these immigrants, the Italians were most numerous, followed by the Spaniards, the French, the Russians, and the Germans; but Britons, Swiss, Belgians, and citizens of the United States were also included.[3]

They soon introduced new methods of agriculture and new and improved farm implements; and it is probable that they were mainly responsible for introducing better breeds of animals, as well as for teaching the natives the value of milk, butter, cheese, and new varieties of crops. For centuries the inhabitants of Argentina had scarcely modified their agrarian and pastoral techniques, but now, after its long isolation, the country felt the effects of a new exposure to advanced ideas and technology. A more effective attack was made upon an environment that had been changed little by the hand of man since the introduction of domestic animals and food plants from Spain in the course of the sixteenth century.

Within a short time, the immigrants not only became the major group of agriculturalists but began to make important contributions to the pastoral industry. Although the Argentine Creoles were responsible for the policies which brought in the immigrants and the alien tech-

---

[2] Tobal, *Lecciones de geografía argentina,* p. 148.

[3] A. B. Martínez and M. Lewandowski, *The Argentine in the Twentieth Century* (London, 1910), pp. 118-120.

nology, and were active in the pastoral transformation, they took only a minor part in the development of the new agricultural régime. The natives of the upper class speedily became a wealthy landed aristocracy who dwelt largely in the cities, ruled the nation, and made important contributions to its literature and art. They reaped enormous profits as landowners and *entrepreneurs*. Rising land values, abundant cheap labor, and a growing world demand for Argentine commodities made them rich. *Pesos* fell like rain into their *sombreros*.[4]

II

While Argentina was winning its independence and perfecting its national organization, several inventions of great utility in subduing the *pampa* were made, chiefly in the United States. Among these, the steamboat and the steam locomotive are thought of at once, but there were others of scarcely less importance: the steel windmill; the reaper, the thresher, and other implements adapted to large-scale agriculture; barbed wire fencing; new processes of preserving meats; and new methods for clipping and utilizing wool.

Many of these inventions were perfected by virtue of the demands of the Anglo-Saxon when he confronted the problem of conquering the great prairies and plains of the North American west. This region not only called them forth in some instances, but used them in such large quantities as to make possible for the first time their production at prices which the men of an analogous region in the far south could afford. With their perfection, Aryan civilization entered a new phase. The treeless and semi-arid plains of the world—in the United States, in Argentina, in Australia, in Russia—began to yield unsuspected treasures.

The first thresher was invented by Andrew Meikle of East Lothian, Scotland, in 1786, but it was not widely used until citizens of the United States became interested in this type of mechanism several decades later. Its perfection and production in large numbers occurred in connection with the introduction of wheat culture into the great American west. By the close of the Civil War manufacturers of the Great Lakes region were ready to distribute it at reasonable prices.[5]

The invention of the reaper, which naturally increased the utility of

---

[4] The best discussion of the agricultural aspects of this immigration will be found in Mark Jefferson's *Peopling the Argentine Pampa* (New York, 1926).

[5] Edward H. Knight, *American Mechanical Dictionary* (New York, 1874), III, *passim;* William T. Hutchinson, *Cyrus Hall McCormick* (New York, 1930), p. 35, *passim.*

the thresher, occurred in 1831. It was in that year that Cyrus Hall McCormick fashioned a machine which cut many acres of wheat a day. Years passed, however, before it could be marketed in large quantities. Not until the population crowded into the prairies and plains of the Mississippi and beyond did the demand for the reaper become sufficient to enable the manufacturer to turn the machines out cheaply and in mass.[6]

"Just when and how men made the transition from dug wells to drilled wells cannot be determined. We are told, however, that the first really deep well was made for the City of Paris, France. It was begun in 1832, and was completed in 1840, and was seventeen hundred and ninety-eight feet deep." Well-drilling on a large scale began in the United States in the decade between 1870 and 1880,[7] with the steam engine employed as the source of power. It was now possible to find abundant water far beneath the surface of the earth, but there remained the problem of lifting it in quantities sufficient for irrigation or for the use of large droves of stock. A pump operated by hand or horse was clearly inadequate. Shortly after 1850, Daniel Halladay, a young mechanic of Ellington, Connecticut, invented a steel windmill which the inhabitants of the great plains of the United States were to find of indispensable utility. By 1873 the new mechanism was being manufactured on a large scale, and by 1880 it had become the prime mover of water in the arid regions of the west. The requirements of the plainsmen had made possible its larger-scale and, therefore, economical production.[8]

Before farming and the raising of livestock can take place conveniently in the same general area, and before scientific breeding can be carried on in a large way in a region far removed from timber and stone, wire fencing, and (in the case of cattle and horses) probably barbed wire fencing, becomes a prime necessity. Barbed wire was first perfected in 1874 by citizens of the United States; and, as in the case of the thresher, the reaper, and the steel windmill, it found a vast market in the trans-Mississippi west.[9]

It was such mechanical inventions as these, operated in the main by immigrant and alien hands, that effected the economic revolution in

---

[6] Hutchinson, *op. cit.*, p. 75, *passim*.

[7] W. P. Webb, *The Great Plains* (Boston, 1931), p. 335.

[8] *Ibid.*, pp. 337-339.

[9] *Ibid.*, pp. 298ff.

Argentina. The exact year when each of them was introduced into the country has not been ascertained. The approximate dates, however, were as follows: in 1844 [10] wire fences began to be used on the *pampa,* and between 1876 and 1908 more than a million tons of wire fencing—much of it barbed wire—were imported; [11] numerous reapers and several threshers were found in the immigrant agricultural colonies soon after 1870; [12] steel windmills first came into general use about 1890, and were brought in in tremendous quantities during the first decade of the present century, when they became "a striking feature of the landscape." [13] More ready access to domestic and foreign markets began to be suppied soon after 1850 with the construction of the first Argentine railroads and with the establishment of the first lines of steamers not only on the rivers of Argentina, but between its ports and those of the leading European countries.[14] And finally, the preservation of meat by refrigeration was introduced by the French and the English during the decade following 1878.[15]

The initiation and progress of railway construction in Argentina deserve more than passing mention. In general, railroads were pioneers of Argentine development. They did not follow the first settlers with their covered wagons. They led the way across the thistle-covered *pampa* or through untrodden forests. The first railway contract was made by the government of the Province of Buenos Aires with certain natives and British residents in the capital. The road was to extend westward from Buenos Aires, and six miles of it (the first railway in Argentina) were ready for operation in August 1857. The provincial government contributed thirty-nine per cent of the original paid-in capital and renounced its rights to dividends until the remuneration of the private investors reached nine per cent. The first locomotive—a second-hand one, part of the surplus left over from the Crimean War—was shipped from London. The first concession made by the national gov-

[10] Tobal, *Lecciones de geografía argentina,* p. 276.

[11] J. D. Whelpley, "Trade Development in Argentina" (U. S. Department of Commerce and Labor, Bureau of Manufactures, *Special Agents Series,* No. 43), p. 51; Clarence F. Jones, *South America,* p. 378.

[12] Jefferson, *Peopling the Argentine Pampa,* pp. 76-77; M. G. and E. T. Mulhall, *The River Plate Republics* (1875), pp. 45ff.

[13] Whelpley, *op. cit.,* pp. 74-76; Jones, *op. cit.,* p. 378.

[14] William Hadfield, *Brazil, the River Plate, and the Falkland Islands* (London, 1854), pp. 1-5; T. J. Hutchinson, *Buenos Aires and Argentine Gleanings* (London, 1865), pp. 39-40.

[15] Tobal, *op. cit.,* p. 312, note.

ernment was granted to William Wheelwright, a citizen of the United States, in April 1855, during the administration of Urquiza. It authorized the construction of a railroad from Rosario to Córdoba. Owing to difficulties in securing capital, construction on this line was not begun until 1863 and it was not finished until 1870. According to the new concession of May 22, 1863, the national government guaranteed interest on the investment for forty years at seven per cent, subscribed to nineteen per cent of the stock, donated a league of land on each side of the right-of-way, and reserved the right to intervene in fixing rates when the earnings exceeded fifteen per cent! Apparently it was difficult to attract British investments into early Argentine railway enterprises. No other road received so much aid, however; and only five others received grants of land. The national government preferred to guarantee interest on capital outlay, the rate being reduced after a few years from seven to five per cent.

After 1870 the construction of railways proceeded rather rapidly. From Buenos Aires and its environs lines began to radiate across the *pampa* in many directions, but they usually terminated in the extremely arid region of the west. From 454 miles in 1870, the mileage increased to 1,563 in 1880, to 5,861 in 1890, and to 20,805 at the end of 1913. The Bolivian border was reached in 1908, the railway connecting Buenos Aires and Santiago, Chile, was completed in 1909, and through train service between Buenos Aires and Asunción was inaugurated in 1913.

Most of the capital for the construction of this vast railway system was French and British, mainly the latter, and the majority of the railways were also owned and operated by the nationals of these countries. In 1896, however, the national government of Argentina began to purchase a few minor roads, and in 1909 it inaugurated the policy of government construction in thinly settled areas.[16]

The railroads received the heaviest foreign investments of any single enterprise in Argentina. But large sums were invested by aliens, during the six decades which followed the expulsion of Rosas, in government loans, real estate and mortgages, banks, meat-packing plants and other

---

[16] The best discussion of Argentine railways in the English language is George S. Brady's *Railways of South America. Part I: Argentina* (U. S. Department of Commerce, Bureau of Foreign and Domestic Commerce, *Trade Promotion Series,* No. 32). See also E. Rebuelto's series of articles in República Argentina, *Boletín de Obras Públicas,* 1911-1913.. A complete collection of Argentine laws *(Colección completa de leyes nacional)* was published by Roldán, Buenos Aires, 1918. Of course the railway laws are included.

industries, and municipal public utilities. The total probably did not fall short of three billion dollars in 1914.[17]

III

Such were the factors that produced Argentina's economic revolution: immigration, foreign capital, numerous mechanical appliances, more carefully supervised breeding of animals, and an increasing demand for food. It was at once the result and the cause of political stability. A large influx of immigrants and foreign capital as well as the introduction of more effective technological equipment, were the result of the promise of tranquillity; and the renewed attack on the environment not only demanded peace and foreign markets, but diverted men's minds from the battlefield and the roving life of the *gaucho*.

Professor C. F. Jones has fittingly described the rapid development and its causes:

> "As external conditions favored immigration, they also aided the improvement of the grazing industry and the invasion of the Pampa by crops. . . . The industrialization of Europe called for more and more of the commodities Argentina could supply. The introduction of refrigeration . . . made it possible for Argentina to realize upon one of her great assets—the pastures of the Pampa. The enormous development of agricultural machinery of all types with interchangeable parts opened the way for the tillage of the land previously utilizable only by the numerous herds and flocks.
>
> "Within Argentina, the animal industry witnessed [underwent] a complete evolution. Water was provided for the herds and flocks; ranges fenced; breeding regulated; pure-bred stock introduced by the thousands; measures taken to control the ravages of the tick; slaughtering and chilling plants constructed; and, most significant of all, alfalfa ranges established on [al] most every *estancia* [ranch]. Consequently, frozen and chilled meats replaced in trade the live cattle, shipped with difficulty, and the *tasajo* [jerked beef], a staple product for centuries. Sheep carcasses, formerly left for dogs and buzzards or rendered into tallow, likewise entered trade in the form of mutton. Of course, wool, hides, and hair continued to move in great volume. With ocean transport, railways, immigration and machinery [,] the production of cereals for export staged a more remarkable advance than the animal industries. . . . Wheat, corn, and flax began to carve great slices out of the vast grazing domain." [18]

---

[17] Max Winkler, *Investments of United States Capital in Latin America* (Boston, 1928), pp. 66-67. The total was nearly four billion dollars in 1918. Prior to 1914, the capital came mainly from Europe.

[18] Jones, *South America,* pp. 312-313.

All these influences and currents not only elevated Argentina from a secondary position among South American countries to first rank in the continent and the Southern Hemisphere, but transformed her into the world's leading area for surplus foodstuffs and raw industrial material. The Argentine Mesopotamia (Entre Ríos, Corrientes, and Misiones, although the latter remained undeveloped) supplied sheep, cattle, flax, and *yerba maté,* with a little lumber; the Argentine *gran chaco* furnished *quebracho* (a wood used in tanneries), cattle, and cotton; the vast arid west produced sugar, wine, and goats; Patagonia supplied sheep, cattle, forest products, and oil (after 1907); the *pampa,* that great food reservoir of the world, produced beef, wool, wheat, flax, oats, corn, and swine; and even bleak Tierra del Fuego pastured hundreds of thousands of sheep.

A few statistics will illustrate the remarkable economic transformation. It may be observed at the outset that the population grew rapidly: from 1,737,000 in 1869, to 3,955,000 in 1895, and 7,885,000 in 1914. The per capita acreage in cultivation was less than half an acre in the first year mentioned, three acres in the second, and nearly eight acres—or a total of more than sixty million acres—in the third.[19] Thirty-one million bushels of wheat were produced in 1890 and one hundred eighty-seven millions in 1912.[20] Ninety-nine million bushels of corn were grown in 1901 and two hundred sixty-three million in 1913.[21] Only about seven thousand bushels of wheat and some three hundred thousand bushels of corn were produced in 1876. Approximately a thousand tons of linseed were grown in 1880 and more than a million in 1913.[22] Three thousand short tons of sugar were produced in 1876 and two hundred four thousand in 1913.[23] The production of wine was slightly less than fifty-seven and one-half million liters in 1895 and more than five hundred million in 1914.[24]

The agricultural invasion of the *pampa* led to no decrease in the number of livestock, except in the case of sheep, which diminished from approximately seventy-four million—an increase of twenty million since

---

[19] Jefferson, *op. cit.,* p. 43.

[20] United States Department of Agriculture, *Yearbook of Agriculture* (1933), p. 409.

[21] *Ibid,* p. 434.

[22] Ernesto Tornquist, *The Economic Development of the Argentine Republic,* pp. 30-31.

[23] Jefferson, *op. cit.,* p. 38.

[24] Tornquist, *op. cit.,* p. 69.

1869—in 1895 to approximately forty-three million in 1914. There were nearly twenty-three million cattle in 1895 and nearly twenty-six million in 1914, while the number of horses and goats almost doubled and the number of hogs increased nearly fivefold during the period.[25] The value of meat exports rose from approximately eleven million dollars in 1894 to over ninety million in 1914. And it should be added that the decline of the flocks, with the consequent falling off in the quantity of wool, has had ample compensation in the improved quality of that product as well as in the better utilization of the carcasses. Argentina's wool greatly increased in total value between 1895 and 1913 despite the decrease in quantity.[26]

The national wealth increased, of course, very rapidly. It was estimated at a billion dollars in 1886, at approximately four billion in 1895, and at fifteen billion in 1914. There was a great disparity, however, in the distribution of both wealth and income. Only slightly more than six hundred seventy-three thousand Argentine citizens owned real estate in 1914 and fifty-four per cent of the workers had an income of twelve hundred dollars per annum or less. Nearly thirty per cent, indeed, had an income of less than five hundred.[27] It was this inequitable distribution of wealth that was largely responsible for the numerous strikes and the general discontent which characterized the two decades that preceded the outbreak of the World War.

Nor was the per capita wealth by any means equally distributed among the provinces. Those of Buenos Aires, Santa Fé, Entre Ríos, Córdoba, Mendoza, Tucumán, and Santiago del Estero were comparatively rich, especially Mendoza and Buenos Aires. The rest were still quite poor.

Increasing opulence naturally brought larger revenues for the national and local governments. The revenues of the national government amounted to only seven million dollars in 1864, but it was more than one hundred seventy million in 1913. The revenues of the fourteen provinces combined were far less, but after a long struggle with poverty

---

[25] Tobal, *Lecciones de geografía argentina,* p. 279.

[26] Tornquist, *op. cit.,* pp. 74, 106. In 1894 the meat exports consisted almost entirely of jerked beef and cattle on the hoof, although they included some frozen beef and more frozen mutton and lamb. By 1914 frozen beef, mutton, and lamb composed nearly nine-tenths of the meat exports. Until 1908, comparatively little chilled meat was produced.

[27] *Ibid.,* pp. 257-259. Apparently the figures on income are based upon the investigations of A. E. Bunge and are for the year 1916. See Bunge's *Riqueza y renta de la Argentina, su distribución y su capacidad contributiva* (Buenos Aires, 1917); and *Tercer censo nacional,* VIII, pp. 323ff.

in the case of most of them, the state of their treasuries began to improve rapidly shortly after the opening of the present century. Their estimated revenues for 1914 were approximately sixty million dollars; the Province of Buenos Aires alone, however, anticipated nearly half of this sum.[28]

IV

Expanding revenues provided funds for larger expenditures on public services, important among these, of course, being a system of education under the support and supervision of the state. Many of the early national leaders had advocated secular education, but little was accomplished until the epoch of Urquiza, Mitre, Sarmiento, and Avellaneda.

These four statesmen, all of them more or less committed to Sarmiento's maxim "to govern is to educate," probably deserve most credit for founding Argentina's system of public instruction. Urquiza had founded the *Colegio* (high school) of Concepción de Uruguay[29] in 1849 before he took up arms against Rosas, and during his term as chief executive of the confederation, as already pointed out, he not only nationalized the *Colegio* of Monserrat and the University of Córdoba, but encouraged the provinces to establish primary schools. Between 1852 and 1860 at least seventeen elementary schools were opened in the provinces under his control, besides an approximately equal number in the seceded Province of Buenos Aires. Under Mitre, Sarmiento, and Avellaneda progress was much more rapid. At least fifty-eight primary schools and six high schools were opened during Mitre's terms; an equal number of high schools, three normals, and some eighty-five elementary schools during that of Sarmiento; and about one hundred and seventy-five primary and three normal schools under the administration of Avellaneda.[30]

Thus the foundation of the public school system was well laid by the time national reorganization had been completed in 1880. Thereafter each year witnessed the opening of many new schools until Argentina, by 1914, possessed one of the best school systems in Latin America.[31] As early as 1884 (by Act of July 8) the federal government

[28] Tornquist, *op. cit.*, pp. 278-287.

[29] Thomas Jefferson Page visited this school in 1853 *(La Plata, the Argentine Confederation, and Paraguay,* London, 1859, pp. 60 and *passim*).

[30] República Argentina, *Censo general de educación* (1909), II, pp. 35-36.

[31] Only those of Uruguay, Costa Rica, and Cuba deserved to rank with that of Argentina.

had established the principle of compulsory education for children between the ages of six and fourteen.

More and more the national government assumed the burden of supporting the institutions of learning. The national constitution requires the provinces to establish primary schools (the first six grades) and does not preclude them from establishing secondary schools and institutions of higher learning; but the federal government nevertheless has borne not only the expense of secondary and higher education, but has contributed ever-increasing subsidies to the elementary schools. In the year 1909, for instance, it supplied nearly two-thirds of the budget for public instruction.[32]

This attack upon general ignorance, a "veritable cavalry charge" as it has been called, resulted in a decided reduction of illiteracy. Illiterates constituted seventy-eight and two-tenths per cent of the population above seven years of age in 1869, but they were only fifty-four and four-tenths in 1895 and thirty-five and one-tenth in 1914.[33]

Compared with the United States and the most progressive nations of Europe, however, Argentina's primary school system still revealed many defects at the end of the first decade of the present century. Despite the fact that a compulsory school law had been on the statute books since 1884, only forty-eight per cent of the children of school age were enrolled in the primary schools in March 1909, and only thirty-eight per cent were regular attendants. Almost half of the buildings consisted of one room, the teachers were paid very small salaries almost everywhere save in the capital and the Province of Buenos Aires, and in five of the provinces more than half of the population above seven years of age was still illiterate.[34]

---

[32] *Censo general de educación* (1909), II, p. 340.

[33] República Argentina, *Tercer censo nacional* (1914), III, pp. 321ff.; Tobal, *Lecciones de geografía argentina,* p. 167.

[34] *Censo general de educación* (1909), II, *passim;* Tobal, *op. cit.,* p. 166. In 1914 only 878,537 children out of a total school-age population of 1,485,785 were enrolled in the primary schools *(Tercer censo nacional,* IX, p. 137), and 2,517 of the 7,881 primary schools occupied a single room *(ibid,* IX, p. 151).

CHAPTER ELEVEN

VICISSITUDES OF POLITICS, 1880-1912

IT SHOULD not be assumed that Argentina achieved complete political tranquillity after the federalization of Buenos Aires in 1880. It is true that the country became more stable than formerly; and far less turbulent than most of the Spanish American republics, but it did not enjoy absolute good order by any means. Its stability was only comparative. Uprisings in the provinces, usually accompanied by armed intervention on the part of the federal government, were frequent. Between 1883 and 1899, for example, some twenty-four instances of federal intervention occurred.[1]

It would also be erroneous to assume that Argentina speedily became a genuine political democracy. In fact, the government continued until 1912 to be controlled by an oligarchy which often imposed itself upon the nation by force and fraud. Fair balloting seldom occurred. After 1912, however, a new group began to rise to power, and in 1916 the oligarchy was temporarily overthrown.

I

For three decades after the federalization of the capital city, the presidents and the members of the national congress, as well as the provincial legislators and governors, were in the main the descendants of the leading families of the colonial and the early national era. Although the revolution for independence proclaimed equality before the law, and although this principle was reiterated by all the Argentine constitutions, provincial and national, little fundamental change occurred in the texture of colonial society, despite the theoretical access of merchants, artisans, and proletariat to public life. "The families which composed the upper stratum of the provinces of the Royal *Audiencia* of Buenos Aires, those whose leading members were denominated the most sane portion of the population of the municipalities and possessed the privilege of being invited to the open *cabildos,* continued," says Matienzo, "to constitute through their descendants the [controlling] social nucleus, somewhat enlarged by the incorporation of newcomers upon whom

[1] Urrútia, *Intervenciones del gobierno federal,* I, pp. 423ff.

fortune had smiled."[2] Ingenieros, who agrees with him, remarks: "Argentine politics during the nineteenth century has been the monopoly of a single social group, the owners of the land, at whose side dwelt crowds of vassals who were neither a middle class nor a proletariat. All the civil contests, all political changes, have been the work of oligarchies belonging to the same class."[3] The ideals of the reformers of the independence period were not made effective. Nor did the young intellectuals who entertained humanitarian and even socialistic views during their exile of the Rosas epoch, ever go farther than a cautious liberalism in later practice. Many of them failed to secure administrative positions or to influence the statesmen of the day, while those who succeeded in politics became moderate or conservative.

The members of this governing class maintained among themselves close social and economic relations, shared common opinions and sentiments regarding the incentives and objectives of individual and collective conduct. Of the national legislative body of this epoch, Matienzo has written:

> "The pensions, the subsidies, and other forms of pecuniary aid with which the budgets are charged are unmistakable manifestations of the oligarchical sentiment which leagues the members of Congress with the rest of the governing class to which they belong. And one may attribute to the same cause a great number of other legislative acts, many omissions of legislation—among them those which affect the workers—, and not a few silences and indifferent attitudes in the presence of facts which in other parliaments would have given rise to frank demonstrations of protest or sympathy."[4]

In the electoral process, the governors of the provinces exerted great influence. They assumed the prerogative of designating candidates for the local and national legislatures as well as for provincial governors and the presidency. And they frequently succeeded in determining the results of the elections.

Matienzo, writing of the period under consideration, remarks that the provincial chief executives "proceed as absolute and exclusive lords in the designation of provincial elective offices." "The members of the legislatures," he says, "enjoy little independence with respect to the governors, to whom they owe their election as a general rule."[5]

---

[2] *El gobierno representativo federal,* pp. 175-176. *Cf.* also p. 81.

[3] *Sociología argentina* (Madrid, 1913), p. 94.

[4] Matienzo, *op. cit.,* pp. 176, 320.

[5] *Ibid.,* pp. 208, 214.

With reference to the choice of members of the national chamber of deputies the ambition of the governors was no less. They usually managed to send to this body their friends or relatives, with little regard for qualifications. A governor of the Province of Buenos Aires obtained a seat in congress for a friend who had entirely lost his voice!

The retiring governor always expected to obtain for himself any seat which might be vacant in the senate. Since the senators were chosen by provincial legislatures which were mere instruments of the governors, one may readily imagine that the senatorial toga could easily be secured unless opposition was confronted in higher quarters. In that case, a federal intervention would be likely to occur.

The provincial chief executive also assumed the right to dictate his successor. He preferred to transmit his power to a close friend or relative, who was supposed to return it to him after the completion of a gubernatorial term; and he often succeeded in doing so. Writing of the period now under review, Matienzo says: "If the retiring governor does not go to the senate, it is because there is no immediate vacancy, and if he does not return to the gubernatorial office it is because he has not the power to do so." [6]

Finally, the governors of the provinces were not without great influence in the choice of the chief executives of the nation. Combined with that of the retiring president, it was usually decisive. The presidential campaign consisted of a series of manipulations designed to assemble a group of governors who were able to control a majority of the electoral votes, each province having twice as many votes in the electoral college as it had senators and deputies in the national congress. To quote once more from the excellent work of Matienzo:

> " . . . The prevalent theory in the Argentine Republic is that the president and the governors lack the right of exerting influence in the designation of deputies, senators, and the rest of the representatives subject to election by the people. Even more, . . . it is professed as a dogma that the members of the executive power lack even the right of opinion in electoral matters. . . .
>
> "Nevertheless, everybody in the Argentine Republic knows that the shortest road to the congress of the nation is open to him who gains the goodwill of the governor in whose province the election must take place, and that it is impossible to elect a president without relying upon the support of the retiring chief executive and the incumbent governors.
>
> "When the election of a president approaches, one computes in

[6] *Ibid.*, p. 204.

favor of each candidate the electoral votes of the provinces whose governors support him. The public makes this calculation as a matter of course.

"The protests in behalf of free suffrage and against the undue interference of public functionaries neither have moral significance nor confront any sanction which injures the reputation of the executive or employee censured. The functionary who violates his promise to abstain from electoral interference, and even the man who is guilty of electoral fraud, does not on this account lose social respect, but continues to enjoy the friendship of persons whom public opinion qualifies as honorable." [7]

Back of the influence of the governors, however, was that of the presidents. During the half-century which followed the inauguration of Mitre, the relative strength of the national and local executives was reversed. The provincial governors became more and more the agents of the presidents. Since this transformation was brought about through the exercise of federal intervention in the provinces, the president's influence in elections will be observed mainly in that connection.

The constitution of Argentina provides that the "federal government shall guarantee to each province the enjoyment and exercise of its institutions"; it gives the national authorities the "right to intervene in the territory of the provinces in order to guarantee the republican form of government or to repel foreign invasion; and when requested by the constituted authorities, to maintain them in power, or to reëstablish them if they shall have been deposed by sedition or by invasion from another province." [8]

In view of the ambitions and tyrannical record of many of the early provincial chiefs, these provisions would seem to have been justified at the time the constitution was framed. It is a fact, however, that many of the numerous federal interventions of the subsequent period were undertaken with ulterior political motives, and that not a few of the provincial uprisings were fomented by the federal authorities in order to have an excuse for imposing their partisans upon the provinces.

Matienzo has described the circumstances in which these political manipulations occurred.

"Whenever the governor is unable to manage the legislature in a peaceful manner, a contest begins in which both entities resort to every device in order to secure the victory. The legislature . . . tries to depose the governor by means of impeachment, and the

[7] *Ibid.*, pp. 322-323.

[8] Articles V and VI.

governor attempts at the same time to obtain new elections for the legislature in order to modify its majority by the introduction of his decided partisans. A large part of the interventions of the federal government . . . have been occasioned by conflicts [of this type]." [9]

Again, dealing more directly with presidential influence in the national elections, Matienzo writes:

" . . . Whenever the number of governors favoring the candidate supported by the president is not sufficient to secure a victory, conflicts or seditions are planned against such of the opposing or indifferent governors as it is deemed most opportune to change. This furnishes a pretext for the national government to intervene and preside over a new gubernatorial election. At times actual federal intervention is not necessary because the sedition triumphs immediately and [the recalcitrant governor is replaced by a more pliable agent]." [10]

Dr. Leo S. Rowe, who has made a special investigation of the Argentine system of government, points out that the president, during the period now under consideration, depended in large measure upon the provincial governors to aid him in securing senators and deputies in harmony with his policy, and that for this reason the national chief executive was often tempted to employ the device of intervention in order to strengthen his political position. Dr. Rowe also observes that the possibility of securing federal intervention was "a constant temptation to the minority party to plan revolutions and to provoke armed disturbances." The "line of least resistance" for the provincial opposition to the governor was that of securing the president's support, a federal intervention, and a new election under the patronage of the chief executive. Thus, minority parties acquired the habit of looking to Buenos Aires rather than depending upon a systematic campaign designed to enlist the sympathy of the people of the provinces, and the constitutional provisions designed to maintain order within these local political entities tended to produce quite the opposite result.[11]

Such political methods would not have been necessary if political

---

[9] Matienzo, *op. cit.*, p. 217.

[10] *Ibid.*, p. 233.

[11] *The Federal System of the Argentine Republic*, pp. 80-81. For a less restrained discussion of the "Régime," consult Alberto M. Etkin, *Bosquejo de una historia y doctrina de la Unión Cívica Radical* (Buenos Aires, 1928), Ch. IV, *passim*.

parties had been well organized,[12] public opinion thoroughly aroused on current issues, and fair balloting assured. But these prime essentials of an orderly political régime did not prevail for two important reasons: (1) the masses were ignorant and inexperienced in self-government; and (2) the oligarchy had little disposition to arouse the people's interest in public affairs, to organize them into parties, or to permit them to make their influence felt at the polls. This attitude on the part of the oligarchy, and their refusal to follow the orderly procedures prescribed by the constitutions, were largely responsible for the turbulent politics of the period in the provinces. The oligarchy refused to submit their political careers and the choice of policies to the free ballot of the electors.

The revolutionary disturbances of the epoch were not confined merely to individual provinces. Within the three decades following 1880, the national executives at Buenos Aires confronted at least three revolts designed to depose them. One president was forced to retire in order to preserve the peace, and two others had serious difficulties with congress.

The main political issues of the period were two: (1) unfair electoral practices, especially when they involved federal intervention in the provinces; and (2) dishonest and otherwise reprehensible use of government funds and credit. Regionalism appears also to have had some weight, despite Matienzo's contrary contention, for neither the littoral nor the interior provinces were ever left unrepresented in the executive power, each region always furnishing either the president or

[12] Parties existed, but they were not highly organized and their membership was confined largely to the members of the old families, although a few of the middle-class intellectuals and men of large means were included. During the early national period, as already indicated, the leaders were divided into federals and unitarians. After the Rosas period other parties appeared, such as the liberals, the autonomists, and the national autonomists. The federals also continued for a time —their last candidate for the presidency was Urquiza, 1868—but the unitarians disappeared with the Rosas régime. The Civic Union Party made its appearance in 1890, and the Radical Civic Union Party in 1892. Subsequently other parties—the socialists, the National Union Party, the progressive democrats, the national democrats, etc.—came into existence. Perhaps the only political organization in Argentina that resembled the two large parties in the United States was the Radical Civic Union Party, or Radical Party, under the leadership of Alem and Irigoyen. Although political issues were not absent, the personal factor was always important. Avellaneda and Roca dominated the National Autonomist Party for many years, just as Irigoyen dominated the Radical Party until it split into two groups shortly after 1922, one of them following Alvear and the other, which assumed the name *Irigoyenista,* remaining loyal to Irigoyen. Matienzo, *op. cit.,* pp. 99ff.; Ingenieros, *Sociología argentina,* p. 86.)

the vice president. Now and then a religious issue flared up, involving religious instruction in the public schools, civil marriage, divorce, or the appointment of a high official of the church; but religious questions were much less serious in Argentina than elsewhere in Spanish America, and people seldom got excited about them.[13]

The protest against electoral practices involved factors that were both regional and personal. The oligarchy excluded from important government positions not only certain members of the prominent old families, particularly the younger men, but also the leaders of rising new families whose wealth and intelligence nurtured political ambitions; and it was in the provinces of the littoral, where social classes were most unstable, that these new families dwelt and had their rise. Families progressed from poverty to wealth in this area because it was most advantageously located for more intensive agriculture and scientific stockbreeding, and because it received the bulk of the immigrants. Nearly all of the parties of protest had their main roots in the capital and the littoral provinces, although they also reached out into the interior, where discontented young men and idealists furnished a favorable soil.

Shortly after the beginning of the present century these two dissatisfied groups—the young aristocrats and ambitious members of the new families—managed to effect, temporarily at least, a fundamental change in Argentine political life. Dissatisfied or idealistic aristocrats, who were eager for power or for a new orientation of policy, effected a combination with the growing middle class, and finally achieved an electoral reform which gave the masses an effective ballot. The result was an influx of new men into congress and the overthrow of the old oligarchy (in 1916) by means of one of the few fair elections in Argentine history.

II

In 1880, the most influential political organization in the country was the Córdoba clique, a league which was composed of provincial governors and their henchmen. The aim of this group was to control elections, maintain the dominance of the great provincial land-owning families, and keep the *gauchos,* the urban proletariat, and the parvenues in their places. They were the more peaceful but none the less autocratic successors of the armed *caudillos* of an earlier period.

President Roca, who owed his election to the support of the clique,

[13] J. L. Mecham, *Church and State in Spanish America* (Chapel Hill, 1934), pp. 286ff.

served their purpose admirably. He preserved the peace; conquered more lands from the Indians on the frontiers; borrowed—or permitted to be borrowed—large sums of money for the construction of railways, the establishment of systems of municipal sanitation, and the improvement of the ports; stressed higher education;[14] and maintained a fair standard of honesty in the use of public funds. Near the end of his term, however, he made the mistake of inaugurating the régime of inconvertible paper money. He appears to have had a foreboding that such a step would be a grievous mistake,[15] but he nevertheless consented to the suspension of specie payments for two years.

In the national election of 1886, Roca and the Córdoba clique imposed their candidate upon the nation. Miguel Juárez Celman, ex-governor of Córdoba and brother-in-law of Roca, received the electoral vote of every province save those of Buenos Aires and Tucumán.[16] The new president was a man without strength of character or administrative ability. His administration was characterized by a flood of inconvertible paper money, reckless borrowing on the part of the national and provincial governments, wild speculation, and shameless graft. Celman's partisans monopolized the offices and filled their pockets. By the end of 1889 the country was in the throes of a panic and on the verge of a revolt.

At this critical moment two men destined to play a conspicuous rôle appeared again upon the Argentine political stage after a decade of obscurity. They were Leandro Alem and his nephew Hipólito Irigoyen. The two had bitterly opposed the federalization of the city of Buenos Aires in 1880, and when defeated, had retired from active politics. They now came forward to organize the opposition against the corrupt Córdoba régime. Of the two, Alem was at this time the more energetic and influential. Born in the city of Buenos Aires in 1842, he was still a small boy when his father was executed for alleged conspiracy. He soon vowed eternal opposition to all autocratic government and dressed in black in memory of his vow. Struggling with poverty, he achieved a modest education, and upon reaching manhood, became an uncompromising enemy of all arbitrary rule and an ardent champion of democracy. "Tall and slim, with a beard reaching to his waist, his

[14] Primary instruction was by no means neglected, but it was not sufficiently emphasized.

[15] When first approached regarding the measure, Roca expressed strong disapproval. "I will cut off my right hand before I sign any such decree." (Akers, *A History of South America,* New York, 1930, p. 68.)

[16] Matienzo, *op. cit.,* p. 149.

striking appearance always attracted attention, while his agreeable manner secured him many admirers and friends." [17] In him the growing middle class and the inarticulate masses found a voice, as they later found a friend in his nephew. But his appeal was not alone to the middle and humbler classes. His denunciation of the régime awakened a response among the aristocracy, particularly the young men.[18]

Early in 1890 a new party, the *Unión Cívica,* took definite form, and toward the end of July Alem carried the Buenos Aires contingent forward to armed revolt. The uprising was soon suppressed, but Celman was forced to resign. He was succeeded by Carlos Pelligrini, the vice president, who was an experienced politician and a native of the capital. Pelligrini made an effort to reduce graft and confront the financial crisis, but found the task greater than he could manage. Recovery from the debauchery of the Celman administration would require more than a decade.

The election of 1892 was preceded by more than a year of political agitation. A considerable number of the oligarchy preferred Mitre as a candidate for the presidency, and General Roca seemed willing to give his adhesion, but the Córdoba clique refused to accept the historical leader of the *porteños* and informed Roca that they would revolt rather than submit to Mitre. Roca, Pelligrini, and Mitre then conferred and agreed upon a nonpartisan candidate, Luís Sáenz Peña, an aristocratic judge of the federal court. The moderate members of the *Unión Cívica* accepted the compromise, but Alem and his more impetuous followers bitterly denounced the *acuerdo.* Demanding a just registration, a free ballot, and a fair counting of the votes, they broke away and formed the Radical Civic Union. They were determined to overthrow the oligarchy even if they had to resort again to arms. Shortly before the election, however, Pelligrini declared a state of siege, arrested Alem and his friends, and afterwards sent them into exile. Of course Sáenz Peña became president!

---

[17] Akers, *A History of South America,* p. 75; Kirkpatrick, *The Argentine Republic,* pp. 188-189; Etkin, *Bosquejo de una historia . . . de la Unión Cívica Radical, passim.*

[18] Prominent among the young aristocracy were Honorio Pueyrredón and Marcelo T. Alvear, both descended from revolutionary heroes. Other members of the party during the earlier period were Vicente López, Aristobulo del Valle, Bernardo Irigoyen (not a relative of Hipólito), Rómulo S. Naón, Julio Moreno, José C. Crotto (an Italian), F. Álvarez de Toledo, and Guillermo Udaonda, many of whom followed Alem into the radical wing of the *Unión Cívica.* (Brief sketches of several of these men are given in Parker's *Argentines of Today,* 2 vols., New York, 1920.)

But the new executive confronted a difficult task. Too honest to suit the greedy Córdoba clique, lacking experience and the backing of a party, he found his congress a most exasperating group of men who became even more unwieldy after Alem returned from exile and took his seat as representative from the Province of Buenos Aires. Alem busied himself with a more thorough organization of his new party and did all that he could to embarrass the executive. By the summer of 1893, four provinces—Santa Fé, San Luís, Tucumán, and Buenos Aires—were in full revolt. The insurgents were soon suppressed, however, by General Roca, who was placed once more in command of the national army, and Alem with his leading partisans was again ostracized. Nevertheless, congress continued to give trouble, and early in 1895 Sáenz Peña, having decided that his position was untenable, handed the reins over to Vice President José Uriburu, a descendant of a notable family of Salta and a son-in-law of General Juan Antonio Arenales, a distinguished soldier of the war of independence. Shortly afterwards, Alem and his friends returned home, but in 1896 the vehement old reformer committed suicide,[19] leaving his nephew as leader of the Radical Party.

In the election of 1898 the oligarchy had no competition for the presidency. Mitre and Roca were the candidates, and thanks to the influence of President Uriburu and the provincial governors, the latter won an overwhelming victory. The radicals abstained from participation in what they considered an electoral farce; Irigoyen tamely continued his teaching in a normal school for girls! In 1904 likewise the oligarchy had a clear field and competed only among themselves, with official pressure determining the election. Manuel Quintana, a venerable politician of the Province of Buenos Aires, became president, his successful running mate being José Figueroa Alcorta, a Cordoban who had been holding office since graduating from the university.

By this time, however, the oligarchy was divided into numerous bitter factions. Five candidates had made the campaign for the presidency, Uriburu, Marco A. Avellaneda, and Pelligrini among them, and nine had sought the office of vice president. Moreover, a few new men, including at least one socialist, had managed to obtain seats in the national chamber of deputies; and Roca, shortly before the end of his term, had proposed an elaborate labor law, known as the González Law —a step which he felt compelled to recommend because of the growing

[19] For an account of his life, see Carlos M. Urien, *El doctor Leandro N. Alem,* a work published the same year that Alem died. *Cf.* Etkin, *op. cit.,* pp. 161ff.

restiveness and violence of the labor group.[20] Taking advantage of a situation which seemed propitious, Irigoyen and his partisans began another revolt. While the leader of the Radical Party attempted to seize the arsenal and master the capital, simultaneous uprisings occurred in Bahía Blanca as well as in four of the six provinces which had received the greatest influx of immigrants and were enjoying the greatest prosperity; namely, Buenos Aires, Santa Fé, Córdoba, and Mendoza.[21] For a third time, however, the insurgents were crushed, and after giving his approval to a labor law which applied to the national capital, Quintana quietly continued the "Régime" until death overtook him in March 1906.

Alcorta, who succeeded to the presidency for the remainder of the term, had difficulties with the chamber of deputies. The elections for the renewal of half of that body had gone against the administration on the day of Quintana's death. The deputies refused either to give their consent to federal intervention in the provinces or to vote the budget, whereupon Alcorta sent the city firemen to close the chamber, declared congress adjourned (January 1908), decreed the continuance of the previous budget, and later proceeded to intervene in several of the provinces. Kirkpatrick says that Alcorta had interviews with Irigoyen, and that the purpose of the interventions was to undermine the landholding oligarchies. Although Alcorta may have been seeking in this manner to gain support from the growing middle class, it is possible that his purpose was not so much a new orientation of politics as a tractable chamber of deputies and a political arrangement that would enable him to dictate his successor.[22]

Roque Sáenz Peña, the official candidate for the presidency, was almost unanimously elected in 1910. The new executive was a member of the oligarchy and the son of a former president, but he was a staunch advocate of electoral reform. His conduct may have been influenced by three considerations: a genuine sense of justice coupled with a desire to make his nation really democratic; a full realization of the growing strength of Irigoyen and his party and of the danger that their further exclusion from participation in the government would lead to

[20] Ingenieros, *Sociología argentina*, pp. 363ff., gives a good analysis of this law, which failed to pass.

[21] The other two were Entre Ríos and Corrientes.

[22] These interventions were discussed by Rowe (*op. cit.*, pp. 76-88). It must be admitted, however, that the candidate Alcorta supported for the presidency, Roque Sáenz Peña, had committed himself in general terms to effective suffrage. (*Cf.* Sáenz Peña's *Escritos y discursos*, Buenos Aires, 1914, II, pp. 16, 26.)

another revolt; and a desire to induce Argentina's more than two million aliens to become citizens by offering them one of the valuable privileges of citizenship.[23] Late in 1910 he recommended to congress a new registration of voters, and in August 1911, a bill making voting secret and compulsory, and granting representation to the minorities. Both measures were passed, the latter after warm and eloquent debate.[24]

In some quarters it was predicted that the law would not be enforced and that elections would continue to be subject to official interference. But under Sáenz Peña and his successor[25] the prediction proved erroneous. The Radical Party, after years of abstention and insurgency, went to the voting booths and elected a third of the chamber of deputies in 1912, won the governorships of Santa Fé, Entre Ríos, and Córdoba shortly afterwards, and elevated Irigoyen to the presidency in 1916.[26] Temporarily at least, Argentina had become a genuine political democracy.

---

[23] See his *Escritos y discursos,* II, pp. 67-141.

[24] See in particular *Diario de sesiones de la Cámera* (1911), III, pp. 113 and *passim.* For the law, consult *idem,* V, p. 266.

[25] Sáenz Peña turned the government over to Vice President Victorino de la Plaza in October 1913, and died in August 1914.

[26] Matienzo, *op. cit.,* p. 111, note. A convenient but somewhat laudatory reference work on the period treated in this chapter is Bucich Escobar's *Historia de los presidentes argentinos* (Buenos Aires, 1927).

CHAPTER TWELVE

CONTEMPORARY ARGENTINA

BY THE opening of the second decade of the present century Argentina had become one of the richest and most progressive nations of Hispanic America. Concrete evidence of this position was revealed by the results of the third national census (1914). The cultivated lands of the republic had increased more than sixtyfold since the year 1869 when the first census was taken, and yet more than eighty-five million head of live stock still grazed on its plains. During the same period its population had increased from considerably less than two million to almost eight million; six of its principal towns[1] had grown from backward villages to modernized cities of from sixty thousand to almost a quarter of a million inhabitants; Buenos Aires had developed from a sprawling, unsanitary, and unattractive town of less than two hundred thousand to a beautiful up-to-date city of a million and a half, the leading Latin city of the Western Hemisphere and one of the great cities of the world; and Argentina's foreign trade had increased from a value of some seventy million dollars to seven hundred million, despite the temporary decline caused by the scarcity of shipping during the first few months of the World War. Hardly begun in 1869, its railway mileage had reached twenty thousand, its telegraph system was excellent, and its telephone and postal services were fairly good. Its public buildings were stately and beautiful, its parks delightful and impressive, and its educational institutions among the three or four best in Latin America. There were five universities[2] with

---

[1] The six settlements and their population for the dates mentioned were as follows:

	Population		
Town	*1869*	*1895*	*1914*
Rosario	23,169	91,669	245,199
Córdoba	28,523	47,609	121,982
La Plata	575	45,410	137,413
Tucumán	17,438	34,305	92,284
Santa Fé	10,670	22,244	64,095
Bahía Blanca	1,057	9,025	62,191

The population of Buenos Aires grew from 177,787 in 1869 to 1,571,614 in 1914. (U. S. Dept of Commerce, *Commerce Yearbook,* 1932, II, p. 338; Tobal, *Lecciones de geografía argentina,* p. 410.)

[2] Namely, Santa Fé, Tucumán, Córdoba, La Plata, and Buenos Aires.

a total enrollment of some eight thousand students. Numerous normal schools, and a secondary and primary educational organization moved slowly but steadily toward a capacity adequate for the accommodation of the nation's children. The percentage of illiteracy was gradually diminishing, and public health was good almost everywhere save in the northwest. Newspapers, periodicals, and public libraries were numerous; the press was free; and the nation had produced a group of scholars and writers which ranked with the best of the New World. All of this development had been due in large measure to the bountiful natural resources of the country and to the generous impact of world economy; but it was in part a tribute to the policies of Argentine political leaders who, while governing the country mainly in the interest of the oligarchy, were as a rule not lacking in patriotism, vision, and administrative ability.

As the nation approached the end of the first century of its independent life, however, it confronted one paramount and urgent problem: the raising of the masses of its people to a higher standard of living. More than thirty-five per cent of the population were still illiterate—in some areas even more than fifty per cent; and in a country of vast extent and sparce settlement, only one-eighth of the inhabitants owned any real estate, while fully half of them were on the verge of poverty and misery. If Argentina was ever to take its place among the world's most progressive countries, its wealth and income would have to be more equitably distributed and its public school system expanded and improved. But its male citizens were now in possession of an effective ballot which they might employ to achieve these much needed reforms as soon as they learned the proper use of the instrument which had been placed in their hands. Much would depend upon wise leadership.

I

The history of contemporary Argentina has been characterized by a period of prosperity and reform followed by one of depression and revolt. The country moved forward for a time at a rapid pace, but was finally halted by the world's economic crisis.

The members of the Radical Party who gained seats in the national congress after the adoption of the electoral law of 1912 soon revealed their influence. The years 1912 to 1915 were marked by several liberal laws, among which the following may be mentioned: (1) a law (applying to the capital and to all of the national territories) prohibiting labor for wages on Sunday, and on May 25 and July 9; (2) a law which forbade the seizure or attachment of wages by creditors; (3) a law fixing employers' liability for accidents in certain enumerated industries and enterprises; (4) a law establishing a national Department of Labor; (5) two laws setting up free employment agencies for labor; (6) a law providing for a national commission to supply cheap houses for workmen; (7) a law requiring pensions for railway employees; (8) a law providing for the more effective sanitation of the capital; and (9) legislation establishing a national postal savings bank. Indeed, it would be almost correct to say that this period witnessed the beginning of labor legislation, for in 1912 the Argentine statute books contained only two laws relating to workmen: one (1905) prohibiting labor for wages on the Sabbath in the city of Buenos Aires, and the other (1907) providing for a Labor Office (*Dirección de Trabajo*).[3]

But these measures were but a beginning. Argentina was at the threshold of a new epoch in which the Radical Party would assume control of both the national and the provincial governments.

In April 1916, a notable election occurred in Argentina. The citizens of the nation, under the provisions of the new suffrage law, freely chose in every province electors who were to select a new chief executive. The old-line politicians pleaded in vain for presidential interference in favor of the conservative candidate. President Plaza refused to follow the traditional policy, and Irigoyen was elected by a narrow margin.[4]

> "The new President was something of a mystery. He lived modestly and alone. Since 1890 he had abstained from parliamentary life, like his fellow-radicals; but by ceaseless propaganda and sometimes by open fighting had opposed the Régimen [Régime]. He gave away in charity the salary which he had received as a teacher in State schools until he was dismissed from Government employment after his armed revolt in 1905. He was no orator,

[3] This legislation will be found in V. Peralta's *Leyes nacionales,* II, pp. 11 and *passim,* IV, pp. 35-40, 151-166. Of course it could not have been passed without the votes of some of the members of the more conservative parties who were doubtless influenced by a sense of justice and by a desire to avoid the nuisance of strikes, which were becoming more frequent every year. (*Cf.* Bucich Escobar, *Historia de los presidentes,* 1927 ed., pp. 395 and *passim.*)

[4] Bucich Escobar, *Los presidentes,* pp. 470-471. The result of the election was as follows (Bucich Escobar, *op. cit.,* p. 482):

Party	*Popular vote*	*Electoral vote*
Radicals	367,208	152
Conservatives	141,083	69
Democrats	131,022	62
Socialists	66,075	14

> and the language of his written pronouncements was involved and obscure. Born and educated in the city, he knew also the life of the Pampa, had sat with cowboys and peons around the campfire, and was everywhere welcome as the friend of the workingman." [5]

In some respects Irigoyen's victory of 1916 was analogous to that of Andrew Jackson in the United States in 1828. An ex-rancher of humble Basque origin, Irigoyen was the first man of the people to be elevated to the Argentine presidency. Like "Old Hickory," he was supremely courageous and defiantly independent; but he was a much better educated man than Jackson.

The task he faced upon assuming his duties as chief executive was not an easy one. He not only confronted the crisis occasioned by the World War, with much social unrest and labor agitation, but he had to administer the government and manage a strong opposition through the aid of a party composed for the most part of men untried in public life and lacking the tradition of public service.

Defying the majority of the leaders of congress, and especially the more conservative group, he kept Argentina out of the war. Perhaps this was because he considered neutrality the best course for his country and feared that participation in the struggle would prevent the achievement of domestic reforms.

His six-year term was prolific in social legislation. He justified in some measure his reputation as a friend of the workers; for, although he sternly suppressed a strike of stevedores in Buenos Aires in 1921, he managed to obtain legislation regarding (1) hours of labor, minimum wages, and the work of women and children in "sweatshops" (*trabajo de domicilio*); (2) pensions for the employees of the municipal public utility companies; (3) the arbitration of industrial disputes; and (4) the reduction of penalties for strikes. In the field of public health he secured a more rigid supervision of drugs, forbade the manufacture or importation of certain poisonous matches, and obtained legislation relative to lepers, as well as a law designed to provide running water and sewer systems for all of the towns of the republic. He also gave public education his generous support, for he encouraged the founding of the University of the Littoral (with branches at Santa Fé, Rosario, Paraná, and Corrientes), as well as the construction of hundreds of new primary schools. Lastly, his administration was signalized by the

[5] Kirkpatrick, *The Argentine Republic,* p. 218.

passage of a homestead law; but little headway was made in breaking up the large rural estates.[6]

Although Irigoyen's contribution to effective and maturely considered legislation may have been disappointing to some of his more impatient partisans, it should be remembered that he was greatly handicapped by parliamentary opposition, by the industrial slump of 1920-1921, and by the blind impetuosity of the labor agitators. He also spent much of his time and energy in securing control, often by dubious methods, of the various provincial governments. In fact, he intervened in every province except Santa Fé, where his political allies had governed continuously since 1912, and repeatedly in some of them, for a total of twenty interventions occurred during his administration. His purpose, however, appears to have been that of securing provincial governments committed to a reform program, and the result of his efforts became apparent during the administration of his successor.

The constitution of Argentina prohibits two successive terms in the presidency, and Irigoyen was accordingly not a candidate in 1922. In that year Marcelo T. Alvear, a moderate radical, was elected chief executive, receiving a large majority over several opponents.[7] The Radical Party appeared to be gaining strength; and yet, near the beginning of the new administration, the party split into two factions, the supporters of the new president and the followers of Irigoyen. The result was virtual legislative paralysis at certain periods.

Although the *Irigoyenistas* accused Alvear of being reactionary, his term was marked by rather progressive legislation. Among the labor laws, the following may be enumerated: (1) a statute regulating night work in bakeries; (2) a decree establishing arbitration boards to deal with railway labor problems; (3) a decree designed to prevent accidents arising from the use of certain types of motors in large-scale agriculture; (4) a law regulating the labor of women and children; and (5) a law providing pensions for employees in banking enterprises. A more general workmen's pension act was passed in 1923, but it proved unsatisfactory to the laborers themselves and was repealed three years later.

---

[6] A moderate statement of the problems and achievements of Irigoyen's first administration will be found in Kirkpatrick, *op. cit.*, pp. 219ff., and in Bucich Escobar, *op. cit.*, pp. 480-510. For a more passionate and laudatory view, see Etkin, *Bosquejo,* pp. 107ff.

[7] The Radical Party polled 458,457 votes, the National Coalition Party a little more than two hundred thousand, the Progressive Democrat Party and the Socialist Party slightly in excess of seventy-three thousand each. (Bucich Escobar, *op. cit.*, p. 518.)

Other legislation provided for an inheritance tax and a special real estate tax—a six mill levy—for the support of the national schools; and the president attempted to prevent the agents of the meat-packers from fixing the price of livestock. Moreover, Alvear brought the railways to an agreement to colonize the lands adjacent to their lines by establishing farmers on small holdings with fixed tenure and ultimate ownership.

It was during the same period also that the conservative interior provinces initiated their labor legislation. Córdoba passed an eight hour law which applied to several industries, and inaugurated old age pensions; Jujuy attempted to regulate certain abuses from which the peons had been suffering; Mendoza provided pensions for the aged and the infirm; and both San Juan and Tucumán stipulated not only an eight hour day in certain industries and mercantile establishments, but minimum wages as well. Tucumán also provided for medical care in its sugar mills; and Salta wrote on its statute books some of the most progressive and extensive labor laws of Latin America—the *Ley Güemes* and others.[8]

In October 1928, Irigoyen returned to the presidency. The election of that year, as Kirkpatrick has remarked, "was a strange one." The candidacy of Irigoyen

> "was announced a week before the election, and was everywhere received with acclamation. He made no speeches, wrote no address, never appeared in public. He was returned by an overwhelming majority on a very large poll, and reëntered Government House an autocrat by the popular will, having issued no programme, but expected by his supporters to initiate a prolific period of progress and constructive liberalism."[9]

[8] Some of this provincial legislation was passed during Irigoyen's first term. For the labor legislation of the period of radical rule, consult *Legislación social de américa latina* (Geneva, 1928), I, pp. 1-113, and Peralta, *Leyes nacionales, passim.*

[9] Kirkpatrick, *op. cit.*, pp. 225-226. In his *Bosquejo* published early in 1928, however, Etkin had set forth with a plethora of words the platform of the Irigoyen wing of the Radical Party. He declared that it represented the popular classes and desired to make their influence felt in the government, in the universities, and in every vital phase of the social order. It demanded that the public functionaries be chosen from among the common people and that the chief executive should personify the ideals of the nation; that the registry of voters be purged of fraud and that there should be absolute liberty of propaganda and voting; that the army of democracy should select the candidates and impose its will upon those chosen to administer the government; and that all of the liberties and guarantees of the constitution be transformed into reality. In the economic sphere it set up the following objectives: "Freedom from the foreign mortgage which weighs down upon our riches. A fair partition of the public domain. Energetic assistance for the producers. Division of the big rural estates. . . . The economic emancipation of the poor classes." (See in particular pp. 294-295.)

His victory was due in part to an effective political machine and in part to personal popularity. But these great hopes were not realized. The economic world was soon adrift, and the great radical leader was in his dotage.

In spite of the brief post-war slump, the period between 1913 and 1929 had been one of great material prosperity in Argentina. Telephone instruments quadrupled in number, the mileage of telegraph wire doubled, new railways were built, towns were modernized, progress was made in the construction of hard-surfaced highways, almost four thousand new school houses were opened, new industries sprang up and old industries expanded, thousands of automobile were purchased, and the value of foreign trade increased by thirty-five per cent. Radical influences in the government may have had little to do with this flourishing state of business, but they were not an economic deadweight. Labor was better compensated than ever before, school attendance almost doubled, public health services were greatly improved, and times were never more prosperous in Argentina. Between 1914 and 1929 the population of the country increased some forty per cent.[10]

II

By the end of 1929, however, the nation began to suffer from the world depression. An agricultural and pastoral nation lying mainly in the temperate zone, its products were sold in competition with those of the United States, Canada, and Australia, and their sale was further hampered by mounting tariff walls. Moreover, Argentina's economic progress was based to a considerable degree upon borrowed capital, and the nation was deeply in debt. A sharp decline occurred in the prices of wheat, flax seed, maize, meat, hides, and wool, which were the country's chief exports. Business and agriculture suffered, unemployment became a problem, strikes were frequent, politics unsettled, and services on the foreign debt difficult to maintain.

Irigoyen's return to the presidency was to prove most unfortunate for his reputation. During the last two years of his first term, he had struggled with a brief economic crisis which interfered with his program of domestic legislation, but now he would confront a world depression without parallel in modern history. The heavy burden of the presidential office was really too much for him. Seventy-five years old and

[10] The data in this paragraph are based upon the *Commerce Yearbook* of the United States Department of Commerce, 1926-1932, Vol. II for each year; and upon the *Statesman's Yearbook* for the same period.

with health impaired, he had yet to learn how to delegate authority and depend upon others to share his work. Distrustful of subordinates, he concentrated in his own hands all political and administrative matters, reducing his cabinet officers to mere figureheads or bureau chiefs, dissolving congress by having his supporters absent themselves from its sessions, absorbing the legislative functions of government, and intervening in five of the provinces. Because of ill-health and the pressure of routine, he left important judicial and administrative posts vacant, local bosses without anticipated rewards, and government bills unpaid. In brief, "a slow paralysis crept through all the Argentine national administration" at the very time when the world business depression commenced to be seriously felt. Men soon began to feel that the situation was intolerable; and all the nation's woes were attributed to a president who had set himself up as a court of last resort for conflicting interests. Not only was he denounced by old political enemies and the followers of Alvear; he also incurred the hostility of railway workers, dock laborers, farmers, and small business men, as well as of industrialists, railway employers, shippers, and exporters. As early as March 1930, there were signs that his power was beginning to weaken; and after the arrival of news of revolutionary movements in other countries of South America, his overthrow was inevitable.

> "On Thursday evening, September 4, there was a demonstration of university students against the Casa Rosada (Government House) . . . , in which one student was killed and several were wounded by the police. Public sentiment was deeply shocked, and the next morning thousands of students marched in solemn, funeral procession through the streets carrying white flags stained with the blood of the victim. Feeling was so tense that at six in the evening the President was prevailed upon to delegate his power to Vice President Martínez. But the public expected resignation; Martínez was but a screen behind which remained the dominating figure of Irigoyen. Friday morning prominent civilians went outside the city to persuade the armed forces and the military school to join them. The navy concentrated in the harbor refused to defend the government. On Saturday morning General José Uriburu [who had decided to support the revolution as early as August 16] delivered an ultimatum demanding the President's retirement. Troops from the suburban barracks started toward the center; cadets from the military academy were joined . . . by students of the university; with the rectors and professors at its head, the gigantic demonstration moved through the principal avenues down to the central Plaza, and the government unfurled the white flag of surrender. A few casualties occurred at the Plaza del Congreso and before the offices of the semiofficial newspaper. But it was virtually a blood-

> less revolution, and in every sense a popular . . . one. It was no barrack uprising, but a spontaneous movement by the people [of the capital, which contains almost a fifth of the population of the republic]." [11]

General Uriburu, who became at once virtually the dictator of Argentina, was an influential figure in the army and the son of the former conservative president. Although supported by a coalition of conservatives, radicals hostile to Irigoyen, and moderate socialists, his government was "composed almost exclusively of persons whose names carry aristocratic connotations," and was dominated by the conservative group. He persecuted the former adherents of Irigoyen, advocated the repeal of the Sáenz Peña Law, intervened in twelve of the fourteen provinces, and postponed the national elections for more than a year. When these were finally permitted on November 8, 1931, General Agustín P. Justo, the nominee of the National Democratic Party—a new organization of conservatives and provincial bosses in the main, but containing a few anti-Irigoyen radicals—came off victorious after a strenuous contest in which Lisandro de la Torre carried the standard of a coalition of progressive democrats and socialists, and neither wing of the Radical Party was permitted to have a candidate of its own. Justo was inaugurated on February 20, 1932.[12]

It was in this fashion that the leaders of the new middle class and the proletariat were overthrown, their reform program suspended half-finished,[13] and their party suppressed. The conservatives were trying to turn the nation back to the old régime. Perhaps it was the end of an epoch.

---

[11] C. H. Haring, "Revolution in South America," *Foreign Affairs,* IX (Jan., 1931), pp. 291-292. Consult also Ernest Galarza, "Argentina's Revolution and its Aftermath," *Foreign Policy Reports,* VII (Oct., 1931), pp. 309-322.

[12] Galarza, *op. cit.;* Haring, "Presidential Elections in South America," *Foreign Affairs,* X (Jan., 1932), pp. 330-331; *La Nación* (Buenos Aires), September 1, 1931, *passim.*

[13] Irigoyen seems to have "kept the faith" until the end. Among the last acts of his administration were: (1) the signing of an eight hour law applicable to all laborers of the republic save those engaged in agriculture, ranching, and domestic service; and (2) the opening of the "People's University," offering opportunities for adult education in courses ranging from elementary subjects to those of university grade. (Peralta, *Leyes nacionales,* Buenos Aires, 1930, II, pp. 229-231; H. L. Smith and H. Littell, *Education in Latin America* (New York, 1934), p. 35.)

III. BRAZIL

By Percy Alvin Martin

CHAPTER THIRTEEN

DOM JOÃO VI IN BRAZIL

THE futility of attempts to divide history into neatly arranged compartments and chapters is now recognized by all historians. To say that a given year definitely ends or initiates an epoch is to misunderstand the laws of historical development. Yet there are certain crises in the history of a nation as in the history of an individual, and a given event may deflect the course of national development into quite different channels. Such an event was the transference of the Portuguese court to Brazil in 1808.

I

For something over three hundred years Portugal had held sway over a large section of tropical South America. According to the traditional account, Brazil was discovered in 1500 by the Portuguese navigator, Pedro Alvarez Cabral, who, while en route to India, was sailing far to the westward in order to avoid the calms off the coast of Africa. Although the Portuguese settlements were for a long time confined to a few isolated communities along the coast, intrepid explorers penetrated so far into the interior that by the end of the eighteenth century Portugal had made good her claim to something over half of the continent. Over this vast territory was gradually spread—somewhat thinly to be sure—the language, culture, and tradition of the Lusitanian motherland.

While the dominant race in this vast colonial domain naturally harked back to Portuguese origins, other elements were represented in the population. At the time of discovery, Brazil was inhabited by a congeries of Indian races and stocks relatively low in the scale of civilization. In the early days of the colony, crossing between the settlers and the indigenous races were frequent with the consequent emergence of the *mestizo*. But this was not all. In order to secure laborers on their plantations, the colonists drew so heavily upon the teeming population of Africa that by the beginning of the nineteenth century nearly one-half of the three million inhabitants of Brazil were negroes. As was to be expected, a considerable mulatto element had meanwhile made its appearance and still further complicated the ethnic complexion of Brazil. Of the number of uncivilized Indians in the remote interior of Brazil we can only offer conjectures, but certainly it did not exceed a million.

While Brazil was thus being explored and settled, the government of Lisbon had been elaborating a colonial policy which, though somewhat less rigid and artificial, was not in its essentials so dissimilar to the system employed by Spain in her American possessions.

Such in fine were the conditions in Portuguese America when the advent of the Braganza family ushered in the first chapter in the history of modern Brazil.

The cause for this shifting of the axis of Portuguese power across the Atlantic is naturally to be sought in Europe. The ruler of Portugal, Dom João, acting as regent for his demented mother, Queen Dona Maria, had endeavored since 1795 to remain neutral in the struggle between Napoleon and Great Britain. But this neutrality, difficult under the best of conditions, became impossible when the French Emperor established in 1806 the continental blockade. Dom João, threatened on the one hand by the British fleet and on the other by the armies of Napoleon, was forced to make a decision. While still in an agony of suspense he read in *Le Moniteur* of November 13, 1807, that Napoleon had decreed that the Braganza dynasty had forfeited its throne and that Portugal was to be divided up between Spain and France.

The news of Napoleon's decision reached Lisbon on November 25, and already Junot's army was advancing upon the Portuguese capital in forced marches. To have offered resistance to the French would have been the counsel of folly. At this juncture Dom João decided on a step which had been discussed on many previous occasions: to move with his court, bag and baggage, to his great trans-Atlantic colony. From one point of view he was hardly a free agent. Actually it was Canning, the British secretary of state for foreign affairs, who brought the event to pass. On his order the British envoy, Lord Strangford, landed at Lisbon on the 27th and repeated orally the virtual ultimatum which had been issued some days previously, namely, that Portugal would have to surrender her fleet to England or utilize it for the transportation of the court to Rio de Janeiro. Strangford intimated that were the latter alternative adopted, the British government would lend the support of its naval forces.

Impaled between the horns of this dilemma, Dom João could do nothing but yield. The character of this monarch has generally been attacked by Portuguese historians who have never forgiven what they style his cowardly desertion of his native land. Brazilian writers on the other hand have done much to rehabilitate this monarch. Especially is this true of Oliveira Lima whose two volume monograph on Dom João has rendered obsolete all previous works on this period. The truth seems to be that Dom João was intelligent, astute, but timid; only with great difficulty could he reach any important decision. But he had the welfare of his subjects, especially the Brazilians, deeply at heart, and most of his actions were justified by events. Certainly his hegira to America was an act of wisdom and not an exhibition of cowardice. As Sir Sidney Smith, the commander of the British fleet, points out in his memoirs, but for the action of the prince at this time Brazil might well have been definitely lost to Portugal. Had Dom João yielded to Napoleon, the British might well have occupied the Portuguese colonies on the pretext that otherwise they would have fallen into the hands of the French.

The actual passage across the Atlantic had its comic as well as its serious aspects. Amid tremendous confusion the royal family, the court, and a multitude of functionnaires—some ten thousand in all—sailed from the Tagus on November 29. The ships were crowded beyond belief; according to Lieutenant O'Neill, who accompanied the expedition, the *Principe Real* had more than 1600 persons aboard. Provisions were scarce, and many of the aristocratic ladies of the court had to sleep under covering made of sail-cloth donated by the sailors of the English fleet. Even in the case of the Prince Regent, it was necessary to cut up sheets to make shirts for him.

After suffering severely from bad weather, including a frightful tempest, the bulk of the fleet arrived safely at Bahia on January 22, 1808. This was the first time that a sovereign of the Old World had set foot on the soil of the New. The good people of Bahia received their distinguished guests with great rejoicing and acclaim, hoping that their city would be raised to the status of capital of the new realm. They even offered to construct a royal palace for this purpose. But Dom João preferred to establish himself in Rio de Janeiro where he arrived on March 7.

The advent of the Portuguese court threw the somnolent colonial city into the wildest confusion. The problem of accommodating the numerous guests was not an easy one. The hospitable *Cariocas,* as the natives of Rio de Janeiro were called, freely threw open their homes to the newcomers, but later had occasion to regret their hospitality as many of their guests showed no disposition to leave. There were even some cases of outright expropriation. Yet despite these transitory hardships the feeling was general that a new day had indeed dawned for Brazil, and the Prince Regent quickly won the affection of his American subjects.

The first acts of the sovereign clearly revealed the changed status of Brazil. During his temporary sojourn in Bahia the prince issued on January 28 the famous decree opening the ports of Brazil to the commerce of all friendly nations, thus abolishing by a stroke of the pen the odious colonial monopoly. Much has been written regarding the responsibility of this act which was destined to have such profound effects upon Brazil. The truth is that Dom João could hardly have acted otherwise. The Portuguese ports were closed by the continental blockade, and Great Britain and, to a certain extent, the United States were the only powers with which Brazil was in a position to trade. England was of course the chief beneficiary of this situation and laid then and there the basis of a commercial preëminence which endured up to the outbreak of the World War.

The abolition of the old Portuguese commercial monopoly was not the only benefit Dom João conferred upon Brazil. Though the Prince Regent was a scion of one of the most absolute of the European kingdoms, the type of monarchy which he established in the New World was the only possible one under the circumstances—a hybrid monarchy, a mixture of absolutism and democracy. In theory the monarchy was indeed all-powerful, but as Oliveira Lima well points out, this absolutism was from the first tempered by the mildness and good nature of the prince. It likewise may be regarded as democratic in its manners, customs, and relations between the ruler and his subjects. It was this type of royalty which reached its apogee under Dom Pedro II, a sovereign who had many traits in common with his grandfather.

II

Space will not permit any detailed account of the manifold changes wrought by the Prince Regent in almost every phase of national life. An elaborate administrative machinery was set up, and was staffed by both Portuguese and Brazilians. Dom João had a real flair for choosing able advisers—men of the type of Palmela and Silva Lisboa. Supreme tribunals were established, and a national bank, the Banco do Brasil, was founded. During the entire colonial period no printing press existed in Brazil; the mental pabulum of the colonists was imported from Portugal. Under these circumstances it is not surprising that two-thirds of the free population was illiterate. As early as May 1808, Dom João established a royal printing press from which was issued the first periodical in the shape of the official organ of the court. During the next few years presses were set up in Bahia, Pernambuco, and São Paulo. Fully as important, in the opinion of Handelmann, as the opening of the ports, was another decree, that of April 1, 1808, removing all prohibitions on industrial activity on the part of the prince's Brazilian subjects. Unfortunately it was not until much later, when foreign capital became available, that this decree became really effective. In subsequent years, 1810-1811, a school of commerce and a military academy opened their doors. In 1814 was placed at the disposition of the public a royal library, the nucleus of the present Biblioteca Nacional. A national museum was created in 1818, as was also a school of fine arts. The latter institution deserves a word of special mention. After the conclusion of peace with France, Dom João invited a number of artists, headed by Lebreton, the perpetual secretary of the Academy of Fine Arts of Paris, to settle in Brazil. Among those who accepted the invitation were Debret, the painter of historical scenes; the brothers Taunay (one a landscape painter and the other a sculptor); Grandjean de Montigny, the architect; and the engraver Pradier. While most of these men were not artists of the first rank they did much to stimulate artistic interest in Brazil.

The liberality accorded foreigners was in fact one of the most significant features of Dom João's enlightened policy. The capital, with a population of 130,000—the largest city at that time in South America—contained some 3,000 Frenchmen alone. Foreigners were permitted to purchase land on the same basis as the Portuguese. Brazil was in fact like a rich storehouse, whose treasures hitherto but dimly suspected, were thrown open to all comers. Scholars and men of letters such as the Germans, Spix, Martius, von Eschwege, and Prince Maximilian von Wied Neuwied; the Frenchmen, August de St. Hilaire and de Freycinet; and the Russian Langsdorff requited Dom João's hospitality by carrying on fruitful explorations of the interior and by writing a number of scientific works and books of travel which introduced Brazil to the world. Immigrants were brought in at government expense and settled in some of the most productive regions adjacent to the capital.

Despite the undisputed advantages accruing from the transference of the Portuguese court, its residence in Brazil was not an unmixed blessing. Though well-meaning, and in many respects able, Dom João was weak and indolent, and made little effort to check the many abuses which sprang up within and without the court. Extravagant sums were spent on the royal table. Provisions had to be made, frequently at the expense of the Brazilians, for a swarm of greedy and avaricious Portuguese nobles and adventurers. Corruption on a large scale invaded the administration. Partly to defray the enormous expenses of the court, the Prince Regent distributed offices and honors by the wholesale. The English traveller Mathieson declares in this regard:

> "The sale of patents of nobility, stars, crosses and *habitos de Christo,* or insignia of the order of Christ and others similar to it, was among the most lucrative expedients for raising money. The rage for these decorations attained a greater height at Rio than it had perhaps ever before done in any country; almost any petty shopkeeper might be seen on the streets on holidays with his *habito de Christo.*"

The historian Armitage declared that Dom João, during his residence in Brazil, conferred more honorary insignia than all the members of the Braganza dynasty who had preceded him. To such an extent did the nobles aspire to bask in the royal favor that according to the American minister, Sumter, it was difficult to find anyone who would accept the position of Brazilian envoy to the United States.

The advent of Dom João witnessed a great change in the social structure of Brazil. On his arrival he found that politically and socially the most powerful element in the colony was the *fazendeiro,* or owner of the estate or plantation known as the *fazenda.* These estates were generally of immense extent and were virtually self-sustaining units; in the words of Dr. Normano, the *fazenda* was in a middle state between a family and a principality. Now that the gold mining, which had played an important part in the colonial economy of the eighteenth century, had become unprofitable, the land was the only source of wealth and power. The transferrence of the Portuguese court began to draw the *fazendeiro* from his rural isolation. In the words of Normano:

> "Not the new economic possibilities but the splendor and luxury of the court attracted the Brazilian agrarian aristocracy. . . . A movement started from all parts of the vast country; the fazendeiro with his wife, sons, daughters and other members of his rustic family, with slaves and servants, came from the bucolic lonesomeness of his estate to the tropical Versailles at Rio de Janeiro. He offered the monarch his services, his experience, his knowledge of the country. In exchange he received participation in power and political influence. There was thus an unwritten alliance be-

> tween the monarchy and the landed nobility—an alliance which ended only with the downfall of the monarchy. The fazendeiro won the victory over his only rival, the Portuguese immigrant, 15,000 of whom had accompanied Dom João to the New World."

Those immigrants who remained in America after the definite separation of Brazil from Portugal were gradually assimilated by the *fazendeiro* until they became integral parts of the social structure of the nation.

III

Dynastic and territorial ambitions led Dom João to embark on two wars which brought him scant credit and no permanent gain. The Prince Regent could not resist the temptation to strike at his enemy Napoleon through the one French holding in South America, and in 1809 an expedition organized in Pará captured the French colony of Cayenne, or French Guiana as it is generally called. Eight years later, however, Dom João was obliged to return it to France in accordance with the decisions of the Treaty of Vienna. The only permanent gain from this foray was the importation of useful as well as rare plants, long acclimated in Cayenne, such as nutmeg, pepper, breadfruit, cloves, and other spices. The shoots of the royal palms, now the glory of the Rio botanical garden, also came from this French colony.

The Portuguese conquests in the south, although much more important and of longer duration, were likewise temporary. Portuguese aspirations for a *point d'appui* on the Plata estuary had been realized at various times during the colonial period through the establishment of the post of Colonia, directly across the river from Buenos Aires. Here, despite Spanish protests, a lucrative smuggling industry had arisen. But now with the seat of the Portuguese monarchy moved to Brazil there were additional pretexts and reasons for expansion to the south. Buenos Aires had risen against Spain in 1810 and there was great disorder in the former Viceroyalty of La Plata. Inroads on the Brazilian frontier province of Rio Grande do Sul by the followers of the great Uruguayan *caudillo* Artigas, provided a welcome pretext for the extension of Portuguese power southward. Dynastic intrigues played their part too; Dona Carlota Joaquina, the faithless and ambitious wife of Dom João, toyed for a time with the idea of becoming the head of the former Spanish possession in the name of her royal brother Ferdinand VII, now the prisoner of Napoleon. Dom João was not unwilling to round out his domains to the south by the inclusion of the *Banda Oriental,* the present republic of Uruguay. Two armies, one sent by land and the other by sea, penetrated the *Banda Oriental,* and laid siege to Montevideo. On the capitulation of this Spanish stronghold in 1817 the *Banda Oriental* was incorporated with Brazil under the designation of *Provincia Cisplatina*—the name being an echo of the *Provincia Cisalpina* of the days of the Roman Republic. But as we shall see later this union of the Spanish speaking Uruguayans with the Portuguese speaking Brazilians was destined to last barely a decade.

Some time before the completion of the conquest of the *Banda Oriental* it was felt that the new status to which Brazil had attained called for some official recognition. By a decree of December 16, 1815, Dom João abolished the few remaining differences in the public law of the two sections of his vast domains, which were henceforth to be known as the "United Kingdom of Brazil, Portugal and the Algarves." This move was suggested, according to Oliveira Lima, by none other than Tallyrand; in any case, however, it was little more than the consummation of a *fait accompli,* for the old colonial government had long since ceased to exist in anything but name. On March 20, 1816, the insane queen, Dona Maria I died, and Dom João was formally proclaimed King of Portugal and Brazil under the title of Dom João VI.

IV

The internal tranquillity which Brazil enjoyed under Dom João VI suffered but one serious break. It could hardly be expected that Brazil would escape the contagion of republicanism which was sweeping over the rest of the continent. The immediate causes of the revolution which broke out in Pernambuco in 1817 were the republican aspirations of a group of Brazilians who were still under the spell of the French and American revolutions, and the growing antagonism between the "sons of the kingdom," *filhos do reino* as the Portuguese were called, and the former colonials. The Portuguese were apt to be overbearing and supercilious and made no attempt to hide their scorn of the Brazilians. A brawl arising over the murder of a Portuguese by a Brazilian soldier led to an uprising which soon became frankly republican and separatist. Emissaries were sent throughout northern Brazil to secure adhesions. A provisional government was organized, a flag adopted, and a number of onerous taxes abolished. Attempts were made to secure recognition from the United States. Although some of the best elements of Pernambuco lent their support to the revolution, it made scant headway elsewhere. When news of the uprising reached Rio de Janeiro the population rallied unanimously to the support of Dom João; volunteers presented themselves in large numbers, and money for the campaign was freely offered. As a result, the royal authorities had little difficulty in quelling the insurrection. Pernambuco was attacked from both land and sea. The prompt surrender of the insurgents did not save them from savage reprisals, and many of the most prominent leaders were put to death with the merest farce of a trial. However little the revolt may have been warranted at the outset, the virulence of the royalist reaction went far to justify the sympathy and even the admiration with which its victims have subsequently been regarded. Oliveira Lima, who has written a convincing *apologia* of Dom João and his reign, characterized it as the only genuine republican revolution in the history of Brazil.

CHAPTER FOURTEEN

THE INDEPENDENCE OF BRAZIL

WHEN the center of Portuguese power shifted from the Old World to the New through the transferrence of the court of the Braganzas from Lisbon to Rio de Janeiro, the independence of Brazil was only a question of time and circumstance. In fact, during Dom João's residence in Rio de Janeiro the monarchial régime had become so thoroughly acclimated in Brazil, and the various institutions implanted in American soil by the sovereign had struck such deep roots that a return to a status of colonial dependency was unthinkable. From this point of view the independence of Brazil really dated from the day that Dom João touched the soil of his great trans-Atlantic possession. The only possibility of permanent union between the two portions of his far-flung kingdom was perfect equality between mother country and colony.

I

Such a consummation, difficult under the best of conditions, was rendered impossible by a series of events in Portugal to which we must now briefly recur. After the departure of the French, that unhappy country had been turned over to the mercies of an arbitrary and tyrannical regency in which British influence under Marshal Beresford predominated. Portugal was indeed in a desperate plight. As a result of the opening of Brazilian ports to world commerce, the formerly lucrative trade between Lisbon and Brazil had almost ceased to exist. The absence of the court aggravated the economic distress, and the refusal of Dom João to return to Portugal aroused great discontent. A revolutionary movement, launched in Oporto in 1820, quickly swept the regency out of existence. There then arose a universal demand for a constitution, similar to that adopted by Spain in 1812. To this end the Portuguese revolutionists conceived the idea of summoning the *Côrtes,* an all but forgotten representative body whose last meeting took place in 1698. Among the most important tasks confronting the *Côrtes* was the adoption of a constitution which would place Portugal in the vanguard of the liberal monarchies of Europe. As the elaboration of such an instrument would necessarily require some time, the governing revolutionary *junta* temporarily adopted, on November 11, 1820, the ultra-liberal Spanish Constitution of 1812.

It was but natural that the liberal or even democratic principles espoused by the revolutionary government in Lisbon should awaken powerful echoes in Brazil. The necessity for some type of constitutional government was generally recognized, although there was a strong absolutist group in Brazil opposed to any kind of innovation which might smack even remotely of democracy. In the midst of this ferment the king as usual hesitated. Of the influences pulling him in various directions that of his son was the strongest. The Prince Dom Pedro was then twenty-two years of age. He was a dashing, brilliant, but rather erratic, young man who partly from conviction, partly because he could read the signs of the times, espoused the cause of liberalism. On February 24, 1821, he read to the crowds massed before the palace a decree in which Dom João unreservedly accepted the constitution to be drawn by the *Côrtes,* although its terms were not yet known. The populace vented its joy by flocking to São Christovão, the country seat of the king, and dragging him to the city. The unfortunate monarch, obsessed with the spectre of Louis XVI, fainted with terror when the crowd removed the horses from his carriages. But he mustered sufficient courage at the end of his journey to ratify the oath made by the prince.

The constituent *Côrtes,* now sitting at Lisbon, rendered at least lip service to Lusitanian solidarity by inviting the Brazilians to participate in the drawing up of the future constitution. A number of deputies were selected to this end; the instructions furnished them reveal clearly the aspirations of the Brazilians at that time: absolute equality, both politically and economically of the two kingdoms, parallel administrative organizations, and the seat of the government to alternate between Lisbon and Rio de Janeiro. As will presently appear, these principles were entirely unacceptable to the Portuguese members of the *Côrtes.*

Both patriotic and dynastic reasons now counselled the return of the king to Lisbon. A longer sojourn in Brazil might spell the loss of his crown and even the total overthrow of the Braganza dynasty. The *Côrtes,* moreover, in its reforming zeal, was embarked on a course of action inimical to Brazil which only the sovereign might hope to check. With great reluctance Dom João yielded to these arguments. During his thirteen years' residence in Brazil the king had enjoyed the few peaceful years of his troubled existence. He was now to face unknown perils, including the crossing of the Atlantic, of which, recalling his previous experience, he was in mortal terror. None the less the decision had to be faced. On April 22, 1821, he appointed his son, Dom Pedro, regent and lieutenant in Brazil, and four days later set sail for Lisbon. The parting was extremely affecting. The king burst into repeated sobs, uttering the word, "Brazil," in truly heart-rending fashion. He distributed decorations and titles to all who asked for them; on his son's breast he placed the insignia of the Golden Fleece. On his hegira he was accompanied by three thousand nobles and court functionaries who carried off everything portable of value including all the specie in the Bank of Brazil. As the ship weighed anchor, he had a premonition of the momentous changes the next few months would bring forth. According to a well-authenticated tradition he turned to his son and declared: "Pedro, Brazil will, I fear, ere long separate herself from Portugal; and if so place the crown on thine own head, rather than allow it to fall into the hands of any adventurer."

II

The departure of Dom João after a residence of thirteen years in Brazil left the fate of the country in the hands of the young regent, Dom Pedro, then twenty-two years of age. In some respects he was well-equipped to face the difficult problems suddenly thrust upon him. He had been raised in Brazil, and as a result inspired confidence in his future subjects. He was impulsive, rash, easily moved to anger, but quick to forget past injuries. With his ardent and romantic temperament he was the ideal "liberating hero" of his people, a rôle which for a time he filled with marked success. On the other hand he was vain, ambitious, and as time went on increasingly reactionary. Later he was to abandon in large part his liberal views—never the result of any deep conviction—and go over bag and baggage to his reactionary Portuguese advisers.

The tasks confronting the young regent in 1821 were indeed formidable. The country was impoverished and the treasury was empty. The Bank of Brazil, on which such high hopes had been placed, was virtually wrecked. The antagonism between the Portuguese and the Brazilians was daily becoming more and more bitter, and Dom Pedro had the delicate task of holding a balance between them. Although the majority of the country was monarchist, the republican spirit, which had flared up in Pernambuco in 1817, was by no means extinct. But most serious of all, Dom Pedro had to face the responsibilities of a separation of Brazil from Portugal, a course of action rendered all but inevitable through the short-sighted and impolitic actions of the *Côrtes* at Lisbon.

III

This assembly claimed, as we have seen, to represent the entire Portuguese realm on both sides of the Atlantic. Of the two hundred members of this body, seventy were to be chosen by Brazil. At first the *Côrtes* was loud in its professions of Portuguese solidarity. In a proclamation signed July 13, 1821, the most high-sounding promises were made to "the South American branch of the great Portuguese family; henceforth the interests of both countries would be inseparable; the Portuguese would not consider themselves free if this liberty was not shared by their Brazilian brethren." In practice, however, events fell out quite differently. Without waiting for the arrival of their Brazilian colleagues the Portuguese members of the *Côrtes* began to legislate on matters vitally affecting the two halves of the Lusitanian kingdom. Symptomatic of what was to follow was a manifesto in which all the misfortunes which had befallen Portugal were traced jointly to the sojourn of the royal family in Rio and the opening of Brazilian ports to the commerce of all nations. The latter measure was attacked with especial bitterness as being largely responsible for the decay of Portugese manufacturing and commerce. It soon appeared that the real object of the *Côrtes* was to recolonize Brazil; to reduce it in other words to a condition of complete dependence on its former mother country. To the statement of the Brazilian deputies that the creation of a separate Brazilian legislative congress was indispensable, the Portuguese deputy, Borges Carneiro, amid frightful uproar, declared that the rebellious prince should abandon the palace of São Christovão where he was "forced to breathe the fetid atmosphere of cowardly and subservient counsellors."

Only a few of the many intemperate decrees of the *Côrtes* need be mentioned. To assure if need be the military subjugation of Brazil, it was provided that the Portuguese and Brazilian armies should henceforth constitute a single body, thus facilitating the transfer of loyal troops to disaffected areas. A little later, practically all the institutions created by Dom João were abolished: the chancery court, the royal treasury, the *junta* of commerce, all went by the board. Possibly the most insulting act of all was a decree of September 29, 1821 ordering Dom Pedro to return to Europe, on condition that before his entry into Portugal he should make a tour *incognito* through England, France, and Spain "in order to complete his political education." Finally, on the Roman theory of divide and rule, the *Côrtes* encouraged the creation of provincial *juntas* which should receive their orders directly from Lisbon.

The Brazilian delegates at Lisbon soon found themselves in a hopeless situation. Among them were a number of men later to be famous in Brazilian history—Antonio Carlos, Padre Feijó, Araujo Lima, and Vergueiro. At the outset, none of them had thought of independence. But now outnumbered and insulted, powerless to arrest the flood of decrees inimical to their country, many of them fled to England. The conviction steadily grew among them that the only salvation for Brazil lay in her complete independence from her former mother country.

IV

When the text of the decrees of the *Côrtes* reached Brazil they were at first greeted with incredulity which quickly gave way to anger and alarm. The immediate result was a great wave of loyalty to Dom Pedro. The patriotic party, recruited largely from republican and revolutionary elements, rallied to the support of the young regent. Brazilians of all shades of political opinion soon came to realize that they were in danger of losing everything they had gained by the residence of Dom João and the court in their midst. Popular ferment increased. "If the object of the constitution is to do us harm, the Devil take the constitution," was a sentiment openly proclaimed on the streets. With the abolition of the censorship, energies hitherto suppressed, made themselves felt. A number of newspapers sprang up, and what was perhaps more important, a flood of pamphlets appeared. Of these latter, the one which produced the greatest impression was by Francisco de Franca Miranda, *O despertador brasiliense*. Its influence might perhaps be compared to Thomas Paine's *Common Sense*. It qualified the legislation of the *Côrtes* as

> "illegal, injurious, and impolitic. Illegal, because it was decreed without the coöperation of our representatives, and consequently without the sanction of the nation. Injurious because it revealed the cynicism with which the *Côrtes* disposed of our existence as if we were a handful of miserable slaves . . . and not an allied kingdom more powerful and with more resources than Portugal herself. Impolitic because it chose this particular moment, when the eyes of the world were on Brazil and Portugal, to make our independence necessary and legitimate."

Other influences also worked in favor of independence. Especially was this true of the Masonic Order, among whose members were many eminent Brazilians, including some members of the clergy. In addition to this secret organization, the *Associação Philotechnica,* a scientific society, exerted itself to the same end under the direction of José Sylvestre Rebello, who later was the first Brazilian minister to the United States.

The conviction gradually became general that on no account should Dom Pedro be permitted to leave Brazil. From Portugal itself, from the intimate friends of Dom João, came intimations to the same effect. Dom Pedro's presence in Brazil, it was declared, was the only means of saving the king, Portugal, Brazil, and himself. The position of the prince, however, was a cruel one, and it is small wonder that for a time he hesitated. If he defied the *Côrtes* and refused to leave he would be taxed with treason; if he returned to Portugal he would be recreant to the trust reposed in him by the Brazilians. He was, in fine, placed in the dilemma of having to choose between the land of his birth and the land of his adoption, and events were to prove that Dom Pedro was Brazilian first and Portuguese afterwards. The correspondence between himself and the king, now published, leaves no doubt as to his absolute sincerity.

Pressure on Dom Pedro to remain in Brazil was now brought to bear from various quarters. His wife, Dona Leopoldina, a former Austrian archduchess, urged her husband to oppose the decrees of the *Côrtes;* and she is entitled to be regarded as one of the founders of Brazilian independence. Emissaries were hastily sent to Minas and São Paulo to secure signatures for petitions imploring Dom Pedro to remain in Brazil. The results exceeded all expectations. All classes of the population joined in begging Dom Pedro to defy the orders of the assembly at Lisbon. The reply from São Paulo was probably written by José Bonifacio, whom we shall meet presently, and is one of the most famous documents in Brazilian history. In terms that a few months earlier would have been regarded as highly treasonable, it set forth in passionate language the grievances of the Brazilian people and flayed the actions of the *Côrtes* in its attempt to destroy the institutions set up by Dom João and to reduce Brazil to the status of a colony. At the same time it beseeched Dom Pedro not to abandon his Brazilian subjects. A petition of similar tenor came from Minas Geraes; as for Rio de Janeiro, the supporters of Dom Pedro steadily grew in number, due in part to the influence of a patriotic organization, the *Club de Resistência,* later known as the *Club de Independência.*

V

In view of what seemed to be the overwhelming demand of his people, Dom Pedro hesitated no longer. On January 9, 1822 he replied to a deputation of the municipality of Rio with the famous sentence: "Since it is for the good of all and for the general happiness, I am ready; tell the people that I shall remain." This declaration is known in Brazilian history as the *"Fico"* (literally "I shall remain"), and is rightly regarded as one of the important milestones on the road toward independence.

The formal refusal of Dom Pedro to obey the orders of the *Côrtes* suddenly brought to a head the latent antagonism between the young regent and the Portuguese garrison in Rio de Janeiro. On January 11, the two thousand men constituting the so-called "auxiliary division" *(divisão auxiliadora)* defied the regent by issuing from their barracks and occupying the Morro do Castello, an eminence which dominated the city. Their object was to force the prince to return to Europe. When, however, Aveliz, their commander, realized that practically the entire city would support Dom Pedro in case of violence, he was persuaded to remove his garrison across the harbor to Nichteroy. But even here his situation soon became so untenable that he agreed to return with his troops to Portugal. In mid-Atlantic he passed a number of transports loaded with reënforcements sent to Brazil by the *Côrtes.* These, too, on their arrival were prevailed upon to return to Lisbon in the same ships which had brought them. Thus by a clever use of pressure and diplomacy Dom Pedro freed Brazil of a most serious menace. Any hope of reducing the Brazilians to obedience by armed force was to prove futile.

By means of the *Fico* Dom Pedro had burned his bridges behind him and had thrown down defiance to the *Côrtes.* Independence, to be sure, had not been declared, but events were conspiring to make it inevitable. The pro-Portuguese cabinet which had favored Dom Pedro's return to Lisbon was dissolved, and on January 16 a new ministry was chosen in which the guiding spirit was José Bonifacio de Andrada e Silva, soon to be known as the "Patriarch of Independence," and one of the outstanding figures in Brazilian history. As Oliveira Lima once remarked, to treat the independence of Brazil with no mention of José Bonifacio would be like discussing the formation of Italian unity with no reference to Cavour.

The Portuguese historian Oliveira Martins has observed that in the eighteenth century such intellectual life as existed in the Portuguese domains was largely the contribution of Brazilians. In the field of scholarship, belles-lettres, and statecraft Brazilians abounded. Colonials might indeed aspire to the highest position in church or state provided they were graduates of the University of Coimbra, then as now, the most important seat of learning in the Portuguese-speaking world. As a consequence, many prominent families sent their sons to Europe to complete their education, where some of them achieved distinction. Of the Brazilians who thus rose to fame none gained the world-wide recognitions of José Bonifacio. This remarkable man was born in 1765 in Santos, the chief seaport of the Captaincy of São Paulo. At the age of fifteen he went to Europe where he remained for the better part of the next four decades. After graduating from the University of Coimbra he travelled from 1790 to 1800 in France, Germany, England, Sweden, Denmark, and Austria. His chief interests were scientific, and he soon won for himself a European reputation in the fields of mineralogy and metallurgy. He became well acquainted with some of the greatest thinkers of the day including Alexander von Humboldt, with whom for years he carried on an active correspondence. He worked with such men as Volta, Priestley, Lavoisier, and de Capital. He discovered several minerals hitherto unknown. He was a frequent contributor to scientific magazines and was a member of the most important learned societies of Europe. On his return to Portugal in 1800 he was appointed to a number of high offices, including a professorship at the University of Coimbra. He led a corps of students against the French army under Junot in 1808. In 1812 he was elected secretary of the Society of Sciences and Letters at Lisbon. But the stupidity and ineptitude of the regency, a mere instrument in the hands of Beresford, caused him to abandon Portugal in disgust. On his arrival in Brazil in 1819 he had in all probability forseen the eventual separation of Brazil from Portugal and was prepared to offer his services and abilities to the cause of independence. In the difficult days to come he was to prove a tower of strength to the young and inexperienced Dom Pedro.

In the new ministry, in which he received great aid from his brilliant brother, Martim Francisco de Andrada, he quickly revealed a full grasp of the situation. His first care was to restore the unity of Brazil, which the *Côrtes* had done its best to destroy, by making the various provinces directly dependent on Lisbon. On February 16, 1822, at the instance of José Bonifacio, Dom Pedro signed a decree inviting the various provinces to send deputies or *procuradores* to Rio to form a sort of council of state to which the government might turn for aid and advice. Such, however, was the state of disunion in Brazil, that only four of the provinces, Rio de Janeiro, São Paulo, Minas Geraes, and Rio Grande do Sul, gave any real support to this proposal. The north, held in subjection by a strong Portuguese garrison, remained aloof. Moreover, the loyalty of the great province of Minas Geraes to Dom Pedro was not entirely above question, owing in part to existence of republican sympathies which went back to the abortive rising against Portugal in 1789.

For the double purpose of quieting disorder and winning the support of the *Mineiros,* as the inhabitants of the province were called, Dom Pedro now took, on the advice of José Bonifacio, a horseback trip through the most densely populated portions of the province. The journey was highly successful. The great *fazendeiros* or landowners almost unanimously pledged their support. One municipal council after another hailed Dom Pedro as the savior of Brazil against the nefarious designs of the *Côrtes.* Everywhere the presence of the young prince aroused sympathy and enthusiasm.

VI

Events now moved rapidly. It was evident that the *Côrtes* was reaping the rewards of its folly. On May 13, after his return to the capital, Dom Pedro accepted the title of "Perpetual Defender of Brazil" proffered him by the municipality of Rio. On June 3 he took a step of far-reaching importance by signing a decree convoking a constituent assembly. In some respects this act may be regarded as the decisive step in the process of separation from the mother country; to be effective but one additional act was necessary: the formal proclamation of independence. This was soon to come.

In August Dom Pedro set out on horseback for a tour through the Province of São Paulo to gain adherents to establish a closer contact with his future subjects as he had done earlier in the year in Minas Geraes. The Paulistas had already given unmistakable evidence of their detestation of the *Côrtes* and their determination that the old colonial régime should never be restored. From every side the prince received evidences of loyalty and devotion. On September 7, while Dom Pedro and his suite were on the banks of a little stream called the Ypiranga in the vicinity of São Paulo, the prince was overtaken by a messenger from José Bonifacio bearing the latest decrees from Lisbon, notably the ones which abolished the Council of *Procuradores* and ordered the prosecution of the members of Dom Pedro's cabinet. There was also a letter from Princess Leopoldina, with the significant sentence, "The apple is ripe; harvest it now, or it will rot." When Dom Pedro realized the full tenor of the decrees of the *Côrtes,* he determined to make the severance from Portugal irrevocable. Suddenly unsheathing his sword he cried: "Comrades, the Portuguese *Côrtes* wishes to reduce Brazil to slavery; we must forthwith declare her independence." Then tearing from his hat the band of Portuguese colors, he shouted, "Independence or Death," a cry that was repeated by the members of his escort. This act culminating as it did the complete and definite break between the mother country and her great American colony, is hailed by the Brazilians as the birthday of their independence.

Dom Pedro now hurried back to Rio where he found that as early as August 20 the Grand Orient Lodge of the Masonic Order had proclaimed the definite and complete separation of Brazil from the mother country. In general it may be said that the rôle of the Masonic Order in these difficult days was a crucial one; Dom Pedro himself had joined the Order at the instance of José Bonifacio, and within its ranks were to be found some of the leading men of the country. On October 12 Dom Pedro was proclaimed "Constitutional Emperor of Brazil," and the solemn coronation took place on December 1. It is to be noted that Dom Pedro was to rule over not a kingdom, but an empire. The choice of the latter term was not due merely to the vast extent of Brazil's territory. A kingdom, even a constitutional one, would signify tradition, even divine right. The empire, on the other hand, signified a revolutionary conquest, a popular acclamation. Thus the new empire of Brazil, ruled over by the scion of one of the oldest dynasties in Europe, had a double origin; hereditary right, and popular choice.

In striking contrast to the course of events followed in Spanish America, the achievement of independence in Brazil came to pass without violence and almost without shock. If, in the words of the French economist, Leroy-Beaulieu, the colony detached itself from the motherland even as a ripe fruit falls from the tree, causes of Brazil's independence must not be regarded as purely fortuitous. The comparative mildness of the Portuguese colonial administration had left no such heritage of resentment as was to be found in Spain's American possessions. The thirteen years residence of Dom João VI had admirably served as a transition between colonial dependency and complete independence. Finally, the enormous disparity between the size and resources of mother country and colony made any effective opposition to independence impossible once the Brazilians were convinced that such a step was logical and necessary. The intransigent and stupid action of the *Côrtes* at Lisbon merely accelerated a movement that sooner or later would have been irresistible.

We may fittingly conclude this study with a quotation from Prince Metternich, the famous apostle of reaction and defender of absolutism. In a remarkable memorandum submitted to the European courts while the *Côrtes* of Lisbon was still in session he declared:

> "The emancipation of Brazil was a necessary and inevitable consequence of the revolution in Portugal. The bonds which united the two kingdoms had become so weak that they depended on nothing more than the unity and strength of the royal power. The crown, shorn of its rights, dignity, and splendor by a group of demagogues, became a phantom in the eyes of the Brazilians. From that time on the pretentions of the *Côrtes* of Lisbon to govern a distant country, fifty times as large as Portugal, necessarily appeared to this country absurd and monstrous . . . and one may be permitted to say that if ever the revolt of a colony against its metropolis has been justified, such was the case of the uprising of the Brazilians against an authority usurped by a revolutionary *junta* which had dethroned and shackled its sovereign and overturned from top to bottom the government of its country." [1]

[1] Oliveira Lima, *Formation historique de la nationalité brésilienne*, p. 174.

CHAPTER FIFTEEN

THE REIGN OF DOM PEDRO I

THE Emperor Dom Pedro I, as we may henceforth call him, had proclaimed independence; before him lay the much more formidible task of organizing the empire and defending it from attack from without and disintegration from within.

I

The news of the *Grito do Ypiranga,* as the declaration of September 7, 1822, was called, had been received with wrath and amazement in Lisbon; naturally the *Côrtes* had no intention of calmly acquiescing in the loss of Portugal's most valuable overseas possession. Hostilities were therefore inevitable, but fortunately they were confined almost entirely to the activities of the Brazilian and Portuguese navies. We have already seen that the Portuguese government had stationed a number of powerful garrisons at strategic points along the Brazilian littoral. The successful efforts of Dom Pedro to dislodge and send back to Lisbon the troops assigned to Rio under General Aveliz have already been noted. There yet remained, however, strong Portuguese forces in the north; here also, were many loyalist elements among the civilian population who would have liked to have erected a kind of Brazilian Canada. Others, with their headquarters in Pará talked vaguely of "an independent Amazonia."

The center of Portuguese resistence was Bahia where a strong force was stationed under General Madeira. An attempt to dislodge the Portuguese by a land attack under Labatut—a Frenchman serving under Dom Pedro—proved a fiasco. Fortunately for the Brazilians the emperor had secured the services of one of the ablest seamen of the day, Lord Cochrane, Earl of Dundonald, who had gained fame through the service he had rendered the Chileans in their struggle for independence. He arrived at Rio on March 13, 1823, and on the 21st was appointed "first admiral of the national and imperial navy." A number of capable and daring British seamen, including Captains Taylor and Grenfell, served under him. Bahia was now actively besieged both by land and sea, and on July 2 General Madeira surrendered and agreed to return with his troops to Lisbon. He was accompanied by a large number of Portuguese merchants who because of their reactionary ideas feared reprisals had they remained in Brazil. Lord Cochrane also liberated Maranhão and Pará; Portuguese ships on the high seas were relentlessly pursued by Cochrane's captains, and some were even captured in sight of their own shores. With the capitulation of the Portuguese garrison at Montevideo, the rule of Dom Pedro was accepted throughout the length and breadth of Brazil.

II

The expulsion of the last of the Portuguese garrisons did not by any means end the difficulties confronting the young emperor. Internal problems of even greater magnitude were pressing for solution. The new empire was quite without experience in the practice of self-government while the character of Dom Pedro I was, as we have seen, an amalgam of conflicting qualities. While professing a sincere attachment to liberalism he was at heart arbitrary and dictatorial. With the qualities of high courage and noble conception of public duty were coupled a capriciousness and an obstinacy of temper and a growing laxity of private morals. The disastrous results of these shortcomings were not, however, to appear until later.

The constituent assembly convoked on June 3, 1822 met amid great rejoicing on May 3 of the following year. José Bonifacio and his brother, by virtue of their abilities and prestige, were in a position largely to influence its deliberations. The delegates consisted of the intellectual and moral élite of Brazil. They were recruited from magistrates and judges, members of the higher clergy, professors, high government functionaries, and the like. It is worth noting that this assembly contained thirty-three future senators, twenty-six ministers of state, eighteen presidents of provinces, seven councellors of state, and four regents. Unhappily, they were, with rare exception, abysmally ignorant of parliamentary practice, and their competency as administrators was almost nil. At the same time many of them were imbued with humanitarian and philanthropic ideas which led to interminable and fruitless debates on such subjects as the emancipation of negro slaves, improvement of the lot of the Indians, foundation of universities, and the like.

Unfortunately, the Andrada brothers, particularly José Bonifacio, did not use their power altogether wisely. The emperor, whom they were too prone to regard as a sovereign of their own creation, chafed at their dictatorial measures. And it must be admitted, in all conscience, that the actions of the ministry were in many cases high-handed. The whole tone of the assembly was extremely nationalistic, which in the present instance, meant anti-Portuguese. Among the delegates were several men who had sat in the *Côrtes* at Lisbon and were still burning with resentment at the treatment they had received. A proposal to expell from Brazil all Portuguese suspected of hostility to national independence was sponsored by José Bonifacio's brother, Martim Francisco, the most brilliant orator in the assembly. This project naturally brought down upon the Andradas the hostility of the extreme royalist party and the suspicion of the emperor.

Weary of dictation, Dom Pedro at length yielded to pressure and on July 17 dismissed the ministry. As a consequence the Andradas went over to the opposition. From the defenders of the government they became its most caustic and unsparing critics. They founded a periodical called *O Tamoyo*—the name of an Indian tribe hostile to the Portuguese—and as the paper was clever and well written it gained wide influence. The emperor, quick-tempered and passionate, bitterly resented the conduct of the Andradas and drew closer to the Portuguese and royalist elements. The assembly in turn was ambitious and extremely jealous of its prerogatives with the natural result that its relations with the emperor became more and more strained.

Thoroughly incensed at the conduct of the assembly and his erstwhile ministry, Dom Pedro determined to get rid of them both. He may well have had in mind the example set by his hero Napoleon on the 18th Brumaire. Assured of the loyalty of the army, which had recently been reënforced through the incorporation of the Portuguese prisoners-of-war taken at Bahia, Dom Pedro ordered a concentration of troops about the palace of São Christovão where the assembly held its meetings. This body, sensing the blow about to fall, declared itself in "perpetual session" and defied the emperor. Yet these mock heroics availed it nothing. After the famous "night of agony" one of Dom Pedro's officers forced his way into the chamber and read a proclamation dated November 12 in which the assembly was accused of having been false to its oath "to defend the integrity of the empire, its independence and my dynasty," and was accordingly dissolved. The deputies left the building amid the general indifference of the populace. At the same time the Andradas and a number of deputies were arrested, placed on shipboard, and sent to France. As Dr. Oliveira Lima once remarked, one of the greatest gains from the dissolution of the constituent assembly was the series of lyric poems and caustic political letters written by José Bonifacio during his exile in France.

The assembly through its factiousness and intemperate actions had forfeited the sympathies of all of the royalist and many of the liberal elements of the capital. It had, however, one great achievement to its credit: the completion of a constitution, which after all, had been the chief reason for its existence. As we shall see in a moment, the efforts expended on this instrument were not entirely wasted. Moreover, the condemnation of the assembly was by no means general, nor did all of the provinces acquiesce in its dissolution. A revolution flared up in Pernambuco, where the embrace of the revolt of 1817 still smouldered, and an ambitious attempt was made to launch a so-called "Confederation of the Equator." But this movement was put down in 1824 with comparative ease by loyal troops and the fleet under Lord Cochrane, and the ringleaders were executed. The suppression of disorders in the north was succeeded by general apathy and a willingness to follow the lead of the emperor. In the words of the famous Brazilian publicist, Theophilo Ottoni: "It was believed in 1824 that there were no more antidotes against despotism."

III

As has already been suggested Dom Pedro was at heart an absolutist. But he had learned much during the past two years and he realized fully that an attempt to restore an absolute monarchy of the eighteenth century type would spell the loss of his throne. Too much water had flown under the bridge since the departure of his royal father. In fact in the very proclamation by which the constituent assembly was dissolved he declared that he would summon another body to prepare a constitution that would be "twice as liberal" *(duplicadamente mais liberal)* as the one which he had just rejected. In a later proclamation he attempted to justify his actions; the arrest and banishment of the Andradas, he declared, was due solely to his desire to avoid anarchy.

> "The salvation of the country, which is confided to me, as the Perpetual Defender of Brazil, and which is the supreme law, has required these measures. Have confidence in me as I have in you, and you will see that our internal and external enemies will alike beg our indulgence. Union! Brazilians, union! Whoever has adhered to our sacred cause, and made oath to the independence of the empire, is a Brazilian."

On November 26, 1823, a council of state of ten persons appointed by Dom Pedro was commissioned to draw up a project of a constitution. This body worked under the personal inspection of the emperor with such rapidity that its labors were completed on December 11. The project was not, however, submitted to a new national assembly as Dom Pedro had promised, but to various municipal councils *(camaras)*. When a majority of these had given their approval the emperor, the empress, and the great dignitaries of church and state took the oath to the new constitution (March 25, 1824).

The Constitution of 1824 is one of the most important and significant public documents ever issued in Hispanic America. With slight modifications it served as the fundamental charter of Brazil up to 1889 when the monarchy was succeeded by the republic. It will, therefore, repay careful study, but it seems more logical to defer the analysis of its chief provisions until we examine the constitutional and parliamentary life of the empire under Dom Pedro II. At this point we may merely indicate some of the important respects in which it departs from the constitution elaborated by the assembly of 1823. At the outset it should be made clear that both documents, considering time and circumstances, were extremely liberal in character. In this respect Dom Pedro was as good as his word. The most striking differences had to do with the imperial attributes. The Constitution of 1824, like the *Chartre* of Louis XVIII, had been granted by the ruler to his subjects; while the earlier instrument was the work of a popularly elected assembly. The "moderative power" of the emperor, a constitutional innovation described as the key to the whole system, was perhaps the most striking addition, and will be discussed in detail later. Among the faculties it conferred upon the emperor was the right of dissolving parliament, a power denied him in the earlier document. The first constitution declared that the acceptance of a foreign crown would *ipso facto* bring with it the renunciation of the Brazilian throne. The absence of this provision in the latter instrument introduced serious complications as we shall see presently. Though the earlier constitution gave the Catholics a privileged position in the state, other beliefs were explicitly tolerated and non-Catholics were granted the right of suffrage. In the later constitution only Catholics could vote; this provision lasted until almost the end of the empire.

IV

The foreign relations of the newly created Brazilian empire now demand our attention. It is obvious that the recognition of Brazilian independence by Portugal was an imperious necessity before the new empire could take its place in the family of nations. But the authorities in Lisbon proved obdurate. In the spring of 1823 the *Côrtes,* now hopelessly discredited, had been dissolved and Dom João was once more the absolute ruler of Portugal. Since the unwarranted demands of the *Côrtes* had been the occasion of Brazilian independence, the Portuguese government not unreasonably felt that the Brazilians might under the changed circumstances be willing to come back into the Portuguese fold. Accordingly, in the fall of 1823 two envoys, the Count of Rio Maior and Luis Paulino de Oliveira Pinto da França set sail for Brazil to effect a reconciliation. But their reception by the Brazilians was far from cordial. When they were forced to admit that they had no authorization to recognize the independence of Brazil they were ignominously shipped back to Lisbon. The rejection of these overtures caused much bad blood in Portugal, and it was not until March of the following year that negotiations were opened for peace. As was to be expected England played the rôle of mediator. Since the seventeenth century, as is well known, Portugal and Great Britain had been closely bound together, both politically and economically. In the case of Brazil, England had laid the basis of her commercial preëminence as early as 1808. It was distinctly to the interest of the British Crown, therefore, that enduring peace be established between the two branches of the Lusitanian family. Dom Pedro sent to London one of his ablest diplomats, Marshal Felisberto Caldeira Brant Pontes, later known as the Marquis of Barbacena. George Canning, the all powerful foreign secretary, played the part of mediator. But negotiations soon came to an impasse as Portugal's assertion of sovereignty and Brazil's demand for independence proved irreconcilable. Canning now took matters in his own hands. He sent Sir Charles Stuart, the accomplished British ambassador at Paris, on a special mission to Lisbon to explain to the Portuguese that Great Britain found herself constrained through her own interest to recognize the independence of Brazil, and that he, Stuart, would proceed to Brazil to negotiate to this end. Canning added, however, that he preferred to take this step after Portugal had herself accepted the *fait accompli* of Brazilian independence. After protracted negotiations Portugal yielded to the inevitable; by a treaty signed August 29, 1825, Portugal formally recognized the independence of her former colony. As a partial *quid pro quo* Brazil agreed to assume a debt of £1,400,000 contracted by Portugal with great Britain in 1823 and to pay Dom João £600,000 for his private property and palace in Brazil.

Portugal was not, however, the first foreign power to extend recognition. That honor was reserved for the United States. In a sense this step had already been anticipated through the residence from 1810 to 1820 of United States ministers in Rio at the court of Dom João. Late in 1823 Dom Pedro appointed as chargé d'affaires to Washington one José Rebello, who arrived at his post in April 1824. At once a difference in President Monroe's cabinet developed on the wisdom of extending recognition to an empire, as it might encourage monarchy to gain a foothold on the free soil of America. Others argued that the United States was more interested in the fact of independence than in any particular form of government. Since, however, the United States had recognized several of Spain's former colonies two years earlier it could hardly do less with Portugal's former possession. Formal recognition was accordingly extended to Rebello on May 26, 1824.

V

The reign of the first emperor of Brazil, which began as we have seen under what were on the whole brilliant auspices, ended all but disastrously. The high favor in which Dom Pedro was held in 1822 and 1823 began to suffer an eclipse. Many of the liberal elements in Brazil never forgave the emperor for the dissolution of the constituent assembly and the banishment of the Andradas. Dom Pedro's refusal to summon parliament until 1826 aggravated the discontent, and the public authorities were in many cases as arbitrary and ruthless as under the old colonial régime. To these causes of unrest at home were added the serious loss of prestige which the emperor suffered as a result of his disastrous foreign policy. Many felt that the recognition of Portugal and Great Britain had been purchased at too high a price and that the various commercial treaties to which Brazil was a party were onerous and unfair. But the chief grievance was against the emperor's activities in the regions bordering on the Río de la Plata.

It will be recalled that Dom João had annexed the *Banda Oriental* (the present republic of Uruguay) which was incorporated into the Portuguese domains under the title of the Cisplatine Province. But many of the Uruguayans—as we may call them by way of anticipation—chafed under Portuguese control, and led by their heroic chieftain, Artigas, maintained for several years a desultory though savage resistance against the invaders from the north. In the end, Artigas was forced to seek asylum in Paraguay, and the province was seemingly pacified. But the calm was only on the surface. The leaders of the patriotic party in Uruguay only waited an opportunity to expel the foreigners, while Buenos Aires was eager to reincorporate the *Banda Oriental* into Argentina. Early in 1825 the immortal "Thirty-Three" Uruguayans sallied forth from Buenos Aires, crossed over to Uruguay, and raised the standard of rebellion. The country rose *en masse;* the Brazilians were everywhere defeated save in Montevideo. Realizing, however, their relative helplessness against Brazil, the Uruguayan patriots appealed to Argentina for aid. The request was readily granted and the *Banda Oriental* was incorporated with Buenos Aires.

The Brazilians as a whole had no stomach for a war with Buenos Aires but still less did they desire to lose the rich Cisplatine Province. For Dom Pedro the maintenance of the territorial integrity of the empire was a point of honor and the action of Argentina was promptly followed by a declaration of war. In the main, the ensuing struggle turned out disastrously for Brazil. An attempted blockade of Buenos Aires by the Brazilian fleet greatly exasperated the neutral powers, especially Great Britain, whose commerce with Buenos Aires suffered severely. The extent of British interests is shown by the fact that as early as 1823 the value of British exports to South America reached the then formidable sum of £5,600,000, a considerable portion of which was destined to the Platine countries. Nor was Brazil able to render her blockade effective. The navy which Cochrane had built up a few years earlier proved no match for the Argentine fleet commanded by an Irishman, Admiral Brown. Only one important land engagement was fought, that of Ituzaingó (1827). Although Brazilian military critics are wont to qualify the battle as indecisive, certain it is that the imperial commander, the Marquis of Barbacena, was obliged to abandon the field, and the Argentines regarded the engagement as a victory. Both belligerents were weary of war; neither was apparently strong enough permanently to incorporate the *Banda Oriental* within its own territory. A treaty of peace was, therefore, signed under English auspices in 1828, which guaranteed the existence of Uruguay as an independent state. The dream of the Portuguese and later of the Brazilians of extending their domain to the Plata estuary had definitely vanished.

VI

Though the war aroused little enthusiasm in Brazil its failure brought disappointment and increased the unpopularity of the young emperor. But long before the conclusion of hostilities his favor had begun to warp. Liberal circles had never really forgiven him the dissolution of the constituent assembly of 1823, and his refusal to summon Parliament until 1826 naturally heightened discontent. In 1824 Dom João died. When the news of the king's death reached Brazil, Dom Pedro assumed the title of the King of Portugal, and though he finally abdicated in favor of his eight-year-old daughter, Dona Maria da Gloria, many of the Brazilians were convinced that he planned eventually to reunite the two branches of the House of Braganza, naturally to the detriment of Brazil. Certain it is that he tended to draw closer and closer to his Portuguese advisers.

When finally the assembly met in 1826 the emperor encountered a vigorous opposition composed of liberal monarchists, who were partisans of the British parliamentary system, with a sprinkling of federalists and republicans. From almost the first there existed strained relations between the emperor and parliament, particularly in the lower house. The functions of the executive and legislative branches of the government were ill-defined; each claimed more than the other was willing to grant. Dom Pedro considered any reflections upon the government as a personal affront. On the other hand the emperor treated the chamber with scant courtesy. He was wont to choose his ministers from the senate or even entirely outside of parliament. The ministry felt no responsibility to the chamber. It neither submitted its reports to the lower house nor did its members attend its debates. Yet progress towards some form of parliamentary government was constant as the power of the lower house steadily increased; in fact Dr. Oliveira Lima considers this emergence of the parliamentary system as an outstanding event of the reign of the first emperor. In 1827, for instance, the chamber refused to pass a government bill fixing the naval forces; in 1828 it refused to sanction the budget, and in 1829 it went so far as to pass a motion of censure of the ministry.

The increasing friction between the lower chamber and Dom Pedro encouraged the emperor to rely more and more on an unofficial set of advisers who are sometimes dubbed the "Kitchen Cabinet." Chief among these was a certain Domitilla de Castro, usually known in Brazilian history as the Marchioness of Santos. The influence of this Brazilian Marquise de Pompadour was very real. Ministerial councils were held in her residence, and she changed the membership of the cabinets according to her caprices. The influence of the emperor's beautiful mistress was regarded with great disfavor by most of the Brazilians, and it was currently believed that the death of the Empress

Leopoldina was hastened by the humiliations she was forced to endure at the hands of her rival.

The unpopularity of the emperor reached its height in 1830. Cabinets succeeded each other with disconcerting rapidity. The federalist-republican elements—the so-called *exaltados*—steadily grew at the expense of the moderates. The July Revolution in France and the abdication of Charles X had profound repercussions in Brazil and tended still further to undermine the prestige of the emperor. The influence of the press at this juncture must be taken into account, for it had gradually risen to a position of influence. At the beginning of Dom Pedro's reign it had been virulent. It tarnished many characters and destroyed many reputations. Soon, however, a tone of dignity began to appear. The most famous of the papers at this time was the *Aurora Fluminense,* edited by Evaristo da Veiga, a former bookseller who had secured election to parliament. He was absolutely honest. His moderate, liberal, and sane views won for him and his paper great power. Dr. Oliveira Lima is of the opinion that he was chiefly responsible for saving the monarchy in 1830. The situation was in fact so critical, the prestige of the dynasty was at such a low ebb, that the influence of Evaristo was sufficient to turn the scale.

VII

The year 1831 opened with forebodings. Anarchy was rife. Indiscipline was general. The country was dissatisfied with everybody and everything. Foreign troops retained by Dom Pedro as mercenaries excited distrust. The Brazilian troops themselves had little discipline. A contemporary writer speaks of "sinister bands of negroes and mulattoes going about with daggers, pretending to maintain order, but in reality fomenting disorder." The pretext for the revolution of 1831 was the dismissal on April 6 of his cabinet of Brazilian ministers and the nomination of six of his nobles, "the cabinet of marquises," all of them very unpopular. This action aroused an immense popular ferment which threatened to assume the proportions of a revolt unless the former ministry were reinstated. A section of the army itself joined the populace. Dom Pedro was now forced to yield to circumstances. At two in the morning of April 7, without asking the advise of any one or consulting his ministry, he wrote out his abdication:

> "Availing myself of the right which the constitution concedes to me, I declare that I have voluntarily abdicated in favor of my dearly beloved and esteemed son Dom Pedro de Alcantara."

The last moments of the reign of Dom Pedro were on the whole dignified; in the words of the French chargé d'affaires, Pointoise, "he knew better how to resign than to reign." One of his last acts in Brazil was to recall from exile the aged José Bonifacio and appoint him tutor of his children. With his empress and his daughter, Dona Maria da Gloria, he sailed for Europe on the English ship *Warsprite,* leaving the young Dom Pedro II, then four years of age, to continue the Braganza dynasty in the New World. With the departure of Dom Pedro one may say that Brazil severed the last link that bound her to Portugal.

Despite his weaknesses and inconsistencies Dom Pedro I on the whole deserves well of Brazil. Under peculiarly trying and even desperate circumstances he had won the independence of his adopted country and secured for her an honored place in the family of nations. Though at heart an absolutist he had the wit and intelligence to realize that the New World could no longer be hospitable to a monarchy of the eighteenth century type, and he was responsible for the promulgation of a liberal constitution under which the Braganza dynasty, acclimated in America, might live on and prosper for well over half a century longer.

CHAPTER SIXTEEN

THE PERIOD OF THE REGENCY, 1831-1840

THE nine years of the regency have not inaptly been characterized as the storm and stress period of Brazilian history. During these years the forces of stability and cohesion within the empire were put to the severest test. The abdication of the emperor in 1831 was followed by a wave of anarchy which, sweeping over the entire country, made itself felt especially in the provinces of the extreme north and south. For a time there seemed reason for the belief that these tendencies towards disintegration would cause Brazil to follow the fortune of a number of the Spanish American republics and break up into separate states even as the Republic of Great Colombia—one of the most genial creations of Bolívar—had dissolved into New Granada, Venezuela, and Ecuador.

I

For three years, from 1831 to 1834, the country was governed by a triple regency which made futile efforts to put down the growing disorders in the provinces and to curb the lawlessness and insubordination of the army. In this task it derived great assistance from Father Diogo Antonio Feijó, who as minister of justice revealed not only an exceptional political capacity but also boundless energy and determination. He dissolved the insubordinate elements in the army and created in their place the national guard, composed for the most part of civilians in sympathy with the new régime. Three parties were struggling for supremacy. The liberal monarchists (*Partido Liberal Moderado*), of whom Evaristo da Veiga and Bernardino de Vasconcellos were among the guiding spirits, remained in power from 1831 to 1837. They were obliged to wage a bitter struggle against the federalists (*Partido Liberal Exaltado*), who were almost all republicans, and the reactionaries (*Partido Restaurador*). Of this latter group the Andrada brothers, who had as we have seen returned from exile and were reconciled with Dom Pedro, were the leaders. The reactionaries demanded the return from Portugal of Dom Pedro and were anxious to restore the past. They were, however, in a minority and after the destruction of the Military Club *(Sociedade Militar)* and the death of the ex-emperor in 1834 the party ceased to have any great importance.

The chamber of deputies in 1834 adopted heroic measures to check the growing disorders. The triple regency was abolished in favor of a sole regent to be elected by the nation at large. To satisfy the legitimate aspirations of the liberal monarchists for a larger degree of local autonomy the so-called Additional Act (*Acto Addicional*) was passed at the same time. This amendment to the constitution abolished the council of state—which was later restored—and replaced the provincial councils by local elective assemblies. The proposal of the federalists that the presidents of the provinces be elected by the provinces themselves was fortunately rejected, largely through the efforts of Evaristo. Such action, if taken at this time, would almost certainly have resulted in the break-up of the national unity of the empire.

II

As sole regent was elected the most energetic and possibly the ablest statesman in Brazil, Father Feijó. Feijó had already served a long apprenticeship in politics. As one of the deputies from São Paulo at the *Côrtes* at Lisbon he had eloquently defended the rights of Brazil. Though a priest, he was far from being ultramontane, and at various times had opposed the doctrines of the celibacy of the clergy. His activities as minister of justice have already been noted. He had energetically seconded the efforts of Evaristo da Veiga who had organized a "society for the defence of liberty and national independence" to serve as a counterpoise to the organizations sponsored by the reactionaries and the federalists. This organization of Feijó and Evaristo, with branches throughout the provinces, had great influence on public opinion and acted as a powerful cohesive force against the disruptive propaganda of the federalists.

As regent Padre Feijó governed barely two years, but he made his influence felt in almost every field of national life. The great Brazilian novelist, Euclydes da Cunha, describes him as "the providential hero of Carlyle." While he succeeded in restoring a semblance of order in the provinces of the north, particularly Pernambuco and Pará, he was unable to cope with the rebellion which broke out in Rio Grande do Sul and which lasted nearly a decade. This southern province was influenced in many ways by the *gaucho* spirit which had assumed such sinister forms in the neighboring republics of Argentina and Uruguay. Even today it is not entirely extinct. The present revolt, frequently known as the *"Guerra dos Farrapos,"* was frankly separatist in tendency and constituted the most serious internal menace which Brazil had to face during the entire period of the empire. It will be discussed again when we take up the early years of the reign of Dom Pedro II. It is interesting to note that the rebels included in their ranks at this time young Giuseppe Garibaldi, then an exile from Italy. The regent also had to contend against a bitter opposition in parliament.

After the death of Dom Pedro I, the reactionaries united with a fraction of the liberal monarchists and began to call themselves the Conservative Party. It was in frank opposition to Feijó who was supported by the remaining liberal monarchists, henceforth to be known as the Liberal Party. Thus came into being the two great political parties whose vicissitudes supply most of the material for the subsequent parliamentary history of the empire.

III

Confronted by this hostile coalition and no longer in command of a majority of the lower house Feijó resigned in 1837, being succeeded by Araujo Lima, later known as the Marquis of Olinda. Unfortunately the conservatives under Araujo Lima showed no greater capacity for government than their predecessors. The guiding hand of Evaristo da Veiga had been removed by death; the seemingly interminable war in the south took on even greater proportions. National disintegration became more and more ominous. Realizing that some kind of rallying point was necessary, the Liberal Party early in 1840 launched an agitation for the declaration of the majority of the young emperor, Dom Pedro II; this despite the fact that the move was clearly unconstitutional. Though Dom Pedro was barely fifteen years of age he already gave evidences of maturity and exceptional capacity. It was known that he was quite willing to assume the responsibilities of government. Under these circumstances the movement quickly gained momentum; the nation at large, weary of the futile efforts of the regency to preserve national unity hoped to find in the person of the emperor a symbol to which all the elements in the nation might rally. The liberals, therefore, had little difficulty in securing from the chambers, united as a national assembly, a declaration of majority (July 23, 1840). A deputation waited upon the emperor in the palace and obtained the famous *quero já* ("I am quite ready") from Dom Pedro. From now on, for the space of almost half a century, Brazil was to be governed by the last and greatest of the American branch of the Braganzas.

IV

It would be a mistake to regard the regency as a fallow period in the evolution of Brazilian nationality. Despite internal commotions the government displayed considerable strength and had to its credit a number of positive achievements. As we shall see later a vigorous effort was made to grapple with the thorny problem of the slave trade. In 1833 was voted a code of criminal procedure, in which the spirit of a constitutional régime was combined with the old Portuguese legislation. Shortly before the abdication of Dom Pedro I the death penalty for political crimes was abolished. In spite of appearances to the contrary it was a period in which the prestige of the monarchy steadily grew while republicanism as represented in the separatist and frequently anarchical tendencies of the federalists lost ground. The bulk of the liberals were freed from the fetish of republicanism. The Brazilian people as a whole gained an apprenticeship in self-government. The historian Nabuco[1] declares that in some respects the epoch of the regency represented the high watermark of public life in Brazil. The patriotism of this period had something of a Puritan stamp. Only men of great ability, high sense of public duty, and austere morality could have steered the ship of state through the troubled waters. As Nabuco well puts it: "The glory of Feijó is to have upheld the supremacy of the civil government; the glory of Evaristo da Veiga is to have saved the monarchical principle; that of Vasconcellos to have reconstructed authority." In conclusion it should be noted that many of the outstanding figures in the reign of Dom Pedro II secured their political education in the decade between 1830 and 1840.

---

[1] *Um Estadista do Imperio* (Rio de Janeiro, n. d.) vol. I, *passim*.

CHAPTER SEVENTEEN

THE REIGN OF DOM PEDRO II. THE INTERNAL ORGANIZATION OF THE EMPIRE

IN MANY respects the reign of Dom Pedro II, covering as it did the greater part of the second half of the nineteenth century, constitutes the most interesting and fruitful period in the entire history of the nation. The almost fifty years of this emperor's rule witnessed the growth of Brazil from a country racked with revolution, striving to adapt the monarchical principle to the New World conditions, to one of the foremost powers in Hispanic America, respected in both the New World and the Old. It is generally conceded that the remarkable progress of Brazil, during a period of almost unbroken peace, was due in no small degree to the ability and statesmanship of Dom Pedro II. A brief analysis of the character and qualifications of this remarkable man may fittingly serve as an introduction to his reign.

I

In appraising the character of the young emperor of Brazil, due account must be taken of his early education. Committed from early childhood to the care of conscientious but rather pedantic tutors he saw little or nothing of the traditional court life; besides he was too young to be affected by the dissolute circles which surrounded his father. It was quite natural, therefore, that he should have preferred the library to the court, the laboratory to the parade ground. He was an omnivorous reader and possessed an almost insatiable intellectual curiosity. As José Maria dos Santos points out in a recent book, he was very early in life exposed to the great political and humanitarian ideals of the eighteenth century.[1]

His moral ideas came in the final instance from Bacon and Descartes through the works of Locke, Shaftsbury, Leibnitz, Montesquieu, Adam Smith, David Hume, and Jeremy Bentham. José Bonifacio, the first tutor of Dom Pedro and of his sister Dona Januaria, was strongly imbued with the principles of the *Encyclopédie*. A composition written

---

[1] *A politica geral do Brasil* (Rio de Janeiro, 1930), p. 23.

by Dom Pedro as a boy of ten in 1833 has as its tenor the following: "In proportion as man becomes more important in society, the greater obligation he has to labor for his associates." Such might have been the motto of Dom Pedro throughout his long reign.

He has been charged with being a dilettante, a royal dabbler, rather than a scholar. There is perhaps some basis for this accusation. In his endeavor to embrace the entire field of knowledge he could become really proficient in none of the sciences or arts. Yet his interest in things of the spirit was no affectation. He never missed a session of the Historical and Geographical Institute, a venerable body which will celebrate its centenary in 1938. Scientists and visitors of distinction were always assured a hearty and sincere welcome by Dom Pedro. The exploration of Agassiz in the Amazon basin were followed by the emperor with eager and genuine interest; he was in fact never more happy than when conversing with men of letters or scientists. Though not lacking in personal distinction, Dom Pedro was always simple, modest, and democratic. His generosity and magnanimity became proverbial. His domestic life was happy and above reproach. In matters of religion he displayed a broad tolerance and though nominally a Catholic was in reality a latitudinarian. Yet he was the first to insist on the rights of the state whenever he was convinced that they were threatened by encroachments of the church.

Dom Pedro, both during and after his lifetime, has not been without his bitter detractors. Paradoxical as it may seem, this mild-mannered and liberal sovereign has been accused of being both a tyrant and a despot. The grounds for this charge we may consider when we take up the political institutions of the empire. It also may be said that his very qualities as a scholar and a man of letters may have adversely affected his views as a statesman. It is possible that his interest in the moral progress of the nation caused him to pay insufficient attention to its material advance. He failed for instance, as we shall see presently, to appreciate the transcendent importance of immigration, a social and economic necessity in such an immense, thinly-populated country as Brazil. There were times when he seemed to show insufficient appreciation of the work of the great financier and economist, the Baron of Mauá. A sympathetic but acute observer, Dr. Vicente Quesada, Argentine minister to Brazil in the eighties, was impressed by the inordinate amount of time the emperor devoted to visiting schools, scrutinizing examinations, and the like. The emperor's interest in astronomy, to the neglect, it is alleged, of more terrestial matters, was frequently satirized in cartoons appearing in the comic papers of the epoch. Yet, after all, these were but minor defects which threw into greater relief the character of one of the most remarkable figures produced by Hispanic America, the "emperor-scientist" as he was called by Pasteur, the "prince-philosopher" in the words of Lamartine, or the "grandson of Marcus Aurelius" as he was dubbed by Victor Hugo.

II

Naturally it was not until some years after his accession that his qualities as a ruler began to make themselves felt. Although the declaration of majority relieved the political tension, the heritage of civil strife bequeathed by the regency lasted nearly a decade longer. The most burdensome of these heritages was naturally the revolution in Rio Grande do Sul; in fact the *Guerra dos Farrapos,* as it was called, was the most serious revolutionary movement that the empire had to face. As already noted, the rebellion began under Feijó, and had as its cause, apparently, merely local political rivalries. The geographical situation of Rio Grande do Sul, bordering on both Argentina and Uruguay, singularly favored this revolt, which for a time aimed at nothing less than the separation of this favored region from the rest of the empire. The insurgents, when pursued, easily found refuge in foreign territory. Here they suffered little or no molestation. They were even able to secure arms and supplies, for these neighboring republics were interested in the propagation of the rebels' republican ideas, and particularly interested in the weakening of the empire, whose immense dimensions terrified them.

We have neither time nor space to discuss the details of this struggle. It may merely be noted that on one occasion the rebels felt sufficiently strong to declare themselves absolutely independent and founded the short-lived republic of Piratinim under the presidency of one Bento Gonçalves. It was not until the government of Dom Pedro sent General Luiz Alves de Lima e Silva, the future Marshal Duke of Caxias and the greatest soldier of the empire, into the disaffected area that the movement was finally crushed. A vigorous campaign, followed by an offer of full amnesty, brought the rebels to terms, and thus the most serious menace to the unity of the empire ceased to exist in 1845. A short-lived revolution in Minas Geraes, of which one of the most conspicuous leaders was Theophilo Ottoni, was put down in 1842, while the rebellion of 1848 in Pernambuco—a belated flaring-up of the smouldering hostility between the Brazilians and the Portuguese—represented the last attempt to challenge the authority of the central government. From this time on the empire enjoyed absolute internal peace, in vivid contrast to its turbulent and faction-torn Spanish American neighbors.

III

The Brazilian empire was governed by the Constitution of 1824 to which reference has repeatedly been made. Considering the circumstances of its origin it was extremely liberal in character. This instrument had been rapidly drawn up, as we have seen, by a special committee appointed by Dom Pedro I after the dissolution of the constituent assembly of 1823. According to Armitage, one of our chief authorities of this period, the origins of the new documents were to be found in the constitution of the year previous, the ultra-liberal Portuguese Constitution of 1822 (for example the veto of the emperor), the fundamental code of Norway, the document which issued from the French Constitutional Assembly of 1791, and above all the project proposed in writing by Benjamin Constant as a modification of the *Chartre* of Louis XVIII of France. Freedom of speech, of the press, and of religion, and equality of all citizens before the law were guaranteed.

The powers acknowledged by the constitution—all of which were delegations of the nation—were four: executive, legislative, judicial, and modernative. The first of these was lodged in the emperor, who was styled "Constitutional Emperor and Perpetual Defender of Brazil." His person was sacred and inviolable; he was exempt from all responsibility, and enjoyed all of the privileges and prerogatives ordinarily associated with constitutional sovereigns. The powers of the emperor were exercised through the medium of a ministry appointed by him and nominally responsible to him. But even under Dom Pedro I the chamber of deputies had begun to extend the scope of its prerogatives. As early as 1847 we find the emergence of the prime minister, and with the growth of the parliamentary system the ministry became responsible to the lower house.

The emperor was assisted by a body known as the council of state. This organ had been abolished by the Additional Act of 1834 but was restored in 1841, shortly after the declaration of the majority of Dom Pedro II. Modelled somewhat after the French council of state, its members, whose number could not exceed ten, were appointed by the emperor for life. Their advice was sought, though not necessarily followed, on all matters falling within the province of the executive. Especially was this true on subjects relating to war and peace, negotiations with foreign states, and the exercise of the modernative power, of which more anon. The position of a member of the council of state —who enjoyed the title of "councilor" *(conselheiro)*—was one invested with great dignity, and the calibre of this body was remarkably high. Their written decisions, or *pareceres,* were in many cases valuable contributions to the administrative or constitutional law of the empire.

The legislative power was vested in the general assembly *(assemblea geral)* consisting of two bodies, the chamber of deputies and the senate. The members of the lower house held office for four years and were chosen by provincial electors, themselves elected by universal suffrage, though with a literacy, and until almost to the end of the empire, a property qualification. While the chamber of deputies possessed its analogue in practically all constitutional monarchies, the senate in its organization and functions included a number of features so striking as to lead an English authority[2] to declare that for almost half a century it was one of the most successful upper chambers in the world. The number of senators was fixed at half that of the deputies; they represented the provinces, each province having from two to six members according to population. During the greater part of the empire the number of senators was sixty. The senators were nominated by the emperor from a triple list submitted to him by the provincial electors and held office for life. Dom Pedro exercised his prerogative of nomination with great scrupulousness and rare impartiality. In some cases the same names were submitted and rejected six or seven times. Partly on this account the general level of ability and intelligence of the upper chamber was very high. It became the supreme ambition of every public man to enter this body. Although a number of mulattoes and negroes were chosen members of the lower house it was tacitly understood that only persons of white birth were eligible to the senate.

Naturally this body had its detractors. Republicans and other enemies of the monarchy described it as an oligarchy. Much was made of the emperor's right of rejection, and the "fatal pencil *(lapiz fatidico),* by which the emperor deleted the names of senators of whom he did not approve, became famous. But if the senate was an oligarchy it was an impartial, enlightened, and dignified one. Curiously enough the chief drawback of the system lay in its complete success. Owing to its composition and organization the senate was apt to be so far removed from party dissensions and current political discussions as to become unre-

---

[2] H. W. V. Temperley, *Senates and Upper Chambers* (London, 1910), p. 218.

sponsive to public opinion. Again, candidates rejected by the emperor frequently became implacable opponents of the monarchy. Finally the consciousness of its superiority over the lower house aroused a resentment which was frequently directed against the monarchy or even the emperor himself.

By all odds the most unique feature of the Constitution of 1824 was the so-called moderative power. Article 98 declares:

> "The moderative power is the key of the whole political organization and is entrusted exclusively to the emperor as supreme chief and first representative of the nation, that he may incessantly watch over the maintenance of the independence, equilibrium, and harmony of the rest of the political powers."

The chief attributes of the moderative power were the nomination of the senators as just described, the convocation of the general assembly or parliament whenever the good of the empire might require it, the sanction of the decrees or resolutions of the assembly, the dissolution of the lower house, the nomination of ministers of state, and the granting of amnesties. Critics of the empire would have us believe that Dom Pedro wielded the moderative power not wisely but too well. Under cover of this authority he was accused of having set up a kind of veiled and irresponsible despotism to which the name of *poder pessoal* (personal power) was too loosely applied. In the appointment of his ministers he constantly aimed, it was charged, at maintaining a certain equilibrium between the two great political parties in order that the balance of power might remain in his own hands. A chamber of deputies hostile to the ministry might easily be dissolved, and thanks to the electoral system then in vogue another more complacent one elected in its place.

It is now recognized that these attacks are somewhat wide of the mark. Under the social and political conditions then prevailing in Brazil the emperor could hardly have avoided the exercise of the *poder pessoal* which was thrust upon him by the force of circumstances. We can now clearly see that the smooth functioning of the machinery of government year after year without a serious breakdown was due in large measure to the tireless vigilance of the emperor. Despotic, Dom Pedro may have been at times. Not always were the susceptibilities of his ministers or of parliament duly safeguarded. But above the interests of parties, of cabinets, of the dynasty itself, was the higher interest of the nation; this was the lodestar by which the actions of the emperor were guided; this the touchstone by which he judged both men and events. In the phrase of the Brazilian historian, Oliveira Lima, "if there was any despotism it was the despotism of morality."

As in most civilized countries the judiciary was independent of the other branches of the government. The judges held office during good behavior; their procedure was determined by both civil and criminal codes. In the capital there existed a supreme court of justice, while in each of the provinces, as well as in the capital, there was an appellate court. The members of the supreme court were "learned judges" chosen from the appellate courts by seniority, and like the members of the council of state had the title of "councilor." In general it may be said that the administration of justice in the higher courts was conducted on a high plane, and there were comparatively few complaints of corruption or miscarriage of justice. The same cannot always be said of the appellate courts or of the locally elected justices of the peace.

Probably the least satisfactory feature of the imperial system was the government of the provinces. The Constitution of 1824 as originally drafted made very little provision for local autonomy. In each of the provinces a council was appointed entirely destitute of any real authority but with the privilege of suggesting needed legislation. According to the Additional Act of 1834 these councils were converted into legislative assemblies with a certain amount of power in purely provincial matters. On the other hand the governors or presidents of the provinces were the appointees of the emperor and held office merely during his good pleasure. While such a system acted as a salutary check on the centrifugal forces at play during the earlier years of the reign of Dom Pedro II, the conviction steadily gained ground in the latter days of the empire that the well-being of the provinces was being sacrificed to the bureaucratic tendencies of the central government. In the program of the Viscount of Ouro Preto, the last prime minister of the empire, appeared the provision that the presidents of the provinces were to be elected by direct suffrage in their respective administrative units and were to be chosen by the emperor, in agreement with the senate, from a triple list. The term of president was to be for nine years and the other two citizens on the list were to act as vice presidents. Nothing came of this plan as the monarchy was overthrown this same year. In general it may be said that one of the causes for dissatisfaction with the imperial régime was the small amount of autonomy allowed the provinces. Thus federalism versus centralization eventually became a genuine political issue.

From one point of view the Brazilian empire may be regarded as a democracy with a permanent president. President Mitre of Argentina styled it the "crowned democracy of America." On receiving the news of the collapse of the empire President Rojas Paul of Venezuela declared: "The only republic which existed in America has come to an end: the empire of Brazil." *(Se ha acabado la única república que existía en América: el imperio del Brasil.)*

IV

During the greater part of the empire two political parties, the liberals and the conservatives, strove for control of parliament. Both of these parties, as has been noted, came into being during the stormy period of the regency. Brazilians are wont to find a certain parallel between these two parties and the organizations of similar name in Great Britain. While it will not do to force the analogy, undoubtedly a certain parallelism does exist. Both in their programs and their ideals the two great Brazilian parties presented a striking contrast to the political alignments of the majority of the Spanish American republics where such parties as did exist were almost always based on personalities rather than principles.

The conservatives styled themselves the representatives of law and order. They were opposed to revolutions based on purely political motives. They regarded political centralization as indispensable to the maintenance of the integrity of the empire, and were consequently opposed to the extension of local autonomy. They likewise were in favor of high suffrage qualifications and the independence and immovibility of the judiciary.

The liberals on the other hand piqued themselves on being the exponents of progress and from time to time advanced programs of social and political reforms, chief among which were greater decentralization and extension of the suffrage. They committed the error, however, of sharing the odium of responsibility of a number of revolutionary disturbances, notably that of 1842 in São Paulo and 1848 in Pernambuco. As a consequence they became discredited and from 1848 to 1860 Brazil was governed by a number of cabinets called "cabinets of conciliation" *(conciliação)*. The soul of this movement was Carneiro Leão (later the Marquis of Paraná) who succeeded in including in his cabinets former liberals of the type of Limpo de Abreu (Abaeté), Pereira (Bom Retiro), and Paranhos (the Viscount of Rio Branco), as well as traditional conservatives such as Nabuco de Araujo and later Wanderley (the Baron of Cotegipe). This new orientation met with the approval of public opinion and the press and had full support of the emperor. The period of "conciliation" lasted until 1860 when the Liberal Party was revived partly through the efforts of Theophilo Ottoni—a sort of stormy petrel of Brazilian politics—and Francisco Octaviano and Saedanha Marinho, all of whom were elected to the lower house. At first known as the Progressive Party *(O Partido Progressista)* it came to embrace the old historical liberals, and by 1869 it had evolved into what might be called the new Liberal Party, which under this traditional name lasted until the end of the empire. Its chiefs were Nabuco, Zacharias, Silveira Lobo, Theophilo Ottoni, and Francisco Octaviano. Nabuco, a distinguished senator and chief par excellence of the new party, drew up a program of twelve articles, which on account of their importance are worth summarizing.

1. Responsibility of the minister for the acts of moderative power.
2. The adoption of the maxim: "The king rules but does not govern" *(O rei reina mas não governa)*.
3. The organization of the council of ministers in accordance with the two preceding rules.
4. Decentralization in the true sense of self-government, elaborating the Additional Act, especially as regards the freedom of the provinces and municipalities.
5. The maximum liberty as regards commerce and industry, with the resulting extinction of the privileges of monopoly.
6. Effective guarantees of the liberty of conscience.
7. Full liberty of the citizens in the foundation of schools and methods of instruction.
8. Independence of the judicial power, and more particularly the independence of the magistrates.
9. Unity of jurisdiction as guaranteed by the Constitution of 1824 with the consequent derogation of all administrative jurisdiction.
10. The council of state to be a mere aid *(mola auxiliar)* to the administration and not a political body.
11. Reform of the senate in the sense of suppressing its immovable features.
12. Reduction of military effectives in time of peace.

The program also included a reform of the system of election, of the judiciary, and of the police; the abolition of recruiting (its place being taken by the enlistment of volunteers); the substitution of the municipal civic guard for the national guard; and finally the abolition of slavery, first by liberation through "free birth" *(liberação do ventre escravo)*, later through gradual emancipation. It is to be noted that before the fall of the empire most of the reforms included in the program of 1869 had been accomplished. Even some form of federation would probably have been adopted but for the *coup d'état* of 1889.

There still remains to speak of the Republican Party. Prior to the organization of this avowedly anti-dynastic party there were comparatively few militant republicans, at least subsequent to the regency. The Frenchman, Gambetta, and the Spaniard, Castelar, were the real godfathers of the Brazilian Republican Party, which issued its manifesto on December 2, 1871, on the birthday of Dom Pedro II. Gambetta sent a letter of encouragement somewhat in the style of Victor Hugo. Castelar, with the proverbial Spanish courtesy, sent a specialist in conspiracies, who explained to the nascent party the secret of revolutions and insisted on the maximum importance of a *means of escape,* which he warned should never be lost sight of. In point of numbers the new party was very small but it included within its ranks a number of persons of future importance. Among these may be mentioned Quintino Bocayuva, who was the first minister of foreign affairs of the republic in 1889; the illustrious jurisconsult, Lafayette Rodrigues Pereira, author of a celebrated treatise on international law; Aristides Lobo, a kind of Jacobin who under the provisional government was minister of the interior; Salvador de Mendonça, a man of letters and subsequent minister to the United States; and Rangel Pestana, a doctrinaire publicist who was sincere, persuasive, and honest. A small group of the liberals adhered to the anti-dynastic program of the republicans, including Campos Salles, subsequently president of the republic, and Americo Braziliense, later president of the State of São Paulo. As already intimated the party always remained numerically weak; only in the provinces of São Paulo and Rio Grande do Sul did it have a solid organization and was able to secure the election of its candidates to the lower house. Campos Salles and Prudents de Moraes—the latter the first civilian president of Brazil—were elected deputies.

The political life of the empire was on the whole pitched on a high plane. The imperial officials were generally noted for their probity and ability; many left office poorer than when they entered it. Public opinion, voicing itself in the press and popularily elected assemblies, could hardly be said to exist in the sense that it does in the United States and the more advanced countries of Europe. The percentage of illiteracy was high, the populace except in the urban centers were widely scattered, and the people generally were apathetic. The literacy test and the property qualifications made the electorate small. Yet the growth of the parliamentary system shows clearly that the government was becoming increasingly responsive to public opinion. Even under Dom Pedro I the lower house had exerted its authority; under the regency the parliamentary system had its real beginning; and by 1847, as we have already seen, the prime minister or premier had the sole right of choosing his colleagues, and the ministry held office only as long as it could command the majority of the chamber of deputies.

As a check on the possible encroachments of the parliament on the executive, the emperor had as a weapon the right to dissolve the lower house. Yet as a matter of fact from 1823 to 1881 but ten dissolutions occurred. It is generally conceded that Imperial Brazil presented a striking instance of the successful working of the parliamentary régime. By and large, parliament represented the rule and opinion of the cultivated classes and the influence of traditional authority. In certain regards, conditions in Brazil were not so dissimilar to those in England before the passage of the Reform Bill of 1832. It is a striking testimony both to the tact and ability of the emperor as well as to the vitality of Brazilian political life that the ablest men of the country embraced politics as a career. A roster of the members of Dom Pedro's thirty-six cabinets reveals a list of statesmen and administrators of which any nation may be proud.

CHAPTER EIGHTEEN

THE REIGN OF DOM PEDRO II. THE FOREIGN POLICY OF THE EMPIRE

THE diplomatic history of the empire from 1840 to 1889 constitutes one of the most interesting chapters of Brazilian history. During the half century of Dom Pedro's reign, Brazil found herself involved in diplomatic controversies with Great Britain, the United States, and a number of South American nations. We may more appropriately consider Brazil's difficulties with Great Britain when we come to take up in the next chapter the suppression of the slave trade. Relations with the United States, if discussed in detail, would constitute a treatise in themselves. We shall accordingly confine our survey to only a few of the more significant aspects of the subject. This succinct treatment is the more justified as we fortunately have at our disposal the scholarly work of Professor Lawrence F. Hill on United States relations with Brazil.[1] As regards Brazil's relation to her South American neighbors, the story is indeed a complex one. Touching elbows, so to speak, with all but one of the republics of South America, it was inevitable that Brazil should be affected by the controversies among her neighbors, more particularly on the south. On two different occasions, Dom Pedro II was obliged to intervene in the affairs of the Platine Republics.

I

During the best part of the thirties and all of the forties of the nineteenth century, Juan Manuel de Rosas was the undisputed master of the Argentine Confederation. He harbored ambitious plans. He dreamed of nothing less than the reconstruction of the old eighteenth century Viceroyalty of La Plata. This meant in effect the control of Uruguay, Paraguay, and possibly even Bolivia or Upper Peru by Buenos Aires. Naturally, such a program was bound to bring him into collision with adjacent countries. As regards his great neighbor on the north, it was natural that he should look upon the empire of Brazil as his secular enemy. Unfortunately, in such an atmosphere of suspicion and ill-will, pretexts for hostilities were never lacking.

---

[1] Durham, 1932.

The little republic of Uruguay, directly across the Platine estuary, was logically marked out to be the first link in the chain of vassal states which Rosas hoped eventually to bring under his control; this despite the fact that by the treaty of 1828 the independence of the *Banda Oriental* had been guaranteed by both the Argentine and Brazilian governments. Fortunately for the plans of the Argentine despot a willing instrument was at hand in the person of one Manuel Oribe, aspirant for the presidency of Uruguay, and leader of the so-called *Blanco* faction. Opposed to him was Fructuoso Rivera, head of the *Colorados* and the friend of Brazil. In the civil war which ensued Oribe, counting on Rosas' support, succeeded in dominating almost all of the countryside of Uruguay, shutting up his opponent in a nine-year siege of Montevideo, the capital. To the other enemies of Rosas was soon added Urquiza, the powerful *caudillo* and perpetual governor of the Argentine Province of Entre Rios. Urquiza, Rivera, and the Brazilians determined to make common cause against the Argentine dictator. The war which broke out in 1851 proved to be of short duration. When the Brazilian General Caxias began to dispose his troops for the invasion of Argentina, he was promptly joined by the forces of Urquiza and the pro-Brazilian factions in Uruguay. The siege of Montevideo was raised and Oribe surrendered without condition. Under the protection of a Brazilian squadron the allied forces crossed the Paraná River and on February 3, 1852, Rosas suffered a major defeat at Monte Caseros. Argentina was now freed from her worst despot. Although Argentina profited immeasurably by the elimination of Rosas, Brazil herself derived little benefit from this invasion of the Platine basin. While she had freed South America from a real menace, her actions left an unfortunate legacy of suspicion among her neighbors.

II

Of much greater importance than the campaign against Rosas was Brazil's participation in the Paraguayan War, which lasted from 1865 to 1870. The motives for this long and sanguinary struggle are still a matter of dispute among historians. It is my opinion that the ultimate cause was the overwhelming vanity and ambition of the Paraguayan ruler, Francisco Solano López. The history of the landlocked republic of Paraguay is in point of fact the most tragic of any of the nations of America. During the better part of the seventeenth and eighteenth centuries, the inhabitants of this region, consisting for the most part of Guaraní Indians, lived under the beneficent control of the

Jesuits who, gathering them in their famous missions or "reductions," converted the entire district into a sort of an American Arcadia. In the nineteenth century the same spirit of blind obedience inculcated by the Jesuits enabled the dictator, Francia, to isolate Paraguay from the rest of the world and rule it as his private preserve from the years 1814 to 1840. Upon the death of this gloomy dictator the power passed into the hands of a prosperous and ambitious *hacendado,* Carlos Antonio López. Though in all domestic matters as absolute as Francia, López did maintain contacts with the outside world and actually opened a short railway line, a link in the present route from Asunción to Buenos Aires. He was followed in 1862 by his son, Francisco Solano López, one of the most sinister figures produced by Hispanic America. The vanity of the younger López was exceeded only by his ambition. Absolute ruler of the state, with a treasury brimful and an army well equipped and blindly obedient, he determined to play a preponderant rôle in South American affairs. The almost chronic civil war in Uruguay, coupled with the designs, real or alleged, of Brazil on her southern neighbors, supplied him with ample pretext.

The Paraguayan War, one of the greatest catastrophies in the history of South America, was due, therefore, to the ambition of the Paraguayan dictator and to a lesser extent to the Brazilian policy of intervention in the troubled affairs of La Plata. The grievances of the Brazilians were indeed substantial. Some thirty thousand residing on both sides of the southern frontier suffered severely from the anarchical conditions in Uruguay. The president of the latter country, Aguirre, who began his terms of office in 1864, was a representative of the *Blanco* Party and as such paid scant heed to the Brazilian protests. Opposed to him was the pro-Brazilian faction of the *Colorados.* Feeling his position insecure, Aguirre began to cast about for possible allies, and through his minister of foreign affairs, Herrera, made overtures looking to an alliance with both López, the Paraguayan dictator, and with Urquiza, the governor of the Argentine Province of Entre Rios. Two able Brazilian diplomats, Saraïva and Silva Paranhos, generally known as the Viscount of Rio Branco, failed to reach a satisfactory agreement with Aguirre or secure reparation for injuries to Brazilian subjects and property. Convinced of the futility of further diplomatic negotiations, the imperial government finally determined to intervene in Uruguay in favor of the *Colorado* candidate for the presidency, General Flores, against Aguirre.

Hostilities with Paraguay were not slow in breaking out. López, already suspicious of Brazil, was greatly incensed that his offers of mediation in the Uruguayan imbroglio had been treated with scant courtesy. He determined therefore to lend aid to Aguirre and attack Brazil. Without even a declaration of hostilities he seized the Brazilian merchant steamer, the *Marquez de Olinda,* on November 11, 1864, while on its way to the great interior Brazilian province of Matto Grosso, and made prisoner the governor of this province, Colonel Carneiro de Campos. Not content with this patent violation of international law, he proceeded to lay waste Matto Grosso, which the imperial government was at this time quite powerless to defend. Dom Pedro II really had no option but to declare war against him, which he did, reluctantly, early in 1865.

López was extremely anxious to come to the aid of his friends, the *Blancos* in Montevideo, and thus safeguard what he called "the equilibrium of La Plata." At the same time he hoped to deliver a mortal blow at Brazil by an invasion of her southernmost province of Rio Grande do Sul. To accomplish these ends it was necessary to throw an army across the Argentine Province of Misiones. On January 14, 1865, he asked permission of President Mitre of Argentina, which was promptly refused. López, none the less, insisted, and Argentina promptly declared war against him. In thus defying the two greatest nations of South America, López would at first sight appear insane. Paraguay had at this time a population of barely a million, while the combined populations of his enemies were ten or twelve times this number. But the odds were not all on the side of the allies. López had an excellent army of sixty thousand men on whom he could rely implicitly, while the total force of sixteen thousand Brazilians was for the most part scattered through provincial garrisons. The Argentine army was even smaller. A number of competent Brazilian engineers and soldiers had helped train the Paraguayan army and had assisted López in erecting the apparently impregnable fortress of Humaitá at the confluence of the Paraná and Paraguay rivers. Furthermore, Argentina was rent with domestic quarrels between the unitarians and the federalists, the latter being particularly strong in the two provinces of Corrientes and Entre Ríos. Finally, Rio Grande do Sul was, in López's judgment, chronically ripe for revolt. Thus the dictator might hope for a quick victory of the Paraguayans, allied with the unitarians of Argentina, the *Blancos* of Uruguay, and possibly the dissenting elements in Brazil's southernmost province.

In all of these calculations the tyrant of Paraguay proved to be badly mistaken. Urquiza, on whom he had pinned such high hopes, remained loyal to President Mitre, at least to the extent of remaining neutral. Corrientes refused to join him. Rio Grande do Sul, despite its turbulent past, remained faithful to the empire. The Uruguayan *Blancos* were badly worsted by the *Colorados* under Flores, who promptly joined the allies with his faction. The army which López had imprudently thrown into Rio Grande do Sul was defeated by the Brazilians and forced to surrender at Uruguayana.

López now resolved on his only logical plan of campaign, namely, a defensive war. Securely protected by the two rivers and his great fortification of Humaitá, he could for a time, at least, bid defiance to his enemies. The allies in turn had already, on May 1, 1865, signed a treaty of triple alliance in which they agreed not to lay down their arms until López had been eliminated. This treaty, with its numerous clauses, was to be kept rigidly secret, but unfortunately for the allies a copy was smuggled to England, where it was published by Lord Russell in a parliamentary Blue Book.

As in the case of the World War, few if any foresaw a struggle of any great length or magnitude. Bartolomé Mitre, the general-in-chief of the allied armies, was the first to be deceived. In a proclamation to the Argentines on the declaration of war, he declared, "Señores, in twenty-four hours we shall be in the barracks, within fifteen days on the march, within three months in Asunción." As a matter of fact, the Paraguayan capital was not captured until four years later.

Despite the apparently disinterested aims of the allies, the treaty of the triple alliance on its publication provoked throughout the rest of South America, the United States, and Europe much indignation; particularly was this true after López and his prime minister, Borges, began to launch a clever and effective propaganda in favor of Paraguay. The feeling became general that a small and defenseless country was being strangled by powerful and greedy neighbors. Peru took the lead in a kind of international protest and went so far as to break off relations with Brazil. Chile openly encouraged Argentine revolutionists whose machinations seriously embarrassed the Argentine government. Bolivia set about to mobilize her army. On the other hand, Sarmiento, who was Argentine minister to the United States from 1864 to 1866, ably presented the cause of the allies in a number of important papers of New York, while the great naturalist, Agassiz, who was in South America at this time, also endeavored to create in the United States sentiments favorable to Brazil.

The actual events of the war we shall take up very briefly. Early in the summer of 1865 López suffered a crushing naval defeat at Riachuelo, a small stream near Corrientes. As this was the most important naval engagement in the war, it deserves a passing mention. On paper the leading combatants were not ill-matched. The Paraguayan and Brazilian fleets each consisted of eight ships. Argentina participated with but a single vessel, the *Guarda Nacional.* The victory was won through the brilliant offensive of the Brazilian admiral, Barroso, who so skillfully maneuvered his flagship, the *Amazonas,* that he was able to ram three of the most important of the Paraguayan vessels. He thus anticipated by some months the tactics successfully used by Tegenoff in the Battle of Lissa in the war of 1866 between Austria and Italy. Only with difficulty did the remnants of the Paraguayan fleet find refuge behind the fortress of Humaitá. The allied victory was, as a matter of fact, of the utmost importance. Had the Brazilian fleet been destroyed, Buenos Aires would have been at López's mercy.

During the course of 1866 the allies slowly advanced up the Paraguay River for an attack on Humaitá and eventually on Asunción. Some distance downstream from Humaitá was the fortress of Curupaity, against which the entire army was hurled. The attack, which took place on September 22, was unsuccessful; the allies were forced to retreat with a loss of over four thousand, while the Paraguayans lost only two hundred and fifty men. A long period of inaction followed, caused partly by dissensions among the allies, but chiefly due to the ravages of disease. Finally, in 1868 the fortress of Humaitá was successfully passed and on January 5, 1869, Asunción was occupied. The struggle ended at length with the death of López at the little stream of Aquidabán, near the Brazilian frontier, on March 1, 1870.

The war was, in almost all respects, disastrous. Paraguay was left a shambles. According to the Spanish scholar Posada, the population shrank from a million and a third to a third of a million. As the male population had been so largely killed off, polygamy gained a kind of quasi-legal sanction. One may even say that the country has not yet entirely recovered from this frightful holocaust. For Brazil, the war was barren of results. Over fifty thousand men, which the empire could ill spare, were killed. The cost in money easily reached a half billion dollars. Save for the removal of López, who had been a constant threat to the peace of his neighbors, the empire had little or nothing to show for this vast expenditure of blood and treasure. Argentina alone profited by the war. Once the scene of hostilities was removed from her border she became more or less disinterested in the military aspects of the struggle. In fact the brunt of the campaign, during the latter part of the war, rested almost exclusively with the Brazilians and their commanders, the Duke of Caxias and the emperor's son-in-law, the Comte d'Eu. Argentina's chief contribution to the common cause was the furnishing, with profit to herself, of supplies and munitions.

Two further episodes of the war deserve mention. The first was the unfortunate land offensive of the Brazilians against the Paraguayans who, as we have noted, early in the war had occupied the remote province of Matto Grosso. The distance from Rio de Janeiro was so enormous that the expedition required two years to reach its goal, the city of Cuyabá. Even then the depleted Brazilian force was obliged to retreat, owing to the numerical superiority of the Paraguayans and the lack of provisions. This disastrous retreat, a veritable Anabasis, happily found its Xenophon in the person of Viscount of Taunay whose work, *A retirada de laguna,* eventually became a classic in Brazilian if not in world literature.

The second episode was the attempt of the United States to mediate in the struggle, a *démarche* which is described in great detail by Professor Hill in his book on the diplomatic relations between the United States and Brazil. Late in 1866, when the war seemed to have resolved itself into a stalemate, the government at Washington sent to each of the warring nations a circular offering mediation. More specifically, it proposed a cessation of fighting and a congress to be held at Washington for the discussion of the terms of peace. The offer was accepted by López with avidity, but was peremptorily declined by the Marquis of Caxias, commander-in-chief of the allied forces. He declared that the allies would never treat with López, whose elimination was a *sine qua non* for the discussion of peace, and a little later a reply of similar tenor was handed to the United States minister at Rio, J. Watson Webb, by the imperial government. Various reasons for this refusal have been offered. If we are to believe Webb, peace at any other price rather than complete victory meant an end to Dom Pedro II and the monarchy. This contention has some merit, for the emperor had indeed committed himself and his dynasty deeply. Then there was the conviction held by many in authority that López was an impossible person to deal with and that he could not be trusted. There was also the distinctly sordid influence of many Brazilian and Argentine contractors who were deriving lucrative profits from the war. Finally, there existed in South America a certain distrust of the United States, heightened by the indiscreet and ill-timed actions of our envoys, Webb and Washburn, the latter being our minister to Paraguay.

III

Of the remaining foreign relations of the empire, only two call for mention: difficulties with the United States over the navigation of the Amazon, and the friction caused by the favors accorded by the Brazilian government to the Confederate corsairs during our Civil War.

During this conflict the United States was represented in Brazil, as we have seen, by General James Watson Webb, who owed his position to his friendship with William H. Seward, our secretary of state. Webb was a prominent newspaper man and an ardent member of the Republican Party, but totally lacked any diplomatic finesse. His knowledge of international affairs was rudimentary in the extreme. On August 1, 1861, the empire announced its neutrality in the Civil War and a little later, following the precedent set by England and a number of European powers, recognized the Confederates as belligerants. This recognition caused great umbrage in the United States. The policy of the imperial government almost immediately induced serious complications. In September 1861 the Confederate privateer *Sumter* entered the northern port of Maranhão to take on a supply of provisions and coal, over the protest of the United States consul. This led to an exchange of somewhat acrimonious correspondence between Webb and the Brazilian minister of foreign affairs, Senhor Taques, in which Webb roundly denied to Brazil the right to recognize the Confederates as belligerents; and the Confederate cruisers which continued to enter Brazilian harbors he characterized as pirates. While the status of the *Sumter* was still a matter of dispute, news reached Brazil in the spring of 1863 that the *Alabama,* commanded by Captain Raphael Semmes, had played fast and loose with Brazilian neutrality by utilizing the Brazilian island of Fernando de Noronha as a base of supplies. It seems that the raider, who had captured a number of prizes, had seized six United States whalers as they were returning from a voyage to the South Atlantic. In reply to Webb's emphatic protest, the Brazilian foreign minister disavowed the action of the commander of the island, who was removed from office for having given improper aid and countenance to the *Alabama.* At the same time the cruiser was ordered to leave Brazilian waters on threat of internment. As the Civil War approached its close the tone of Webb's communications became stronger, and early in 1864 the minister informed Secretary Seward that Brazil was prepared to see destroyed within her ports any Confederate vessel discovered there by a United States warship.

Although this was probably a case of wishful thinking on the part of Webb, the opportunity to test the soundness of his views soon appeared. The *Florida,* which in the previous year had put into Bahia, once more entered this harbor for the purpose of securing water and provisions and of repairing her machinery, and over the protests of the United States consul, was allowed by the governor of the province forty-eight hours for this purpose. Before the expiration of this period the United States warship *Wachusett* under the command of Captain Collins entered the harbor, captured the *Florida,* and towed her to Hampton Roads as her prize. Excitement ran high in Brazil, and there was great indignation at the arbitrary action of the commander of the *Wachusett.* The Brazilian chargé at Washington, on instructions from his government, demanded a public repudiation of the acts of Captain Collins, a formal apology, the dismissal of the offending officer from the United States service, a salute of twenty-one guns in the harbor of Bahia, the liberation of all prisoners aboard the *Florida,* and the return of this ship to Bahia. With the exception of the last request all of the demands of Brazil were met by Secretary Seward, who recognized that in this flagrant violation of international law any other position would be untenable. When it came to returning the *Florida* to Brazil, however, it was found impossible to comply with this demand as the vessel had been "accidently" sunk in Hampton Roads.

The conclusion of the Civil War naturally brought to an end the tension caused by Brazil's attitude towards the southern raiders. At the most, this friction was but a temporary departure from the long tradition of friendship between the two countries. It is possible too that Dom Pedro's recognition of the empire of Maximilian in Mexico attributed to the strained relations of the period.

IV

We now turn to a brief consideration of one of the most curious, not to say fantastic, episodes in the relations between the two countries. The reference is to the influence of the United States in the opening of the Amazon to world commerce. About the middle of the century attention was centered on the problem largely as the result of the energy and untiring propaganda of a Lieutenant Matthew Fontaine Maury, an officer of the United States navy, and generally regarded as the leading hydrographer of his time. Between the years 1849 and 1855

Maury set forth his views regarding the Amazon Valley and its importance in numerous articles which appeared in such important papers and reviews as the *Southern Literary Messenger, The National Intelligencer,* and *De Bow's Review.* A number of these articles were republished in pamphlet form with the title of *Letters on the Amazon and Atlantic Slopes of South America.* Maury's vehement interest in this subject may be illustrated by the quotation of a single paragraph from this pamphlet.

> "We want nothing exclusive up the Amazon: but we are nearest the Amazon, or rather to the mouth of it, than any other nation . . . And therefore it may well be imagined that the execrable policy by which Brazil has kept shut up, and is continuing to keep shut up, from man's—from Christian, civilized, enlightened man's—use the fairest portion of God's earth, will be considered by the American people as a nuisance, not to say an outrage. . . .
>
> "This certainly is the question of the day. The problem of the age is that of the free navigation of the Amazon and the settlement of the Atlantic slope of South America. It is to draw after it consequences of the greatest importance, results of the greatest magnitude. It is to stand out in after times, and among all the great things which this generation has already accomplished, as *the* achievement in its way of the nineteenth century. The time will come when the free navigation of the Amazon will be considered by the people of this country as second in importance, by reason of its conservative effects, to the acquisition of Louisiana, if it be second at all; for I believe it is to form the safety valve of the Union."

Despite the fantastic views of Maury, his reputation as a hydrographer and a scientist secured for him a wide hearing. It should be noted also that his views were greatly reënforced by the popularity of the two volume report of the explorations of Lieutenant Herndon which was published in 1853. This intrepid officer, who was a kinsman of Maury, had been associated with Lieutenant Gibbon in a thorough reconnaissance of the Amazon under the auspices of the United States government. His report was one of the most widely read government papers of the time.

The propaganda of Maury began to bear fruit. The government itself began to take an active interest in the opening of the Amazon. At first, however, all efforts were met by a Brazilian *non possumus.* In fact there was a good deal of suspicion of the motives of the United States, due to the recently concluded Mexican War and the filibustering expeditions to Cuba and to Central America. It was even feared that once United States citizens had established themselves in the southern continent they would introduce their own institutions and eventually demand annexation to their own country.

In the final instance propaganda in Brazil in favor of the opening of the Amazon was largely inspired and guided by a single individual, the publicist and writer, Tavares Bastos. Although this man is all but forgotten in Brazil today, at one time his pen wielded a very considerable influence. Long interested in the improvement of commercial relations between the United States and Brazil, he had secured a copy of Lieutenant Herndon's report and had read with avidity the letters of Maury which appeared in the *Correio Mercantil* of Rio de Janeiro. While quick to detect the exaggerated features of Maury's arguments, he differed absolutely from the bulk of his fellow countrymen in regard to the Amazon. Instead of following a suicidal policy of exclusion, the Brazilians should, in his judgment, obey the dictates of common sense and enlightened self-interest by throwing open to the world the Amazon Valley whose natural resources he depicted in the most glowing colors. Despite the opposition of the conservatives, his efforts began to bear fruit. He secured as a recruit Brazil's greatest lyric poet, Gonçalves Dias. During the course of the year 1861 he printed a series of letters in the *Correio Mercantil,* which, published in the following year in book form under the title of *Cartas do solitario,* enjoyed a large circulation. These "Letters of the Hermit" were supplemented by a series of notable speeches delivered in parliament. Both in his writings and his speeches he pled for a more enlightened policy in reference to the Amazon.

The government began to change its attitude. In his annual report for 1864 the minister of foreign affairs stated that the opening of the Amazon was desirable and that the government had resolved "to extend the freedom of navigation to the flags of all nations." The reform was shelved for a time owing to the ultra-conservative and obstructionist attitude of the council of state, although José Antonio Saraïva, then minister of marine, espoused Tavares Bastos' views. The distinguished jurisconsult, Nabuco de Araujo, made an eloquent plea before the council. Brazil, he pointed out, by insisting on the free navigation of La Plata could not consistently withhold the same privilege for the Amazon. The great scientist, Professor Luis F. Agassiz, at a banquet held on June 25, 1866, enlarged on the wonders of the Amazon Valley and stated that the first means necessary to the development of this region was the opening of the river to navigation. The final act, as drawn up by Nabuco, provided that after September 7, 1867 the Amazon should be free to the merchant ships of all nations as far as the frontiers of Brazil. Of the tributaries, the Tapajos was to be open to Santarem, the Madeira to Borba, and the Rio Negro to Manaos. The Tocantins was to be open to Cameta and the São Francisco, lying entirely outside of the Amazon basin, to Penedo. It is worthy of note that on December 17, 1868 Peru followed the example of Brazil and declared her rivers open to all nations. The Amazon, including its most important tributaries, was now free from mouth to headwaters.

V

In the course of this chapter we have touched upon most of the major problems in the field of foreign relations under Dom Pedro II. Naturally there remain a number of others of secondary importance which we must pass over in silence. Some reference, however, should be made to the Confederate exiles to Brazil. During the years immediately following the close of our Civil War, between three and four thousand Southerners established homes in the Brazilian empire. This voluntary exile, accompanied in many cases by great hardship, was due partly to the disappointments growing out of the defeat of the South and the sufferings which the Southern people had to face under Reconstruction. The fact too that these *émigrés* might find a home in a country in which slavery was legalized offered a strong attraction. The Brazilian government extended a hearty welcome to these Confederates and endeavored to provide them with suitable sites for their colonies. Despite the fact that a few of these settlements, notably in the provinces of Espirito Santo and São Paulo, could claim a fair degree of prosperity, the majority of these ventures were unsuccessful. As time went on, many of the settlers returned to the United States, while the remainder were little by little absorbed into the Brazilian population. Even today, however, a few direct descendents of these Confederates are to be found in the interior of the state of São Paulo.[2]

---

[2] Full details on this interesting topic are given by Professor L. F. Hill, *op. cit.*, Chapter IX.

CHAPTER NINETEEN

SLAVERY AND ABOLITION. THE COLLAPSE OF THE EMPIRE

THE most serious social and economic problem which the empire had to face sprang directly or indirectly from the institution of slavery. The slave trade and its abolition at the beginning of the reign of Dom Pedro II, and negro emancipation as the empire approached its decline, were subjects in which the ruler and the nation alike took a passionate interest.

I

The importation of negroes into Brazil was almost from the first regarded as both logical and necessary. The Portuguese colonists were convinced that only through the aid of servile labor could their hold on the colony be permanent. When the settlers discovered that the indigenous races were unsuitable for their purpose they quite naturally turned to the teeming populations of Africa. One of the most recent writers on the subject, Dr. Pandiá Calogeras, estimates that the average annual importation of negro slaves rose to forty-four thousand in the seventeenth century and to fifty-five thousand in the eighteenth.

Three centuries of unrestricted slave trade had left an indelible stamp on the ethnic complexion of Brazil, and there is good reason to believe that on the eve of Brazilian independence the number of negro slaves exceeded the white population. As is well known, the initiative for the destruction of this infamous traffic came from Great Britain. Her own slave trade abolished in 1807, England, for motives that have been characterized as both philanthropic and philistine, turned her attention to the worst offender among the European powers, the Kingdom of Portugal. It was generally regarded as to the financial interest of England, already hard hit in her American colonies by the abolition of the traffic, to remove the menace of an unrestricted slave traffic between Portugal and Brazil. At the Congress of Vienna, Great Britain brought pressure to bear upon Portugal to sign a treaty abolishing all slave trade north of the equator. But this was not all. In 1817 additional conventions were signed which stipulated that the warships of each country should have the right of search and visit of any merchant vessel operating north of the Line which might be suspected of having slaves on board. Slavers captured under such conditions were to be brought for adjudication before two mixed tribunals, one in Sierra Leone and the other in Brazil, established *ad hoc,* and these provisions were to remain in effect fifteen years after the complete abolition of the traffic.

After the independence of Brazil, Great Britain insisted that her conventions signed with Portugal applied to Brazil as well. Though the Rio foreign office objected to this view, it really was helpless. In return for the recognition of the Brazilian empire by Great Britain in 1825, the Rio de Janeiro government accepted the terms of the Anglo-Portuguese agreements of 1817 and promised that at the end of three years after the expiration of the treaty the slave trade should cease utterly, and all ships engaged in the traffic after that date would be considered as pirates. The treaty was ratified March 13, 1827, and as a consequence the traffic became illegal after March 13, 1830, either below or above the equator. As a natural corollary to this treaty the Brazilian general assembly passed a law on November 7, 1831, which declared that all slaves illegally imported into Brazil automatically became free.

For the next two decades no serious efforts were made by the Brazilian authorities to carry out the provisions of the treaty of 1827. Public opinion, with rare exceptions, not only tolerated but approved of the traffic with which the economic welfare of the country was held to be involved. It has long been known that citizens of the United States, taking advantage of the refusal of our government to sign with Great Britain a treaty granting mutual right of search, were involved in the traffic, but thanks to the recent investigations of Professor Hill of the Ohio State University in the archives of our state department the extent of this participation has been established. One paragraph from the dispatch sent by Minister Proffit under date of February 27, 1844, to our government is worth quoting.

> "It is not a fact to be distinguished or denied that the slave trade is almost entirely carried on under our flag and in American vessels sold her [that is, Rio de Janeiro] chartered for the coast of Africa to slave traders. Indeed the scandalous traffic could not be carried on to any extent were it not for the use of our flag, and the facilities given by the chartering of American vessels to

carry to the coast of Africa the outfit for the trade and the materials for purchasing slaves."

The traffic was cruel and gruesome in the extreme. Ruy Barbosa, one of the greatest orators produced by Brazil, in a speech before the chamber of deputies declared: "If Dante Alighieri had lived in the eighteenth century, he would have placed the limit of human suffering, the lowest circle of his Inferno, in the hold of a slave ship." In almost equally emphatic terms, José Bonifacio, the "Patriarch of Independence," had, as early as 1823, vigorously but futilely attacked the traffic.

Although no absolutely accurate statistics of the number of slaves illegally introduced into Brazil are available, the detailed reports of the British diplomatic and consular agents furnish some notion of the extent of the traffic. The yearly average of the decade 1842-1852 was well over thirty-two thousand. Other estimates are much higher—Nabuco placed it at fifty thousand per year—and it is quite possible that nearly a million of these unfortunates were brought to Brazil in violation of the law. The eminent Brazilian historian, Dr. Oliveira Lima, told the writer that as a young man he knew personally many negroes born in Africa.

The tension between Great Britain and Brazil over the latter's inability or unwillingness to suppress the traffic all but led to a break in diplomatic relations when in 1845 the Rio foreign office announced that the abolition convention of 1827 had expired and would not be renewed. Faced with the unpleasant necessity of bringing additional pressure to bear on the Brazilian empire, Lord Aberdeen, the secretary of state for foreign affairs, introduced in 1845 a bill into parliament providing for the trial of all cases of vessels carrying on the slave trade by British admiralty or vice-admiralty courts instead of the mixed commissions sitting at Sierra Leone and Rio de Janeiro. The resentment of the imperial government at the action of Great Britain was intense. In a ten-page official protest the Brazilian minister of foreign affairs declared that the Aberdeen Bill violated "the most clear and positive principles of international law," and constituted an infringement upon the sovereign rights and independence of Brazil. The famous Sir Richard Burton, who spent a number of years in Brazil, qualified this law as one of the greatest insults ever inflicted upon a weak by a strong people.

The first results of the Aberdeen Bill were indeed deplorable. The number of slaves illegally imported increased rather than decreased until in 1848 the number exceeded sixty thousand. In 1850 Great

Britain resorted to even more drastic measures by issuing orders to her cruisers to enter Brazilian territorial waters, including ports, rivers, and bays, and seize all ships fitted for the slave trade.

The situation had become intolerable to all patriotic Brazilians. Dom Pedro II, keenly sensitive, as always, to foreign criticism of Brazil, declared that he would prefer abdication to continuance of the traffic. That the slave trade finally came to a sudden and spectacular end was due in large part to the energy of the minister of justice, Eusebio de Queiroz, the author of the famous law of September 4, 1850. This act reaffirmed the traffic to be piracy, established the right of seizure on the mere grounds of equipment for the trade, provided that clearance papers were to be granted only to those ships bound for Africa which gave security for the total value of the ship and cargo, and finally ordered that those implicated in the traffic should be tried, not before juries from which acquittal was almost certain, but before admiralty courts enjoying the full support and authority of the imperial government. The law was carried out with such effect that by 1852 importations ceased. Great Britain finally repealed the Aberdeen Bill in 1869.

II

In Brazil as in the United States a sharp distinction was drawn between slavery and the slave trade. The second half of the nineteenth century was well on its way before there arose in Brazil any serious agitation against slavery as such. For a long period it never occurred to the bulk of the Brazilians that as an institution slavery was really open to attack; it was in fact almost regarded as a part of the order of nature. The state itself bought and sold slaves and employed their labor to lighten the charges on the budget. Convents and monasteries held slaves; they were supposed to be the property of St. Loyola or St. Benedict. Orphan asylums bought negresses as nurses for foundlings. Unscrupulous doctors advertised for wornout slaves, set them on their feet again, and sold them at a handsome profit. There even seem to have been instances of slaves owning slaves.

As to the condition of the negroes in the heyday of slavery, authorities differ, although the evidence is fairly conclusive that the lot of the slaves was in general a relatively mild one. The kindly, easy-going temperament of the Brazilians prevented them from being harsh masters. In the cities, household servants were in the main treated kindly. The overwhelming majority of the slaves, however, were to be found on the great plantations in the interior. Here a certain patriarchical relationship existed between the master and slave. Yet instances of abuse, cruelty, and neglect were not lacking; especially was this true on plantations left in charge of overseers by their absent landlords. Here were occasionally paralleled the worst conditions in ante-bellum Mississippi and Louisiana.

In a number of respects slavery in Brazil differed from slavery in the United States. In general it may be said that in the former country a greater liberty was allowed the slaves, especially in the cities. Not only on Sundays but also on the numerous religious holidays they were allowed to rest. Frequently the owners gave the slaves entire disposition of their time, on condition that they turn over a fixed, lump sum from their earnings. These men, known as *negros de ganho,* were left more or less to their own devices. They were accustomed to organize themselves into bands of workers and offer themselves as porters, stevedores, or longshoremen. They were preceded by a kind of musician who urged them on by shaking a quantity of buckshot in a gourd; at the same time they encouraged each other by a kind of rhythmic chant sung in unison. Slaves were often permitted to instruct themselves, and if the slave had the time or the ambition it was frequently possible for him to gain the rudiments of education which would pave the way for eventual freedom.

Perhaps the most striking feature of the status of the negro in Brazil was the opportunity opened to freedom. Caste and social distinctions based on color are much less sharply drawn in Brazil than in the United States. Former slaves or their descendents, if they possessed the requisite ability, found almost every career open to them. Sons of slaves might enter the army or navy, become lawyers, doctors, professors, artists, or clergymen. In the latter days of the empire several negroes or mulattoes were elected to the chamber of deputies.

III

It was not until the sixties that the emancipation movement began to make serious headway. The emperor himself was opposed to the whole system of slavery but the rôle which he played in the emancipation movement was passive rather than active. Many members of the Conservative Party—and to a somewhat less extent was this true also of the Liberal Party—were recruited from plantation owners who regarded slavery as an economic necessity. It was natural, therefore, that Dom Pedro should hesitate to antagonize this influential class which formed one of the chief supports of the dynasty.

The outcome of the Civil War in the United States naturally gave encouragement to the opponents of slavery. Apologists of the institution had long pointed to the United States as a country in which slavery flourished and was legally protected. In fact our minister, R. K. Meade, in an interview with Dom Pedro late in 1859 declared that the common institution of slavery was fixed and deeply rooted in the soil of the two nations and that this fact established "an affinity between them" and insured "for mutual defense a unity of action and feeling that" would "prove invincible in the future." But after the Emancipation Proclamation and the defeat of the South, Brazil had the melancholy distinction of being the only important country in the world in which slavery was legalized. This sense of moral isolation was increased by the petition sent in July 1866 to Dom Pedro by the French abolition society, begging him to use his influence to bring about the extinction of slavery in Brazil. Among the signatures were such names as Guizot, the Prince de Broglie, Laboulaye, Montalembert, and Henri Martin. In reply the emperor, through his minister of foreign affairs, assured this group of distinguished French humanitarians that "the emancipation of the slaves . . . is only a question of form and opportuneness." And in his speech from the throne in May of the following year Dom Perdo stated to his representatives:

> "The servile element in the empire cannot fail, at an opportune time, to merit your consideration. While respecting existing property rights . . . the important interests involved in emancipation must receive your careful attention."

Despite the studied moderation of this pronouncement, the effect was almost revolutionary. Overnight, slavery had become the most important domestic problem of Brazil. Logically, to the liberals should have fallen the honor of putting through the two great bills of 1871 and 1888, the former destroying the source of slavery, the latter abolishing the institution. In 1869 the liberals had in point of fact inscribed in their program the emancipation of the slaves. Yet by a curious and perverse irony of fate both of these measures were passed by conservative governments. Such anomalies are not unknown in other countries, as for example the English Reform Bill of 1867 which, sponsored by the liberals, was finally passed by the conservatives—the famous "leap in the dark" of Lord Derby.

An actual beginning towards gradual emancipation was made in 1866 when the Marquis of São Vicente, with the full approval of the emperor, laid before the council of state a draft of a bill to this end. The absorption of the energies of the nation in the Paraguayan War caused this project to be shelved, but in 1871, in the face of the most strenuous opposition, the Rio Branco Bill, called after the Viscount of Rio Branco, the conservative prime minister, was passed by parliament. This act, generally known as the law of "free birth" *(ventre livre)* was one of the great milestones on the road towards abolition. It provided that all children born of slave mothers should be free, facilitated manumission, and created an emancipation fund the proceeds of which were to be applied annually to a number of slaves. But by the terms of the bill, the children of slave mothers—the so-called *ingenuos*—might under certain conditions be required to labor for their mothers' owners up to the age of twenty-one.

At first the Rio Branco law met with general acquiesence, but this period of relative indifference to the slavery question lasted barely seven years. The bill, like most palliatives, really satisfied no one, and dissatisfaction with the measure really became vocal in 1878 with the return to power of the Liberal Party.

In the group of able and brilliant young men who consecrated themselves to what was then a most unpopular cause, one name stands out preëminent, that of Joaquim Nabuco. Nabuco sprang from one of the old aristocratic planter families of Pernambuco and was the son of the distinguished jurisconsult and cabinet minister Nabuco de Araujo, an account of whose life and times he subsequently wrote. Sacrificing apparently both his political and professional career, he embraced with almost demoniacal fervor the cause of the million and a half negroes still in bondage. The problem, as Nabuco soon came to see it, was one, not of gradual emancipation, but of complete and unconditional abolition. Eventually his great services to the nation became recognized. Under the republic he shared with the younger Rio Branco the distinction of making a settlement of some of Brazil's thorny boundary controversies. As the culmination of his career he served brilliantly as the first Brazilian ambassador at Washington where he died in 1910.

In 1880 Nabuco become president of the influential Brazilian Anti-Slavery Society *(Sociedade brasileira contra a escravidão),* and in 1883 he wrote a remarkable book called *O Abolicionismo,* perhaps the most devastating arraignment of slavery and all its works ever published in Brazil. Naturally the inadequacies of the Rio Branco law were stressed. In one of the most telling paragraphs Nabuco pointed out that a negro child born the day before the signing of the bill might become a mother in 1911 of one of the *ingenuos* who would remain in provisional slavery until the year of grace 1932. Much of the book was devoted to the now recognized commonplace that in the final instance slavery is more detrimental to the slave owner than to the slave. He drew a gloomy but arresting picture of the political, economic, social, and religious effects of slave labor, and with a wealth of illustrations, well-buttressed by facts, endeavored to prove that slavery was poisoning the wellsprings of national life.

The propaganda in favor of complete abolition began to bear fruit. A number of abolitionists, including of course Nabuco, were elected to parliament. In 1883 the province of Ceará freed its slaves; in 1885, Amazonas. The two great political parties could no longer ignore the question; in 1885 under the ministry of Dantas—whom Nabuco compared to Gladstone—a bill passed parliament for the liberation of all slaves over sixty-five. But the agitation instead of decreasing took on greater proportions. The abolitionists carried on their campaign in presses, parliament, and public meetings. The contagion reached the slaves themselves; in certain parts of the great province of São Paulo they began to desert their plantations *en masse,* and troops despatched to capture these runaways practically refused to carry out their odious task. In 1888 Dom Pedro II, failing in health, sailed for Europe leaving Princess Isabella, his daughter, to act as regent. Isabella was in favor of complete and immediate abolition, although one of the most astute of Brazilian statesmen, Cotegipe, warned her that such a course might sound the death knell of the monachy. Her most serious mistake was her failure to recommend to parliament that an indemnity be granted the slaveholders. Apparently she felt that a great moral issue such as this should not be placed on a monetary basis, while the slaveholders themselves, with a delicacy little short of quixotic, were loath to mention the fatal word, indemnity.

On May 13, 1888, amid indescribable enthusiasm, parliament passed the measure forthwith extinguishing slavery in Brazil without compensation to the owners. The full significance of this historic moment was summed up by Nabuco who declared before the chamber of deputies on May 7:

> "This is not the moment for party controversy, for we are approaching what is incomparably the most solemn hour of our history. The present generation has never before experienced such depths of emotion and to find a parallel we must turn back to the exultation felt by our fathers on the proclamation of independence.

For us Brazilians the year 1888 is a landmark in our history even greater than was 1789 for France. It is literally a new nation that is born."

By the Act of May 13 nearly three quarters of a million slaves with a legal value of nearly a quarter of a billion dollars were given their freedom.

IV

We now address ourselves to a brief consideration of the momentous changes which took place in 1889. At first sight the collapse of the Brazilian empire seems inexplicable. It was generally assumed in Europe, and to a lesser extent in the United States, that the Braganza dynasty had become thoroughly acclimated in Brazil, and that the wisdom and statesmanship of Dom Pedro II were largely responsible for the half-century of peace and progress which had become the envy and admiration of Brazil's South American neighbors. Under such conditions the overthrow of the empire and the banishment of the emperor seemed not only unwise but ungrateful. Yet to those familiar with the deeper currents of Brazilian political life, the collapse of the monarchy came as no surprise. By the abolition of slavery without compensation to the slave owners the monarchy lost one of its chief supports. Yet the power and influence of the former slave owners may be exaggerated. We have already alluded to the important rôle played in Brazilian life by the *fazendeiro,* or great land owner, and we have seen that there was an unwritten alliance between the monarchy and the landed nobility. The majority of the nobility, which in 1883 included one duke, five counts, thirty-nine viscounts, and two hundred and sixty-eight barons, was largely recruited from this class which until the rise of the industrial elements constituted the only important political power in the country. Then as the industrial class from the time of Mauá began to assume prominence, came the gradual disintegration of the power of the *fazendeiro.* From this point of view, if we are to accept the views of Dr. J. F. Normano, the revolution of 1889 was not caused merely by the abolition of slavery, but because the gradual eclipse of the *fazendeiro*—always one of the strong props of the monarchy—left the political organization of the empire without the necessary economic backing.

With some show of reason it may be said that the new elements in Brazilian economic life never received the same cordial support by the emperor accorded to the *fazendeiro.* As early as the fifties this economic shift in the life of Brazil began. By the sixties it was well under way. The guiding spirit was Ireneu de Souza, the Baron of Mauá, who in the sixties was responsible for most of the economic creations in Brazil: banks, railroads, factories, steamship lines, and the pushing further westward of the Brazilian frontier. In fact the enthusiastic biographer of Mauá, Alberto de Faria, has not hesitated to characterize him as one of the three greatest men of the empire, the other two being Caxias and Dom Pedro II. Joaquim Murtinho, the great minister of finance under the republic, went so far as to declare, "There was in this country a man so illustrious that one can say without error that he personified his time. This man was Mauá." Unfortunately Dom Pedro never appreciated Mauá at his true value, partly, perhaps, because the illustrious financier was opposed to the Paraguayan War. In any event the emperor did not accord sufficient importance to these new economic forces which were slowly altering Brazilian life; especially was this true of white immigration which in the later decades of his reign began to make rapid headway, and in the great coffee province of São Paulo was commencing to supplant slave labor.

The clergy, which in most European kingdoms has been strongly monarchial and which in Brazil might have been another pillar to the throne, had been antagonized by the imprisonment in 1874 of the bishops of Pará and Pernambuco for their attempts, illegal under the laws of the empire, to expell members of the Masonic Order from a kind of benevolent institution known as "brotherhoods" *(irmandades)*. This is a subject on which a great deal has been written and probably the last word has not yet been said. The Republican Party, launched as we have seen in 1871, though numerically small, kept up an intermittent agitation and aided in undermining the loyalty to the empire. It was wont to ring the changes on the phrase: "The monarchy is an exotic plant on the America continent." The disintegration and sterility of the two great political parties for which the emperor was held partly responsible tended still further to lower the prestige of the monarchy. Thoughtful Brazilians came to believe that the liberals and conservatives had abandoned their earlier ideals in favor of a sordid opportunism. The *volte-face* of the conservatives in 1888 when they espoused the cause of emancipation, gave rise to the most cynical commentaries. And yet it must be said that the last cabinet of the empire, that of Ouro Preto (liberal) showed itself fully equal to the demands of the time by its espousal of a comprehensive reform program which included such a large degree of decentralization that the empire would have been all but federalized. It also provided for the extinction of the moderative power of the emperor. So highly was the credit of Brazil held in the money marts of Europe that the *milreis* actually rose above par. On the other hand, during the waning of the empire Dom Pedro was a weary and, for months at a time, a sick man. Towards the end, his attitude in regard to public affairs was colored with a certain scepticism which at times approached fatalism. He made little real effort to stave off the catastrophe with which he might have seen his dynasty was menaced. Unfortunately, too, the heiress to the throne, Princess Isabella and the Prince Consort, the Comte d'Eu, the grandson of Louis Philippe of France, were both unpopular. Despite the aureole which surrounded the head of *Isabel a redentora* as signer of the emancipation bill of 1888, she was charged with being a tool of the clergy; against the count nothing could be alleged save his reserved, somewhat formal, bearing and the fact that he was a foreigner.

Some allusion must be made to the positivistic philosophy of the Frenchman Auguste Comte which in the seventies and the eighties had a great vogue among the Brazilian intellectuals and through a distortion or misunderstanding of Comte's teaching furnished them with a theoretical justification for a republic. Finally a passing reference must be made to the virulent and at times unscrupulous press. Freedom of the press was at all times complete under the empire, and there can be little doubt that this liberty was abused through unscrupulous and untrue attacks on the emperor. Dr. Oliveira Lima even goes so far as to say that in the last days of the empire Ruy Barbosa, through his campaign in the *Diario de Noticias*, did more than any single individual to overthrow the throne that Evaristo da Veiga had done so much to strengthen in 1831.

Despite the causes of discontent with the existing régime, the empire might have lasted many years longer had it been able to count on the support of the army. The truth of the matter is that the Brazilian army, although it had given a good account of itself at various times, especially in the Paraguayan War, was never a model of discipline; both at the beginning and the end of the empire it did not scruple to intervene in purely political matters. Unfortunately, too, certain factions and leaders of the army became convinced that they were the victims of grave injustices on the part of the imperial government. In Brazil the officers were freely elected to parliament where they found a ready forum for their grievances, alleged or real. But when their specific complaints are subjected to a closer scrutiny they shrink to pitiable dimensions. The censuring of two officers by the minister of war for ventilating their grievances in the press, the dispatch of certain regiments whose loyalty was not above suspicion to the distant Province of Amazonas, clashes between soldiery and the police—such were the acts, most of them of a purely disciplinary character, which formed the burden of the complaints of the disgruntled elements. The real grievance of the army was of a somewhat different character. Partly to relieve the drain on the imperial exchequer, partly because he had himself strong pacifist leanings, Dom Pedro after the Paraguayan War not only decreased the size of the army but permitted it to wane in influence. Militarism in the sense that it existed in certain of the Spanish American republics was repugnant both to the emperor and to the bulk of the Brazilian people. It is significant that the great majority of the ministers of war were civilians. The unprejudiced investigator is forced to the conclusion that the real grievance of the military was the refusal of the government to grant the army a privileged position in the state. Had Brazil possessed a strong military tradition, had the army been content to eschew politics and confine itself to its proper rôle of providing for national security and defense against foreign attack, it is improbable that any serious issue would have arisen.

It was not until the early autumn of 1889 that the disaffected elements of the army made common cause with the republicans. Hitherto, opposition had been directed against the government and more particularly against the ministry in office and not against the dynasty as such. That the plans of certain recalcitrant officers were diverted into frankly revolutionary channels was due in large part to the efforts of Lieutenant-Colonel Benjamin Constant Botelho de Magalhães, professor of mathematics in the military school at Rio de Janeiro. Benjamin Constant, as we may call him according to the Brazilian custom, was one of the most ardent votaries of positivism in Brazil and a fanatical republican. Held in check by no dynastic scruples or loyalty to Dom Pedro, he made it his task to forge the accumulated grievances of the army against the government and particularly the cabinet of Ouro Preto into a weapon capable of demolishing the monarchy. Early in November he won over the leader of the aggrieved faction of the army, General Deodoro da Fonseca, a veteran of the Paraguayan War, and one of the most important military men in Brazil.

On November 11 the plot was worked out in detail at Deodoro's home. Most of the future members of the provisional government were present. The overthrow of the monarchy was definitely decided upon "as a measure of urgent necessity for the salvation of the country and the only possible means of restoring the army." Until almost the day of the revolt, Ouro Preto, the prime minister, failed to realize the gravity of the situation. On November 13, Floriano Peixoto, who was adjutant-general of the army and the recipient of the full confidence of the prime minister, wrote to Ouro Preto: "At this hour your excellency must have observed that plotting is taking place in certain quarters. Attach no importance to it. . . . Trust the loyalty of the military leaders who are on the alert. I thank you once more for the favors you have deigned to bestow upon me." Such eleventh-hour measures as Ouro Preto took proved inadequate. When, on the early morning of November 15, 1889, the Second Brigade revolted, the remainder of the army quickly joined it. Armed resistance being futile the ministry handed in its resignation to the emperor.

Summoned by telegraph from his summer residence at Petropolis, Dom Pedro on his arrival at Rio made desperate efforts to form a new cabinet. But even while these deliberations were taking place the republic was proclaimed at the municipality and the provisional government was organized with General Deodoro da Fonseca as its chief and Benjamin Constant as minister of war. On the 16th, Deodoro formally notified Dom Pedro of his deposition and banishment from the country within the space of twenty-four hours. The reply of the aged emperor is worth quoting:

> "In view of the representation delivered to me today at three o'clock, I resolve, yielding to the force of circumstances, to depart with all my family for Europe tomorrow, leaving this country beloved of us all, and to which I have striven to give constant proofs of deep-seated affection during almost half the century during which I filled the position of chief of the state. In departing therefore I, with all my family shall always retain the most tender remembrances of Brazil and offer ardent prayers for her greatness and prosperity."

Before daylight on the morning of November 17, the imperial family was forced to embark on the *Alagoas,* which under convoy of a Brazilian man-of-war set sail directly for Europe. After a brief sojourn in Portugal, the emperor, already failing in health, removed to Paris where he died, less than two years later, at the modest Hotel Bedford.

The proximate cause of the collapse of the imperial régime was a barrack-room conspiracy participated in by only a fraction of the army whose grievances were skilfully exploited by a small group of determined men bent on the establishment of the republic. The ultimate cause was the slow crumbling of the foundations on which the stability of the empire depended. The monarchy had gradually ceased to be identified with the nation in the minds of the majority of the Brazilians. It had become a thing apart, encompassed with a growing isolation, an object of respect but incapable of arousing save in a restricted class any feeling of self-sacrifice or devotion.

Whatever, therefore, may be the verdict of history on the motives and ideals behind the revolution of 1889 it is reasonably clear that sooner or later the coming of the republic was inevitable. An American empire was inexorably fated to become more and more of an anachronism. Yet he would be quite wanting in historical perspective who, with his eyes fixed only on the achievements of the republic, would ignore the beneficent rôle which the empire played in the national development of Brazil. Thanks to the ability, patriotism, and rugged honesty of Dom Pedro II the monarchy rendered the nation inestimable services. It supplied the cohesive force which prevented Brazil from falling prey to anarchy and possible dismemberment. Under its ægis Brazil took her place among the most cultured and liberal countries of Hispanic America. Yet after all, perhaps the greatest service rendered by the empire was to afford the Brazilian people, decade after decade, a large and fruitful apprenticeship in the practice of self-government within the confines of liberal constitutional monarchy. Thus were laid, solid and enduring, the foundations on which the success of the republic had ultimately to depend.

CHAPTER TWENTY

BRAZIL FROM 1889 TO 1894. THE PROVISIONAL GOVERNMENT AND THE NAVAL REVOLT OF 1893

THE empire was overthrown without a struggle and practically without bloodshed. The new provisional government not only encountered no opposition but apparently it could count on the enthusiastic support of the most influential elements of the nation. Telegrams of adhesion poured in from the farthest confines of Brazil. Those who were hostile to the new régime went into voluntary exile or maintained a discreet silence. Yet there were not lacking keen observers who detected certain artificial elements in this enthusiasm. It is significant that the populace at large, once the initial fervor had cooled, regarded the new government with a mixture of indifference and cynicism. As the events of November 15 began to stand out in their true perspective it became increasingly clear that the revolution was not the protest of an oppressed and downtrodden people against a hated despotism, but that the advent of the republic was not so dissimilar to the typical Spanish American barrack conspiracy or military pronunciamento. In a letter written on November 15 and frequently reprinted, Aristides Lobo, later minister of the interior, declared:

> "I should like to call November 15 the first day of the republic but unhappily I cannot do so. What has taken place is one step—perhaps not even that—towards the advent of a great era. . . . At present the stamp of the new government is purely military. This is strictly logical. The work was theirs and theirs alone, for the collaboration of the civilian element was almost nil. And the people stood by stupefied *(bestialisado)*, dumbfounded, without an inkling of what it all meant. Many honestly believed they were beholding a parade."

I

As head of the provisional government was naturally placed General Deodoro da Fonseca, the hero of November 15, who largely owed his advancement to the personal friendship of the deposed emperor. The bulk of Deodoro's first cabinet was necessarily largely made up of civilians, recruited chiefly from the leaders of republican propaganda during the last days of the empire. As minister of foreign affairs was chosen Quintino Bocayuva, a well-known journalist and head of one of the factions of the Republican Party. The portfolio of justice was held by Campos Salles, a prominent Paulista, later president of the republic. The ministry of agriculture, commerce and public works was placed in charge of Demetrio Ribeiro, a young engineer who represented the turbulent positivist group in Rio Grande do Sul. Aristides Lobo, whom we have already met, was chosen minister of the interior. The important post of minister of finance was entrusted to Ruy Barbosa, a distinguished orator, publicist, and scholar, later recognized as the most erudite man in Brazil. Benjamin Constant was naturally minister of war and Vice-Admiral Wandenkolk minister of marine. Although the future was to show that the cabinet was far from homogeneous its formation met with general approval.

The tasks confronting the provisional government were fraught with difficulties. The empire had been overthrown; it now remained to create the republic. On the whole the beginning was good. On November 16 the government issued a long decree providing for the extinction of the imperial system, the abolition of the life senate and the council of state, and the dissolution of the chamber. Moreover, "the provisional government recognizes and respects all of the national engagements contracted during the preceding régime, the existing treaties with foreign powers, the domestic and foreign public debt, and other legally constituted obligations." On the same day was issued decree Number 1 which created a federative republic with the official name of the United States of Brazil. Among the many other decrees of importance were: the summoning of a constituent assembly for the formulation of a new constitution, the separation of church and state, a general naturalization decree which provided "that all foreigners resident in Brazil on November 15, 1889, are Brazilian citizens" unless they should make a declaration to the contrary before the proper municipal authorities, and a decree instituting civil marriage. The precipitancy with which some of these measures was passed caused much dissatisfaction.

The new republic quickly took its place in the comity of nations, particularly after Ruy Barbosa's assurance that all existing engagements should be respected. On November 20, only five days after the overthrow of the empire, Argentina and Uruguay took the initiative in recognizing the republic; on the 13th of December it was the turn of Chile, though it was not until the 29th of February 1890 that recognition came from the United States. The European governments were still more conservative, and with the exception of France and Portugal, withheld their recognition until the end of the year.

The sincere but mistaken zeal of certain members of the provisional government led to unfortunate and unforeseen results in many directions. The important post of minister of finance was, as we have seen, entrusted to Ruy Barbosa, the caustic critic of the financial policy of the Ouro Preto cabinet. Ruy was born in Bahia, the Brazilian Virginia, which had given so many statesmen to the empire: Rio Branco, Saraïva, Zacharias, Cotegipe, Dantas. He belonged to what Dr. Normano called the Anglo-Saxon current of tradition in Brazil. His father, Dr. João José Barbosa de Oliveira, was the follower of the cult of English and North American models. Not by accident did the young Ruy use the *noms de plume* of Grey and Lincoln in his contributions to the *Jornal do Commercio*. And with the advent of the republic Ruy attempted to apply the North American principles of banking and finance to Brazil. He greatly admired Alexander Hamilton but lacked the great North American's sense of the practical and possible. As minister of finance he had to meet a flood of applications for the granting of the privileges of emission of paper money. The first of his banking laws, that of January 17, 1890, reveals clearly the influence of the United States banking system. Feeling it his duty to quicken the economic forces of the nation and place Brazil squarely on the highway of progress, he divided the country into three zones, each to be provided with a new bank empowered to issue paper money within its own district. The total issue authorized amounted to the enormous sum of 450,000 *contos,* at the rate of exchange then in force approximately a quarter of a billion dollars. This immense sum was to be guaranteed, not by a gold reserve, but by government bonds or *apolices,* purchased by the banks in installments and deposited as security in the national treasury. These banks thus supplied with funds were to be granted a long list of financial, industrial, and commercial privileges—loans to agriculturists, formation of companies, construction of railroads, introduction of colonists, and the like. The scope of the activities of these banks was a mixture of a bank of issue and a *crédit mobilier*. It was unsparingly condemned by the more conservative European critics, including the great French economist, Leroy-Beaulieu.

For reasons which it would be profitless to discuss in detail Ruy Barbosa was unable to carry out his financial program in its entirety. During the succeeding months he was obliged to issue so many decrees modifying or supplementing the act of January 17 that by the end of the year his earlier policy had undergone a complete reversal. For a system of emission based on *apolices* granted to certain regional banks was substituted a mixed system which permitted the issue of paper money guaranteed by both government bonds and a gold reserve. The policy of decentralization was abandoned, and by the decree of December 7, 1890, there was created a great banking institution known as the *Banco da Republica* with authorization to issue up to 500,000 *contos*—a *contos* was worth some $500.00 with exchange at par—against the deposit of one-third of this amount in gold in the national treasury. We find thus a complete *volte-face* in Ruy's policy: from liberty of banking to monopoly, from the basis of *apolices* to that of metal, from regional banking to centralization, all within the space of a single year.

The full effects of this unstable—and as events proved—disastrous, financial policy did not appear until the great financial depression in 1892. For a time the inflation of the currency, far beyond the real needs of the country, brought about an era of fictitious prosperity not unlike that in the United States in the years immediately preceding the Wall Street crash of 1929. During several months the Brazilians lived in a kind of fools' paradise. Hundreds of companies were organized, ostensibly to exploit the resources of the country, in reality to cater to the craze of speculation which swept Brazil from end to end. From all parts of the nation speculators and promoters flocked to the capital, which became a kind of South American Monte Carlo. Many professions and occupations were virtually abandoned. Physicians and lawyers left their practices, *fazendeiros* their estates. All were dazzled by the prospect of easily acquired wealth. For this species of gambling and stock-jobbing a special term was invented, *ensilhamento*.

Many of the worst financial abuses of these years should not be laid at the door of the minister of finance. Conditions were frankly abnormal. Brazil was ruled by a military dictator who did not scruple to exert his authority and override the wishes of his ministers. On his own confession Ruy Barbosa was obliged to tolerate many "financial aberrations" and countenance dubious transactions against which his better judgment rebelled. Particularly was he powerless to check the wave of extravagance which invaded every department of the government. Finally it should be emphasized that the most zealous efforts of Ruy could not prevent a certain amount of downright fraud. With the wholesale printing of paper money counterfeiting was easy. There are even instances of the same firm printing two sets of notes, one of which was turned over to the banks and the other put into clandestine circulation. Ruy perhaps unwittingly sowed to the wind; his successors were to reap the whirlwind.

II

In the light of subsequent events it is clear that a mistake was made in deferring the definite organization of the republic for over a year after the overthrow of the empire. This is a mistake, however, to which the Brazilians are prone, as is shown in the long interregnum following the revolution of 1930. In the present case this long period not only permitted the growth of bitter personal rivalries and irreconcilable factions, but it made possible the advent of a military dictatorship infinitely more irresponsible and arbitrary than anything under the empire.

Although the civilian element was well represented in the government, it soon became evident that in all serious conflicts of authority the military had the whip handle. During the long and kindly rule of Dom Pedro II the Brazilians had acquired an ingrained dislike of militarism, but now to their dismay and alarm they beheld the army gradually usurping a privileged position in the state. Salaries of privates and officers were greatly augmented; the number of higher officers was increased far beyond the real needs of the country; the powerful Military Club was presented with valuable property belonging to the nation. Promotions were the order of the day. Deodoro accepted the title of "Generalissimo of the Forces of the Land and the Sea," a distinction usually accorded only to the commander of allied armies during a campaign. The patent of brigadier general was bestowed upon all of the civilian members of the cabinet, despite the fact that a number had never shouldered a musket. And all of this came at a time when Brazil was at profound peace with her neighbors.

The higher officers found it profitable to enter politics. On the shallowest of pretexts local civilian authorities were ousted and members of the army put in their place. For a time, ten out of the twenty states of Brazil had military governors. As the military became more avid for power it became more contemptuous of legal or constitutional restraint. Pretorian methods of government became the order of the day. The freedom of the press came to exist only on sufferance. A single instance will suffice. Learning that a plan was on foot to wreck the plant of the *Tribuna,* an anti-administration organ, Campos Salles, the minister of justice, informed Deodoro that certain members of the army were implicated in the plot. The marshal, as he was now called, gave formal assurance that no such attack would take place. Yet on the night of November 29, 1890, the office of the paper was invaded by a mob in which a number of officers figured conspicuously. The press was totally destroyed and one of the operatives was brutally murdered. This was but one of the numerous incidents which led to friction between Deodoro and his ministry which finally insisted on resigning as a body on January 21, 1891. A new ministry, presided over by a certain Baron of Lucena, a personal friend of Deodoro, took its place and soon became exceedingly unpopular. In fact by many Lucena was considered the *âme damné* of Deodoro.

III

During the course of these dissensions the constituent assembly, whose convocation was one of the chief tasks of the provisional government, had been holding its meetings. The electoral machinery had been so thoroughly controlled by the new minister of the interior, Cesario Alvim, that the composition of this body, which first met on November 15, 1890, was a foregone conclusion. All of the delegates were republicans of one kind or another; out of the total membership of three hundred and one, one hundred and thirty-eight were "historical republicans," that is, those who had supported the republican propaganda in the last days of the empire. The competency of the assembly was strictly limited. The principles of federalism and the form of the legislative branch of the future government were placed outside the realm of discussion. As for the constitution itself, the assembly did little more than make minor revisions of a draft drawn up by Ruy Barbosa, who in turn drew his inspiration chiefly from the Constitution of the United States.

The new instrument was formally promulgated on February 24, 1891. Since it has been replaced by the new Constitution of 1934, only a few of its more important features need be discussed here. It states specifically that the nation is composed of the former provinces united into an indissoluble union called the United States of Brazil. The executive, legislative, and judicial departments are modelled rather closely on our own, and are in theory correlative. A president and vice president are elected for four years, not as with us by an electoral college, but by direct popular vote. The president has, according to the constitution, powers analogous to our own executive, including the appointment of a cabinet which is responsible only to him. Experience was to show, however, that the presidents often wielded an authority which completely dwarfed the powers of congress. Brazil, in fact, was an excellent example of a presidential type of government of an extreme form. The legislature was such as we might expect in a federal type of government: a house of representatives, whose members are elected for a term of four years on the basis of population; and a senate, consisting of three members from each of the states and the federal district holding office for nine years. Perhaps the most striking departure from our own constitution is in the organization of state government. Among the powers expressly granted the states, is the right to levy export taxes. As is well known this power is forbidden both to the state and federal governments by our own constitution, but is extensively used in Brazil. In fact a number of the states, notably São Paulo, derive the bulk of their governmental revenue from this one source.

The experience of the next four decades was to show that the Constitution of 1891 was not entirely suited to the conditions in Brazil. In practice the executive ofttimes wielded a power rarely, if ever, assumed by Emperor Dom Pedro himself. Jealousies among the states were rife. Militarism from time to time raised its ugly head. The freedom of the individual was frequently suspended. One brilliant writer, Senhor José Maria dos Santos, in his work, *A politica geral do Brasil,*[1] goes so far as to find the chief cause of Brazil's subsequent difficulties in the substitution of the federal type of government, with an all-powerful and at times despotic president, for the parliamentary system of the empire under which the Brazilian people enjoyed a degree of liberty unique in the history of Hispanic America.

IV

The adoption of the new constitution left the constituent assembly free to perform its last act—the election of a president and vice president for the ensuing four years. Had the election taken place a few months earlier, but one candidate for chief magistrate would have been seriously considered, namely, Deodoro da Fonseca. His honesty, the distinction he had won in the Paraguayan War, and above all the fact that he was virtually the founder of the Brazilian republic, all conspired to render him the logical choice as chief magistrate. But the pretorian methods employed by the government and the license granted the military had brought about a revulsion of feeling. The conviction began to gain ground that the next executive should be a civilian. The

[1] Rio de Janeiro, 1930.

elements opposed to Deodoro put forth as an opposition candidate Dr. Prudente de Moraes Barros, a distinguished lawyer, a republican of long standing, and a son of the great State of São Paulo. It is not necessary to enter into the details of the campaign. The election took place on February 25, 1891, and resulted in the choice of Deodoro for president and Floriano Peixoto, one of the high officers in the army involved in the revolt of 1889, as vice president. The total number of votes cast was two hundred and thirty-four and of these Deodoro received one hundred and twenty-nine and Prudente twenty-seven.

To many unacquainted with the deeper current of Brazilian political life the result of the election was a disappointment. For fifteen months Brazil had been subject to a dictatorship in which the military had ridden roughshod over the rights of civilians. And now that the nation was to assume the responsibilities of self-government, the constituent assembly refused to select a civilian and insisted on retaining in power the man most closely identified with the odious features of the provisional government. To understand the action of the assembly one must remember that Deodoro still had his strong partisans while many regarded his choice as the lesser of two evils. There was a fairly widespread conviction that a majority vote in favor of Prudente would be followed by a revolt in the army, the dissolution of the assembly, and the proclamation of Deodoro as dictator.

Events were soon to show that Deodoro had profited little from his experience as head of the provisional government. He failed to understand the spirit of the new constitution or properly to gauge the attitude of the Brazilian people. Straightforward, frank, accustomed to obedience, imperfectly schooled in politics, he was ill-equipped to cope with the problems confronting the young republic and easily became the dupe of men less scrupulous and more able than himself. The administration began under two handicaps: a ministry, that of the Baron of Lucena, which the nation at large regarded with profound distrust, and an unsympathetic congress which soon became bitterly antagonistic to the executive. At length the tension between the legislative and executive branches of the government became so great that the president decided to cut the Gordian knot by the proclamation of an out-and-out dictatorship. On November 3, 1891, Deodoro signed a decree providing for the dissolution of congress and the assumption of dictatorial powers by the president. When congress attempted to meet the following day the entrance to the palace of São Christovão was blocked by a military guard. Martial law was declared, and the press put under a strict censorship. This *coup d'état* was defended by Deodoro in a long proclamation, in which, after attacking the actions of congress as calculated to endanger the safety of the republic, he asserted that the government had evidence of widespread monarchical plots and that conspirators were aiming at an armed revolution.

In his recourse to violence and illegality to end the conflict between the executive and congress, Deodoro failed to carry the country with him. His veiled reference to monarchical plots frightened or deceived no one. Opposition at once began to raise its head. In São Paulo where the republican sentiments were strongest, the federal deputy and ex-minister of justice, Campos Salles, published a scathing attack on the manifesto of Deodoro and the alleged motives for the *coup d'état*. In Rio Grande do Sul, the traditional hotbed of revolution, the garrisons in the more important towns rose against Deodoro and forced the governor to resign. A fraction of the army and all of the navy fell away from the government. On November 23, 1891, Admiral de Mello, a leading naval officer, assumed command of the warships stationed in the harbor of Rio and ordered their guns trained on the city. The president was in no mood to offer further resistance. Ill in body, a prey to the deepest despondency, he determined to withdraw from his impossible position. On November 23 he issued a brief manifesto recalling his services to the country and stating that in order to avoid a fratricidal struggle he had determined to resign in favor of the vice president. General Floriano Peixoto quietly assumed the duties of the presidency by virtue of his office, and Deodoro retired into private life, practically forgotten until his death which occurred the following August.

V

The overthrow of the dictatorship was acclaimed as the beginning of a new era, and the restoration of constitutional government through the accession of Floriano caused general satisfaction. To be sure, the antecedents of the vice president were such as not to command the unqualified support of the better elements in Brazil. It was no secret that his well-known opposition to Deodoro had been based fully as much on personal as upon political motives. It was remembered too that as quartermaster-general of the army he had proven faithless to the emperor in the tragic days of November 1889. Finally, it was not forgotten that he had been closely identified with the military elements whose excesses the Brazilians had such good reason to deplore. On the other hand it was hoped that he had profited by the lessons of the past two years and that the new administration would follow strictly constitutional lines.

The political horizon, apparently so serene, soon became obscured. It developed that Floriano's methods of government differed little in practice from those of his predecessor. In order that the various states should not become foci of attacks on his régime—all of the twenty states except Pará had adhered to Deodoro's *coup d'état*—he aided the local groups to overturn their state governments and oust their presidents or governors. This illegal act aroused enormous resentment, but if we are to believe the historian Calogeras, it may be justified on the grounds of sheer necessity. He did little or nothing to introduce economy in public affairs or to improve the difficult financial situation which he had inherited from Deodoro. When on April 6, 1892, thirteen generals appealed to him for a new presidential election as the only method of allaying the existing discontent, Floriano ordered them placed on the retired list. One of his first acts was to summon congress which, thanks to his control of the majority, proceeded to approve all of his acts, including the deposition of the state governors. At this time a controversy arose which did much to inflame public opinion. Should there be a new election for president or should Floriano remain in power until November 15, 1894? According to Article 42 of the constitution the former alternative should be adopted since the constitution stated explicitly that a new election should take place if the vacancy in the presidential office occurred during the first two years of the presidential term. Others, including Floriano's supporters, claimed that by virtue of certain transitory dispositions of the constitution he was entitled to rule during all of Deodoro's term. Congress appointed a commission which pronounced against a new election.

Floriano's favor throughout the country began to wane. In Rio de Janeiro, Minas, Matto Grosso, São Paulo, Amazonas, and Maranhão occurred sporadic uprisings, all of which were suffocated, but in July 1892 there flared up again the civil war in Rio Grande do Sul. We cannot take up in detail this conflict. Suffice it to say that conditions were ripe for revolt. During the three years of the republic the state had been ruled by no less than nineteen governors. In the present uprising against Floriano and his partisans more was at stake than a local rebellion. The legitimacy of republican institutions was called into question due partly to the influence of the former monarchical senator, Gaspar da Silveira Martins. The headquarters of the "federalist" revolution, as it was called from one of the articles of its political program, was close to the Uruguayan frontier and frequently Brazil was invaded by armed bands from across her border. One of the most famous of these was the *gaucho* leader, Gumercindo Saraïva, the "king of the pampas," whom we shall meet later. Finally, it should be recalled that resentment against the vice president was particularly strong in the navy which had looked with a jealous eye on the privileged position which the army had usurped since the overthrow of the empire. It was symptomatic that in April 1893 the minister of marine, Admiral Custodio José de Mello, resigned his portfolio and in a public letter severely criticized the conduct of the executive.

Luckily for the vice president there was little real unity among his opponents. These latter consisted of disgruntled politicians of all stripes and colors, many naval officials, and a few monarchists. The great cohesive force in this heterogeneous group was the distrust and dislike inspired by Floriano himself.

VI

Finally on September 6, 1893, the long threatened revolt of the navy took place. Admiral de Mello raised the standard of rebellion on board the armored cruiser *Aquidaban* in the harbor of Rio de Janeiro. He justified his action in a long manifesto in which he accused Floriano of mutilating and violating the constitution, and of fomenting civil war. Moreover, by opening the exchequer to bribery and corruption he had, declared de Mello, brought the country to the verge of bankruptcy.

The action of de Mello was greeted with approval by practically the entire navy and by a number of prominent civilians, including many members of congress, who promptly joined the admiral on his flagship. It was generally assumed that the revolt would be of short duration, that Floriano would tender his resignation, and that steps would be taken for a new election. In fact, the condition of the success of this plan lay in its speed and effectiveness. It was somewhat naïvely assumed that the vice president would conveniently eclipse himself much as Deodoro had done.

Those who argued thus failed lamentably in their appraisal of the character of Floriano. Whatever faults the vice president may have possessed, indecision and cowardice were not among them. Supported by the army and the majority of congress he determined on the most energetic resistance. The defenses of both the harbor and city of Rio de Janeiro were strengthened, batteries were mounted on various hills commanding the bay, the members of the national guard were called out, and orders were placed in Europe and the United States for the purchase of ships with which to attack the revolting fleet. With the sanction of congress martial law was declared in various parts of the republic. Those known to be in any way sympathetic with the revolt were promptly incarcerated. As will readily be imagined many of the most prominent citizens of Brazil suffered temporary imprisonment.

From the very beginning of the revolt a curious situation developed. The entire harbor, with the exception of a number of the islands, was in the hands of the navy, while the city of Rio de Janeiro and the shore defenses were under the control of the government. Thanks, however, to the size and effectiveness of the insurgent fleet, de Mello was in a position, by bombarding the city, to make the position of Floriano if not untenable at least highly precarious. This menace held over the capital was by all odds the most effective potential weapon in the hands of the rebels.

Unfortunately for the rebels they found their hands tied almost from the first. At the outbreak of the revolt there were stationed in the harbor of Rio de Janeiro naval forces of the United States, France, Italy, Great Britain, and Portugal. A German warship, anchored off the capital during a portion of the revolt, refused to coöperate with the remaining foreign units. Realizing that the interests of their nationals would be gravely injured by the bombardment of the city, and alleging at the same time the higher interests of humanity, the foreign commanders, in a conference assembled on October 1 announced in a note addressed to de Mello that "they would oppose by force, if necessary, any enterprise against Rio de Janeiro." At the same time they secured from Floriano an assurance that the cannon would be removed from the batteries which had been placed at various points in the city for the purpose, eventually, of blowing the fleet out of the water. While this agreement was kept by the commanders of the revolting fleet it was apparently later violated by the government. That this intervention by the foreign powers, though dictated in part by motives of humanity, contributed to the collapse of the revolt admits of no possible doubt. Both the government of Floriano, which gladly acquiesced in the action of foreign powers, as well as the intervention itself, have been flayed by the writer Joaquim Nabuco in his work, *The Foreign Intervention During the Revolt (A intervenção estrangeira durante a revolta)*. The author also defends the thesis that the powers in depriving de Mello of one of his most important weapons at least should have granted the rebels the rights of belligerents. Had this right been accorded they could have instituted a legal blockade of the harbor of Rio de Janeiro.

Finally the prestige of the rebels was still further lowered by the action of the United States commander, Vice-Admiral Benham, who refused to recognize a barred zone drawn up in the harbor by the rebel commander in which ships were forbidden to discharge their cargo. Benham went so far as specifically to authorize two United States merchantmen to go to the wharves within the barred zone, and informed the Brazilian admiral that if interferences were attempted he would open fire on the insurgent squadron. As the United States fleet, consisting of five warships, the *New York, Charleston, San Francisco, Detroit,* and *Newark,* was far superior in power to the Brazilian squadron, the demand was naturally complied with.

The many incidents of the revolt, some of them of a highly picturesque and dramatic character, may be quickly summarized. At daybreak on the morning of December 1, de Mello in his flagship the *Aquidaban* braved the fires of the fortresses São João and São Sebastião at the entrance of the harbor and sailed southward to establish contact with the anti-government forces which under Gumercindo Saraïva were operating in southern Brazil. The command of the insurgent fleet was assumed by Admiral Luiz Felipe Saldanha da Gama, a man who had won marked distinction in his long career in the Brazilian navy. At the beginning of the revolt he had been in charge of the Naval Academy, but at length early in November, he cast his lot definitely with the insurgents. In a proclamation issued at the time, da Gama professed monarchical leanings but it would be a mistake to assume that on this account the purpose of the revolt was a monarchical restoration. It was not. At the most da Gama came out in favor of a plebiscite to determine the future form of the government of Brazil. Even so the manifesto was a mistake as it brought further confusion and dissension into the ranks of the insurgents. On the other hand such was the nobility of da Gama and such was the disinterestedness of his aims that it is no exaggeration to say that for several months it was only his personality which kept the revolt alive.

The only possibility of the success of the insurgents lay in the closest coöperation between the navy and the land forces operating in southern Brazil. It was hoped that these forces, in which the bands of Saraïva figured prominently, would advance northward against the capital, gathering momentum and recruits as they went. Although the insurgents did gain possession of Desterro, the chief seaport of Santa Catharina, where a provisional government was organized, there was no realization of the critical condition of the navy under da Gama. The march northward which might have saved the revolt was indefinitely delayed, thus permitting Floriano to organize resistance in São Paulo and other points in the interior. Meanwhile, the fleet at Rio was being reduced to a pitiable plight by the continual pounding of the various land batteries in which guns of a high calibre had been mounted. At the same time the government was making frantic efforts to assemble a squadron with which to oppose da Gama. At length, on May 7, 1894, a nondescript fleet, purchased in the United States and Europe by the agents of Floriano at an enormous price, and manned by a motley crew of Europeans, Argentines, Chileans, and citizens of the United States, arrived off the mouth of the harbor of Rio and prepared if need be to attack da Gama.

On March 11, 1894, the Brazilian commander, realizing the futility of further resistance, offered to surrender on condition that his officers should be permitted to leave Brazil and that the lives of the men be spared. Although the minister of foreign affairs as well as the representatives of Portugal, England, France, and Italy agreed that these overtures were acceptable, Floriano rejected them on the grounds that the government could not accept proposals from rebels. On the morning of March 12 the government announced that within forty-eight hours it would undertake energetic operations against the insurgents, utilizing all of the forces at its disposal. The result was a wild stampede on the part of the populace to abandon the capital.

Admiral da Gama had no intention of engaging in a struggle which could only result in the annihilation of the forces under his command. On the 11th of March he asked permission for himself and his men to seek asylum on the two small ships of the Portuguese sqaudron under the command of Captain Castilhos. Such permission was granted, and during the forenoon of the 13th the *Mindello* was invaded by the refugees, an act clearly visible from the other ships in the harbor as well as from the heights of the city. But the government insisted on carrying out its plans; beginning at noon and continuing for an hour and a half the abandoned ships and deserted strongholds of the insurgents were subjected to a terrific bombardment. By nightfall the government forces were in possession of the entire harbor.

The act of Captain Castilhos in granting asylum to the refugees aroused the fury of Floriano. When the Portuguese commander refused to surrender his guests an effort was made to persuade Great Britain to bring pressure to bear on the government at Lisbon. In his reply the British secretary for foreign affairs intimated that her majesty's government would not surrender refugees who had sought asylum on British ships under similar circumstances and that it "would be excessively impolitic" on the part of the Brazilian government to press the matter further with the government of Lisbon. Despite this admonition Floriano insisted on severing diplomatic relations with Portugal, and they were not restored until March 1895. The subsequent conduct of Floriano showed that Castilhos was well-advised in not turning over the refugees to the victors.

The triumph of the government over the insurgents in the harbor of Rio de Janeiro made the collapse of the rebellion inevitable. Gumercindo Saraïva attempted to retreat from Paraná to Rio Grande do Sul but his forces were cut off and he himself was killed. Admiral de Mello's position became desperate. He succeeded in manoeuvering the remnants of his fleet into Argentine waters where he surrendered to the local authorities.

Admiral da Gama, who had sought asylum on the Portuguese fleet, was taken by Castilhos to Buenos Aires, as it was not possible to convey the Brazilians to Europe. Here many of them escaped, including da Gama. In an engagement with the government troops da Gama was defeated and committed suicide. His body was horribly mutilated. Captain Castilhos was tried and acquitted by the supreme court at Lisbon for his share in these unhappy events. The four-volume work which he wrote in his defense entitled *Portugal and Brazil* is one of our best sources for the revolution.

The collapse of the revolt was followed by terrible reprisals. Many of the participants in the rebellion were executed after the merest farce of a trial. Punishment was even inflicted on those who had no share in the revolt but were known to be hostile to Floriano. During the revolution some of the most prominent men of Rio were held *incommunicado* in prisons which remind one of the *piombi* of Venice. While a number of atrocities were perpetrated without the knowledge of the vice president, Floriano cannot be absolved for responsibility for many of the worst acts of what was virtually a reign of terror.

VII

The legal term of office of Floriano Peixoto came to an end on November 15, 1894. Up to the very end predictions were freely made that the vice president, supported by the army, would refuse to surrender his office. To his credit it should be added, however, that he paid no attention to these promptings and quietly turned over the power to his successor, Dr. Prudente de Moraes Barros, at the appointed time.

The character and administration of Floriano still call forth the most divergent views among Brazilian writers. Like his predecessor he was a military despot with all the defects of that type of ruler. Constitutionalism as understood in Europe and the United States had little place in his scheme of things. He governed Brazil as he might have commanded a regiment. Yet it can hardly be denied that he rendered the nation very real service. Like a true soldier he stuck to his post to the very end when a man of less determination might have faltered. The leaders of the naval revolt may command our sympathy and admiration but their triumph would probably have launched Brazil on an endless cycle of civil wars and revolutions. From this point of view, Floriano, with all his faults, deserved well of his country.

CHAPTER TWENTY-ONE

THE HISTORY OF BRAZIL FROM 1892 TO 1914. THE CIVILIAN PRESIDENTS

APPARENTLY better days were at hand for Brazil. The successor of Floriano, as we have seen, was Dr. Prudente José de Moraes Barros, a distinguished lawyer, a republican of long standing, and a son of São Paulo. We have already met him as the unsuccessful contender with Deodoro for election as first constitutional president of Brazil. It was at once made clear by the acts of the new executive that he intended to follow a line of policy as far removed as possible from that of his predecessors. He is accordingly sometimes spoken of as Brazil's first civilian president. He appointed a strong ministry, every member of which, like himself, had a reputation for probity. His important minister of finance, Dr. Rodrigues Alves, was subsequently president of the republic.

The situation in Brazil was indeed difficult. The military elements were thoroughly dissatisfied with Prudente and his methods and threw as many obstacles as possible in his path. The state of the finances, a legacy of his predecessors, was deplorable. The international situation was threatening, with acute boundary controversies with Argentina over the so-called Misiones district, with France over French Guiana, and with Great Britain over the Island of Trindade (not to be confused with the British colony of Trinidad off the mouth of the Orinoco). Prudente was making encouraging progress in the settlement of these vexatious problems when his program was badly disarranged by one of the most curious and sinister episodes in the history of Brazil: the so-called Canudos affair. To this we must briefly address ourselves.

I

The interior of the northern states of Pernambuco and Bahia is made up in part of a strange and mysterious region known as the *sertão,* which means the wooded, back-lying highlands. It is a semi-arid plateau region, afflicted with frequent droughts, with a climate ranging from stifling hot days to chilly nights. The flora chiefly consists of thorny trees and plants known in Brazil as *caatinga,* a Tupi word signifying "bush" or "scrub." R. B. Cunningham-Graham, in his book entitled *A Brazilian Mystic* has drawn a graphic picture of the strange inhabitants of this strange region.

> "All these conditions, together with the isolation in which they have lived for three hundred years have left their impress on the population, making them a race apart—a race of centaurs, deeply imbued with fanaticism, strong, honest, revengeful, primitive, and refractory to modern ideas and life to an extraordinary degree."

The ancestors of the *sertanejos*—as the inhabitants of the *sertão* are called—originally came from good Portuguese stock. But from the earliest colonial times the Portuguese crown neglected the *sertão,* because its only industry was cattle-breeding, in favor of the rich sugar plantations along the coast or the gold mines in distant Minas Geraes or Matto Grosso. There was some intermarriage with the Indians, and later a slight fusion with the negroes. These crossings made the *sertanejo* a still more pronounced type. This backward, ignorant, and isolated community, a little like the more remote, mountainous portions of our own Tennessee or Kentucky, has always been prone to gusts of fanaticism, and it needed only a leader to arouse these benighted people to the heights of a peculiarly dangerous religious frenzy. Such a man was one Antonio Maciel, known to his devoted followers as Conselheiro, or "the Counsellor."

Antonio Vicente Mendes Maciel was born in the *sertão* of Ceará somewhere about the year 1842. As a youth he was timid and retiring and there seems to have been nothing about his young manhood to distinguish him from the thousands of lawyers' clerks and employees of small storekeepers throughout northern rural Brazil. When he was in the twenties an event occurred which completely altered the tenor of his life. Reports of this tragedy vary greatly. According to the one which has received widest circulation his mother cherished a deep enmity against her daughter-in-law. She alleged the woman was unfaithful. To prove her charge she simulated the appearance of her daughter-in-law's lover. Maciel, coming upon this supposed rendezvous, killed both women. He was tried for this double murder but after a short imprisonment was released.

For ten long years he disappeared, another John the Baptist, somewhere in the desert wilds of the *sertão*. When he returned to civilization he was, in the striking phrase of Euclydes da Cunha, "an old man of thirty." He was not mad, and yet not altogether sane, but probably just on that borderland in which dwell saints and visionaries. His fame began to grow, miracles were attributed to him, and presently he was surrounded by a motley horde of followers. These took the name of *Jagunços,* a rough equivalent of "bravos," and soon became noted for their cruelty and fanatical devotion to their leader. They made their headquarters in an abandoned ranch or *fazenda* known as Canudos in the interior of Bahia.

A collision between these fanatics and the civil authorities of Bahia was sooner or later inevitable. Canudos had become an asylum for many of the worst elements of the province. The governor and the religious authorities of Bahia, incensed at the defiant attitude of Conselheiro and his followers, ordered them to vacate Canudos. On their refusal a body of provincial militia was sent against this stronghold and was repulsed. The struggle soon reached such proportions as to make necessary federal reënforcements. An expeditionary body under Colonel Moreira Cesar was overwhelmingly defeated and Cesar himself was killed. The entire county was now raised to a high pitch of excitement. The wildest rumors circulated. It was freely stated that Conselheiro and his men were aiming at a monarchical restoration. Prudente was taxed with being criminally negligent. The followers of the late Floriano Peixoto began to raise their heads. The stability of Prudente's government was seriously menaced. Into the various military campaigns necessary to subdue Canudos we cannot enter. The government continued to pour troops into the region until by September 1897 no fewer than thirteen thousand men were in the field, led by the minister of war himself. Under his direction the attack on Canudos was so skillfully conducted that the settlement was finally captured to the accompaniment of a frightful massacre of the *Jagunços* and the death of Conselheiro. Peace was restored to the troubled *sertão* but at a heavy sacrifice. The various expeditions had been costly in men and money, and the already parlous state of the national finances was further aggravated.

The entire Canudos campaign is one on which Brazilians can look back with very little satisfaction. With a greater degree of tact and understanding the war might have been avoided. The state and national authorities had to pay a heavy price for the neglect of these brave but ignorant dwellers of the *sertão.* One Brazilian told the writer that instead of soldiers, nurses and physicians should have been sent to minister to the rebels. The only lasting good which came out of this whole unhappy business was the enrichment of Brazilian literature by the greatest of its regional novels, *Os Sertões,* by Euclydes da Cunha.[1]

The campaign in the north was accompanied by a dastardly attack on the life of the president. On November 5, 1897, Prudente went to the former war arsenal to welcome a body of troops returning from Canudos. A common soldier attempted to kill him but was overpowered by the bystanders. During the scuffle the minister of war, Marshal Carlos Machado de Bittencourt, popularly known as the "Gold Marshal" *(O Marechal de Ouro)* was stabbed and died shortly afterwards from his wounds. The impression caused by this criminal attack was tremendous. The would-be assassin, who promptly committed suicide, was of course in the employ of higher-ups. Martial law was declared and many arrests were made, including three senators and four deputies. Other suspects escaped in foreign ships. If morally the exaggerations and excesses of the parliamentary opposition and the recrudescence of militarism were responsible for this crime, its perpetrators far overshot the mark. The enemies of Prudente, whether innocent or guilty, were avoided by everyone; parliamentary opposition virtually ceased, and the last year of the president's administration was calm. Prudente is remembered in Brazilian history as an honest and capable executive, possibly too rigid and unyielding in his views, who courageously faced a number of difficult problems not of his own choosing. He is now recognized as one of the great figures of republican Brazil.

II

Manuel Ferraz de Campos Salles (1898-1902), the second civilian president of Brazil, was like his predecessor, a son of São Paulo, and was president of that state at the time of his election on March 1, 1898. His motto was "peace and economy" *(paz e economia),* and he strove with some success to translate these ideals into acts. Even before he assumed office he had gained a certain initiation into Brazilian national finance. His predecessor, as we have already seen, was reaping the financal whirlwind sown by the provisional government and aggravated by the expenses incurred in the Canudos campaign. In fact, the last year of Prudente's term found the country at the end of its financial rope. There was no money in the treasury to meet the interest on Brazil's foreign obligations, and bonds were declining in the London

[1] "From the point of view of economic history the drama of Canudos belongs to the long series of events leading to the opening of the interior of the country and the moving of the frontier." Normano MS.

market. Under these circumstances Prudente requested the president-elect to proceed to Europe and to make some arrangement with Brazil's creditors that would avert the calamity of a suspension of payments. This mission Campos Salles performed with brilliant success. His engaging presence, his patent sincerity, and his promise that Brazil would mend her ways financially made him *persona grata* in the London financial marts, particularly with the Rothschilds, the chief bankers of Brazil. Through his skillful negotiations was arranged the famous funding loan —called in Brazil *o funding*—of June 15, 1898. By the terms of this loan Brazil was able to dispose of her bonds at par for a total of £8,613,717, a financial success equalled only once before in the history of the country. These bonds were to bear interest at five per cent with one-half per cent amortization, and run for sixty-three years, the loan being secured by the collection in gold of import duties. And what was fully as important, interest payments in species were to be suspended for three years—their place being taken by bonds—and amortization suspended for ten years. Thus did Brazil enjoy a financial breathing spell of which she stood in sore need.

The administration of Campos Salles is chiefly remembered for the faithful and successful execution of the measures needed to put the credit and finances of the country on a sound basis. The honors are to be divided, however, with his minister of finance, Dr. Joaquim Murtinho, one of the ablest financiers produced by Brazil. In many ways Murtinho was the antithesis of Ruy Barbosa. Ruy was impassioned, brilliant, cultured, but erratic. He still had laurels to win for Brazil at the Second Hague Conference, and like our own Henry Clay he unsuccessfully aspired to the presidency. Murtinho, physician and scientist (he had specialized in chemistry), was calm, logical and insistent. He was born in distant Matto Grosso. He had something in him of the level-headed French provincial. He fought savagely against inflation through the issue of paper money, and as Dr. Normano has pointed out, his attempts at financial equilibrium recall vividly the contemporaneous activity of the great Russian minister of finance, Sergius Witte. He went so far as to burn large quantities of the paper currency, and when the first specie payments were due under the funding loan in 1901, there was deposited in gold in London more than enough to meet Brazil's obligations.

During Campos Salles' administration Brazil was represented at the second International Conference of American States at Mexico City. Her relations with Argentina were strengthened through an elaborate exchange of visits with President Roca. The difficult boundary controversy with French Guiana was settled in a manner highly advantageous to the nation. This latter episode, however, we may more conveniently discuss when we take up as a whole the settlement of Brazil's boundary disputes.

III

The third and perhaps the greatest of the civilian presidents was Dr. Francisco de Paula Rodrigues Alves, like his two predecessors, a son of São Paulo. Under the empire he had been deputy of his province, had been federal senator in the early days of the republic, and was president of São Paulo at the time he was elected to the office of chief magistrate of Brazil. Thanks to his ability, energy, and intelligence his four years in office (1902-1906) were perhaps the most prosperous in the history of the republic. Had it not been, however, for the marvelous recuperative power of Brazil and the foundations laid by his predecessors his achievements would hardly have been possible.

Perhaps the greatest accomplishment of Rodrigues Alves was the transformation of Rio de Janeiro into one of the most beautiful capitals in the world. Despite also the fact that the city had a population of 600,000 and was the capital and metropolis of Brazil, it had many of the aspects of an overgrown colonial town. The business section of the city was badly congested and ill-served with narrow streets; the possibilities of a superb waterfront were totally neglected, and the harbor facilities quite inadequate for Brazil's growing commerce. All of this was to change. Under the able direction of Dr. Francisco Pereira Passos, prefect of the Federal District, a magnificent avenue known as the *Avenida Rio Branco* was cut through the heart of the congested business district; strictly modern port-works were installed; and along the ocean and bay was flung a system of magnificent boulevards. Rio de Janeiro at length became worthy of its incomparable natural setting.

Still more was accomplished. At the beginning of Dr. Rodrigues Alves' term of office, Rio was one of the most unhealthy cities in the Western Hemisphere. Yellow fever, which had probably been imported from Africa around 1850 by one of the ships engaged in the slave trade, had become almost endemic. While the Brazilians themselves had acquired a certain amount of immunity, the disease was especially virulent among the foreign elements, particularly the diplomatic corps. During the Brazilian summer (from December to February) those who could took up their residence in the elevated and healthy city of Petropolis, located just over the rim of the coast range. It has been estimated that from 1850 to 1889 yellow fever caused the death of no less than 15,557 persons, the majority between the ages of twenty-four and forty-five. As late as 1894 there were 4,852 cases, and in 1902, the year that Rodrigues Alves assumed power, there were 982 deaths. It was alleged that Brazil was polluting all of Hispanic America. According to official statistics the average mortality per 1,000 inhabitants in the urban zone in and about Rio de Janeiro for 1902 was 28.86.

With the appointment of Dr. Oswaldo Cruz to the highly responsible post of director of public health, the measures for the extinction of yellow fever took on a new direction. Dr. Cruz had been a disciple of Pasteur and had followed with close interest the successful efforts of the United States to cope with tropical diseases in Havana and the Canal Zone. He had become convinced that disinfection and isolation, though important in themselves, were ineffective and that the transmission of the disease was by the stegomyia mosquito. He, therefore, requested the government to pass drastic sanitary regulations and secured authorization to form a brigade of 1,500 men—popularly known as "mosquito-killers"—which forcibly, if need be, cleaned up infected spots. Despite opposition and ridicule, Dr. Cruz, supported by the president, carried on his campaign ruthlessly and efficiently. The results were spectacular. In 1903, the year the campaign was initiated, the number of deaths had dropped to five hundred and eighty-four, in 1904 to forty-eight, in 1908 to forty, and for the year 1909 no deaths were reported—this despite excessive heat and the arrival of some 46,000 immigrants. In its gratitude the government constructed a model laboratory on the outskirts of the city which is known as the *Instituto Oswaldo Cruz.*

IV

The administration of Rodrigues Alves is also notable for the settlement of some of Brazil's most vexatious boundary disputes, and the subject as a whole may well be discussed here. On the advent of the republic, Brazil had controversies with most of her neighbors. The district known as the Misiones *(as Missões)* had been the object of dispute with Argentina for some time. An attempt to settle it was made as early as the treaty of Madrid of 1750, and was renewed under Dom Pedro II, who just at the end of his reign proposed the arbitration of the United States. Under the provisional government, attempts were made to settle the dispute by direct negotiations but the Brazilian congress refused to ratify a treaty signed by Quintino Bocayuva in

1890. The question was finally submitted to the arbitration of President Grover Cleveland, who rendered his decision on February 5, 1895, during the presidency of Prudente de Moraes Barros. Brazil's cause was brilliantly represented by José Maria da Silva Paranhos, baron of Rio Branco and son of the Viscount of Rio Branco, author of the famous law of "free birth" of 1871. The award was almost wholly in favor of Brazil. There were also difficulties with the French republic over the boundaries with French Guiana, but this difficulty was likewise settled by arbitration by the Swiss federal council. The claims of Brazil were set forth by Rio Branco, and the decision which was handed down in 1900 was also regarded as favorable to Brazil.

Partly as a result of these triumphs Rio Branco was selected by Rodrigues Alves as minister of foreign affairs, a position which he held during the administration of four presidents, until his death in 1912. One may say that his policy had a double object: to increase Brazilian prestige abroad and to further continental harmony. Shortly after his appointment all of his tact and skill were needed for the solution of one of the most thorny problems which Brazil has ever been called upon to grapple. Not all of its details are even yet fully known. The reference is to the controversy with Bolivia over the Acre district.

The district of the Acre is a roughly triangle-shaped territory, lying adjacent to the head waters of the Amazon River, particularly to the east of its confluent, the Javary. The inhabitants at this period were mostly Brazilians who had trekked into this region on account of the terrific and long-continued droughts of Ceará. The writer, Ildefonso Albano, has given us a graphic picture of this hegira.

> "This slow, patient, and heroic work consumed the flower of the population of northeastern Brazil. But the new *bandeirantes,* obscure and persistent, bore through the Amazon forests, advance, and gain ground day by day. The number of the victims runs into thousands, but the conquered soil becomes Brazilian. The Acre won with the rifle is Brazilian, because Brazilian are the remains of the human skeletons which whiten that vast cemetery. This is the modern epic poem, written . . . with ink of blood but in letters of gold."

Although a portion of this region was claimed by Brazil, the greater part of the territory belonged to Bolivia. The attempt on the part of the Bolivians to establish in 1899 a customhouse at Porto Alonso on the Acre was the occasion of a revolt on the part of the inhabitants who set up the independent state of Acre *(Estado Independente do*

Acre), with the eventual hope of annexation to Brazil. Naturally the Bolivians sought to put down the revolt, and a vessel with arms and supplies was fitted out in Europe and was despatched by way of the Amazon directly to Porto Alonso. The Brazilian authorities, however, refused transit to this vessel over Brazilian waterways. Partly as a consequence, tension between Bolivia and Brazil steadily grew and there was a real likelihood of an outbreak of hostilities. Especially was this the case after the Bolivians in 1901 turned the Acre over to the so-called Bolivian Syndicate, an Anglo-American concern, invested with almost sovereign rights over the region. This act was the occasion for a second insurrection in the Acre, and renewed appeals to the government of Rio. With some difficulty, and after many negotiations, the Brazilian authorities, with a payment of £110,000, induced the Bolivian Syndicate to withdraw from the Acre. There now remained the still more difficult problem of dealing with the government of Bolivia. Here Rio Banco showed great skill. By the treaty of Petropolis of November 17, 1903, Bolivia ceded to Brazil her claims to the Acre for the sum of two millions pounds sterling and agreed to construct about the falls of the Madeira River the Madeira-Mamoré Railway, thus giving the vast hinterland of Bolivia access to the Amazon valley and the Atlantic. There were other clauses as well, chiefly of a commercial nature. Such importance did Rio Branco attach to this treaty that he cabled the text to Professor John Bassett Moore of Columbia University before he would sign it.

The other achievements of Rio Branco may be briefly noted. He reorganized and strengthened the foreign service. He insisted that Brazil be adequately represented at international gatherings, particularly of a Pan American character. In the year 1905 he obtained for his country the first South American cardinalate, the Archbishop of Rio, Dom Joaquim Arcoverde de Albuquerque Cavalcanti, being raised to this dignity. He was directly responsible for the negotiation of a notable series of arbitration treaties. He took the unusual step of persuading congress to grant to Uruguay joint jurisdiction over the boundary waters of the Juguarão River and Lake Mirim. Through his efforts the Brazilian legation at Washington was raised to the rank of an embassy. He believed in the Monroe Doctrine but felt it should be maintained collectively by all the American nations. He was the greatest minister of foreign affairs of the Brazilian republic and his death on February 10, 1912, was regarded as a national calamity.

Aside from the holding of the Third Pan American Conference in

Rio de Janeiro in 1906, made notable by the presence of United States Secretary of State Elihu Root, one other event of international significance occurred during the presidency of Rodrigues Alves. Since the middle of the nineteenth century there had existed a sporadic controversy with Great Britain over the boundaries between Brazil and British Guiana. In 1901, the last year of the Campos Salles administration, the problem was submitted to the King of Italy for arbitration. The rights of Brazil were ably presented by Joaquim Nabuco. In his decision, however, Victor Emmanuel III rejected the claims of Brazil based on priority of discovery, and declared that possession was effective only when *non interrompue et permanente,* a condition, he alleged not fully met by Brazil. He finally declared that since it was not possible, owing to lack of geographical data on the region, to divide the contested territory into two parts equal in extent and value, he would follow the lines traced by nature, preferably the watershed. The consequence of this decision was a loss of from half to two-thirds of the territory claimed by Brazil. It was a keen disappointment to the nation and naturally to Nabuco, although it reflects no discredit either on his diligence or his ability.

IV

The administration of Dr. Affonso Augusto Moreira Penna (1906-1909) may be passed rapidly in review. Unlike his three predecessors he was not a Paulista but a native of the great state of Minas Geraes. During the empire he had been active in politics; he had represented Minas in the constituent assembly; had served as vice president of his native state and vice president of the republic in 1903. His administration is remembered for a number of achievements of Brazil in both the foreign and domestic fields. In 1907 took place the Second Hague Conference, to which Dr. Ruy Barbosa was sent as the head of the Brazilian delegation. In the work of the various commissions as well as in the plenary sessions Barbosa played a conspicuous and at times brilliant part. His chief fear was that the right of the smaller nations, particularly those of America, should not receive their full recognition. His numerous speeches, cabled to Brazil, were followed with passionate interest and great pride by the Brazilian people.

The international relations of Brazil with her great South American neighbor Argentina were perhaps less happy at this time, due in part to Brazil's naval program. As a result of the destruction of the *Aquidaban* through an accident in 1906, Brazil's navy had been reduced to a single obsolete ship, the *Riachuelo.* Such a situation, in the opinion of the government, called for remedy. The year 1908 will be memorable in the history of Brazil as marking the inauguration of her modern naval policy. When it became known that she had placed orders in England for a number of warships, including at least two dreadnoughts, there was a great sensation and much speculation as to the purpose of these ships. It was declared by many that the navy was intended to be used against Argentina, Brazil's most formidable rival in South America. Dr. Zeballos, the Argentine ex-minister of foreign affairs, and a noted publicist, was the mouthpiece of this type of criticism, and there was a disposition in certain quarters to discover an intense rivalry, if not hostility, between him and Rio Branco. Fortunately, any feeling of hostility between the two countries was largely confined to the less responsible members of the press and was not of long duration.

One of the outstanding achievements of Affonso Penna was in the domain of finance. Brazil had long suffered from fluctuations in her currency in terms of foreign money. For the double purpose of stabilizing the rate of exchange and of gradually putting Brazil on a gold basis, there was opened in December 1906 the *Caixa de Conversão,* or bank of conversion. Its chief function was to issue paper money against gold deposited with it at a fixed rate of fifteen pence, or about thirty cents in gold for each *milreis*. This institution soon proved its usefulness, and had conditions remained normal would have been of inestimable benefit to the country. By 1912 the convertible notes of the *Caixa da Conversão* had risen to more than two-thirds of the value of the inconvertible paper. Unfortunately, the outbreak of the World War brought the usefulness of the *Caixa* to an end. Immense issues of unsecured paper had to be issued at that time to help Brazil tide over the crisis, and the notes of the *Caixa* all but disappeared from circulation.

President Penna did not live to complete his term of office. He had never enjoyed robust health and died on June 14, 1909. The remainder of his term, approximately a year and a half, was filled out by the vice president, Dr. Nilo Peçanha, whom we shall meet again later as minister of foreign affairs when Brazil became involved in the World War.

Since the advent of Prudente de Moraes Barros in 1894 Brazil had been governed by a series of able civilian presidents. The curve of progress had been steadily rising. Some of Brazil's most difficult political, diplomatic, and economic problems had apparently been successfully solved. The excesses of the early days of the republic and the civil war of 1893 seemed like some hideous nightmare. The future was apparently unclouded. The next four years were to show, however, that such optimism was hardly justified and that Brazil had still far to go on the road towards real democracy.

V

The campaign of 1910 was a memorable one in the history of the republic. Since the days of Prudente, or even earlier, the outgoing president, through his control of the electoral machinery, and by virtue of his position in the dominant political party, had usually succeeded in nominating his successor. President Affonso Penna was no exception to the rule. He had selected as his successor his able minister of finance, David Campista. But his choice was not agreeable to the political party in control, known as the Republican Conservative Party. To rid themselves of Campista, its leaders suddenly conceived the importance of a nominating convention to be appointed by congress whose majority they controlled. To this procedure the delegates from São Paulo, Minas Geraes, and in part from Bahia refused to agree, alleging that since congress was the final arbiter of elections it could not fairly put forward for nomination its own candidate. Nonetheless, the convention met and nominated Marshal Hermes da Fonseca, nephew of Deodoro, the revolutionary chief of the republic and first president. His nomination was partly due to the influence of an astute and able political boss from Rio Grande do Sul, one Pinheiro Machado.

It is clear now that the nomination of Hermes represented a retrogression in Brazilian politics. As secretary of war under President Penna, Hermes had shown some military capacity, but he was poor presidential material. Although the lines were at first not clearly drawn, it became evident as the campaign progressed that the old military element was striving once more to gain political supremacy. Such an attempt could not pass unchallenged. The representatives of the three bolting states and some others now determined to nominate an opposition candidate. Brazil was accordingly divided into some one thousand electoral districts, each entitled to send a delegate. Five hundred and twenty-eight such delegates met at the *Theatro Lyrico* on May 22, 1910, and at the first regular nominating convention in the history of Brazil the *Civilista* Party was born. As standard-bearer was chosen Ruy Barbosa, the minister of finance in the provisional government, the father of the constitution, the representative of Brazil at the Second Hague Conference, and probably the most learned and eloquent public man in Brazil.

As candidate of the new party Ruy Barbosa stumped the country, a procedure hitherto unknown in Brazilian political life. In his numerous and brilliant speeches he flayed the concentration of power in the hands of an irresponsible political clique, he attacked the failure of the so-called representative government really to represent the people, and finally inveighed in the strongest terms against the menace of the military. When the election took place Hermes won by 233,882 votes over 126,-292 given to Ruy Barbosa. The supporters of Ruy asserted that they had been defrauded of the election through corruption and duress at the polls. The writer has interviewed a number of Brazilians on this point and confesses that he is unable to reach any conclusion.

As was to be expected, the four years of Hermes' administration (1910-1914) was a marked decline from the high level set by the civilian presidents. Hermes was a soldier but he had neither the prestige of his uncle, Deodoro, nor the persistence of Floriano. He was kindly, good-natured, and prone to follow the counsels of those who last had his ear. Of administrative ability he had little. Corruption and extravagance began to invade the administration. Although outwardly the civilians held the majority of public offices, in reality the influence of the military became more and more paramount.

The financial policies of Hermes proved to be disastrous. An attempt to valorize coffee in São Paulo has been attended, as we shall see later, with a qualified success. When the rubber industry, the chief support of Amazonia, was threatened with ruin through extravagant and faulty measures of production and above all through competition of the plantation grown rubber of the Far East, an ambitious scheme of subvention and aid was launched, the so-called *defesa da borracha*. This attempt to "valorize" rubber proved to be a total and costly failure and brought discredit on the government of Hermes.

Despite these financial aberrations the four years from 1910 to 1914 witnessed an almost uninterrupted progress in the economic development of the country. Immigration was encouraged through government subvention and other means; everywhere was raised the cry of *falta de braços* ("lack of hands"). During the years 1911, 1912, and 1913 immigration reached the record figures of 136,000, 180,000, and 192,000 respectively. During Hermes' term of office nearly 3,000 miles of railway was added to existing systems. Yet all of this progress was accompanied by a mounting national debt, and it need occasion no surprise that the financial situation in Hermes' last year of office became so difficult that in 1914 he was forced to an issue of inconvertible paper money, and on October 19, 1914 a second funding loan had to be contracted in London. But the responsibility for these last disastrous financial expedients must not be laid wholly at the door of Hermes. Before the end of his term of office the European War had broken out, and in the financial dislocation which followed, Brazil was bound to suffer. To a consideration of this great catastrophe and its effect on Brazil we now address ourselves.

CHAPTER TWENTY-TWO

THE WORLD WAR AND ITS AFTERMATH

THE four years of the World War coincided with the presidency of Senhor Wenceslau Braz Pereira Gomes. Though he had been the candidate of the same forces that had supported the candidacy of Hermes da Fonseca, namely the so-called Republican Conservative Party, he was a civilian, a native of Minas Geraes, and an administrator of ability. As president of his native state he had acquitted himself with distinction. As vice president during Hermes' term of office he had been the object of insult and slanders, but he had held his peace under extreme provocation. His abilities and forbearance were now to stand him in excellent stead.

I

The immediate effect of the war on Brazil was disastrous. The price of coffee and rubber, which had already begun to sink, went lower. In common with a number of other Hispanic American countries Brazil derives much of her national income from import duties, and these were naturally much curtailed; in fact the value of imports for 1914 fell to but a little over half the value in the preceding year. The economic and financial situation was further aggravated by a corresponding decline in exports, taxes on which formed one of the chief sources of revenues of a number of the Brazilian states. New sources of revenue had to be tapped, but when these proved to be inadequate, Brazil fell back once more on the vicious expedient of issuing unsecured paper money. As already intimated, the activities of the *Caixa da Conversão* had to be suspended. Under these adverse conditions the government found it impossible to meet the interest on its foreign obligations. As out-and-out repudiation was in every way undesirable, in October 1914 an agreement was made with Brazil's foreign creditors for a funding loan of fifteen million pounds sterling, the bonds of which met the interest due on the foreign debt until 1917 when regular specie payment was resumed.

It is not my intention to take up in detail the financial history of Brazil during the four years of Wenceslau Braz's administration.

Thanks in part to the vigorous and able policy of the minister of finance, Dr. Pandiá Calogeras, the most difficult of the problems were solved. Every effort was made to reduce public expenses. Through revision and special arrangements, contacts and responsibilities to which the government was a party were cut down some 500,000 *contos,* which meant a saving of about one hundred million dollars at the current rate of exchange. The large floating debt was consolidated. The quotations on the public debt, both in Brazil and abroad, remained high. Of course, this relatively favorable financial showing was due also to the expansion of exports after 1915 and the growing demand on the part of the United States and the Allies for Brazilian products.

II

Of greater interest to us is the diplomatic and political history of Brazil during this difficult period. On the outbreak of the war in 1914 Brazil quite properly declared her neutrality. This did not mean, however, that she was indifferent to the struggle. The sympathies of the vast majority of the Brazilians gravitated towards the Allies and particularly towards France. The cultural indebtedness of Hispanic America towards France was particularly marked in the case of Brazil. Her educational system had been largely based on French models, and French textbooks were widely used in the higher schools. For most Brazilians, France was a sort of second *patria.* The remaining European Allies also had their strong partisians in Brazil. Commercial and financial relations with Great Britain had been intimate and of long standing, as we have already seen. After the entry of Italy into the war the large Italian population, especially in the coffee state of São Paulo, naturally espoused the cause of the Allies. For sentimental reasons the unhappy plight of Belgium aroused great sympathy in Brazil. On the other hand there were large and influential Teutonic elements in Brazil, due to heavy immigration around the middle of the nineteenth century. In fact, the minister of foreign affairs, Dr. Lauro Müller, was the son of one of these German colonists. As early as 1915 sympathy for the nations composing the Entente crystallized into an organization known as the Brazilian League for the Allies, with Ruy Barbosa as president. Prior to Brazil's participation in the war the league confined its efforts to the creation of new currents of sympathy for the Allies and to the alleviation of suffering in the stricken regions of Europe. After Brazil entered the war it naturally greatly expanded its activities; perhaps its most useful service was its intensive campaign of public education on the issue of the war.

Causes of friction between Brazil and Germany early began to multiply. The growing intensity of the ship famine stimulated sentiment in favor of the requisition of the forty-six German vessels lying idle in Brazilian harbors, a course of action persistently urged by the powerful and influential *Jornal do Commercio.* Brazil was one of the few Hispanic American powers possessing a merchant marine of respectable proportions, and with the existing dearth of shipping found it profitable and even necessary to maintain regular communication with Europe. But on January 31, 1917, as is well known, the imperial German government announced the blockade of the coast of the Allied countries enforced by a system of unrestricted submarine warfare. This act led to a vigorous protest on the part of the Brazilian government, which left to the imperial German government "responsibility for all events which may happen to Brazilian citizens, merchandise or ships, as a result of abandonment of the recognized principles of international law."

No attention was apparently paid to this protest. On April 5, 1917, one day before the United States declared war on Germany, a German submarine sank the Brazilian ship *Paraná* off the coast of France without warning of any kind. The indignation of the Brazilian populace was intense. In the light of its previous declaration the government could do no less than sever diplomatic relations, an act which took place on April 11 when Herr von Pauli, the German minister, received his passports. The vigorous action of the government met with general approval in Brazil. It was also calculated to strengthen the traditional friendship between Brazil and the United States, since the attitude of Brazil was quite in harmony with the hope expressed by President Wilson on our suspension of diplomatic relations that "other neutral powers will find it possible to assume the same position as that assumed by the United States of America."

There was a growing feeling that the mere severance of diplomatic relations would have to be followed by more drastic action. The government itself gave intimations that changes in Brazil's official status were impending. The resignation on May 3 of Lauro Müller as minister of foreign affairs and the assumption a few days later of this important portfolio by Dr. Nilo Peçanha, the ex-president of the country, clearly revealed a stiffening of the attitude of the administration. Still more significant was a special message to congress of President Wenceslau Braz on May 22, designed to clarify an anomalous position which had arisen between Brazil and the United States. The North American republic had declared war against Germany on April 7, and four days later Brazil, as we have seen, severed diplomatic relations. In spite of this action the Brazilian government on April 25 issued a decree proclaiming Brazil's neutrality in the war between the United States and Germany. The alleged reason for this decree was the unwillingness of the executive to proceed further without the sanction of congress. In his message of May 22 the president stated:

> "The government could go no further than this; but the Brazilian nation, through its legislative organ, can . . . adopt the attitude that one of the belligerents [that is, the United States] forms an integral part of the American continent; and that to this belligerent we are bound by a similarity of political opinion in defense of the vital interests of America and the principles accepted by international law."

This revocation of neutrality was duly sanctioned by congress, and the decree was signed by President Wenceslau Braz on June 1, 1917. This act is rightly regarded as an event of real significance in the history of Brazilian-United States relations. Friendship between the two largest countries of North and South America had become a tradition reaching back nearly a century. It will be recalled that the United States was the first foreign power to recognize the Brazilian empire, this event taking place on May 26, 1824. During the fifties there was some friction between the two countries over the opening of the Amazon to the world's commerce, and in the early sixties a controversy arose over the attitude of the imperial authorities towards Confederate raiders. These periods of coolness were happily short-lived. In the latter days of the Civil War, President Lincoln, on refusing offers of mediation from some of the European powers, is reported to have declared that if mediation should ever be acceptable it would only be that of the Emperor Dom Pedro II of Brazil. When the *Alabama* claims were submitted to arbitration by the United States and Great Britain, Dom Pedro named one of the arbitrators, the Viscount of Itajubá. Dom Pedro's visit to the United States in 1876, his journey to California, and the keen interest he took in our educational institutions are still remembered. On the establishment of the republic in 1889 the United States was the first great power to recognize Brazil. At the present juncture the Brazilian government went to particular pains to point out the true significance of the revocation of Brazilian neutrality. The pertinent sentences in President Wenceslau Braz's note have been frequently reprinted but they merit repetition here.

> "The Republic has thus recognized that one of the belligerents is an integral part of the American continent and that we are bound to this belligerent by a traditional friendship and by a similarity of political opinion in the defense of the vital interests of America, and the principles accepted by international law.
>
> "Brazil never had and still has no war-like ambitions, and if she always abstained from any partiality in the European conflict, she could not remain indifferent to it, when the United States was drawn into the struggle without any interest therein, but in the name alone of respect for international law, and when Germany extended indiscriminately to ourselves and other neutrals the most violent acts of war.
>
> "If hitherto the relative lack of reciprocity on the part of the American republics has withdrawn from the Monroe Doctrine its true character, permitting a scarcely well-informed interpretation of the prerogatives of their sovereignty, the present crisis, by placing Brazil, even now, at the side of the United States, in the critical moment of the world's history, continue to give our foreign policy a practical form of continental solidarity—a policy indeed which was that of the old *régime* on every occasion on which any of the other friendly sister nations of the American continent were in jeopardy."

During the summer and early fall of 1917 a number of acts of the government presaged Brazil's early entrance into the war. On June 1 a decree was signed by the president for the utilization of German ships lying in Brazilian harbors, and on the following day they were taken over by the government, which was at pains to state that it was a question, not of confiscation but of utilization in accordance with the principles of the Hague Convention of 1907. This was a distinction which later, at the Peace Conference, was to cause Brazil no little embarrassment. On June 28 the president signed a decree revoking Brazilian neutrality in the war between Germany and the principal allied powers. The Brazilian merchant marine, augmented by the ex-German ships, were now guarded by the war vessels of both the United States and the Allies. The situation was of course fraught with alarming possibilities. On October 23 word reached Brazil that the steamer *Macau* had been torpedoed off the Spanish coast by a German submarine. On the next day the president sent a special message to congress; after noting that all told four Brazilian ships had been sunk, he declared that by these acts a state of war had in effect been imposed on

Brazil and that it only remained for her to take such action as might be necessary "to maintain uninjured the dignity of the nation." On October 26 congress passed all but unanimously a resolution which "recognized and proclaimed the state of war initiated by the German government against Brazil." Thus did Brazil, alone among the South American republics, definitely and unequivocally, align herself with the United States and the Allies in the World War.

It must be admitted that from the military and naval point of view the participation of Brazil in the war was rather platonic. Aside from a few aviators, no Brazilian soldiers were to be found on the western front. This fact was due largely to the dearth of transports and the fact that considerable sections of the army were employed to check possible disorders in Brazil. The navy was somewhat more active. Immediately after Brazil's entry into the war it assumed partial responsibility for the patrol of the South Atlantic. In the summer of 1918 a fleet composed of scout cruisers and destroyers under the command of Admiral Pedro Max de Frontin was given exclusive charge of the patrol of certain portions of the African coast much frequented by Allied ships proceeding from South America. Late in the autumn the fleet was transferred to the Mediterranean for more active service; it arrived at Gibraltar on November 10 but the armistice signed the following day put an end to all hope of further operations against the enemy.

III

In the domestic life of Brazil the war wrought a number of important changes. At the suggestion of the president, congress passed on November 16, 1917 the so-called War Law *(Lei da Guerra)*, investing the government with a number of extraordinary powers of which perhaps the most important was the authorization to declare any part of the republic in a state of siege. This provision was particularly aimed at the suppression of possible disorders in the three southern states of Panamá, Santa Catherina, and Rio Grande do Sul, where the bulk of the German population was concentrated. A great deal had been written before the war, and much of it foolishly, regarding the alleged designs of Germany on southern Brazil. Yet it was not all vaporings of Pan German chauvinists. In 1910 the eminent economist, von Schmoller, in his work *Handels und Machtpolitik* wrote:

> "We must desire that at any cost a German country containing some twenty or thirty million Germans may grow up in the coming century in South Brazil—and that, too, no matter whether it re-

mains a portion of Brazil or becomes an independent state or enters into close relationship with our empire. Unless our connection with Brazil is always secured by ships of war, and unless Germany is able to exercise pressure there, our future development is threatened."

At first sight there appears to have been some reason for German alarm. A population of Teutonic extraction estimated at from a quarter to half a million seemed to be firmly entrenched in one of the most fertile regions of the republic. German immigration, much of it officially subsidized, had come into Brazil in considerable quantities, especially around the middle of the nineteenth century. And with the repeal in 1896 of the von der Heydt rescript of 1859, which had prohibited subsidized immigration, there had come a new influx of German settlers and businessmen.

In reality the persistence of certain centers of German nationalism in the three southern states was due to a considerable extent to the neglect shown by the Brazilian authorities. In the more compact communities little attempt was made to assimilate the foreign elements. In matters of education the state authorities were especially delinquent. Schools, many of them the recipients of subsidies from Germany, were subject to practically no state control. In some districts not even the third generation of these German settlers could speak Portuguese. It was small wonder, therefore, if Brazilian life and culture were often looked upon with indifference if not contempt by the descendants of these German immigrants.

Under these circumstances the Brazilian government easily persuaded itself that southern Brazil represented a real danger spot. A number of regiments were despatched to these regions and martial law was declared in the three southern states as well as in Rio de Janeiro, São Paulo, and the Federal District. Newspapers and letters were censored and eventually newspapers printed in German were suppressed. Some seven hundred Germans were interned.

These forehanded actions of the authorities, though inevitable, were probably unnecessary. In the light of events it can hardly be doubted that the sympathies of the Teuto-Brazilians, especially those of the second and third generations, inclined towards Brazil. Even before Brazil formally entered the war, protestations of loyalty from widely separated districts poured in on the government. Only in the larger coast cities, such as Rio Grande do Sul and Porto Alegre, where the large business houses were in the hands of the Germans, did Brazil's entry into the war cause any strong reaction in favor of Germany. In the final instance the German menace in Southern Brazil was potential rather than active. A decisive defeat of the Allies and the United States in the war, coupled with the advent to power in Germany of the Pan German elements, might conceivably have spelled for Brazil the loss of one or more of her southern states.

The law of November 16, 1917 (the war law) had a number of other provisions of some importance which cannot be discussed here. It provided for the cancellation of contracts with the enemy, and the sequestration of enemy goods, and the liquidation of or control *(fiscalização)* over German financial, commercial, and industrial enterprises. In carrying out this law the executive showed a moderation which was lacking in the case of a number of belligerents; especially was this true as regards the German banks to which special concessions were granted. On the conclusion of the war these various enterprises were turned back to their owners with the minimum of friction.

The most important contribution of Brazil towards the winning of the war was the increase of her foodstuffs and the placing of them at the disposition of the Allies and the United States. Much of this would have been done even had Brazil remained neutral, but the process was doubtless accelerated by entry into the war. In this regard a few statistics are enlightening. The export of beans, which in 1915 had slightly exceeded $24,000 in value, rose in 1917 to over $10,000,000; the value of the sugar exported in the same period showed an increase from $3,000,000 to $17,000,000; and most striking of all, refrigerated beef registered an increase in value from slightly over $1,500,000 to over $15,000,000. Obviously some of this increase is to be attributed to the rise in prices. Yet in the case of chilled beef, at least, the increase in quantity was almost equally imposing. In 1914, one ton was exported; in 1915, 8,500 tons; in 1916, 33,600 tons; and in 1917, 66,400 tons. The distribution of these food supplies was, after August 1918, placed partly in the hands of a Commission of Public Alimentation, at the head of which was Dr. Leopoldo de Bulhões, the able minister of finance under President Rodrigues Alves.

IV

Among the Hispanic American powers entitled to representation at the peace conference, Brazil easily played the most important rôle. As head of her distinguished delegation was Senator Epitacio Pessôa, former member of the supreme court and later president of Brazil.

Among the other members were Dr. Olyntho de Magalhães, Brazilian minister to France; Professor Rodrigo Octavio L. de Menezes, one of the foremost legal authorities in South America and the secretary-general of the delegation, and Dr. Helio Lobo, Brazilian consul-general in London and a recognized authority on the diplomatic history of Brazil. It was assumed by many that Ruy Barbosa would be one of the delegates, but unfortunately personal and political difficulties prevented his appointment.

Despite the fact that Brazil was represented on a number of important committees, notably on the committee on the League of Nations, her interests in the conference were largely confined to two questions, for her, of major importance. These were the settlement by Germany for the stocks of Brazilian coffee seized by the late imperial government in various ports in its control, and the disposition of the forty-three German vessels which Brazil had requisitioned and utilized during the war to alleviate the shipping famine. The first of these questions was easily settled by the German government's agreement to place at the disposal of the Brazilian government the proceeds of the sale of this coffee on the signing of peace.

The second question proved to be both complicated and vexatious. Of the Brazilian ships taken over by Brazil, thirty had been leased to France at what the Brazilians regarded as very reasonable terms. When the subject of the ex-German ships was broached in the conference the Brazilian delegates insisted that Brazil should be allowed to retain the ships. This contention was rejected by the finance commission of the conference. M. Loucheur, minister of reconstruction and chairman of this commission, informed Senhor Pessôa that the commission was determined to distribute among the allies, in proportion to their losses, all those ex-German ships which had been sequestered or requisitioned by the belligerent and neutral nations. As Brazil had suffered comparatively few maritime losses she would naturally gain very little by this arrangement.

Naturally the proposed action met with the determined opposition of Senhor Pessôa and his colleagues. France, he asserted, had acknowledged Brazil's title to the ships when she had leased them. He further pointed out that the United States had also tactitly recognized Brazil's right of ownership when she offered to buy the vessels from Brazil. Senhor Pessôa went so far as to write directly to Lloyd George and President Wilson, stating to the former that Brazil would refuse to sign the peace treaty if it should embody the decision of the finance commission in regard to the ships. As a matter of fact the Council on March 8, 1919 adopted a protocol giving the allied and associated governments the full right of property and use of the ships "captured, seized, or retained during the war." President Wilson and Lloyd George signed this without reservation. Not so Clemenceau, who accepted it only in so far as it applied to the United States.

This action by the French premier was naturally ill-received in Brazil and resulted in a feeling of resentment against France and all her works. The Brazilian delegation, meanwhile, refused to abate in the slightest degree its demands. Finally, after some hesitancy, the French government retreated from its intransigent position and on May 2, 1920 fully recognized the claims of Brazil. Thus was solved to the full satisfaction of the South American republic one of the thorniest international problems bequeathed to Brazil by the war. Brazil's participation in and withdrawal from the League of Nations we shall take up in a slightly different connection.

V

The term of Wenceslau Braz expired only four days after the armistice. His elected successor was Rodrigues Alves who had already served with such distinction in the presidency from 1902 to 1906. This is the only instance in Brazilian history of a president being chosen for a second term; in fact, the Brazilian constitution specifically forbids reëlection except after the lapse of at least one term. Unhappily Rodrigues Alves, already in his seventieth year when elected president, was too ill to assume office. Hence the vice president-elect, Dr. Delphim Moreira da Costa Ribeiro, automatically became the chief magistrate. On January 16, 1919 President Rodrigues Alves died, and according to the requirement of the constitution a new presidential election took place in April. The caucus or convention of the Republican Party departed from its customary procedure of selecting a son of São Paulo or Minas Geraes and chose Dr. Epitacio da Silva Pessôa, a native of the little northern state of Parahyba. He had held a number of important federal offices, including that of justice of the federal supreme court. He was, as we have seen, serving as head of the Brazilian delegation at Versailles at the time of his election. He was opposed by Ruy Barbosa, who had twice before, in 1910 and 1914, unsuccessfully run for the presidency.

The three years of Epitacio Pessôa's administration in many ways represented a hectic and abnormal period in Brazilian history. Brazil, like other countries, rode for a time high on the wave of post-war prosperity. The money marts of the United States were now thrown open and Brazil increased her already large foreign debt by seventy-five million dollars borrowed from the United States. The internal and floating debts also vastly increased. A good deal of this money was used wisely. During the war much needed internal progress had been neglected. The railroads had fallen into a critical state and badly needed funds for rehabilitation and additional equipment. Public education, port and irrigation works, the recurrent problem of droughts in the north, all demanded attention and justified heavy expenditure. For the first time in Brazilian history — if we except Dom João VI — rulers of European states honored Brazil with their presence. The visits of King Albert and Queen Elizabeth of Belgium and of the President of Portugal were the occasions for extravagant expenditures. In 1922 Brazil celebrated fittingly the centenary of her independence with a great international exposition at Rio de Janeiro, the most notable event of the kind that had ever been held in Hispanic America.

The last months of Dr. Epitacio Pessôa's presidency were critical ones. Not all of the vast expenditures which he had incurred were wisely or economically administered, and were partly responsible for a severe financial crisis resulting in the decline on the exchange value of the *milreis* and the abandonment by the government of some of its grandiose projects, such as the electrification of certain portions of the state-owned Central Railroad. The political situation also became menacing. In March 1922 took place the election of the new executive. The official candidate was Dr. Arthur da Silva Bernardes, president of the State of Minas Geraes. For a variety of reasons, into which we cannot enter, this was the most bitterly contested election which up to this time had been held in Brazil. Nilo Peçanha, whom we met once before as acting president from 1909 to 1910, and later as minister of foreign affairs during Brazil's participation in the war, opposed him. After Dr. Bernardes' election the defeated group, known as the reaction *(A Reacção),* led by Nilo Peçanha and a number of disgruntled elements in the army headed by Hermes da Fonseca, planned to seize power by a military *coup d'état,* making Hermes provisional chief even as his uncle had been back in 1889. The plot was nipped in the bud through the energetic action of President Pessôa, but he failed to prevent the fortress of Copacabana, under the command of Hermes' son, from firing upon the city the night of July 5, 1922. The fortress was soon reduced to submission and the revolt may be looked upon as one of the last desperate attempts of the military and a group of disloyal civilian politicians to get back into the saddles as they had in 1889 and 1910.

VI

Partly for reasons just outlined the four years of Dr. Bernardes' administration were critical and troubled ones. The president was able and energetic but he was disliked by many elements of the population. Everywhere there was a feeling of *malaise*. A state of siege was repeatedly declared in various parts of the republic. There was a growing lack of mutual understanding between the executive and the army.

The most serious challenge to the authority of President Bernardes came from the great coffee state of São Paulo. The revolt which took place in the summer of 1924 was sponsored by the same disgruntled elements which had been behind the uprising of 1922. The revolution took the government by surprise, and the rebels under General Isidoro Dias Lopes were able to occupy the city of São Paulo without bloodshed. President Bernardes promptly proclaimed a state of siege in the states of São Paulo and Rio de Janeiro and in the Federal Capital, and called upon the various loyal states to send troops to Rio de Janeiro. He was handicapped by his desire not to subject the great city of São Paulo to the horrors of bombardment, but on July 28, 1924 finally succeeded in forcing the rebels out of São Paulo after an occupation of three weeks. They proceeded to separate into small bands and were run to earth without difficulty by the federal troops. The collapse of this short-lived rebellion was hailed with satisfaction through most of Brazil and it was hoped that the military and subversive elements had definitely been scotched.

One important event in the field of foreign relations deserves to be chronicled in the history of this unfortunate quadrennium. As one of the victorious belligerents, Brazil affixed her signature to the Versailles peace treaty and became one of the charter members, as it were, of the League of Nations. Elected to membership in the Council she played a creditable if not important part in the deliberations of that body. The first intimation of a crisis in Brazil's relation to the league came in 1926. It will be remembered that the famous Locarno treaties were to come into effect only when Germany became a full-fledged member of the League, and it was assumed by everyone that she would be given a permanent place on the Council.[1]

[1] Brazil apparently was in full agreement with this point of view as late as July 1925, as appears from a confidential memorandum adressed by the Brazilian

Early in 1926 a change took place in the attitude of the Brazilian government. For reasons which are not entirely clear, Brazil determined to demand a permanent, not elected, place on the Council. This demand was coupled with the statement that should this request be denied she would use her veto power to exclude Germany. The first intimation which Europe had of this intention was a despatch from the Rio correspondent of the Paris *Temps* published on February 24, 1926. This intelligence caused both surprise and indignation. In the English house of lords none other than Lord Robert Cecil declared that this policy of demanding concessions by means of a threat was contrary to the whole spirit of the League. The Belgium minister of foreign affairs went so far as to use the word *chantage* or blackmail. There was endless speculation concerning Brazil's motives. Some declared that Mussolini was behind her, others the Vatican or Germany. Still others declared she had the support of the United States in whose favor she had agreed to vacate her seat in case that country joined the league.

Such suggestions are really fantastic. As a matter of fact, since 1921 Brazil had manœuvered for a permanent seat on the Council. At that time the Chilean representative, Señor Agustín Edwards, brought her name before the Council. The matter was broached on various other occasions, and now with the changes in the size and constitution of the Council coincident with the admission of Germany, apparently Brazil's golden opportunity had come.

The official point of view we set forth by the Brazilian ambassador, Senhor Mello Franco—who throughout these negotiations was but the mouth-piece of the Rio foreign office—in speeches which he delivered before the League on March 17 and before the Council on June 10 respectively, and in a long telegram or *exposé* prepared by the Brazilian government and read by him at the latter date. The thesis of Brazil was that the exclusion of America from permanent membership in the Council is odious from the fact that such representation is accorded the other continents. Europe has three places and the inclusion of Germany brings them to four; Asia has one representative; Africa and Australia are likewise represented, as the dominions constitute "an integral part of the political system of the British empire." [2] Hispanic

government to the members of the Council: "It is certain that the entry of Germany into the Council depends only on her request for admission to the League, since all the states with seats in the Council have replied favorably to the memorandum which the German government has sent them on this subject." José Carlos de Macedo Soares, *O Brasil e a Sociedade das Nações* (Paris, 1927), p. 115.

[2] This argument is a weak one, for by the same token America would be represented through the Dominion of Canada.

America, on the other hand, with seventeen states belonging to the League has no permanent representative on the Council. In voicing this demand, however, Senhor Mello Franco pointed out with some inconsistency that Brazil had never arrogated to herself the right of representing on the Council her sister states of America. The official telegram stated also that the absence of the United States from the place reserved for her on the Council makes the *démarche* of Brazil all the more imperative.[3]

In making this demand Brazil had placed herself in an impossible position. Senhor Mello Franco's speech on March 17 failed to convince the members of the League of the justice of Brazil's cause. M. Briand went so far in his address on March 17 as to hold Brazil responsible for a "humiliating paralysis" in the activities of the League. Realizing that it was a question of submission to the League or withdrawal, the Brazilian government elected the latter course. On June 14 Senhor Felix Pacheco, the Brazilian minister of foreign offairs, telegraphed Sir Eric Drummond, the secretary of the League, Brazil's resolution to retire from this body in accordance with Article I of the covenant. Since then Brazil has limited her activity in Geneva to participation in the work of the Labor Bureau and to certain other non-political activities of the League.

As the Brazilian government has never seen fit to explain further its actions at this time, it is impossible, at least for the writer, to explore further the real motives of the withdrawal. Senhor Macedo Soares, who has written a book on this subject, insists that Brazil's foreign policy had been transformed into the unworthy instrument *(baixo instrumento)* of her internal policy. In other words, the government, that is the executive, desired to divert attention from what was going on at home to events at Geneva. The writer is unable to substantiate the correctness of this view. He can only state that to him it seems extraordinarily unfortunate that Brazil, who had always prided herself on her success in settling international difficulties by peaceful means, should have voluntarily withdrawn from an organization avowedly created for this purpose.

[3] The *Diario Official* for June 12, 1926, stated that ambassador Morgan presented to President Bernardes his congratulations on the attitude of Brazil. This statement was formally denied by the United States consul in Geneva and by the members of the United States delegation to the Disarmament Conference. *Journal de Genève,* June 17, 1926.

CHAPTER TWENTY-THREE

CONTEMPORARY BRAZIL

IN CONCLUDING this discussion we shall attempt a brief summary of the history of Brazil during the past decade. The survey will include the revolution of 1930 (the only successful revolt in the history of the republic), the uprising of São Paulo of 1932, the achievements of the provisional government under Dr. Getulio Vargas, and an analysis of some of the more striking features of the new constitution which has just been adopted. At best, the survey will be tentative and fragmentary. Full data are obviously lacking, and the nearness of events makes impossible anything like a true perspective.

I

We may pick up the threads of our narrative with the year 1926. As successor of Dr. Bernardes was elected Dr. Washington Luis Pereira de Souza, minister of justice in two previous administrations and governor of São Paulo from 1920 to 1924. In these various positions he had acquitted himself with unusual competency. Such, in fact, was the confidence which he inspired that his election was generally hailed as the dawn of a new and better era for Brazil.

The first three years of the new administration were reasonably prosperous. The president took energetic measures to cope with Brazil's perennial financial difficulties. He attempted to stabilize the *milreis,* increase the nation's gold reserve, balance the budget with a surplus, consolidate the floating debt, and, finally, increase the country's favorable balance of trade by "defending" coffee, which amounted to over seventy per cent of Brazil's total exports.

For a time these measures enjoyed a fair degree of success, but they proved ineffectual to exorcise the economic and political crisis which overwhelmed Brazil at the end of his administration. In the fatal year 1930 South America was visited by an epidemic of revolutions from which Brazil could not escape. To a brief consideration of the causes and development of this movement in so far as it affects Brazil we now address ourselves.

During the course of this discussion attention has been called to the fact that the larger of the Brazilian states enjoy a degree of influence in national affairs of which we in the United States have little conception. The state executives usually are known as presidents and are assisted by a cabinet modelled somewhat on that of the federal government. The states enjoy wide powers, including the right to levy export taxes, to contract foreign loans, and to grant sweeping concessions. Many of them in practice have almost the powers of autonomous principalities. They may even have their own military forces; the militia of São Paulo, for instance, constitutes a veritable state army. It was natural that between these states jealousies and rivalries should appear, particularly as regards their influence in the affairs of the national government. An unwritten law has grown up to the effect that no state may furnish a president for two consecutive terms. With but two exceptions the presidency has, since the revolution of 1889, alternated between representatives of the states of São Paulo and Minas Geraes. In recent years, however, other states have begun to assert their claims, particularly Rio Grande do Sul, whose wealth, influence and population have greatly increased since the advent of the republic. The president of the republic plays no passive rôle in these assertions of "state rights." As head of his political party—usually the only one in the country—he has naturally great influence on the choice of his successor. As a matter of fact, such is generally the case throughout Hispanic America.

The campaign for the election of 1930 was hardly under way when the governor of Minas Geraes, Dr. Antonio Carlos de Andrada, regarded by many as the logical candidate for the presidency, threw his support to Dr. Getulio Vargas, the governor of Rio Grande do Sul, and minister of finance for a short time under Dr. Washington Luis. Not unnaturally, Dr. Vargas looked to the outgoing president for support, but on July 25, 1929, Dr. Washington Luis declared that he would lend his influence to the candidacy of Dr. Julio Prestes, the governor of São Paulo.

In thus defying the unwritten law regarding the presidential succession, Dr. Washington Luis was doubtless perfectly sincere. He could allege in his defense that seventeen states had agreed to support the candidacy of the governor of São Paulo. It is possible that he was honestly convinced that the election of another Paulista was necessary, in the words of the party platform, as a "guarantee of the continuation of policies which during the present four-year administration have contributed to the greatness and glory of our institutions." Unfortunately for Dr. Washington Luis, this point of view met with no general acquiescence throughout the country. The opponents of Dr. Prestes proceeded to sink their various rivalries and under the designation of "liberal alliance" lined up behind Dr. Vargas. In the election which took place on March 1, 1930, the announced votes were 1,089,949 for Dr. Prestes and 735,032 for Dr. Vargas. Although the leaders of the alliance publicly agreed to abide by the result, the majority of the members of this organization voiced great dissatisfaction. Hostility against Dr. Washington Luis and his protégé, Dr. Prestes, spread throughout the country. Against the outgoing president were charged his refusal to grant amnesty to the revolutionists of 1922 and 1924, his responsibility for the difficult economic situation, and above all, his attempt to foist his own successor on the country.

Such in brief was the political background of the revolution. There were, of course, economic bases for the revolt. It may be recalled that the post-war years had witnessed a vast increase in Brazil's foreign indebtedness, encouraged it must be said in all conscience, by our own bankers. According to *Moody's Investment Service,*[1] the total foreign indebtedness of Brazil, including federal, state, and municipal loans, amounted at that time to the enormous sum of $1,181,000,000, of which some three-fourths was owed by the federal government. Service on this foreign debt, together with the return on foreign capital investments, was placed somewhere between $175,000,000 and $200,000,000. These large remittances could, of course, be met only by a favorable balance in Brazil's international trade or by further borrowing. The export balance for 1929, however, amounted to barely $40,000,000 and for 1930 a trifle over $50,000,000. The situation was aggravated by the large internal debt amounting to at least a quarter of a billion dollars. President Washington Luis, though he had effected some economies, was forced to continue the pernicious practice of additional foreign loans. With the coming of the world depression in 1930, such sources were automatically closed.

The most important single factor in Brazil's economic crisis was coffee. As is well known, Brazil furnishes from one-third to one-half of the world's production of this article. Thanks to this happy situation, the country enjoyed for a time a quasi-monopoly of this commodity, and within certain limits could dictate prices. It could do this, however, only with government assistance, and at various times the federal and state authorities have been called upon for the "valorization" or "defense" of coffee. The ultimate result has been a vast amount of over-

[1] July 17, 1930.

production. By November 1930, for example, the amount available in São Paulo for export was estimated at 26,600,000 bags of 132 pounds each. This was a million bags more than the entire world consumption in 1929 and twice the amount of Brazil's normal export of this commodity. An organization known as the Coffee Institute was created in 1928. By means of foreign loans it endeavored to hold the surplus coffee out of the market and keep the price at a high level, but in 1930 the situation got beyond its control. No more foreign loans were possible. Prices dropped catastrophically, and many of the planters were ruined. So great was the economic importance of coffee that almost every phase of Brazil's life was adversely affected. The responsibility for this situation was naturally laid at the door of the government.

Such in brief was the political and economic background of the revolution which broke out in September 1930. The details of this struggle we shall necessarily omit. Fortune seemed to favor the government forces, when on October 4, 1930 a number of generals in Rio de Janeiro rose against President Washington Luis and gave him but half an hour to resign. He refused and was held prisoner until November 20, when he was allowed to embark for Europe. Exactly one month after the outbreak of the revolt a provisional military *junta* turned over the office of chief executive to Dr. Getulio Vargas. The *gauchos* of Rio Grande do Sul kept their promise to tether their horses at the foot of the obelisk fronting the Monroe Palace. One episode of the revolution deserves to be noted. Just before the collapse of the government forces, United States Secretary of State Stimson placed an embargo on the arms intended for the revolutionists. This act was naturally ill-received in Brazil and for a time caused some coolness between the new government and the administration at Washington.

II

The provisional government remained in power for something over three years. Its activities were to affect almost every phase of national life. The basis of its program appeared in the platform of the liberal alliance, published as early as July 21, 1930. The following are the most important items:

1. A general amnesty to include all persons exiled for participation in the revolutions of 1922 and 1924.
2. The right of the people to select their own chief executive without interference from the president and politicians in power.
3. A recommendation in favor of the compulsory vote.

4. The necessity for a secret ballot and other methods of eliminating fraud, and the establishment of severe penalties for infractions.

5. That the chief executive of the nation be not allowed to accept the leadership of a political party.

6. That public instruction should be more widespread.

7. That hygiene should be carefully promoted.

8. Aid not only to coffee but to agriculture.

9. Protection to industries and other production in order to increase the favorable merchandise balance, "as it is estimated that the international balance of payments shows a deficit of at least one hundred million dollars annually."

10. To carry on the financial policy of the Washington Luis administration: stabilization of the currency, balancing of the budget, and increase of domestic production in an attempt to increase the surplus in the balance of trade.

Dr. Vargas, who in effect possessed dictatorial power, proceeded at once to dissolve the national congress and the state legislatures and municipal councils. The place of the state executives was taken by men known as "interventors," appointed by Dr. Vargas himself. As the personal representatives of the executive, these officials were granted wide discretionary power. Unfortunately, many of them were young military officers without political experience and their rule occasioned much dissatisfaction. Their power soon waxed so great that they became known as *O partido dos tenentes* (the party of the lieutenants). Especially was their rule resented in São Paulo which, as we shall see, revolted against the central government in 1932.

Dr. Vargas was on the whole happy in his choice of members of his cabinet. As minister of justice was appointed Dr. Oswaldo Aranha. Many regarded him as the strong man in the cabinet. Later he became minister of finance and then ambassador to the United States. Dr. Afranio de Mello Franco, former head of the Brazilian delegation at Geneva, received the portfolio of minister of foreign affairs. In this position he showed marked capacity, particularly in his successful efforts to bring about the settlement of the Leticia controversy between Colombia and Peru. He has been seriously proposed as a candidate for the Nobel peace prize. As head of the newly created ministry of labor was appointed Senhor Lindolfo Collor, former deputy and journalist. The veteran political writer, Dr. Assis Brasil, was chosen minister of agriculture, while a well-known Paulista banker, Senhor José Maria Whitaker, was selected for the important post of minister of finance.

Before taking up the accomplishments of the government of Dr. Getulio Vargas, we must in a parenthesis refer to an event which for a time threatened to jeopardize the success of the revolution. The reference is, of course, to the revolt which broke out in the State of São Paulo in the summer of 1932. The great coffee state had particular occasion to complain of the course of the revolution of 1930. The interventors and other officials sent by the government at Rio apparently failed to rise to the level of the responsibility and their actions aroused intense opposition. It is alleged that a number of these men were intent only in furthering their own interests. The Paulistas objected to the mounting expenses of both the state and federal governments to which they were naturally heavy contributors. Since the state contributed something like thirty-three per cent of the funds in the national treasury, it felt that it should receive a more equitable treatment. Even in normal times, however, only four and one-half per cent of its contribution is expended in the state. So bitterly did the Paulistas resent the attitude of the government at Rio that the local political parties as well as every class of the population, formed the so-called "united front" *(frente unica)* against the national government. In order to regain their own autonomy and also, as one writer put it, to "reconstitutionalize" the country, they determined to take up arms. At the outset of the revolt they were led to believe that they could count on the support of Rio Grande do Sul and Minas Geraes. The uprising took place on June 9, 1932. At the last moment, Senhor Flores da Cunha, the interventor in Rio Grande, abandoned São Paulo and went over with all his forces to the national government. Minas Geraes also left her former ally in the lurch and directed her troops against the state of São Paulo. None the less, São Paulo continued the struggle. In point of troops engaged, it was one of the most serious revolts in the entire history of Brazil. At the outset, the federal forces consisted of more than 70,000 men against 28,000 of the revolutionaries. In the face of this menace, the city and state rose, as it were, *en masse*. Volunteers to the number of 200,000 offered themselves, of which it was possible to equip barely a fifth. The capital of the state was transformed into a veritable arsenal for the manufacture of arms and ammunition. Even women and children feverishly labored for the success of the movement. The belligerents possessed the largest and best equipped armies that have ever taken the field in South America. The revolution lasted eighty-three days. Early in August the federal forces surrounded and cut off the Paulistas, and forced them to yield to overwhelming odds. It is the opinion of the Paulistas that had it not been for the defection of Colonel Herculano de Carvalho, commander of the state army, São Paulo would have been victorious. Yet the Paulistas believe that their enormous sacrifices had not been in vain. They allege that their heroic resistance to the dictatorship resulted in a different orientation in the government with the consequent adoption of a number of important reforms, including the convocation of a national constituent assembly. It is their conviction, too, that the representatives of São Paulo in this body were responsible for many of its most salutary measures.

Whatever may have been the results of this abortive revolt in São Paulo, certain it is that the federal government treated the conquered province with great consideration. No executions or reprisals took place. The leaders of the movement, including the last interventor, Dr. Pedro de Toledo, were exiled to Europe, but were subsequently amnestied. The federal government even assumed the debts which São Paulo had contracted during the revolt, and has done everything possible to undo the effects of this unhappy civil war.

Before we take up our brief analysis of the constitution, certain accomplishments of the provisional government in other fields should be touched upon. Dr. Vargas had issued a multitude of decrees, some of immense importance. Perhaps the most noteworthy are those abolishing interstate taxes, eliminating a number of useless holidays (leaving only six recognized by the federal government), appointing a commission to study the reform of the judiciary, limiting the production of sugar to equalize the supply and demand of this crop, and a variety of decrees attempting to cope with the ever-present problem of coffee. This latter topic deserves a word of further elaboration. In 1932 it was provided that no coffee trees should be set out for three years, despite the fact that an international coffee congress assembled at São Paulo in 1931 had refused to agree to the Brazilian plan of reduction of planting. A succession of decrees beginning with May 1931, provided for the progressive destruction of the inferior grades of coffee. By June 30, 1934, no less than 29,140,665 bags had been destroyed. Whatever one may think of the wisdom of this measure, it is clear that had it not been put into operation something like 45,000,000 bags of unsold coffee would have been on hand at the time of harvesting the 1934-1935 crop. Such is the bitter fruit of over-production. The government has fully recognized that the chief remedy for this state of affairs is the encouragement of crops which will partially replace coffee. As a consequence, it has furthered the growth of citrus fruits, the production of silk, the development of the hardwood industry, and in general the more intelligent exploitation of Brazil's many resources. In this connection, it is to be noted that the government of Dr. Vargas was very sympathetic towards the Ford rubber plantation on the Tapajos River in the State of Pará.

Among the other accomplishments of the Vargas administration are those dealing with labor legislation, child welfare, and recurrent droughts in northern Brazil. Decrees were even passed looking towards the eradication of leprosy, which is a scourge in certain of the more backward portions of the country. Not the least important of the decrees issued by the new government are those which provide for the partial resumption of interest payment on dollar loans of the Brazilian federal government, states, and municipalities, beginning with 1934. The terms of these decrees are rather complicated but in general they include a resumption of payment from one hundred per cent on certain types of federal loans to seventeen and one-half per cent on certain state and municipal loans. This latter percentage, however, steadily rises until the year 1937, when the whole subject will be reopened. In general it may be said that in this respect the provisional government has made heroic efforts to meet its international obligations within the limits of its capacity. So many and wide-sweeping have been the changes introduced into the fabric of national life that the term *Republica Nova* (New Republic) has been used to designate the new régime in contradistinction to the Old Republic inaugurated in 1889.

There now remains a consideration of the greatest achievement of Dr. Vargas' administration, namely the new constitution promulgated, as we have seen, in July 1934. The steps leading up to the adoption of this document may briefly be recapitulated. On May 3, 1933, Dr. Vargas, as provisional president, signed a decree calling for the election of a constituent assembly. There is some evidence that his hand was forced. As has already been suggested, one of the chief results of the Paulista revolt of 1932 was to force the government back into constitutional channels. More particularly, however, the decree of May 3 followed a political agreement negotiated by Dr. Aranha with the leaders of Rio Grande do Sul, who had withdrawn their support from the government because of Dr. Vargas' refusal to call the constituent assembly. The provisional president had defended himself on the grounds that the country was not yet ripe for such a move.

Elaborate preparations had been made for the election of members to this body. More than 1,200,000 voters out of a total population of

42,000,000 were registered. Women for the first time in the history of Brazil were granted the suffrage, and twenty per cent of the total votes were cast by them. This large voting strength was the more remarkable when compared with past elections which seldom exceeded 200,000 voters. It may be noted that the well-known feminist, Dr. Bertha Lutz, ran for a seat from the federal district, but was defeated; the only woman deputy elected was Dr. Carlotta de Queiroz from São Paulo. More than fifty political parties appeared at the polls. Two hundred and fifty-four delegates were finally elected for the assembly which met at the Tiradentes Palace (the former chamber of deputies) on November 15, 1933. Of these, two hundred and fourteen were chosen by popular election and forty by labor, trade, and professional organizations. The great majority of the members had had little experience in public life. Only two former deputies were present, both veterans of the constituent assembly of 1891, namely Dr. Assis Brasil of Rio Grande do Sul and Dr. J. J. Seábra from Bahia. As president was chosen Dr. Antonio Carlos de Andrada, former governor of Minas Geraes, an aspirant in 1930 for the presidency. The congress opened with a lengthy report by Dr. Vargas giving a detailed account of the three years of his stewardship. It is worthy of note that this able exposition was well received by the deputies from São Paulo. The assembly proceeded on November 16 to ratify the sweeping discretionary powers assumed by Dr. Vargas on October 24, 1930.

The delegates found placed before them the draft of a preliminary project drawn up by a commission of thirty-one members appointed by Dr. Vargas on October 27, 1932. This commission included many well-known figures, such as Mello Franco, Assis Brasil, José Americo, Oswaldo Aranha, and General Goés Monteiro. As was to be expected, the assembly was divided over a large number of issues. The lengthy debates, some of which were very able, it would be profitless to discuss here, as the final decisions of the assembly were naturally embodied in the constitution. On July 15, 1934 the approved copy of the final draft was published, and the following day the new constitution was promulgated. It consisted of a forty-four page document as against the twenty-six pages of the Constitution of 1891. On July 16 the dictatorship of Dr. Vargas formally ended.

Before dissolving, the constituent assembly elected the new constitutional president of the republic for the next four years. Of the two hundred and forty-eight votes cast, one hundred and seventy-five went to Dr. Vargas, fifty-nine to Dr. Borges de Medeiros, the veteran political leader of Rio Grande do Sul, and four to the minister of war, General Góes Monteiro. The remaining votes were scattered. On July 20, Dr. Vargas was formally inaugurated in the Tiradentes Palace, and took the oath of allegiance to the new constitution. The constituent assembly automatically became the first chamber of deputies and was to exercise the powers of the senate until that body could be elected. On July 24 a new cabinet was appointed which, however, included a number of men who had served in a similar capacity under the provisional government.

III

We shall now attempt a brief and necessarily inadequate analysis of the outstanding features of the new constitution. The document opens with an account of the organization of the federal government. In general it may be said that the powers granted the federal government do not differ materially from those of the Constitution of 1891 save that they are more explicitly stated and cover a somewhat wider domain.

A considerable number of articles relate in detail the powers of the states. Here again there are few striking departures from the earlier instrument. The advent of the automobile is suggested by the provision that the states shall have exclusive power to collect imposts on consumption of combustibles used in explosive motors. In time this gasoline tax—for such it is in effect—will considerably augment the revenues of the various states. Though repeated efforts were made to secure the abolition of export taxes, this reform partially failed, owing to the fact that a number of states had virtually no other important source of revenue. It is to be noted, however, that one of the transitory provisions of the constitution states that excess export taxes levied by the states shall be reduced, beginning January 1, 1936, gradually at the rate of ten per cent a year until the constitutional rate of ten per cent *ad valorem* shall have been reached.

The faculties of the president are carefully defined, and efforts are made to check what is sometimes called the hypertrophy of the executive power. Particular efforts are made to place a curb on the president's right of intervention by carefully specifying when such a right may be invoked. It is to be noted, however, that the president is specifically authorized to intervene in the states to reorganize a state's finances when for more than two years it has passed service upon its funded debt, or to assure the observance of the state's constitutional principles. In the latter case, the executive must secure permission of the federal supreme court. When necessary, the chamber of deputies shall name the interventor or authorize the president to do so. Intervention does not suspend the operation of state laws except those that have brought it about, and then only temporarily. It will be seen that the restraints placed upon the president's right of intervention are much more detailed and specific than in the Constitution of 1891.

The legislative power consists of a senate and chamber of deputies. The latter is to be elected by universal suffrage, equal and direct, except for those deputies who represent professional classes. The number of deputies popularly elected is not to exceed one for each 150,000 inhabitants up to twenty deputies, and from this limit on, one for every 250,000 inhabitants. One of the most striking constitutional provisions has to do with the other type of deputies representing professional classes. They are to be chosen by indirect vote of their professional associations according to four categories: agriculture and stock-raising, industry, commerce and transportation, liberal professions and public functionaries. The number of this category of deputies may not exceed one-fifth of the deputies chosen according to population. The chamber of deputies may summon before it any minister of state to supply information respecting his particular department. This right of interpolation is to be found in a number of Hispanic American constitutions, notably that of Argentina. The presidential veto may be overridden by an absolute majority of both houses instead of by a two-thirds vote of those present in each house, as required by the Constitution of 1891.

The senate calls for only a brief reference. It consists of two representatives from each state and from the federal district, elected for eight years. Its meetings take place the same time as the chamber of deputies, save that between sessions of the national legislature one-half of its membership acts as a permanent committee. In general the senate is designed to preserve administrative continuity, to act as a coördinator of federal powers, and to watch over the constitution. Among its exclusive faculties is the appointment of certain officials, especially the consultative members of the tribunal of accounts, the attorney-general of the republic, and the chiefs of diplomatic missions. Otherwise, the senate has more or less equal power with the chamber in the field of general legislation.

Some account must be accorded the technical councils (*conselhos technicos*) attached to each ministry. Here we have, perhaps, a rough equivalent to our own so-called "Brain Trust." The organization and function of these bodies still await appropriate legislation. The constitution provides, however, that half of these technicians shall be recruited outside of the personnel of the respective ministers. They must, however, in all cases be specialists in the subject on which they are to offer advice. The minister is forbidden to adopt any decision within his exclusive competency contrary to the unanimous advice of the council attached to his office.

As regards the election of the executive, a few innovations may be noted. The election is to be direct, secret, and by a majority of popular votes. It is specifically provided that congress may no longer canvass the presidential vote. Instead, this important task is undertaken by a special body known as the *justiça eleitoral,* and the result is given to the country by a delegation of this body, presided over by the vice president of the supreme court. An entire chapter of the constitution provides for this system of "electoral justice," administered by a hierarchy of tribunals. It may be noted in passing that the regular federal judiciary remains practically unchanged.

One of the major sections of the constitution deals with the economic and social order. Here we have thirty-eight articles, some nationalistic, others socialistic in character. Only a few will be touched upon here. The economic order must be organized in conformity with the principles of justice and the necessities of national life in such manner that all Brazilian citizens may lead a dignified existence. Within these limits, economic liberty is guaranteed. The public powers shall ascertain periodically the level of the standard of living in various sections of the country.

Federal concessions must be obtained for the industrial use of mines, mineral deposits, and hydro-electric energy, even though these may be in private possession. These concessions are to be granted exclusively to Brazilians or to enterprises organized in Brazil. The board of directors of such companies must have a majority of Brazilians, resident in Brazil. Subsoil resources and waterfalls constitute property distinct from that of the soil when used for industrial exploitation. Here we see, probably, an echo of similar provisions in the Mexican Constitution of 1917. It is of interest to note that one article declares that all insurance companies shall eventually be nationalized. As a step to this end, foreign companies operating in Brazil must be converted into Brazilian concerns.

One article deals with immigration. It is provided that the entry of immigrants into Brazil will be subject to the restrictions necessary to guarantee the "ethnic integration" of the immigrants, who in no year shall exceed in number two per cent of their total nationals resident in

Brazil during the last fifty years. During the course of the debates of the constituent assembly the charge was freely made and denied with equal vehemence that this provision is directed against the Japanese, of whom there are now some 200,000 in Brazil.

As is usual in documents of this character, there is a long list of "transitory dispositions." A few will be noted. The first term of the president shall end on May 3, 1938, and he may not immediately succeed himself. As in the Constitution of 1891, the question of the location of the future federal capital is broached. The president of the republic is required to appoint a commission which shall report its findings to the chamber of deputies which in turn "will choose the proper location and without loss of time shall take the necessary steps for the transfer of the capital." This having been done, the present Federal District shall become a state. Nothing is said about the location of the capital in Goyaz as contemplated by the Constitution of 1891. Finally, an article provides that a plan of national reconstruction shall be immediately formulated. This is perhaps the closest approach to the mention of "planned economy" to be found in the constitution.

IV

In conclusion, the writer will assay the difficult task of hazarding a few comments on this new instrument. Naturally these remarks, based on a document promulgated so recently, make no claim to being authoritative.

In view of the membership of the constituent assembly, which included a great many "advanced" groups, the constitution is a remarkably conservative document. A number of the articles represent, in my opinion, distinct gains over the Constitution of 1891. The additional guarantees against abuses of the state of siege and the restraints placed upon the personal power of the president are salutary if they can be enforced. These restraints, however, will be ineffectual if the house and senate abdicate their constitutional powers as they have frequently done in the past. Among other forward steps are the secret ballot, equal suffrage, compulsory registration, and a magistracy which should provide for a better electoral system and insure honest returns from the polls.

Among the members of the constituent assembly were a number of Fascists. Their efforts were chiefly directed to the creation of a Fascist and authoritarian "supreme council" modelled somewhat on the body of similar name in Italy. This proposal, however, was defeated, and out of the violent discussion emerged a senate and not a council. This was due partly to the efforts of the representatives of São Paulo.

Innovations of a more questionable character are the extension of the legislative capacity of the union, provisions for professional representation in the chamber of deputies, an excessive economic activity granted to the public powers, and finally an exaggerated nationalism which if carried out will work a real hardship on foreigners carrying on a legitimate business in Brazil.

There are also a number of miscellaneous provisions which might more appropriately have been covered by statute law. Such are the restrictions on immigration, the prohibition of divorce, articles relating to the hours and status of labor, and the rights of squatters who have remained on land for ten years to receive up to ten hectares (about twenty-five acres).

Critics of the new constitution declare that all of the important reforms might have been secured through a simple revision of the document of 1891. This may be true, but the political situation in Brazil rendered such a consummation impossible. All things considered, the work of the constituent assembly may be regarded as reasonably satisfactory. The new constitution, to an extent which was certainly untrue of the earlier instrument, reflects present-day idealogy in the social and economic domains, while the political innovations tend on the whole to provide for a government which is more responsive to public opinion than has hitherto been the case.

Apparently Brazil is at last supplied with a fundamental charter, adequate to the needs of a great progressive people, with whom the rights of the nation and the well-being of the citizens are safeguarded against possible encroachments from both without and within the state.

IV. CHILE

By Isaac Joslin Cox

CHAPTER TWENTY-FOUR

THE STRUGGLE FOR POLITICAL INDEPENDENCE, 1808-1818*

I

CHILE is a land of contrasts.[1] It stretches for some twenty-six hundred miles along the west coast of lower South America. At no point is it more than two hundred miles wide, and its average width is considerably under half that figure. Climatically it is also a country of contrasts. Its northern area comes nearer being a desert than any similar portion of the earth's surface. Its southern portion, according to report—whether well founded or not—has thirteen months of rainfall during the year! On its eastern boundary rises Aconcagua, the highest peak in the New World, while near its shoreline the bed of the Pacific Ocean sinks to one of its lowest depths.

---

* Each of the following chapters bears witness to the painstaking labor of Luís Galdames. Without his scholarly synthesis of the multitudinous tomes that make up the written annals of Chile, foreign commentators would be unable to grasp the progressive sweep of its development or its own youth to gain a true perspective of their inspiring historical background. His *Estudio de la historia* first appeared in 1906; the seventh edition was published in 1929. For almost a full generation, therefore, it has held its own as the leading school text of that country. It is to be hoped that the translation of this work, which is now ready for the press, will shortly be available for English readers.

No one author, however facile or discerning, will suffice to explain the development of Chile during the past century. Hence the writer has not hesitated to call upon his friend, the late Alberto Edwards, and upon Alberto Cabero, Carlos Keller, Daniel Martner and many others to help in this halting interpretation of their national history. To them and to the host of others who have made his two visits to their land so pleasant and profitable, he extends his heart-felt thanks.

[1] For the physical background of Chile and for its population, one may consult Augustín Edwards, *My Native Land* (London, 1928), C. F. Jones, *South America* Ch. 4 (New York, 1930), and R. H. Whitbeck, *Economic Geography of South America,* Chs. 7, 8 (New York, 1930). A convenient summary of the country's outstanding features is to be found in the Fourteenth edition of the *Encyclopedia Britannica,* article "Chile." Cf. also G. F. Scott Elliott, *Chile: Its History and Development* . . . (London, 1907). A very suggestive but brief picture of the influence exerted by the different classes of Chilean society is to be found in Carlos Keller R., *La eterna crisis chilena* (Santiago, 1931) Ch. I; and of the influence of the physical background in Santiago Macchiavello Varas, *Política económica nacional* (Santiago, 1931) I, Ch. II.

Despite its great length, a comparatively small portion of the land contains the bulk of its people. With abundant mineral resources, water power, timber supply, its natural wealth is still largely unrealized and the national income is badly distributed. Agriculture, for the greater part of four centuries, determined its economic development; but its minerals, particularly nitrates and copper, have recently attracted greater attention.

The core of the country consists of the central valley lying between the Andes and the sea and stretching from Coquimbo to Concepción, a distance of some six hundred miles. This is preëminently an agricultural zone although the northern portion of it is broken and irregular in contour. This region enjoys a Mediterranean climate, one which can produce the vine and the orange, but one in which wheat and other grain yield abundantly and livestock also flourish. In the north of this favored area lie the semi-arid regions which at the upper extremity merge into the Desert of Atacama. This is the mineral producing area of modern times, where are found the *salitreras,* the barren stretches that produce the nitrates, and the extensive copper deposits that virtually set the price of that metal in the world's markets. These industries have within recent decades brought in a laboring population which gives to the country some of its most pressing social and economic problems. To the south of Concepción lies the heavily forested area upon which the country draws heavily for its lumber supply. Below this extends the long and lowering line of the Andes, reaching westward at intervals to send offshoots into the sea, where they form the forbidding southern archipelago, which finally terminates in Tierra del Fuego (the Land of Fire).

Varying as greatly as the land are its people. Before the white man came, scattered tribes of Indians gave it a sparse population. Those of the northern inhabited areas were partially under the control of the Inca empire. Farther to the south came the Araucanians, the most warlike tribe of South America. The Incas never subdued them, nor did the Spaniards, who came later, succeed much better. From this indomitable race came a portion of the blood-stream that flows in the veins of modern Chileans, mixed, of course, with other Indian elements. Joined with this indigenous stream is the blood of the Spanish conquerors, themselves a race of stubborn fighters, representing all classes of Iberians but prevailingly drawn from the south of the peninsula. Later in the colonial period the early colonizers were reinforced by contingents from the north of Spain: Basque, Navarrese, Catalonian, Galician, and other sturdy groups that made their impress on the commercial and industrial life of the colony.

From these two main currents, Iberian and indigenous, arose, therefore, the population that occupied Chile at the end of the colonial period. By 1800 the Indian tribes of the northern and central regions had been exterminated or absorbed by the Spanish conquerors. The Araucanians still held their own in southern fastnesses, subject only to occasional slave raids or spells of missionary zeal. As a result of the union of the white and red, there existed an extensive *mestizo* element which made up the mass of the common people. In all the country on the eve of independence there may have been five hundred and thirty thousand souls. A hundred thousand of these were the savage Araucanians. Most of the remaining population lived between La Serena in the north and the river Biobio in the south, a region that was shortly to be divided into three provinces: Santiago, the central one, containing the capital of that name with Valparaiso its chief sea port, accounted for more than a quarter million people; Coquimbo, made a separate province in 1811, had seventy-five thousand inhabitants; and Concepción, the southern province, also created in 1811, had one hundred thousand people. About twenty-five thousand individuals were to be found around the settlement of Valdivia, lying still farther to the south, and on the island of Chiloé.[2] These last named settlements were under the direct jurisdiction of Peru.

For three centuries Chile had been a conquest land, where the Spaniards had established themselves as masters and where they had sought, by forcible means, to make the natives serve them. As a result of this policy, the population economically was divided into two general classes: the *latifundistas* and the *campesinos*.[3] The former, a relatively small class, were descendants of the original grantees to whom the country had been assigned under the *encomienda* system. In the later colonial period many of these original lines of descent had been broken by more recent arrivals from Spain who gave to the ruling class certain bourgeois characteristics. It represented a combined commercial and agricultural oligarchy characterized by its practical bent and its sense of proportion. Through the management of its estates, it had learned how to deal with people and to command them. Conservative by nature and tradition,

[2] These estimates are from Carlos Keller R., *Sinopsis geográfico-estadística de la república de Chile* (Santiago, 1933), p. 39.

[3] For a suggestive summary of the origins and chief characteristics of the Chilean people, cf. Alberto Cabero, *Chile y los chilenos* (Santiago, 1926), Chs. II and III.

it was opposed to sudden change. It was neither saintly nor fanatic, but esteemed and supported the church as an agency to keep the people mild and obedient. Such was the landholding aristocracy that was to direct the war for independence.

The *campesinos,* forming the vast majority of the population, were composed of two general groups: the *inquilinos,* or retainers on the big estates, and the *peones,* or free laborers who wandered from one part of the country to the other. The relation between both of these groups and their masters was regulated by force, modified somewhat by the irregular sex relations from which the *mestizo* class had sprung. These were the men who worked on the estates and in the mines, but whether laboring in one task or the other, their general condition was the same. Life was restricted to the satisfaction of the most elementary necessities. Without higher aspirations, they were, in most cases, attached to the soil on which they labored. A few, more miserable still, wandered about in search of seasonal work. Still fewer found employment in towns.

Life in colonial Chile was essentially rural. Santiago, the chief center, had barely thirty thousand inhabitants and no other town more than five thousand. The Chileans were a people in whose life mining played a very secondary part only. Such a population might have continued to vegetate indefinitely had not an accident thrown upon them the necessity of self-government.

The system of colonial control under which they lived had a definite legal basis established by the motherland, and was devised to meet the wishes of the metropolis rather than the needs of the colony.[4] Nevertheless, such was the conservatism of the people and their distrust of innovations that metropolitan control, despite its abuses, might have continued unchanged for decades. Among these abuses the most galling were restrictions upon commerce which made the colony a mere trading post for gathering supplies for Spain. Furthermore, the country, perhaps without appreciating it, labored under a system of intellectual repression which kept it in ignorance. There was more definite complaint over the preference in administration given to recently arrived Spaniards, and there were frequent protests against the complexity of laws and the delay in administering them. Moreover, the mother country was held responsible for the general misery of the lower classes although

---

[4] The grievances of the colonists against Spanish control are summarized in Luís Galdames, *Estudio de la historia de Chile* (7th ed. Santiago, 1929), Ch. VI, and in the general historical texts relating to Latin America.

much of that was directly due to the means by which the landed proprietors enforced their mastery over their retainers.

To these clearly-felt grievances one might conceivably add certain ideas of political philosophy current in other parts of the world. Yet it is doubtful if a population almost wholly illiterate was greatly concerned about Rosseau's *Social Contract* or the writings of the Encyclopedists. A few choice spirits, indeed, succeeded in smuggling in some of these prohibited works and discussed them in secret with their friends. These discussions were given point by rumors of revolt in the English colonies to the northward and of uprisings in Europe, but such clandestine information affected only a relatively small portion of the Chilean people. The movement for independence there had virtually no precursors, at least in the sense of those who, from the beginning of active life, consciously directed their efforts toward emancipation. Napoleon Bonaparte rather than the political philosophers initiated the movement for independence.

II

Chile was Spain's most remote American dependency, but even so the people were thrown into consternation by the tidings that reached them early in 1808.[5] The people of the mother country, they learned, had risen against the incompetent Charles IV and his hated minister Godoy, and had forced the king to abdicate in favor of his son Ferdinand VII. This news was received with rejoicing, for the unknown young prince then aroused hopes of national betterment. Shortly after, they learned that both the new king and the old had been forced by Napoleon to renounce the throne of Spain, and that the conqueror had turned the mother country and its colonies over to his brother Joseph. This series of insults led the Spanish people to rise *en masse* against the intrusive régime, and it likewise aroused the colonists of Chile to a defense of Spain's interests as well as their own. They instituted processions in the towns, and, with fitting ceremonies, renewed allegiance to the legitimate king and vowed death to the usurper. The bewildering happenings in the peninsula apparently aroused a universal expression of loyalty in the

---

[5] From this point to the end of the chapter the narrative is based largely on Galdames, *op. cit.*, Ch. VI. Cf. also A. S. M. Chisholm, *The Independence of Chile* (Boston, 1911) and A. U. Hancock, *A History of Chile* (Chicago, 1893). A coöperative series of intensive studies dealing with the period and written by an earlier generation of historians will be found in *Historia jeneral de la república de Chile desde su independencia hasta nuestros dias*, 5 vols. (Santiago, 1866-1882). The standard work for this and the succeeding chapter is still Diego Barros Arana, *Historia jeneral de Chile*, 16 vols. (Santiago, 1884-1902), volumes VIII-XVI.

distant colony. But at the same time these events served to awaken a division among its people that in time was to lead to independence.

Napoleon had already sent emissaries to the American colonies demanding allegiance to his brother Joseph. The princess regnant of Portugal, who with her husband, João VI, was now domiciled in Brazil, likewise offered her royal protection to the neighboring colonies, in case Spain should remain conquered. The bewildered colonists learned that in Spain the people were organizing against the invaders through local committees or *juntas* and felt that similar action was incumbent upon them. Such a proposal aroused among their leaders a marked difference of opinion. One group, largely made up of imperial officeholders and of recent arrivals from Spain, remained uncompromisingly attached to the mother country and expressed the greatest confidence in her ability to resist foreign domination; the other, which found its principal supporters among the members of the municipal council or *cabildo* of Santiago, were more doubtful of Spanish success and in the event that the mother country fell permanently under Napoleon's control were prepared to establish an independent government in Chile.

We may assume that these sentiments, in the beginning, represented tendencies rather than definite programs. One group was dubbed "revolutionary," although its members professed the most strict fidelity to Ferdinand VII, while the other was regarded as favoring either the Princess Carlota or Napoleon and was labelled accordingly. As a matter of fact, the grouping simply emphasized the rivalry that for a long time had existed between the Chilean Creoles and the peninsular Spaniards. As secret discussion continued, the division between the two became more bitter, particularly so because of the inept character of the colonial executive, Francisco Antonio García Carrasco.

This ruler displayed little political power and less tact. He was an accident in office. At the beginning of 1808, his predecessor suddenly died and García Carrasco succeeded by virtue of the fact that he chanced to be the highest military official in the colony. He was an old man who had spent his life in camp, particularly in the vicinity of Concepción, far removed from the center of government. His secretary, Juan Martínez de Rozas, constituted Carrasco's best qualification for office. A man of education, Rozas had served as legal adviser to the intendant at Concepción and later was in charge of the *intendencia*. He was also a man of considerable private fortune. As adviser to Governor Carrasco, he tried to draw that official toward certain reforms that would preserve peace in the colony, but finding himself unable to effect these reforms he had withdrawn from Santiago and returned to Concepción, where he began to agitate among the more intelligent people of the vicinity for a complete change of government.

Meanwhile, the inept governor alienated in turn the influential groups of the colony—first by appearing to favor the reform element, by which course he offended the members of the royal *audiencia* and the leading clergy; and later by turning against the liberal elements but without regaining the confidence of the opposing group. In his reactionary course he issued decrees forbidding conversation about affairs of state and tried to expel the few foreigners who were in the country. Point was given to his severity by reports of revolutionary movements in the neighboring colonies. Spurred on by these rumors, and fearing that similar uprisings would take place in Santiago, he arrested three of the leading householders of the city and prepared to send them to Peru. This led to protests from the principal inhabitants, voiced by the *cabildo* of Santiago, the royal *audiencia,* and by leading churchmen and men of affairs, and caused the irresolute governor to revoke his order of banishment.

At the same time news came to Santiago that at Buenos Aires an open town meeting had deposed the viceroy and established a local *junta* there. This caused Governor Carrasco to reverse his policy and reorder the prisoners sent to Peru. This new turn of policy caused a general uprising in Santiago, marked by assemblages in the plazas, parades in the streets, and demonstrations against the governor. These manifestations continued for nearly a week when through the representation of the royal *audiencia* the governor, July 16, 1810, was persuaded to resign.

His successor, a representative of one of the older families, bore the title of Conde de la Conquista. He was a man of over 80 years, and despite his excellent reputation and good intentions, was unable to still the tumults. After some two months of effort, marked by growing enmity between the *cabildo* and the royal *audiencia,* the newly-appointed governor determined to resign. Secret and continuous agitation in favor of local action thus bore fruit. An important contribution to this result was an anonymous writing entitled *A Political Christian Catechism,* which was being secretly circulated at this time. This document was the work of a cleric, Camilo Henríquez, who took occasion to recall to his fellow citizens the grievances that they had suffered from the mother country and the little faith that they could put in any promise of reform. In concluding, he called upon them to come together in an open *cabildo* where they might form a provisional *junta* to take charge of affairs of the colony, but to take this action in the name of King Ferdinand and to resist all attempts at foreign domination.

His appeal aroused an equally vigorous rejoinder from the clergy. But despite their opposition, the old governor was led to convene the proposed open *cabildo,* representing the most important elements of the colony, and this body, to the number of about three hundred and fifty, convened on September 18, 1810, "on a spring day redolent with sunshine." Before the assembled multitude the aged executive arose and definitely offered his resignation. After some discussion, punctuated by shouts of "we want a *junta!*", the resignation was accepted, and a motion presented to nominate the governing body. This was adopted by acclamation. The assemblage similarly approved a prepared list of nine names for membership in the *junta.* These represented the leading factions, official and unofficial, of the colony. The Conde de la Conquista was a mere figurehead, soon removed by death from his trying situation. Another member, the archbishop of Santiago, was then absent from the colony and never served at all. These vacancies left the Creole element of the *junta* in a decided majority.

The city showed its appreciation of the day's work by illuminations and improvised serenades to the members of the *junta.* Two days later the administration and the governing body amidst salutes of artillery took a solemn oath of obedience to Ferdinand VII. In Concepción a similar demonstration took place, with the former secretary of the government and also member of the *junta,* Martínez de Rozas, assuming charge. Like action occurred in other centers. Thus was inaugurated the first step toward independent government in Chile.

III

Fundamental measures at once occupied the attention of the new governing body: it must defend itself against possible reaction, and it must raise revenues and provide an armed force. In the tasks thus presented it welcomed the coöperation of its fellow *junta* of Buenos Aires. In the course of some months it organized fifteen hundred men, ill-armed and worse clothed. It opened the ports of Chile to commerce and thereby acquired necessary revenues. Its most important act, however, was the decision to hold elections for deputies to a congress representing the entire colony. This undertaking was further complicated by the news that the general *junta* in Spain, operating in the name of Ferdinand VII, had appointed a new viceroy for La Plata provinces, and that its appointee would attempt to take possession of the government there by force. The imperilled *junta* at Buenos Aires sought aid from the body at Santiago, which in turn ordered a supply of gunpowder to be sent across the mountains and enlisted recruits for service there.

On the morning appointed for the election of delegates to congress, the city of Santiago beheld an outbreak against the *junta*—a countermove stimulated by the royal *audiencia*. The revolt failed promptly, and its leader was executed at dawn the following day. The attempt led to the dissolution of the *audiencia* and the assumption by the *junta* of all necessary powers of government. Its most serious concern was now to provide for the proposed national congress. This body was to be made up of forty-two deputies of which Santiago was to have twelve and Concepción, the next largest jurisdiction, three. The members were to be chosen by the *cabildos* from a list of the most honorable men in each locality. Under these regulations, the elections occurred in all except the capital where the process was held up by the mutiny mentioned above.

On the first day of May, the date set for the opening of congress, the deputies from the provinces were present and ready to exercise their functions. But Santiago had not yet chosen its representatives. The others, unwilling to wait, asked the *junta* to admit them to its sessions, and when this request was granted, the *junta* became a more general deliberative assembly. This move was largely due to the personal influence of Martínez de Rozas. It arrayed against him the *cabildo* of Santiago and spurred the city on immediately to choose its quota, which, added to the general representation, constituted what was termed the "executive directorate" of the colony. This new body was to control affairs until the formal opening of congress; and reinforced by those from Santiago, the majority of its members assumed charge with the determination of overthrowing the policy of Rozas. It filled offices with conservative men, created a court of justice of like character, and in various ways tried to establish a more moderate policy than Rozas had favored. It thus paved the way for the formal opening of the first national congress.

This event fittingly took place July 4, 1811, and was accompanied by parades, a special high mass, and a sermon delivered by Father Camilo Henríquez. The members took an oath to protect the Catholic religion, to obey Ferdinand VII, and to defend Chile and its recently created institutions. Then came a formal session of congress presided over by Martínez de Rozas, who delivered a patriotic address and resigned his office to his successor. At night there was an illumination of the city and appropriate fireworks.

IV

In the assembly thus created, there were three distinct currents of opinion. The majority of the members were men of conservative ideas who were still disposed to remain attached to the mother country, provided that certain reforms were assured them, such as freer trade and the right to select delegates to the Spanish *Cortes*. Affiliated with this moderate group were a few reactionaries who wished to reëstablish the fallen régime. Opposed to this combination was another faction, less numerous but bolder, that aimed at a republic. Rozas headed this group. Associated with him were Manuel de Salas, a noted economist and philanthropist, and Bernardo O'Higgins, destined to become an important leader in subsequent events. O'Higgins was then thirty-three years of age, son of the former Governor of Chile and Viceroy of Peru and of an unmarried mother, who belonged to one of the principal families of the country. O'Higgins had received a good education which also included travel and study in England. Here he came in contact with Francisco Miranda, the forerunner of Hispanic American independence, and imbibed many of his revolutionary ideas. Confirmed in these views by his contacts with Martínez de Rozas, and endowed with wealth, education, and a handsome presence, he entered the first Chilean Congress with a prestige that soon put him at the front of the Radical Party.

Very shortly, however, this group found itself deprived of power. The conservative members gave it no representation on the executive *junta,* which was to take charge of public affairs until a national constitution could be prepared. In protest against this action, twelve members of congress retired from this body and were beginning to agitate against it when a military *coup d' état* changed the course of events. This resort to violence was directed by a young officer, José Miguel Carrera, a scion of one of the most wealthy and influential families of the country. His father and two brothers had taken part in the previous popular movement, and when José Miguel returned to Chile he more than seconded their efforts. His previous career had already given his family some trouble, but his open and frank character readily attracted the sympathy and adherence of the younger radicals. Like other young Creoles who in recent days had acquired European experience or education, Carrera eagerly embraced the movement for independence. It was natural, therefore, that he should aim to gain control of congress. Assisted by his two brothers, (who were like himself officers of high rank in the local militia), he won over the military forces, appeared before the hall in which congress was seated and forced that body to adjourn unconditionally. He then replaced the conservative deputies by men of radical stripe, altered the complexion of the local *cabildo* in Santiago, and in coöperation with other leaders forced similar action throughout the country. With the backing of the new members he then formed an executive *junta* of five, of which he was the head.

With the *junta* and congress under his control, radical legislation promptly followed. This provided for judicial and administrative reform, including a supreme court of justice. The sale of municipal offices was prohibited, the Inquisition overthrown, certain parochial fees suppressed, and as a crowning act, African slavery was abolished. This last act, of course, would affect few, for it applied simply to children born thereafter in the province. But limited as it was, Chilean writers claim that it was the first step of the sort taken in the New World. In addition, congress provided for free trade, for publicity of its acts, for secularized cemeteries, and broke off relations with Peru. Furthermore, it placed upon paper a complete system of public education and of universal military service.

Carrera's hand-picked assembly also appointed a special commission to prepare a constitution, but before definite action could be taken to that end, they were rendered futile by Carrera's own action. Neither he nor his brothers had been given sufficient attention to satisfy them; therefore, they found a pretext to declare previous elections invalid and, by an appeal to the lower elements of the population, were able to gather a mob for the purpose of overthrowing congress. That body was forced to convene another open *cabildo* in which all elements of the population, not excluding the most influential, were invited to take part. All affairs were, however, entrusted to a new *junta* of three, representing the three provinces of the country, with José Miguel Carrera at its head. O'Higgins was its second member, but he and the third accepted membership unwillingly. In November 1811, a new conspiracy broke out against the three brothers. Carrera then formed a third military mob, forced congress to dissolve, and from this point on assumed all authority.

His dictatorship, however, aroused resistance throughout the country. Opposition was centered largely in Concepción where Martínez de Rozas refused to recognize his authority. In response to this challenge, Carrera sent thither a body of troops. Civil war seemed imminent, but at a conference held on the banks of the Maule River, he and Carrera temporarily came to terms, and a later revolution provided for the supremacy of Carrera and the exile of Rozas.

It was during this period of Carrera's supremacy that the first distinguished visitor from North America, Joel Roberts Poinsett, reached Chile. His arrival aroused hopes of prompt recognition from the United States, and Poinsett, of course, did little to dispel this impression. He coöperated heartily with Carrera in many of his measures, including the establishing of a printing press and the project for a new constitution. A fellow-American of Swedish descent introduced this press, and on it, with Camilo Henríquez as editor, was printed the first paper, *La Aurora de Chile*. Few acts of these early days aroused more popular demonstration than the appearance of this sheet. It was a fitting token of the new age that was dawning for Chile. Henríquez and a small group of leaders associated with him exerted themselves to start other cultural agencies, including a National Institute. This was to replace the medieval establishments that hitherto had offered Chile its educational opportunities. These measures and others of similar character occupied the attention of the authorities until 1813 when peril from the north threatened to overthrow the government and its sponsors.

V

Up to this point the pathway of the revolution had been altogether too smooth. This was due to the fact that the mother country was too thoroughly engaged at home to pay much attention to distant colonies. The situation with regard to Peru, however, was quite different: the viceroy there had not only retained his authority intact, but was enabled to take measures against revolution in the neighboring colonies. Directing his efforts first to the provinces of La Plata, he continued campaigns there until his forces finally met defeat near Tucumán. Simultaneously he sent a force to the island of Chiloé. Shortly after its arrival there an anti-revolutionary movement in neighboring Valdivia brought that city under control of the Spanish commander. From this point the latter advanced northward and forced Concepción to surrender. These movements brought about a restoration of allegiance to Ferdinand VII in the occupied territory, and by March 1813 all Chile south of the Maule was in possession of the royalists.

News of these events did not reach Santiago until April. Public clamor immediately called for defense against the threatening invasion. Yielding to this outcry, Carrera, assisted by his brothers, by O'Higgins, and by another Irishman in Chilean service, Juan McKenna, forgot personal quarrels and united with the other radicals or "patriots" as they were now called, to fight their common peril. The contest then became one of unspeakable cruelty. Robbery, pillage, torture, and useless murder became the rule on both sides. As the recruits for each force came largely from the immediate country, fighting took on all the aspects of implacable civil war.

Carrera as commander so mismanaged the campaign for the patriots that at the end of the winter (August 1813) he met with disastrous defeat. The *junta* that directed affairs deprived him of his command and placed O'Higgins at the head of the army. Before he could reorganize his forces, news reached Santiago that the royalists had captured Talca and were on their way toward the unguarded capital. The terrified *junta* named a supreme director and prepared to meet the onset. McKenna and O'Higgins gathered forces in an attempt to protect the threatened city. Each in turn administered defeat to the royalists and then continued his march northward to place his army between the invaders and the capital. Thus they saved the latter city, but Concepción during 1814 remained in royalist possession.

At this juncture a British naval captain, Hillyar by name, attempted to arrange a truce between the belligerents. Great Britain was the ally of Spain in Europe, and at the same time British interests were being served by the insurgents who had opened their ports to general trade. It was natural, therefore, that the British captain should intervene in the hostilities on the west coast. His offer was welcomed by both groups in Chile, and in May 1814, patriots and royalists signed a treaty on the banks of the Lircay. Under its terms Chile was to recognize the sovereignty of the King of Spain. Hostilities were to cease and prisoners to be exchanged. Spanish forces were to leave the country and deputies were to be chosen to the Spanish *Cortes*. Meanwhile the patriot authorities were to remain at their posts.

The truce was acceptable neither to the rank and file of the patriots nor to the Peruvian viceroy. Moreover, the patriots fell out among themselves. The Carrera brothers, who had been captured by the royalists, now made their escape. When they reached Santiago and learned of the prospective peace, they effected another military *coup*, and José Miguel Carrera again found himself at the head of affairs. His action was based upon a resolution to continue the struggle at all hazards.

The new dictator immediately banished McKenna and called upon O'Higgins to submit to his rule. Far from obeying, the latter gathered his forces and started for Santiago to overthrow the usurper. Checked by Carrera's brother, Luís, O'Higgins was preparing to renew the attack when he learned that another force from Peru had landed to the southward and was advancing in his rear. The new threat led him to propose to Carrera that they unite against the new invader. In view of the common danger, his offer was accepted, and O'Higgins, late in September 1814, took up a defensive position at Rancagua. Here he was beseiged by the royalists, and, unrelieved by Carrera, was, after a stubborn defense, forced to abandon the town. Some five hundred of its defenders followed O'Higgins in a sortie and the major portion of them succeeded in escaping across the Andes to Mendoza.

The fall of Rancagua registered the overthrow of the earlier insurgent movement and put an end to what later writers called the "Old Fatherland." This period from 1810 to 1814 beheld the taking of initial steps in self-government, but no formal declaration of independence. Energetic minorities proposed reforms that were never put in force, largely because of lack of means or unfortunate quarrels among the leaders. Nevertheless, these proposals stimulated the survivors to persevere in the aspirations aroused by the quadrennium of local rule.

VI

The two and a half years that followed are spoken of as the "Spanish Reconquest." Three days after Rancagua, the Spanish commander, General Mariano Osorio, at the head of his victorious royalists entered Santiago amid the acclaim of the multitude. The Spanish commander at first displayed leniency, but nevertheless sought forcibly to undo the work of the insurgents. Local tribunals, made up from the *cabildos,* were given the task of examining the loyalty of the inhabitants. Under this scrutiny, many of the leading patriots were banished to the island of Juan Fernández. These repressive acts naturally produced reaction among the people, which was still further stimulated by the cruelty of subordinates. Discontent was heightened by the distinction made between troops brought from Peru or Spain and those of Chile. The sequestration of the property of leading insurgents did not suffice to meet the expense of the restored régime, so resort was had to extraordinary contributions. The institutions that had been abolished under the insurgent rule, such as the *audiencia,* and the Inquisition, reappeared. Free trade was suppressed. In one respect the royalists imitated the insurgents by establishing a paper of their own. These repressive measures of Osorio were still further augmented under his successor,

Marco del Pont. This ruler, seemingly more like a social lion than a frontier soldier, was a man of cool, implacable cruelty. He established tribunals, "brief, summary, and secret," that soon succeeded in turning even loyal supporters against him.

Meanwhile, across the Andes, General José de San Martín, of the Argentine forces, was forging the weapon that was to break the royalist hold on Chile. Joined by O'Higgins and other refugees, whom he welcomed as associates, San Martín from discordant forces was slowly bringing into shape a real army. At the same time, a free lance Chilean, Manuel Rodríguez, was also helping to undermine Marco del Pont's prestige. In the course of a few months Rodríguez established his own reputation as a guerrilla leader and made his exploits the theme of countless legends.

In February 1817, San Martín was ready to undertake the next stage of his main campaign against the royalists of southern South America. Although aimed ultimately at Peru, he first planned to overthrow opposition in Chile. After considerable maneuvering, designed to deceive his opponents, he and O'Higgins lead the bulk of the patriot forces directly across the Andes. All plans were so carefully laid that the difficult march was successfully accomplished, and on February 12, 1817, the mystified royalist commander was signally defeated in the battle of Chacabuco. On the following afternoon the vanguard of the victorious army arrived in the capital. On the following day, San Martín and O'Higgins were received there with every manifestation of joy. The former was offered the command of the state, and refusing to accept it, O'Higgins was proclaimed supreme director.

Chacabuco assured the success of the third and final step in Chilean independence. Like their royal master in Spain the representatives of the restored régime had "learned nothing and forgotten nothing." When, therefore, their authority was once fully broken, no considerable feeling of loyalty remained latent in the province. Marco del Pont and his minions had done their work all too well. From the portentous south the royalists might still threaten, but the patriots, confident of final triumph, on February 12, 1818, fittingly celebrated the anniversary of Chacabuco by issuing a formal declaration of independence. At Maipú, in the very outskirts of Santiago, they made this declaration good, April 5, by a second and final rout of the royalists. This hard-won victory meant that the "New Country" was to maintain itself and that its supporters now stood on the threshold of uninterrupted national existence.

CHAPTER TWENTY-FIVE

THE PERIOD OF POLITICAL TURMOIL, 1818-1833

I

THE early years in all Spanish American republics were marked by political turmoil. Chile differed from its neighbors only in the fact that it was subject to a briefer period of disturbance than they.[1] Its good fortune was determined in large part by the character of its population. This, we have noted before, consisted of two main groups, the landholding aristocracy, reinforced somewhat by mercantile and mining elements, and the *mestizo* mass, largely found in the country districts where it formed the tenant class on the great estates or the wandering *peones*. In towns the servants of the leading families, the mechanics, and other skilled laborers, and some of the smaller shopkeepers likewise belonged to this servile mass.

In winning independence, the Chilean aristocracy had changed little. Yet it should have changed, were its members as a class to undertake the task of carrying on a republican government. It is true that in early Chile, as in Rome, the word "republic" means little except the absence of a dynasty in the state.[2] But the new nation had adopted the word and its people must in some measure take on the responsibilities that accompany it. The class that had brought about political separation from Spain was now faced with the necessity of building up adequate political institutions. To this task they brought very limited resources. As a group they displayed considerable ability in managing their estates and in directing the labor of a servile class. A few of their number had a local reputation for culture and civic service. More of them were ready to present plans for constitutional development and still more were able to assume on occasion military functions. As a whole, however, those who must now direct the development of Chile lacked initia-

---

[1] Galdames and Hancock are useful for this period; also Barros Arana and the *Historia jeneral*. Among special works Ramón Briseño's *Memoria histórico-crítica del derecho público chileno* (Santiago, 1849) still has value. Cf. also Luís Galdames, *La evolución constitucional de Chile* (Santiago, 1927), vol. I, 1810-1833.

[2] Cf. Alberto Edwards, *La fronda aristocrática en Chile* (Santiago, 1928), p. 31. The late Señor Edwards was one of the most noted political philosophers of contemporary Chile.

tive. Nor could they meet this lack with extreme piety. Chile, therefore, might become a republic in name only—an entity subject to a crude local aristocracy and threatened by intervention from abroad. Yet its aristocratic sponsors must be credited with a fixed desire to create an adequate government. The fifteen years between the declaration of independence and the Constitution of 1833 bear abundant witness to this desire. They were, indeed, years of turmoil and bloodshed, but they were likewise years of constitutional experiment that were more promptly crowned with success than anywhere else in Spanish America.

Even before 1818 the devotees of a constitutional government had made their proposals.[3] None of them proved effective, largely because of the confusion that marked the period of active hostility. Likewise, before the declaration the spirit of orderly government was in evidence. After the battle of Chacabuco, Bernardo O'Higgins became supreme director of the republic. Primarily chosen to that office because of his military reputation, he demonstrated executive ability from the outset. He was handicapped by quarrels with the followers of Carrera. That leader and his brothers had aroused bitter hostility against themselves, both in Chile and in Argentina, to which they ultimately fell victims. O'Higgins was held responsible for their deaths, and also for the assassination of Manuel Rodríguez, the guerrilla chieftain whose popularity was so widespread in Chile. The weight of the accusations proved in the long run a stubborn source of trouble to the supreme director.

Another ever-present worry was the unsatisfactory financial condition of the country. The necessary expenditures in carrying on campaigns more than used up the increased revenues from customs duties and from the confiscation of royalist property. Naturally during the period of warfare, agriculture and mining had not flourished; nor when the enemy was finally driven from Chile did military expenditures lessen. O'Higgins contributed largely to the support of the campaign of his friend San Martín against Peru. This made necessary continued high taxes during the greater part of his administration. Moreover, in the extreme south it was necessary to continue operations against small royalist bands. These demands, plus the growing expenses of the governing personnel, made it impossible to balance the budget or to undertake any marked retrenchment in public expenditures. During the last

[3] Cf. Briseño, *op. cit.* and Galdames, *La evolución constitutional;* also Alcibíades Roldán, *Las primeras asambleas nacionales, 1811-1814* (Santiago, 1890). Señor Roldán has served his country long and well, both as professor of law in the University of Chile and as cabinet minister.

few months of his rule, the supreme director undertook through an agent in London to negotiate a loan abroad. The terms offered were difficult, but as low as could then be expected. This loan later led to an interesting experiment with the tobacco monopoly, of which more anon.

II

O'Higgins also stirred up resentment against himself by suppressing all titles of nobility in the country and by forcing some of the wealthy residents to tear down the coat of arms which decorated their houses. He also attempted, but unsuccessfully, to do away with primogeniture. He stirred up further opposition by proposing to take over some of the church property and by creating a cemetery for dissenters. He also tried without much success to regulate cockfights and bullfights, public processions and carnivals, and the worship of certain images. These attempts checked the development of more positive measures. He established a theatre in Santiago, improved the streets, provided a new market place, promoted the digging of canals, and greatly improved the public health and general appearance of the capital. Valparaiso became a port of three thousand inhabitants. In these two cities and elsewhere, he organized a more adequate police force, and outside the cities did much to break up banditry. In the field of education, he reopened the national institute, established a public library, and provided for Lancasterian and other schools in the capital and larger towns. Books were freely admitted and the press encouraged. But in spite of these well-meaning measures, he aroused against himself increasing opposition.

In his foreign policy the director was more fortunate. He did not succeed in getting papal recognition, but formed an alliance with the governments of Peru and Colombia and kept up cordial relations with Argentina. The independence of the country was recognized by Brazil, Mexico, and the United States. The government maintained a diplomatic agent in England through whom a necessary loan was arranged.

These events were largely brought about through the director's personal initiative. But his good sense and his energy did not commend him to the ruling class of the country. O'Higgins never really affiliated with the oligarchy that sought to control the country from Santiago. When he formally assumed power in 1818, he gave the country a constitution which provided for a legislative senate of five members, through whom he should exercise power, and a supreme judiciary tribunal. He also promised to convoke a constituent congress when the country was at peace. But as the years passed he made no move to call that congress. When, therefore, the execution of the Carreras and the enforced contributions made him still more unpopular with the oligarchy and the church, the growing opposition of these factions led him to action. He called for an election of members to an assembly, but all measures to that end were undertaken through pressure from the government and rendered him still more unpopular. The assembly met, however, and provided a constitution which was never put into force. Before it could be promulgated the garrison at Concepción arose in revolt and a little later that at La Serena followed. Ramón Freire, military chief at the former place, assumed leadership in the uprising and marched toward the capital.

O'Higgins at first believed that he could keep disaffection out of Santiago, but in this he was mistaken. When an uprising finally occurred there, February 28, 1823, an open *cabildo* met and demanded his resignation. For a time he refused, but when he found that the garrisons in the city were implicated in the revolt, he presented himself before the open town meeting, and demanded the object of the assemblage. Its leader informed him that they wished him to resign. He dramatically continued his refusal, but agreed to meet with a special commission to discuss the situation; and to this group, after further parley, he announced his willingness to give up authority. The public announcement which readily followed was received with universal rejoicing, and a *junta* of three members was appointed to take over the government. In a dramatic gesture the fallen director stripped himself of the sash which was his insignia of office and then challenged his enemies to accuse him of any public crime. His attitude and the belief that his career had been of real service to the republic, brought him public expressions of commendation. They acclaimed him as patriotic in office as he had previously been on the battlefield, but his days of usefulness to the republic were over.

The provisional *junta* did not long remain in office. Freire, who had headed the revolution, refused to recognize its authority and created a new one which he claimed was more nearly representative of the whole country. This body merely nominated the military chief as temporary supreme director. The choice for this office was a young man of thirty-five years, who had performed important military service, but who had never showed any ability as a statesman. He selected a prime minister, and associated with that official a so-called conservative senate of nine members. This body continued some of the social measures undertaken by O'Higgins, and it gained recognition for the final abolition of

African slavery. Such action had been taken in 1811 but it proved ineffective. This time public opinion enabled the sponsors to carry it out. Other legislation disclosed a general desire to improve public instruction, but for the present went no further. On the initiative of the government a new constituent congress was chosen. At its meeting in Santiago it named Freire supreme director and later adopted a document known as the Constitution of 1823. It was a utopian plan, a confused mixture of the principles of Greek democracy and more modern political thought, and it created a new organism inapplicable to any country. It entrusted the government to a supreme director who was assisted by a council of state to prepare laws and a conservative legislative senate to approve them. A national assembly served only to settle quarrels between the supreme director and the senate. This strange document, however, established the judiciary on a sane basis and permitted the citizens to assemble for elections and for action on the affairs of government. The document prohibited atheists from residing in the country and also forbade priests to hold political opinions. In other ways it attempted strictly to regulate private social life.

This bizarre creation, as might be imagined, lasted less than six months when it was suppressed by Freire. But other matters gave the director more trouble. The financial situation seemed to make it advisable to give to a private corporation the tobacco and other fiscal monopolies. In return the company was to undertake payments on the loan due in London. This concession for the first time brought into public notice the man, Diego Portales, who was later to direct the destinies of the country into more practical channels. As head of this monopoly, Portales did not realize the purpose for which it was created, but it gave him a public machine through which he later came into power.

Another measure which aroused more formidable opposition was the seizure of property belonging to the regular clergy. This action and the removal of the bishop of Santiago from his position for political reasons led to a break with the clergy. A papal vicar who had just arrived to arrange for a renewal of relations with the Vatican also left the country, and the combined results of their opposition was a general condemnation of the director. To a certain extent the Monroe Doctrine then proclaimed by the United States served to counterbalance the effect of this failure to establish relations with the papacy. But it did not save the unpopular director who, in 1826, was forced to abdicate his power.

From this time on Chile existed in full anarchy. Congresses and supreme directors followed each other in futile succession. The congress that received Freire's abdication, adopted in principle the federal organization. This was in accord with the views of one José Miguel Infante. To him the Constitution of the United States was a model, and that constitution with certain modifications, he believed, should be applied to Chile. Under his leadership, therefore, an attempt was made in 1826 to establish the federal system. The country was to be divided into eight provinces, each governed by its own popularly elected assembly. Obviously such an organization did not work in the new republic. Under Spanish rule, the unitary form of government was in vogue. The federal form, favored by Infante, was foreign to custom and to the wishes of the people. The system was discredited before it began, and the lack of funds brought on the revolution that overthrew it. The leader of this uprising rode his horse into the midst of the hall where congress was seated and ordered that body to dissolve. The country was wholly in the hands of its military leaders. But even so, no one of them could maintain himself in power.

By this time the tendencies that were to divide the country into the political parties had thoroughly manifested themselves. There were some who aimed to establish real liberty, who sought to reform the old institutions. Others who supported reaction abhorred all proposals of reform. Infante led the liberals; Manuel Egaña of monarchial inclination, the conservatives. To the liberals was given the name *pipiolos,* which might seem to indicate a person of unstable character who had little to lose. They in turn designated their opponents as *pelucones* from the *peluca* or wig which was a fitting sign of reaction. At this juncture, General Francisco Pinto, who held the office of vice president, undertook to control affairs. He had already given valiant service as a soldier and had served ably as a diplomat in Buenos Aires and London and as minister of state under Freire. He really desired to establish a democratic republic, and when he found that the federal type of government was unsatisfactory he brought together a new constituent congress. The election for this body went overwhelmingly to the liberals and to that body was presented the plan drawn up by a Spanish literateur who then resided in Chile, José Joaquín de Mora. Mora was a man of marked liberal principles which he strove to put into force in several South American countries. The constituent congress adopted his work with slight modifications. It was an ideal document far in advance of the country or even of the times. In one respect, however, it seemed less liberal for it retained the Catholic religion and forbade the public exercise of any other although "no one should be persecuted or molested for his private opinions." The government organized under this constitution gave supreme power to the legislative assembly, which was to form the budget, fix the salaries, make military promotions, and name members of the supreme court. It was likewise to censor the president and his ministers and hold them responsible for acts of government. One fundamental weakness of the constitution was that it continued the provincial assemblies, favored by Infante and other federalist leaders. This rendered the whole form of government as impracticable as that proposed in 1826.

The defects of the new system soon manifested themselves. Early in 1829, members of congress were chosen and the liberals received a substantial majority. Pinto was elected to the presidency, but a dispute arose over the office of vice president and in settling this question, the members of congress passed over the two who received the highest vote and selected a third person who belonged to their party. This led to a dispute with the disgruntled conservatives who forced the resignation of Pinto. Then followed a new revolution in the south headed by Joaquín Prieto, one of the discarded candidates for the vice presidency. Starting as usual from Concepción he advanced toward Santiago and met the government troops a little way from the city in an indecisive battle. A truce was followed by an agreement to place the forces of the country under General Freire, but the agreement lasted a short time only. The conservatives distrusted Freire because of his former liberal connections. They organized among themselves a *junta* which conferred military leadership upon Prieto. Freire prepared to resist this move. Gathering a force in the north, he transferred it to the southward, where his army encountered that of Prieto at Lircay, April 17, 1830, and was totally defeated. This battle was decisive. It ended the long period of political experimentation and marked the definite triumph of the conservatives. Prieto became the first of the autocratic rulers who for the next three decades directed the government of Chile.

The successful general gained the presidency, but he was not the strong man of his administration. That rôle belonged to Diego Portales. By refraining from seizing the presidency and by retiring for a time from public office, Portales showed that he preferred principle to personal aggrandizement. Born in Santiago in 1793, Portales had taken no part in the struggle for independence nor did he mix in politics until the fall of O'Higgins. Engaged in trade from his youth, he had received a very haphazard education, and he did not attract public attention. His first political enterprise was the administration of the tobacco monopoly, which we have noted above. The monopoly failed, but the organization gave him a party machine and also an influence in public affairs that virtually made him leader of the Conservative Party. Through correspondence and a propaganda sheet, Portales developed an organized attack on the various administrations of the liberals. He was a devotee of order and stability, and to the realization of these ends devoted the remainder of his life. He accepted a cabinet appointment shortly before the encounter at Lircay, a position which gave him real control of affairs. He coöperated in the campaign of Prieto and contributed materially to the latter's success. He was likewise instrumental in transferring the victor of that battle to the presidency. Naturally, therefore, in Prieto's administration he received the recognition to which his genius entitled him. Peace and stability became his watchword. He had combined with the militarists to overthrow an inefficient liberal government, and he now proposed to control the military hero in order to insure his coveted strong rule. He must in the long run make government conform to reality. Devoting himself first to the restoration of peace, he suppressed uprisings with a strong hand, and controlled all expression of public opinion in the forum or in the press. With order thus established he then turned his attention to the form of government.

Under his leadership a new constitutional assembly was brought together in 1831, and after two years' deliberation brought forth, May 25, 1833, a constitution that derives its name from that year. This constitution, largely the work in detail of Mariano Egaña, placed political power definitely in the hands of the landed aristocracy and rendered their property and privileges for the time being inviolate. At the same time it provided that members of this class who were willing to accept the cardinal principle of Portales should be equal before the law and maintain equal rights in respect to public office and employment. In fiscal matters the country was to carry on with a balanced budget. The legislative body was to be selected with the approval of the chief executive through his control of the electoral machinery, and local government was to be under the same supervision. Apparently, therefore, military power was to be transformed into civilian control but without losing its essential features. This was the system that was to inaugurate autocratic control. It was personified in the president, but administered for the benefit of the landed gentry. Thus while republican in form, Chile definitely became an oligarchy.

The Constitution of 1833 had then the virtue of not being an imitation, and it was not composed by mere idealists. It conformed more or less to the nature of the Chilean people and met the necessities of the time. It recurred to the principles of authority exemplified in colonial administration, and thus formed as a writer tells us an "appropriate bridge between 1810 and 1830." It also made Chile a "state in form," as defined by Spengler.[4]

---

[4] Cf. Alberto Edwards, *Fronda,* pp. 47, 58. His *Bosquejo histórico de los partidos políticos chilenos* (Santiago, 1903), Chs. III and IV, is likewise useful.

CHAPTER TWENTY-SIX

THE AUTOCRATIC REPUBLIC, 1831-1861

I

PORTALES represents, as one of his admirers has said, a near approach to the dictum of Carlyle regarding great men and the course of history.[1] In a few months, apparently, he changed the whole character of Chilean development and gave that nation a stability that none of its neighbors enjoyed. This was due to the fact that he recognized as no other contemporary statesmen the necessity for tranquility and order and hence sought to make progress gradually and with little change in the habits and thoughts of the people.

Chile had doubled its population since 1800. The half million of that date had, despite warfare, disease, and political disturbances, increased to more than a million by 1835. The greater portion of them were still found in the country, although the population of the cities was increasing rapidly. The capital, Santiago, in 1830 had about forty-eight thousand people and Valparaiso, the chief seaport, about half as many. Despite the growth of these cities and of lesser towns, they were still unlighted and unsanitary, and the urban population still continued the simple social customs of the colonial period. For amusement, the evening party within doors or the church procession outside still held first place, modified by an occasional theatrical performance or by a concert by the philharmonic orchestra. With respect to food supply, dress, and personal habits, little outward change could be noted among the better class. As for the poor, they still lived in the same miserable huts, wore the same scanty garb, and ate the same restricted list of foods, if they dined at all, as their forebears ate one or two generations earlier. In general, agriculture was beginning to yield somewhat to mining as a source of wealth. But the former still continued first in importance.[2]

It was such a people that fate and Portales summoned Prieto to govern. The first few years of his administration were by no means

---

[1] A. Edwards, *Fronda,* p. 41.

[2] Galdames, *Estudio,* Ch. VIII. The present chapter is based largely on this portion of Galdames' text.

peaceful. There were several conspiracies which forced the president to make use of the extraordinary powers incorporated in the new constitution. Prieto was the man to use these powers to the utmost. Primarily a military leader, he was acceptable to the oligarchy and on occasion could act against his enemies with moderation as well as firmness. Physically he made a good figure in public life, hence he attracted certain reactionaries who were glad to bolster up his administration. Through it all, he was willing to be guided by his great man whether the latter was in office or in retirement. Hence he afforded a convenient instrument to carry out the policy of Portales.

The latter in 1830 secured the services of Manuel Rengifo as minister of the treasury. A good financier and a man of high character, Rengifo held the office for four years. By strict economy in expenditures and by dismissing useless employees, he was able to effect considerable savings, and then by better regulation of the revenues to bring about an increase in receipts. He endeavored to make Valparaiso the best port on the Pacific, and measurably aided the commerce centering there. He adopted a protective policy for national industry and agriculture by laying customs duties upon certain manufactures, wheat, and cattle. He attempted to break up prevalent contraband trade by reducing or abolishing excise taxes. He dealt with the national debt, both domestic and foreign, in a way to satisfy the creditors and to establish the financial reputation of his country. When in 1835, through political intrigue, he was driven from office, he had completely reorganized national finances, increased revenues from one and a half to two million *pesos,* and materially lowered the debt.

These results had not been accomplished without arousing some opposition. Other questions brought further division into the government councils. The policy of Portales in excluding from the government all his opponents naturally failed to meet with universal approval. Men of more liberal spirit found fault with his intolerant course and with the predominance of the clergy in state affairs. In the cabinet, Rengifo represented a conciliatory spirit. His most significant opponent was the minister of interior, Joaquín Tocornal, a resolute servant of church and of autocracy. The moderate faction, as the period for electing a new president approached, issued a newspaper called *El Philipolita* (The Friend of the Common People) in behalf of the candidacy of Rengifo. This brought him into opposition to General Prieto who was a candidate for reëlection, and likewise attracted the support of some of the *pipiolos,* who were recovering courage after years of repression. Portales, who for some time had not been in office, saw with regret the appearance of this division and feared its effect on his general policy. When, therefore, the moderates proposed by legislation to restore to service the military officers who were dismissed in 1830, he decided it was time for him to act. On the night after the national holiday, September 18, 1835, he suddenly appeared in the government palace and assumed the war portfolio. Rengifo was surprised and resigned. Tocornal was transferred to the treasury department, and Portales combined the war portfolio with that of the interior. Thus was crushed what might have provoked a disastrous political controversy. Portales was once more openly in office at the head of a double ministry and even more powerful than in 1830.

The incident, which was after all a mere cabinet intrigue, might have assumed national proportions, but Prieto was reëlected without opposition. His opponents refrained from going to the polls. Thus was established the precedent of the ten year administration which was followed by Prieto's three successors. It was not hard for the chief of state to gain reëlection. For he nominated the mayors and members of municipal councils, the governors, intendants, judges, and other local officials. They in turn saw to it that the electorate received the certificates which each citizen had to present when voting. Citizens of twenty-five years who knew how to read and write and who had fixed property or income, or later, who were enrolled in the national guard, were permitted by the constitution to exercise the suffrage. In the towns the national officials, and in the country the landowners, saw to it that those who possessed the necessary qualifications were enrolled as voters, and what was more important, that they cast the right ballot. Thus voting was determined more by geographic areas than by individual preferences. The president, through the minister of the interior, sent the necessary instructions to these local agents, commending for the suffrage certain individuals or instructing the officials to prevent others from electioneering. Under the circumstances it was not hard for the chief executive to secure a loyal congress, especially when one might serve as senator or deputy while holding another public office. This method, sanctioned by the Constitution of 1833, lasted with little change for more than a half century. Consequently the opposition in congress was largely a negligible factor. Such conditions were inevitable in a country where the people lacked political knowledge, but the system had the advantage of keeping governments stable.

II

Shortly after Prieto's second term began, a serious quarrel arose between Chile and Peru. This was ascribed to an unsuccessful attempt by Freire to overthrow Prieto's government. Returning from exile in Peru, he landed on the Island of Chiloé, in order to start his campaign, but was defeated and captured before he began serious operations. Condemned to death, he was permitted instead to go again into exile. The defeat ended his political career.

This useless attempt against his system greatly exasperated Portales. To him Freire was the arch-culprit of disturbance, and when he and other revolutionists were released by the courts, he intervened to secure more severe sentences. Furthermore, Portales professed to see in the uprising the machinations of General Andrés Santa Cruz, the president of Bolivia and recently self-appointed Protector of the Peru-Bolivian Confederation. Santa Cruz proposed to combine these two countries under his jurisdiction, and he affected to believe that Chile would oppose the union. Portales, indeed, feared such a move and apparently was awaiting a chance to interfere. Freire gave him the necessary pretext. The fact that O'Higgins was also an exile in Peru further aroused his animosity against that nation and its new head. In addition to this charge of intervention, Portales could point to the fact that Peru had not met its portion of the expenses incurred some fifteen years before by the liberating army under San Martín. This expedition had been paid for in part by the debt incurred in England, so Peru's failure to meet its share bore with double weight upon Chile. Hence the exasperated and distrustful Portales had an additional reason for resentment against his northern neighbor. Years before, some of the Chilean statesmen had predicted for their country a mediatizing position between Argentina and Peru. In a political, as well as a physical sense, Chile was to become a sort of Switzerland for South America. In his resentment, however, Portales lost sight of this possible intercessory rôle and determined to force his rival into war.[3]

As a first step he sent two ships to Callao to seize the vessels of the Peruvian navy. His agent secured possession of these ships by surprise and then entered into negotiations with Santa Cruz. The latter preferred to leave the ships with the captor rather than proceed to hostilities. The agent returned to Valparaiso in triumph, bringing the captured vessels and also a Chilean envoy whom Santa Cruz had arrested

[3] Gonzalo Bulnes, *Historia de la campaña del Peru en 1838* (Santiago, 1878).

in his first impulse of rage and then released. The Bolivian preferred temporary submission to open hostilities.

Such a victory, however, did not suit Portales. He wanted to crush his enemy, not to give him a chance for further plotting against the Chilean government. He disapproved of the treaty, therefore, and then asked congress to authorize a declaration of war against Peru because of the outrage committed by arresting, even though momentarily, a Chilean envoy. His own agent, in seizing the Peruvian fleet, had committed a far worse outrage; but Portales lost sight of that in his determination to pick a quarrel with Santa Cruz. The counsels of Peruvian refugees in Chile strengthened his purpose. They persuaded him that should a Chilean army reach Peru, it would stimulate a formidable uprising against his rival. Accordingly, he despatched a second expedition under Mariano Egaña, with instructions to make such demands upon Peru as to force that country into war. Egaña carried out his task to the letter, and when the impossible demands were refused issued a definite declaration of war in September 1836.

When news of this declaration reached Santiago, Portales immediately assumed mastery of the situation. The entire republic was declared in a state of siege, and he was given unlimited powers to conduct the war as he saw fit. He immediately redoubled his activities and necessarily so. His previous repressive measures, coupled with what many thought was an unjust attitude toward Peru, led to innumerable outbreaks against him. These he repressed with his accustomed severity. Answering resistance with still greater threats, he strove to meet the peril by creating subordinate tribunals to judge by military law all who disturbed public order. Thus was initiated a veritable reign of terror in the midst of which the country was called upon to invade Peru.

At the beginning of June 1837, the dictator was reviewing a body of troops in camp near Valparaiso when the officers in charge arrested him and declared themselves in open rebellion. The mutineers started to convey him toward Valparaiso. The garrison at that port tried to resist them. On the morning of June 6, while fighting was under way, the officer in charge of the distinguished prisoner gave the order for his assassination; this was quickly carried out and as quickly produced widespread reaction throughout the republic. The murder was the result of no definite plan for improving conditions and it removed in an hour of peril the one figure who seemed able to command the situation. The tyrant of the moment before became an idolized martyr. The war that had aroused the last opposition against him now fired the national will and the country prepared to carry on the campaign so shockingly interrupted.

The first expedition proved a disaster. The Peruvian people did not rise in arms as their exiled representatives in Chile had predicted. Rather, they surrounded a small Chilean force that had seized Arequipa, forced it to capitulate and sign a treaty under which the Chileans were to recognize the Peru-Bolivian Confederation, withdraw from the invaded country, and return the ships previously seized.

Such a treaty of course served to arouse general indignation. The government disavowed it, ordered Peruvian ports to be blockaded, and prepared for a second campaign. This expedition under General Manuel Bulnes, a nephew of the president, was more successful. When the Chilean force landed north of Callao, the upper provinces of Peru rose in revolt. Aided by these insurgents, Bulnes in the course of a few months won the decisive battle of Yungay, January 20, 1839—a battle which destroyed the confederation of Santa Cruz before it had a chance to get well under way. Moreover it established abroad the reputation of Chile as a fighting nation, and a well-organized one. The event seemed to justify the motto of the country "By reason or by force."

III

The war also made its successful leader the next president of Chile. General Bulnes took his seat in 1841, and thus for a second time a military hero became the titular head of the country whose civic aim was order and stability. Like his predecessor, the new executive displayed other than military qualifications. He was simple minded, sincere, conciliatory and generous—withal a man of good common sense. What he lacked in definite instruction, he supplied by rare intuition.[4] Conservative as might be expected, he exerted himself to remove local disaffection, and in the early years of his administration was remarkably successful in achieving his purpose. Amongst other measures he gave O'Higgins permission to return from exile, but that leader died in 1842 before he could take advantage of it.

One of the important moves of the new administration was to recall Rengifo to the treasury.[5] Through the efforts of this minister, economy and prosperity became general in the country. Agriculture was devel-

---

[4] Alberto Cabero, *Chile y los chilenos,* p. 215.

[5] Cf. Daniel Martner, *Estudio de política comercial chilena é historia económica nacional,* I, pp. 205 *et seq.;* also Cabero, p. 290. The figures in the following paragraphs are based on Martner.

oped through the introduction of machinery, the opening of new roads, and the formation of a National Society of Agriculture. Foreign commerce increased rapidly with the introduction of steam navigation. New mineral resources were discovered, especially silver, copper, and coal, and for a time Chile figured as the foremost copper producer of the world. The fiscal policy of the country, already greatly helped by commercial treaties with the United States, Peru, and France, was still further stimulated by the treaty of 1843 with Great Britain, which was partly dictated by the policy of free trade. Rengifo also succeeded in refunding the British debt, first contracted under O'Higgins, on terms satisfactory both to the creditors and to the country.

Trade and revenues advanced simultaneously. Systematic statistics of foreign trade began in the mid-forties when nearly a half of the total commerce of the country was with England and a sixth with the United States. The figures show consistent gains. Beginning in 1845 with a total value of more than 16,600,000 *pesos,* they reach more than twenty-two millions by 1849 and twenty-eight millions in 1851. With some fluctuations, foreign trade continued to increase during the next ten years, rising at the end to more than 47,642,000 *pesos.* The revenues reflect this gain. Starting with more than three million *pesos* in 1845, which is twice the figure for 1831, they reached nearly four and a half millions by 1851 and seven and a half millions in 1860. Some of the later increase was due to the market for foodstuffs, opened by the discovery of gold in California and Australia—a market which in each case proved to be but temporary. A third or more of the income was derived from customs duties, with the tobacco monopoly and the *diezmo* (subsequently modified) occupying the next favored places. New mines, better instruction in mining methods, and the opening of steamship lines to Europe helped both trade and revenues. The national debt, although placed on a satisfactory basis, kept pace with both. In 1850 it showed a total of nearly 8,900,000 *pesos,* of which five-sixths represented the foreign debt. In 1860 the entire debt ran to over fifteen millions, and in about the same proportion. Foreign obligations had been increased by a loan of 7,700,000 *pesos* for the construction of railroads.

In general, the efficient ordering of national finance, public and private, formed the crowning achievement of Chile's autocratic régime. But the cultural development of the country was by no means neglected. In 1842 congress by law established the National University. The same year saw the appearance of two ephemeral literary reviews, each conducted by a literary society under the inspiration of a future intellectual leader, José Victorino Lastarria. Stimulated by such influences, a journal, *El Seminario,* soon appeared, a welcome, though short-lived, literary medium for an expanding circle of Chilean youth. Another publication of the period, *El Crepúsculo* ("Twilight"), brought to one of its contributors, Francisco Bilbao, an assured position in the national literature, expulsion from the National Institute, and temporary banishment from the country. His *Sociabilidad chilena* ("Chilean Sociability") was too "blasphemous and immoral" an attack on the church for the authorities to ignore. Chile, for them, was still in a twilight which Bilbao's pen, too early arrested, was doing much to lighten.[6]

In the same year, 1844, Lastarria inaugurated a more judicious line of literary production. His dissertation on the social influence of the Spanish conquest and the Spanish colonial system was the forerunner of a long line of historical studies to be presented before special annual sessions of the university. More philosophical than factual, it drew criticism as well as praise upon its young author, but it set him apart as a prospective intellectual and political leader.

Much of this mental ferment of the early forties was due to foreign influence. The tyranny of Rosas, in the neighboring republic, brought to Chile a select and most helpful Argentine immigration. Most prominent among these refugees was Domingo Faustino Sarmiento, editor for a time of *El Mercurio* of Valparaiso, and founder and first director of the normal school of Santiago. Also prominent in literary as well as in political circles was José Joaquín de Mora, who in the early thirties conducted a private *liceo* for boys, while his wife taught one for the girls of Santiago. More potent than Mora or Sarmiento in the literary development of Chile was the learned Venezuelan, Andrés Bello. Coming to Chile in 1829, after serving that country and his native land as consul general in London, Bello devoted the remainder of a long life to his adopted country. He was named as first rector of the university despite the efforts of the clergy to have one of their own number put in that strategic place. From that time until his death, Bello was recognized as the intellectual dean of Chile. With an enormous output in the fields of pure literature and of philology, he also formulated the civil code of the country and sought through his wide correspondence to make over the grammatical structure of the Spanish language. Unable to obtain general acceptance of his views, he did fix his peculiar orthog-

---

[6] Cf. Pedro N. Cruz, *Estudio sobre la literatura chilena,* I, Chs. I-III; also Alfred Coester, *Literary History of Spanish America,* Ch. VI.

raphy on his adopted country for several decades. More significant still was his impress upon the youth who were to direct public affairs in the latter part of the nineteenth century.

The educational system quickly responded to these new impulses. The National Institute, under the rectorship of Manuel Montt and Antonio Varas, trained men both for secondary teaching and for political careers. Under Varas its instruction became more definitely scientific in spirit. The three secondary schools of the thirties had become six by 1842, and eight a few years later. At La Serena, in the northern mining district, the secondary school offered instruction in chemistry and mineralology under a Polish scholar, Ignacio Domeyko. A school of arts and crafts and one of agriculture existed in Santiago, along with a newly founded school of architecture and painting and a conservatory of music. Somewhat later the distinguished German botanist, Armando Philippi, took up his work in Chile.

Private "colleges" or seminaries, to the number of ten, supplemented the work of the public *liceos* in the forties. Fifty common schools, attended by some three thousand pupils, represented the educational opportunities of two hundred thousand children of school age. This pitiful showing will account for the low rate of literacy in the country. But another ten years was to witness substantial progress in education.

IV

The administration of General Bulnes was on the whole a tranquil and productive period during which the national credit was strengthened abroad and internal affairs were administered with regularity and general approval. Furthermore, Bulnes did much to extend national prestige by taking possession of the Straits of Magellan and establishing there the southernmost settlement in the southern hemisphere. This act aroused protests from Argentina and started a series of boundary controversies that were to last for more than half a century. The president also encouraged foreign immigration, and the first contingents of German settlers reached the country before the close of his administration. He finally settled outstanding questions with Peru and, in 1844, obtained recognition from Spain, thereby bringing about a modification of the national anthem and building up harmonious relations with the Vatican. Simultaneously, he started a series of disputes with the church by favoring toleration and permitting an open press discussion of the practice. Moreover, slight modifications of earlier religious ceremonies showed that the influence of the church in public affairs was waning. More serious still were the controversies carried on with the bishops of Santiago and Concepción, who were beginning to struggle against this loss of prestige.

This tendency, becoming more marked toward the end of the administration led to division in the Conservative Party. Some of the younger element led by Manuel Antonio Tocornal and Antonio García Reyes took a less uncompromising attitude with respect to the province of the church. In the depleted liberal ranks arose a group of intellectual leaders, guided by José Victorino Lastarria, who espoused a series of reforms tending to weaken the authority of the executive, to liberate the press, and to bring about an independent suffrage; in short, to make Chile a true republic "popular and representative."

Many of the principles espoused by this group were derived from the French revolution of 1848. In 1849 a number of these younger men, including Tocornal and García Reyes, secured seats in congress. This was an important assembly because it was to decide the election of the next president. Already the contest had caused a division in the cabinet. The minister of the interior, in preparing the list of members for this congress, had put in too many from his own family and from among his protégés. The president and most of his advisers, who were united in behalf of the candidacy of Don Manuel Montt, remonstrated without success against the action of their colleague. In certain centers a real contest developed between the supporters of Montt, who was also a member of the cabinet, and the henchmen of the offending minister. From this time on, congress became more of a debating society without, however, breaking the hold that the aristocracy exerted over its members. Montt, though of a comparatively poor country family, was a thorough supporter of the existing conditions, and as the designated candidate for the presidency, let no chances interfere with his prospects.[7]

This protest, as it might be so designated, formed a significant step in the parliamentary development of Chile. For a time it promised even more. The cabinet seemed to be working at cross purposes. The president gave no sign to indicate his wishes, and the country was un-

---

[7] The political events of this period are well summarized in A. Edwards, *Fronda,* Chs. XI-XIII and in his *Partidos políticos,* Chs. VI-VIII. The same author gives a more detailed study in *El gobierno de Don Manuel Montt 1851-1861* (Santiago, 1932). This last book, published in the year of the author's death, represents a fragment of a greater work covering a hundred years of Chilean history. Cf. also Cabero, pp. 217-222. Unsympathetic sketches of Portales appear in J. V. Lastarria, *Don Diego Portales* (Santiago, 1896), and B. Vicuña Mackenna, *Don Diego Portales* (Valparaiso, 1863).

certain how to vote. Manuel Camilo Vial, the neopotic minister, resigned and the president filled his place with Antonio Varas, the most intimate of Montt's supporters and thus assured the latter's success.

The incident, however, was not wholly closed. The spirit of opposition thus engendered in governmental forces stimulated the younger liberals to definite action. Imitating their Paris mentors, the more radical among them resorted to barricades or to processions that ended in hostile clashes. Their demands were supported by the Society of Equality—a series of clubs designed "to teach the people to use their inalienable rights," and also to train them in rioting. In support of these ideas one Eusebio Lillo edited a journal called *El Amigo del Pueblo* ("The Friend of the People").

The leader of this movement, Lastarria, was the young son of a banker, born in Chile and educated in Paris, where he beheld the disturbances of 1848. His associate was Francisco Bilbao, recently returned from his five years of exile abroad. These upper-class proletarians joined with the liberals to bring about a change in the presidency. They opposed Montt's candidacy with such fervor that the government determined to suppress the society, and in August 1850 broke up a night session of one of the clubs. In reply, the Equalitarians, under the leadership of Bilbao, began manifestations against Montt and the government. Before the end of the year the society was dissolved and further organizations of the sort prohibited. Making use of its extraordinary powers, the government declared a state of siege, stopped opposition papers, and exiled the leaders, including Lastarria and Bilbao. This repression served to spread the mischief rather than to stop it; disorder broke out in the provinces, and on April 26, 1851 there was a bloody uprising in the capital which cost the lives of more than one hundred persons. Peace was then reëstablished.

These repressive measures did not check electioneering activities. General José María de la Cruz, cousin of the president, was put forward by the liberals as their candidate. He was of course unsuccessful, for he carried only Concepción and La Serena. Montt was elected by an overwhelming majority but his success did not end the contest. Early in September of that year, in the two opposing centers, an uprising occurred in favor of General Cruz. Bulnes who had come into the presidency ten years earlier and who had carried on his high office in the midst of general peace thus ended his administration in a revolutionary outbreak. The new president had therefore to crush the movement, and the retiring president, resuming his military functions, quickly carried out this task. He broke the first serious challenge to the autocratic system at the battle of Loncomilla, December 8, 1851, when two thousand dead and fifteen hundred wounded (significant proportion!) were left upon the field. Shortly afterward the revolution in the north was likewise suppressed.

V

The new president thus encountered a stormy introduction, but it was a threat that called forth an equally energetic response. Unlike his two predecessors, Montt was a civilian, but an even greater and more uncompromising devotee of discipline than they. Of country birth and educated at the National Institute, he owed his rise wholly to hard work and study. For five years, 1835-1840, he was the rector of the Institute and then entered the chamber of deputies, which immediately made him its president. In the same year, General Prieto made him minister of the interior and thus he directed the presidential election of Bulnes, whom he later served as minister of public instruction, and as his chief said, "proved a most active assistant." When in turn he was elected to the chief magistracy, he brought to that office, despite his forty-two years, a comparatively long public experience. His own training and his career as educator had given him the schoolmaster outlook on life. An admirer of the autocratic system, although largely its servant rather than its director, Montt was a follower of Portales and like that leader an unquestioning representative of law and order. For ten years therefore, he faced with firmness and equanimity the subversive elements that had arisen since the time of Portales. His administration proved a period of social and economic progress, but in the midst of change he sought to preserve the significant features of the preceding régime and to keep them from being overwhelmed in the tide of new interests.

His rule though turbulent was not unproductive. He enlarged and improved public administration. He continued valuable public works and added to them. He began the railroad from Santiago to Valparaiso and also one to the southward, improved the highways, and completed a telegraph line. He put through these improvements against the opposition of those who saw in them the end of their privileges. Santiago, the capital, received a completed penitentiary, an insane asylum, and a congressional palace. Along the coast appeared new warehouses, wharves, and lighthouses. Savings banks were established to encourage thrift and a mortgage loan bank to stimulate agriculture. The tithe, a colonial ecclesiastical levy in kind, was replaced by a more productive tax on the revenue from real estate. His administration also saw the end of entailed estates, a reform that had been undertaken by O'Higgins, a generation before. He encouraged colonization in the south, and a new port bearing the president's name was established to promote German immigration in that quarter.

Despite measures to curb disorder and to limit discussion that might lead to it, Montt gave due attention to cultural matters. More than five hundred public schools were founded during his decennium; the total number of cultural institutions, public and private, reached nine hundred, attended by some forty-five thousand pupils. The Society for Primary Instruction, a private organization, helped to bring about this growth. The government started schools for training women teachers and improved the one for schoolmasters. It furthered the founding of public libraries and the development of technical education. The country now boasted of ten secondary schools, of which the National Institute still maintained the lead.

As in the preceding decade, cultural advance owed much to foreign representatives. Domeyko and Philippi continued their scientific pioneer work. They were now reinforced by two eminent French scholars: Amando Pissis, a geologist and map maker, and J. G. Courcelle-Seneuil, who introduced the study of economics into the law course. Sarmiento published an important work on public instruction before returning to Argentina, and this was followed in the late fifties by a more important study, *Primary Instruction in Chile: What It Is and What It Ought tc Be.* Its author, a Chilean largely self-taught, was Miguel Luís Amunátegui, later more famous as a historian and statesman. An astronomical observatory, started under North American auspices, was acquired by the government and placed in charge of a German mathematician. More significant still was the completion, in 1855, of Bello's *Civil Code of Chile,* the crown of twenty years of personal effort.

The general social conditions of the country did not keep pace with its material and cultural advance. Sanitary conditions were deplorable. Smallpox and scarlet fever made great inroads among the lower classes of the cities, although a voluntary charity commission sought to aid the government in combatting these plagues. Beggars thronged the streets of the towns, while highwaymen terrorized the countryside. Robbery and assassination occurred all too frequently. Portales dealt with criminals with the same severity as with political offenders, but the barred carts of his day afforded very inadequate means for detaining them. Under Bulnes there was an increase in the police force and an improvement in its personnel. Under Montt was completed a penitentiary and an insane asylum.

The mid-century saw the beginnings of assisted immigration, especially from Germany. These immigrants were largely settled in the district of Llanquihue, where Puerto Montt soon became an important receiving center. They proved to be an industrious element and in a short time their farms, tanneries, packing houses, and breweries began to move northward into the former Araucanian country, where a new Germany began to reproduce itself. In the early fifties Chile sent its own contingent of emigrants to California, where their experiences on the whole were far from being pleasant or profitable.

In general, the period of conservative control was a time of slow social evolution. The great landed proprietors still continued to monopolize agricultural interests although the abolition of primogeniture in 1852 promised to break up class solidarity. The cities were growing and becoming more attractive. Santiago boasted of a hundred thousand inhabitants by 1861; Valparaiso of sixty thousand. The growth of these two cities, not to mention that of smaller towns, shows a strong tendency toward urbanization, more intense civic pride, and culture. The introduction of steam navigation, the improvement of highways, the building of bridges, and the beginning of railroads, all helped the tendency toward closer centralization. General culture expressed itself more definitely in the cities where schools abounded and where literary expression was more favorably received. Wealth continued, of course, to dominate the situation, but learning, ability, and civic virtue were also influential. By 1860 a new aristocracy, in which the business group dominated, was beginning to make itself felt. This was made up of mine owners from the north and the commercial element of towns and cities.

This social development, of course, had its effect on the political system. In fact many of the newer features in the latter may be directly traced to the new spirit of social consciousness which now began to make itself felt. This showed itself nowhere more clearly than in the attitude toward ecclesiastical control. It affected the relation of the church and state where the laws permitted the marriage of nonconformists without Catholic rites, but compelled priests to witness the contract. The law of civil patronage also gave the government jurisdiction over parish priests when carrying out their duties. The age at which candidates could enter clerical orders was likewise raised to twenty-five years.

With a man of Montt's temperament one would anticipate cordial relations with the church. That institution did indeed share in the general prosperity in the country and its budget was augmented year by year. But during the mid-period of Montt's presidency occurred a serious break between the government and the hierarchy. A minor dispute arose over the expulsion of a sacristan from the cathedral. This led to the suspension of two canons who thought it was undeserved. The suspended prelates appealed to the supreme court which revoked the decision. The archbishop protested against the opinion of the tribunal and thus provoked a sharp exchange of notes between himself and the minister of worship. Montt supported his minister for he placed obedience to law above every other consideration. His attitude subjected him to severe criticism on the ground that he was trying to discredit the Catholic religion through its highest representative in Chile. From this time on the Conservative Party was definitely divided into two groups, one supporting the government and hence gradually acquiring the name of nationalists, while the other continued to support the church in its pretended exemption from civil control. Moreover, the administration faced numerous complaints from foreign nations. These were based largely on injuries suffered by the citizens of those countries during general disturbances such as the revolution of 1851. As a result of the controversy, the government adopted the law of civil responsibility which in cases of sedition held individual persons responsible for any excesses committed.

The administration which began with an armed revolution faced another at its close. Public opinion was now arraying itself against the excessive authority of the last quarter century. The government was accused not only of repressing free speech and the press, but of using its influence to continue definitely its representatives in office. The powers bestowed upon the president enabled him to imprison or banish opponents, although his supporters regarded them as pledges for the security of person and property. The presidents fully believed that the bulk of the population was still unprepared for a representative type of government, so they opposed, as premature, reforms suggested by the liberals. To the criticisms of these opponents was added that of the reactionary conservatives, angered by the dissolution of entailed estates and by the disputes between the executive and the archbishop of Santiago. So far did this conservative faction carry its opposition that they were led before the close of Montt's second term to join forces with the liberals. Thus the two extremes combined; the new liberals who replaced the *pipiolos* of 1829 allied themselves with the remnant of the *pelucones* who had at the earlier period opposed them. This liberal-conservative fusion, known as the coalition, not only opposed Montt but arrayed itself against the proposed successor. Their motto was "Order within Liberty." They demanded this liberty because they found themselves in opposition to the existing government.

On the other hand, the more moderate liberals and conservatives, uniting to support Montt and his friends, assumed the name of nationalists and presented as their motto "Liberty within Order." This group was called the Montt-Varista Party; its prospective leader was Antonio Varas, the head of Montt's ministry during his first term. In more than one way, he was Montt's devoted follower. Born some eight years after that executive, he had, like him, attended the National Institute, had become a professor there, and had served as Montt's vice-rector. When Montt became minister, Varas became rector; when Montt passed from the minister of justice to that of the interior, Varas succeeded him in the former office. When Montt was a candidate for the presidency, Varas was the minister of the interior who managed the election; so that it was generally believed, when Montt approached the end of his presidency, that Varas would succeed him. Upon Varas, therefore, was concentrated all the wrath of the liberal-conservative fusion.

Varas was an intelligent and distinguished man, a lawyer and an engineer, who in the press, in legislative assembly, and in the ministry had shown qualifications which fully entitled him to the presidency. His candidacy, however, brought about a revolution in 1859. An earlier proposal to banish those involved in past uprisings led to the launching of a periodical known as *La Asamblea Constituyente.* Its chief contributors were Manual Antonio Matta and Benjamín Vicuña Mackenna. It advocated numerous reforms in the constitution, and from the Union Club of Santiago distributed propaganda to that end in all parts of the republic. Attempts to suppress demonstration against the government were unsuccessful; one hundred and fifty persons who gathered in the Union Club, in violation of government orders, were arrested, and Santiago and near-by provinces were declared in a state of siege. By January 1859, insurrection began in numerous provincial towns. The most serious point of opposition was Copiapó where Pedro León Gallo, a rich mine owner, raised an army at his own expense and for a time dominated the area. He was, however, finally overcome in April 1859. Below the settled area to the southward, the Araucanians arose in revolt and were not defeated until after a campaign of two years. Furthermore, in 1861 a grave financial crisis threatened the country. This was due in part to these disturbances, but more to the fall in the price of wheat. The temporary demand for Chilean foodstuffs caused by the gold discoveries, had greatly benefited the landowners and led to overproduction in the country; hence the crisis which fell upon it in 1861. With this economic threat added to previous disorders, the election of Varas became a critical issue. No doubt the government could have advanced him to the presidency, but at the cost of serious internal strife. Hence that leader took the more patriotic course of declining that high office. With the withdrawal of his name and the substitution for him of José Joaquín Pérez, a politician of the National Party who was acceptable to the opposition, the election passed off peacefully and on September 18, 1861, Montt handed over to him the coveted but provocative office. Chile was about to enter a new era.

CHAPTER TWENTY-SEVEN

THE LIBERALIZED REPUBLIC, 1861-1886

I

ON SEPTEMBER 18, 1861, Don José Joaquín Pérez succeeded Montt as president. A man of moderate ideas and of conciliatory temperament, he represented the national *milieu*. He was a minister, as one writer put it, "of serenity and egoism, of equanimity and inertia, of learning and knowledge of men, with disdain for ideals, of good sense and of highest malice, of rectitude and political opportunism."[1] He had had a wide diplomatic experience with some general travel both in the United States and Europe, and likewise had served during the two preceding administrations as minister and councillor of state. Yet his association with Montt's administration was not so close as to render him unacceptable to other political factions. Selected as a compromise candidate, although connected with the Nationalist Party, he entered upon his duties as a sort of representative of the combined moderate liberal and conservative groups.

Starting out with hopes of harmony and goodwill, he soon found it necessary to break with the nationalists and with some of the more advanced liberals. This divided him from the liberal-conservative fusion that had put him into office and, shortly after he began his duties, brought about a change in his cabinet and a definite alignment with the more advanced groups. Thus Pérez became a liberal in spite of himself—a type of the executives that were to succeed him. Generally these were timid as administrators but able to give a certain impulse to the material evolution of the country. From this time on, therefore, the administration begins definitely to act with parties rather than to use a party as a personal instrument with which to dominate the country.[2] The president becomes a sort of arbiter among political factions, which in turn tend to

---

[1] A. Cabero, *Chile y los chilenos,* p. 222.

[2] For the course of political events during this period of political change, consult A. Edwards, *Fronda,* Chs. XX-XXVI, and his *Partidos políticos,* Chs. IX-XI. The narrative as before parallels the *Estudio* of Galdames, Ch. IX. From this point on the sources of Chilean history are much more scattered. We are beyond the era covered by the "great" historians who wrote during the last half of the nineteenth century.

form temporary unions to curb him or through him to direct national affairs.

In the early sixties a new political group, composed of the more advanced liberals, definitely detached themselves from their fellows and formed the Radical Party. Its members repudiated fusion with the conservatives that had brought about the election of Pérez and later allied themselves with the nationalist group. The party pretended to live up to the dictum of a contemporary political philosopher in that "it was scientific in its foundation, methodical in its conduct, positive in its ideals, organic in its principles, in its measures and in its purposes." [3] One of its leaders was a rich mine owner by the name of Gallo. The brothers Matta[4] in their paper, *La Voz de Chile,* presented the program of the party, namely, "reform of the constitution, laical instruction, administrative decentralization and electoral liberty." After all, it will be noted that this program represented a middle class philosophy rather than an extreme move to the left. It was one of the forces that later contributed to the establishment of parliamentary government.

In the congressional election of 1864, party combinations definitely expressed themselves in what seemed diametrically opposed groups. On one side, the radicals, who protested against an autocratic government, united with the nationalists, who most strongly supported that form of control. While their opponents were made up of conservatives, who were strong supporters of the church and its privileges, and the moderate liberals, whose chief watchword was opposition to the influence of the church in the state, politics in Chile, as ever, made strange bedfellows. But the incongruous elements did not long repose on the same couch. Party disputes for a decade or more had arisen on constitutional questions. Now, apparently, they began to develop a new technique, and religious questions replaced mere constitutional ones; although, as one commentator mentions, religious issues simply helped to democratize the constitution.[5]

II

Whatever the purpose of these party disputes of the sixties, they were for a time halted by the threat of foreign war. By the middle

[3] Cabero, p. 223.

[4] For sketches of these famous brothers and of other political leaders of the period—sketches that are often biased, but expressed in vigorous and fascinating style—consult Don Justo and Don Domingo Arteaga Alemparte, *Los constituyentes de 1870* in *Biblioteca de Escritores de Chile,* Vol. II.

[5] A. Edwards, *Fronda,* Ch. XXIV.

of the decade a serious controversy had arisen between Peru and the mother country. Spain had never recognized the independence of its former colony. So the controversy precipitated a discussion in which Peru felt that its national dignity was insulted. The Peruvian administration, therefore, refused to make terms with the commander of a fleet sent to demand reparation. In retaliation, the Spanish commander seized the Chincha Islands—a blow to the Peruvian treasury as well as to national pride. This ultimately led Peru to a formal declaration of war againt Spain. Meanwhile the threatening peril had, in 1864, brought about a proposed American Congress with a prospective alliance among the republics of the west coast. In Chile the controversy provoked demonstrations against the Spanish minister, and these in turn caused the irritated Spanish naval commander to demand an immediate apology. Chile's reply to the fiery correspondence was a declaration of war against Spain, and an appeal for national unity to which the people promptly responded.[6]

Chile's attitude was in effect a vicarious sacrifice to South American unity. In a naval skirmish that followed, the Chilean sloop, *Esmeralda,* captured the Spanish schooner, *Covodonga.* This defeat, followed by the suicide of the Spanish admiral, proved in the end a costly victory. For the new Spanish commander, Méndez Núñez, when ordered to retire from the Pacific, bombarded the port of Valparaiso and inflicted on that unarmed city a damage of some ten millions of dollars. The net result was that Chile lost confidence in the Monroe Doctrine as an insurance policy for defenceless ports. An American war vessel, then on the coast, had retired from the harbor before the bombardment began, and the efforts of the American minister and others to prevent that useless atrocity had proved unavailing. It was some years before Chile and its sister republics settled the dispute with the former mother country, but in the meantime the Chilean government had taken measures to increase the naval strength of the country and to bring about a better organization of its war forces. The Radical Party, indeed, wished to use the incident to demonstrate the need for a confederation among the former Spanish colonies, but the time was not ripe for such an intimate bond.

III

From Pérez the country expected a tranquil administration. Barring the above brush with Spain and a few other untoward incidents, he did

[6] For an excellent summary of this incident cf. H. C. Evans, *Chile and its Relations with the United States,* pp. 86-96; cf. also W. S. Robertson, *Hispanic-American Relations with the United States,* pp. 147-149.

not disappoint them. Economically a tranquil administration meant one in which railroads and telegraph lines would be extended and public revenues increased. Receipts were in fact doubled. At the outset, however, there was a drop in trade, due possibly to the disturbances of the period, but the general economic trend was upward. Certain new legislation of the period was to have an important affect on the economic situation. A new railroad law, still in existence, was adopted in 1862. A new ordinance for the customhouses appeared two years later. Foreign vessels under this law acquired complete liberty in the coasting trade. Agriculture was given special encouragement. The state proposed to take over the railroads. Further efforts were also put forth in the field of colonization, especially in Germany. A commercial code was established in 1865, followed eleven years later by a mining code. The trade at this mid-period of the sixties still showed England as the most important nation with which Chile dealt. Peru came second, in 1855, outstripping the United States, even with the addition of California.[7]

Foreign capital now became an important agency of material progress. Much of the money was used to exploit the nitrate and guano areas of the north, still in the possession of Peru and of Bolivia. The Caracoles silver mine, also in Bolivian territory, lent itself to swift but prolific speculation. The brief but useless war with Spain affected trade and revenues but little. In 1866 Chile, through the house of Morgan and Company, added ten million *pesos* to the national debt, but three years later paid the last installment of the original one contracted under O'Higgins. The external debt in 1870 stood at 27,843,000 *pesos* and the internal debt at 8,786,000 *pesos*—a total of about nineteen *pesos* per head. The foreign trade was then approaching fifty million *pesos* and the national income eleven and a half million *pesos*.

This highly creditable showing was due in large measure to the skillful administration of the treasury under Alejandro Reyes and Melchor Concha y Toro. The latter proved a functionary of originality and real initiative. He it was who suggested an income tax—to be adopted many years later—and advised a tax on inheritances. Like other progressives, he favored dropping the *alcabala,* but that measure also had to wait twenty years. Nevertheless, the two years of his incumbency,

---

[7] In the Chilean trade statistics for the period, California appears as a separate item. Cf. Martner *op. cit.* I, pp. 254, 283, *et passim.* This is the basic work for the economic phases of the period.

1868 and 1869, represent the high water mark for the period in fiscal affairs.

With public revenues doubling themselves every ten years, the government was able to encourage the building of railroads and of telegraph lines, improve the public service, open up new areas for settlement, and extend all means of communication. It could also devote more attention to primary and secondary schools and reform the curricula of the older institutions. The National Institute took on new life under the able administration of Diego Barros Arana. He did much to popularize the study of history, particularly of the Americas, and through his books and his teaching carried on a more effective campaign for liberalism than any political leader of his day. Public teaching now began to show the influence of Auguste Comte. This was another contribution of the Institute which now furnished most of the teachers for the *liceos* of the country.

IV

Pérez, like his three predecessors, served two terms in the presidency. Elected as a nationalist, but as a compromise candidate, it was inevitable that he should break with his lukewarm supporters at the first change in 1862 in ministry and turn to the "fusionists," the moderate liberals and clerical conservatives, when forming a new cabinet. This surprising move, ratified in the congressional elections of 1864, threw his former supporters, the nationalists, into opposition; but fortunately the head of the new cabinet, Manuel Tocornal, proved a temporizing influence. One of the few *pelucones* still in public life, he was able through his personal prestige to command universal respect and to moderate the hostilities of political factions. The war with Spain forced him from power and he died shortly afterwards. His death deprived the conservatives of a leader and left the path of succession open to two of the younger aristocrats, Domingo Santa María and Federico Errázuriz. Like many of their generation, ambition, if not conviction, had led them into the liberal ranks. Both, since 1849, had experienced the woes of opposition; both aimed at the presidency, and both ultimately reached their goal. Santa María's claims for office were, for the time being, ignored. Errázuriz as minister of war made a good record in the difficulty with Spain. He was a nephew of the archbishop, and the favored candidate of the administration. Characterized by his opponents as a time-server, his recent services entitled him to consideration by the fusionists and Pérez. Pérez, ever seeking the easiest course, gave him the support of the administration. The elections of 1867 confirmed the fusionist hold on congress and his succession seemed secure.[8]

Political affairs, however, were taking a turn distinctly less personal. Public attention was now being directed toward religious questions. The people at large were not becoming more pious, but rather more politically minded, and religious issues were more comprehensible than deeper constitutional principles. Hence Chilean politics for the next twenty years, while memorable for important constitutional changes, seem closely wedded to religious discussion. The union proved unavailing, however, to soften political asperities.

The controversy began in 1865. Some advanced groups brought about the passage of the law which sought to explain Article 5 of the constitution. The "explanation" permitted private worship to non-Catholics and such people could also carry on private schools for the education of their children. This act virtually established liberty of worship in the republic, although failing to meet the demands of the more liberal elements. It did, however, arouse the reactionary clericals to intense opposition. Meanwhile, younger men among the nationalists had founded "reform clubs" for the purpose of developing a wider program—a program that sought to curb the power of the president as well as the social influence of the church. Their efforts were furthered by the abolition of the law of civil responsibility which had been aimed at those who assisted in uprisings against the government.

Political agitation reached a climax in 1868. Tocornal was now dead and the Conservative Party thereby leaderless. The headship of the liberal-conservative fusion, which had chosen and still supported the Pérez administration, was taken by Errázuriz. His former associate, Santa María, supported another candidate, an old-time conservative, who was also acceptable to the more radical elements. This combination, forerunner of the later liberal alliance, proposed to give preliminary battle to the government in the congressional elections of 1870. Their purpose was still further strengthened by the attempt of the fusionists to curb the power of the supreme court. The house of deputies, under clerical prodding, brought in a motion to impeach the judges, of whom, their former enemy, Manuel Montt, was chief. President Pérez kept aloof from the struggle and fortunately the senate rejected the accusation. The president then called a moderate liberal, Miguel Luís Amunátegui, to head a new ministry. Political factions

[8] Arteaga Alemparte, *op. cit.*, p. 134.

were permitted to form their combinations without hindrance, and the executive refrained from interfering in the ensuing elections.

The congress chosen in 1870 was, therefore, of unusual character. Fusion triumphed because no other element presented a strong opposition; but at least a third of the members belonged to other groups. While this body did not bring about in form a new constitution, it accomplished during the next three years a number of significant changes that really entitled it to the definition "constituent." These changes were due more to the development of social and economic forces in the country than to definite political purpose.

The first task before the new congress was the presidential succession. As a preliminary measure, congress adopted a law forbidding a president to succeed himself. The opposing factions also maneuvered to defeat Errázuriz, but, despite their efforts, he was successful by a substantial majority.

V

The new president, Federico Errázuriz Zañartu, was an aristocrat of forty-six years of age, a member of an old Chilean family, enterprising and active, honest, simple-minded, and inflexible. He had early attracted attention for his ardent liberalism and had shown administrative ability both in congress and in various ministries. In the course of time, he had moderated any former radical tendencies and now was regarded, although a liberal because of family and class influences, as one of the strong supporters both of the church and of the aristocracy.

One of the first questions that came before the administration concerned freedom of instruction. Paradoxically this principle was espoused by the clerical faction. The tendency of the last few decades in education as well as in politics had shaken the hold of the church on public opinion and now it found itself obliged to assume a principle against which it had ordinarily fought. The clerical-conservatives naturally desired to carry on education according to their ideas. Many of their leaders were opposed to the vogue of natural science which had been introduced into the state system, where religious instruction was no longer obligatory. They wished their seminaries and other private institutions to be given equal public recognition with the state institutions. For this purpose in the fusion cabinet of Errázuriz, the post of public instruction was given to a reactionary conservative, Don Abdón Cifuentes, who as minister of public instruction issued a decree in 1872 by which the graduates of private seminaries were exempt from supervision by the National University. Under this ruling, institutions were created for the purpose of issuing certificates, and the abuse caused such a scandal that within a year the decree was repealed and Don Abdón was forced to resign from the cabinet.

This scandal definitely forced the Conservative Party out of the government and kept it out for the next twenty years. The reform elements now presented for consideration certain "theological" questions. One of these proposed to do away with the "ecclesiastical privilege" which permitted the clergy to be tried by their own tribunals. Another was to secularize the cemeteries by putting them under state control. Hitherto all formal burying places were under church control, but the new law by inference would permit nonbelievers to be interred in them. Still another measure provided for "civil marriage" by which matrimonial measures were placed under the state. A fourth question, to which these measures led, was the ultimate separation of church and state.

The Radical Party favored all of these proposals. The Conservative Party, at least the reactionary portion of it, was as heartily opposed to them. These two factions therefore represented the poles of the conflict, while the liberal and national parties were divided over the issues. The clergy, of course, looked upon the proposals as a blow to their influence and wherever possible exerted themselves against the hated action. Thus the conflict became one between an ultramontane group and the faction that was played up as "red." The intensity of the struggle checked somewhat the waning power of the president. The nationalists and a few of the more moderate liberals sided generally with the Catholic faction while the bulk of the liberals went over to the radicals. This alliance prevailed in the Errázuriz administration, and the president, despite his moderate tendencies, went with the alliance.

The devotees of the new plan triumphed only in part. In the law of the tribunals, promulgated in 1874, ecclesiastical privileges were suspended in civil and in criminal clauses. Furthermore, the privileges of the cemeteries were open to dissenters. These measures were carried despite the protest of the archbishop of Santiago and the threat of excommunication against liberal and radical legislators; but for the present congress made no changes in civil marriage nor did it force the separation of the church and state.

In a sense these ecclesiastical questions opened the way for direct constitutional changes, upon which leaders of the Radical Party were no less determined. The campaign which for a considerable time had been carried on against the power of the executive now began to have effect. In 1874 it was enacted that certain public employees could not at the same time hold legislative positions. The extraordinary powers of the president were restricted. The house of deputies placed some of its members on the "conservative committee" which acted during the recess of congress. The personality of the council of state was modified so as to give congress rather than the president the control of this body. These and similar measures gradually worked to make the control of congress over the ministry more complete. Furthermore, there were extensive changes in the electoral system. The control of elections was taken from municipal councils, which were then under the direct control of the executive, and placed under certain boards representing the larger taxpayers. The cumulative vote was introduced for selecting members of congress and municipal electors. Minority parties now had a chance to secure representatives in either body. These changes were effected under the personal direction of the minister of the interior, a liberal politician. Aside from the one change in 1872, the original cabinet continued in office and pursued a consistently liberal policy.

Errázuriz pushed on public works and means of communication, and greatly beautified the cities. More significant still were the efforts of Vicuña Mackenna, who as intendant of Santiago modernized the city and converted its noisome central hill into the beauteous Santa Lucía Park. One Cousiño also ceded to the public a magnificent park. These, together with new streets and plazas, the introduction of tramways, horse drawn and supported by private foreign capital, greatly changed the appearance of the capital. In the last years of his administration the country faced a serious financial crisis. The public debt, charges on which ate up a large part of the income, showed a heavy deficit. New mines gave out after a brief period of yield. The nitrate and guano industries of the north suffered from the exactions of the Bolivian and Peruvian governments. This caused a decrease in commerce and resulted in widespread personal loss. Hence it was in the midst of an intense depression that he had to turn over the administration to his successor, Aníbal Pinto.[9]

The new chief of state was a man fifty years old, son of the executive of the *pipiolo* period. He was historically both an aristocrat and a liberal, a man of solid reputation, culture, and political experience, but not of colorful career.[10] His selection likewise represented a new devel-

[9] Cf. Martner, II, pp. 357 *et seq.*
[10] Cabero, p. 228.

opment in politics. The liberal ranks, as the election approached, were divided between Miguel Luís Amunátegui, a famous historian and teacher who represented a tolerant liberalism, and Pinto. In order to determine the party's choice, a convention was brought together and in that body, with the influence of the administration back of him, Pinto triumphed. Then he had to face at the polls a second rival, Benjamín Vicuña Mackenna. The latter, well known as a historian and as a public administrator, was a man of deserved popularity. His friends, after the failure of the party to accept him, formed an organization of their own that called itself "liberal democrat" and carried on an exciting public campaign which, however, proved powerless against official intervention. Pinto, therefore, came into power with an overwhelming majority.

The immediate problem before the new president was to meet the economic crisis. His administration began with a general cut in expenditures, including appropriations for the army and navy and for the civil service. The government contracted a domestic loan and raised taxes, including a new inheritance tax. These increased exactions were rendered somewhat more tolerable by a new method of appraising lands. This combined policy of economy and increased taxes did not help private sufferers upon whom the panic pressed with increasing force. Foreign exchange still further drained the country of specie, and to meet the situation the government, in 1878, resorted to paper currency, a financial crutch that it has never been able to discard.[11]

The reforms of the previous administration were continued in a law making judicial offices incompatible with membership in congress or in the administration. The tobacco monopoly was likewise suppressed. Secondary and higher education were bettered by the law of 1879. The main issues of Pinto's administration, however, occurred in the foreign field, and these will be reserved for the following chapter.

Pinto remained in office until 1881, when the struggle with Bolivia and Peru was already settled in favor of Chile. This victory induced the conservatives to present the successful general, Manuel Baquedano, as their candidate for the presidency. In spite of his excellent reputation, none of the liberal factions would endorse his candidacy. After the recent constitutional reforms, political leaders were unwilling to follow a military chieftain. The administration threw its influence in favor of Domingo Santa María. For many years he had aspired to

[11] An adequate sketch of the rôle of paper money in the history of Chile is Frank Whitson Fetter's *Monetary Inflation in Chile* (Princeton, 1931).

the presidency, and in his ambitious course had trafficked with most of the leading factions. In his earlier days as a revolutionist, he opposed the administration of Montt. Exiled for that cause, he had spent some time traveling in Europe, and on his return had served as deputy, senator, and minister. During the War of the Pacific, he held the posts of minister of foreign relations and of the interior. With energy, experience, ambition, and intrigue he became the reluctantly accepted candidate and was successful at the polls. Despite his recent liberal connections, he represented the social and political traditions of old Chile. He was devoted to the ideal of authority and believed thoroughly in the supremacy of the aristocracy.[12]

VII

Conditions favored the new executive far above his predecessor. The country was now victorious in war, both to the north and to the south. While the bulk of the army was engaged in Peru, the last war with the Araucanians broke out and it was necessary to carry on a definite campaign against those Indians. With this successful Indian campaign, a new section of the country was thrown open to settlement. At the same time the victors in the north brought under national control the productive nitrate regions there. Each of these acquisitions furnished outlets for the growing population of Chile as well as for foreign immigrants. With this territorial and economic gain, it was possible to carry on public improvements and to increase compensation for public employees. Thus Santa María was relieved of serious fiscal problems, and at the same time his country had acquired prestige as a leader among the nations of the southern continent. Revenues more than doubled within five years after the war, and this increase in wealth and prestige gave promise of a peaceful administration.

Santa María was fated by nature to command, and his arbitrary use of the powers still remaining to the executive speedily disgusted his more moderate followers. Their opposition seemed to render advisable further resort to official intervention in the elections. Such resort, which proved largely unnecessary, caused him to favor further discussion of the persistent religious questions.

In 1878 occurred the death of Archbishop Valdivieso who had headed the Chilean church for many years. With a wide reputation for virtue

---

[12] Arteaga Alemparte, *op. cit.*, p. 9; Carlos Walker Martínez, *Historia de la administración de Don Domingo Santa María* (Valparaiso, 1889) treats of political affairs in detail.

and charity, he had faced the politico-religious issues in a harsh and unyielding manner. The government, therefore, desired to fill his place with one who would harmonize relations between church and state. It selected a certain canon, Taforó by name, but its candidate did not receive papal sanction. Nor did the pope yield after he had sent a special legate to examine affairs. The government, therefore, gave the legate his passports and the latter, in 1883, left the country, accusing the government of being anti-religious. Naturally, congress, where the Liberal Party had an overwhelming majority, answered the challenge by bringing forward certain measures against the church. As a result of the discussion, which again failed to bring about separation of church and state, the liberal majority secured a law creating secular cemeteries and also a law establishing civil marriage. In theory this deprived the clergy of much of its control of family relations and each of these laws passed in 1884 was hotly opposed as sacrilegious. In practice they proved much less detrimental to the secular power of the church than its devotees had feared.

In addition congress extended its reforming zeal to constitutional questions. It authorized congress to pass a law over the presidential veto by a two-thirds majority. It extended suffrage to every Chilean citizen who could read and write, and it took away from the intendants and governors much of their local power, giving it to the subordinate jurisdictions. Thus the campaign for more liberal measures in church and state begun some twenty years before was in large measure realized.

VIII

From the tortuous materialistic politics of the liberal régime one turns with relief to a review of its literary output. Bello died in 1865, but his influence still prevailed in the country. The whole Spanish world, at his death, acclaimed him as critic, poet, and jurist of local and international fame. A strong rival but more limited in his field of expression was Lastarria, professor of the Institute, mid-century parliamentarian, and occasional cabinet minister, whose legal and philosophical works are still of substantial value and whose critical ability made its impression on his time. In this respect, he was more fortunate than Bilbao who stimulated the progressive spirit of Chilean literature, but whose exile and premature death in 1866 largely put an end to his influence.

These men, however, had a stimulating effect on the youth of their time. Prominent among those who showed historical bent were the two brothers Amunátegui. We have already noted the activities of

Miguel Luís in the political world; his brother, Gregorio Victor, was a noted physician, who coöperated so effectively with Miguel Luís that it is extremely difficult to determine the share of each in their combined study of the colonial and revolutionary periods. Along with these talented brothers, one must class Benjamín Vicuña Mackenna, who wrote history with a charm equal to his public and professional activities. He likewise devoted himself to the period of revolution and the subsequent years. Greatest among the historians of this period was Diego Barros Arana. Educated in the Institute, and later its director, he produced a textbook, *A Compendium of the History of America,* which well illustrated his idea of the combined annals of American states. He edited as well the general history of Chilean independence and of the War of the Pacific, but his masterpiece, to which he devoted thirty years of patient effort, was his sixteen volume *General History of Chile,* a work which told the story up to the days of 1833. Like Bancroft, his latest revision appeared on the eve of his death, and like McMaster he added a final chapter to his great history in his monumental work on the administration of Bulnes.

These are the leaders in the historical field, but a host of others have added works devoted to special institutions or periods. Among them were Don Crescente Errázuriz, archbishop of Chile, who wrote much of church activities during the Spanish conquest; Ramón Sotomayor Valdés, who wrote an excellent history of General Prieto's administration; and Gonzalo Bulnes, military historian, who described the campaigns of his father and also produced a monumental study of the War of the Pacific. Better known, perhaps, than they, both for his extraordinary production and for the wide field of his investigation, was José Toribio Medina, an investigator of great merit, a bibliographer in all fields of Hispanic American history, and especially known for his stupendous researches concerning the Inquisition and the colonial press. These men, with the legal writers of the day, have done much to establish Chile's reputation in the field of substantial literature.

Lighter literature also presented its devotees. Prominent among them we may name José Joaquín Vallejo, better known under the pseudonym, "Jotabeche," who wrote articles for the press, which after his death were published in book form as a tribute to his literary merit.[13] A prominent novelist was Daniel Barros Grez whose *Pipiolos e pelucones* was an important social study as well as interesting history of the early national

---

[13] Coester, *Literary History,* p. 200.

period. More prominent as a work of pure literature is Alberto Blest Gana's *Martín Rivas*. This is a satire on contemporary manners both among the rich and the poor, and the story holds its readers well despite its length and philosophizing. An important contemporary of Blest Gana was Martín Palma who died in 1884. A free-thinker, his anti-clerical bias appears in many of his writings. As a novelist he sought to improve public taste by attacking many current customs. His style and his method was followed by Liborio E. Brieba and others who attempted the historical novel with success.

Poets were not lacking among these earlier writers. Eusebio Lillo wrote the national hymn. Guillermo Blest Gana and Luís Rodríguez Velasco excelled in sentimental and exquisite verse. Guillermo Matta was a philosophic poet, somewhat rude in verse but of extraordinary productivity. Eduardo de la Barra was a well-known poet, philologist, and debater. Most distinguished among the pupils of Bello was Salvador Sanfuentes who early attracted his master's attention, and after diplomatic service abroad returned to become general secretary of the university and a member of the cabinet and congress. In the midst of his public career he found time to demonstrate to foreign critics that poetry could flourish in Chile. Like the novelists, his themes are largely drawn from the history of the country, particularly of the colonial period. The work of these men was in some measure duplicated by the poetry of Doña Mercedes Marín de Solar which was mainly concerned with family life.

To these we must add representatives of painting and sculpture. Pedro Lira, one of the earliest, is best known for his painting "The Founding of Santiago." Rafael Correa is likewise a painter of whom the nation is proud. Among the sculptors are to be noted Nicanor Plaza with his "Caupolicán" and Eugenio Árias, who carved the group "Daphne and Chlóe." The works of these and other artists were shown in the annual exposition inaugurated in 1884, and later their masterpieces were housed in the Academy of Painting and Sculpture. Deserving young men of talent were being sent to Europe to complete their artistic education, and this was likewise true of certain pupils of the National Conservatory of Music and Oratory, although this institution has not placed an equal mark on Chilean genius.

IX

The census of 1885 gave the country two and a half million people, with an estimated addition of three hundred thousand during the next six years. The preceding decade, despite war and depression, had shown a substantial growth in external forms of national wealth. Foreign trade had risen from fifty-eight millions to more than eighty-one—an expansion due in part to the introduction of paper money. Exchange fluctuated between forty-five and thirty pence to the *peso*. Pinto's financial minister, José Alfonso, handled his difficult task of war finance with dexterity. The country emerged from warfare to an era of fiscal betterment. The national income was doubled, even when expressed in a *peso* that had fallen a third in value.[14]

The eighties represent a period of remarkable industrial growth. The nitrate region afforded a source of governmental income and national wealth hitherto undreamed of. Foreign trade increased prodigiously, fast enough in fact to cause apprehension that it had reached too high a figure for the resources of the country. Great Britain continued steadily at the front in this trade, while the United States reached a position just about equal to that of Peru. With that country after the Treaty of Ancón, and with Argentina, Chile sought to improve commerce, generally on a basis of freer exchange. These were fat years, with the government doubling and tripling its income, now varying from fourteen to eighteen *pesos* per head, and exerting itself to bring new industries into the country, and to improve those already under way.

President Santa María was an active and sagacious man with wide experience, so with the new income at his disposal and with the spirit bred by military success, he could hope for a prosperous administration. His minister of finance, Pedro Lucio Cuadra, handled his task much as Rengifo had done a half century before. With trade approaching a hundred million *pesos* a year it became necessary to revise the treasury department, to introduce a better system of accounting, and to improve the mint. There was, of course, some expectation of returning to normal monetary conditions, but such hopes were doomed to disappointment. National and personal income was mounting too rapidly for that. Although the government sought to regulate treasury operations and to control expenditures for public works, to reorganize under a new law of 1885 the railway system, and by controlling expenditures through budgets to refund previous obligations, it found itself unable to hamper, much less to direct, the materialistic spirit that had been evoked.

---

[14] Martner is still the standard authority for the economic development of the period.

Certain improvements were to be noted in rural life. The tenant on his little holding was still in evidence, as was likewise the wandering *peon* and his misery.[15] But there was more connection between town and village and the country, hence more shifting in the working population; better living conditions on the farms and estates, more schools, finer clothes, and more chance for diversion. In the country it is true that progress was less evident than in the cities, but food was more plentiful, privileges more widespread, and life on the whole more tolerable.

Santiago, the capital, now claimed a quarter million people. This and the other cities accounted for a third of the total population, including a considerable admixture of foreigners. In the chief urban centers, fashionable life with its theatres, clubs, promenades, and opportunities for display assumed a decided modern tinge. Santiago, of course, took the lead. Materially and in an architectural way it was much improved. It was a more beautiful city, more comfortable and healthful, with better residences—some of palatial character—broader, better paved streets, and running water, sewers, and sidewalks. Fire and police protection gave added sense of security. The rise in national wealth gave opportunities for cultural facilities at home and for travel abroad.

The working population of the cities likewise benefited from the economic expansion, but in a smaller measure. Salaries and wages were about doubled in the course of fifteen or twenty years. From this working class also came a large part of the patronage for taverns, jails, and hospitals. Alcoholism was still a prevailing vice. Crime seemed to increase, and much of this unfavorable showing was attributed to drunkenness. Hospital accommodations, although improved, were still far from satisfying public needs. There was talk of improving social conditions through encouraging savings-banks, increasing instruction, and improving public hygiene. There was also talk of vigorous repression, but little was done to meet the ravages of strong drink or to repress the universal vice of gambling. Thus Chile, as it approached the end of the nineteenth century, could pride itself on great improvements in its political, social, and economic life, but these advantages were far from being equally or justly distributed. To this task Chile of the twentieth century must devote itself, but before the country could do so it was once more called upon to settle an overshadowing political issue.

---

[15] An important study of the Chilean people is Alejandro Fuenzalida Grandón, *La evolución social de Chile* (Santiago, 1906). The author's thesis that the early Spanish settlers were almost wholly of Visigothic descent is untenable.

CHAPTER TWENTY-EIGHT

THE WAR OF THE PACIFIC AND ITS AFTERMATH, 1879-1929

I

AMONG the legacies that Spain left to her former possessions was that of disputed boundaries. This was more or less excusable, for during the greater part of the Spanish régime there was no real necessity for defining the limits between these separate colonies. Rather, the method of procedure was for the Spanish authorities to designate a certain administrative center, when the population required it, and attach to that center outlying communities as they were formed. For this reason the subordinate units of the various viceroyalties were made up of clusters of settlements, rather than well defined areas. When, therefore, the various republics began marking out their limits with more precision, they often discovered wide stretches of territory over which two or more might extend irregular claims. This was the situation with respect to the area known as the Desert of Atacama.[1]

As already noted, this region was one of the most nearly rainless spots on the face of the globe. It was one of the barriers that contributed to make early Chile a veritable island. When, in the Constitution of 1833, Chile first ventured to define its area, the northern limit was put down simply as "The Desert of Atacama." Thus the nation itself, as late as 1833, failed to indicate a definite limit for its claims. In this uncertain area her sovereignty promised to conflict with that of Bolivia and Peru, especially with the former, when the region acquired sufficient economic importance.

The mid-century put a new phase on the conflict. As the explorers of the early forties pushed farther away from the trails that crossed this desolate region, they encountered two unexpected sources of wealth—the guano deposits along the coast, left there for untold years by the numerous wild fowl of the region, and the nitrates and the mineral salts of the interior deposited in some early geological era and still lying

[1] Isaiah Bowman, *Desert Trails of Atacama* (New York, 1924) gives an interesting and scholarly description of the disputed area. Cf. also Jones or Whitbeck *op. cit.*

unleached near the surface. These commercial fertilizers were scattered in irregular patches over the coast and the *pampa,* the name applied to the central valley of the desert. Exploring parties found the exploitation of both difficult because of the almost total lack of water in this dry area where no green thing grew naturally. Neither the Bolivians, who claimed most of the territory where the guano was found, nor the Peruvians, who claimed the area to the northward where were the best deposits of nitrate, had made much use of these natural resources. Both, it was found, were of considerable commercial value, and the demand for them, both in the United States and in Europe, after 1840 was increasing each year. The explorers and promoters in their exploitation were for the most part Chileans, but behind them stood the British capitalists and, melancholy note, French and American commercial rivals, the latter two operating occasionally through Peru, rather than through Chile. Thus, the situation was no mere economic setting, but presented complications of international purport as well.

In a diplomatic way Chile had already involved herself with her neighbors. In addition to the earlier war with Peru and the alliance with that nation and Bolivia against Spain in the sixties, Chile had growing boundary disputes with Argentina, and feared that her rivals might take advantage of the altercations with that power to bring the Platine confederation into the quarrel.

II

Thus an area that for centuries had been noted as a barrier suddenly acquired sufficient economic importance to become a matter of international concern. In 1866 Chile and Bolivia sought to settle this question.[2] They agreed upon the twenty-fourth parallel of south latitude as the limit between them, but they also arranged to share the proceeds of the mineral wealth lying between the twenty-third and twenty-fifth parallels.

---

[2] Sir Clements R. Markham in *The War between Peru and Chile, 1879-1882* (London, 1882), pp. 81-92 reviews the causes of the war with a strong bias against Chile. The rest of the volume gives the story up to the date of publication. Of similar character is Victor M. Maúrtua, *The Question of the Pacific* (Trans. by F. A. Pezet, Philadelphia, 1901). B. Vicuña Mackenna, Gonzalo Bulnes, and Diego Barros Arana have written in detail on the Chilean side. The arbitration at Washington in 1921-25 gave each contestant a chance to submit documents in unlimited detail to support its contentions. A few of these documents are edited by W. J. Dennis in *Documentary History of the Tacna-Arica Dispute* (Iowa City, 1927). A summary of the nitrate war, its causes and subsequent negotiations is in *Tacna and Arica* (New Haven, 1931) by the same author. No phase of South American history since independence has called forth such a volume of publication.

Shortly after this pact, extensive deposits of nitrate were found near Antofagasta, and still later the important Caracoles silver mines were discovered in the same region. Promoters from Chile obtained from the Bolivian government the right to exploit this mineral wealth under what they considered difficult terms, and shortly Chilean laborers and capital were well scattered throughout the region, where soon the port of the city of Antofagasta was rivaled by other mining centers. These promoters opened roads, brought in a water supply, built railways, and in other respects made the desert habitable.

These improvements were tolerated by Bolivia because of the fiscal income derived from them, but with a certain amount of jealousy. The rulers of that mountain country were too much occupied with local personal disputes to appreciate the industrial development that took place there, but they seemed determined to derive the highest possible income from it. Naturally, therefore, they found cause for dispute over the terms of their joint agreement, and, according to the Chilean writers, made exactions upon the promoters that the latter found difficult to meet. To their demands and protests the Bolivian authorities made little concession, and finally, in 1874, Chile agreed to give up to Bolivia all territory north of the twenty-fourth parallel on condition that the industrialists of the region should not be burdened with new taxes.

In the meantime the dispute had been taking another direction. Peru also entered into the controversy. Her territory of Tarapacá contained extensive nitrate deposits which Chilean promoters were developing as they had developed those of Bolivia. The Peruvian government of that period, however, maintained a disturbed existence that was wasteful to its natural resources. Hence, keen-eyed prospectors from France and the United States saw in the nation's growing bankruptcy a chance for private speculation, and undoubtedly encouraged Peru to take hostile measures toward those who were exploiting Tarapacá. In this way the government might possibly stave off bankruptcy. Hence, its changing authorities, as well as those of Bolivia, had what they regarded as common cause against Chile, and in 1873 the two countries signed a treaty of offensive and defensive alliance. Obviously, this joint action was directed against Chile, and the existing quarrel of that nation with Argentina led the allies to hope that the Platine country would likewise be induced to unite its interests with theirs.

The financial situation in Peru led that government to attempt the nationalization of the nitrate region. The proprietors of mineral holdings were to be forced to sell them to the state; but Peru did not have the means to pay for them. An attempt to float a loan in Europe for this purpose was not successful. They expropriated these holdings of the Chilean prospectors, however, under an agreement to pay on time. This was the situation in the year 1878. Peru and Bolivia were in alliance, supposedly a secret one, although like many diplomatic secrets the purport of the agreement was known to Chile. That government had by no means contented itself with mere protest. Ever since the threat from Spain ten years before, Chile had been improving her armed forces, spurred on, we may imagine, by the outcome of the Franco-Prussian War in Europe. In the contest looming up before her, Chile did not propose to play the part of France. Hence, its government was ready to act when the crisis came. In 1878 a new military adventurer seized the government of Bolivia. More familiar with arms than economics, he was easily persuaded by his advisers, including some from Peru, to act in Antofagasta as that nation had done in Tarapacá. The allies evidently believed that Chile could not oppose this action by force, and that if she did, they might persuade Argentina to join them and thus hem in the resistant power with a circle of hostile enemies, each of whom would profit at Chile's expense.

Bolovia's new executive, Hilarión Daza, therefore, issued a decree levying a new tax on the Chilean nitrate company. That organization attempted to arbitrate the question, but the Bolivian dictator, striving, on the advice of his councillors, "to regain possession of the nitrate plants," refused to yield. The dictator then placed an embargo on the company's property and advertised it for public sale. Just before the auction was to occur, however, Chilean forces landed at Antofagasta, took possession of the town, raised the Chilean flag, and thus formally started the War of the Pacific. This was in the middle of February 1879. Most of the inhabitants of the region were Chileans and hence welcomed the coming of their fellows. The small Bolivian garrison and the few Bolivian employees of the region could put up no adequate resistance.

III

The occupation of Antofagasta led first to a declaration of war on the part of Bolivia. Peru offered its mediation, but its representative was taunted with the treaty of alliance and the government of Chile refused to consider the offer until that treaty should be abrogated. It followed this refusal, in April 1879, with a declaration of war against both allies.

The forces of the combatants were apparently unequal. Peru was a country of between two and one-half and three million people, and Bolivia had about two millions. In numbers, therefore, they seemed double the strength of Chile, but neither in the character of their people nor in preparation for the conflict were they as ready to meet the issue. The Chileans recognized the possibility that Argentina might assist her rivals and hastened to make a settlement with that power. Chile's representative at Buenos Aires succeeded in staving off immediate hostilities and finally in 1881 effected what seemed a definite settlement of their quarrel. Argentina, therefore, was not numbered among the open enemies of Chile in this conflict.

After the initial occupation, the Chileans experienced no difficulty in overrunning all the territory belonging to Bolivia. When Peru entered the conflict, however, there came a pause in land operations. It was necessary to secure dominion on the sea before military campaigns could be carried on farther to the northward. The first naval encounter occurred at Iquique May 21, 1879. Two Chilean vessels, the *Covadonga* and the *Esmeralda,* were blockading that port. While thus engaged, two Peruvian ships, the *Huascar* and the *Independencia,* attacked them. The Chileans were no match for their rivals, but the commander of the *Esmeralda,* Arturo Prat, made up his mind to resist, declaring that his flag should flutter in its place as long as he lived. He called on his sailors to fulfill their duty. They replied with a vigorous "Viva Chile" and for more than three hours the unequal contest continued. The Peruvian commander of the *Huascar,* Miguel Grau, started to ram the *Esmeralda,* when Prat, waiting for that encounter, ordered his men to board. They did not hear his command, but he, accompanied by a single sergeant, jumped on the deck of the other vessel where they both fell, riddled with bullets. At a second clash one of the lieutenants, accompanied by a few sailors, likewise leaped on the deck of the *Huascar* and met a like fate. A third ramming sent the *Esmeralda* to the bottom, although in such shallow water that her flag still waved defiance above the waves to the victorious enemy.

For the Peruvians, however, this victory was a disastrous one. The *Independencia,* sister ship of the *Huascar,* started in pursuit of the *Covadonga.* The latter vessel sought the shallower water near the coast and when after a three-hour chase the *Independencia* tried to ram the Chilean vessel, it struck a reef near at hand which crushed in its prow and completely grounded it. The *Covadonga* then turned on her pursuer, now unable to answer its fire, but was in turn chased away by the victorious *Hauscar* that, as we have seen above, had prevailed over the *Esmeralda.* The *Covadonga,* however, succeeded in making its escape to Antofagasta. Chile had lost an old worn-out vessel, but Peru, in the *Independencia,* had suffered the shipwreck of its finest iron-clad.

This was the celebrated fight off Iquique, which, despite its loss, still represents the crowning naval exploit of Chilean history. The nation still honors the memory of Captain Prat and his associates in that unequal combat.

For a time, however, Chile suffered still further loss. Shortly after, one of its transports carrying a whole army corps with arms and munitions was seized by the Peruvians. This caused a protest against the naval authorities and a change in the Chilean naval command. For several months Grau, with a single effective vessel, the *Huascar,* and another minor craft terrorized the Chilean coast; but his day of reckoning occurred off the point of Angamos, October 8, 1879, when the *Huascar* and her companion ship fell in between two Chilean squadrons. The *Almirante Cochrane,* crack ship of Chile, engaged the *Huascar* in a terrific combat at close range. Both vessels were ironclads and this was the first significant test of that type of ship. With the early discharges from the *Almirante Cochrane,* Grau was blown to pieces by a shell which burst against the armored tower from which he directed his vessel. Two other officers speedily met their death, and when the fire of another Chilean vessel reënforced that of the *Almirante Cochrane,* the Peruvian ship was surrendered by its crew. This victory, followed up by minor captures, gave Chile the mastery of the ocean. But the resistance maintained by Grau and his associates formed a page in Peruvian history equally glorious with that of Prat in the annals of Chile.

IV

This naval victory enabled Chile to undertake the second important campaign, centering around Iquique, during which it secured possession of Tarapacá. The presidents of Bolivia and Peru joined forces, under command of the latter, and proposed to hold Iquique against the invaders. The capture of this place would be no mere occupation. The campaign must be carried on over extensive deserts, utterly lacking in provisions or water supply. Nevertheless, the Chilean forces landed at Pisagua, a short distance above Iquique, won a brilliant victory there and then pressed on to a post near the city, where they were equally successful. Meanwhile, the Peruvians in turn, with a force twice as large, moved northward to meet the enemy, while General Daza with the Bolivians advanced southward from Tacna. Thus they purposed to catch the Chilean division between two fires, but the commander of the latter, moving too promptly for them, defeated the Peruvians in November 1879, and shortly afterward occupied Iquique. It was then but a matter of mopping up to secure possession of the entire territory of Tarapacá. This defeat aroused the population both in Peru and in Bolivia, and in addition to military reverses, both countries faced a revolution which displaced the executives of both and brought to the head of Peru a popular and energetic leader, Colonel Nicolás de Piérola. A man of like type secured control in Bolivia, and the two countries prepared to resist further invasion of their territory.

Early in 1880 the Chilean troops took the offensive, and soon thirteen thousand of them under the command of Manuel Baquedano landed in the vicinity of Arica, the chief port of the Tacna-Arica region. Tacna was occupied within two months after many a bloody battle in which the casualties approached five thousand dead and wounded. Shortly after, the port of Arica was blockaded by the Chilean fleet and threatened by the victorious army. Most of the fighting occurred on a massive flat-top mountain overlooking the sea. The Peruvian defenders had dynamited the slopes of this mountain and the first charge of the Chileans met a deadly reception. They rallied, however, and infuriated by their earlier losses carried the heights at the point of the bayonet. Colonel Bolognesi, the brave Peruvian commander, died in action. His men either fell with him or were taken prisoners. This campaign added still further to the misfortunes of the allies.

At that juncture other nations sought to intervene in the struggle.[3] England offered its mediation, and Chile accepted the offer, but Peru refused. The United States offered its good services. The allies accepted and Chile also, but without much expectation of success. In October 1880 representatives of the fighting nations and of the United States met on the deck of an American cruiser and sought to bring the struggle to a close. The Chilean representatives insisted among other conditions upon the definite cession to itself of Antofagasta and Tarapacá. The allies, trusting in the mediation of the United States, refused any proposal for the cession of territory, preferring to continue the hopeless struggle. Chile from that point determined to make it a war *à'outrance,* and determined to dictate terms in Lima.

Following the fruitless conference at Arica and a few destructive

[3] For intervention during the struggle cf. Dennis, *Tacna and Arica* Ch. V, H. C. Evans *op. cit.,* and W. S. Robertson *op. cit.,* pp. 149-153.

raids along the Peruvian coast, the Chilean army of thirty thousand men was landed, early in 1881, in the vicinity of Lima. With this threat of invasion at the capital, the Peruvian dictator, Piérola, bestirred himself to raise a defensive force. The country over which the invaders had to advance was difficult, and this fact plus the determined spirit of resistance on the part of the Peruvians made the last important campaign a bloody one. On January 13 the Chileans carried the fortifications of Chorillos at the point of the bayonet. Two days later, after ineffectual attempts at a truce, they occupied Miraflores. In both these battles the unseasoned Peruvians put up a brave but losing fight in which many of their leading civilians perished. On January 15 the victorious leader of the Chilean forces, Baquedano, entered Lima in triumph. Meantime, its population had sacked the capital while the survivors of the two defeats destroyed what was left of the fleet and government property.[4] A mere handful of forces retreated into the mountains to carry on for two and one-half years longer a useless guerrilla warfare. The contest was prolonged in part because of quarrels among the Peruvian leaders. After stiff resistance on the part of Piérola, another militarist, Cáceres, succeeded him. For a time he gained some slight success in the north, but in the long run was forced to make terms with the victors. In the midst of this sporadic warfare a small Chilean force entrapped in the town of La Concepción carried on a determined fight for more than twenty hours before the inevitable massacre occurred. This event on July 9 and 10, 1882, is still celebrated as one of the heroic days in the national history of Chile.

V

Shortly after the occupation of Lima a prospect for peace arose through the influence of the Chilean commander at that capital. One Francisco Gracía Calderón was chosen as provisional president of Peru and entered into negotiations with the Chileans. When it came time to sign the treaty, however, he refused because it provided for a cession of territory. In this refusal he was encouraged by the attitude of the United States, where the state department was now under the leadership of James G. Blaine. Blaine was at that time interested in Pan American affairs and was hoping to bring about a Pan American meeting at which should be discussed closer trade relations between the na-

---

[4] As might be anticipated the campaigns around Lima and the subsequent negotiations involving the United States have given rise to much controversy. Cf. Evans, pp. 100-119.

tions of this continent and measures to arbitrate quarrels. Naturally the War of the Pacific came up for consideration, and Chile on its part opposed the meeting of such a congress. A political turn in the United States, caused by the death of President Garfield, drove Blaine from office and the proposed Pan American meeting was indefinitely postponed. This change was undoubtedly a distinct advantage to Chile, for the American government, under a new secretary of state, took a decidedly neutral position in the South American quarrel.

Finally in October 1883, after General Miguel Iglesias became head of the government of Peru, a peace conference took place at Ancón, a small town north of Lima. The ensuing treaty brought to Chile the ownership of the Province of Tarapacá and temporary control for a period of ten years of the provinces of Tacna and Arica. With respect to the two last named areas, there was a special provision that at the end of ten years a plebiscite should be held in them to determine their permanent ownership. If the people decided to remain under the control of Chile, that country should pay Peru ten million *pesos*. If, however, the decision was to return to Peru, the payment was to come from the latter country. Furthermore, it was agreed that the claims of Chileans who had been injured in the war should be arbitrated. This treaty with Peru was followed some months later, in 1884, by a truce with Bolivia, signed in Valparaiso, by which the province of Antofagasta was definitely left under the sovereignty of Chile. Thus, through failures of the two unfortunate allies to attract the support of Argentina, through the bravery of the Chilean forces aided by good leadership and thorough preparation, through the division of councils in the allied republics and civil commotion in each of them, and through the vacillating policy of the United States, Chile came through the most significant struggle in South America with substantial additions to its territory and a great increase in national prestige. The little republic that at the beginning of its national history had prophesied for itself a neutralizing policy in South American affairs now emerged as the most conspicuous example of triumphant militarism.

By the terms of the treaty noted above, a plebiscite was to be held in the provinces of Tacna and Arica at the end of ten years to determine their permanent status. As the designated period approached, Peru had by no means reached a stable political condition, but that alone would not have prevented action in respect to these provinces. The provision for the plebiscite was undoubtedly determined by the chaos that reigned in Peru at the conclusion of the war and by the necessity for some pledge of security to Chile. Possibly, too, Chile expected to keep the provinces definitely but wished to conceal the acquisition through the taking of the plebiscite. The region was under her control and, while in itself of little economic importance, it might serve as a bulwark against invasion of the rich nitrate area farther south. Later, Chilean writers claimed that the two provinces represented security for a further indemnity which they thought Peru should pay. The latter country had nothing to offer in the treaty of Ancón but further territory. Hence, they took over the area as such a pledge. It was to prove doubly unprofitable. Only a very small fraction of it could be profitably cultivated and it contained no minerals of importance; hence there was little hope of any addition to the national wealth through the possession of it. Furthermore, it was a continued threat against peace on the west coast of South America. The necessary military measures to hold it proved a perpetual bill of expense to the possessor.

In 1893 negotiations were attempted to settle the fate of the two provinces. They failed largely because neither government could agree upon the terms of the plebiscite. Who could vote in such an election? Only those who lived in the two areas while they were under Peruvian control? That was the position taken by Peru. Or should the population then in the provinces be allowed to participate? Chile favored such a solution, but Peru opposed it because, as its representatives claimed, the Chilean authorities during their control of the region had forced many former Peruvians into exile and had colonized the country with Chileans. Very likely they were right in these charges, but at the time neither country was willing to yield to the other, so the attempt to hold a plebiscite failed.

VI

Nevertheless, the question remained an open sore in Latin American diplomacy. No measure of general interest, no attempt at a common gathering, could be presented without assuring Chile that arbitration of territorial disputes would not be a subject of forced discussion. If any such proposed gathering met the demands of Chile, it was likely to lead to the abstention of Peru. Hence all proposals for Pan American gatherings must be carefully worded and cautiously pursued in order to secure delegations from each of these republics. Furthermore, the continuing question was the bane of politics in both countries. Organizations were formed in all of the principal Peruvian cities to agitate for the recovery not only of Tacna and Arica, but also of Tarapacá. Their propaganda was greatly furthered in each locality by the presence of refugees from the conquered provinces, refugees whose numbers were continually increasing through those who were forced out of the region by Chilean methods of control. The stories of atrocities fed the hatred of the people in general and often influenced the attitude of public leaders. On the other hand, equally vigorous propaganda was carried on in Chile, not merely in favor of holding the regions definitely ceded, but the two frontier provinces. They were needed, military leaders affirmed, in order to assure the safety of Tarapacá and Antofagasta. Certain civilians tried to show that the two little areas might be made more productive and that Chile could obtain from them subtropical fruits that would not grow elsewhere in the country. Thus the retained provinces served not only as a bone of contention between the two republics, but as a continually disturbing element in local politics.

Frequent efforts were made to settle the question. One proposal was that it should be submitted for arbitration to the Queen Regent in Spain, but at that time, 1898, that estimable lady had other matters to occupy her attention; besides Chile lost its desire to settle the question after coming to terms with Argentina over other boundary disputes.[5] Suggestions to divide the provinces between them proved unacceptable. In 1912 a plebiscitary commission proposed by Chile was rejected by Peru. During all of this period it is doubtful if any political leader in either country could have survived a definite proposal to settle the matter.

To make a long story short, but to bring in at this point the final settlement, may we add that in the period after the World War measures were taken that finally brought about a solution.[6] Chile was finding the dispute a continual handicap to herself, and under the leadership of President Alessandri in 1920, aided by the mediation of the United States, the question of the plebiscite was submitted to the latter government for arbitration. Each side prepared its case *in extenso,* and, after some delay, early in 1925 President Coolidge announced a decision in favor of a plebiscite. Forty years had passed since the signing of the treaty and during that time the population of the provinces had greatly changed. But it was determined that all former natives of the provinces and the lineal descendants of such could participate in the election, together with legal residents of two and a half years' standing. Members of the military and of the civil service, wholly Chileans, were to be excluded. The decision seemed fair to both parties, but as

[5] Cf. Dennis, *Tacna and Arica,* p. 196.

[6] *Ibid,* Chs. X-XII.

Chile was to maintain control of the region and police it, there still remained a possibility of trouble.

Such proved to be the case. Stories of Chilean atrocities continued to arise, and the testimony from neutral sources tended to confirm them. Finally General Pershing, who had been elected as the neutral member of the commission of three in charge of the plebiscite, withdrew in disgust. His successor after more months of wrangling declared a plebiscite impossible, and the solution in June 1926 seemed as far away as ever. But hope in a settlement still persisted. Negotiations under the auspices of the United States were resumed in Washington. Finally in 1929 the two countries signed a definite treaty. Chile was to retain Arica, but on the bay where that town is located was to designate another place for a port for Peru. The latter country was to receive Tacna. Thus the dispute between these countries after so long a period of delay came to what seems a reasonably good solution.

With respect to Bolivia, Chile reached another type of settlement. The truce of 1884 continued without serious change for twenty years. In 1904 the two countries signed a definite treaty by which the province of Antofagasta was yielded to Chile in perpetual sovereignty, while Chile agreed to construct a railroad from Arica to the Bolivian capital, and to permit the transport of Bolivian goods on this railway without payment of customs duties to Chile.[7] Fifteen years after the completion of the railway, Chile was to turn the portion within Bolivian territory over to that country together with a money indemnity. Thus Bolivia secured a sort of outlet to the Pacific, the kind that she already had obtained through the Peruvian port of Mollendo. Naturally this did not meet her full demands and in the general settlement of the issues closing the World War, Bolivia tried to obtain for herself something that would resemble the Polish Corridor to the Baltic. But neither in the Peace of Versailles nor in subsequent measures of the League of Nations did she secure the adoptions of her program. The railroad, begun shortly after the treaty of 1904, ultimately reached La Paz in 1913, and fifteen years later, in accordance with the terms of the treaty, Chile definitely deeded to Bolivia the portion within her limits.

Such is the solution of the issue aroused by the War of the Pacific. That the solution was thoroughly satisfactory to the people of the countries concerned, no one will contend. It afforded a certain security to each, and left the major portion of the disputed territory in the possession of Chile. Along with this territory, however, it was to leave other

---

[7] *Ibid,* p. 198.

questions, social and economic, that were of compelling influence in the subsequent development of the country. The acquisition of the nitrate fields brought such increasing revenues that it encouraged careless—not to say worse—methods in government expenditures and too exclusive a reliance on a single source of national income. In the chief nitrate center, Iquique, discontented political elements, some seven years after the war, were to find a refuge that would at once afford money for their machinations against the central government and men with whom to overcome it.

CHAPTER TWENTY-NINE

THE CONFLICT BETWEEN THE PRESIDENT AND CONGRESS, 1886-1891

I

POLITICAL control, under the liberalizing tendencies of the last three decades, had alternated between president and congress. These fluctuations seemed rather to respond to the character of the chief executive than to any real change in public opinion. By direct methods Errázuriz prevailed over congress, while the mild views of Pinto almost provoked parliamentary anarchy. Santa María sought to reëstablish presidential power, often by unscrupulous methods, but before the end of his administration he beheld the gathering of forces that were to overthrow the authority he had so vigorously wielded.

The opposition revealed itself in the congressional election of 1885.[1] This contest would not only determine the membership of the new congress, but the choice for president the following year. Hence every recourse at the command of the executive was used to secure a majority and insure the presidential succession. Bribery, fraud, violence, characterized all of the elections in doubtful districts, and the fraudulent returns themselves in many cases were lost, destroyed, or altered by executive decree. Through these strong-arm methods, plentifully gilded where necessary, the chief executive obtained a competent but distrustful majority. Many of the more independent in spirit among them, and those less accustomed to official favor simply were waiting for a good chance to ally themselves with the president's enemies.

The Conservative Party presented a convenient nucleus about which the opposition might group itself. Buffeted and chastened by the controversies of the last fifteen years, its leadership was now aided by recruits from rejuvenated theological seminaries, well prepared for wordy conflict and well led by a notable aristocrat, Manuel José Irrarázaval. His wealth enabled him to furnish the fighting funds. His learning, his sound character, his sincere convictions, made him a leader they were

[1] Carlos Walker Martínez, *op. cit.,* furnishes the details for Santa María's part in the struggle. Cf. also A. Edwards, *Fronda,* Chs. XXVII-XXIX and *Partidos políticos,* Ch. XII, and Cabero, pp. 229-233.

proud to follow, and one who commanded much respect among the liberal factions. The party, therefore, gained additional seats in the stormy congressional election, largely at the expense of the radicals, and, in the session that followed, were prepared to battle with the president over the choice of a successor. In this struggle they anticipated further recruits from the very ranks of their liberal opponents.

Over the selection of a candidate the liberal-nationalist alliance was inclined to split into three factions. The most numerous and the most docile favored José Manuel Balmaceda, leader in recent "theological" reforms, able diplomat and cabinet member. As minister of the interior he held a favored position over his rivals, and President Santa María, although originally preferring another, came to the support of his powerful minister. The major part of the liberal element naturally followed a candidate who had so eloquently favored their policy on clerical issues, while the nationalists looked upon Balmaceda as one who most nearly met their specifications for a strong executive. Their support, therefore, even if for personal reasons not given willingly, plus presidential influence, promised to carry the day.

But the enemies of Balmaceda were not yet ready to give up the fight. Early in January 1886, the conservatives, with the aid of radicals, independent liberals, and personal friends of other candidates, started a filibustering debate over the bill for appropriations. During four days while the parliamentary wrangle continued the government was virtually at a standstill. Balmaceda's opponents hoped, through the threat of an interminable session, to force him to withdraw as a candidate, but Don Pedro Montt, president of the house of deputies, after strong encouragement from Don Antonio Varas, president of the senate, declared the debate closed. Thus he relieved the country of a serious political crisis and saved the candidacy of Balmaceda. Incidentally Montt's ruling gave rise to much criticism, but it seems to have established an important constitutional precedent with respect to the closing of debate.

II

President Balmaceda assumed office on September 18, 1886. At that time forty-five years of age, he had spent some twenty years in public life. Trained in the seminary at Santiago, he seemed destined for the priesthood, but on leaving the hall of learning forsook both a clerical career and his early faith, entered politics, and became liberal in his party allegiance and a consistent opponent of ecclesiastical privileges. Member of a well-known family, rich, distinguished in appearance and with a certain remarkable facility for words, graceful and brilliant in delivery, he speedily became the most notable orator of his day, and his addresses in the chamber of deputies, before reform groups, and in public assemblies were greatly in demand. A natural leader, he was too aristocratic by birth and temperament and too insistent upon his personal dignity and political views, to gain general popularity. Yet he attracted and retained a personal following that served him devotedly during his troubled administration and still professed attachment to his cardinal principles.

Balmaceda recognized the force of the elements that had opposed his election, and entered upon his administration with an attempt at conciliation. He selected a cabinet that should, from his point of view, "reconcile the great liberal family." But this cabinet lasted only two months, and a second one, in which he allotted two seats to the opposition, speedily followed it into dissolution. The president then attempted to conciliate conservatives by settling the dispute over the appointment of an archibishop and thus reëstablished outward relations with the papacy. But not even this concession, although accompanied by increased appropriations for the church, availed to bring about harmony. By temperament and by training Balmaceda did not belong to the aristocratic class from which he had sprung, nor was he prepared to head the new social forces that were even then beginning to affect the hitherto inert Chilean masses. He stood, without perhaps fully realizing his rôle, for the full measure of presidential power, for that element in the state which represented the monarchial tradition—a tradition that dated back to the colonial period, that had felt the restorative touch of Portales and the repressive watchfulness of Manuel Montt. Fate had made Balmaceda the belated champion of monarchial tradition, now disguised but scarcely debilitated, in the garb of presidential authority.[2]

Opposing him was the Chilean aristocracy, heirs of an even stronger tradition. Their ancestors had accepted the system of Portales sixty years before, because it promised to save them from a worse one—from fruitless constitutional experiment or open military dictatorship. The legal pact, devised by Portales and defended by Montt, had preserved them from the worst ills that afflicted their neighbors. The formula of Portales had lost, during the last three decades, much of its original force. Santa María, and now Balmaceda, sought to recover its pristine

---

[2] Cabero, p. 231. Cf. also J. Bañados Espinosa, *Balmaceda, su gobierno y la revolución de 1891* (Paris, 1894); Joaquín Nabuco, *Balmaceda* (Santiago, 1914); and Fanor Velasco, *La revolución de 1891* (Santiago, 1925).

strength without fully realizing, it may be, what they were contending for or whether, amid changed conditions, it would continue to work. Their opponents were equally in the dark; yet they strove, albeit blindly, to keep their class privileges and to restrict the president's functions within still narrower limits. Once the executive office had seemed their chief support; now it threatened to hamper them. They could not discard it altogether, but they would link it to their will by subjecting it to a system of psuedo-parliamentary control.

Many leaders of this group were then and thereafter flattered by some slight resemblances between the society of contemporary Chile and that of England in the late eighteenth and early nineteenth centuries.[3] These comparisons seemed to apply more definitely to the aristocratic group in each country than to any other common feature. Political power in England rested with that group and was definitely expressed through the responsibility of the cabinet to parliament. One could find in Chile, from the days of Montt onward, a few political events that seemed to indicate a growing sense of dependence upon congressional majorities. Such interpretation followed rather than accompanied the event, but it was now freely made to bolster up the pretensions of the aristocracy.

Against such a weakening of presidential authority, Balmaceda resolutely set his face. Nevertheless he tried to carry on government through party combinations, and in the course of his administration experimented with some fourteen different cabinet groupings. At one time his advisers were all drawn from the liberal factions; at another from the three principal parties, excluding the conservatives. On occasion he definitely recognized this last named group. He once attempted to form a cabinet made up of his personal followers only, and on another occasion contented himself for a short time with one made up entirely of his opponents. These fluctuations in the ministry did not strengthen the harassed president with congress. At the end of four years he could count on only a relatively small minority of that body.

III

From the story of this barren struggle for political control, let us turn to the positive accomplishments of the period. The steady increase in revenues which nearly doubled in four years enabled the president

---

[3] Cf. Paul S. Reinsch, "Parliamentary Government in Chile," in *American Political Science Review* III, November 1909, pp. 506-538. For a criticism of Reinsch's view, cf. A. Edwards, *Fronda*, p. 63.

to undertake extensive public works and to increase salaries. Railroads and bridges were constructed, highways were repaired and marked out, telegraph lines were extended throughout the country, and cities were enabled to institute an adequate water supply and erect commodious local buildings. There was during this period a veritable orgy of construction under a newly-created ministry of public works.[4] A tribunal of accounts provided for the inspection of public expenditures. The external debt, expressed in a *peso* valued at eighteen pence, reached the figure of eighty millions. The internal debt was reduced, but this reform did not extend to the suppression of paper money. Expenditures for the army and navy were increased, new vessels were purchased in Europe, and a new system of instruction on the Prussian plan established compulsory military service for the country. Certain old taxes including the *alcabala* were suppressed and a new system of taxation established that was designed to make levies more nearly equal throughout the country. These material improvements, with the accompanying appropriations, helped to strengthen Balmaceda in his contest with the aristocracy.

As in the preceding decade, public instruction received favorable attention. This was due in part to the freer press of the period and in turn gave that press a wider circle of readers. During the seventies, also, the law for censoring books, dating back to the time of Portales, had been repealed. In 1879, under Pinto's administration, the government had adopted a regulation for reorganizing and developing the facilities for secondary and higher education. More striking progress occurred during the next ten years. In 1889 the Pedagogic Institute was founded for the purpose of preparing teachers of secondary education. With the new institution there was introduced the concentric plan of studies, a favorite device followed by the disciples of Comte. New *liceos* for girls as well as for boys now appeared, and in connection with the National Institute, a dormitory accommodating a thousand students was established. Admission to this institution, however, was still primarily a class privilege. At the end of Balmaceda's administration in 1890, there were more than fifteen hundred public and private schools attended by some eighty thousand students of both sexes. In respect to numbers, this exhibited a gratifying advance in the course of a half century, and it promised a cultural foundation of genuine character; but it represented accommodations for less than one-fourth

[4] Cf. Galdames, *Estudio,* Ch. IX and Martner, *Politica commercial,* II, pp. 452-488, for the outstanding phases of development during this period.

of the scholastic population. The National Institute and the *liceos* provided for the future governing class of the country; normal schools for men and women prepared primary teachers for the country in general. The church through the control of the bishops educated many young men for the priesthood or for ordinary life. Many private *colegios* also contributed to the cultural growth of the country. A multitude of lawyers, engineers, physicians, dentists, and pharmacists revealed the increase in professional instruction, and in 1888 the establishment of the Catholic University in Santiago gave a rival and complementary institution to the state university.

Among the multiplying cultural advantages, we may point out the appearance of libraries and museums, the furthering of scientific, artistic, and literary societies growing out of earlier groups dating back to the mid-century. Concerts and public lectures stimulated scholarly pursuits and their influence extended into the political circle. The daily and periodical press showed the same cultural tendency. In 1860 there were two substantial dailies in the country, *El Ferrocarril* in Santiago and *El Mercurio* in Valparaiso. Thirty years later the capital had seven dailies, and there were twenty in the different cities of the republic, with many others of less frequent issue. The telegraph service and the extension of railroads permitted a wider distribution of these papers. Prominent among the newspaper writers of the period were two brothers, Justo and Domingo Arteaga Alemparte,[5] but they were simply leaders among a host of others. Nearly all of the professions carried on reviews, and there were likewise occasional publications of general literary or scientific character. The university published its *Anales,* and *Revista Católica* showed the literary purpose of the church.

IV

During more than half of the seventies, the country was in the midst of a financial depression. This forced the government to resort to paper money, and the *peso* speedily fell to about half its original value. This depreciation was followed by a corresponding increase in prices which bore most heavily upon day laborers and middle class clerks. These groups now began to agitate for better living conditions and on occasion resorted to strikes and violence. This ferment among the laboring classes found expression in the rise of the Democratic Party. Originally made up of a small group founded in 1887 to take part in

[5] Roberto Huneeus contributes a critical but sympathetic study of the two brothers in his Introduction (pp. vii-lxii) to *Los constituyentes de 1870.*

the turbulent political struggles, the party soon fell under the intelligent and firm direction of Malaquias Concha, a noted lawyer. By the turn of the century it became an important factor in national life. For the present it simply added one more complication to the political tangle.

With these changes, and with further lowering of the suffrage to include males twenty years of age, the president was in sympathy. As his administration progressed, he found it more necessary than ever to resort to measures that would gain him new friends. Sincerely devoted to what he thought the good of the country, but equally insistent on his personal prerogatives, he alienated the more prominent aristocrats; but through personal charm and public largess continued to gain in general popularity. The mass of the people were little interested in political contests among high-placed rivals; they were all too ready to follow a popular autocrat whose course promised material betterment. Thus Balmaceda approached the end of his administration fully confident that he had served his country well and that he could hand it over to a successor of his own choice.

It was this confidence in his personal strength that led to Balmaceda's undoing and to the overthrow of presidential authority. The congressional elections of 1888 were carried out with the customary resort to fraud and bribery. Balmaceda, nevertheless, permitted the election of some who were not his mere creatures. The various liberal factions retained their proportional strength; the conservatives gained more seats than they had had in twenty years. In this congress the choice of the next president became at once the absorbing question. The nationalists and the various liberal clans who would ordinarily follow the president's wish, were now divided into two major groups headed respectively by Augustín Edwards and Eduardo Matte.[6] In view of this division among his nominal supporters, Balmaceda ventured to bring out a candidate of his own, Enrique Salvador Sanfuentes.

The choice was a man of good family connections, but of untried ability. Perhaps the president suggested it as a measure of discipline for the liberals; perhaps he designed it as a bid for conservative support. Certainly Sanfuentes was himself something of a conservative. But whatever the purpose, the president alienated the nationalists and most of the liberals and failed to win the conservatives. The last named party, under the leadership of Manuel José Irrarázaval, was now aiming at a program of freedom in local control that was utterly incompatible

[6] A. Edwards, *Fronda*, p. 176.

with Balmaceda's course. Hence, the president found himself facing a congress in which he had no supporters but those attached to himself through executive favor and patronage. Nevertheless, he determined to pursue his course to the end.

The year 1889 witnessed a virtual alliance between Augustín Edwards and Eduardo Matte against the president. Cabinet changes by which Balmaceda sought in turn to gain these powerful leaders followed; then came attempts to rule through a cabinet made up from his diminishing personal following, then through a cabinet headed by his favored candidate. At the opening of congress in May, the president in his message set forth his constitutional views. He was contending, he claimed, for an independence and an equilibrium among the fundamental powers of the state. At the same time he paid tribute to the classic liberal ideals.

Balmaceda was in some measure following the course of Montt in 1860, but the country, or at least those who directed its elections, had left that precedent far behind. The legal advantage in the forthcoming struggle rested with congress, and that body was in no mood to listen to the president's eloquent argument. His plea, indeed, was based on familiar constitutional ground, not on the compelling force of pressing social and economic needs. Each of the parties to this quarrel tried to justify itself from past history. There each found precedents that drove it to a decisive but barren contest from which neither the contestants nor the country at large were greatly to profit.

The immediate advantage rested with Balmaceda's opponents. Congress refused, while the president retained Sanfuentes at the head of the cabinet, to approve the law for collecting taxes. It was the weapon used against Santa María in 1886, but now wielded by a majority of that body, not a minority. Without money government must cease. The archbishop of Santiago intervened and, through his mediation, Balmaceda agreed to form a cabinet acceptable to congress and that body to vote the necessary appropriations. The truce, however, was not lasting. In October 1890, he replaced the cabinet foisted upon him by another composed of his personal friends. Congress adjourned without adopting the budget or providing for the maintenance of armed forces beyond January 1, 1891. It definitely cast the gauge of battle before the president.

V

That stalwart executive was equally determined to test his power. He omitted to summon congress to pass the budget; that would have meant abject surrender to its leaders. He determined to put his principle to a conclusive test. On January 1, 1891, arrived the fatal day when the country was without a tax law. Balmaceda issued an executive order declaring his intention to collect taxes under the budget of the preceding year. His opponents in congress under the leadership of the president of the senate and the president of the chamber of deputies joined forces with Captain Jorge Montt, in command of the navy, and issued a proclamation declaring the president deposed from his office and threatening all who should pay taxes or obey his commands. In 1891, therefore, the quarrel between the president and congress had come to hostile clash and each was appealing to the country for support in the ensuing conflict. The congressional leaders departed to Valparaiso, united with the naval commander, and sailed northward to Iquique. Here they had at their disposal the revenues of the surrounding nitrate region and the laborers from the nitrate plants. While the army for the most part remained true to Balmaceda, his opponents with the resources of the northern conquered provinces were able to purchase war munitions and to improvise an army that eight months later, in the battles of Concón and Placilla, overthrew the forces of the dictatorial president and established the power of the congressional opposition. Among the results of this strife, which cost ten thousand casualties and a hundred million *pesos,* was the immediate resignation of Balmaceda, the sacking of the cities of Valparaiso and Santiago, and the establishment of the congressional majority in power. Balmaceda, who had taken refuge in the Argentine legation, committed suicide on September 18, 1891, the legal end of his administration. He left to his followers a manifesto known as a "Political Testment," in which he sought to explain and justify his acts and to inspire them with a desire to continue the principle of separation of powers for which he had contended.

VI

The civil war of 1891 was measurably hastened and furthered, if not directly caused, by the acquisition of the nitrate provinces to the north. From the war also emerged serious diplomatic controversies with the United States.[7] James G. Blaine, once again secretary of state in the northern republic, was represented in Santiago by an intimate personal friend, Morris P. Egan, a New York politician. Egan showed himself,

[7] Cf. H. C. Evans, *Chile and its Relations with the United States,* Ch. X. The narrative follows Galdames' *Estudio,* Ch. X. Hancock's narrative ends with the events of this chapter.

so the congressionalists claim, altogether too favorable to Balmaceda and his adherents. At any rate the Irish-American representative had evidently bet on the wrong horse, and found himself at the conclusion of hostilities *persona non grata* with the successful party. His attempt to fight prevailing British interests in Chile had ended disastrously.

The civil war also provoked a second unfortunate incident. The *Itata* was sent to the United States to procure a supply of arms for the insurgents. Suspected by the authorities, the vessel was under detention in San Diego, when it slipped out of the harbor, loaded the arms, and started for Iquique, pursued by two United States war vessels. Fortunately they did not overtake their prey, but the congressional leaders, not wishing to incur the open hostility of the northern republic, delivered to the pursuers both ship and cargo and bought other arms abroad. Thus the incident provoked nothing more threatening than a change in markets. More serious, however, was the charge that an American naval captain had first reported the landing of the congressional troops at Quinteros Bay, just before the final decisive battles. The officer involved definitely denied the charge and there is no reason to doubt his word. But in public belief it constituted another count against the neutrality of the United States.

The situation was still further complicated by rioting which occurred in Valparaiso in the fall of that year. The United States cruiser *Baltimore* under command of Captain—afterwards Admiral—Schley of the later famous controversy, was then visiting in Valparaiso harbor. Some of her sailors on shore leave, as was frequently the case, fell into disputes which led to a serious encounter with the local policemen. In the *melée* one sailor was killed, others wounded, and a considerable number arrested. Those detained were promptly released, but the local investigation dragged on and the sailors under detention reported treatment that aroused a popular demand in the United States for explanation and apology. Coming on top of the Egan incident and on the eve of a presidential election, the incident served to inflame the fighting spirit of the United States. Secretary Blaine promptly took measures to secure an apology and the indemnity that would likely be forthcoming. President Harrison, without consulting his secretary of state, demanded an immediate apology from the Chilean government, made the matter a lengthy topic in his annual message, and, when immediate reparation was refused in an unacceptable cablegram from Chile, the incident became the subject of a special message to congress in which Harrison assumed a decidedly warlike tone. Chile was, of course, in no position to reply in kind and shortly thereafter offered the necessary apology and agreed to pay damages to those injured and to the family of the dead sailor to the extent of $75,000. Thus ended this untoward incident which may be regarded as another international complication arising from the War of the Pacific.

The disturbances above mentioned affected in many cases the foreign merchants who lost no time in presenting extensive claims for indemnity. None caused so violent a quarrel as the *Baltimore* affair. Most of them affected British citizens and after some negotiations, Chile made an agreement with Great Britain by which such claims were submitted to tribunals of arbitration made up of one representative from each country and a third member. This commission after examining the claims declared most of them null and reduced materially the others which were then paid. Through this action Chile in time asserted the principle, practiced by European states, that "governments are not responsible for injuries occasioned to foreigners because of any internal disturbance whatever, when its constituted authority has done its utmost to avoid them." Citizens of other countries in such cases have the same recourse as citizens of Chile, namely, formal resort to the courts of the country. Thus her civil strife exerted a material influence on Chile's international position.

CHAPTER THIRTY

THE PSEUDO-PARLIAMENTARY RÉGIME, 1891-1914

I

CHILEAN historians designate the three decades that follow the civil war of 1891 as the "Democratic Republic." More realistic writers might term it—at least for a brief period—the restoration of the oligarchy. Members of the landed gentry who had called themselves conservatives and others who called themselves nationalists and liberals, had permitted representatives of a growing middle class, who called themselves radicals, to join forces with them in a move to overthrow a too dictatorial president. In this limited sense only, can the civil war be called "democratic." It removed an executive hitherto popular, who for a few months was proceeding in an unconstitutional manner. The contest seemed absolutely untouched by social influences that even then were faintly beginning to make themselves felt in contemporary Chilean life and thirty years later were to form the main planks in the program of another executive who dared challenge aristocratic supremacy.

The internecine contest turned on barren constitutional theories. To the victors the outcome proved equally profitless. No longer did a Manuel Montt direct them, nor even one of the lesser executives of the liberalized régime. The congressionalists had triumphed; congress was now the devoted instrument of the aristocrats and they proposed to make the most of their success. But one can find little in the political manipulations of the next thirty years that suggests popular government.

Apologists for the political system that followed seek to draw comparisons with British procedure. In both, a landed aristocracy manipulated the machinery. In both, the earlier aristocrats were reinforced by commercial and industrial leaders who in turn assumed equal pretensions. But in England the type of government that ultimately emerged was one increasingly responsible to public opinion. In this respect the landed and industrial directive group in Chile, and its small but increasing middle class, fall far short of the British prototype. Public opinion remained largely inert while politicians trafficked among themselves for temporary supremacy. The revolt of 1891 simply established the control of an "Aristocratic *Fronda*," and this new group speedily demonstrated its inability to cope with the forces that it sought to control.[1] Thus by sweeping aside the power of the president, the main prop of the government in earlier Chile, the attempt at reaction frustrated itself and the country became subject to a new period of administrative uncertainty, such as had characterized the first cycle of national life. That it provoked less turmoil than seventy years earlier, was due to the presence of certain economic and social factors that the inept oligarchs were unable to recognize.

II

Congress established its supremacy and apparently in a constitutional manner. In reality, the system that followed represented a conspicuous change in the government. Supposedly the way was now free to establish a parliamentary system. What actually took place was the supremacy of an elective oligarchy. Members of congress were really plutocratic commanders. A seat in either house was a sort of title of nobility to be won more by wealth than by personal qualifications. The parliamentary system was simply a play of parties in which irregular combinations busied themselves with the spoils of office without much regard to professed principles.

To the control that congress now assumed, two measures especially contributed. One was the cumulative vote which had already been established by law, but was now put into formal action. This assured any party group of reasonable size its representation in congress. A second measure that added to the influence of the congressionalists was the establishment of the autonomous commune. This deprived the executive of the control earlier exercised over the elections and turned them wholly over to party organizations. These two measures did much to prevent electoral intervention that had formerly determined the occupant of the presidential chair and the holders of congressional seats. Another earlier law establishing what was known as parliamentary incompatibility helped also to check the power of the executive. Under it legislative offices were closed to all employees paid by the state.

The law of the autonomous commune[2] divided the country into a large number of minor jurisdictions, each to be directed by a municipal

[1] A. Edwards, *Fronda,* Ch. XXIX.

[2] Galdames, *Estudio,* Ch. X. The materials for a narrative history of Chile from this point on are very fragmentary.

council. The members of this council were to hold office for three years and were placed in charge of public health, the cleaning and embellishment of towns, the promotion of education and of industry, and the maintenance of a police force. These measures would, it seems, call out local pride in such a way as to contribute to a healthful political tone in each community, but it was speedily apparent that the revenues placed under the control of the communes were inadequate to meet their demands. Hence, it was necessary in case of ordinary, as well as extraordinary, expenditures to appeal to the central government for further appropriations. Under the new system, however, this appeal was made to the party leaders, rather than to the president. Hence, centralization continued, but responsibility was divided among groups of politicians.

From another standpoint the commune also favored political parties rather than the president. The communal councils enrolled the citizens for voting and designated the names to be placed on the local ballot. This power extended to all candidates for office—communal, provincial, and national. The president of the republic could not interfere with councils in their tasks, hence he retained little power to influence their choice. On the other hand, party leaders in the capital named the candidates as definitely as the president earlier had done, but less openly; hence such measures were less subject to public scrutiny. Abuses inherent in the presidential system, such as arbitrary instructions, false writs, the suppression of votes, the use of military force, disappeared, but bribery became more prevalent. Money controlled the elections. The parties did not seek to send their most capable men to congress but the richest, those who could best pay for an election. If ability should be united to fortune, that was good; but if not, the fortune must be available. By the end of the first decade of the twentieth century an election for a deputy might cost from twenty to one hundred thousand *pesos,* while an election as senator from two hundred thousand to a million *pesos*. The amount depended on where the district was placed and on the resources of the adversary. In time, the custom of vote selling became so pronounced that if candidates by agreement tried to prevent the practice, they brought mob violence down upon their agents. The masses of the people became convinced that it was the "duty" of a candidate to bribe his electors.

Under this system elections were still determined in Santiago through combinations of party leaders. The increasing number of parties interfered with successful parliamentary procedure. The original conservative and liberal cohorts had long since split up into warring fragments. From the ranks of the former had come the nationalists, retaining many features of the old *pelucón* group, but asserting the supremacy of the state over the church. When the liberals began to gain politically, they first sloughed off the radicals, and then those that retained the original name subdivided. A portion claimed to be doctrinaire liberals, still fiercely opposing whatever smacked of clericalism in politics, while the great majority of them favored a strong president and were firm supporters of Santa María and of Balmaceda. Oddly enough they called themselves democratic liberals. Still others of liberal persuasion, styling themselves "free" or "unattached," gave comfort and support to Balmaceda's enemies. But defeat did not long disrupt his following. They reappeared in force during the congressional election of 1894, and by craftily combining with other political groups, gained more than their share of office and patronage.

III

The evolution of the above party groups is in keeping with Chilean traditions. Politics, in that country, had been a sort of aristocratic sport, a welcome alternative to horse-racing or gambling. Toward the end of the eighties appeared the Democratic Party, an aggregation of different character. Its purpose was to present a program in favor of the laboring class, but for the first ten years or so it did not play any considerable part in the political game. An attempt to model this party on the lines of French socialism miscarried, although by 1906 the group began to support strong social measures. Still later one portion of its membership became frankly communist.

Through subdivision these parties carried on as seven or more separate entities.[3] Obviously no one of them was able to control a majority vote in congress. Party measures, therefore, could be adopted only through political combinations. These generally took the form of two major divisions—the liberal alliance, and the liberal-conservative fusion. The alliance was generally made up of the radical group (really middle class) and the doctrinaire and free liberals. The fusion was usually

---

[3] A. Edwards, as usual, affords helpful interpretations for contemporary political events in his *Partidos políticos,* Ch. XIII, and more extensively and philosophically in his *Fronda,* Chs. XXX *et seq.* Manuel Rivas Vicuña, in "Campañas presidenciales," a series of articles published in *El Mercurio,* January and February 1925, goes minutely into the shifting details of party politics from the administration of Jorge Montt to that of Alessandri.

made up of the conservatives, nationalists, and democratic liberals. These combinations were by no means stable, and after 1894 the democratic liberals, by occupying a middle position, exerted considerable influence in determining administrations and hence in filling public offices. None of the political parties consistently adhered to principles. While these appeared in party platforms and were frequently professed in public speech, the real considerations that determined the selection of candidates were largely personal and economic. As an economic measure was really of national concern, it was, when carried into congress, frequently declared an open question upon which a person might argue as he pleased without compromising his party or causing internal division. The main purpose that influenced public life was to hold office and to enjoy the fruits thereof. Men who understood this program controlled affairs.

The presidential candidate was selected by a combination of parties, and the cabinet of the president after election was still dominated by this combination. Members of the cabinet had to obtain the consent of party leaders before accepting a seat therein, and, if the demands of the party seemed to warrant it, they could, after accepting, be forced to resign and thus disrupt the cabinet. With this division in authority there is little wonder that parliamentary responsibility became a by-word and responsible government the sport of political factions. The leaders of the party were the real ministers, but they were more concerned with popular issues that would carry elections than with decisions based on so-called "party principles." It was possible, therefore, to arouse considerable discussion on questions which touched upon education and religion, but comparatively little upon the serious social and economic questions which constituted the really important measures of state.

IV

It may be well to review briefly the main political events of these thirty years through the personality of the presidents. They, as we have seen above, no longer constituted the great men of state. Virtually such men no longer appeared in public life. Nevertheless, the character of the executive who initiated the parliamentary régime gave a certain amount of confidence. Don Jorge Montt did not belong to the family of the great Manuel.[4] He was a naval officer with a good record, but was in no sense remarkable. He was benevolent, frugal, honest, and

---

[4] Cabero, *Chile y los chilenos*, pp. 237, 238.

extremely scrupulous with respect to public funds. Simple in his tastes, he performed no theatrical feats but carried out his duties correctly and tactfully. He had no practical experience to guide him in the new tasks, nor was he familiar with the new methods of political control. He lacked acquaintance with public men; therefore, he committed certain errors which his good sense led him to correct promptly. He readily sought the advice of various leaders for he was himself exempt from vanity and belonged to no party group. With this equipment he carried on the government tranquilly and in a legal manner, so that for the first time there were free elections in Chile, and thus those who were defeated in 1891 were permitted to enter congress in considerable numbers after the election of 1894. He administered the country without graft and without undue interference with subordinates. After retiring from office he took up a minor position which he filled with the same devoted attention to public welfare. Friends contributed a house in which he lived, and when he died he left no greater estate than the prize money which had come to him in his naval career.

Despite his moderate course, cabinet changes were frequent during his administration. When the time arrived to elect a new congress in March 1894, he refrained from interfering, with the result that a combination of the Balmacedists with a portion of the radicals gained twenty-six seats and became the second group in congress. The conservatives led with twenty-nine; the moderate liberals gained fifteen seats and the radicals twenty-one. From this time on, therefore, the government had to ally itself with the more liberal forces. This necessitated frequent changes in party alignment and added to the general political confusion.

The revolt against Balmaceda had financed itself through letters of credit on London based on the resources of the nitrate region. These and other obligations incurred in the civil strife had now to be converted into more permanent forms of debt. To this task and to the restoration of the gold standard, the minister of the treasury, Enrique MacIver, energetically devoted himself.[5] It was not until May 31, 1893, that he secured the passage of a law setting the end of 1899 as the date for beginning to replace paper money with coin. That law, however, was never enforced. The value of the *peso* was now definitely placed at

[5] Martner, *Política comercial,* II, pp. 488-525 is still the main source of information for economic matters. Santiago Macchiavello Varas *op. cit.* occasionally applies general economic principles to specific national issues. F. W. Fetter *op. cit.,* reviews the course of economic development from the standpoint of monetary inflation.

eighteen pence—about forty per cent of its original value; internal loans were floated for immediate needs, and some minor changes were made in the system of coinage. Neither the will of the people nor international monetary conditions permitted more drastic financial legislation.

Foreign trade was greatly disturbed during 1891 when it barely exceeded twenty-nine million *pesos*. Four years later it registered above a hundred and forty-two millions and in the interval fell only once below a hundred millions. National income was somewhat adversely affected by turning part of the sources of taxation over to the municipalities. The receipts for 1891, however, were 55,723,000 *pesos* and they did not fall below that sum during the next four years, despite the conversion of the debt, the regulating of the *peso,* and the general financial depression. For this creditable showing in trade and income, the export tax on nitrates was largely responsible. Greater dependence on a single source of revenue led to a simpler fiscal mechanism and to less careful budgetary methods. Generally speaking, the ministers of finance failed to measure up to the standard set by their great predecessors. With such frequent change in personnel as was entailed by continual rotation in office, this decline in reputation is not surprising.

V

In 1896 Federico Errázuriz Echauren, son of the executive of the early seventies, became president.[6] His election was accompanied by charges of faking returns for the delegates who nominated him and of bribing electors without stint. Even with this dubious aid, his election was disputed in congress, and it was necessary to resort to a tribunal of honor which declared him elected by two votes. Several of his relatives figured among these electors. Under the circumstances he found it necessary to break with the executive tradition of recent years and to use political offices and public contracts more freely to pay party obligations and to advance his personal views. Such a course alienated many; hence he was continually impelled to seek new supporters and to change ministers frequently.

The younger Errázuriz, nevertheless, was an energetic, and in many respects, an able administrator. He possessed personal charm that readily gained friends and gave real prestige to his administration. Distinguished for his good humor and good taste, he knew human weak-

---

[6] Cabero, pp. 238-240.

ness and human passion and was able to utilize these qualities in others to his own advantage. Simple in person and manner he attracted and held friends by a certain subtlety of action. He could punish military men who seemed inclined to revolt. He could drive from public office functionaries who tried to stir up trouble. His most famous feat, however, was to further the settlement of the long-continued boundary disputes with Argentina.[7]

These controversies began with the occupation of the Straits of Magellan in 1849. Argentina also laid claim to the southern tip of the continent. The disputes that then arose dragged on until during the war with Peru. Chile and Argentina then came to an agreement as to the division of the Patagonian area. The major part of the territory was to go to Argentina; the Straits of Magellan in its whole extent, to Chile. The Andean boundary of the two countries was to be formed by "the highest peaks that divide the waters." Unfortunately when they came to run the line it was found that in many cases the watershed did not correspond with the highest peaks. In claiming the line of the peaks, Argentina might in some cases have extended to the Pacific. Chile naturally resisted this claim and hence the line was not actually marked. In 1898 the dispute threatened to bring on an armed crisis, but after some consideration of the matter the disputants agreed to submit the question to the arbitration of England. As a gesture of friendship in connection with this agreement President Errázuriz of Chile visited General Julio Roca, the President of Argentina, in the Straits of Magellan where the two executives dramatically met in what was known as "the embrace of the Straits."

Coincident with the dispute in the south another arose in the north. This concerned a portion of the country derived from Bolivia—an elevated, irregular, mountainous table-land known as the *Puna* of Atacama. Supposedly it was a land of great mineral wealth although no one has yet proved it to be so. Hence this mountainous desert region seemed another likely cause of serious trouble between the two countries. It was, however, referred to the minister of the United States in Argentina, William I. Buchanan, and in 1898 he gave a decision which really divided the territory. Some two-thirds of it fell to Argentina and the remainder to Chile. This decision, like most compromises, produced discontent in both countries. The people of Chile blamed their president for "giving up the *Puna*," and those of Argentina in similar manner

---

[7] Galdames, *Estudio,* Ch. X.

complained of their executive. The press on both sides took up the quarrel, and newspapers in each country began to accuse the other of exercising sovereignty prematurely in the disputed territory and even of diverting streams of water.

In the meantime the British arbitrator proceded slowly towards a settlement of the southern question. A commission under Colonel Thomas Holdich [8] took four years to make a careful survey of the disputed region. Public agitation in each country spread from the press to congress and thence to the people. During 1901 war seemed more threatening than ever. Both countries were assembling military and naval armaments and arranging to buy vessels. It required all the tact and good humor of President Errázuriz and the military force of General Roca to hold back their respective peoples. The successor of Errázuriz continued a conciliatory policy. As a result Chile and Argentina in May 1902, signed new treaties to settle by arbitration all existing differences between them, and other controversies which might arise in the future.

These treaties have a significance beyond the mere questions involved, for they constitute the first general arbitral treaties signed by modern nations. The two agreed not only to arbitrate all differences that might arise between them, but they also hit upon a formula by which they might secure naval and military equality. Neither of the nations for a period of five years was to acquire any new war vessels, and subsequent acquisitions were to be made by mutual agreement. It was this feature which attracted attention throughout the civilized world and marked a new step in the development of international relations. By a supplementary act Chile agreed to maintain neutrality in affairs on the Atlantic side that concerned Argentina, and Argentina made a similar declaration with respect to Chilean affairs on the Pacific. Several months later the decision of King Edward VII with regard to the southern boundary was announced. It was a compromise, for he divided the disputed area into two almost equal parts. Thus a series of disputes that had lasted for more than a half century were in 1902 brought to peaceful settlement. The event was graphically commemorated in the erection of a fitting memorial, the "Christ of the Andes," at the point where the principal mountain pass crosses the border line of the two countries.

Two years later, as we have noted elsewhere, Chile came to an agree-

---

[8] T. H. Holdich, *The Countries of the King's Award* (London, 1904).

ment with Bolivia which gave her undisputed control of the Province of Antofagasta and established the political and commercial relations between the two countries on a better footing. Bolivia, however, was not satisfied with being shut off fully from the sea and hence, some fifteen years later at the conclusion of the World War, strove to revive her claim for a western outlet.

VI

Errázuriz had been elected in 1896 by a combination of liberals and conservatives. His political methods and his forceful suppression of public discontent over the boundary settlements caused a new political alignment. The liberal alliance, in 1901, drew from the supreme court to the presidency one of its most notable judges, Don Germán Riesco.[9] A man of domestic tastes and a judge of high integrity, he was not forceful enough to make a strong executive. He lacked political experience, nor did he act with decision to stem the tide of corruption then existing in Chile. His administration, therefore, was an age of wild speculation. Corporations, many of them fraudulent, were formed to seize lands in the south or in the nitrate area of the north. Many of these crooked deals could only be carried through in collusion with subordinate officials. Thus the country was treated to the spectacle of a president, personally honest and well-meaning and interested in reform, but completely surrounded by self-seeking politicians and contractors whom he was unable to control; one who spent too much time over the letter of the law and not enough over the deeds of those who were to administer it. Some of those who, during this period of peculation, made their fortune, most heartily condemned similar practices twenty years later. Riesco was elected by the liberal alliance, but shortly afterward the inconstant liberal democrats broke from him and forced him to approach the conservative coalition. As a result of these changes, his presidential period of five years was marked by seventeen separate ministries. The most significant acts of his administration, therefore, were concerned with foreign affairs and particularly with concluding territorial disputes with Argentina and Bolivia.

Trade and governmental expenditures commenced to mount during this period.[10] Chilean consuls abroad made particular effort to expand the market for nitrate, and in 1906 forty per cent of the revenue was

[9] Cabero, p. 240.

[10] Martner, II, pp. 551-589. Cabero, *Libro* III, *Cap.* III affords suggestive comments on the economic developments of the period. Cf. also Fetter, *passim.*

derived from this one source. The government made extensive efforts to increase commerce with its South American neighbors with but little result. England and the United States afforded the country its best markets, with Germany rapidly becoming a dangerous rival for the former. The consumption of foreign goods was increasing, although the government attempted a vacillating protective policy. By 1900 the national income, expressed in *pesos* of eighteen pence, exceeded a hundred millions a year, while the total foreign trade was three times as much. In 1906 these figures were respectively a hundred and thirty-six millions and four hundred and fifty millions. The latter part of Riesco's administration was a time of relative quiet and of material gain. The inflation of the credit, the measures for developing foreign trade, and appropriations for railways form the outstanding economic measures, for which, however, the government can take unto itself little credit. Even in distributing public appropriations, party leaders exercised more influence than the executive.

One of the problems that confronted Riesco was the possible resumption of specie payments. By this time the system of paper money had been in operation more than twenty years and could not lightly be changed, especially under Chile's preposterous parliamentary government. The landed proprietors, whatever their party designation, were essentially conservative in money affairs. A fluctuating paper currency best fitted in with their heavily mortgaged estates. Thus we have the unusual spectacle of a paper money system, not merely continued but greatly increased under conservative control. With increasing commerce and a rise in the price of copper and nitrates, it would have seemed relatively easy to bring about the resumption of specie payments. The foreign situation seemed threatening at the turn of the century, so it was not difficult to postpone conversion until October 1903, and then to January 1905. Before that date the general spirit of speculation and the demand of labor for better living conditions, led to further issues of paper money and the postponement of resumption until 1910. Thus passed another favorable opportunity to reëstablish the gold standard.

VII

By 1906 the country was heartily disgusted with the workings of the parliamentary system which had rendered the president pusillanimous and congress inefficient. Even the party leaders were determined upon some change, and this transformation was to be brought about largely through the action of independent electors. The man selected by this group, composed of conservatives, nationalists, and moderate liberals, was Don Pedro Montt, son of the president who ruled in the fifties. The reputation of the father still persisted in the country and was furthered by the character of the son. He was known as a man of good education, of honorable career, active, forceful and self-effacing. With the prestige afforded by family connections and long experience, the country anticipated from him a strong administration, one that would give to the presidential office something of its former power, attract to it men of outstanding ability, and enable them to bring about a material and moral regeneration of the country.

Various factors conspired to defeat this aim. Shortly before he took office occurred the great earthquake which destroyed so much of Valparaiso. Then followed the financial crisis of 1907 which once more caused a scarcity in the country and brought on demands for still further assistance from the government. This led to another emission of paper money in August 1907. Attempts on the part of the executive to bring about specie payments were defeated. The president vetoed an act to postpone resumption, but congress passed it over his veto. Both the years 1908 and 1909 produced deficits. The situation with regard to exports was on the whole not favorable although it gradually improved in spite of the panic. As one minister of the treasury pointed out, only a little over twenty-five per cent of the exports of the country represented the healthy production of national goods. Altogether too large a proportion was expressed in terms of nitrates and copper. While Chile enjoyed a monopoly of the first named, its people could not appreciate the force of this statement. It is interesting to note that the United States had a trade with Chile considerably over one hundred million *pesos* in 1910, being surpassed by Great Britain which still maintained first place, and by Germany. The national debt in 1910 exceeded a hundred and seventy-nine million *pesos,* of which a hundred and fifty million was represented by issues of paper money.

Montt's administration, therefore, did not meet expectations. Perhaps he was, as one of his contemporaries remarked, "more of a statistician than a statesman." [11] Certainly he was tireless in his attention to administrative details, many of which he should have trusted to subordinates. But with all his good will and energy he was unable to overcome the defects of a corrupt political system or to meet the ravages

[11] Cabero, p. 242.

of the disease that ultimately carried him off. The great work of his administration was the beginning of the longitudinal railway, which was to unite the most northern ports of the republic with Puerto Montt, the gateway named after his father. Much was anticipated from this railway as a link between the agricultural south and the industrial north; but transportation still continued cheaper and more expeditious by sea. As a public work the railway added more to the country's debt than to its defense. Montt also had the satisfaction, if such it proved, of opening the Trans-Andine Railway in 1910. He and his party used it to cross to Argentina, where the executives of the two countries celebrated together, in May of that year, the hundredth anniversary of the movement for independence in southern South America. Before the return celebration in Santiago, however, President Montt died while on a trip to Europe in search of medical attention. His untiring efforts to improve conditions did much, contemporaries believed, to shorten his life.

VIII

The death of Montt abroad was followed within a few weeks by the death of the minister who succeeded him. The second bereavement occurred in September on the eve of Chile's centennial celebration. Already the visitors from abroad had gathered in the capital, and after mature consideration the government determined to proceed with the festivities as planned. They took place under the direction of Emiliano Figueroa Larrain, minister of the interior, who assumed in turn the provisional presidency. The quiet succession of these two men in office showed visitors the essential stability of the Chilean people.[12]

In addition to celebrating its centennial, Chile had also to choose a new president. In view of the double affliction suffered by the country the political leaders determined, if possible, to avoid a serious contest. The liberal convention came together and designated as its candidate Ramón Barros Luco, a statesman of half a century of administrative experience, a man of common sense and of dignity in public appearance.[13] He was one who could listen to heated discussions and then at the proper moment dryly propose an acceptable solution. According to popular belief he settled the most serious matters of state while dozing, but his solutions were deliciously humorous. At any rate, he did not bury himself in details of administration as did his predecessor,

---

[12] Galdames, *Estudio,* Ch. X.

[13] Cabero, p. 243; A. Edwards, *Fronda,* p. 213.

but contented himself with pointing out the general line of procedure. All political parties united to put him in office. Thus in the critical year marked by death and the centennial celebration, the people of Chile avoided the dangers of a harsh political campaign.

But this moment of political quiet was not permanent. Twenty years of pseudo-parliamentary government had wrought a change of heart in the people;[14] but new influences were beginning to be felt in the country at large and they were marked by proposals of a social character, even tending towards communism. Strikes were more common. Some of the leaders who appreciated their significance began to speak more freely of necessary labor legislation. The movement of the population from the central and southern regions to the north, the coming in of foreign capital in large measure, the active contact afforded by railways, steamship lines, and telegraphic service, linked Chile more closely with her neighbors and with North American and European countries. The prospective opening of the Panama Canal gave promise of closer relations with more distant centers. A law, passed in January 1914, provided for the autonomous organization of the railways. Commercial treaties did much to change the course of trade and gave promise, under favorable conditions, of a substantial increase in its total.

The social and economic problems of the period were becoming more complex. One of Chile's leading financiers, Guillermo Subercaseaux, tried with some associates to found a national party that should avoid questions that were merely political or religious in character and confine itself to significant economic issues. Unfortunately he and his handful of followers exerted comparatively little influence upon general political programs. To the labor organizations of a beneficiary type, that had existed in the country since 1853, were now added those of more militant character. In 1909 the Labor Federation of Chile was organized, with subordinate councils throughout the country, and immediately it began to direct strikes in the coal and nitrate regions. It favored an extensive program embracing mutual aid, propaganda against alcoholic liquors, the advancement of education, an eight-hour law, arbitration of disputes, and friendly relations with the public authorities.

After 1900 a few more foresighted leaders showed interest in the laboring masses. Their efforts were directed, however, more toward the amelioration of specific evils than their prevention. Of this type

---

[14] Abraham König, *La constitución de 1833 en 1913* (Santiago, 1914), affords an adequate critical résumé of the political situation, with some suggestions for improvement.

may be mentioned the "League against Alcohol" and certain agencies to care for destitute children. To some extent the government paralleled this work by enacting measures against disease. In 1906 it passed a law for better housing conditions, which marked the first direct intervention by the government in a social question. In general, however, the country was still unprepared for adequate social legislation. Nor could improvement be expected under the existing government. Barros Luco's favorite motto was, according to report, "politics is the art of the possible."[15] Under him, therefore, executive power did not increase. In many respects it approached its greatest point of weakness. Apparently the leading parties were able to divide public offices to suit themselves. Ministries often lasted no longer than two or three months. Congress became definitely a scene of confusion, showing alike its own incapacity and the weakness of the president. Some force outside Chile seemed necessary to arouse its people to a sense of their own shortcomings.

Contemporary literature afforded additional evidence that an era was passing. No writers directly stimulated literary production nor so dominated it as had Bello and Lastarria in their time. The former with the Arteaga brothers, the Mattas, and others who had so profoundly influenced political thought and æsthetic taste were now dead. Victor Hugo's later verse, the poems of De Musset and of the Spaniard, Gustavo Becquer, readily found their imitators in *fin de siècle* Chile. Rubén Darío, the Peruvian, José Santos Chocano, and the Mexican Gutiérrez Nájera attracted their devotees. Yet the local product, withal, became more definitely indigenous. Indicative of the new spirit is Gabriella Mistral whose contemporary verse, though mournful in theme, is vibrant with the spirit of the new age. Poetry, it is true, still kept traces of the exotic; the stern character of the Chilean yielded to it grudgingly. He did better with respect to the descriptive sketch and the legend—forms of literary expression to which his life and surroundings entice him; but he still displayed his best efforts in political and historical writing.

Alberto Blest Gana, the American Balzac, began with the turn of the century a second productive period. From Paris, where he spent the last years of his life, he turned once more to interpret in his novels the history and manners of his native land. Other contemporary novelists also found congenial themes in the exploits of the War of Inde-

[15] Vicuña Subercaseaux, *El socialismo revolucionario y la cuestión social en europa y en Chile* (Santiago, 1908).

pendence, or in the traditions of banditry so widely current, or in the conflict with Peru and the career of Balmaceda. Others, of whom Daniel Barros Grez is chief, satirized contemporary life in the style of Cervantes; still others like Vicente Grez—novelist, poet, and journalist—developed a more careful technique in physical description and psychological analysis. Something of the anti-clerical spirit of contemporary political life appeared alike in poem, sketch, and novel. With the opening of the new century, the short story, often frankly imitating Maupassant, brought commendable artistic skill to the delineation of various types of Chilean life. Pedro Antonio González, whose *Ritmos* helped introduce Darío to Chile, and most of his contemporary versifiers have gone, but they blazed a pathway in national literature that the present generation gladly follow.

In 1886 Vicuña Mackenna passed from the scene, leaving behind him a voluminous historical output. Barros Arana continued to produce until the eve of his death in 1907. Still active and still productive to the end of the third decade of the century was Toribio Medina, who crowned a life of fabulously fruitful labor by leaving his magnificent historical collection to the National Library of Chile. The elder Amunátegui, dying in 1888, left the educational and historical tradition of the family to Domingo Amunátegui Solar. General Bulnes continued his historical labors unabated and from 1927 to 1931 rounded out the changing phases of a busy life as ambassador of Chile to Argentina. Works on law, philosophy, history, and education combine to make memorable the career of Valentín Letelier. Alejandro Fuenzalida Grandón essayed biography, as did many of this period, and touched on the intellectual development of the country in his *La evolución social de Chile* which represented the results of a lifetime study. His theory of the Germanic origin of the Spaniards who settled Chile is not tenable, but the data he so toilsomely gathered have value for the student.

Of Alberto Edwards, recently deceased, of Luis Galdames, Alberto Cabero, Carlos Keller, and Daniel Martner the footnotes of the present work abundantly attest. Emphasizing as they do the Chilean tendency to historical and legal writing, their work likewise shows the influence of contemporary economics and social philosophy. Honored as interpreters of their country's past and present, they may be regarded as prophets of its more hopeful future.

CHAPTER THIRTY-ONE

SOCIAL FERMENT AND REVOLUTION, 1915-1925

I

TO CHILE the World War proved both a quickening influence and a handicap. It caught the country without a merchant marine and without neighbors who could supply the lack of transport. With few European vessels available for commerce and altogether too many bent on war, Chile, at the beginning of hostilities, found it difficult to ship its products or to maintain its neutrality.[1] In this respect Germany caused greater trouble than Great Britain, although the latter nation committed the most striking trespass upon Chile's sovereignty. For decades Chile had maintained close commercial relations with Great Britain, as English, Scotch, and Irish patronyms among its people attest. Furthermore, its navy had a long traditional connection with British service. On the other hand, German colonists and their descendants were plentifully scattered over southern Chile and were beginning to penetrate all phases of Chilean life in other sections. Since 1891 Prussian methods and traditions had set the pace for the army, which in uniform and equipment closely patterned itself after the model set in Potsdam.

Outside the country Chile was looked upon as favoring the Central Powers. At the outset, indeed, German methods in coaling and provisioning the fleet in the south Pacific proved particularly annoying both before and after the destruction of the English fleet under Craddock. When, in turn, the fleet of von Spee met defeat and the English pursued and sunk a German vessel among the Juan Fernández Islands within Chilean waters, the offending nation rendered prompt apology for the insult. After this incident no serious question arose between Chile and the nations actually at war. In interpreting its obligations, its ministers even went beyond the requirements laid down at the Hague conferences. Its course, in view of possible British and German predilections, was difficult and in a corresponding degree commendable.

[1] See P. A. Martin, *Latin America and the World War* (Baltimore, 1925). Cf. also Galdames, *Estudio*, Ch. X *passim*.

As the war progressed, public opinion veered strongly to the side of the Allies.

The slump in trade presented a more difficult problem.[2] Lacking the means to move exports, the stocks of nitrate, copper, wool, and other products simply piled up at the ports. Trade was at a standstill; ruin impended over banker and merchant; starvation threatened the laborer and his family. Early in 1915 naval operations ceased to imperil commerce on the west coast. The copper and nitrate of Chile began to find their way to the battle front of western Europe. The opening of the Panama Canal facilitated this traffic and brought the country into more direct contact with the United States. The total of foreign trade, in 1917, exceeded a billion *pesos*—a figure heretofore undreamed of and altogether too large to represent a healthy development.

II

The election of 1915 was carried by the conservative coalition in favor of Juan Luís Sanfuentes. It was a violent struggle where the president-elect was in his element. He has been termed a genuine representative of existing conditions in Chilean politics. He was not a statesman but he had wide experience in business and unusual skill in political combination. He knew how to shuffle men and parties with dexterity, and to attract a following by means of pelf and promises. Stout, strapping, ruddy, and smiling he suggested the landed proprietor rather than the widely discussed politician. Suspicious even of the combination that had elected him, he tried to create still more political factions, but in this he was not successful. As chief of the democratic liberals, he had managed previous governments as he willed. Now as president he found himself caught in the same nets that he had often woven for others.[3]

With little vision as to the real necessities of the country and without definite proposals for meeting the economic and social crises which came upon it, the president left these problems largely to his swiftly changing cabinet. His administration, hampered at times and helped at others by the World War, simply sought, therefore, to extenuate the evils caused by that strife rather than to effect any great change in policy. Hence it promised to have little permanent impression on the country. At the end his adversaries charged him with attempting

[2] Martner, *Política comercial,* II, pp. 620, 650.

[3] Cabero, *Chile y los chilenos,* pp. 244, 245.

to intervene in the elections, contrary to recent practice, while both students and laborers held him responsible for acts of persecution visited upon them. President Sanfuentes, be it said, was by nature a conservative, the last of a long line of administrators who saw in every proposed change a real peril to personal and class interests. A fit executive for the liberalized republic of a half century before, he was unequal to the task of guiding it through the social and economic maze in which he found himself. That was a task for one of far different antecedents and training.

For Chile the aftermath of the World War was of greater importance than the conflict itself. The armistice closed the market for Chilean products and left the country financially stranded amid a plethora of unsalable exports.[4] *Oficinas* in the nitrate region shut down, dispossessing thousands of laborers with their families, whom the government had to feed and shelter and transport to other sections of the country. After a brief recovery in 1920 Chile plunged into a still deeper slump from which the prospects of emerging seemed hopeless. Contemporary politics seemingly had no remedy to offer. The numerous parties, even those of recent origin, seemed on the point of dissolution. The confusion may have been due in part to the wider suffrage introduced before the bulk of the population was trained to use it properly. Most parties were simply political groups gathered around an outstanding personality, who, possibly, owed his position to his intellectual and moral character, but the chances were that he had gained it through the use of money. From top to bottom political practice was shot through with corruption and its widespread influence poisoned all the sources of power. The ordinary forces that divided men, the tendency toward conservatism or toward liberalism, had become so thoroughly scattered that instead of forming two major parties, some seven or eight made an appeal to the people, an appeal that was based more on bribery than on reason.

Future developments were already beginning to declare themselves. In 1915 Arturo Alessandri had been elected senator from Tarapacá as a member of the liberal alliance. As a law student he had written a thesis which had showed advanced social views, but since 1907, when he first entered the chamber of deputies, he had kept these views under cover and had kept closely in touch with the more conservative coalition. In 1915 he achieved the senatorship and was also mentioned as a presidential candidate. In the senate he showed himself a vehement

[4] Martner, II, p. 655; Cabero, pp. 245-252, 385.

opponent of President Sanfuentes and as such, for some months in 1918, he headed a liberal-radical cabinet which attempted to simplify the method of closing debates in congress. Both in and out of office he was tireless in advancing his pretensions to the presidency. In the end he wore down the resistance of the liberal alliance and became its accepted candidate.

It was a period of political crises. The congressional election of 1918 more than met the expectations of the liberal alliance; it even caused some of the leaders a certain dismay. A new era was dawning in Chilean politics—a period in which social and economical influence must replace the time-worn wrangles of the past. The election of 1920 was largely to turn on these issues and demanded a candidate who was in accord with them. Alessandri seemed the man of the hour. Hence the alliance reluctantly accepted him, hoping that success would measurably modify his program and permit the old practices to continue unchecked.

III

Alessandri was, and still is, an enigma.[5] Almost childlike in certain characteristics, his energy, virility, and brilliance formed a powerful attraction for the multitude. Frank and open in manner, generous and impulsive, true to his friends and vehement toward his enemies, he attracted enthusiastic followers and raised up for himself equally bitter enemies. No man in recent public life in Chile has been more discussed than Alessandri. He always seemed to act more through impulse than through conviction or reason. In parliament he spoke correctly and well; before a crowd he was able to carry his hearers by his enthusiastic pleading or fiery denunciation of his enemies. Perhaps there was something of his Italian descent to explain his career and character, but certainly he exerted a popular influence equalled by no South American of his day.

From the beginning of his senatorship he had espoused the popular side. As a candidate he entered upon the formal campaign in 1920 in an unusual manner. Hitherto those seeking this high office had depended for their election solely upon party combinations. Alessandri had his party backing, but he determined also to make an open campaign. His opponent was Don Luís Barros Borgoño, a man of liberal convictions, an academic orator but one who lacked popularity. He belonged to the

---

[5] Cabero, pp. 252-257 and personal interviews. The writer made a visit to Chile in 1922 and a more extensive one in 1926.

higher classes and might be represented as an embodiment of the decadent oligarchy. Hence by a direct campaign among the people, Alessandri might hope to gain the election. Accordingly he introduced the whirlwind methods which are more common in the northern countries than in South America. His oratory swept the multitudes from the nitrate deserts of the north to the wooded slopes of the south. Never had the country heard such an appeal; never such a torrent of eloquence in behalf of popular measures. It was an attempt to arouse the people, as serious as it was unusual.

Victory for a time remained uncertain. Alessandri and his supporters then menaced the country with strikes and popular agitations, charging that his opponents were trying to steal the election from him. As usual the final word was to be given by congress. That body, unable to solve the conflict, appointed a Tribunal of Honor. The group of three examined carefully the returns from the various provinces. Fraud appeared on both sides and there were many evidences of corrupt political practices, but in the long run the Tribunal decided that Alessandri's rivals had been more guilty of corrupt practice than he, and gave the election to him by one vote. In reality Alessandri typified the new social and economic forces too well to be turned down at the last. His enemies feared him more, deprived of office, than when given apparent control of affairs. They were unwilling to grant the legislation that public opinion now demanded; they felt able to thwart any leader who should attempt the task. "Let Alessandri try," they reasoned, and let him bear the brunt of failure.

The president's control of affairs, it soon appeared, was more apparent than real. He had set for himself, as he later assured the writer, a threefold program: to settle matters at issue with Peru; to balance the budget and stabilize national finance; and to put in force important measures of social legislation. But he found himself handicapped by the opposition of the senate. Legislation that he proposed was rejected by that body and with each rejection came a cabinet change. Hence, it was impossible to carry through any measures that depended upon congressional action.

IV

Shortly after assuming office, the president did succeed in carrying through the preliminary steps submitting to arbitration the Tacna-Arica dispute. This depended largely upon executive measures. Meanwhile, there occurred a second important slump in national finance, the second since the close of the World War. The market for nitrate fell off so greatly that the national income was reduced; operatives were thrown out of work and from the north came further migrations of the unemployed laborers with their families to show the people of central Chile the depths of economic misery. Most of them did not need such an object lesson to realize that depression rested over the country. The closing of the nitrate plants shut off the market for grain and other food stuffs of central and southern Chile, so that hard times fell upon the estates of central Chile and the farms of the south, as well as upon the laboring populations in the commercial centers. The year 1922 represented an extremely low point in national well-being. In the following year there was some improvement due to measures taken by the government to aid the nitrate producers, but this did not promise permanent results.

The laboring classes of the north especially felt pinched during this period of scarcity. When the *oficinas'* only source of livelihood shut down, they were dispossessed and driven from their wretched homes, deprived of their scant personal belongings, and turned out to wander in barren deserts, unless happily the government should transport them elsewhere.[6] These nitrate workers constituted a pitiful exhibit of privileged exploitation. Toiling through burning days and chilling nights, in a desolate land that afforded provender for neither man nor beast, their wages at best barely sufficed to feed and clothe and shelter them and their families. On their labor rested a large share of the revenues of the government and the bulk of the swollen fortunes of a new industrial economy. Now with the source of wealth and wages gradually drying up, they and their employers, not to mention the country at large, faced an almost hopeless future. The desert would no longer tolerate them; other industrial centers, even their former homelands, seemed scarcely less repellant.

The employers, indeed, put forth some effort to soften the rigors of the situation for those whom they could still employ. Impressed by the welfare work carried on in the copper plants of Chuquicamata and El Teniente, *La Associación de Productores de Salitre,*[7] in 1921, formed a department of welfare that in the next three years devoted over forty-one million *pesos* to this purpose. This effort largely expressed itself in better housing for employees and in better medical and sanitary serv-

---

[6] Cabero, p. 385.

[7] *Ibid.*, p. 394.

ice. Other mining companies, including those in the coal producing areas, imitated this good example.

As may be inferred, these efforts barely touched the labor problem, nor had the government turned its attention seriously in that direction. A pioneer law in 1906 had suggested the need for better dwellings for laborers, but a decade passed before it was followed by legislation providing for seats and rest periods for commercial clerks, for precautions against accidents, for provision for those injured while at work, for facilities for nursing mothers while employed, for free Sabbaths, and on the state railways for retirement and insurance funds. In 1920 a general loan fund was created by law.

This legislation, it will be observed, interfered very little with individual regulation of industry. President Alessandri was not content with such modest measures, and in 1921 submitted a project for a labor code that should limit working hours, forbid child labor and regulate the work of women, provide for insurance against accidents, disease, and old age, recognize unions and organize coöperative societies, and guarantee to individual employees retiring allowances and the right to combine with their fellows.

Such an extensive social program, if put in force at once, would prove extremely costly to industry. As a countermove the senate presented a project for general labor legislation. Congress, seeking to play politics with both plans, did nothing. More than once the disgusted president was on the point of resigning his thankless task. Budgetary conditions gave him further trouble. The three years from 1916 to 1918, inclusive, had shown a surplus, but each of the five to follow bore a deficit, despite some reduction in expenses for 1921 and 1922. In the six-year period ending in 1920, expenses had mounted from 172,826,000 *pesos* to more than 264,000,000—an increase due in part to the bad distribution of public funds, but still below the needs of the population. The service on the public debt absorbed more than a third of the appropriations, and salaries and pensions another third, leaving altogether too small a sum for public works and public welfare.[8]

V

The president and his followers expected much from the congressional elections of 1924. He determined to bestir himself in order to

[8] Martner II, pp. 662-674 gives a detailed account for the early part of Alessandri's administration. Cf. also *Current History*, XIX (Jan. 1924), p. 676.

secure a majority in support of his measures. For thirty years the president supposedly had not interfered in elections, but Alessandri did not hesitate to collect a group of followers for a general campaign through the country on pretext of inaugurating an industrial exposition in the south. In his addresses he violently attacked the senate and the leaders of the national union, the conservative combination that was entrenched there. On his return he repeated this attack, directing it especially against the senatorial majority that ventured to flout public opinion. He was now determined to curb that hostile majority through fundamental changes in the constitution. Like Balmaceda before him he would fight the reactionary forces by enlarging the power of the president.

He did not content himself with mere speeches. Directing his followers to break up and disperse the gatherings of their opponents, he made ready to use the army and the national police force in his own behalf. His efforts naturally aroused the intense opposition of his enemies; but with the political machinery in his hands he would be able to carry the elections. The bitterness of strife, however, seemed to point either to a dictatorship or to anarchy. Consequently his enemies attempted to make a bargain with him by which they agreed to accept in part his reforms if in return he would not use the army and police in the election. The conservative forces claimed that they were prepared to carry out their part of the bargain but that the president did not remove his partisan functionaries or refrain from using armed force. What he wanted was a majority in both houses of congress and a majority that would enable him to establish a firm rule and to carry through his measures. To accomplish this worthy purpose he believed that the end justified the means. With his more popular appeal and by using the military and resorting to violence at the polls, he carried the election and secured the required majority in both houses of congress.[9] His enemies claim that he could have gained this end without such means, but at any rate he had succeeded and was prepared to take advantage of his victory.

Disappointment again awaited the reforming president. His own followers now failed him. The congress of 1924 was in general a body of much lower grade than previous congresses. Its members were apparently more interested in getting jobs for their friends and in voting themselves a salary, than in balancing the budget or adopting social

---

[9] Cabero, pp. 258-260; A. Edwards, *Fronda,* Ch. XXXVIII; *Current History* Vols. XIX-XXI *passim.*

legislation. Accordingly its sessions during the months of 1924 were devoted to sterile harangue while behind the scenes revolution gathered headway.

VI

The president's methods had accomplished one thing, at least—he had made the country politically minded. The people at large were disgusted with congress; their chief executive apparently could not help them. His bitter opponents of the national union plotted at once to get rid of him and of the discordant and distrusted congress, hoping to use the unpopularity of that body as a cloak to conceal the reactionary dictatorship at which they aimed. Recent changes of government in Italy and in Spain afforded them a model for procedure They had at hand the instrument for their purpose—the army. It was a very different body from the force that had gained the victory over Peru and Bolivia. Long years of peace had affected its discipline. It was top-heavy with officers and filled with discontent. There had been previously a few symptoms of insubordination but these had been readily suppressed. The disgruntled leaders of the national union believed, however, that they could gain the army to their cause, especially as younger officers were discontented at the scant prospect for promotion and the soldiers had been unpaid for several months. The condition within the armed forces of the republic betokened serious trouble, but the scheming oligarchs believed they could make any ensuing disturbance serve their own purpose.[10]

But universal discontent was moving too fast for them. The greed of congress, plus its general ineptitude, hastened the course of events. In view of the financial stringency, which affected all branches of public service, the president had proposed an issue of paper money to the extent of 110,000,000 *pesos.* Despite popular discontent and disordered finances which affected all sections of the country, not to mention evidences of insubordination in the capital itself, congress voted to give its members for the first time an annual salary.[11] Hitherto, service in congress had been regarded as an honorable privilege. Pay was to be obtained secretly, if at all, through contracts and appropriations, but in the old days there had been no hint of scandal of this sort. In more recent times such charges are all too common. But the spectacle of congress-

---

[10] Cabero, p. 262. Among the groups of the liberal alliance, measures were under way to oppose the president. A. Edwards, *Fronda,* p. 240. Cf. *Current History,* XXI, (Nov. 1924) pp. 271, 272.

[11] Edward suggests that Alessandri proposed this to keep his followers in line. *Ibid,* p. 245.

men in the midst of general distress dallying over important social issues and using an emergency fund to vote themselves a salary stirred up furious resentment throughout the country. This sentiment found expression, on the nights of September 2 and 3, 1924, in a disquieting manner. Some of the younger officers from the Santiago garrison, listening from the galleries to the debates of the senate, voiced their disapprobation of proceedings in no uncertain manner. Their course seemed designed to provoke an "incident," but they were evidently not working in collusion with their superiors. The latter needed more time to develop their plot.

The minister of war made a move to discipline the youthful culprits but without success. Public opinion seemed to applaud the demonstration. Thus encouraged, on the night of September 4, some four hundred officers met at the military club and formulated a demand on the government for an increase in salary and for more rapid promotions, and also asked the president to veto any act giving a salary to members of congress. President Alessandri was not unmindful of what was going on. He summoned to the palace one of the most prominent leaders among the younger officers, assured him that he sympathized with their demands, and asked the group to support his own projects for reform, promising in return to help their program. "If the army is with me," he affirmed, "I am with the army. Don't forget that I count on the aid of public opinion." [12]

On the next morning these officers designated some of their number to form a military *junta,* and empowered the body to publish their pronouncement in the name of the army. They also approved petitions which were to be presented to the president—petitions, be it noted, that were largely prepared by himself. This military *junta* in the afternoon went to the palace, asked for a change in the cabinet and the acceptance of the program agreed upon. In the course of the interview one of the more impetuous of their number intimated that he and his companions demanded a change of the ministry. The president repelled this forceful insinuation with dignity, and the incident closed. He offered, however, to veto the law for parliamentary pay, accepted the

---

[12] Cabero, pp. 264 *et seq;* Edwards, Ch. XXXIX. The narrative that follows is based largely on these two sources, supplemented by the files of *El Mercurio.* Cf. also E. Monreal, *Historia completa y documentada del periodo revolucionario 1924-1925* (Santiago, 1927). Consult also Clarence H. Haring, "Chilean Politics, 1920-1928," in *Hispanic American Historical Review,* XI (February 1931), pp. 1-26. See the files of *Current History,* XXI *passim* and especially Earle K. James, "Chile's Bloodless Revolution," XXI (Dec. 1924), pp. 370-376.

resignation of the ministry and charged General Altamirano to form a new cabinet, believing that thus he would stamp out sedition. Later, he called in the general and asked him about rumors that Altamirano's assumption of power was in keeping with a premeditated plan to drive the president from office. The general denied this and affirmed that his purpose and that of his proposed associates was to restore a normal constitutional situation, to aid the executive and congress, to bring about a rapid approval of the budget and of laws for military and social reform. At midnight on September 6 the president called a member of the military *junta* to ask that body to present a new set of petitions that would provide for a real change in parliamentary system and the substitution, therefor, of one definitely restoring the power of the president.

This request brought a reaction which convinced Alessandri that he could no longer control the situation. The army in reality feared him even more than congress and proposed to remove him and establish its own power. Accordingly on the eighth Alessandri presented his resignation because he recognized that the military was now in control. The senate on the ninth refused to accept this, but in the meantime Alessandri had taken refuge in the American embassy and on the tenth was escorted by the American minister and a representative of the military *junta* to the Argentine frontier. Meanwhile the minister of the interior formally turned the government over to a *junta* composed of two generals and an admiral. On the eleventh that body formally took charge of affairs and dismissed the incompetent congress, but not before its terrified and bewildered members had adopted, without debate, the measures of reform over which they had wrangled for months.[13]

VII

The series of events that forced Alessandri from office constituted no mere *coup d' état;* they indicated the passing of the inadequate parliamentary system that for more than thirty years had misgoverned the country. Despite the gravity of this change in government, it was accomplished without any serious resistance on the part of the people. There were some slight manifestations by the friends of Alessandri, but in general he departed without any serious expression of regret. His popularity had apparently vanished in the course of a few hours. His efforts had failed to establish in the people at large any idea of

[13] Jorge Gustavo Silva, *Nuestra evolución político-social* (Santiago 1931), pp. 44, 82.

social solidarity, nor would his going affect the more intellectual classes. They realized that the country was ill and needed substantial attention, but Alessandri had failed to convince them that he was able to administer the cure.

The military *junta* that now took charge issued a proclamation to the country on September 11 explaining its action and expressing its intention to seek remedies for the general ills. Its members sought to ingratiate themselves with public opinion by giving a democratic tendency to the movement headed by them, forgetting that democracy and militarism make poor bedfellows. They promised to maintain public liberty, forgetting also that liberty maintained by force no longer is liberty. They tried to keep their movement free from political parties when all public men of Chile were affiliated with one or another of the existing organizations. In their desire to do something they gradually drifted into an alliance with the reactionary elements embodied in the unionist ranks. Hoping to proceed in a constitutional way, they appointed a ministry of civilians headed by the leading law professor of the university, but that body resorted to decrees to carry out its policy rather than ordinary legislation and naturally met with resistance. It turned political opponents out of office and dissolved municipal governments—both measures necessary perhaps for immediate efficient administration but apparently giving the negative to its professions of constitutional rule. As time went on the members of the military *junta* and their supporters showed an increasing tendency to meet the reactionary views of the national union.

A crisis portended when a dispute between the cabinet and the *junta* led the former to resign. Moreover, the younger officers in the army felt that their claims were being neglected. The parties that made up the liberal alliance were anxious once more to play the political game. The *junta* had promised a convention to modify the constitution but such action seemed indefinitely postponed. With general discontent making itself felt, the two forces that might join in expressing it gradually came together. The younger officers demanded a change; the liberal alliance wished to bring it about through their leader. He, however, was in exile. Accordingly, they united to recall him.

On January 23, 1925, a group of the younger officers, led by Major Carlos Ibañez and Major Marmaduque Grove, took possession of the palace and forced the *junta* to resign. For a time the officers of the navy seemed inclined to resist this uprising, but instead gave way to prevent civil war. The new *junta* then took charge and invited President Alessandri to return and assume direction of affairs. The exiled president was then in Rome but hastened to accept their invitation under conditions. His cablegram read:

> "I esteem indispensable the immediate establishment of civil government formed by men fully in the confidence of the general opinion of the country and whose patriotic antecedents may be a secure pledge that they will know how to put aside passion and particular interests and, throwing a veil upon the dolorous events of the past, may direct their action to the reëstablishment of harmony and to obtain the indispensable reforms which the constitution requires." [14]

The new *junta* of government that was in charge until Alessandri got back had a difficult task to perform. There was much discontent in the country and much need for efficient action to improve affairs. The old officers of the army and the politicians of the national union were naturally discontented. It was necessary to banish many of them. Groups of public employees organized to bring about better conditions for themselves. Moreover, certain newspapers were openly criticizing the turn of affairs. The *junta* proceeded to close these newspaper offices, to suppress revolts in certain regiments, and to exile some politicians of the national union. In order to attract the bureaucrats and the army they passed decrees raising the salaries of public employees, in some cases to double or treble former compensation. To help the junior officers of the army, they retired in the course of seven months nine generals of division, seventeen brigadiers, and nineteen colonels, and advanced a large number of the others two grades. They also decreased the period of service from forty to thirty years.[15] These were the most conspicuous acts of the second military dictatorship that followed the fall of Alessandri. The double overturn resulted in revolution which expressed itself in legislation, one in which ink was spilled instead of blood.

VIII

Shortly afterwards, Alessandri returned to Chile. His arrival was an apotheosis. The mob poured forth to welcome its idol. Alessandri as usual had the ready word for those who thus rapturously welcomed him. He spoke moderately but with purpose. "The party that I govern with will be the party of the nation, the party of public good, the

---

[14] Cabero, p. 271; Edwards, Ch. XL. *Current History*, XXI (March 1925), pp. 933, 934.

[15] Cabero, pp. 272, 273.

party of those who love Chile. I will not accept dictatorship. I will seek the coöperation of all the social forces."[16] Noble words these, but the president, thus recalled, seemed soon to forget them. When he made a ministry it was composed of liberals, his personal friends. None of the representatives of the national union were included in it nor some of the more powerful groups of the liberal alliance. He did not welcome many offers of coöperation which looked toward a restoration of normal civil life. He proceeded to issue certain decrees augmenting the salaries of those employed in public instruction. More effective were his measures with respect to public finance. The second military *junta* had already invited Professor E. W. Kemmerer of Princeton University, with a commission of experts, to make a survey of the finances of the country, and the work was carried on after the return of Alessandri. In keeping with the recommendations of the commission, decrees were issued during August and September establishing the gold standard for the country at a valuation for the *peso* of six pence; providing for a Bank of Chile similar to the Federal Reserve Bank of the United States to control the currency, for a general banking law, and for a general budget law. These measures, the fruits of extensive and careful studies by financial experts, did not differ greatly from earlier local proposals, but they came now with the backing of highly paid outsiders.[17]

More significant than these were the measures taken by the restored president to reform the constitution.[18] At the time, this document boasted an age of ninety-two years, second only to that of the United States. Under it, early Chilean leaders had established peace and order, had brought about a financial stability that had persisted even during the ineffectual parliamentary régime. In the course of its existence the constitution had been modified, but no one had dared greatly to change it. Alessandri took up this task. Among the changes that he proposed were those to take away from the senate its political powers, to authorize the president to dissolve the chamber of deputies, to create the office of vice president, to decentralize administration, to separate church and state, to enact a progressive income tax, to suppress parliamentary incompatibility, and to separate members of the ministry from congressional posts. In order to accomplish these changes, the president summoned a consultative commission over which he presided. This was

---

[16] *Ibid,* p. 274.

[17] Kemmerer in *Current History,* XXII, pp. 115, 642, 980.

[18] Cabero, pp. 275-280; Edwards, pp. 263-267.

to represent the people of all parties and of all political tendencies. In this commission very little discussion occurred. The president, supported by efficient helpers, presented tentative constitutional articles, and these after formal consideration were adopted substantially in accordance with his views. He was thus able, with a minimum of friction, to incorporate in his proposed constitution what he regarded as the main features of "presidential government."

This commission was supposedly to pave the way for a general popular assembly which should discuss and adopt the constitution. As the months went on, however, and opposition had a chance to express itself, its sponsors feared that a formal convention would give rise to political disturbance. Therefore, the president determined to content himself with the action of the consultative commission and submit the document prepared by it to a general plebiscite. Of course such an election was little more than an endorsement of the finished product. It was virtually a choice between that and the old system, and with ballots definitely colored to guide the mass of voters the new constitution received a comfortable majority. Many of the older political parties refused to take part in the vote so that less than half those inscribed on the rolls participated in this plebiscite. At any rate the president secured the formal endorsement of the new pact, and that approval registered the passing of oligarchic rule for Chile.

CHAPTER THIRTY-TWO

DEPRESSION AND ECONOMIC RECOVERY, 1926-1931

I

THE first step to be taken under the new constitution was the election of a president.[1] Candidates for the office immediately appeared in Alessandri's cabinet. When he intimated that all such should resign, they complied with the exception of the minister of war, Carlos Ibáñez, now sporting the title of Colonel. When Alessandri invited him also to resign he refused. Thereupon President Alessandri presented his resignation October 1, and thus left office before the end of the period for which he was elected five years before. As a characteristic stroke he turned the government over to Luís Barros Borgoño, who had been his opponent in the contest of 1920. The supporters of Ibáñez began to waver, so that officer announced that he would also resign, if within a week the various political factions could agree upon a joint candidate. They accepted his challenge and named their candidate within two days. In view of pressing social and economic issues, their choice, Emiliano Figueroa Larrain, the "national" candidate, represented the class that had dominated the country before 1920. He had held the chief executive office *ad interim* in the trying days of 1910, but conditions had greatly changed during the intervening fifteen years and many doubted his ability, despite his intelligence, good will, and undoubted patriotism, to cope with contemporary problems. Nevertheless, a dubious civilian seemed preferable to an out and out militarist, so they acquiesced in Don Emiliano's candidacy, or as it proved, his personal sacrifice.

Thus confronted with a national choice, Ibáñez, after some hesitation, renounced his own candidacy—but not his ministerial office. His manifest unwillingness to withdraw, however, appeared in a manifesto to the army. In this he noted that certain political groups—evidently he had in mind the radicals and the more liberal elements—were not satisfied with Figueroa; hence the election should be postponed until

[1] Cabero, *Chile y los chilenos,* pp. 280-287 and A. Edwards, *Fronda,* Ch. XLI, give succinct accounts of these critical events. Cf. also *Current History,* XXIII (Nov. 1925), p. 263, (Dec. 1925), p. 417.

the party situation was cleared up. But the forceful colonel had not yet shown that he was indispensable, either to his fellow ministers or to prospective military and naval associates, so with obvious misgivings he and they accepted the general choice.

It soon appeared that acceptance was not universal. Dr. José Santos Salas, whose work as minister of hygiene had attracted attention, was put forward by some of the more radical labor elements, with perhaps some encouragement from the military. Despite their vigorous campaign, Figueroa received an overwhelming majority in the election on October 25. The defeated elements attempted to nullify the result by proclaiming a general strike in Santiago and by stimulating disorder elsewhere, but in vain. Borgoño kept the subversive elements in check, and on December 23 turned the government over to the legally elected president. Before he left office he added still more to the list of laws established by decree. This emergency legislation provided for numerous changes in administrative methods and substantial increases in all official salaries.

II

With renewed hope accompanying him, President Figueroa took over office. His administration, however, was destined to register failure. He was in many respects a "gentleman of the old school" and was well versed in the established political procedure. Wealthy, he did not need to encourage graft in public life. In fact, he preferred to remain on his farm rather than attempt to direct the political forces of the new régime. Supposedly, under the presidential system, he was to control his cabinet and for a time he presided over one of marked ability. But political parties were still in existence and still eager for the spoils of office. Nor could congress keep from tinkering with the intimate affairs of the executive. His ministers were responsible to him alone, but party leaders in discussions among themselves and in congress often tried to influence policy, and failing in that to force the resignation of the ministry. Hence the administrative situation was not greatly improved over the days of Alessandri.[2]

One of the purposes of that president had been to settle the outstanding questions with Peru. Early in 1925 President Coolidge had rendered his decision in favor of a plebiscite. The attempt to hold one

---

[2] The above paragraph is based on personal observations made in Santiago in 1926, supplemented by interviews and newspaper reports; cf. also *Current History,* XXX, *passim.*

failed, and by June 1926 the commission at Arica had broken up and the country was faced with a continuance of the long drawn out dispute. The administration naturally had to accept responsibility for this failure.[3] Many of the measures for regulating conditions of labor proved too costly to be put in force. The attempt to control prostitution and other social regulations stirred up contemptuous opposition. The railway situation, the care of public markets, the regulation of finance, unrest in educational circles—all induced groups in congress to oppose the new administraton. Strikes among the laborers were answered by strikes among the students. The social program as a whole failed to meet public expectation. Discontent continued unabated. The government could please neither of the extreme groups in congress, and the two together were able to hold up important measures of policy, including the budget. Only in the separation of church and state did the government seem to make progress, and that was due largely to the fact that subsidies were to continue for a five-year period. No serious attempt was made to present a workable municipal program, nor to reduce the number of unnecessary public employees, nor to find adequate revenues for the mounting government expenditures.

The administration, confronted by the growing difficulties, changed ministries. For a time this seemed to mend matters, but not for long. The strong man of the cabinet was Colonel Ibáñez, who had directed the second military *coup d' état,* and who had been forced to withdraw his candidacy for the presidency. He had served in the war office under Alessandri and Borgoño and continued under Figueroa. His post enabled him to guide the internal affairs of the administration and direct outside movements. The general change in the cabinet in November 1926 left him unmoved. Figueroa could not form a ministry without him. Finally the president gave in to his stubborn subordinate, and in February 1927 made him the head of a new cabinet without requiring him to surrender his control of the military. Ibáñez was now in the position of dictator, a position that he promised to utilize to the utmost in curbing radical manifestations.[4]

Then followed a period of subdued but effective terrorism. Political leaders from Alessandri to the most rabid communist were proscribed,

[3] H. C. Evans, *Chile and its Relations with the United States,* pp. 205-220.

[4] Cf. n. 2. From 1927 on the files of *Chile,* the organ of the Chile-American Association are available, as well as those of *Current History,* vols. XXV *passim* and H. T. Collings, "Chile's New Anti-Bolshevist Government," XXVI (April 1927), pp. 108, 109. The *New International Year Book,* 1927 (New York, 1928), Article "Chile" affords a convenient summary of events.

banished to the lonely islands of the Pacific, or forced into exile. Any opposition to the autocratic measures of Ibáñez led to immediate punishment. Among the exiles were conservatives, communists, radicals, liberals, and democrats. Some proscriptions took the form of special government missions, but their effect was none the less mournful. The new dictator made a thorough sweep among his opponents. When the president's brother, who was the presiding judge of the supreme court, attempted to curb the dictator's purpose to clean up the judiciary, he was ordered under arrest in his own home and later banished from the country.

III

Before his brother's exile occurred, President Figueroa, in April 1927, retired from office. He was no longer able to continue in a position so thoroughly intolerable to him and apparently so useless for the country at large. First withdrawing from the capital "on a vacation," he later presented his resignation.[5] Ibáñez, as head of the cabinet and vice president, now entered upon the full discharge of executive duties, more openly indeed but not less effectively than before. He found several extensive jobs of house-cleaning awaiting him. He opened up abuses in public expenditures and in public contracts and handled them without mercy, subjecting offenders to fines, imprisonment, or banishment. He introduced new methods of control. He made substantial reductions in the number of useless public employees. In the railway service, which he found honeycombed with corruption, he changed the directing personnel and discharged many of the subordinate employees. Local administration was thoroughly overhauled and regulations adapted to meet the demands for public betterment.[6] He sought in innumerable ways to carry out educational reforms without, however, making much progress. Apparently Chile had found the man who could meet the social and economic needs of the hour.

Ibáñez was no paladin of civic betterment. That rôle belonged rather to the twice-exiled Alessandri, whose fiery pleas for the laboring masses had borne fruit in legislation adopted in 1924 on the eve of his first withdrawal from the country. During the following year he and the military *juntas* added to and greatly improved this legislation, although

[5] *Chile,* April 1927, p. 115, and May 1927, p. 188. Cf. Harry T. Collings, "Chile's New Government," in *Current History,* XXVI (July 1927), p. 639.

[6] The files of *El Mercurio* (Santiago) furnish much of the information for this chapter. Cf. also N. A. N. Cleven, "Suppression of Opposition in Chile," in *Current History,* XXVII (February 1928), p. 732.

much of it turned out to be unworkable in practice. Financially, as well as politically, 1926 was a year of uncertainty. Employers who could barely keep their plants going were little inclined to add materially to their operating expenses in order to further utopian social legislation. Hence, neither Alessandri nor Figueroa, nor for that matter any of their successors, ever beheld this program fairly under way. For years to come it was to remain merely an ideal. Perhaps it were well to enact comprehensive laws in behalf of insurance, hours of labor, old age pensions, conditions surrounding employees, provisions for clerks and household servants, and the multitude of other matters affecting labor, as was done in the stirring months of 1924 and 1925; but if contemporary political reforms failed to work, in spite of comparatively long experience in that field, what could be expected from this mass of social legislation, foisted suddenly upon the country during these critical months? Chile needed social as well as financial and political reform, but not in such allopathic doses.[7]

A similar result obtained in the field of sanitation. The public was unprepared to accept so vigorous a regimentation of private conduct, as Doctor Long prescribed. In fiscal affairs, however, reforms made a better showing. The measures proposed by the Kemmerer Committee in 1925 gradually got under way. The Central Bank of Issue began operations early in January 1926, and at the new value of the *peso* (six pence), began to check undue speculation in foreign exchange, as well as to provide more stable issues of currency.[8] The government still had to resort to loans in order to meet deficits, to put its fiscal system into operation, and to assist the Mortgage Bank. Notwithstanding continued quiet in general business and a decided slump in the sale of nitrate—conditions which affected the early months of 1927—banking operations continued easy.[9] The foreign debt at the end of 1926, including short-time loans, stood at 1,230,811,481 *pesos* and entailed an interest charge of 148,276,179 *pesos*[10]—altogether too large a part of the nation's obligations. In the interval since 1913 the annual budget had more than doubled and gave promise of a deficit, by the end of 1926, approaching two hundred million *pesos*. The national railways alone showed an improved revenue since 1922, an improvement partly due to the decreased

---

[7] Jorge Gustavo Silva, *Nuestra evolución política-social,* pp. 44 *et seq.*

[8] *Current History,* XXIV (September 1926), p. 955.

[9] *Chile* for 1927 *passim.*

[10] *Ibid,* April 1927, p. 153.

valuation of the *peso*.[11] From the railway administration, too, Ibáñez was able to draw a new corps of administrators with which to improve the general public service.

IV

The touchstone of economic well-being was, as usual, the nitrate industry. The year marked a serious fall in production and exports. In 1913, which may be taken as a convenient norm, the shipment of nitrates reached 2,738,339 tons, the output of a hundred and twenty-seven plants. Thirteen years later, twenty-eight plants, all that were then in operation, produced a hundred million tons less—some sixty-two per cent of the earlier figure and approaching the low point reached in 1921 and 1922.[12] Obviously something had to be done for the country's chief industry and source of revenue.

The situation was well-nigh desperate. Chile's pet product faced world-wide competition from synthetic nitrate—a competition largely engendered by the World War, and rendered formidable when that conflict ceased. An association of nitrate producers, formed in 1919, had attempted to meet lessening sales by pro rata assignments among its members, but that meant skimpy returns for all, including the government. A reduction in the cost of manufacture, estimated as high as fifty per cent, promised to help somewhat, but this charge formed a relatively small part of the total expense incurred in carrying the product from the *caliche* beds to the consumer in the United States and Europe. Joint propaganda in behalf of nitrates, paid for in small part by the treasury and the rest by the producers, had aided more; still more helpful was the payment advanced by the state to each producer who kept his plant working—a system first introduced during the war and continued thereafter—and by a pool or association of buyers, which at one time kept back from the market a million tons of nitrate. Through an agreement with the government these immense stocks were disposed of at a reduced price, so that production might be put on a normal basis. This policy caused a further unfavorable reaction in 1925 and 1926. In September of that year less than forty plants were in operation.

The general attitude of the government toward the industry had been that of the contented consumer toward the cow. Concern for the operatives began to reveal itself during the war and perforce continued after the conflict, as the number of operating plants steadily dwindled

[11] *Ibid*, May 1927, p. 176.

[12] *Ibid*, p. 175.

and the fiscal returns grew less. The producers bestirred themselves to agitate for a lowering of the export tax, hoping thereby to recover their vanishing markets; but few treasury officials could see their way clear to renounce what still seemed too easy a source of revenue. Yet they all professed a readiness "to do something" for the nitrate industry and its dependents.

In the midst of this uncertainty there sounded a hopeful note. After years of experimentation, the Guggenheim Brothers, Yankee capitalists long associated with copper, announced a new and cheaper process for producing nitrate. They stood ready to invest untold millions in the industry and, in addition, to take over all nitrate deposits and lend money to firms who would introduce the new process into their plants and enter a working agreement with the Guggenheims on a preferred stock basis. The North American promoters were simply to hold the common (and controlling) stock.[13] Although the proposal took on some of the aspects of a Trojan horse, neither the perturbed government nor the bankrupt producers were in a position to reject it. The government, at least, professed itself ready to make any sacrifice in order to regain the nitrate market for Chile.

V

It was under such conditions that President Figueroa yielded office to General Ibáñez—promotion had been prompt for him!—and retired to his beloved estate. For some weeks his successor continued to exercise power as vice president, and then on May 22, 1927, through an election virtually unopposed, became the regular president for a six-year term.[14] His task did not, however, change in character. He must continue the policy of cleaning up affairs which he had inaugurated, and in addition bring about a permanent betterment in national finance and in the general means of livelihood. His rule, though strict, seemed for a time to promise results. He had started out to settle the problem of radicalism and he initiated his program in no uncertain terms. Anarchism and communism could no longer exist in Chile. Workers who were quiet and law-abiding might have confidence in the government, but mere agitators engaged in scattering Bolshevistic and unpatriotic doctrines were to be suppressed "without regard for the exaggerated value attributed to freedom of thought." The people must yield him

[13] This and the two preceding paragraphs are based on statements in *Chile,* April 1927, pp. 133, 136, 142, 151; and *Ibid,* May 1927, p. 175.

[14] *Chile,* May 1927, p. 188.

their faith and confidence. Assured of that he promised to purify the public service, to introduce economy, and to form a new corps of officials from tried servants. He proposed to strengthen the defenses of the country, to increase its production, to reconstruct its finances under the Kemmerer Plan, and to balance the budget. The process, he assured his fellow citizens, would be painful but necessary, but he did not point out the greatest sufferers, the masses of the people.

The new president needed voters but not political parties. Hence he made voting compulsory—a good majority was flattering even to a single candidate—but declared party organizations useless. For years they had been losing their hold on the people and had only been kept up by tradition and the exertions of their chieftains. In this statement he was not far wrong. All recent tendencies—he evidently had Spain and Italy in mind—had been toward consolidation. Political liberalism was dead. There might be more coherence in conservatism because of the religious element therein, but with the separation of church and state, upon which he was firmly resolved, even conservatism as a political factor would disappear. The wage-earning classes should not commit the mistake of tying up to any of the old parties nor yield to the solicitations of mere agitators.[15]

VI

Thus announcing his policy of consolidation, with himself as the key man of the state, the American Mussolini in July 1927, began his regular administration. With an excellent set of cabinet officers, he continued the reforms already under way. He reorganized the naval service, hitherto a less dependable arm of the consolidated state, and thus got rid of worn out chiefs and removed the distinction between the line and engineer officers. He united the local police and the *carabineros* in a single force under his immediate command—a useful instrument for quick action or future unrest—and increased its size beyond that of the army itself. He promised not to interfere with the judiciary in its regular functions, but expressed his intention to punish ruthlessely all offenders against public order, whether they succeeded in carrying their intentions into effect or not.

Ibáñez was devoting himself to a practical program, whose moving principle was force. With a few words of meaningless commendation, therefore, he dismissed the elaborate sanitary code devised by Dr. Long, and confined his program of social betterment to dwellings for laborers

[15] Message of Ibáñez in *Ibid,* June 1927, pp. 213, 223, 224.

and better food for the public in general. Some months after the new administration was inaugurated, Professor Kemmerer visited Chile and gave his approval to fiscal conditions in general. A review of the industry of the country since 1870 revealed a gratifying growth in the number of manufacturing establishments which had nearly doubled within the last twenty years.[16] A disqueting footnote to this progress was afforded by a memorial from groups of workmen complaining that the policy of protection had been frequently adopted to benefit a few producers at the expense of the many consumers. The petition particularly stressed the advantages of a "free cordillera," [17] that is, free trade with Argentina.

The new president carried through a plan for territorial reorganization that consolidated a number of the provinces and shifted the departments to the manifest advantage of public service. In the congressional election of 1929 he distributed the congressional representation from these subdivisions so as to favor the major party in each and avoid a real contest. Such procedure had advantages for a dictator, nor was it unacceptable to the old-line leaders, who were content to have the more radical elements kept from voting. The new territorial subdivisions would further a "clean up" campaign, simplify a program of public works, and enable the central government to distribute funds and check upon them more readily.[18]

VII

For years the general unrest of the country had reflected itself in the educational system.[19] The good work of the late nineteenth century, reinforced by legislation in 1907 and in 1917, was shown in the primary schools which in 1920 reached the number of thirty-five hundred and accommodated some three hundred thousand pupils. During the decade, attendance rose more than fifty per cent, due in some measure to a law of compulsory education adopted in 1920. This again represented an ideal rather than an attainment. In equipment, administration, teaching personnel, and general spirit the decade witnessed other substantial advances in secondary, normal, and higher instruction, both as regards the teaching staff and the student body. These institutions continued

---

[16] *Ibid,* October 1927, p. 187; Nov. 1927, p. 221.

[17] *Ibid,* p. 227.

[18] *Chile,* May 1929, p. 202; *Current History,* July 1929, p. 695.

[19] This section is based on personal observations and interviews in 1922 and 1926 and on articles appearing in *Chile,* November 1927, p. 213; March 1928, p. 103.

to supply instructors for the country at large and to train men (and an increasing number of women) for public service. All phases of the work had been stimulated by educational assemblages held in Santiago in 1902 and 1912; hence the proposal of another educational congress in 1927 awakened universal interest.

Despite improvements, a general desire for better and more practical instruction prevailed in the country. To meet this, Enrique Molina, after careful study in Chile and abroad, had in 1917 opened the University of Concepción, a "free" establishment in the sense that it is under no state or ecclesiastical control. Like some of the earlier revolutionary movements emanating from the southern city, it had vitally affected pedagogic conditions to the northward, and made its director an outstanding educational leader of the country. In 1922 and again in 1926 the routine of university life at the capital was greatly disturbed by strikes on the part of students, many of whom saw hope in the southern experiment. General dissatisfaction with existing conditions accounted in some measure for these manifestations which originated in friction with the university administration; but in each case the students affiliated with labor organizatons or espoused some contemporary social problem. In 1926 their contentions centered largely around reforms in education. Teachers interested in regular and more ample compensation took up the cry for reform. The result was an important educational gathering in Santiago in the following year, from which its sponsors anticipated much improvement. Congress, which had likewise been led to discuss the absorbing topic, passed a law reorganizing the entire educational system. Under it, technical public instruction was to be directed by a general superintendent, with councils of education for the major divisions of the field, each under its special director. University and secondary instruction was to be separated and primary education decentralized. Briefly, public teaching was to be professionalized.

Doctor Molina was summoned from Concepción to put the new scheme in force, but in the course of a few months friction developed between him and the minister of education; the former withdrew from his interrupted task and many features of the new plan were forthwith discarded. During the next two years, however, the ministry began a frontal attack upon illiteracy by starting the construction of six hundred primary schools—an attack all too soon frustrated by the overshadowing economic crisis. The partially completed structures remain, however, as monuments to the universal desire to lessen the numbers of the unlettered. Adult instruction contributed to the same end. The compulsory law governing primary instruction, pased in 1920, was finally to be put in force in December 1930. In 1931 the country, despite economic and political handicaps, could point to a provision for six hundred thousand pupils and claim an average literacy of fifty-six per cent[20]—a creditable showing when one considers the handicaps, political, social, and economic, under which the country has labored during the preceding century. Further cause for hope was presented in the Santa María Endowment, a large fund left by a Chilean philanthropist living in Paris, for the establishment at Valparaiso of a high-class technical school. This institution, which opened its doors on December 20, 1931, closely follows German methods and bids fair to supply what was a serious lack in the country's educational opportunities.[21]

VIII

The church in Chile during the past half century has responded to contemporary influences. The development of the Catholic University is a case in point. The literary reputation of its outstanding prelates, particularly the present archbishop of Santiago, is another. The church has profited from the increase in wealth, both in its material equipment and in the extension of its work. The separation of church and state under the Constitution of 1925 is a reality that betokens better conditions for both. Thanks to a more charitable attitude on the part of both, the final step was taken without arousing the bitter controversies of fifty years before. While one may detect a growing laxity in respect to church practices, especially among the men, the vast majority of the people are fundamentally religious and professedly Catholic. The work of the church must now be carried on by voluntary contributions, and this in many cases includes personal service, particularly in respect to charitable work, on the part of numerous laical organizations for young people and adults. The number of Protestants increases slowly, nearly all communicants of this faith being found among foreign residents or in organizations more or less following foreign models. Nevertheless Protestantism has exerted no inconsiderable influence in the field of education and of private charity.

In respect to landowning, Chile is far from making substantial progress. In 1928 some five hundred and thirteen persons, less than one-half of one per cent of all the landowners, were reported to own sixty

---

[20] *Sinopsis geográfico-estadística de la república de Chile* (Santiago, 1933), p. 87; *Current History*, XXXI (March 1930), p. 1206.

[21] *Chile*, July 1928, p. 251.

per cent of the land in private hands; two and a half per cent of all landed proprietors possessed seventy-eight per cent of the arable land. Some 63,483 small farmers held two and a half per cent only of such land, and they made up some sixty-six per cent of the reputed owners. With such persistent inequality in a fundamental occupation, Chile must wait long for an adequate development of its rural life. The extension, by Ibáñez, of credits to general agriculture showed itself in the increased production of grain and other crops in 1928.[22]

In other respects, too, this year showed material prosperity. Gains were reported in mining operations and in bank reserves. Shipments of nitrate surpassed the banner year 1917. Chile reached eighth place among the coal producing nations of the globe. The country was able to borrow money abroad for road-building and other public works at a lowered rate of interest. Investments of capital from the United States showed a jump in twenty years from twenty-five million dollars to more than five hundred millions, although Great Britain was still ahead in the total amount invested and was gaining in respect to annual trade.[23]

IX

The general improvement was reflected in a new issue of gold bonds, in January 1928, to be devoted in part to railway construction, particularly to the electrification of the lines between Valparaiso and the capital. Extensive improvements were begun in the various ports of the country. By October the government could report a prospective surplus of twenty millions in a budget of more than nine hundred and forty millions. The revenues from internal taxes and from the railways were higher. Estimates for 1929 indicated that both income and expenditures would exceed a billion *pesos,* with the customs duties furnishing more than half of the income. A revised income tax promised to relieve the nitrate industry of its disproportionate part of this burden.

This industry still presented the weakest point in Chilean finance. Despite sales associations and measures to popularize the natural product, artificial nitrates continued to gain in the general market. The critical situation of the industry in 1926 had led to the creation in 1927 of a general superintendency of nitrates and mines that should direct and develop measures in its behalf. For the next three years, however,

---

[22] *Chile,* October 1928, p. 352; December 1928, p. 492.

[23] Summary of report of Carl Ackerman, Commercial Attaché of the United States, in *Chile,* March 1929, p. 119; April 1929, p. 146.

little general improvement occurred. There was some increase in local production and in the amount exported, but this gain fell far behind that of the world at large. The Guggenheim interests absorbed the major number of local plants and finally united with itself the Lautaro interests, the leading British combination. The combined producers were inclined to hold the government measurably responsible, through its export tax, for the plight of the industry. The government, in turn, held wasteful methods in production and selling as equally responsible for the poor showing of recent years. Coöperation, however, promised better results than mutual recrimination, and this spirit led in July 1930, to the organization of "Cosach" *(Compañía de Salitre de Chile)* which gave even more substantial promise of betterment. This company was designed to establish a national monopoly that should include all local producers and at the same time regulate the company's relations with the treasury. The government, in fact, became an equal partner in the country's chief industry, as owner of half of the capital stock and the sharer in its prospective profits. After four years, during which a certain income was guaranteed to the government, it was to receive merely a return on its stock not to exceed six per cent. Thus national income was to rise or fall with the fortunes of this monster corporation.[24]

The success of this experiment in corporate finance rested on international factors beyond Chilean control. If Cosach could form with the producers of synthetic nitrates a world-wide cartel, capable of controlling general prices, all would be well. A general loan contracted in New York was to finance the enterprise. This effort to prop up the nation's chief resource proved abortive. By July 1931 all attempts to bring about world agreement in prices failed, and this failure proved the last blow to the declining power of Ibáñez.

---

[24] *Chile,* February 1929, p. 87; *New International Year Book,* 1931, (New York, 1932), article "Chile."

CHAPTER THIRTY-THREE

REVOLUTION AND REVERSION, 1930-1934

I

THE administration of General Ibáñez rested upon a combination of military force and public largess. The latter depended upon mounting revenues and ability to borrow abroad, and expressed itself in public works, including roads, port works, the electrification of railways, sewage and water systems, and new school buildings. In 1928 the government had started a program of this sort that contemplated an expenditure of two hundred million *pesos* a year for the next six years. It expected to raise this extraordinary budget through long-time foreign loans. Judging from recent experiences such a plan seemed easy, but the authorities soon found themselves facing requests for similar largesses in behalf of the army and navy. Yielding to these, the extraordinary budget increased threefold and threatened to become a burden that the country could not meet even in good times.[1]

But times after 1929 were not good, even in Chile. The president and his cabinet, however, seemed unmindful of the universal financial peril. Not until May 1930 was a proposal made to reduce the budget by some forty million *pesos*—a reduction that was to be doubled the next year; but this suggestion was not acted upon. Another minister of finance, Julio Philippi, later in 1930 predicted the inevitable crash, but only courted his own dismissal. Three ministries in close succession tried to straighten out the intricate tangle, but in vain. The failure was due as much to the unwillingness of the president to permit a curtailment in expenditures as to the lack of coöperation elsewhere. The executive seemed unable to consider retrenchment when confronted by clamorous beneficiaries.

With public largesses dwindling and disappearing, he must perforce make greater use of his military power. In the earlier stages of his

---

[1] C. H. Haring, "The Chilean Revolution of 1931," in *Hispanic American Historical Review*, XIII, pp. 197-203, gives details of the overthrow of Ibáñez, based on personal observation. Cf. also *Current History*, XXXIII and XXXIV, *passim*, and especially Henry Grattan Doyle, "Chilean Dictatorship Overthrown," *Ibid*, XXXIV, (Sept. 1931), pp. 918-922.

rule, General Ibáñez, though ruthless in suppressing opposition, had generally observed constitutional requirements. Later he resorted more freely and frequently to the army and police force, and to banishment. His autocratic course, coupled with growing financial difficulties, aroused wide discontent. In February 1930 he assumed extraordinary power for a period of six months. In September occurred an attempted revolt in Concepción which was quickly suppressed. The trial of one of the civilians concerned in this outbreak caused demonstrations by the students, already incensed at the suppression of their council. The president responded by closing the university and arresting numerous other civilians. The fall of fellow despots in Peru and Argentina gave impetus to these demonstrations against Ibáñez, but the Chilean executive continued to ride the gathering storm. With the new year congress and the president attempted to meet difficulties by deportations, rigid censorship, and extraordinary military expenditures, coupled with some reductions in public salaries.

Even now the president failed to measure the full strength of the opposition. In July 1931, he appointed a new cabinet under Pedro Blanquier and definitely promised to support its recommendations as to economy and the restoration of civil rights. This "people's cabinet" resigned within a week, charging the president with failure to keep faith. Obviously he could no longer depend on popular support.

II

The month of July brought serious financial blows upon the harassed dictator. From New York on July 12 came news that Chilean nitrate had fallen in price four and a half dollars a ton, because Cosach had failed to come to terms with the producers of the synthetic nitrates. The government at once announced the suspension of service on the foreign debt,[2] Blanquier, as noted above, resigned at the end of the week, and Francisco Garcés Gana essayed for a second time the thankless task of attempting to bolster up falling finances and a tottering dictatorship. Minor clashes were occurring on the streets. The students began their customarily active—some would say over-active—part in public disturbances. On July 23, when the cabinet of Garcés Gana retired, they barricaded themselves in the National University, hung out a banner with the word *Libertad* inscribed upon it, and from

[2] *New International Year Book,* 1931, p. 192.

the windows appealed to the people to help end the despotic rule.[3] Thus incited, the passersby began to wreck streetcars, twist off lamp posts, smash windows, and commit other acts of violence. The disorder in the capital was copied elsewhere. In Concepción a public mass meeting demanded the resignation of the president. In a final effort he summoned a new cabinet, frankly military in complexion, which expelled the riotous students from the barricaded university, and killed two of them in the process. Some twenty deaths occurred during three days of rioting, while the number of wounded exceeded two hundred.

Obviously civil war or abdication was the only outcome. The death of a prominent young physician decided the issue. The medical association of the city declared and enforced a general strike. The lawyers and the engineers followed suit. Then the teachers, including members of the university faculties, took similar action, moved thereto by the killing of a professor. Finally the labor organizations, despite their indebtedness to Ibáñez for favorable social legislation, joined the professional classes in demanding his resignation. Urban life approached a standstill.[4]

On Sunday morning, July 26, the dictator-president gave up the office and later fled across the Andes—the first of Chile's executives to leave his post without formal permission. A universal but orderly demonstration of joy followed his departure—a demonstration that culminated in an enormous outpouring at the funeral of two late victims of the disorder. The hated police withdrew for some days to their barracks, while the mercurial students, male and female, assumed the task of directing traffic and preserving some semblance of order. In general the whole train of incidents showed essential solidarity in public sentiment. The Chilean people would suffer much to preserve the status quo; they would resort to violence only when conditions became intolerable; they would return to orderly living at the first opportunity.

Next in legal succession to Ibáñez stood his brother-in-law, the president of the senate, but he was forced by public opinion to resign at once in favor of Juan Esteban Montero, whom he had made minister of the interior. Montero, a noted law professor and a member of the earlier Blanquier cabinet, had made a favorable impression on the country by insisting on freedom of speech. He now accepted the provisional

---

[3] H. Ochoa Mena, *La revolución de julio* (Santiago, 1931), pp. 103-114. Diego Múñoz in his novel *La avalancha* (Santiago, n. d.) describes the events of this uprising in graphic form.

[4] Ochoa Mena, pp. 135-179; Haring, *op. cit.*, pp. 201-203.

presidency, but announced that he would not be a candidate in the election of October 4. Despite his prompt disclaimer he was elected president on that date by a large majority over his nearest competitor, Arturo Alessandri. His support came largely from the Civic Party, a new organization in which the students were prominent. This group refused to follow Alessandri, whom the more radical elements supported, or Ladislao Errázuriz, a leading conservative.[5]

III

The new president took office on December 4 under auspices that were far from hopeful. A professional man and not a politician, and no self-seeker, he presented a marked contrast to his predecessor. But the difficulties confronting him seemed almost insurmountable. He had promised to give especial attention to the unemployed, who now were estimated to number from eighty to a hundred and twenty-five thousand. His program included resumption of payments on the foreign debt as soon as possible, a continuation of strict economy in expenditures, and a careful study of the nitrate industry upon which national prosperity so largely depended. Public opinion was especially aroused against Cosach because of the expense involved in its management and because it was so definitely directed by foreign interests. Ibáñez, it was claimed, had betrayed the country's birthright: the creation of Cosach was the leading crime of his dictatorship. Public opinion also demanded the punishment of those who were guilty of extreme cruelty in attempting to put down the recent revolution.

Montero's course, from the outset, was beset with difficulties. His attempt to reduce expenses, which he shared himself to the extent of fifty per cent of his salary, was not popular. A discussion in congress of the gold standard started a great rise in prices and a run on the Central Bank of Chile. In order to keep down foreign exchange, by reducing importations, the government attempted in March to ration the supply of gasoline. This brought on a strike among the taxi drivers of Santiago and led to a fall of the cabinet and the proclamation, April 6, 1932, of martial law. In the midst of prevailing dissatisfaction, Alessandri brought together a group of the more radical parties to demand the dissolution of Cosach. The formation of this group was followed by the election of Alessandri, on April 10, as senator from

[5] *New International Year Book,* 1931 and 1932, Article "Chile," and *Current History* for the above years give the main facts of Montero's brief administration. Cf. *Ibid,* XXXVI, (July 1932), pp. 477-480.

Tarapacá. To many this event suggested a repetition of the political career that had begun in that province seventeen years before. In this same April, Carlos Dávila, former ambassador of Chile to the United States, issued a manifesto in which he advocated a form of state socialism, and claimed that the government could take over and operate the means of production and distribution under the present constitution. On the nineteenth of the same month congress passed an act temporarily suspending the gold standard.

Workmen were being discharged until the number out of work reached a hundred and twenty-five thousand—twelve times the usual number of unemployed. Another nitrate conference at Lucerne, Switzerland, failed to come to an agreement. Cattle shipments from Argentina ceased, and the shortage of freight caused the closing of the Transandine Railway. The gathering forces of unrest proved too much for Montero. His administration was overthrown in a nearly bloodless revolution, June 4, 1932, and Carlos Dávila essayed the perilous task of directing the government. Dávila had returned to Chile in the preceding July. In March he had been arrested on a charge of conspiring against the government, but was released. A second arrest was ordered in April, but he kept in hiding and from his place of concealment issued the proclamation mentioned above. Montero had striven valiantly to preserve law and order and maintain the financial integrity of the country. All acknowledged his sincerity, courage, and honesty. In a last effort to prevent another revolution, he had even offered to make Alessandri his premier; but this concession proved unavailing.

The revolution engineered by Dávila broke out in the aviation school from which the insurgents entered Santiago in trucks escorted by airplanes.[6] The military and police generally remained neutral. The air corps, which had assisted Montero to put down a revolt of the Chilean navy in September 1931, now turned against him. The president had sent his personal representative to take charge of its barracks but without success. Nothing but his complete elimination would satisfy the revolting masses. When thus threatened with force and denied military support, Montero refused to resist, but also declined to resign. His opponents had come "to take command of the country" and they must assume full responsibility for their violent action.[7]

---

[6] See accounts cited in the above note; cf. also Manuel Aranguiz Latorre, *El 4 de junio* (Santiago, 1933) and Alfredo Guillermo Bravo, *El 4 de junio; el festín de los audaces* (Santiago, 1933). The former was Montero's secretary.

[7] Cf. Bravo, pp. 42-57 for a restrained and sympathetic discussion of Montero's course, and his action in this crisis.

IV

Dávila immediately took charge, and on June 6 issued a statement in which he said that his new government did not contemplate drastic measures and would make no changes of importance except to establish better international relations, particularly by recognizing Soviet Russia. Declaring his belief that Chile could not come out of the present depression under a capitalistic system, he proposed to introduce progressive state socialism, but without molesting private property. Despite this declaration, on June 9 he expropriated all credits and deposits of foreign currency in Chilean banks, replacing them by *pesos* at the rate of sixteen and one-half to the dollar. This announcement led to protests from the American and British representatives. The course pursued by Dávila was surprising because, while representing the Ibáñez government in Washington, he had, as late as July 1930, advocated encouragement to foreign capital. Another surprising aspect of the situation was Dávila's alliance with Colonel Marmaduke Grove, a pronounced radical and bitter enemy of the Ibáñez régime. This alliance at least seemed to assure the country that the former dictator would not be restored. The students and working classes generally supported the new government. On June 8, however, a mass meeting of the unemployed demanded that the exclusive Club of the Union should be turned over to them as a place for social gathering. At the same time it was reported that worker's councils were taking over the Chilean savings banks and that nuns were being expelled from their convents.[8]

Then followed a series of kaleidoscopic changes that, for the time, put Chile in the same class with its most unstable neighbors. On June 12, Dávila was driven from power and restored five days later. The interlude, for which Colonel Grove was chiefly responsible, represented a demand for more extreme socialistic measures; the prompt restoration to office bespoke an alliance of Dávila with more conservative groups. It was difficult to maintain one's balance in the midst of this political seesaw, but for three stormy months Dávila attempted it. The ups and downs of the period recall the troubled era of the century before, with modern means of transport to speed up political change.

---

[8] *New International Year Book,* 1932, article "Chile." Cf. Henry Grattan Doyle, "The Chilean Scramble For Power," in *Current History,* XXXVI (Aug. 1932), pp. 591-595. For a critical discussion of the plans of Dávila, Grove, and their associates cf. Bravo, pp. 91-113. Another view, especially favorable to Grove is presented by the latter's brother Jorge in *Descorriendo el velo* (Valparaiso, 1933).

Banishment was, of course, the alternative to precarious rule. Grove was sent to Juan Fernández, while his supporters protested in sympathetic strikes and irregular disorders. The government ran trains with the military and resorted to a temporary curfew in order to suppress street rioting. Fiscal regulations threatened disruptions within the cabinet which favored more constitutional measures. Dávila announced a convention, to meet in September, for revising the constitution on socialistic lines. He sought to cut expenses in the army and navy, a proposal which aroused the officers of both services. His obvious purpose was to pursue a middle course between the extreme left and the right, now much less extreme than formerly.

An unexpected visit from General Ibáñez did not tend to settle affairs. Arriving in Santiago July 6 by airplane, he conversed with Dávila on the seventh and publicly announced that his visit had no political significance. Two days later he attempted to head a revolt, failed, and forthwith returned to Argentina. Two months later Dávila appointed him as ambassador to that country. The appointment might serve as a gilded exile for the unquiet general, and leave the distraught Dávila free to subsidize industry through new issues of paper money, and to regulate exports through a Foreign Commerce Institute. A National Socialist Legion ("the White Shirts") was organized to protect the Dávila régime from communistic or conservative threat, from student uprising or labor strike.

Proposal and precaution were alike futile. On September 13 Dávila's "hundred days" came to an end when the head of the air force overthrew him and then proceeded to quarrel with the commander-in-chief of the army over the provisional presidency. Both men were eliminated by the end of the month, when the president of the supreme court took charge. The country had no desire for military rule, even for a limited time. A provisional civilian government assumed the direction of the ensuing presidential campaign. In the formal election, held on October 30, the country turned once more to its former idol, Arturo Alessandri, who was elected over three opposing candidates by a substantial majority and who far outdistanced his nearest competitor, Colonel Marmaduke Grove. The country, after fifteen months of turmoil, was in a conservative mood and its chosen chief was the erstwhile radical of the early twenties; but conservatism, aside from the die-hard element, had drifted to the banner of the moderate socialists. Alessandri's "practical" socialism seemed more acceptable than the extreme views of Colonel Grove.[9]

V

Calling on his fellow citizens to coöperate in a truly national administration, Alessandri, in his inaugural address of December 24, 1932, expressed his faith in civilian rule under the Constitution of 1925. His program also favored decentralization in government. This political plank, reminiscent of earlier party struggles, was matched by promises to deal with more pressing problems: to lessen unemployment; to aid agriculture, industry, mining, and commerce; to readjust the *peso;* and to solve the problems connected with nitrate and copper. In reply to this extensive program, his leading opponent, Colonel Grove, declared in a manifesto his intention to continue fighting for the socialistic ideal. To him the election of Alessandri merely indicated that the traditional parties, under a different banner, had recaptured their former position in the state.

Grove's manifesto was an earnest declaration of his intention. In August 1933, he was arrested for his subversive activities and banished to a southern province, but he still constituted a center of danger to the new administration. Communistic activities, late in February, had caused the arrest of some labor leaders. These threats led to the organization of the *milicia republicana,* which repudiates fascism, but pledges support to constitutional government. Its counterpart is found in the National Socialist Party, a movement more frankly Nazi in aim. The former organization claims to be well armed, but despite its promise of protection, the president felt impelled, December 13, 1933, to ask for a grant of extraordinary powers to suppress possible outbreaks.

General conditions to some extent favored Alessandri's economic policy. The year 1932 had shown a decrease in imports and exports to about a fourth of the figures for the preceding year. Exports picked up slightly in 1933 (from 350.3 million *pesos* to 368.1 millions), while imports fell off still more (213.8 million *pesos* to 181.6 millions). This decrease may be explained in part by the need to check imports, since with the fall in value of the *peso,* foreign exchange had largely ceased. The restriction in turn encouraged domestic manufacturing, and this local growth, plus governmental effort to employ men in mining and

---

[9] *New International Year Book,* 1932 and 1933; *Current History* and *El Mercurio* (Santiago) for the same years. The same references apply to the following section.

in agriculture, brought better times to the laboring classes. The fall of the *peso,* however, had added materially to the cost of living. Some slight improvement in the export of nitrate and copper had not materially helped these industries. Only thirteen per cent as many men were engaged in the production of nitrate in 1933 as in 1929. During the year, measures were taken to liquidate Cosach and replace it by a new selling corporation. A new blast furnace, opened at Corral in September 1933, gave Chile a unique position among South American republics in the production of iron and steel for domestic use.

The budget, although expressed in depreciated coin, showed marked improvement. The year 1932 had closed with a deficit of about three hundred and four million *pesos,* due in large measure to expenses carried over from 1931 and to the upheavals of the next year. The estimates for 1933 called for a budget of over nine hundred and forty-five millions that was virtually balanced at the end of the year. This included more than two hundred millions for public works and public relief. The 1934 budget was authorized at a little under 830.5 million *pesos.* In view of the fall in the value of the *peso,* this decrease over previous budgets is the more remarkable. The total public debt, internal and external, at the end of 1932, was 3,850.7 million *pesos,* of which more than 2,800 millions was due abroad. Service upon the latter ceased during the year, but was continued, although with some delay, on the internal debt.[10]

VI

Fate has been kind to Alessandri. His return to the presidency may signify—without venturing into prophecy—that his fellow countrymen recognize him as a determining figure in their history, one that is worthy to stand beside Portales, Manuel Montt, and Balmaceda as an exponent of his time and as director of his country's immediate destiny.

Whoever hopes to meet the demands of the hour must show characteristics that distinguished all three of these illustrious leaders. Gifted with eloquence equal to that of Balmaceda and endowed with far wider sympathies, Alessandri still shows marvelous power to sway the multitudes, and more to the point, to secure response from liberal minded conservatives. He apparently knows better than any other contemporary how to interpret the general demand for social betterment and how to use it to his political advantage. But mere response to popular

[10] See *Current History,* XXXVII (Dec. 1932), p. 344, and XL (Aug. 1934), pp. 597-599.

urge is not enough. On occasion, too, he must suppress violence with the ruthless energy of Portales; at all times he must display the firm attachment to law and order that distinguished Manuel Montt. Yet withal, he must recognize that not every expression of discontent breeds treason, nor does legal precept or constitutional amendment wholly meet the plea of social justice.

During the last two decades both president and people have learned much. National well-being, for instance, can no longer rest wholly on nitrate alone. Industry must become reasonably varied, stimulated thereto, if necessary, by moderate protective duties. But such protection must be devised so as to arouse a minimum of protest from foreign competitor or domestic consumer. Nor can the income from common industry be diverted so largely to the use of a chosen few, whom blood, or brains, or newly-acquired wealth have favored above their fellows. The day of the governing oligarchy is gone.

Nevertheless it was a day in which the Chilean may well take pride. It produced Diego Portales and Manuel Montt. They were men who interpreted the destiny of the country in terms of material growth, and achieved it. Order to them was heaven's first law and Chile's prime necessity; hence it was embodied in its constitution and enforced with all the power at their command. The answer was the age that they dominated—an age in which were applied or reëstablished those agencies of commerce, of industry, of culture, and of faith that were to preserve much of the country's colonial heritage and assure its future progress.

To their iron rule succeeded a freer régime. Individuals exercised less power. Parties replaced presidents in the direction of national policy. Responsibility became more diffused, custom less binding, wealth more enticing. Material expansion ruled the market place and the chancellery; "religious" questions prevailed in the forum and in the press. Old moralities disappeared, corruption permeated public life and vitiated business transactions. With a great price Chile obtained its barren liberalism, its pseudo-parliamentary system, its northern deserts with their distracting mineral deposits, its southern forests no longer the haunt of the doughty Araucanian. Balmaceda paid part of that price with his life; so did hosts of his fellow countrymen. There was less drama in their supreme sacrifice, more drudgery and toil in their fruitless daily round, more disillusion at the end of an era. With the turn of the century the oligarchy was still in the saddle, national resources were still being pilfered or subject to prodigal waste.

Under the surface, however, new social forces were being engendered. In part they were the by-product of the materialistic age, and in part the offspring of other forces, cultural and moral, that still persisted in the Chilean character and occasionally were given vent in school, in press, in public debate, and in more varied religious and social agencies. The masses were moving—blindly through bitter strikes, in a more orderly fashion through mutual aid, through self-training, through political organization, through public opinion at length aroused to the perils of selfish class interests. Hastened by the coming of the World War, these new social and political elements simply awaited their destined leader.

He offered himself, as we have seen, in the tumultuous days of the post-war period. He offered himself—but, it seemed, in vain. The country, it is true, now boasts of a new constitution, bolstered up by a mass of social legislation. But a people is ill-advised to trust its future wholly to legal enactment. A more democratic spirit must pervade both precept and practice—a spirit based on social justice and cultural advantages for all, with a more equable division of national wealth. It remains to be seen whether those who direct the country's immediate future are able to grasp this truth and apply it or whether its under-privileged class must be driven further afield in search of a more abundant life.

Alessandri alone cannot meet this problem, nor did Ibáñez solve it with his policy of repression, nor Figueroa with his trust in *laissez-faire*. Nor will any other relying wholly on personal prestige, class connections, military force, or material prosperity. The country cannot continue to live in the realm of restricted privilege and achieve its solution. Communistic theory promises still less as a social panacea. Only through coöperation—as inclusive as the country's limits and as widespread as its interest—can the people of Chile achieve a future worthy of their past, and fully measuring up to their opportunities.

V. APPENDICES

APPENDIX A

THE POSITION OF ROSAS IN ARGENTINE HISTORY

By Stetson Conn

I. The Background of the Power of Rosas

THE object of this brief sketch of Rosas is to give some incidents in the life of the great dictator and to show his position in Argentine history.

First, the background of Rosas' power must be taken into account. This rested on five factors: ancestry and extensive personal relationships, personal wealth, popularity among the masses, fame as a military leader, and reputation as a known conservative.

Juan Manuel José Domingo Ortiz de Rosas, to quote his full name, was born on March 30, 1793, in Buenos Aires at 94, Calle de Cuyo. He was the descendant of an aristocratic family of northern Spain. His great-grand uncle had been governor and captain-general of the Province of Buenos Aires in the first half of the eighteenth century, and his grandfather had emigrated to the Plata region to serve as an aid to this uncle. There Rosas' grandfather and father married into leading Spanish families; the father of Rosas was a captain in the royal forces and later caretaker of the royal property in the viceroyalty. Rosas himself married into a well-known family with many connections. He was the eldest of twenty children, ten of whom lived to maturity and who furnished Rosas with numerous other valuable connections. Thus he was related to, or a friend of, many of the most wealthy and influential families in the Province of Buenos Aires.[1]

The second factor to be considered is the personal wealth of Rosas. He showed great aptitude for business in his youth, being made sole manager of his parents' extensive holdings at the age of eighteen. He inherited nothing from his own parents, but received a considerable property from those of his wife. At the age of twenty, he set out to earn his own living, with marked success. About the same time, Rosas

[1] Adolfo Saldías, *Historia de la confederación argentina* (Buenos Aires, 1881-1887), Vol. I, pp. 11-17. A similar account is contained in Manuel Bilbao, *Historia de Rosas, 1810-1832* (Buenos Aires, 1868).

married Encarnación de Ezcurra y Arguivel, a woman of forceful and ambitious character. Rosas entered into a partnership with Juan N. Terrero and Luís Dorrego, forming the house of *Rosas, Terrero y Cía.*, which by 1817 had built up strong connections not only in Argentina but along the Atlantic coast, especially at Rio de Janeiro and at Havana, through its export business. In 1815 the partnership established one of the first *saladeros,* or meat-salting plants, and this led to the development of a lucrative export business in salted meats. In 1817 the government at Buenos Aires ordered the *saladeros* closed, and this led to the first conflict of Rosas with the central government. This *saladero* enterprise stopped, or at least restricted, Rosas and his associates turned to ranching and purchased large tracts along the River Salado, then the southern frontier of the province. Rosas renewed his partnership with Terrero in 1821, and this continued until 1838. At the time of his elevation to the governorship, Rosas was one of the richest men in the country, and his estate of Los Cerrillos, along the Salado, covered 470,000 acres or about 735 square miles.[2]

Rosas had established himself as a popular leader of the country districts before he accepted the governorship. He was the idol of the *gauchos,* and the self-professed protector of the lower classes, including the negroes. He himself had led the rude life of the *gaucho,* and learned all the feats of *gaucho* life. He was an expert horseman, and it is said that he never asked his men to do anything which he could not do himself. He had a widespread reputation for fair and honest dealing, although he was a strict disciplinarian. He was, moreover, a handsome man, of great physical strength, and a tremendous worker. He had further enhanced his popularity along the frontier by assuming the rôle of protector against the wild Indians, and he was much esteemed and respected by the friendly tribes.

Rosas had fought as a boy against the English in 1806 and 1807, but he took no further part in military life for the next decade. He then formed a company of militia to protect the frontier against the Indians, and on the eve of the troubles of 1820, he was a *commandante* in the militia, under General Rodríguez. During this year of anarchy, Rosas fought with Dorrego against López of Santa Fé, and afterwards with General Rodríguez at Buenos Aires; he took a leading part in the suppression of the revolt against Rodríguez which was initiated in the city in the first part of October, and he was the popular hero of the day. Through the succeeding decade, he took part in several expeditions

[2] Saldías, *op. cit.,* Vol. I, pp. 19-27.

against the Indians, and was a military idol of the masses and in command of the country militia in 1829, with the rank of colonel. It must be said, however, that Rosas was not a skillful military strategist, and against well-trained forces never showed himself to advantage.

Lastly, Rosas was a known conservative, and seemed to be an ideal tool for the conservative classes. He was a strong, though not fanatical, supporter of the church, and an exponent of federalism and of the rights of the country as opposed to the efforts of the city reformers. Apparently he was the man for the wealthy conservatives to support to end the anarchy which existed in 1829, and also to stop the reform efforts of the unitarians. After Rosas came to power, he became so powerful that he dominated the situation personally, but as late as 1832 he was considered merely the means by which the conservative classes maintained control.[3]

Thus, with this background as a personal leader and as a conservative, Rosas was supported financially as well as by other means in his campaign against Juan Lavalle, and with the bloodless triumph over the latter, through a truce in the summer of 1829, his elevation to the governorship was a foregone conclusion. He combined the strength of a *caudillo* with that of an aristocratic conservative, and this fact explains the almost unanimous support which he possessed in the first decade of his dominance.

II. Rosas in Power

To understand the political situation in 1829 it is necessary to review the conflict of the preceeding years between the so-called unitarian and federalist parties. The unitarian reform movement under Bernardino Rivadavia had had as its eventual objective the education of the country and the development thereof to a point where it could be truly democratic and self-governing; but in the interim, the direction of the nation was to be in the hands of the upper class only, and the unification of city and country under their control was necessary. Neither Rivadavia nor his followers were ever in true contact with the masses nor did they count on their adhesion for the success of their enterprise. Their plan was not only to set up a new democratic system, but to suppress the reactionary forces such as the local military leaders (the *caudillage*) and also the church. The opposition to the unitarians under Rivadavia was not from one class only (the *caudillos* and frontiersmen). It

[3] William R. Manning, *Diplomatic Correspondence of the United States: Inter-American Affairs, 1831-1860* (Washington, 1932), Vol. I, Doc. 70, pp. 132-133.

found expression in the movement of Dorrego, a man of high ideals, who sought to build up the Province of Buenos Aires first, in preference to the visionary national unification of all of the Plata region. To his support there came many of the leading men of the time, especially from the city. And to his own faction there gravitated two other factions—the *caudillos,* who were the popular idols of the masses and who could count on their support, and the reactionary conservatives of the higher classes, such as the Anchorenas, who resented the attacks on the church and the influx of revolutionary social ideas. Under this combined opposition, the unitarianism of Rivadavia must fall, for it did not have popular support. While the strength of the federalists was so powerful, the strength of Dorrego as the leader of his party was not, since he had to rely for support on the *caudillos* and conservatives, who had joined with him to further their own ends; without them he would have to fall, and he lacked the support of these classes which was later accorded to Rosas.

The end of the war with Brazil saw the return in 1828 to Buenos Aires of a victorious army of veteran soldiers, who had never been beaten in battle and many of whom had served in the Andean campaigns. They had no sympathy with the masses, or with their provincial spirit which had conquered unitarianism. They laughed at the provincial militia of the *caudillos.* They wanted honor and power, and were willing to follow a leader like Lavalle in opposition to the federalists. Lavalle had the backing of many unitarians besides the veteran troops, and his revolution of December 1828, was an easy military success; but it had no permanent base. It had neither popular support nor a permanent plan of action, and it in no wise crushed the popular movement that had overthrown Rivadavia. The revolution of Lavalle could no more stem the tide of provincial spirit and popular control through local leaders or overcome the prejudice of the reactionary groups of the upper strata than could the Directory in 1820 or the unitarians in 1827.[4]

Thus was the stage set for the advent of Rosas. He allied himself with Governor López of Santa Fé against Lavalle and marched on Buenos Aires. Lavalle, in the face of superior numbers and the hostility of the city at his back, was forced to withdraw. An interim government was assembled, and the provincial legislature which had been disbanded the preceding year was called together. This body chose

---

[4] G. F. Rodríguez, *Contribución histórica y documental* (Buenos Aires, 1921-1922), Vol. III, pp. 3-16.

Rosas as governor in December 1829, granting him extraordinary powers, and also voted him the rank of brigadier-general and the title of "Restorer of the Laws," meaning the laws of the confederation, as opposed to the unitary laws of Rivadavia and his followers.

Rosas drew his support, as heretofore explained, from two opposing groups, the aristocratic conservatives on the one hand, and the mass of the people on the other. The former group had no particular sympathy with the latter. The result was that Rosas' own political ideals, such as they were, must have been compromised, and it is difficult to determine what his true purposes were at the time of his election.

It does seem, however, fairly certain that Rosas from the beginning attempted and generally did govern in favor of the mass of the people, who heretofore had had no political rights or support from the ruling governments. He did this as a guardian, maintaining the attitude of a paternalistic autocrat, but he had their almost unanimous support and never resorted to measures that were oppressive to the lower classes. One of the most violent critics of Rosas has written: "It seems to me unquestionable that Rosas governed in favor of the uncultured and semibarbarous majority which peopled the country and which supported the *caudillos.*" [5]

During the first governorship, Rosas had two great problems to solve, first, that of extricating the government from the financial straights in which he found it, and second, that of suppressing the military revolts in the interior. He had two alternatives in solving the first difficulty: either to find new sources of revenue, or to curtail drastically governmental expenditures. He chose the latter course, with the result that many activities of the government were suspended, and governmental support for others, such as the University, was withdrawn.[6] The second problem was solved by personally leading an expedition in 1830 and 1831 which aided in quelling the interior revolts. These collapsed when General Paz, their leader, was captured by López of Santa Fé, the ally of Rosas, to whom he was turned over. Paz was kept prisoner by Rosas for seven years, and then released in 1838; he immediately began to fight Rosas again.[7]

---

[5] Ramón de Castro Estreves, *Rosas ante la historia* (Buenos Aires, 1931), p. 111.

[6] Ernesto Quesada, *La época de Rosas* (Buenos Aires, 1898), Chapter 7.

[7] F. A. Kirkpatrick, *A History of the Argentine Republic* (Cambridge, Eng., 1931), pp. 143-144.

III. The Mazorca

After completing his three year term in 1832, Rosas retired, and undertook a campaign against the southern Indians. In the three year interval before his choice as governor in 1835, the Federal Party remained in control, but soon split into factions. In the factional strife in the fall of 1833, Rosas' successor, Balcarce, was overthrown through a conspiracy hatched by the most partisan supporters of Rosas, backed by the reactionary conservatives; it is claimed that Rosas' wife was the leader of this almost bloodless revolt, and that she kept her husband in touch with events and acted as his agent during the period in which he was absent from the city. In this revolt, the partisans of Rosas started an organization which became known as *La Sociedad Popular Restauradora,* which initially was a political club formed to back Rosas' selection as governor with dictatorial powers.[8]

This organization in its later years became known, at least by the enemies of Rosas, as the *Mazorca,* and it has been bequeathed a most sinister reputation. This name is supposed to have originated in a poem by Rivera Indarte, written in 1835, which appeared under an illustration of an ear of corn, reading as follows:

> "This ear of corn which here you see
> In ruddy dress of greenish husk
> Has sunk into the depths of hell
> The Unitary faction.
> And thus you may with true devotion
> Thus murmur to your inner self
> Oh draw me from this great commotion
> Oh Sacred Federation. . . ."

The author of this fervent tribute subsequently became a bitter enemy of Rosas; it is said that the origin of his disaffection was a refusal by the *Sociedad Popular* to admit him to its membership.[9]

In 1835 the *Mazorca,* to use its more familiar name, took an active part in the ceremonies which accompanied Rosas' installation as governor "with the sum total of public power." [10] It was at this time a fanatical partisan organization, but with a membership which included many well-known and esteemed citizens of Buenos Aires. Indeed,

---

[8] Martín V. Lazcano, *Las sociedades secretas, políticas, y masónicas en Buenos Aires* (Buenos Aires, 1927), Vol. II, p. 218.

[9] Adolfo Saldías, *Buenos Aires en el centenario de la revolución de mayo* (La Plata, 1910), Vol. I, p. 257.

[10] See Antonio Zinny, *Historia de los gobernadores de las provincias argentinas* (Buenos Aires, 1880), Vol. II, p. 120.

membership was granted as a great honor. Rosas had no part in the organization of this society, but probably was in no way adverse to its activity.

The real notoriety of this organization originated in its activities in the years 1838-1842, the critical period in the rule of Rosas. To this society was assigned the work of "classification" of all of the opponents of the government. This system of listing the political records of dissenters did not necessarily mean persecution against them, if they took no further action in opposing the power of Rosas. But the mere preparation of such a list by a strong partisan organization, in a period of intense emotional feeling due to the attacks upon the country, led to violence against the suspects. Thus, beginning in 1838, acts of terrorism occurred sporadically, and in two brief periods, in October 1840 and April 1842, there was widespread and inexcusable violence. In each instance there is no evidence to show that Rosas instigated this terrorism, and it was suppressed at once when he issued edicts to that effect, but it seems likely that he did not desire to stifle this wave of barbarism entirely, and wished to grant it temporary leeway in these brief periods to serve as a vent for popular feeling.

Who were the perpetrators of these acts? The enemies of Rosas have indiscriminately laid them at the door of the *Mazorca,* picturing it as a mysterious, terrible, and brutal body. But the names of all of the members of the society through these years are known, and many, if not most, of these are of well-known and respected citizens of Buenos Aires, whom it seems impossible to picture as assassins and cutthroats. It seems far more likely that the classification of suspected opponents, mixed with the intense feeling among the illiterate mass of the people and the laxity among the police, resulted in undirected attacks by the lower classes, and murder and violence on a considerable scale. Perhaps some of these attacks were instigated by the *Mazorca* or some of its individual members. But unorganized terrorism often accompanies a tottering government, (as was that of Rosas in September 1840), and it is probable that the dictator and his friends permitted such terrorism, rather than instigated it.[11]

Whether the *Mazorca* was or was not responsible for the terrorism of 1840 and 1842, the stigma attached to its name by the writings of the unitarians of Montevideo resulted in its being discredited at home,

---

[11] For an anti-Rosas account of the work of the *Mazorca,* see Zinny, *op. cit.,* pp. 149 and 158. For a more favorable account, see Saldías, *Historia de la confederación argentina,* Vol. II, pp. 202-203.

and while it continued in the following years, it was an innocuous and unimportant club.

IV. Personal Characteristics of Rosas

Rosas himself was notable particularly for his stern character and indomitable energy. Like Philip II, he knew everything that went on in the country; he read every dispatch, studying and deciding upon it; the immense official archives of the epoch show many marginal annotations in the hand of Rosas, even on the most insignificant documents.[12]

Although emotional in some respects, Rosas lacked a sense of humor and charity which might have tempered the severity which won him such ill-fame. He never smiled, except with a grim humor which boded ill rather than good. Perhaps his most striking eccentricity was the fact that he always kept at his side two buffoons, for diversion, like a medieval king.[13] Rosas was fond of practical jokes, sometimes of a grim nature. It is related, apparently with authority, that he once made a wager with one of his subordinates that he could make the British minister help prepare his dinner for a certain evening. To accomplish this, he requested Manuelita, his daughter, to pound corn with a heavy wooden instrument in a passage through which the minister had to pass on an expected diplomatic visit to Rosas. The minister arrived as expected, and being an admirer of Manuelita as well as a British gentleman, he begged her to allow him to aid her in her task. This she did, probably not aware of the stratagem that Rosas had planned (for she was domestic, and led a simple life which did not make such a task unusual); and Rosas won his wager. Incidentally, this is the only incident which I have found which might exemplify the supposed contempt and discourtesy which Rosas has been accused of displaying toward diplomats, and this was certainly not a very serious affair.

In personal appearance, Rosas was light complexioned, a *rubio,* a term applied to those with florid complexion and light eyes, indicating a descent from the pure Gothic race without any intermixture of Moorish or Jewish blood; and this race was held in much esteem by the common people of both Spain and South America.[14] He was clean shaven. In conversation, Darwin remarked that he was enthusiastic,

---

[12] Quesada, *op. cit.,* p. 69.

[13] Charles Darwin, *Journal of Researches . . . during the Voyage of H. M. S. Beagle round the World* (New York, 1873), p. 74. This book was first published in England in 1845.

[14] Manning, *op. cit.,* Vol. I, Doc. 70, p. 132.

sensible, and grave.[15] One of the best pictures that has been drawn of him is that of A. de Brossard, an attaché of the French legation, written after a six-hour interview with Rosas in 1847.

> "General Rosas is a man of medium height, quite stout, and apparently endowed with great physical vigor. His features are regular; he has a light complexion and blond hair, and does not at all resemble a Spaniard. One might well exclaim upon beholding him 'here is a Norman gentleman.' His physiognomy is a remarkable mixture of craft and force. He is generally tranquil, and even mild; but upon occasion, the contraction of his lips gives him a singular expression of deliberate severity. He expresses himself with much facility, and as one who is a perfect master of his thoughts and words. His style in conversation varies; now he uses well-chosen and even elegant phrases; again he indulges in trivial expressions. There is perhaps a little affectation in the way he expresses himself. His remarks are never categorical; they are diffuse and complicated by digressions and incidental phrases. This prolixity is evidently premeditated and intended to embarrass the interlocutor. In truth it is quite difficult to follow General Rosas in the detours of his conversation. The dictator showed himself by turns to be a consummate statesman, an affable individual, and an indefatigable dialectician, a vehement and passionate orator; as the emergency arose, he displayed with rare perfection, anger, frankness, and bonhommie. One realizes that, when encountered face to face, he could intimidate, or deceive, or seduce." [16]

This is certainly a remarkable portrait drawn by one who could not have entertained an altogether friendly feeling toward Rosas. It shows us that the governor was no ordinary man, but one of rare capacity.

Rosas had three children, one of whom died in infancy: a son, Juan, lived to maturity, but there is almost no record of him; the second child, Manuelita Rosas, lived with her father, and after the mother's death in 1838, acted as "first lady." Manuelita was not beautiful, but was a young lady of rare charm and gentle disposition, quite a contrast to her stern father. Her father opposed her marriage, even to the son of his own business partner, Terrero, and it was not until she went into exile in 1852 that she married the latter. Rosas was never reconciled to his daughter's marriage, and always lived apart from her in England.[17]

---

[15] Darwin, *op. cit.*, p. 74.

[16] Translation of W. S. Robertson, "Foreign Estimates of the Argentine Dictator, Juan Manuel de Rosas," *Hispanic American Historical Review,* May 1930, quoting French diplomatic records.

[17] See Carlos Ibarguren, *Manuelita Rosas* (Buenos Aires, 1926), on the family relations of Rosas.

To a considerable degree, the Puritanical character of Rosas acted as a restraint upon the gay and somewhat frivolous society in Buenos Aires. Ostentation in clothes and in display of all sorts was discouraged, not by edict in most cases, but by example and suggestion, for Rosas' power was so great that his suggestions had the power of edicts. It is said that one of the reasons for the decrease in the popularity of Rosas in the latter years of his rule was his uncomfortable severity and restraint upon the social life of the city. Nevertheless, it should not be thought that life was without any pleasure and entertainment under Rosas. He developed a large estate at Palermo, on the river bank above the city, and made it into a great public park, surrounding his residence, with beautiful gardens and other attractions. All were free to enter, and it was customary for society to ride out to Palermo evenings (on horseback, the universal means of transport), and dancing and parties were held at which there was a mingling of diplomats, the aristocracy, and some from the lower estates. But Rosas did cut down on the number of public holidays, and on the public festivals in the city, which he considered wasteful, and thus he alienated the support of the rather carefree and pleasure-loving lower classes.[18]

V. Rosas in Exile

Before the battle of Caseros, Rosas had arranged means for fleeing the country through the British legation. He accordingly was conveyed to Southampton on a British warship, and was received there with the honor due his rank and renown.

For twelve years Rosas lived in a small hotel in Southampton. In 1864 he moved onto a small estate outside the city (known as the Burgess Street Farm) and, although he was now 71 years of age, he undertook to personally operate this farm. He lived there until his death on March 13, 1877, following the contraction of a cold which developed into pneumonia. He lived alone, save for his servants and farm help, in his later years; his daughter lived in London, as previously stated.

Writers have generally remarked upon the poverty of Rosas while he was in exile, but this poverty was only relative. He received an income sufficient to support himself, from friends and relatives, amounting to about 420 pounds annually; he had been permitted to sell one

---

[18] J. Power, *History of the Argentine Republic* (Buenos Aires, 1892), quoting a contemporary account by Dr. Daniel Kelly, a British resident of Buenos Aires. See especially pp. 42-44.

of his smaller estates before his property was confiscated in 1853, and he is said to have received 100,000 pesos for this. General Urquiza, with whom Rosas maintained an extensive and friendly correspondence after his exile, offered him financial assistance in 1858, and Rosas finally agreed to accept this. In 1865 he received from Urquiza 1,000 pounds, and this is supposed to have been continued as an annual payment at least for several years.[19]

Of the several accounts of interviews with Rosas during this period that have been published, that of Alberdi, one of his veteran unitary opponents, and one of the greatest of Argentine scholars, is especially interesting. Some of its most interesting portions may be quoted.

> "Last night I met Rosas. I agreed to meet him at the house of Mr. Dickson. . . . His respectful attitude to the nation and its national government, has made me less resentful toward him.
>
> "He was speaking in English with the ladies when I entered. Mr. Dickson presented us and he shook hands with courteous words. A little afterwards, he spoke to me aside, seated in chairs placed by him. He charged me with assuring General Urquiza the truth of what he said, as his representative: 'That he strongly recognized his righteous and just attitude towards him [Rosas], that if today he possessed something to live on, he owed it to his [Urquiza's] efforts.'
>
> "He renewed to me his assurances of respect and submission to the national government.
>
> . . . .
>
> "He spoke much. He spoke English, poorly, but without hesitation and with facility.
>
> "He is jovial and friendly in society. After dinner, when the ladies had left, he spoke much of politics; almost always he addressed himself to me, and several times he came to my side. He called me *señor ministro* and sometimes *paisano;* otherwise by my name. He had just finished reading all that which the boat of the day before yesterday had brought about his suit. He was not on account of this less jovial or happy. 'They summon me by edicts,' he said. 'Am I crazy enough to go to hand myself over so that they may kill me?' [This refers to the suit over the confiscation of his personal property, and of a court summons for him to personally testify with regard thereto.]
>
> "He denied to Buenos Aires the right of judging him. . . . He

[19] On the exile of Rosas, and his financial aid from Urquiza, see the pamphlet of Martiano Leguizamón, *El ocaso del dictador* (Buenos Aires, 1917). See also Saldías, *Historia de la confederación argentina,* Vol. V, p. 340. The *Papeles de Rosas* (La Plata, 1904-1907), Vol. II, edited by Adolfo Saldías, contain much of Rosas' rather extensive correspondence while in exile.

said that the Government, the Sovereign or Superior Authority to which he alludes in it [his Protest in the above mentioned suit], is the Government of the Nation or Confederation, not that of Buenos Aires.

. . . .

"He spoke with moderation and respect of all of his opponents, including de Alsina.

. . . .

"He spoke much of horses, of dogs, of his liking for English life, of his present poverty, of his economies, of his horse, and of English horses.

"He is no ordinary man. He fits well into society. He had the easy and accustomed manner of a man who is used to seeing the world from the top. But, nevertheless, he is neither a blusterer nor is he arrogant, and perhaps for this itself, he is respected by the lords of England; by the most cultured and finest people in the land.

. . . .

"He told me that he brought no silver from Buenos Aires, but he had brought his historic papers, in whose authority he rested. He said that he kept his own opinion, without prejudice to his respect for the authority of the nation.

"After Balcarce, no *porteño* in Europe has treated me better than Rosas last night, as a representative of the Argentine Confederation." [20]

Rosas was not unhappy during his period of exile. He was well received in England, and had many friends. He cherished particularly a personal friendship with Lord Palmerston. He had brought as many of his personal papers with him as he could gather on his hasty departure, and always believed that future judgment would vindicate his rule and acknowledge his position in Argentine history.

VI. The Results of Rosas' Rule

In estimating the results of Rosas' long period in power, one cannot overlook its shortcomings; it was a period of political turmoil, and lack of government revenue as well as reactionary ideas prevented any marked social or intellectual progress.

In education, there was small progress; there was some progress in establishing schools for the lower classes, but the scarcity of money

---

[20] *Rosas (en el destierro)*, letter of Juan B. Alberdi of October 18, 1857, published in *Grandes escritores argentinos* (Buenos Aires, 1927), Vol. II.

and the hatred of the intellectual classes, who were leading the émigré attacks on Rosas, prevented the support of higher education.

There is not much evidence of social progress, other than the establishment of internal law and order, which was accomplished. An interesting exception was the introduction by Rosas of smallpox vaccination on a large scale, among the country classes and Indians. Again the lack of money prevented the government from carrying on social improvements and agencies.

Economically, the country did advance, though comparatively slowly. But the great increase in Argentine population and economic activity did not begin until after 1870, two decades after the fall of Rosas.[21] But even during the disturbed conditions of the epoch of Rosas, the business of the country expanded. The quantity of principal exports quadrupled between 1837 and 1851, and the value of these more than doubled. Imports increased only one-third in value from 1825 to 1851, but more than double in quantity.[22] Due to the expansion of the country and the long period of foreign blockade, the number of cattle trebled, increasing from three or four millions to ten or twelve millions.[23] Internal trade prospered under Rosas, so that in 1850, when the governor went through the usual process of declining his reëlection, the British residents of Buenos Aires, who were principally engaged in trade, petitioned him to continue in power.

While the period of Rosas saw the evolution of no new political institutions, it did have important and valuable political results. Its two great accomplishments were the elimination of the provincial *caudillos,* and the consequent establishment of a feeling of nationalism among the Argentine provinces. When Rosas was installed in power, Argentina was a theoretical confederation of practically independent states,[24] and when he departed, it was a unified state, united by his personal power and prestige, although it took another decade of strife to finish the process of amalgamation.

VII. The Judgment Upon Rosas

To learn the truth about Rosas, and to understand his position in and influence upon the foundation of the Argentine Republic has been

---

[21] J. H. Williams, *Argentine International Trade Under Inconvertible Paper Money, 1880-1900* (Cambridge, Mass., 1920), p. 27.

[22] Sir Woodbine Parish, *Buenos Ayres and the Provinces of La Plata* (London, revised edition, 1852), pp. 357 and 361.

[23] Parish, *op. cit.,* p. 357.

[24] See the letters of F. Baylies, U. S. Chargé at Buenos Aires, of July 24 and August 13, 1832, Docs. 70 and 75, pp. 129 and 146, in Manning, *op. cit.,* Vol. I.

the task of many modern Argentine historians. For such study, there are two types of sources: the voluminous writings of his unitarian opponents, written acknowledgedly in many cases by men who felt that "the end [the overthrow of Rosas] justifies the means"; and the literary and official writings of the Federals, which were scanty and admittedly greatly censored.[25]

With the fall of Rosas, his opponents came to power, but they could not, nor dared not, admit then that their previous writings were untruthful. This would have denied the propriety of their French alliance and the constant encouragement of foreign opposition to their own country.[26]

> "How, then, can one know the truth? There was left a final recourse: to collate, and to transcribe the official archieves. . . . But no one ignored the fact that Rosas, on embarking for England—he, the rich man of the provinces, whose own fortune, before it was confiscated by the government, was perhaps the largest in the country—did not carry money, for he was poor, without means [after getting to England], but he did pack up many of the archives of the government to take with him, with the intent that posterity would be able to know the truth of his long dictatorship; he was not able to carry it all; time was short, and he left entire cabinets full of papers, and many boxes in the possession of private individuals. Rosas feared that the conquerors would destroy the archives in order to perpetuate mystification and erase the possibility of contravention to their writings; he was not mistaken; the first succeeding government of Buenos Aires hastened to 'classify' all the papers of the period which it could find, to make a part of them into huge piles in a house on the Calle Moreno, and to perform a monstrous 'auto de fé' with the purpose of destroying even the footprints of the past." [27]

Modern judgment has greatly modified the viewpoint on Rosas; as long ago as 1898, Kirkpatrick, a not very friendly critic, wrote:

> "Rosas gave the first real solid government to Argentina. He practically secured internal peace—with brief interruptions—to a country torn by incessant revolutions and civil war. He was the creator of the Argentine Confederation—by force, perhaps; but force was the order of the day; and he arose from among a crowd of *caudillos,* party chiefs, half-soldiers, half-brigands, mostly as despotic in spirit, as regardless of law and restraint, as contemptuous of human life as Rosas himself was. To him more than to

[25] Quesada, *La época de Rosas,* p. 43.

[26] Quesada, *op. cit.,* p. 43.

[27] Quesada, *op. cit.,* pp. 43-44.

anyone it is due that Argentina is one country instead of containing half a dozen rival and discordant republics." [28]

How did Rosas himself view his dictatorship? While in exile, he repeatedly expressed confidence that time and history would recognize his true position. He had no illusions about the results of his government, nor did he ever try to shift the blame for any of his errors or excesses to others. But without further comment on his position in Argentine history, this study may be concluded with a transcript of an interview held with him by the father of Ernesto Quesada, who was an Argentine diplomat, in February 1873, at which young Quesada was present and took down as best he could Rosas' statement. This declaration of Rosas is replete with his political ideas. Quesada's father first asked the question: "Why did you not establish yourself as head of a constitutional government, when you could have so easily done so . . . ?" To this Rosas replied:

> "That was my ambition, but I spent my life and my energy without being able to realize it. I mounted to the governorship while the country was gripped in anarchy, divided into hostile and recalcitrant groups, dismembered already in part, and other portions in process of dismemberment, with neither a stable government in international affairs, nor with an internal national organization, without experience in government, converted into a thorough chaos, with the most complete subversion of ideas and ideals, and with the political parties furiously hating one another; a hell in miniature. I decided that if it did not modify its foundations, our great country would definitely disintegrate into a chain of petty republics without importance and waste themselves thusly in the future: too much already had the colonial viceroyalty been broken up! The Province of Buenos Aires, nevertheless, had a real basis of governmental organization and of orderly habits. I proposed to reorganize the administration, consolidate the economic system, and, little by little, see that the other provinces should do the same. If the Unitarian Party had allowed me to breathe I do not doubt that, in a little while, I would have carried the country towards a complete normalization; but it was not possible, because the opposition was permanent and in the neighboring countries the émigrés organized constant invasions. It was thus that my whole period of government was spent in defending myself from these conspiracies, these invasions, and the foreign naval interventions; this consumed the resources and prevented me from subduing the *caudillos* of the interior to a more normal and tranquil status. Furthermore, the habits of anarchy, developed in

[28] F. A. Kirkpatrick, "Rosas," *Cornhill Magazine*, London, Oct. 1898, p. 530.

twenty years of governmental strife, could not be modified in a day. It was necessary first to govern with a strong hand in order to guarantee security to life and to labor, in city and country, and to establish a system of order and tranquillity which would allow the exercise of a real republican life. . . . I soon understood, however, that I had undertaken a task superior to the strength of a single man. . . . Those who have berated my tyranny and have suspected that I enjoyed the sensation of power, are but defamers, since I lived in sight of everyone, almost in a house of glass, and renounced all that which was not constant work on never ending business. The most scrupulous honor in the management of public moneys, absolute dedication to the service of the state, unlimited energy to decide upon acts and to assume full responsibility for such resolutions, required the people to have confidence with me, for which reason I was able to govern for so long. With my personal fortune and that of my wife, I could have lived privately with all the flatteries which money could attract, and without the least worry; I preferred to renounce that and to deliberately convert myself into a slave of duty, consecrated in absolute and disinterested service to my country. If I have committed errors—and there is no man who does not commit them—I alone am responsible. But the reproach of not having given the country a constitution seems to me always futile, because it is not enough to dictate a *cuadernito* [little notebook], as Quiroga called it, but to apply it and to solve its difficulties; it is necessary first to prepare the people for it, creating habits of order and government, because a constitution ought not to be a product of an illusive dream without reflecting the needs of the country. Always I have disliked the farce of paper laws which cannot be carried into practice. The base of a constitutional system is the exercise of suffrage, and this requires not only a sane public that can read and write, but who feel that the vote is a right, and, at the same time, a duty, so that each elector knows whom he ought to elect; in the United States itself very much was left to be desired when I left my government, as my minister Alvear communicated. On the contrary, the elections of legislatures and governments were iniquitous farces and they were tools of the cliques of interlopers, accompanied by scoffing from others and among themselves, fomenting corruption and villainy, breaking down character and disturbing everything. One cannot put the cart before the oxen; it is necessary to domesticate the latter, to habituate them to the yoke and goad, so that they can draw the cart after them. It is necessary, likewise, before dictating a constitution, to implant in the people habits of government and of democratic life, which is a long and heavy task; when I retired, because of Caseros—for I had previously prepared everything so that I could absent myself, packing papers and reaching an understanding with the British minister—the country found itself perhaps already partially prepared for an attempt at constitutional government. And you know that in spite of that, there still passed a good ten years in the conflict of desires between the city and the country population, with Buenos Aires separated with respect to the Conferedation. . . ."

"Then," interrupted my father [the elder Quesada], "you were tired of the work of such a long rule. . . ."

"Certainly. There is no man who can stand a similar task too long a time. It is an honor to be the first servant of the country, but it is a formidable sacrifice, which reaps only ingratitude among contemporaries and among those who immediately succeed them. But I have a tranquil conscience that posterity will justify my effort, because without this continued sacrifice of mine, the state of anarchy would still be present, as one can yet observe it today in other sections of America. For the rest, I have always believed that forms of government are a relative matter, since a monarchy or republic can be equally excellent or pernicious, according to the state of a particular country; this is the real kernel of the question: to prepare a people so that they can have a suitable form of government; and for this, that which is needed is men who are true servants of the nation, statesmen of merit and not mere common office-holders, since, under any constitution, if there are such men the problem is solved, and if there are not, any constitution is useless and dangerous. The cry of constitution, which ignores the condition of the country, is an empty word. I could never understand this fetish for a written constitution which does not reflect practical life, but the opinions of the doctrinaires; if such a constitution does not reflect the real life of a people, it will always be useless, no matter what assembly or governmental decree sanctions it. And at the risk of scandalizing you, I will say that for myself, the happiest form of government would be the paternal, intelligent, disinterested and tireless autocracy, energetic and resolved to secure the happiness of the people, without favorites. For this reason never did I have any [constitution]; I sought to realize the single ideal of a paternal government, in the epoch of transition in which I handled the government. . . . I have always scorned the petty tyrants and the local *caudillos,* who hide in the shadows; I have always admired the autocratic dictators who have been the first servants of the people. That is my great title; I have wished always to serve my country, and that was my plan, and the responsibility for the measures employed to accomplish it is mine alone. To prescribe a constitution was a secondary matter; the primary thing was to prepare the country for it—and that is what I believe I have done!" [29]

---

[29] Quesada, *La época de Rosas* (1923 edition), appendix, pp. 229-233.

APPENDIX B

SOME BRITISH ACTIVITIES AND INFLUENCES IN ARGENTINA

By Alfred Hasbrouck

THE early nineteenth century saw the complete military failure of British arms to take and hold Buenos Aires, and the downfall of Spanish power in that city and in the whole of La Plata region; but its subsequent years saw an increasing familiarity with the language and customs of Great Britain, and a phenomenal development of that nation's social influence, commercial prestige, and financial power in the Argentine capital. This spread of English cultural and financial prevalence, so evident in the present twentieth century, may fairly be called the British Reconquest, keeping in mind that this term does not imply in any way military or political control.

The fact that the colonists unaided by the Spanish Viceroy or royal troops had protected themselves and driven out the British invader in 1806 and 1807, opened their eyes and made them realize that they no longer had need of the protection of the mother country. When, therefore, in 1808, Ferdinand VII of Spain was driven from his throne by Napoleon, and Joseph Bonaparte was crowned as King of Spain by his brother, it became necessary for the colonists to decide whether they should transfer their allegiance to this new king or should set up an independent government of their own. The leading spirits among the colonists, believing that they had proved themselves competent to stand alone, had on May 25, 1810, in open town meeting *(cabildo abierto)* deposed the viceroy and organized a new council of government *(junta)*; and on July 9, 1816, at Tucumán, delegates from the several provinces had issued a Declaration of Independence for the United Provinces of the Río de La Plata. Meanwhile, many of the British officers and merchants had remained in that land, had married Argentine girls, and had raised families, the descendants of which have exerted strong influence in the political, economic, and social life of the new republic throughout the nineteenth century, and until the present day.

When the independence of La Plata was recognized by England, Englishmen and Scotchmen flocked to its shores, hoping to make their fortunes. British travelers were the first to carry back reports of the natural richness of this land. Among these were some who published books describing their explorations and experiences: John Miers in 1818, Captain Basil Hall in 1820, and Captain Head in 1825. The authors of the well-known *Letters from South America,* John and William Parish Robertson, who came as merchants at the time of the British invasion, must also be mentioned as having later founded on their *estancia* of Monte Grande a colony of 200 Scotch families. Many of these pioneers remained and grew up with the country. Other less hardy souls ventured their wealth in investments for developing in the young country cattle and sheep ranges, railroads, steamship lines, newspapers, banks, factories, and department stores. Steadily and perseveringly these British colonists and investors increased their own wealth as the country prospered, until they became a weighty factor in the financial and economic life of the republic.[1]

When in 1825 Argentina signed its first trade treaty with a foreign power, Great Britain was that power. Then Darwin came to investigate its flora and fauna, and Captains Stokes and Fitzroy charted its coasts. By 1831 there were 5000 Britains in Buenos Aires. In 1885 British imports and exports to and from Argentina totaled $35,000,000, and in 1910 they reached a total of $300,000,000.[2] Statistics of immigration for the years 1857 to 1910 show that the number of English coming to Argentina was 46,796, as compared with 1,994,740 Italians and 1,013,737 Spaniards.[3]

---

[1] Although Argentine trade figures and other statistics could easily be quoted to prove British influence, these facts make dry reading and will be employed only when their use cannot be avoided. Statistics and other data have been obtained from the following sources: *Buenos Aires Herald,* Buenos Aires, 1933-1934; *Buenos Aires Herald, British Empire Trade Exhibition Number; Buenos Aires Herald, History and Activities of the North American Colonies of Argentina; Buenos Aires Herald, Year Book and Directory, 1931; Comments on Argentine Trade,* published by The Chamber of Commerce of the United States of America in the Argentine Republic, Vol. XIII, No. 8, March, 1934; *Guía Expreso Villalonga,* Buenos Aires, May, 1933; *Guía Peuser Metropolitana,* Buenos Aires, May, 1933; Michael G. Mulhall *The English in South America* (Buenos Aires & London, 1878); M. G. & E. T. Mulhall, *Handbook of the River Plate* (Buenos Aires & London, 1892); *The Review of the River Plate,* Buenos Aires, 1933; Luís D. Rodríguez, *La Argentina en 1912* (Buenos Aires, 1912); and Carlos M. Urien, and Ezio Colombo, *La república argentina en 1910,* 2 vols. (Buenos Aires, 1910).

[2] *Buenos Aires Herald, British Empire Trade Exhibition Number,* p. 19.

[3] Luís D. Rodríguez, *La Argentina en 1912,* p. 33.

Mulhall says that in 1878 there were 30,000 British residents in Buenos Aires and that the property they owned amounted to several millions sterling. This authority also divides the epochs in the growth of British population in Buenos Aires into four.[4]

The first epoch dates from the overthrow of Spanish rule in 1810, when the country was first opened to trade with Britain. In 1823 there were 3500 British residents and forty English business firms. The second epoch began with the treaty with England signed in 1825. In this period was founded Robertson's Scotch colony. From 1825 to 1830 there was an influx of Irish who came to work in the *saladeros* (salt meat establishments) of Brown, Dowdall, Armstrong, and others. At that time 200 Irishmen settled in Buenos Aires. In the third period, beginning in 1835, a large number of Irish sheep farmers also entered the country. Finally after the fall of the dictator, Rosas, in 1852 there began a fourth period of commercial activity in which British capital was invested in railways, telegraphs, steamships, cattle raising, banks, and various industries.[5]

In addition to the English, Scotch, and Irish settlers, Welsh immigrants flocked to the shores of Argentina. In 1863 the government, in order to populate its southern territories, offered to give fifty square miles to every 200 families. These settlers were to be free from taxation for ten years, but were to protect themselves against the Indians. A contract was also entered into whereby 3000 were to come from Wales within ten years to settle the Welsh colony of Chubut. Two years later the first group of such colonists, 132 in number, sailed from Liverpool. In 1870 the legislature of the Province of Santa Fé conceded thirty-four square leagues to the banking firm of Thompson, Bonar & Co. for the establishment of the Alexandra Colony in the *gran chaco*.[6]

English engineers came out to investigate the possibilities of extracting the precious metals and other minerals in South America. As early as 1824 the Famatina (Rioja) Mining Co. was founded in London, but this venture, as well as the English mines at Potosí (Bolivia) and Uspallata were financial failures owing to expensive methods of working, jealousy toward foreigners, and troubles from civil wars. After the fall of Rosas and the establishment of a stable government,

---

[4] Michael G. Mulhall, *The English in South America*, p. 335.

[5] *Ibid.* pp. 417, 433.

[6] *Ibid.* pp. 434-443.

better success was obtained. During the 1870's, mines at Hilario, Gualilán, and Chalecito proved profitable to Englishmen, but mining in Argentina has not attracted the favorable attention of British residents or investors, as have the other forms of activities to be mentioned.[7]

In 1822 the first bank *(casa de moneda)* was founded in Argentina by a number of English and Argentine merchants. Four years later it was reorganized as the Bank of the United Provinces, on the board of directors of which were Joshua Thwaites, James Britain, and James Barton. In 1863 the London and River Plate Bank was opened. In 1880 the English Bank of the River Plate was founded, but this failed during the financial crash of 1891.[8] At the present time (1934) British banking facilities are concentrated in the Anglo-South American Bank, the London and South American Bank, and The Royal Bank of Canada. In this connection may be mentioned the services to Argentine finances of Dalmacio Vélez Sarsfield, an Anglo-Argentine, who reformed the Provincial Bank of Buenos Aires in 1853, and who as minister of the interior encouraged the construction of 5,000 miles of telegraph line and in 1873 opened the Río Cuarto Railway.[9]

Many of the government telegraph lines were constructed under contract by Englishmen: 3110 miles for the national government by Charles Burton; 415 miles for the provincial government of Buenos Aires by a Mr. Traut; and 620 miles for the Transandine line by Clark & Co. with subsidies from the Argentine and Chilean governments. The River Plate Telegraph Co., a commercial line, was built and managed by John Oldham.[10]

A survey of the history of railway development in Argentina shows the importance of British influence. British rails and locomotives, which had been used during the Crimean War and had been salvaged after that war, were shipped to Buenos Aires and installed in a line from Plaza del Parque to Floresta. Although this first railway, completed in 1857, was due to Argentine initiative, it later was bought by a British syndicate and became the Buenos Aires Western. All succeeding railways, with few exceptions, have been constructed with British capital. In 1929 the total British capital invested in railways in Argentina amounted to $1,405,613,664, while capital other than

---

[7] *Ibid.* pp. 445-450; M. G. & E. T. Mulhall, *Handbook of the River Plate,* p. 52.

[8] Mulhall, *Handbook,* p. 35.

[9] Mulhall, *The English in South America,* p. 391.

[10] *Ibid.* pp. 506-507.

British so invested was only $495,900,000; and out of the total of 39,087 kilometers of railways, 26,310 belonged to British-owned companies. Among the latter may be named, beside the Buenos Aires Western, the Central Argentine, the Great Southern, the Buenos Aires and Pacific, the Central Córdova, the Entre Ríos, and five others; while among the otherwise-owned railways there are eight, including the Great Patagonian, the Santa Fé, and the Rosario-Belgrano Port Railway. Thus sixty-seven per cent of railway mileage was built with British capital, and seventy-four per cent of all capital invested in railways in the country is British.[11]

In Buenos Aires the principal subway line, the Subterraneo, is British owned, as are the ninety-nine tram routes controlled by the Anglo-Argentino, which operates all the tram lines in the city except the five routes of the Port and Dock Trams, the five routes of the Tranvías Eléctricos del Sud, and the twenty-two routes of the Compañia Tranvías Lacroze.[12]

As regards water transportation, large first-class steamers carrying passengers and mails connect Buenos Aires and England with a vessel each way every week, alternating between the Royal Mail and Blue Star lines. Freight steamers carrying passengers also sail at frequent intervals, operated by the Lamport & Holt Line and Houlder Brothers & Co. (Argentina) Ltd. The Furness-Prince Line sends passenger steamers, flying the British flag, each way every other week between Buenos Aires and New York. Ships of the Donaldson South American Line sail from Glasgow and Liverpool once a month, and those of the National Steamship Line maintain a regular cargo and passenger service from Liverpool. Other British lines touching at Buenos Aires on the way to other South American ports are the British Steam Navigation Company, Calcutta-River Plate Line, River Plate-Liverpool Line,

---

[11] *B. A. Herald Trade Exhibition Number,* pp. 31-32. Page 32 of this publication gives the following instructive table concerning British owned railways in Argentina.

Year	*Length in kilometers*	*Percentage of total kilometers*	*Capital in gold dollars*	*Percentage of total capital*
1865	148	60	3,754,898	70
1880	1,279	51	38,332,073	61
1895	11,077	78	398,333,486	82
1912	23,725	73	961,444,885	78
1929	26,310	67	1,405,613,664	74

[12] *Guía Expreso Villalonga,* May 1933, pp. 56-64; *Guía Peuser,* pp. 52-80.

and the Nelson Line.[13] The excellence of the steamship service under the British flag is reflected in the trade reports.

From a publication of the Chamber of Commerce of the United States of America in the Argentine Republic may be learned the fact that during the first two months of 1934 the total value of exports to the United Kingdom was 68,112,311 paper *pesos* as against 16,910,141 to the United States, 17,819,889 to France, and 21,498,686 to Germany; and the total value of imports during this period from the United Kingdom was 34,454,798 paper *pesos* as against 21,498,191 from the United States, 15,741,288 from Germany, and 8,024,902 from France.[14]

In 1911 the total trade between Argentina and the United Kingdom amounted to 108,637,430 gold *pesos,* as compared with 52,353,390 with the United States and 65,862,211 with Germany.[15] Since the value of livestock and agricultural products exported from Argentina far exceeds the value of all other exported products, it is well to inquire into the ownership of the sources of these products.

Owing to the natural adaptation of its vast *pampas* for the ranging of cattle, stock breeding and the production of meats, hides, and wool are undoubtedly among the most important industries of Argentina. Although the introduction of cattle began with the earliest Spanish conquerors, and the making and exporting of dried and salted beef was carried on by citizens of the republic from its first days, progress in this industry was hampered by the deterioration of the quality of the native stock due to inbreeding and lack of selection. It was the British stock breeder who set an example of improving his herds by importing animals selected for the purpose of breeding them with the *criollo* (native) animals, with a view toward improvement of meat and wool. Among the earliest of those who saw the value of the Lincoln breed of sheep was John Gibson who came in 1819. He also imported Cotswolds, Cheviots, Leicesters, and Romney Marshes to improve the sheep on his *estancia,* "Los Ingleses," in Tuyú. John Hannah and Thomas Lloyd Halsey continued this good work with such success that the former has been called "the founder of the sheep-breeding industry" in Argentina.[16]

John Miller is said to have imported the first Shorthorn bull. The

---

[13] All these lines carried advertisements in the *Buenos Aires Herald* during 1933-1934.

[14] *Comments on Argentine Trade,* vol. XIII, No. 8, pp. 52-53.

[15] Rodríguez, *op. cit.,* p. 31.

[16] *British Empire Trade Exhibition Number,* p. 119.

breeding of better grade cattle was fostered likewise by other Englishmen, among whom may be mentioned James and William White, Wilfrid Latham, George Bell, and James Ritchie. Richard B. Newton introduced wire fencing. He was among the founders, and became one of the first vice presidents, of the Argentine Rural Society. In this society and elsewhere Argentine and British stock raisers continued to develop high-bred cattle, devoting especial attention to Shorthorns. The annual Rural Society livestock show has become one of the most important business and social events held in Buenos Aires.

For the exportation of beef and mutton, some better method of preservation than that of drying in the sun and salting had to be developed. In 1876 Robert MacAndrew began freezing meat in small quantities and made a successful shipment of ten tons from Argentina to London. The first *frigorífico* (cold storage plant) in Argentina was built in 1882 by Eugenio Terrason. For the next ten years only four more such plants were constructed, but then there ensued a rapid development of this industry, especially by the North American meatpackers, Armour, Swift, and Wilson. One of the first plants built at Las Palmas in 1886 by Hugh Nelson, of James Nelson and Sons, was later operated by the English and Dutch Meat Company. While British have lagged behind North American interests in the meat packing industry in Argentina, at the present day the Frigorífico Anglo claims to be "the greatest packing house in the world, is entirely British controlled, and supplies Argentine meat to the British market by means of the most complete system of meat distribution that has ever existed." [17]

In spite of this paucity of British cold-storage plants in the country, a comparison of the destinations of Argentine meat shipments is convincing. During the year 1930, as against 269,785 carcasses of mutton, 24,337 of lamb, and 1,347,039 quarters of beef shipped to Europe, and 19,649 carcasses of mutton, 4,349 of lamb, and 83,143 quarters of beef shipped to "various destinations" (probably including the United States), the shipments to the United Kingdom amounted to 1,211,707 carcasses of mutton, 3,994,575 of lamb, and 5,751,719 quarters of beef. Thus it will be seen that the Argentine meat industry is largely influenced by the preponderence of British trade.[18]

The number of large retail and department stores under British ownership and management in Buenos Aires shows the attractiveness

[17] *Ibid.*, p. 115. This statement appears in the advertisement of the Frigorífico Anglo.

[18] *Buenos Aires Herald Year Book and Directory,* 1931, p. 79.

of British-made goods to the Argentine buyer. Outstanding among the best shops in the capital are the large department stores known as Harrods Ltd., Gath & Chaves, and Casa Tow (all of which are believed to be controlled by the English firm of Whiteway Laidlaw & Co.), and McHardy Brown & Co.'s department store. There may also be mentioned Lacey's for sporting equipment, Mappin & Webb for jewelry and British silverware, Maples & Co. and Thompson Muebles for furniture, Cowes & Co. for sporting goods, S. T. Leith for Portland cement, A. G. Prudence for British machinery, J. C. Ross & Co. for British athletic goods and suitings, and the Dwight P. Robinson Engineering and Construction service, as well as the British controlled Compañía Unión Telefónica.[19]

Among the hospitals of Buenos Aires there are seventeen municipal, eight national, thirty-two private, and six foreign. Of these last, two are British owned and controlled—the Britanica and the Anglo-American Private Hospital. The former of these, commonly called the British Hospital, was founded in 1857 by private subscription at a cost of $36,000. The present building erected in 1867 contains five wards providing twelve beds each.[20]

The Church of England service is celebrated in St. John's Pro-Cathedral, All Saints Church (Quilmes), Hurlingham Church Hall, Saint Peter's Anglican Church (Flores), and St. Saviour's (Belgrano); the Scotch Presbyterian service is held in St. Andrew's Scot's Church, Quilmes Scot's Church, Belgrano Scot's Church (Dr. Smith Memorial), Escalada Scot's Church, and Temperly Scot's Church; the Methodist Episcopal service is held in the so-called American Church; and the Christian Science Service is held in the First and Second Churches of Christ Scientist. As will be noticed, all of these churches, except the three last named, are distinctly British.

Referring to the fiftieth anniversary of the Buenos Aires English High School, the *Buenos Aires Herald* of March 3, 1934, said: "The institution was formed in what may be called the early days of the community, and has played a great part in the formation of sound character among the thousands of Anglo-Argentines now in our midst. A school has much influence in creating an honest and energetic community." Other such schools, where instruction is in English and based on English educational requirements, include Oates College at Hur-

[19] *British Empire Trade Exhibition Number,* pp. 139ff.

[20] *Guía Expreso Villalonga,* May 1933, pp. 10-11; Mulhall, *Handbook,* p. 604.

lingham, for boys; St. Georges College, founded at Quilmes in 1898, for boys under twelve; St. Andrews Scotch School, for boys and girls; Northlands, at Olivos, a boarding and day school for girls; St. Margaret's School at Belgrano, a boarding and day school for girls; and the Belgrano High School. The only strictly North American school is the American Grammar and High School (a department of Colegio Ward), a boarding and day school for boys and girls which offers a four-year North American secondary school course of study and a college preparatory course for entrance into the colleges and universities of the United States.

In Buenos Aires there are published thirty-eight daily (morning and afternoon) newspapers. Among these there are ten foreign language newspapers, comprising two in German, one in French, two in Italian, one in Syrian, two in Hebrew, and two in English. At the present time these two English language papers are *The Standard* which is the "Doyen of the Argentine Press" having been founded in 1861 by M. G. and E. T. Mulhall, and *The Buenos Aires Herald,* which was founded in 1876 and boasts of having "more than treble the net circulation of any English-language journal in South America." The earliest English-language newspaper was *The British Packet and Argentine News,* which was first published in 1826 as a weekly, but disappeared about forty years later owing to its inability to meet the competition of *The Standard.*[21]

Undoubtedly these newspapers, schools, and churches must exert a powerful influence upon the community in which they flourish. While, as has been seen, this influence is partly North American, it is really overwhelmingly British. This becomes strikingly evident to the traveler or resident from the United States who notes that all those with whom he talks English, either Englishmen, Anglo-Argentines, or even Argentines, speak English with the soft English inflection, using English idioms, and that he is himself recognized at once as a citizen of the United States by his "North American accent"; in every case he is expected to use "O. K." and other slang expressions taught by the North American motion pictures.

Many English words have been transferred bodily into the Spanish spoken in Argentina. Among such words are "futbol," "club," "golf," "mitin" (meeting), "box," "sport." Most of these words pertain to sports, yet few if any baseball terms are heard. In the field of sport

---

[21] *Buenos Aires Herald Year Book, 1931,* pp. 84-85.

the character of a nation is expressed. The Englishman is known throughout the world for his sportsmanship, and the Argentine has in this respect proved himself an apt pupil. As a criterion of social life and culture, the sports which are popular among all classes may be taken.

By tracing the history of sports in Argentina, it will be learned that cricket and horse racing were first introduced by British officers serving in the command of General Beresford at the time of the conquest in 1806. For this we have several statements of Major Gillespie, such as "At Esquina a repose of some days was allowed us; full pockets and vacant time revived the national diversions of horse racing and cricket, for which we always carried the materials." "At San Ignatius, near Córdova, the ground was too rugged and uneven for cricket." "While at San Antonio de Areca, the author and other British prisoners enjoyed as pastimes fishing, cricket, hunting, and riding."[22] Even after the British troops were driven out by the Reconquest, cricket was played wherever there were enough Englishmen to form a team.

About 1831 a Cricket Club was founded in Buenos Aires, and matches were from time to time played between two teams called the Greens and the Pinks. Although this club ceased to exist within a couple of years, it was revived in 1861 as the Buenos Aires Cricket Club. During this interim, two other clubs, the Albion and the Anglo-Porteño, enjoyed a short-lived popularity.

Within three years of its organization, the Buenos Aires Cricket Club had established itself on its present grounds at Palermo (the extensive and beautiful park and sports section of the city of Buenos Aires) and was providing opportunities for its members to play games among themselves and occasionally to match their skill against teams from the suburban towns. Although during the last decade of the nineteenth century, games were played with teams from Brazil and Chile, international matches were not common until the beginning of the present century, when teams from England came to play against the Argentine teams, and the latter went to Brazil and Chile every few years.

While a few of the members of these Argentine teams and clubs were Argentines and Anglo-Argentines, it must be admitted that the great majority of members were British. The Britisher, wherever he may be isolated throughout the world, returns in spirit to the land of his birth by playing his boyhood games, among which cricket was the

[22]Gillespie, *op. cit.*, pp. 139, 184, 195.

favorite; but somehow this game does not seem to appeal to men of other nations, and the Argentines have never adopted it as a favorite sport.[23]

Horse racing, on the other hand, does afford an outlet for the Latin's love of betting and is well suited to a pastoral country like Argentina. Since, as will be remembered, stock raising is one of the leading industries of the country, it is not surprising that those interested should try to improve the racing qualities of horses by the introduction from England of thoroughbred horses and mares for breeding purposes. This was begun as early as 1857, and continued to attract a constantly increasing number of enthusiastic *estancieros* (ranch owners) until the Jockey Club was founded in Buenos Aires in 1882 and the present Hippodrome at Palermo was opened. The races at Palermo and those encouraged elsewhere by prizes offered by the Jockey Club have made horse racing one of the national sports. The Jockey Club is now one of the wealthiest and most exclusive clubs in Buenos Aires. Although its membership contains various foreign names, it is distinctly an Argentine institution, for the wealthy *estancieros* of the country have taken into their own hands the fostering and control of horse breeding and racing, a sport introduced by a handful of British officers in 1806.

Although at the present time there are several golf clubs in the suburbs of Buenos Aires, such as those at Lomas, Hurlingham, Belgrano, and Flores, as well as at Córdova and Mar del Plata, it cannot be said that the Argentines have supported this sport as enthusiastically as have the British residents. They have, however named a suburban station on the Central Argentine Railway, "Golf."[24] As far as the records show, it is believed that the Buenos Aires Golf Club (the first club of its kind in Argentina) was organized in 1892 by a Mr. Scroggle and a number of his Scotch friends who played on an improvised course.

In polo the Argentine and Anglo-Argentine players may certainly be said to hold their own with teams from the United States and England. The names of the Lacey brothers are heard wherever that sport is mentioned. The names of Argentine tennis champions are likewise not unfamiliar in international circles.

Of all forms of sport, football has obtained the greatest hold in Argentina, and has done most to mold the character and physique of

---

[23] Much of the information about sports has been taken from an article on that subject in the *Buenos Aires Herald, Year Book and Directory, 1931.*

[24] Other station names showing British influence are Hurlingham and Temperly.

the Argentine youth. In both forms, Rugby and association, it is played everywhere throughout the nation, and because of the favorable climate, during almost every month of the year.

Association football (or "futbol" as it is spelled in Argentina) is the favorite form of the game. Clubs and leagues throughout the country are devoted to this sport, and football fields have been laid out by the large department stores, primarily for the use of employees. On nearly every Saturday, Sunday, or holiday, matches between local teams are played on these semi-public fields or on public grounds belonging to the municipality. Since the minister of public education has made the practice of athletic sports obligatory, ordinarily an hour a day is set aside in the public schools for the practice of association football by the school boys.[25] On the outskirts of every match and on almost every vacant lot, boys are to be seen practicing the game in as close an imitation of their elders as their limited facilities will permit. If among these boys there is no proud possessor of a real football, a tennis ball will do, or even a cap, a coat, or a rag rolled into a wad will serve the purpose of being kicked about or butted with the head. What baseball is to the North American urchin, association football is to the Argentine small boy. It is an instinct with them both, the only difference being that while the North American uses his hands to catch or throw the ball, the Argentine uses his feet or head to kick or butt it. It is a common sight to see a half-grown youth or even a middle-aged man, when a ball comes his way by chance on the street, lift the ball into the air with his heel and then butt it with his head.

The first Association Football Club was organized in 1867 by British athletes. By 1894 there were six clubs in the Argentine Association Football League, and almost every year thereafter matches were played with British or South African visiting teams. In the matches for the South American championship between 1916 and 1929 the teams representing Argentina have held their own against those from Brazil and Uruguay, the Argentines having won four matches to the Uruguayans' six and the Brazilians' two. Playing for the Lipton Cup between 1908 and 1929, Argentina has won on four occasions to Uruguay's seven, while there have been four ties.[26]

The first recorded match under Rugby Union rules was played in 1874 on the Palermo Cricket Grounds, but the local Rugby Union was

---

[25] *British Empire Trade Exhibition Number,* p. 143.

[26] *Buenos Aires Herald Year Book, 1931,* pp. 52-53.

not founded until twenty-five years later. Rugby football, or "rugger," is a popular game with the Argentines, but it is not so universally played by both young and old as is the game called "soccer" (association football). The players of rugger consider themselves as among the elite and just a little bit more exclusive than those who are devotees of soccer. The River Plate Rugby Union affords opportunities for matches among the local clubs and with visiting British or other foreign teams.

In order to encourage sports and to provide time for their universal practice there was promulgated on September 29, 1932, the Law of the English Saturday *(Sábado Inglés)*. This law provided that no employees shall be required to work after 1 p. m. on Saturdays; that they shall not suffer any reductions in their salaries on account of the enforcement of this law; and that infractions of this law shall be punished by a fine of ten to fifty *pesos* for each person required to work beyond the hour specified, with a minimum fine of fifty *pesos* for each establishment violating the law.[27]

In calling this the Law of the English Saturday, the Argentine government tacitly admitted that in establishing the long week-end it was following the English custom; but without being forced by law to do so, the Argentines of nearly every social class, by pausing from work at 5 o'clock to take tea, and by delaying their dinner hour until late in the evening, show the strong British influence controlling their daily lives.

---

[27] Law No. 11640 in *Leyes nacionales sancionados por el congreso argentino durante el periodo legislativo de 1932.*

APPENDIX C

THE BOUNDARY SETTLEMENTS OF BRAZIL

By Raul d'Eca

WITH the possible exception of the Union of Soviet Republics, Brazil has a greater number of what one might call next door neighbors than any other nation on earth. She borders on all the politically independent or dependent unities of South America except two—Chile and Ecuador—and even the latter at one time claimed a boundary with Brazil in a territory which later came under Colombian sovereignty. The settlement of all these numerous boundary questions [1]

[1] The existing material on this subject being very large, it is not possible to give here more than a few of the outstanding items. Among the source material may be mentioned the *Relatorios* or Annual Reports of the Ministries of Foreign Affairs of the countries involved, the cases or memoirs presented to the arbiters of the several arbitrated disputes, the arbitral decisions, and such collections of documents as: Miss F. G. Davenport, *European Treaties Bearing on the History of the United States and its Dependencies* (2 vols. Washington, 1917), Carlos Calvo, *Recueil des traités,* etc. (7 vols. Paris, 1862), J. F. Borges de Castro, *Collecção dos tratados,* etc. (8 vols. Lisbon, 1856-58), Cardoso de Oliveria, *Actos diplomaticos do Brazil* (Rio de Janeiro, 1912), Hildebrando Accioly, *Actos internacionaes vigentes no Brazil* (Rio de Janeiro, 1927), and De Angelis, *Colección de obras y documentos,* etc. (Buenos Aires, 1836, v. IV). Both the *Anales de la Biblioteca Nacional de Buenos Aires,* and the *Revista do Instituto Historico e Geographico Brasileiro* contain scattered source material printed at one time or another. In John B. Moore's *History and Digest of International Arbitrations to which the United States has been a Party,* vol. II, is found an abridged translation in English of the Brazilian and Argentine cases presented to President Cleveland in the *Misiones* dispute.

Among the most notable secondary works on this matter may be mentioned the following: Carlos A. Aldao, *La cuestión de Misiones ante el presidente de los E. Unidos de América,* New York, 1894; J. A. Puente Arnao, *Historia de los límites del Perú,* Lima, 1927; J. Caetano da Silva, *L'Oyapok et l'Amazone, question brésilienne et française,* 2 vols. Paris, 1899; A. Perez Figuerola, *Nuestra cuestión de límites con el Brazil,* Lima, 1905; Thiers Fleming, *Limites e superficie do Brazil e seus estados,* Rio de Janeiro, 1918; F. I. M. Homem de Mello, *O Oyapok: divisa do Brazil com a Guyana Franceza, á luz dos acontecimentos historicos,* Rio de Janeiro, 1899; Jorge Juan and Antonio Ulloa, *Dissertación histórica y geográfica sobre el meridiano de demarcación entre los dominios de España y Portugal,* etc., Madrid, 1749; A. de Lapradelle and N. Politis, *L'Arbitrage anglo-brésilienne de 1904,* Paris, 1905; João Pandiá Calogeras, *A politica exterior do imperio,* 2 vols. Rio de Janeiro, 1927-28; J. M. Quijano Otero, *Límites de la república de los E. U. de Colombia,* 2 vols., Seville, 1881; and A. J. Uribe, *Cuestionẽs internacionales, económicas, políticas y sociales,* Bogotá, 1925.

constitutes one of the most interesting pages in the history of Brazil and may be said to have occupied a considerable portion of the time of Brazilian diplomats from the date of independence to recent years, besides a good deal of the time of Portuguese diplomats during the period when Brazil was a Portuguese colony. Thanks to these unremitting efforts, the boundaries of Brazil are all today complete and well-defined. They have not yet, however, all been surveyed and marked, although the work is progressing rapidly and, no doubt, will end soon. In this connection one must remember that the work of surveying and marking the boundaries of such a vast country, particularly in certain sections of tropical jungle the access to which is, even today, arduous and dangerous, is, in itself, a most notable enterprise.

In the present paper an attempt will be made to give only a general outline of the main events connected with the subject, since it would be impossible to do otherwise considering the vastness of the topic. For the proper understanding of the historical significance of Brazil's boundary controversies, one must go back to the very beginning of some of them, starting with the disputes between Portugal and Spain for the control of the newly discovered lands beyond the seas. The study may be divided into three main periods: 1. the disputes between Portugal and Spain and France concerning Brazil and attempts to define the boundaries of the latter (1452-1822); 2. the efforts of the Brazilian Empire to define its boundaries (1822-1889); and 3. The final settlement during the now so-called Old Republic (1889-1928).

I

It will be recalled that about the middle of the fifteenth century, due to a number of factors which it is irrelevant to mention here, Portuguese navigators began to feel their way down around the African coast on what to us today seem ridiculously small vessels, until eventually they reached India in 1498. Six years earlier, moved by the same general impulses but taking an opposite direction, Spanish navigators under the leadership of Columbus, came to the shores of what was supposed to be for many years that same fabulous land. News of this remarkable feat came as a blow to the Portuguese dreams of expansion and exclusive possession of the wealth of the Indies. Against such possibility they had tried to safeguard themselves by keeping secret all their nautical progress and above all by securing what they considered perfectly good patents of ownership under the form of Papal Bulls. Of these, several were issued which gave to the Portuguese kings an exclusive grant of all regions discovered and to be discovered by their sailors south of Capes Não and Bojador and towards Guinea, and all those which were to be found on the south coast and on the west side of Africa; other Christians were, under the penalty of excommunication (the severest penalty which any good Christian of those days could think of), prohibited from trading in those regions. It is not difficult to imagine in what state of mind King Dom João II of Portugal and his Court may have been when on March 4, 1493, Columbus entered the Tagus on his return trip to Spain with the somewhat colored news of having reached the Indies on his voyage to the West.

The dispute that ensued between the sovereign of Portugal on the one hand and the sovereigns of Castile and Aragon on the other, was eventually settled by a treaty signed on June 7, 1494, known as the Treaty of Tordesillas. By this treaty a conventional line was agreed upon, straight from Pole to Pole, passing at a distance of 370 leagues west of the Cape Verde Islands; all lands discovered or to be discovered to the east of such a line would belong to the Crown of Portugal and lands discovered or to be discovered to the west of the same line would belong to the Crowns of Castile and Aragon. Within ten months the "Line of Demarcation," as it was called, should be properly surveyed by astronomers and navigators of both contracting parties and marked wherever possible. This treaty, as it is well known, had superseded a Papal Bull issued the previous year providing for a similar dividing line in the Atlantic, but less favorable to Portugal.

The Line of Demarcation was never surveyed as provided by the Treaty of 1494 and in fact could not be, so meager and incorrect were the notions of the geographers of those days concerning the earth and its size. By modern calculations it would have passed at 47° 32′ 56″ west of Greenwich. After 1500, when Portuguese navigators discovered the northeastern corner of South America, well within the zone assigned to Portugal by the Treaty of Tordesillas, a long, bitter, and hopeless dispute started between the two Iberian crowns, which indeed was never definitely settled.

For a number of years the absence in South America of an accepted dividing line between the domains of Portugal and Spain did not bother anyone, since the Spaniards were quite busy searching for precious metals on the western coast and the Portuguese did not go very far away from the sea on the eastern coast. But eventually, daring *bandeiras* of the Portuguese and their Brazilian descendants marched to the conquest of the hinterland, explored the low mountains of the central plateau of Brazil, descended the great rivers which flow northward towards the mighty Amazon and southward towards the River Plate, reaching as far as the rich lands of Matto Grosso in the west, Paraguay in the south, and Rio Negro in the north. These extraordinary incursions of the people of Brazil made absolutely necessary some sort of agreement on limits between the two Iberian crowns. But it must be noted here that a great deal of this expansion of Brazil took place during the sixty years in which Portugal and Brazil, as well as all the other Portuguese colonial possessions, were under the sovereignty of the kings of Spain. This, however, only complicated matters, since in 1668, when Spain recognized once more the independence of Portugal, the treaty of peace signed between the two crowns provided that Brazil should have the same boundaries as she possessed before the war, and no one knew what those boundaries really were. The only previous agreement between the two crowns had been the Treaty of Tordesillas. On the other hand, the Portuguese were now in control of a far greater territory than the old demarcation line would allow.

This uncertainty gave rise, in the latter part of the seventeenth century, to a serious quarrel between the two Iberian crowns concerning the ownership of the left bank of the Río de la Plata, where the Portuguese had built a town and fortress in 1679, known as Colonia do Sacramento, and from where they carried on a very profitable smuggling business with the Spanish colonists of the region. In 1681 a serious attempt was made to determine whether the town was either within the Portuguese or Spanish spheres as defined by the Treaty of Tordesillas; but after scholarly discussions concerning the size of the earth, the length of one degree of longitude on the equator, and the point from which to start measuring the 370 leagues of the treaty—the contracting parties had not specified which of the islands of Cape Verde Archipelago they meant—the geographers and navigators entrusted with the commission gave up in despair. During the wars of the Spanish Succession, troops from Buenos Aires attacked and destroyed Colonia. The Treaty of Utrecht gave back to Portugal the town and the fortress, or whatever was left of both, and their territory. This agreement, however, was interpreted by the Spaniards as meaning the town itself, the fortress, and the surrounding lands within reach of cannon shot.

In 1750, when Portugal was ruled in the name of King Dom José I, the all-powerful minister of state, the Marquis of Pombal, negotiated with the government of Ferdinand VI of Spain a treaty of limits. This treaty, which was signed at Madrid and which for the first time seriously attempted to define the boundaries of Brazil, recognized the actual territorial possessions of each party in South America, with the exception that Portugal ceded to Spain the much-attacked and reconstructed town and fortress of Colonia; and Spain, in return, ceded to Portugal a certain territory on the left bank of the Uruguay River, north of the Ibicuhy, where a number of Indian villages, seven in all, and called for that reason the Seven Missions of the Uruguay, had been founded by Jesuit missionaries during the latter part of the seventeenth century.

This treaty proved, however, equally unpopular among the Portuguese traders and smugglers of Colonia, whose profitable business would naturally have disappeared, and among the Jesuit missionaries who controlled the Indian villages. When the mixed boundary commissions provided by the treaty attempted to survey the line, they encountered all sorts of difficulties, including armed opposition from the Indian inhabitants of the Seven Missions. It took some time before these Indians could be subdued. But other complications appeared: the boundary commissioners quarreled among themselves as to the identity of certain rivers mentioned in the treaty, and the commissioners in charge of the survey in the north, after many months of difficult traveling through the jungle, either never met at all or met only to quarrel and separate. In Europe, the Jesuits exerted all their influence to obtain the abrogation of the treaty, and finally, when Carlos III succeeded Fernando VI on the throne of Spain, a convention was signed between the Portuguese and Spanish governments in 1761 providing for the suspension of boundary surveys in South America until a new treaty could be negotiated.

In 1777, after the downfall of Pombal, another treaty was in fact signed between Portugal and Spain which, purporting to be a preliminary treaty, attempted to define anew the boundaries of Brazil. This treaty, signed at San Ildefonso, established approximately the same boundaries as defined in 1750, except that it gave to Spain both the town and territory of Colonia and the Seven Missions of the Uruguay, thus moving the southern boundary of Brazil a trifle northwards.

Commissioners were again appointed to survey and mark the boundaries, but they quarrelled *ad infinitum* and accomplished nothing. A particularly violent dispute arose among the members of the commission in charge of the survey between the Uruguay and Iguassú rivers in the south, about a certain river known as Pepiry-guassú, which had already been surveyed by the commissioners under the Treaty of 1750. The Spanish commissioners now insisted that the survey made in 1758-59 was not correct since the real Pepiry-guassú of the treaty was another river which one of them had just found a little more towards the east, giving, therefore, to Spain a few more square miles of territory.

Things were still unsettled when in 1801 Spain, as an ally of France, declared war against Portugal in consequence of the refusal of the Portuguese government to enforce Napoleon's continental system against Great Britain. The preliminary Treaty of 1777, never carried out, was now considered abrogated by the Portuguese, and during the next few years, while the struggles for independence took place in Spanish America, nothing was done to settle the boundary questions of Brazil, except possibly in the region of present-day Uruguay, which formed part of Brazil as the "Cisplatine Province" from 1821 to 1828.

Before passing on to the second part of the study, brief mention also must be made here of the dispute which arose between Portugal and France as to ownership of the lands between the Amazon and Oyapok rivers known as *Terras do Cabo do Norte*. This dispute started as far back as the latter part of the seventeenth century, when traders from Cayenne traveled as far south as the Amazon and the Jary rivers, within what the Portuguese considered their own territory. In 1688 a small party of French soldiers appeared before Fort Araguary on the banks of the river of the same name and claimed the territory for the King of France. The Portuguese commander answered that the well-known boundary of his master's domains in that region was the river known to the Portuguese as Vicente Pinzon and to the French as Oyapok.

During the following years the diplomacy of Louis XIV attempted by threats to secure from Portugal the recognition of French sovereignty over the disputed region. At Utrecht (1713) France was compelled to recognize as belonging to Portugal all the territory between the Amazon and the Oyapok or Vicente Pinzon. But the question did not end then. After 1763 the French became very active in South America intending to compensate themselves for their losses elsewhere. They established at several strategic points north of the Amazon small settlements which the Portuguese soon destroyed. During the revolutionary and Napoleonic periods a number of treaties were forced upon the government of Portugal, recognizing ever increasing claims of France in the disputed region. These treaties were, however, declared void by the Prince Regent, later King Dom João VI, in 1808, after the transference of the Portuguese court to Brazil. A Portuguese expedition conquered Cayenne which remained under Portugal's control until

1814, when, by the treaty of the Peace of Paris, Portugal assumed to return to France the whole of the French Guyana as it was on January 1, 1792. This provision encountered opposition on the part of the Portuguese government, since it would have given to France a portion of territory considered Portuguese, but occupied at that time by the French. This clause of the Treaty of 1814 was later modified by an article of the Final Act of Vienna (1815) providing that Portugal should return to France the whole of the French Guyana north of the Oyapok River, the mouth of which lies, said the article, between 4° and 5° degrees N. latitude. In spite of this clear definition of the boundary, the question remained open until decided by arbitration later on, as will be seen.

II

In 1822, the year of her declaration of independence from Portugal, Brazil found herself with her boundaries still undefined. The empire set itself from the beginning to remedy this situation, and in its dealings with the neighboring nations used, as a rule, fairness and common sense. Thus in 1825 the government of Pedro I issued a decree disapproving and declaring null and void the act of the provisional government of the Matto Grosso Province, which, on its own initiative, had ordered an armed force to enter the Province of Chiquitos, later part of Bolivia, in order to annex it to Brazil at the invitation of the royalist governor of that province then in revolt against the patriotic government established in the territory by Bolívar. This decree is of great importance because it shows the general policy of the empire towards the neighboring countries. It declared that the acts of the governor of Matto Grosso were "entirely contrary to the principles of public law recognized by all civilized nations," and that Brazil always would guide herself "by the soundest commands of justice, seeking the greatest good of the nation which it governed without injury to the rights of others."

In this spirit, and basing in general its claims on the principle of the *uti-possidetis,* the governments of Pedro I and his son endeavored, although in the main unsuccessfully, to settle the boundary questions of Brazil.

The dispute with France over the Oyapok or Vicente Pinzon River, the acknowledged boundary between Brazil and French Guyana, continued to occupy the attention of the Brazilian ministry of foreign affairs. In 1840, after attempts by France to establish forts in the region of Amapá, south of the Oyapok, the two governments agreed to send mixed commissions to survey the boundary in accordance with the provisions of the Treaty of Utrecht on this matter. Later on, the French government suggested that it would be of no use to send commissioners to survey the boundary until the two governments had first agreed as to the real meaning of the treaty. The two governments promised to respect the *status quo* in the disputed region, and from 1841 to 1856 Brazilian and French plenipotentiaries met at Paris to discuss the matter. Written memoirs were prepared by both parties presenting their respective claims. Later, the discussion was carried on orally, France claiming that the Oyapok or Vicente Pinzon was the Carapouri or northern branch of the Araouari (Araguary), and the Brazilian representative asserting with equal vigor that it was the present-day Oyapok. Brazil offered compromise lines which were refused by France, and at last the Brazilian plenipotentiary was instructed to break off negotiations due to the uncompromising attitude of the government of Napoleon III. The *status quo* of 1841 continued to be respected by both nations until eventual settlement of the dispute in 1900.

While this dispute with France was going on, another one, no less complicated, arose concerning the line between Brazil and British Guyana. In 1835-37 a German explorer, R. Schomburgk, appeared in the region of the upper Rupununi and stirred up trouble. He was impressed with the living conditions of the Indian inhabitants and asked the protestant bishop of Barbados to send a missionary to the region. A man named Youd was sent in 1838. While Schomburgk was still there, a Brazilian expedition arrived to recruit Indians for the navy, and the explorer was filled with indignation at the manner in which the recruits were taken. Returning to the coast, he wrote a memorial to the president of the Society for the Protection of British and Foreign Aborigenes, expressing for the first time his doubts concerning the rights of Brazil to any territory east of the Pacaraima Mountains and Rupununi River, and suggesting that the watershed between the affluents of the Essequibo and the Amazon rivers would make a better boundary between Brazil and British Guyana. With this suggestion the Reverend Youd entirely agreed, since it would also make the natives British subjects. In 1839 a Brazilian police force expelled the missionary from the region.

By 1841 the British government was ready to act. It ordered a survey of the region made and a map drawn, copies of which were to be sent to the governments of Brazil and Venezuela, the latter also being interested in the matter. The British government also demanded that the Brazilian authorities evacuate the territory which it now claimed as its own. Brazil, to avoid an armed conflict, ordered her officials to withdraw under protest. Protests were also presented to the foreign office in London, together with a proposal to neutralize the disputed region until a definitive settlement of the dispute might take place. This was accepted by the British government in 1842. But the question remained unsettled for nearly sixty years thereafter.

The third serious dispute concerning limits during this period was with the Argentine republic. The first negotiations for the settlement of the boundary between Brazil and Argentina did not take place until 1857, when the great Brazilian diplomatist, José Maria da Silva Paranhos, later Viscount of Rio Branco, entered into negotiations with the government of the Argentine confederation at Paraná, then its capital. Silva Paranhos addressed a memorial to the Argentine government offering as a basis for settlement the *uti-possidetis* of both parties and the Treaty of 1777 between Spain and Portugal where its provisions agreed or did not conflict with the actual possessions of either country. The Brazilian empire, said Silva Paranhos, wanted to define its boundaries with its neighbors in a friendly manner. Brazil did not need any more territory than she already had. Fortunately, he added, the boundary of Brazil with Argentina, as defined by the Treaty of 1777, did not differ from the actual possessions of either country.

Eventually, on December 14, 1857, a treaty was signed between the two governments adopting the same boundary as provided by the Treaty of 1777. It was further declared, in order to avoid any possible controversy, that although well-defined in Article 1, the rivers mentioned in it were those surveyed in 1759 by the commissioners of Spain and Portugal under the Treaty of 1750.

This treaty raised considerable opposition in Argentina because the old controversy as to the identity of the Pepiry-guassú River, which formed part of the boundary between the two countries, was taken up again by some Argentine publicists. Besides that, General Urquiza, then president of the Argentine confederation, wanted to induce the Brazilian government to help him in subduing Buenos Aires, with which he was at war. The government of Dom Pedro II refused to be involved in the struggle, and the Argentine government failed to exchange ratifications of the treaty. From 1859 to 1876 nothing was done regarding the matter due to the unsettled political conditions prevailing in the Río de la Plata region. In 1876 negotiations were renewed in Buenos Aires, but at this time the Argentine government contended that the survey of 1759 was incorrect, offering to submit the question to arbitration. The dispute reached then a somewhat bitter stage, each side claiming jurisdiction over the disputed territory and creating administrative provinces there and protesting against similar action on the part of the other government.

In 1885 a new treaty was signed providing for a new survey of the disputed rivers and intervening territory. Both parties further declared that they would try to settle the question in a friendly manner. The survey was started in 1887 and did not end until after the republican régime had been proclaimed in Brazil. Meanwhile, in 1889, an agreement was signed at Buenos Aires providing that if the two parties were unable to reach an understanding within ninety days from the termination of the survey provided by the Treaty of 1885, the dispute would be submitted to the arbitration of the president of the United States of America or of any other friendly nation. We shall see, in the third part of this study, how this question finally ended.

The boundary negotiations with the other neighboring nations were carried on without definite settlements except possibly in the case of Paraguay and Uruguay.

In 1828, when the independence of Uruguay was recognized by Brazil, a convention was signed between the commanders of the Brazilian and Uruguayan troops establishing the boundary between the two countries temporarily by the Quarehim and Jaguarão rivers. This agreement was not ratified due to the political disorder prevailing in Uruguay for a number of years after the recognition of her independence. By 1845 the government of Uruguay began to endeavor to secure from Brazil a definitive settlement of the matter and the grant of the right to navigate and trade in Lagoa Mirim and the Jaguarão River which formed part of the boundary between the two countries. Brazil refused to recognize such right to Uruguay and eventually, in 1851, a treaty of limits was signed based on the principle of the *uti-possidetis* and reserving to Brazil the exclusive navigation and trade of the lake and river above mentioned. This treaty was accompanied by a declaration of the minister of foreign affairs of Brazil to the effect that the exclusive rights of navigation recognized by the treaty to Brazil would not prevent Brazil from admitting, by a special concession and under certain restrictions, Uruguayan craft to the navigation and commerce of Lagoa Mirim and the Jaguarão River. In 1857 a convention was signed between the two countries whereby Brazil declared that she recognized in principle the convenience of opening the navigation of Lagoa Mirim and the Jaguarão River to Uruguayan craft, but pending the completion of certain studies, the negotiations on the subject would be postponed until a more adequate time. The Uruguayan congress refused to ratify this treaty.

Concerning Paraguay, a convention on limits was signed between Brazil and Paraguay in 1856 providing for the appointment of a commission to study the question of boundaries between the two countries. But negotiations were stopped by the war which Brazil, Argentine, and Uruguay were forced to wage against the dictator López from 1865 to 1870.

In the treaty of offensive and defensive alliance signed between the three governments in 1865, the contracting parties assumed to respect and maintain the Paraguayan territorial integrity. In 1870, at the end of the war, when preliminaries of peace were signed, it was provided that before definitive treaties of limits and peace were negotiated between the allied powers and the permanent government of Paraguay, the latter should have an opportunity to be heard and to present its titles to certain territories also claimed by Argentina and Brazil. Subsequently, in a conference held at Buenos Aires between the allied powers, it was further agreed that in case of differences of opinion concerning territorial matters, some proper and peaceful mode of settlement should be adopted.

Brazil attempted to arrive at some common basis of collective negotiation, but when finally in October 1871 the representatives of the four nations gathered in Asunción to discuss the definitive treaty of peace and limits, the Argentine envoy became dissatisfied with developments and decided to withdraw, leaving behind a proposal for indefinite adjournment of the negotiations. Under the circumstances, Brazil accepted the invitation from the Paraguayan government to negotiate a separate treaty of peace and limits. This treaty was finally signed in December of 1871 and transmitted to the government of Argentina, which protested against such a separate agreement.

In 1872 another treaty was negotiated and signed defining the boundary between Paraguay and Brazil except in the section between the Apa River and Bahia Negra, confining a territory then, as today, claimed by both Paraguay and Bolivia.

With Peru, Brazil started diplomatic relations in 1826, when Don José Domingo Cáceres, first consul general and chargé d'affaires of Peru at Rio de Janeiro, presented his credentials to the government of the Emperor Pedro I. Cáceres suggested the negotiation of a treaty of limits and the appointment of a mixed commission to study the whole matter and gather the necessary data. Brazil accepted this proposal, but before it could be carried into effect, the Peruvian representative withdrew from the Brazilian capital.

In 1841 a treaty of peace, friendship, commerce and navigation was signed at Lima between the two nations. In it they declared, recognizing the importance of settling the question of their common boundary, that they had agreed to enter into negotiations for that purpose, adopting as the basis of settlement the *uti-possidetis* of 1821 and also agreeing to exchange territories or pay indemnities that might be deemed necessary and just in order to define the dividing line by the most natural and lasting boundaries. This treaty failed to secure ratification from the Peruvian congress, but ten years later (1851) a convention was signed and duly ratified by both parties defining a section of the boundary between the two countries and creating a mixed commission to survey it. In spite of repeated requests from Brazil, the Peruvian government did not appoint commissioners to survey the line as provided by this convention.

In 1858 another convention was signed at Lima whereby the two parties agreed to appoint within one year the members of the surveying commission referred to in the Treaty of 1851. Only in 1863, however, did the Peruvian commissioners arrive at Manaos, the meeting point of all the commissioners. Even then, the Peruvian commissioners endeavored to discuss, before proceeding with the survey, certain mistakes which they claimed had been made in the definition of the boundary in 1851. As the Brazilian commissioners insisted that they were not authorized to discuss the matter, the chief of the Peruvian commissioners left for London, alleging ill-health.

Eventually in 1866 the survey of the line between Tabatinga and Apaporis was started, a slight change being suggested and approved in 1874 by the two governments on the Iça or Putumayo River. The Colombian government protested against the settlement between Peru and Brazil in this section, claiming ownership of the territory west of that line.

Concerning the line to the southeast of the sources of the Javary River, Peru suggested that negotiations be entered into at Lima between Brazil, Peru, and Bolivia, since the territory was claimed by both Peru and Bolivia. Brazil refused to do this, maintaining her right to negotiate with each country separately; and when in 1867 Brazil reached an agreement with Bolivia, Peru protested.

In 1885 Peru denounced the Treaty of 1851. This denunciation was accepted by Brazil except in regard to the articles defining the boundaries between the two countries, which were considered perpetual. But later the Acre question necessitated a new agreement between Brazil and Peru, as will be seen.

Venezuela, in 1841, invited Brazil to define their mutual boundaries; but due to the political conditions in that country, nothing was done until 1852, when a treaty of limits, fluvial navigation, and extradition was signed at Caracas. This treaty failed to receive the necessary ratification from the Venezuelan congress, and in 1859 another treaty was negotiated, signed, and this time ratified by both nations, providing for the same line as defined in 1852.

Venezuela did not appoint the surveyors provided by the treaty until 1878. In that year, after some discussion concerning alleged mistakes in the definition of the boundary by the Treaty of 1852, the commissioners of the two nations made the survey of a small section of the boundary. As the Venezuelan commissioners refused to finish the survey, the Brazilian commissioners completed it alone, and in 1884 the Brazilian government sent to Caracas the general map drawn by its own commissioners. The Venezuelan government answered six years later, declaring not to accept the survey made by the Brazilian commissioners alone.

After 1892, when the controversy between Venezuela and Colombia was decided by arbitration, Brazil ceased to confine with Venezuela in the region where the line had been jointly surveyed. In this manner the boundary between Brazil and Venezuela remained totally unsurveyed until after 1905.

From July 9 to 25, 1853, a number of meetings took place in Bogotá, Colombia, then New Granada, to negotiate a treaty of limits between Brazil and that country. Eventually a treaty was signed, but it was not ratified by the congress of New Granada.

In 1859 negotiations were started anew, Brazil insisting that the only basis possible for the boundary settlement between the two countries was the *uti-possidetis* of the independence period. New Granada, however, insisted that the treaties of 1750 and 1777 between Portugual and Spain should also be taken into consideration.

In 1881 the Colombian government sent to Rio de Janeiro Prospero Pereira Gamba to negotiate a treaty of friendship, limits, commerce, and navigation. But Gamba left the city before finishing the negotiations. He presented, however, a more conciliatory proposal which eventually became the basis of the settlement between the two countries.

In 1881 Colombia suggested that the question be submitted to arbitration. Brazil replied that if upon the settlement of the question between Colombia and Venezuela the former were to still confine with Brazil in the region in dispute, Brazil might accept the arbitration proposal.

With Ecuador, Brazil signed in 1853 a treaty of extradition. At the time when this treaty was negotiated, there was an exchange of views, included in a protocol, to the effect that the principle of the *uti-possidetis* would be accepted by both nations in the negotiation of a treaty of limits if Ecuador were to win the dispute which she then had with her neighbors concerning the territory between the Amazon (here called Marañon) and the Japurá rivers.

In 1834 the Bolivian minister at Rio de Janeiro presented a project of boundary settlement with Brazil based on the Treaty of 1777. This project was rejected by the Brazilian government. Again in 1851 negotiations were started on the matter, but the political unrest in Bolivia prevented any settlement from taking place. Later, in 1859, Brazil declared that she would negotiate only on the basis of the *uti-possidetis*. After a few more attempts, a treaty of friendship, limits, navigation, commerce, and extradition was signed between the two countries in 1867, defining their common boundary. This treaty was protested by Peru on the ground that it involved certain territories claimed by her.

In 1883, when Brazil declared her intention to abrogate the Treaty of 1867 with the exception of the articles concerning the boundaries, Bolivia proposed some changes in the line between Bahia Negra and Rio Verde, alleging the need of direct access to the Paraguay River. But Brazil did not accept this proposal.

III

In the third part of this study note may be taken of the final and definitive settlement of the various boundary questions of Brazil. There is no doubt that with the establishment, in November 1889, of a republican régime in Brazil, that country's international situation in the continent was considerably improved, since in the eyes of the neighboring nations, all of which had adopted a republican form of government at the time of their independence, the old monarchial régime spelled imperialism, even if somewhat pared down for the time being by the wisdom and peaceful dispositions of the Emperor Pedro II. The change of form of government was hailed everywhere in this hemisphere with joy, and one is inclined to believe that this sentiment of good will helped, at least in some cases, to bring about the final settlement of the boundary disputes of Brazil with her neighbors.

In no case was this so well exemplified as in the final settlement with the Argentine republic. Immediately after the proclamation of the republic in Brazil, the Argentine minister at Rio de Janeiro entered into negotiations with Quintino Bocayuva, then minister of foreign affairs of the Brazilian provisional government, for a definitive settlement of the boundary dispute between the two countries.

Contrary to the traditional standing of Brazil in the matter, the provisional government of Brazil now decided to accept a compromise line in the region of the *Misiones*. This was probably due to fears of foreign intervention in favor of the ex-Emperor Pedro II, to the revolt in the Province of Rio Grande do Sul, and to the good will shown by Argentina in recognizing the new régime in Brazil prior to any other nation.

The treaty settling the dispute was signed at Montevideo on January 25, 1890 amidst great expressions of joy. But as soon as the text of the treaty was generally known in Brazil, public opinion arose in indignation against it, and the Brazilian congress refused to ratify the agreement by the vast majority of one hundred and forty-two to five.

The treaty signed between the two countries in 1885 provided, as has been seen, that the dispute would be submitted to arbitration if not amicably settled within ninety days from the end of the survey provided by the same treaty.

In April of 1892 the two parties addressed themselves to the president of the United States, then Grover Cleveland, requesting him to act as arbiter in the dispute, which President Cleveland consented to do. The two governments entrusted the preparation of their cases to distinguished diplomats: Brazil, to Baron de Aguiar d'Andrade and Argentina to Dr. Nicolás Calvo. Both these gentlemen died before having fulfilled their duties and their places were taken respectively by José Maria de Silva Paranhos, Baron of Rio Branco, and Estanislau S. Zeballos, both of them ranking very high among the most eminent statesmen of their countries.

The cases of the two governments fill several volumes of well-documented argumentation. One cannot attempt here to go into detail about the cases. In a few words, both nations agreed as to most of the boundary line between their respective territories; the only section in dispute and which was not submitted to arbitration, was that lying between the Uruguay and the Iguassú rivers, Brazil claiming certain streams and Argentina other streams slightly more to the east. The territory in dispute was not more than 12,000 English square miles in size. But the national honor of two proud nations was at stake, and the question assumed tremendous proportions in the eyes of the citizens.

The Argentine case attempted to prove that the survey of 1759 had been erroneously made and that the two rivers to which the Treaty of 1750 referred were not those surveyed by the commissioners of 1759, but others discovered later on by the Spanish commissioners under the Treaty of 1777, and found a little more to the east. Brazil, on the other hand, attempted to prove that the commissioners of 1759 had surveyed the right rivers as provided by the Treaty of 1750 and confirmed by the Treaty of 1777.

The award of the arbiter was delivered to the parties on February 6, 1895. It was a short document in which the arbiter declared after careful examination of all arguments, documents, and evidence presented, that the boundary between the two countries should follow the two rivers claimed by Brazil. This award was respected by both parties, and a protocol signed on August 9, 1895 provided for the survey. Three years later (1898) a general treaty of limits was signed embodying the settlement of the whole boundary between the two nations. Thus ended one of the boundary disputes of Brazil which at several times threatened to involve the nation in armed conflict.

To the Baron of Rio Branco is undoubtedly due the success of the Brazilian thesis. A passionate student of Brazilian history, he ransacked, either personally or through agents, the archives and libraries of the Old World in search for documentation. He was fortunate in finding at Simancas the original of the special instructions to the boundary commissioners of 1758, which enabled him to prove that the Argentine allegation that the characteristics of one of the rivers involved in the dispute which were supposed to be included in such instructions were not there at all; thus he destroyed the strength of the Argentine argument.

Before becoming minister of foreign affairs of Brazil, the Baron of Rio Branco had another opportunity of defending the interests of his country in another celebrated boundary dispute. On April 10, 1897, after a number of unpleasant incidents had occurred in the disputed area between Brazil and French Guyana, a treaty of arbitration was signed providing that the federal council of Switzerland would be asked to act as arbiter in the dispute. The Baron of Rio Branco was entrusted with the preparation of the Brazilian case. The controversy hinged on whether the present-day Oyapok River was the Oyapok, Japoc, or

Vicente Pinzon mentioned in the Treaty of Utrecht (1713), as interpreted by Article 107 of the Final Act of Vienna (1815), and by the Convention of Paris of 1817 as well as by other documents. Brazil attempted to prove that it was; and France ended by declaring that it was not possible to ascertain whether it was or not, and invited the arbiters to decide the dispute by means of a compromise line.

The arbitral sentence, issued on December 1, 1900, comprised in a thick volume containing a very clear statement of the question, declared that the present-day Oyapok *was* the true boundary between French Guyana and Brazil.

This encouraging result led Brazil to entrust to arbitration the settlement of still another difficult boundary dispute, this time with Great Britain over the boundary in the Guyanas region.

After protracted negotiations to settle this matter, the two governments, at the suggestion of the British foreign office, decided to submit the dispute to the arbitration of the king of Italy, Victor Emmanuel III. The *compromis* defining the dispute was signed on November 6, 1901.

The Brazilian government chose Joaquim Nabuco, another notable Brazilian statesman, to prepare its case. The claim of Brazil was based on priority of discovery and exploration of the disputed region by subjects of the kings of Portugal, whose rights Brazil inherited at the time of independence. The British claim, on the other hand, asserted that the region in dispute had been first explored by the Dutch and later transferred to Great Britain.

The arbitral award, delivered to the parties on June 6, 1904, rejected both claims as insufficiently proven and offered a compromise line, which was accepted with slight modifications agreed upon later by the two parties. The treaty defining the boundaries between the two nations was not, however, signed until 1926, due to circumstances not connected with the question.

Two other important settlements, with Bolivia and Peru, were also successfully negotiated by the Baron of Rio Branco as minister of foreign affairs of Brazil. After the War of the Pacific, Brazil signed with Bolivia, on February 19, 1895, a protocol providing for the survey of the boundary between the two countries as defined by the Treaty of 1867. It was during the survey of the boundary that one of the Brazilian commissioners discovered a slight error in the survey previously made of the sources of the Javary River. This mistake was eventually rectified by both nations.

Meanwhile a serious situation had arisen in the region to the south of the line, from the Madeira to the sources of the Javary, agreed upon by the two parties. This region is rich in rubber, and since 1878 many Brazilian *seringueiros* had settled there. By 1903 there were some 80,000 Brazilians in the region of the Upper Purus and Upper Acre, unquestionably Bolivian territory. Exports of rubber from this region were quite large, and since Brazil collected high duties on the product when brought in from foreign territory, a great deal of smuggling took place, depriving both Brazil and Bolivia of a considerable amount of revenue. The Bolivian government with the consent of Brazil established custom-posts at strategic points even north of the boundary line agreed upon between the two countries. In 1899 the *seringueiros,* disgruntled with the attitude of the Bolivian authorities, staged a revolt under the leadership of a Spaniard named Luís Gálvez. After expelling the Bolivian authorities, they declared themselves independent from Bolivia, calling their state *Estado Independente do Acre.* The Bolivian government protested at Rio de Janeiro against alleged help furnished to the Acre rebels by the authorities of the Brazilian states of Amazonas and Pará. But it was difficult to prove that the government officials alluded to had actually helped the revolt, although, no doubt, arms and munitions were furnished to the *seringueiros* from Brazilian territory.

At this point a few nationalistic Brazilian leaders began to suggest in congress, in the press, and elsewhere that the line as defined by the Treaty of 1867 should be interpreted as including the region of the Acre. These Brazilian expansionists suggested that the question be submitted to arbitration, but the Brazilian government, well knowing how groundless this claim was, refused to do so.

Eventually in 1900, the Bolivian troops were able to subdue the rebellion and the question seemed ended, when the following year the Bolivian government granted to an Anglo-American syndicate a concession to administer and exploit the Acre region in the name of Bolivia. The syndicate was to possess vast political powers, besides exclusive rights of trade and exploitation of the region. The Brazilian government protested against this concession and demanded its abrogation, alleging that such a grant of political authority in a region so difficult of access, meant a dangerous situation for the neighboring states. In general, public opinion in South America condemned this act of Bolivia as not quite in accordance with general policies of the continent. The *Acreanos* took advantage of this situation and revolted once more against the Bolivian authorities, but this time under the leadership of a Brazilian by the name of Placido Castro. When it became known that a military expedition was to be sent against the *Acreanos* under the command of General Pando, then president of Bolivia, the minister of foreign affairs of Brazil, Baron of Rio Branco, made public a circular he had sent to all Brazilian representatives abroad in which he condemned the Bolivian concession as unworthy of the American continent and declared that Bolivia had no right to enter into such an agreement with a foreign syndicate concerning a territory the sovereignty of which was then in dispute with neighboring countries. The Brazilian chancellor further declared that since Bolivia was sending an expeditionary force to the disputed region, Brazil would do likewise. A few days later Brazilian troops were ordered to enter the disputed region for the declared purpose of policing it until a final settlement of the question was reached.

Due to the attitude of the Brazilian government, the syndicate did not find it easy to secure the required capital for their enterprise, and so they were willing to sell out their rights to Brazil for the amount of £100,000, this in spite of a clause in their agreement with the Bolivian government prohibiting the syndicate from transferring the contract to any foreign state or government.

As the forces of General Pando advanced and bloodshed seemed imminent, a *modus vivendi* was fortunately signed at La Paz on March 21, 1903, providing for the occupation of the disputed region by forces of the two countries until final settlement of the question. Finally, on November 17, 1903, a treaty was signed at Petropolis, near Rio de Janeiro, whereby the two parties, taking as the basis of their agreement the provisions of the Treaty of 1867, declared their willingness to exchange certain portions of territory in order to establish the dividing line by lasting natural boundaries. Brazil was to pay to Bolivia the sum of £2,000,000 as indemnity for territories ceded by the latter country and was to negotiate directly with Peru regarding the boundary in the territory then in dispute between Peru and Bolivia. Brazil also assumed the obligation to build a railroad connecting the Madeira to the Mamoré, so as to provide an outlet for merchandise exported from or imported into Bolivian territory. The indemnity above mentioned was paid in London to Bolivian agents in 1904 and 1905. The railroad, known as the Madeira-Mamoré, built by an American concern, and one of the most daring pieces of engineering in the whole world, was opened to traffic just before the World War.

Subsequently other agreements were necessary between Bolivia and

Brazil to readjust the boundary. On Christmas Day, 1928, a general treaty of limits was signed between the two governments defining in a definitive manner their mutual boundaries on the basis of the agreement of 1903.

The settlement with Peru was also a difficult one. Peru, like Brazil, protested against the Bolivian concession of such extensive rights to a foreign syndicate in a region the sovereignty of which was then in dispute. In 1902 Peru and Bolivia agreed to submit their dispute to the arbitration of the government of Argentina.

When in 1903, Brazil and Bolivia settled their dispute as to the Acre territory, Peru declared that she still maintained her claims to part of the territory involved, and suggested negotiations on the matter. Brazil refused to enter into such negotiations, considering the question closed by her agreement with Bolivia. Eventually, however, in 1904 the governments of the two nations signed a provisional agreement providing that they would enter into negotiations concerning the boundary in the Acre region, and if they were unable to reach an understanding, the question would be submitted to the mediation or arbitration of some friendly power. Not until 1909 was a settlement agreed upon between the two parties. On September 8 of that year the two governments signed a definitive treaty of limits which brought the dispute to an end.

Other agreements on limits negotiated by Brazil may be briefly mentioned. With Ecuador a conditional treaty was signed in 1904, whereby if that country were to confine with Brazil after the settlement of her dispute with Peru, the boundary should be the same as provided in the convention signed at Lima, in 1851, between Peru and Brazil. After 1916, when Ecuador recognized Colombian sovereignty over that territory, this treaty became void.

With Venezuela, a protocol was signed in 1905, declaring as definitive the survey made in 1880 in common by the commissioners of the two countries and providing for the verification of the survey made in other sections by the Brazilian commissioners alone.

With the Netherlands, although there was never any dispute concerning the traditional boundary between Brazil and Dutch Guyana, a treaty was signed in 1906 defining that boundary, and providing for its survey.

To Uruguay, Brazil decided to grant equal rights of navigation and trade in Lagoa Mirim and the Jaguarão River, this being embodied in a treaty signed at Rio de Janeiro in 1909. The boundary between the two countries was modified accordingly. This generous concession on the part of Brazil was hailed in South America as notable proof of the equitable and friendly spirit of that country towards her sister republics.

With Paraguay it was necessary to negotiate another agreement concerning a section of the boundary which had not been included in the settlement of 1872. A treaty signed at Rio de Janeiro in 1927 defined the boundary between the mouth of the Apa River, on the Paraguay River, and Bahia Negra.

The boundary with Colombia was partially settled in 1907 by a treaty of limits, which, however, said nothing concerning the line in the region between Tabatinga and Apaporis. This region was also claimed by Peru and Ecuador, but in 1916 Ecuador withdrew her claim and in 1922 Peru ceded to Colombia a certain strip of land just west of the line as defined in the Treaty of 1851 between Peru and Brazil. Considering the Treaty of 1922 between Peru and Colombia prejudicial to her interests, Brazil protested against it at Lima.

As soon as the news of this reached him, the Colombian ambassador at Lima, Dr. Uribe, called on the president of Peru and interviewed Dr. L. S. Rowe, Director General of the Pan American Union, then in Lima, and upon suggestion of both, advised his government by cable to authorize the Colombian minister at Washington, Dr. Enrique Olaya Herrera, to enter into negotiations with the secretary of state of the United States, then Mr. Hughes, and with the Brazilian representative at Washington, to obtain the withdrawal of the Brazilian protest against the Treaty of 1922. He further suggested that all influence be brought to bear to secure the ratification of the Treaty of 1922 and that the Colombian government authorize Dr. Olaya to accept, as soon as the treaty had been ratified, the line Tabatinga-Apaporis on condition that Brazil grant to Colombia the freedom of navigation in the Amazon, Putumayo, and all tributaries of those rivers.

This suggestion was well received by all concerned, and on March 4, 1925 Dr. Hernan Velarde, ambassador of Peru, Dr. Olaya, minister of Colombia, and Souza Leão Gracie, *chargé d'affaires* of Brazil, met, at the invitation of Secretary Hughes, in one of the rooms of the state department at Washington and agreed, at the suggestion of Mr. Hughes, that Brazil was to withdraw her protest to Peru on account of the treaty between Peru and Colombia signed in 1922; that Colombia and Peru were to ratify the Treaty of 1922 as soon as possible; and that Colombia and Brazil were to sign a treaty defining their common boundary by the Tabatinga-Apaporis line and granting each other the right of navigation in the Amazon, Putumayo, and their affluents.

In December of 1927 the Peruvian congress ratified the Treaty of 1922, the instruments of ratification being exchanged in Bogotá on March 19, 1928. On November 15, 1928, a treaty was signed at Rio de Janeiro between Colombia and Brazil embodying the Washington agreement. In this manner ended, in a truly Pan American spirit, an old and dangerous controversy.

Thus it may be seen that by 1928 Brazil had completed the task of defining her boundaries in a definitive way. It was a long and arduous process. Considering the difficulties involved, it was, on the whole, a remarkable diplomatic victory or series of victories for Brazil. In only one dispute, that with Great Britain over the boundary in the Guyanas, did Brazil receive less than she claimed. One cannot help admiring the courage, tact, and spirit of equanimity of her statesmen so abundantly shown during the long negotiations connected with these disputes and of which we have in this paper given only a mere outline.

INDEX